Microsoft® Word 2013 BIBLE

Lisa A. Bucki

WILEY

Microsoft® Word 2013 Bible

Published by
John Wiley & Sons, Inc.
10475 Crosspoint Boulevard
Indianapolis, IN 46256
www.wiley.com

Copyright © 2013 by John Wiley & Sons, Inc., Indianapolis, Indiana

Published simultaneously in Canada

ISBN: 978-1-118-48812-6
ISBN: 978-1-118-65771-3 (ebk)
ISBN: 978-1-118-68436-8 (ebk)
ISBN: 978-1-118-65764-5 (ebk)

Manufactured in the United States of America

10 9 8 7 6 5 4 3

For general information on our other products and services please contact our Customer Care Department within the United States at (877) 762-2974, outside the United States at (317) 572-3993 or fax (317) 572-4002.

Wiley publishes in a variety of print and electronic formats and by print-on-demand. Some material included with standard print versions of this book may not be included in e-books or in print-on-demand. If this book refers to media such as a CD or DVD that is not included in the version you purchased, you may download this material at http://booksupport.wiley.com. For more information about Wiley products, visit www.wiley.com.

Library of Congress Control Number: 2012956414

Microsoft®
Word 2013
Bible

This book is dedicated with love to my husband, Stephen Poland,
who honors me daily with his loving and supportive presence in my life.

About the Author

Lisa A. Bucki learned about personal computers and software in the trenches at an up-and-coming Indianapolis PR firm in the late 1980s, teaching colleagues to navigate the brave new world of DOS and WordPerfect, as well as showing clients how to create their own publications in PageMaker, one of the first desktop publishing programs. After moving into the computer book and technical writing field in 1991, she edited or managed hundreds of titles on technology topics as diverse as PC basics, operating systems and utilities, memory management, desktop software, desktop publishing, and even random dot stereograms.

She has also written and/or contributed to dozens of computer books (and stopped bothering to count long ago), but notably was the consolidating writer and editor for *Microsoft Office 2013 Bible* and its prior editions. In addition to book authoring, Bucki has written or collaborated on dozens of multimedia and online tutorials. She has covered a variety of software and technology subjects including Photoshop, FileMaker Pro and Keynote for the Mac, iPhoto, Fireworks and Flash from Macromedia, early versions of Windows, Microsoft Office applications including Project, and digital photography. She has also written software reviews and profiles of online retailers and products for popular online deals site Offers.com, as well as serving as that site's Money Monday blogger for a period. In her consultant and trainer role, Bucki primarily provides instruction in the use of Microsoft Project but has also conducted Word and Excel training courses. In her spare time, she dabbles in creating handmade tile and minds the dogs, the chickens, and the garden along with her husband, Steve, in the wilds of Western North Carolina.

Credits

Acquisitions Editor
Mariann Barsolo

Project Editor
Kelly Talbot

Technical Editor
Dave Johnson

Production Editor
Rebecca Anderson

Copy Editor
Liz Welch

Editorial Manager
Mary Beth Wakefield

Production Manager
Tim Tate

Vice President and Executive Group Publisher
Richard Swadley

Vice President and Executive Publisher
Neil Edde

Associate Publisher
Jim Minatel

Project Coordinator, Cover
Katie Crocker

Compositor
Craig Johnson, Happenstance Type-O-Rama

Proofreader
James Saturnio and Jennifer Bennett, Word One New York

Indexer
Ted Laux

Cover Image
© Aleksandar Velasevic / iStockphoto

Cover Designer
Ryan Sneed

Acknowledgments

Every book project of this magnitude relies on a team of professionals to transport it from concept to reality. Many thanks to Jim Minatel and to Carol Long, who kept me in their contact lists as a potential resource for this project and others. My deep appreciation extends to Mariann Barsolo and Pete Gaughan, who managed the work both at the 10,000-ft. level and the 100-ft. level, and kept me on track during the challenging patches.

Special thanks go to Kelly Talbot, the development editor who lent his thoughtful commentary about improvements, and technical editor, Dave Johnson, whose careful checks of my work helped find flaws that otherwise might have fallen through the cracks. Editorial team members Rebecca Anderson and Liz Welch played an essential role in enforcing consistency and accelerating the schedule to bring a readable book to you in the fastest timeframe possible.

Contents at a Glance

Contents

Contents

Contents

Contents

Chapter 12: Getting Smart with Text: Building Blocks, Quick Parts, Actions (Tags), and More 327

Contents

Contents

Part V: Improving Document Setup and Look   493

Chapter 16: Setting Up the Document with Sections, Headers/Footers, and Columns . . 495

Contents

Part VII: Making Documents Work for You

Chapter 22: Data Documents and Mail Merge 671

Contents

Contents

Contents

Contents

Introduction

Welcome to the *Microsoft Word 2013 Bible*. Like all books in the Bible series, you can expect to find both hands-on tutorials and real-world practical application information, as well as reference and background information that provides a context for what you are learning. This book is a comprehensive resource on Word 2013 (also known as Word 15). By the time you have completed the *Microsoft Word 2013 Bible*, you will be well prepared to take full advantage of the numerous enhancements in Word 2013.

The update to Word 2013 is evolutionary rather than revolutionary. Nice touches, like the move to contextual buttons beside selected objects so you can more easily apply layout and formatting changes, provide even more and better ways to work with document content. Word 2013 also provides more ways to collaborate and share, including ways to make your work environment more portable by sharing to your SkyDrive in the cloud so you spend less time copying files to and from thumb drives and more time working.

Who Should Read This Book

The *Microsoft Word 2013 Bible* is a reference and tutorial for Word users of all levels. For the user who is completely new to Word, the early parts of this book will tell you everything you need both to quickly start using Word 2013 and to get the most out of the features it offers. Word 2013 is a full-service word processing program that can do just about anything you need it to do. Often, there are multiple ways to accomplish a given task. This book will show you the quickest and easiest ways to accomplish your mission, while at the same time pointing out the longer-term advantages of using methods better suited to extensibility and repurposing your work.

For new and veteran Word users alike, this book assumes that you have a basic level of computer literacy, as well as some proficiency with the version of Windows that you are using. (Office 2013 is compatible with Windows 7 or Windows 8, as well as Windows Server 2008 R2 and Windows Server 2013, but it does not run on earlier versions of Windows or Windows Server.) It assumes that you're familiar with Windows basics and that you know what *click*, *drag*, and *double-click* mean. It also assumes that you're familiar with basic Windows-wide techniques for selecting, copying, and deleting text. Furthermore, this book assumes that you know the difference between Internet Explorer and Windows Explorer (Windows 7) or File Explorer (Windows 8), and that you know where and what the Windows taskbar and desktop are.

How This Book Is Organized

The *Word 2013 Bible* is organized in a way that reflects both the way users tend to learn Word as well as the relative timing when particular kinds of information and techniques are needed. This book is organized into nine parts. The first four parts are designed to get you up-and-running as quickly as possible, covering things you need to know to start using Word immediately. However, the early parts of the book not only show you the basics, but also offer tips and strategies that will enable you to become an effective Word user. Topics and techniques covered in the early chapters are revisited throughout the *Microsoft Word 2013 Bible*. You'll quickly gain an understanding of how some concepts—such as Heading styles—give you incredible leverage and easy access to sophisticated word processing techniques and features.

Part I: Welcome to a New Word

Part I begins with things you need to know in order to become comfortable and fully proficient with Word 2013. The mission of this collection of chapters is to get you over any initial stumbling blocks so you can begin to take advantage of Word 2013's power and enhancements. Part I offers a quick-start chapter especially useful for newbies. For Word veterans, there's a chapter explaining how to find features that otherwise appear to be missing in action. To prepare you to be the kind of power user the *Microsoft Word 2013 Bible* knows you can be, Part 1 offers chapters on making Word work for you, understanding Word's new file format, and learning how to tame and control Word's automatic features.

Part II: Working with Document Style and Content

Part II focuses on the baseline skills that every Word user uses and needs. The chapters here cover essentials such as font and character formatting; paragraph formatting; using styles; cutting, copying, and pasting; finding and replacing text; and using Go To to navigate in a document.

Part III: Improving Document Content and Consistency

Part III focuses on aspects of Word that can make your word processing life proceed more smoothly. In Part III, you'll learn how to use Word's cadre of tools for cleaning up your documents, including checking spelling and grammar, Quick Parts, AutoCorrect, AutoFormat, and more.

Part IV: Illustrating Your Story with Graphics

It takes more than words to make a document. Part IV details the many kinds of elements you can include in documents, and shows you how to decide what to use and when to use it. In Part IV, you'll learn how to insert all kinds of objects, including tables, charts, SmartArt graphics, pictures, shapes, WordArt, and text boxes.

Part V: Improving Document Setup and Look

Part V focuses on how documents are put together, as well as special considerations that depend on the ultimate destination of the document. You'll learn what you need in order to turn out professional reports, newsletters, and brochures—and other specialized document formats. Part V covers page setup, sections, headers, footers, column formatting, page background formatting, templates, themes, and master documents.

Part VI: Enhancing Documents with Reference Features

Part VI covers those elements typically used in what people call *long documents*. It ventures into the wonderful worlds of bookmarks, indexing, hyperlinks, tables of contents (and other tables), footnotes, endnotes, citations, and Word's bibliography feature. If you've used information in one place, this chapter will show you how to reuse that information elsewhere in a variety of purposeful and powerful ways.

Part VII: Making Documents Work for You

Part VII deals with the mail merge feature's ability to create personalized documents, such as envelopes, labels, form letters, catalogs, and directories. You learn to set up or and create data source files and merge their contents with the standard information in the main document. This part also explains how to use fields to automate document content and create forms to prompt appropriate user input.

Part VIII: Publishing, Collaboration, and the Cloud

In Part VIII, you'll learn about Word's and Office's collaboration tools, comments, change tracking, and merging changes from different sources. You also learn about how Word now integrates with your SkyDrive storage in the cloud, or with respect to Office 365 and its SharePoint capabilities. Also covered in this part is integration with other Office applications, such as Outlook, Excel, and PowerPoint.

Part IX: Power and Customization

Part IX concludes the book with the kinds of customizations you can make to Word's interface—not just the keyboard and the QAT (Quick Access Toolbar), but also the Ribbon. Part IX shows you the many ways in which you can hone Word's options and settings to match your own style of working. You'll also learn how to write basic macros to automate repetitive chores.

Conventions and Features

There are many different organizational and typographical features throughout this book designed to help you get the most of the information.

The text uses command shortcuts such as Insert ⇨ Header & Footer ⇨ Header. These Ribbon tab name ⇨ group ⇨ command sequences help you navigate through the Ribbon to find and choose the appropriate command. When referencing contextual tabs, where the first part of the tab name appears on an upper row and the subtab name appears on the lower row along with the normal tabs, an arrow will also appear between the upper part of the contextual tab name and the subtab, as in Picture Tools ⇨ Format. After the first mention in a chapter, the text may refer to the contextual tab by its subtab name only, that is, Format rather than Picture Tools ⇨ Format.

Tips, Notes, and Cautions

Whenever I want to bring something important to your attention the information will appear in a Tip, Note, or Caution.

> **TIP**
>
> Tips generally are used to provide information that can make your work easier—special shortcuts or methods for accomplishing something easier than the norm.

> **NOTE**
>
> Notes provide additional, ancillary information that is helpful, but somewhat outside of the current presentation of information.

> **CAUTION**
>
> Cautions provide information about things to watch out for, whether simply inconvenient or potentially hazardous to your data or systems.

Windows Versions

One key change with Office 2013 is that it must be installed on Windows 7 or 8 (or one of the supported server versions mentioned earlier). Because Windows 8 contains a few important distinctions from Windows 7, I do my best to point out the differences where relevant in this book. Also note that this book was written showing the 32-bit (x86) version of Word 2013. If you are using another version, you might see minor differences on your screen, but everything should function basically the same way.

Where to Go from Here

Of course, no book can possibly tell you everything you're ever likely to need to know about any one computer program. With tens of millions of users around the world using Word 2013, there are going to be things that even the *Microsoft Word 2013 Bible* can't anticipate. Even Word's Help feature may not provide the answers you need. When you come up against a problem that stops you in your tracks, there are places you can go and resources you can tap.

Some of the most useful resources are Microsoft public *communities* or *newsgroups*. These communities are visited by millions of users and are frequented by thousands of experts with many combined years of experience in using Microsoft Office and solving problems in ways that are efficient, effective, creative, and often novel. To tap this vast free resource, begin here:

    http://answers.microsoft.com/en-us

Other tremendous free online resources are the many FAQs and articles created by Microsoft's huge corps of volunteer technical experts known as Most Valuable Professionals. To learn more about Microsoft's MVP program, visit:

    http://mvp.support.microsoft.com

A wealth of helpful content has been assembled by these volunteers in a website that is independent of Microsoft and maintained by MVPs. To begin utilizing the Word-specific offerings, visit:

    http://word.mvps.org/

If you have comments or suggestions for improving the *Microsoft Word 2013 Bible*, please don't hesitate to contact Wiley at:

    www.wiley.com

Part I

Welcome to a New Word

L ike the other members of the Office 2013 suite, Word 2013 has been upgraded to take advantage of new aspects of the Windows 8 operating system, such as user accounts and direct integration with the cloud. Even if you are upgrading from a recent Word version, you will find that Word 2013 includes some surprises along with familiar tools.

Part I begins with things you need to know and want to know about Word 2013. Chapter 1 explains how to get started in Word in both Windows 8 and Windows 7, and introduces the Word 2013 interface. Chapter 2 offers a quick start example how to create and print a document, and from there covers basics such as opening and saving files, making selections, and using views. Chapter 3 advises you how to get the most out of Word by using styles and taking advantage of "power user" techniques that are in fact easily employed by anyone. Finally, Chapter 4 shows you how to tame or take advantage of Word's behaviors that you might consider annoying.

Taking Your First Steps with Word

IN THIS CHAPTER

Learning Word's startup methods

Taking a look at the new Word

Locating and using Word's tools

Understanding the File tab and its purpose

Reviewing Word option settings

Finding Help in Word

Shutting down Word when you've finished working

W ord 2013 and its companion Office programs have been retooled and updated to help you get things done faster. Underneath its streamlined new look, Word integrates smoothly with the new features built into the Windows 8 operating system and Windows 8 devices, though you can use Word on a Windows 7 system, too. (It also runs on Windows Server 2008 R2 and Windows Server 2012, but this book limits coverage to using Word on the end-user versions of Windows.)

Word 2013 keeps the Ribbon interface found in the 2007 and 2010 versions. Its "bang for your buck" improvements show up elsewhere, from a new view that makes it easier to peruse a document, to new templates and guides that make document design faster and easier, to improved PDF handling, to integration with the cloud and your social media services. Even if you know the Ribbon, there's a lot to discover about Word in this book. This chapter kicks it off with your first look at starting Word in Windows 8 (and some in Windows 7), getting around in Word, finding options to customize your work setup, getting help, and exiting the program when you're done.

Starting Word

Your work in Word 2013 begins with starting the program, and there are multiple ways to get that done. This book assumes that you're using Windows 8 in its default configuration. If you're using Windows 7, some actions won't apply, and the text will point them out along the way. Office 2013 applications no longer run on Windows XP or Vista, and although Word 2013 does run on Windows Server 2008 R2 and Windows Server 2012, this book primarily limits coverage to using Word on Windows 8, with some coverage of differences when using it with Windows 7.

Start screen or Start menu

When you install Word 2013 in Windows 8, a *tile* for the program automatically appears on the Windows 8 Start screen. The Start screen appears after you start your computer and sign in to your user account, and it is the central location for accessing applications like Word. The fastest way to return to the Start screen at any time is to press the Windows logo key on the keyboard. You also can point to the lower-left corner of the Windows desktop—which retains the much the same appearance in Windows 8 that it had in Windows 7—until a Start tile appears, and then click it. Here's how to start Word 2013 from the Windows 8 Start screen:

1. **If needed, press the Windows logo key to go to the Start screen.**

2. **Depending on your screen resolution, you may need to point to the bottom of the screen to display a scroll bar and then scroll right to display the Word 2013 tile.** Figure 1.1 shows the Word 2013 tile.

FIGURE 1.1

The Word 2013 tile appears on the Start screen.

3. **Click the Word 2013 tile.** Word opens on the Windows desktop.

In Windows 8, you can sign on using two account types: a local account or a cloud-connected Microsoft account. (Microsoft accounts can be associated with any email address, although older Hotmail or Windows Live accounts, as well as newer Outlook.com accounts are automatically recognized during user setup in Windows 8 and there are no additional steps for creating the account online.) If you want to take full advantage of Word's online, social, and collaboration features, sign on to Windows with a Microsoft account. Then, the first time you start Word, it will use your Microsoft account as your Word account and you should enter that account's information if prompted to activate the program.

NOTE

If your Start screen is too cluttered and you want to remove the Word 2013 tile and use another method for starting Word, you can unpin Word from the Start screen. Press the Windows logo key, scroll right to display the tile, and right-click it. In the commands that appear along the bottom of the screen, click Unpin from Start.

If you're still using Windows 7, you can start Word via the Start menu. To do this, you choose Start ⇨ All Programs ⇨ Microsoft Office 2013 ⇨ Word 2013. Perhaps even easier, you can choose Start, and then type **word** into the search box. When Word 2013 is highlighted under Programs in the results list, press Enter.

NOTE

In Windows 8, you also can use the Search charm to start Word from the desktop (or the Start screen, if you've removed the Word 2013 tile). Move the mouse pointer to the upper- or lower-right corner of the screen to display the charms. Click the Search charm, which is the top charm. Move the mouse pointer off the Search pane that appears, over the scroll bar at the bottom of the screen. Scroll right until you see the Word 2013 tile under Microsoft Office 2013, and click the tile.

Pinning Word to the taskbar

You can place a shortcut for starting up Word 2013 onto the Windows 7 or 8 taskbar. This makes a lot of sense in Windows 8, in particular, because you use File Explorer from the desktop to manage your files. Pinning Word 2013 to the desktop in Windows 8 is a quick process:

1. **Go to the Start screen if needed by pressing the Windows logo key or pointing to the lower-left corner of the screen and clicking the Start tile.**
2. **Scroll right to display the Word 2013 tile, if needed.**
3. **Right-click the tile, and then click Pin to taskbar in the commands that appear along the bottom of the screen.**
4. **Click the Desktop tile on the Start screen, or if you were previously working at the desktop, press the Windows logo key or point to the lower-left corner of the screen and click the desktop tile to redisplay the desktop.** The Word shortcut will be added to the taskbar.

To pin Word 2013 to the taskbar in Windows 7, first start the program from the Start menu. Then right-click the program's taskbar button, and click Pin this program to taskbar in the jump list.

Once you've pinned Word to the taskbar in either version of Windows, simply click the Word 2013 button to start the program.

If you no longer want the taskbar shortcut, right-click the taskbar button and click Unpin this program from taskbar.

Creating a desktop shortcut and shortcut key

You also can start Word from a shortcut icon that you create on the desktop. To create a shortcut in Windows 8 you need to find the program startup file (WINWORD.EXE) for Word 2013. This process works in a similar way in Windows 7, which offers another way to create a less flexible type of shortcut that you'll learn about later.

Although locations vary (depending on user and network settings, for example), the usual default location for Word 2013 in both Windows 8 and Windows 7 is C:\Program Files\ Microsoft Office\Office15\WINWORD.EXE for the 64-bit version or C:\Program Files (x86)\Microsoft Office\Office15\WINWORD.EXE for the 32-bit version.

Working from the desktop, open File Explorer and navigate to WINWORD.EXE following the path just noted. When you find it, right-click it and choose Send To ⇨ Desktop (create shortcut). Close the File Explorer window. On the desktop, locate WINWORD - Shortcut. Double-click the new shortcut icon to start Word at any time.

To improve the shortcut, right-click it and choose Properties. As shown in Figure 1.2, the Target text box shows the path to the program startup file. You can add a program startup switch to this Target entry to customize Word startup; Appendix A covers the available switches. The Properties dialog box also includes a Change Icon button, which enables you to choose a new icon for this shortcut. The dialog box also offers the Shortcut key text box, where you can specify a keyboard combination that you can press to launch Word quickly from the desktop.

To assign a shortcut key, click in the Shortcut key text box shown in Figure 1.2, and press the key combination you want to use. You need to choose a shortcut key combination that's not currently used by Windows or another program. Ctrl+Alt+Shift combinations usually are available, so you might choose Ctrl+Alt+Shift+W for Word. After you press the key combination, click OK to finish assigning it to the shortcut. From there, any time you're at the desktop, pressing the keyboard shortcut combination will start Word.

FIGURE 1.2

The properties for the desktop shortcut enable you to change icons, add a shortcut key, or add a startup switch.

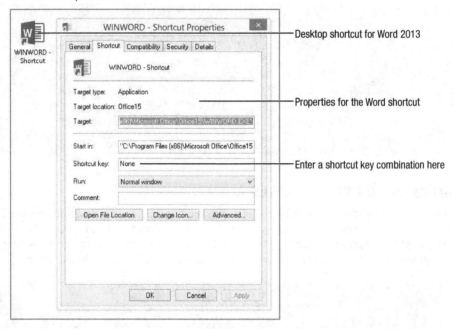

— Desktop shortcut for Word 2013

— Properties for the Word shortcut

— Enter a shortcut key combination here

TIP

To select a desktop shortcut, display the desktop, click anywhere on it, and press the first character of the shortcut's name on the keyboard, such as *W* for *winword*. Repeatedly pressing that key cycles among all shortcuts that begin with that character. Press Enter to launch the program or file associated with the selected shortcut.

If you have multiple desktop shortcuts that begin with the same character, repeatedly pressing the same key still might be tedious. The solution is to rename the shortcut icon. To do this, select the shortcut icon as just described and press the F2 key. Type a new name starting with a different letter to replace the highlighted text, and then press Enter to finish renaming.

Windows 7 offers a faster alternative for creating a desktop shortcut icon to Word. Choose Start ➪ All Programs ➪ Microsoft Office 2013. Right-drag Word 2013 from the menu over the desktop. Release the mouse button, and choose Create shortcuts here.

A shortcut created by this method lacks flexibility, because you can't add a startup switch to the target or change the shortcut icon. However, you can add a shortcut key combination.

TIP

Windows 8 enables you to access a folder that seems to be a legacy version of the Start menu from prior Windows versions. You can copy shortcuts from there to the desktop. Word's Windows 8 "Start Menu" shortcut is found at `C:\ProgramData\Microsoft\Windows\Start Menu\Programs\Microsoft Office 2013\`. You can go directly to this folder from the Start screen (or after selecting the Search charm) by right-clicking the Word 2013 tile and clicking Open file location in the commands that appear at the bottom of the screen. The Word shortcut to copy and paste is *Word 2013*. You could add a shortcut to the `Microsoft Office 2013` folder to the desktop to give you quick access to the startup shortcuts for all the Office apps.

Starting Word from File Explorer

Yet another way to start Word is by double-clicking the icon for a document created in Word 2013 or an earlier version in a File Explorer window on the desktop. Simply click the File Explorer taskbar button, navigate to the desired document, and double-click it. Alternatively, you can select it and press Enter, or right-click it and choose Open.

TIP

In fact, you can open multiple Word files this way—at the same time. Select the first one you want to open, and then Ctrl+click on each additional file you want to open. Then press Enter. This also works in Word's own Open dialog box.

NOTE

File Explorer in Windows 8 is basically the same as Windows Explorer in Windows 7, just updated and given a new name. This book primarily uses File Explorer to keep things simple, but if you are using Word in Windows 7, you can assume that "File Explorer" means "Windows Explorer" in any instructions.

Launching Word and a document via the Web

While you're browsing online, you may find links to documents created in Word, such as white papers, research reports, resumes, fiction works, and more. Clicking a Word document link in a browser window launches Word and opens the document. Keep a couple of cautions in mind when opening documents this way, however. If the file is large, the server is slow, or you are on a slow Internet connection, the download can hang up your browser or appear to hang up Word, in which case you might see a "Word is not responding" error message.

Even more important, however, Word files can carry computer viruses, so unless you have a virus protection program that scans files as they download, you risk infecting your system.

You can reduce the potential risks and problems by right-clicking the document link in question, clicking Save Target As (or your browser's equivalent), and saving the file to a local folder (a folder on your hard disk). Although most (but not all) popular antivirus programs monitor files you open from links, better safe than sorry. After you've saved a file to your hard drive, you can scan it with your antivirus program to remove viruses before proceeding to open the file.

TIP

Any time you open a Word file of uncertain origin, hold down the Shift key as you open the file. This prevents any automatic macros from running. Inspect it for suspicious macros, and once you're sure it's safe, proceed—but cautiously. In theory, this is less necessary in Word 2010 and 2013 than in previous versions of Word, however. When Word detects that a file has come from an outside source (Internet, email attachment, etc.), it can open it in Protected View. If you trust the source of the file, you can click Enable Editing to work with it.

Saving the file also gives you the opportunity to store it somewhere other than with your temporary Internet files. That way, if you need it again later, you won't have to download it again.

Using the Windows 7 Start menu Search box

If you're running Word 2013 from Windows 7, you also can use the Start menu's Search programs and files text box to find and run the program. Click the Start button and type **word** (or **winword** if you need additional parameters or switches) into the Search programs and files text box, and then click the entry for Word under Programs.

Safe Mode

Any time you start Word, you have the option of starting it in safe mode. You might want to do this for a variety of reasons, including the following:

- Word experienced problems and you're trying to diagnose them.
- You need to observe Word's default behavior to help someone else.
- You need to suppress a Word add-in, for whatever reason.
- You're curious about something (my own personal favorite).

To start Word in safe mode, simply hold down the Ctrl key, start Word by double-clicking a desktop shortcut icon or taskbar button for the program (it doesn't work with the Windows 8 Start screen tile), and continue holding the Ctrl key until the dialog box shown in Figure 1.3 appears. Click Yes to continue starting in safe mode.

FIGURE 1.3

Hold down the Ctrl key to start Word in safe mode.

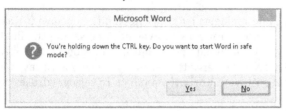

Starting Word in safe mode suppresses a number of Word options and Windows registry settings. Word also does not load add-ins or user settings stored in the default document template `Normal.dotm`. The idea is to prevent user and other customizations from interfering with Word's default behavior. This can be useful in circumstances from diagnosing problems to writing books and articles about Word in which you don't want to confuse your own customizations with Word's normal built-in defaults.

When you are in safe mode, *(Safe Mode)* appears in the program title bar. To leave safe mode, exit Word as described in the final section of this chapter, and then restart Word normally.

> **NOTE**
>
> Starting Word in safe mode is not the same as starting Word using the /a command-line switch. More on this in Appendix A.

The Office Look

In redesigning Windows 8, Microsoft incorporated a sleeker look that would be at home on either tablets or PCs, greater integration with cloud-based features such as SkyDrive, and even more social media functionality. You don't have to spend much time working in the new Word to find that it follows the lead of Windows 8:

- **Sleeker look:** As shown in Figure 1.4, Word's title bar has eliminated the previous 3-D look in favor of flat tabs and a customizable Office Background graphic. The status bar likewise is strictly 2-D and easier to read. The upper-right corner of the screen has an icon you can click to see Ribbon Display Options; for example, clicking Auto-hide the Ribbon puts away all of the onscreen tools and shows you your document head on. Similarly, a new Read Mode displays a document in a format more comfortable for "paging" through it rather than editing. (Read Mode and the Ribbon Display Options are discussed more in Chapter 2, "Diving Into Document Creation.")

FIGURE 1.4

Word's sleek new look helps you focus on your documents.

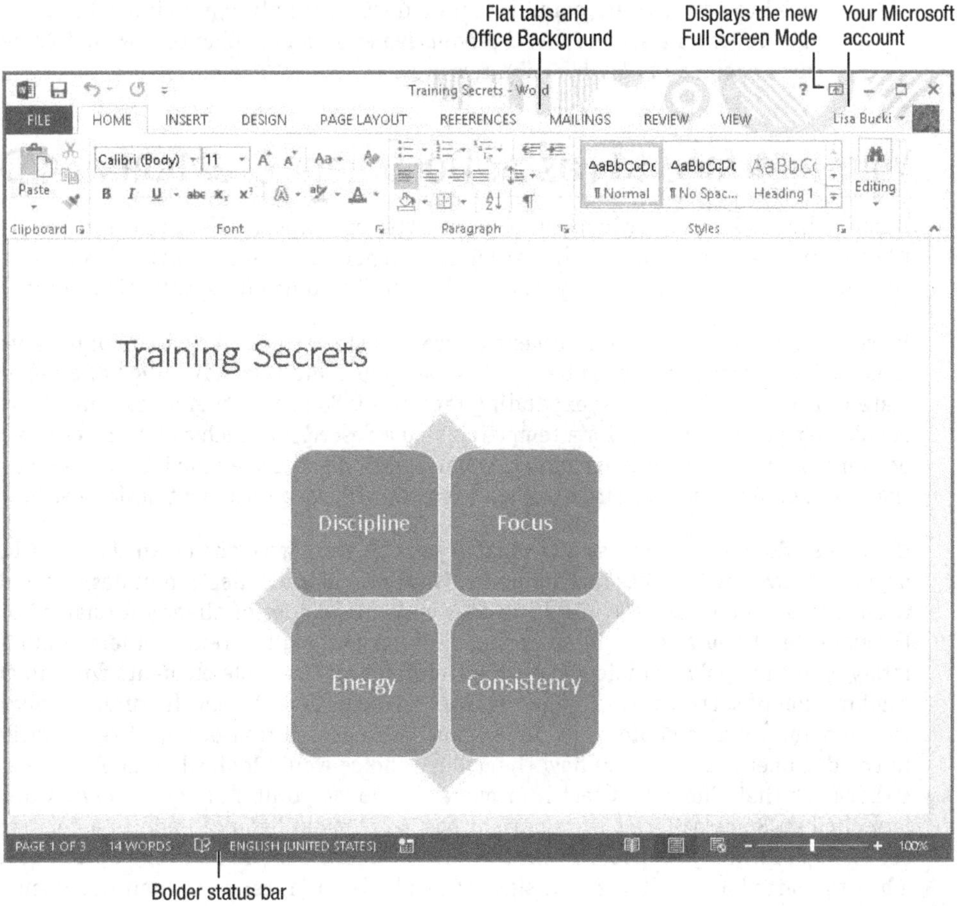

Flat tabs and Office Background

Displays the new Full Screen Mode

Your Microsoft account

Bolder status bar

- **Cloud integration:** The upper-right corner of Figure 1.4 also illustrates that the Microsoft account (or other applicable account type) you use to sign in to Word appears, along with any picture assigned to the account. This means you can save and open documents directly to and from the account's SkyDrive, a feature you'll learn more about in Chapter 2 and Chapter 27, "Collaborating in the Cloud with SkyDrive." Other new features tie into the cloud independent of your account. For example, the new Insert Online Pictures feature enables you to find and add images from Office.com Clip Art, Bing Image Search, or your SkyDrive to a document. Chapter 14, "Adding Pictures and WordArt to Highlight Information," covers the details of this more flexible way to find document images.

- **Social media functions:** The Insert Online Pictures feature also enables you to insert pictures from a Flickr account associated with your Microsoft account. Just

11

make the connection when prompted, and pictures you've shared to Flickr will be available for use in Word documents. And you can more easily share a document saved to your SkyDrive and present a document online, making collaboration with your contacts a seamless and productive experience. Chapters 14 and 27 delve into these social and collaboration features.

Your Interface to Faster Document Creation and Design

If you're like most users, when you begin a letter or a report, the first thing you do is check whether you've ever created a similar letter or report. If you have written and formatted a similar document, then you very likely will open it and use it as a starting point.

However, even if you have a document to use as a starting point, you are only recycling the same look and feel you've used before. Instead, you could take advantage of an existing template in Microsoft Word's ever-expanding repertoire. You can either select one of the more popular templates or search for a template using a description such as letter, resume, brochure, or event planner. Chapter 2 explains how you can find and use a template to create a document that has a professional appearance, even if you don't have a document design background.

If you also do not want to use a template, you can start with the clean slate of a blank document. Even with that starting point, Word provides a collection of designs and tools to save time and guesswork. Word includes built-in *galleries* of already formatted options. For example, if you create a table, rather than formatting the text, borders, and fills separately, you can apply a single table style to format all the table elements with an attractive combination of settings. Most galleries work with the *Live Preview* feature. Simply move the mouse pointer over a choice in a gallery, and the selected text or object temporarily morphs in the document to show you how the gallery choice would look when applied. You can either click that choice to select it or move the mouse pointer along to preview other gallery choices. Some galleries even present special elements you can add to a document page. For example, when you insert a text box into a document, you have the option of inserting a box formatted as a pull quote or sidebar to add design interest to your document. You'll learn about the numerous galleries throughout later chapters in this book.

Word continues to streamline the number of tools onscreen at any time to help you achieve results quickly, rather than combing through myriad tabs and commands to discover possibilities. Depending on what you select onscreen, one or more new *contextual tabs* of options appears. For example, if a picture is selected, the Picture Tools' Format subtab appears on the Ribbon, as shown in Figure 1.5. It offers, among other tools, a gallery of styles for formatting the selected picture, and a preview of the style under the mouse pointer appears for the selected picture. Details about the various contextual tabs appear where applicable throughout the book.

Finally, Word 2013 retains the most powerful design tool of all: themes. The theme defines the document color scheme, fonts, and effects. Changing the theme changes the look of the entire document. Chapter 18, "Saving Time with Templates, Themes, and Master Documents," provides the details about working with themes.

FIGURE 1.5

The Format contextual tab or subtab presents picture formatting options, including a gallery of styles.

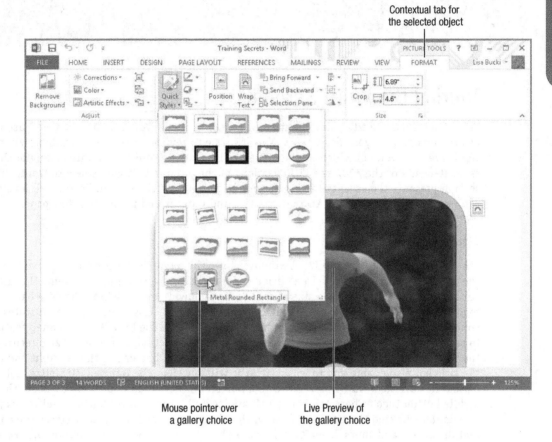

Contextual tab for
the selected object

Mouse pointer over
a gallery choice

Live Preview of
the gallery choice

Using the Word Start Screen

When you first start Word 2013, you'll see a new feature called the Start screen. The Start screen is basically divided into two panes. At the left, you can click a file in the Recent list—which contains files you've worked with in recent Word work sessions—to open it immediately. Or, you can click Open Other Documents below the recent list to navigate to various storage locations and open an existing file. See "Opening an Existing File" in Chapter 2. Finally, you can use the gallery of templates at right to choose a template, as described in "Creating a File from a Template" in Chapter 2. For now, if you're interested in seeing Word's tools, you can click Blank document in the templates at the to open a blank file and look around.

Touring the Word Screen

This chapter has already pointed out a few elements of the Word screen that you'll use to create and enhance your documents. Now it's time to review all the tools available via the Word screen, several of which are identified in Figure 1.6. Word 2013 retains many of the same elements of the 2007 and 2010 versions of the programs. If you're new to Word, this section presents the essential roadmap to help you around the screen. Users of all levels can have an Aha! moment or two via the tips and notes found in the next few pages.

Title bar

The *title bar* at the top of the Word window shows the name of the current document and the program, as in Figure 1.6. In addition to identifying the working document, the title bar enables you to control the size of the Word window. Double-clicking the title bar toggles Word between *maximized* (full screen) and *restored* (less than full screen) states. If you've set your screen to a fairly high resolution and have used the Windows Snap feature to snap a screen to full size or half-screen size, double-clicking the title bar also returns the window to its prior size. The three application control buttons at the far-right end of the title bar also enable you to work with the window size. The left one, Minimize, collapses the current Word window down to a button on the Windows desktop taskbar. The middle button toggles between being a Maximize and Restore Down button, and works just like double-clicking the title bar. Finally, the Close button at the far right closes the current document and shuts down Word if that's the only open document. Pressing Alt+F4 also closes the document window. You also can right-click the title bar to see commands for sizing the window. And, if the window is less than full screen size, dragging a window border resizes the window.

FIGURE 1.6

Word screen elements

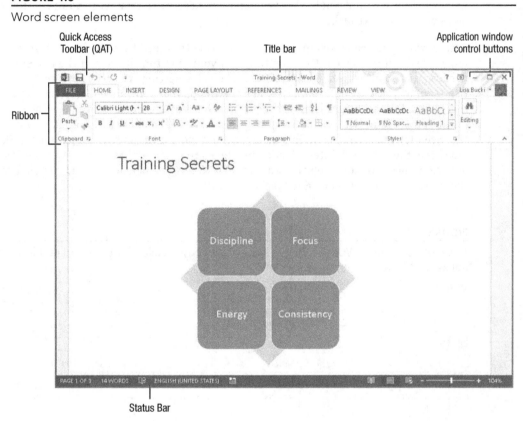

The far-left button at the right end of the title bar is the Help button, with the question mark on it. Clicking it opens Word's Help function, which you'll learn more about at the end of the chapter.

Ribbon

The *Ribbon* appears just below the title bar and is organized to put the tool you need where you need it when you need it. When you click one of the major *tabs* on the Ribbon, the tools you need for specific tasks related to the tab name appear. For example, click the Insert tab to find commands for inserting tables, pictures, and other graphics into a document. Click the Page Layout tab to find choices for setting up the document overall, click the View tab to change views and find other screen settings, and so on. The tabs offer buttons for commands, as well as drop-down menus of settings such as formatting choices, galleries of styles, and other formatting options, as has already been touched on in this chapter.

Each Ribbon tab further offers groups containing related commands. For example, all of the commands for formatting paragraphs appear in the Paragraph group on the Home tab.

Groups help you drill down to the command you need more rapidly, so you can click and move on to the next task.

Exactly what you see in any given Ribbon tab is determined by a number of factors, including your screen resolution, the orientation of your monitor, the size of the current Word window, and whether you're using Windows' display settings to accommodate low vision. Hence, what you see might not always be what is pictured in this book. If your screen is set to a fairly high resolution, you will see the entirety of the Home tab of the Ribbon, shown in the top of Figure 1.7. The bottom image shows the Ribbon at the lower 1024×768 resolution used for the screen shots in this book. You'll notice in the top image that the Home tab shows the Format Painter label in the Clipboard group and more styles in the Styles gallery. At an even higher resolution and/or with Word stretched across multiple monitors, the Home tab would show even more labels and styles.

FIGURE 1.7

At a high resolution, Word's Ribbon displays additional gallery options and text labels (top) not seen at lower resolutions (bottom).

Note that you can customize the tabs that appear on the Ribbon. For example, if you want to create macros to handle certain document formatting tasks for you, you would need to display the Developer tab. Or you may want to hide tabs that you seldom use, such as the Mailings or Review tab. Chapter 30, "Customizing the Quick Access Toolbar and Ribbon," explains how to set up the Ribbon to suit your own needs.

To see what any individual control or command on a Ribbon tab does, simply move the mouse pointer over it. A ScreenTip pops up with a description of the tool. Move the mouse pointer away from the button to hide the ScreenTip.

Ribbon groups

At the bottom of the Home tab shown in Figure 1.7, note the names Clipboard, Font, and Paragraph. These labels identify the command *groups*. Each contains individual tools or controls. You can customize the groups that appear on any Ribbon tab. For example, you might want to add a group that collects all of your most-used commands in a single location. You'll also learn more about this level of customization in Chapter 30.

> **NOTE**
>
> Throughout this book, you may see command shortcuts such as Insert ⇨ Header & Footer ⇨ Header. These Ribbon tab name ⇨ group ⇨ command sequences help you navigate through the Ribbon to find and choose the appropriate command. When referencing contextual tabs, an arrow will also appear between the upper part of the contextual tab name and the subtab, as in Picture Tools ⇨ Format. After the first mention in a chapter, the text may refer to the contextual tab by its subtab name only, that is, Format rather than Picture Tools ⇨ Format.

Contextual tabs

Along with the default set of seven main tabs, additional context-sensitive or *contextual tabs* or subtabs appear depending on what you are working on in the document. For example, if you change to Outline view, the Outlining toolbar, with commands for changing outline levels and more, automatically appears to the left of the Home tab. In other instances, a contextual tab might appear when you select part of a document or an object such as a table. For example, if you choose Insert ⇨ Header & Footer ⇨ Header and insert a header from the Header gallery, the Header & Footer Tools ⇨ Design contextual tab appears, as shown in Figure 1.8.

FIGURE 1.8

When you work with the header, the Header & Footer Tools ⇨ Design contextual tab and its commands appears.

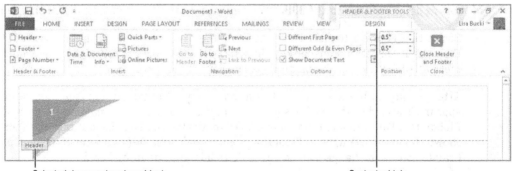

Selected document part or object   Contextual tab

Notice that the right end of the contextual tab in Figure 1.9 has a Close group with a button for closing the tab. Some contextual tabs have such a button, and you have to use it to close the contextual tab. In the case of the Design subtab in Figure 1.8 and many other contextual tabs related to a selected object, you also can deselect or click outside the object, which closes the contextual tab automatically.

In some cases, multiple contextual tabs might appear. For example, when you select a table in a document, the Table Tools appear, with Design and Layout subtabs, as shown in Figure 1.9. In this instance, click a subtab to display its tools. For example, click the Design contextual tab to find the table design choices, or click the Layout contextual tab to find commands for changing the table's layout.

FIGURE 1.9

Selecting some objects, such as tables, displays multiple contextual tabs.

Command keyboard shortcuts or KeyTips

While many users can move fluidly between using the mouse or the keyboard, for the best typists, doing so can actually be a hindrance that slows them down. For such users, shortcut key combinations provide a way to handle formatting tasks and select commands without taking their hands off the keyboard.

In Word 2013 the command shortcut keys are called *KeyTips*, and some users also refer to keyboard shortcuts as hot keys. The keyboard shortcuts remain hidden until you need them. Press the Alt key on the keyboard to reveal them. As shown in Figure 1.10, when you press Alt the letters for selecting the Ribbon tabs and Quick Access Toolbar (QAT) commands appear. From there, you would press the keyboard key for the Ribbon tab you want to display. For example, pressing Alt+H displays the Home tab, Alt+N displays the Insert tab, and so on. The choices on the QAT are numbered rather than lettered, so you would press Alt+1 to select the first button there, Alt+2 the second one, and so on. Note that if you add more choices to the QAT as described later in the book, Word will automatically assign a keyboard shortcut.

Notice that Figure 1.10 also shows the Table Tools ⇨ Design and Layout contextual tabs. Each has a two-letter shortcut key. To display the Design contextual tab, you would need to press Alt+J,T. Pressing Alt+J,L displays the Layout contextual tab.

After you press Alt + a letter to select a tab, a new set of letters and (sometimes) numbers appears. These identify the keys you need to press to choose a command from the displayed Ribbon tab. For example, if you press Alt+P to display the Page Layout tab, the shortcuts shown in Figure 1.11 appear. From there, you could press O if you want to change page Orientation, M to change page Margins, IL to add an Indent, and so on.

TIP

After you press Alt and then a letter to select a Ribbon tab, you can press Tab and Shift+Tab to move forward and backward between the commands on that tab. When you've highlighted the command you want to use, press either the Spacebar or Enter key.

FIGURE 1.10

Press the Alt key to display Word's command keyboard shortcuts.

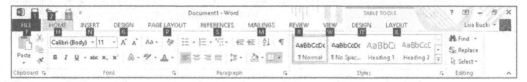

FIGURE 1.11

After you press Alt + a letter to select a Ribbon tab, press the next shortcut keys to select a command.

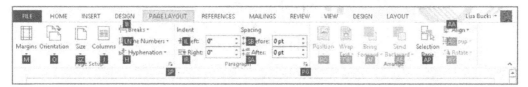

If you decide not to use a shortcut after you've displayed the keys onscreen, no problem. Just press Alt again, click a blank area with the mouse, or press the Esc key once or twice to remove them from the screen.

NOTE

Word also includes an extensive collection of keyboard shortcuts for selecting document text and navigating in a document. You'll learn about these in Chapter 2.

Quick Access Toolbar

I mentioned earlier that you can add a group to the Ribbon to collect all your favorite commands in a single easy-access location. Another and perhaps even faster way to accomplish this goal is to add your favorite commands to the *Quick Access Toolbar*, or *QAT*. The QAT remains onscreen no matter which Ribbon tab is displayed, so any commands on the QAT are available at all times.

By default, the QAT has buttons for three commands: Save, Undo, and Redo. In Figure 1.12, I've moved the QAT below the Ribbon, so you can see these default buttons from left to right respectively. Note that the Redo button is unavailable (grayed out) until you perform an action that Word can repeat. Also, if you move the mouse pointer over the Undo and Redo buttons to see a ScreenTip, the ScreenTip name of each of those buttons changes depending on your last action. For example, the Redo button ScreenTip might read "Repeat Typing."

As shown in Figure 1.12, clicking the Customize Quick Access Toolbar button at the right end of the QAT opens a menu of options for setting up the QAT. You can use the choices above the line on the menu to toggle commands on and off, choose More Commands to access all of the Word commands, or determine whether the QAT appears above or below the Ribbon.

FIGURE 1.12

The Quick Access Toolbar (QAT) always appears, no matter which Ribbon tab you've selected.

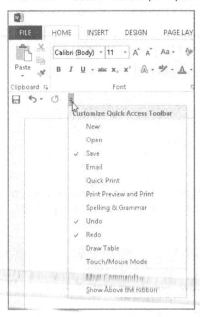

You can add any item from the Ribbon—individual tools, groups, and even dialog box launchers—to the QAT without opening the Customize Quick Access Toolbar menu. For example, right-click Bold in the Font group of the Home tab and choose Add to Quick Access Toolbar. If you add a command such as Bold to the QAT and want to remove it later, right-click it and click Remove from Quick Access Toolbar.

Galleries and Live Preview

In Word and the other Office applications, a *gallery* is a set of formatting results or preformatted document parts. Virtually every set of formatting results or document parts in Word 2013 (indeed, in all of Office 2013) might be called a gallery, although Word itself does not use the word gallery to refer to every feature set. Some, such as the list of bullets, are called *libraries* instead, and the drop-down galleries for selecting colors also may be called color pickers.

Word includes galleries for text styles, themes, headers, footers, page colors, tables, WordArt, equations, symbols, and more. In most cases, you click a button or drop-down arrow to open a gallery, and then click the gallery choice to apply to the selected text or object. Galleries often work hand in hand with the Live Preview feature.

Live Preview temporarily applies the highlighted gallery choice to the current document selection, enabling you to instantly see the results without actually having to apply that formatting, as shown in Figure 1.13. Move the mouse pointer over the different gallery options to display the formatting on the document selection instantly.

FIGURE 1.13

Live Preview showing the Quote style applied to the selected paragraph

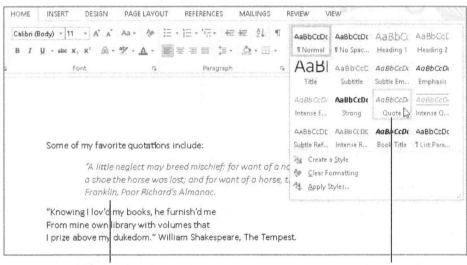

Live Preview of the Quote style   Mouse pointer over the Quote style

Note that not all galleries and formatting options have Live Preview enabled. For example, on the Page Layout tab, none of the Page Setup items produce live previews, nor do its Paragraph group settings. Another time you won't see Live Preview is when working with dialog boxes, such as the Paragraph dialog box. Many of those offer internal Preview areas but do not take advantage of Office 2013's Live Preview capability.

A gotcha in all this newfangled functionality is that sometimes the gallery itself covers up all or part of the Live Preview. This gets old quickly and can negate much of Live Preview's functionality, unless you're blessed with lots of screen real estate.

Fortunately, some galleries and controls have draggable borders that enable you to see more of what you're trying to preview, as shown in Figure 1.14. A handle with four dots indicates when you can resize a control's border by dragging up. If a gallery has three dots in the lower-right corner, that means you resize both its height and width by dragging diagonally.

Once you've determined through Live Preview that you want to apply particular formatting, click the choice in the gallery. If necessary, you can always use the venerable Ctrl+Z (Undo) if you don't like the result.

FIGURE 1.14

Some galleries can be resized to reveal the Live Preview that otherwise would be covered.

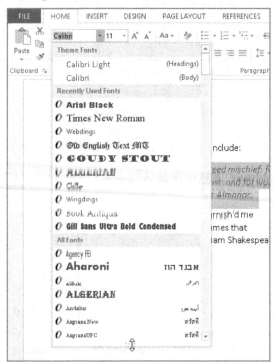

The MiniBar or Mini Toolbar

Another feature in Word 2013 is the *MiniBar,* more formally known as the *Mini Toolbar.* The MiniBar is a set of formatting tools that appears when you first select text. It is not context-sensitive, and it always contains an identical set of formatting tools. There is no MiniBar for graphics and other nontext objects.

When you first select text, the MiniBar appears above and to the right of the mouse pointer, as shown in Figure 1.15. If you move the mouse pointer off the selection, the MiniBar disappears.

FIGURE 1.15

The MiniBar appears when text is first selected.

When the Home tab is selected, the MiniBar might seem superfluous, as all of the MiniBar's commands also appear on that tab. However, consider for a moment how far the mouse has to travel to access the Ribbon commands. With the MiniBar, you only have to move the mouse less than an inch or so to move the pointer to the command you need. For those with repetitive motion injuries, this can save a lot of wear and tear on the wrist.

If you decide that the MiniBar gets in the way, you can turn it off. Even when it is turned off, however, you can still summon it by right-clicking the current selection. If you want to turn the Mini Toolbar off, click the File tab on the Ribbon, and then click Options. Leave the General tab selected in the list at the left, and under User Interface options, click to remove the check beside Show Mini Toolbar on Selection. Click OK to apply the change.

> **NOTE**
>
> Unlike many Ribbon tools, the MiniBar tools do not produce Live Previews of formatting and other effects. If you need to see a Live Preview, use the Ribbon instead.

Shortcut menus and contextual command buttons

If navigating through all the Ribbon tabs still seems like a lot of work to you, Word's *shortcut menus*, also called contextual or pop-up menus, remain. To display a shortcut menu, just select text or an object such as a picture in the document, and right-click or press the menu key on your keyboard. As shown in Figure 1.16, the shortcut menu offers the commands you're most likely to use next for the selected item.

FIGURE 1.16

When you right-click a selection, a context-sensitive shortcut menu appears, along with the MiniBar.

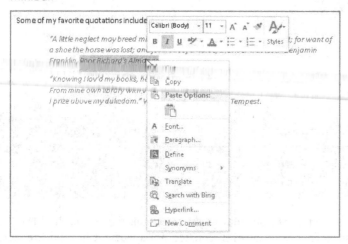

Word 2013 adds a new form of contextual tools to speed your work with some document objects, particularly on a touch-enabled system. When you select some types of objects, such as a chart, one or more contextual buttons will appear to the right of the object. Clicking some of these buttons opens a flyout gallery or formatting options for the selection, as shown in Figure 1.17. Clicking other buttons opens a flyout list of choices that you can click to toggle on and off, as shown in Figure 1.18. Simply click the desired choice in either type of flyout, or deselect the object to hide the buttons.

FIGURE 1.17

New contextual command buttons appear when you select certain objects, such as a chart.

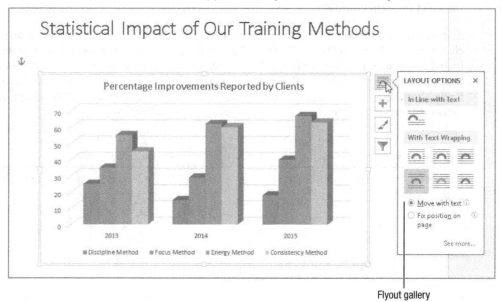

Flyout gallery

FIGURE 1.18

Clicking some of the buttons opens a gallery, as shown in the prior figure, or a list of toggled options, as shown here.

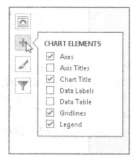

Enhanced ScreenTips

Word 2013 includes the enhanced ScreenTips feature. By default, the ScreenTips for the Ribbon tools and many other screen elements include not just the item name but also a feature description. Enhanced ScreenTips help you find the right tool more quickly and reduce the need to search for help.

A ScreenTip appears when you hover the mouse pointer over a Ribbon command or other choice on the Word interface. Figure 1.19 shows an example. Notice that the ScreenTip includes a shortcut key combination for choosing the specified item. You can customize the ScreenTips by turning off the shortcut key display, turning off the feature description for smaller ScreenTips, or turning off ScreenTips altogether. Chapter 31, "Word Options and Settings," covers setting these and other options throughout Word.

FIGURE 1.19

Enhanced ScreenTips include the name and description for a command or other tool.

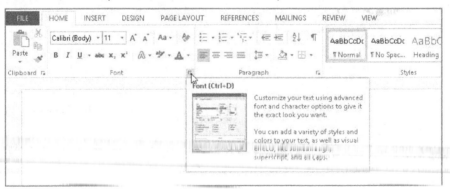

Dialog boxes and launchers

To the right of some group names, a small box button with a diagonal arrow appears. This button is a *dialog box launcher*. Clicking a dialog box launcher opens a dialog box with more detailed options for the commands in the group. For example, if you click the dialog box launcher for the Home tab's Paragraph group, the Paragraph dialog box opens. Point to any dialog box launcher to display a ScreenTip explaining what it does, as illustrated in Figure 1.19 in the previous section.

Clicking the dialog box launcher shown in Figure 1.19 opens the Font dialog box shown in Figure 1.20. Dialog boxes offer scrolling lists, drop-down lists, text boxes, check boxes, option buttons, command buttons, and other controls familiar to most computer users. You can click Cancel to close a dialog box without applying settings, or OK to finalize and apply your choices.

FIGURE 1.20

Dialog boxes enable you to refine formatting and other commands using familiar controls.

Task panes or panes

Similar to dialog boxes, *task panes* (now in Word 2013 more often simply referred to as *panes*) appear onscreen to help you navigate, perform research, apply formatting, and more. Think of them as dialog boxes that enable you to type while they're onscreen. Some of the panes open when you select a particular command such as the Thesaurus, while you toggle others such as the Navigation pane on and off as you work in Word. Still others appear when you select certain items for formatting, such as when you double-click a chart title. Figure 1.21 shows the Format Chart Title pane.

Some task panes appear docked on the left or right side of the document window, whereas others automatically appear undocked. You can undock a pane by pointing to its title until you see a four-arrow move mouse pointer, and then drag it to the desired location with the mouse. Double-click a floating pane's title bar to return it to its docked position. You can display and size multiple task panes onscreen at any time. To close a pane, you can click its Close (X) button at the upper right, or in some cases reselect the command you used to toggle it on.

Other Word features that manifest as task panes include the Navigation pane, the Mail Merge Wizard, Restrict Editing, Dictionary, the Clipboard, and the Reviewing Pane, among others. Later chapters of the book introduce the various panes and when they come into action.

FIGURE 1.21

Word's task panes make commands available while still enabling you to type and make selections in the document.

Status bar

Now we turn to the status bar. Shown in Figure 1.22, the status bar is the bar at the bottom of the Word window. The status bar provides more than 20 optional pieces of information about the current document. Right-click the status bar to display its configuration options.

Do you need to keep track of the word count? Not only does Word update the word count continuously, but if you select text, it tells you how many words are selected, with one of the indicators near the left end of the status bar changing to read *39 OF 69 WORDS* or something similar.

To display the configuration choices shown in Figure 1.22, right-click the status bar. At the top and bottom of the shortcut menu, you can choose options to specify what indicators appear at the left and what view controls appear at the right. In between, it presents choices for turning features such as Track Changes or Overtype on and off. Then close the menu to apply your changes by clicking in the document or pressing Esc.

FIGURE 1.22

Customize the status bar and control several features with the status bar shortcut menu.

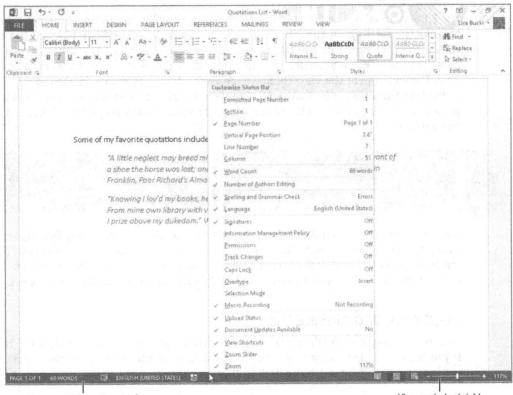

Document information at left   View controls at right

Exploring the File Tab

The File tab in all of the Office 2013 apps works a bit differently than the other tabs. That's because the settings on the File tab enable you to manage the file itself, not the contents within the file, more like the File menu in Word 2003 and other applications with a menu-based interface. When you click the File tab, it displays what is sometimes called *Backstage view*. The contents of the view change depending on the command selected at left; initially it displays the Info choices shown in Figure 1.23. This screen lets you view and add file properties, as well as work with document protection, hidden properties, document issues, and versions.

NOTE

Backstage view is also sometimes just called the "File tab."

Clicking most of the commands along the left side of the File tab—Info, New, Open, Save, Save As, Print, Share, Export, Close, Account, and Options—causes the right pane of the screen to display the choices for that category. For example, if you click Share, as shown in Figure 1.24, options for presenting and publishing a document in the cloud appear.

Displaying and closing the tab

As noted, displaying the File tab is as easy as clicking any other tab. Just click the tab itself. If you decide you don't want to use any of the choices on the File tab and need to return to editing your document, click the Back (left arrow) button at the upper left, or press Esc.

CAUTION

If you click the Close (X) button in the upper-right corner, Word not only closes the File tab, but closes itself, too, which is probably not what you want.

FIGURE 1.23

Manage your file with the File tab choices.

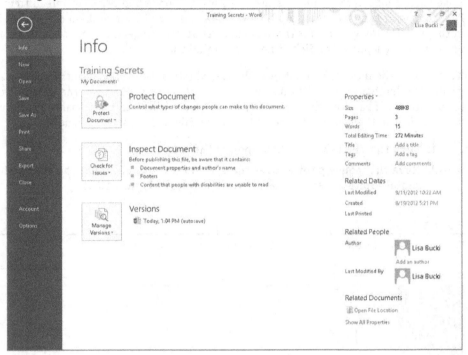

FIGURE 1.24

A cornucopia of online options is found in the Share tab.

Finding recent documents and pinning

Some users might have documents that they want to open and revise or reread frequently. For example, if you have a hot project for a new client and your work on the project is due in the near future, you'll want those documents at your fingertips rather than having to navigate around your hard disk or network to find them.

Word gathers the files you've most recently opened into a Recent Documents list. You can simply display that list via the File tab, and click a file to open it. However, the Recent Documents list updates itself based on the files you open. To ensure quick access to a particular document, you can *pin* it to the Recent Documents list on the File ⇨ Open screen. To do that:

1. **Click the File tab, and click Open at the left.**
2. **Move the mouse pointer over the file you want to pin until you see the horizontal Pin this item to the list icon, shown in Figure 1.25.**

FIGURE 1.25

Pinning a file in Recent Documents gives you fast access.

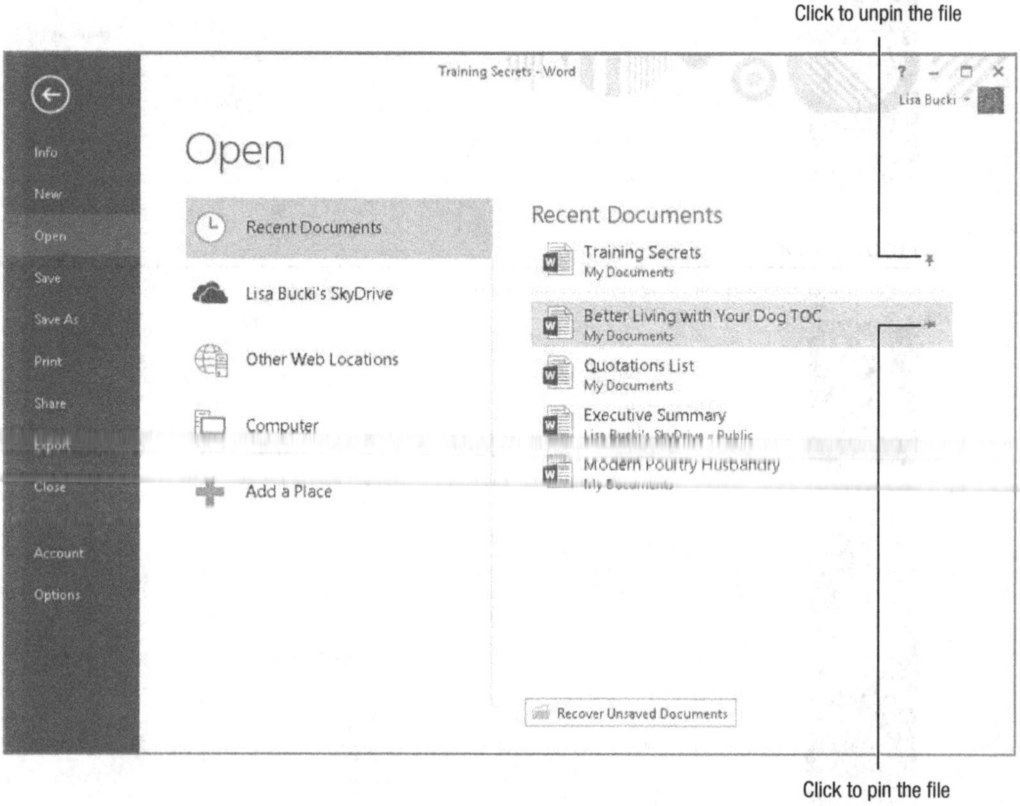

Click to unpin the file

Click to pin the file

3. **Click the Pin this item to the list icon.** The file moves above the line separating pinned and unpinned files, and the pin icon changes to a vertical Unpin this item from the list icon.

Chapter 2 provides more information about using the File menu to open an existing file.

NOTE

You will only see the Other Web Locations choice shown in the middle under Open in Figure 1.25 if you have downloaded and opened a Word document directly from a Web site. If needed you can click Other Web Locations and then click a choice under Recent Folders to re-download the file.

Undoing and Redoing Actions

Figures 1.6 and 1.12 show the Quick Access Toolbar. By default, the QAT has buttons for three commands: Save, Undo, and Redo. As their names suggest, Undo and Redo enable you to rescue your progress if you inadvertently slip up while working. Here's how they work:

- **Undo:** Click the Undo button or press Ctrl+Z immediately to rescind a prior action. For example, if you mistakenly delete some text, the name of the Undo button changes to "Undo Clear," and clicking the button reinstates the text.

- **Redo:** The Redo button is unavailable (grayed out) until you perform an action that Word can repeat. When it's active, click it or press Ctrl+Y to Redo the prior action. Note that the shape and the name of this button change. When it's a round arrow shape, it's called the Repeat button, and clicking it repeats an action such as entering a word you just typed again (in which case the button name is "Repeat Typing). When it's the mirror image of the Undo button, it's the Redo button and clicking it redoes any action you just undid.

- **Multiple undo or redo:** The Undo and Redo buttons both include drop-down list buttons. Click the button to display a list of previously undone or redone actions, and then click an action in the list to undo/redo that action and all the ones listed above it.

Setting Word Options

Word 2013 offers a centralized dialog box for changing Word options. Most beginning users don't need to dive into customizing their Word setup. However, because chapters throughout this book refer to various Word options, take a moment now to familiarize yourself with where the options are and how they are organized. To open Word Options, choose File ⇨ Options to open the dialog box shown in Figure 1.26.

FIGURE 1.31

The Word Options dialog box groups options by category.

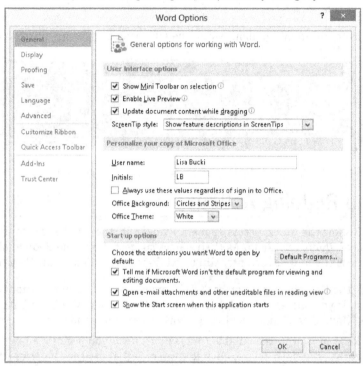

> **NOTE**
>
> I've had to resize the Word window and some dialog box windows to a narrower width to accommodate the book design. The Word Options dialog box will appear much wider for you when you open it.

Finding the option you want

Word's Options dialog has 10 sections, or tabs, on the left. Do not be fooled by the labels Note that one of the tabs is called Advanced. Microsoft's idea of *advanced* might not be the same as yours. What's optional for someone else might be essential for you.

Microsoft's logic is to try to put at the top of the list the controls and options it thinks you are most likely to want to change. The first set, General, is therefore the group it thinks will matter most to the typical user. If you're reading the *Microsoft Word 2013 Bible*, however, you might not be a typical user. Keep this in mind as you look at the 10 tabs.

Another caveat is that the labels aren't even objectively accurate. For example, there is a tab labeled Display. If you don't find the display option you're looking for there, don't give up. Some display options actually reside in General, such as Show Mini Toolbar on selection, Enable Live Preview, and Open e-mail attachments and other uneditable files in reading view.

A number of display options are also sheltered under the Advanced umbrella, including great favorites such as the Show document content options, the Display options (duh!), and Provide feedback with animation (under General). If you're keeping track, there's a General tab, and there's a General section within the Advanced tab. Options are covered in more detail in Chapter 31, but you can also discover a lot of options simply by taking a little time to explore the various tabs.

TIP

If an information icon (an *i* in a circle) appears to the right of one of the Word options, you can point to the icon to display a ScreenTip with more information about the option.

Advanced...versus not advanced?

The Advanced tab, partially shown in Figure 1.27, has 13 major sections. Also depending on how you count, the Advanced tab offers more than 150 different settings, including the Layout options.

Scroll down the Advanced tab a bit, and you can see both the Save and Preserve fidelity when sharing this document sections at the same time. While "Prompt before saving Normal template" seems pretty clear as an option name, others such as "Embed linguistic data" might trip most people up. You can press F1 or click the ? icon at the upper-right corner of the window to use the Help system to search for more information about an option. A section later in this chapter, "Getting Help," explains how to use Help.

TIP

In many instances, but not always, you can find help on what you want by typing the exact feature name (e.g., "embed linguistic data") into the Search box.

FIGURE 1.27

Word's Advanced options contain over 150 settings.

Switching Accounts

As you learned earlier in the chapter, Word is set up to work with the Microsoft account you use to sign on to Windows 8 so that you can take full advantage of cloud features such as SkyDrive, and be able to access your information no matter what device you're using. You may need to work with multiple online accounts in Word to access different storage locations, email accounts, or social media accounts. Or you may want to have separate accounts for work and personal information. Here's a brief description of how to add and select accounts in Word.

Even if you have Windows 8 (or even Windows 7) set up with multiple user accounts, Word by default only uses the one that you were first signed on to when you started and set up the program. If you have other Microsoft accounts already set up with Outlook.com or Live.com and need to switch the account you're using in Word for the first time, follow these steps:

1. **Click your user name at the upper-right corner of the Word window, and then click Switch account.**

2. **In the Sign in to Office box, click either Personal or Organization or School.** If you need to sign in with your Office365 user name, click Organization or School. As discussed in Chapter 27, signing in with your Office365 credentials enables you to use SkyDrive Pro to sync files with your online library or access your Office365 team SharePoint online.

3. **Enter your user name and password at the Sign in screen that appears, and then click Sign in.** Your new account information appears.

After you switch accounts the first time during a work session, Word "remembers" the previous account you used and makes switching easier. When you click your user name and click Switch account, Word displays an Account window with your Current account and a list of Other accounts. Click the desired account under Other accounts to switch back to that account without having to re-enter your sign-in information.

Getting Help

Word retains a hybrid Help system to keep you up and running with your work. While some information is installed with Word on your hard disk, most of the information resides online, so for all practical purposes, you need an Internet connection to ensure you can access the specific Help that you need.

Starting Help is easy: either press the F1 key or click the Microsoft Word Help (?) button near the upper-right corner of the Word window. If you want to browse through Help, start by clicking one of the major topics on the home Help screen shown in Figure 1.28, and then click additional links from there to navigate to a specific topic. Or, to jump more directly to a list of topics that potentially addresses your issue, click in the Search help text box, type a search word or phrase, and press Enter or click the Search help (magnifying glass) icon at the right end of the text box. Then you can click and read a topic in the search results.

To return to the home Help contents at any time, click the Home button that looks like a house. Click the window's Close (X) button to close Help.

FIGURE 1.28

You can browse Help by topic or search for what you need.

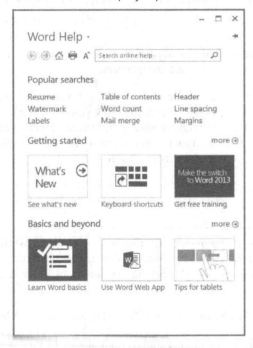

Exiting Word

When you finish working in Word, it's a good practice to close the app just to keep your desktop clutter free. You can use one of these methods to shut down Word:

- Click the File tab, and click Close.
- Click the Word window's Close (X) button at the upper right.
- Press Alt+F4.

If you haven't saved your most recent changes to the document, a dialog box prompts you to do so. Click Save or Don't Save as desired.

TIP

The close methods just close the current document window. If you have multiple Word documents open and want to close them all at once, right-click Word's taskbar icon, and click Close all windows.

Summary

This chapter gave you your first tour of Word 2013. You learned the numerous ways you can start the program and make sure you're signed in with the proper Microsoft account. You've seen how Word has been updated with a sleek, modern look that mirrors other newer Windows 8 apps, while retaining familiar commands and functions like the Ribbon and File tab. The chapter helped you find Word's options for the first time, and you learned how to switch accounts, get help, and exit the program when you finish working. You should now be able to:

- Start and exit Word in Windows 7 and Windows 8
- Identify the key parts of the Word screen
- Use the Ribbon and other Word tools such as panes and dialog boxes
- Undo and redo actions
- Sign in to Word
- Navigate in Help

Diving Into Document Creation

IN THIS CHAPTER

Walking through a document from start to finish

Making a new blank file or using a template

Reopening a saved document

Saving a document

Reviewing file formats and compatibility issues

Navigating in a document and selecting text

Using Word's various views

Making a document hard copy

When a coach teaches someone a new sport, he or she starts with the fundamentals. Eager students often want to skip the basics—especially when in a rush to be productive with new software—and what they miss out on learning now can trip them up later. The first section in this chapter gives a nod to your need to get up and running quickly in Word, showing you how to write and print a letter and envelope in 15 minutes or less. From there, the chapter moves on to discuss the essential skills that will serve you well every time you work with Word 2013. If you're new to Word, this chapter makes getting started painless. If you've been using Word for years, you may not only pick up some tricks you previously missed, but also get an introduction to a few new features in the latest version of Word. You also explore creating files, saving and reopening files, navigating in the text and making selections, viewing variations, and making a printout.

Creating a First Document

If your computer is connected to the Internet, as is more and more the case as high-speed and wireless connections proliferate, you can take advantage of a robust collection of professionally designed online documents to help you create a document. Using one of those as a head start, you can create a terrific-looking document such as a letter in 15 minutes or less. Follow the steps in this section to see how quickly you can get results and create your first document in Word 2013.

Creating and saving a new letter and envelope

The first part of this process involves starting up Word 2013, choosing a template to use for the document, and saving and naming your file. You'll learn about both templates and saving in greater depth later in the chapter, so just relax and follow the steps here for now.

1. **Start Word using the method of your choice as described in Chapter 1, "Taking Your First Steps with Word."** For example, in Windows 8 you can click the Word 2013 tile on the Start screen or use the Search charm to find it. In Windows 7, click Start ⇨ All Programs ⇨ Microsoft Office 2013 ⇨ Word 2013.

   By default, the main template choices for creating a new document appear in the Word Start screen, as shown in Figure 2.1. The FEATURED and PERSONAL choices above the templates in Figure 2.1 do not appear until you have created and saved a custom template as described later in Chapter 18, "Saving Time with Templates, Themes, and Master Documents."

> **NOTE**
>
> You can use the charms in Windows 8 to easily access commonly used functionality, including finding and starting applications or Windows 8 apps. The charms appear at the right side of the screen and include Search, Share, Start, Devices, and Settings. To display the charms, you can move your mouse to one of the right screen corners (or simply touch the right border of the screen on a touch screen); then you can click a charm to select it.

FIGURE 2.1

Create a blank document or choose a template here.

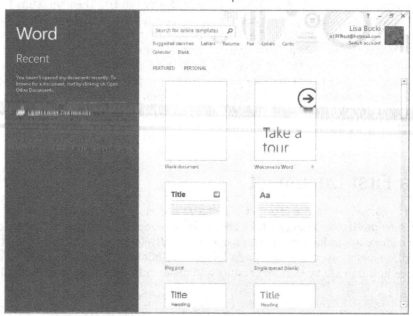

NOTE

If Word is already open or if you have turned off the Word Start screen in Word Options, click File ⇨ New. When I say "click File," I mean for you to click the File tab in the upper-left corner of Word's window. This displays the template choices for creating a new document.

2. **Click in the Search online templates text box, type** letterhead and envelope, **and press Enter.**

3. **In the results that appear, click the Letterhead and envelope template choice.** A small window describing the template appears, as shown in Figure 2.2. If you see More Images and arrow buttons below the template preview image, you can click the arrow buttons as desired to see additional preview images.

NOTE

The templates available online change over time. If you don't see the Letterhead and envelope template, pick any other template that has an envelope and letter or another that appeals to you, and follow those steps that still apply in the rest of this section.

FIGURE 2.2

Word displays a preview and description of the selected template before you download it.

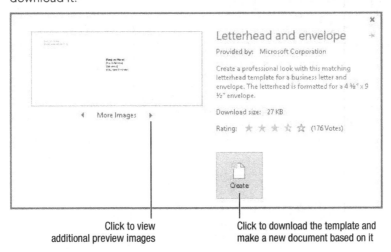

Click to view   Click to download the template and
additional preview images   make a new document based on it

4. **Click the Create button.** The window displays a message that the template is downloading, and then the new document opens onscreen, showing a page for the envelope at the top, and then a page for the letter itself.

5. **Click File ⇨ Save As.** The Save As choices appear.

6. **Click Computer in the middle pane, and then click Documents in the right pane under Computer.** (If you don't see Documents, click Browse.) This opens the Save As dialog box, where you can specify a name for the letter file. The temporary name in the File name text box is selected by default.

7. **Type** Practice Letter for Word 2013 Bible, **and then click the Save button.**

8. **If you see a message box informing you that the document will be upgraded to the newest file format, click OK.** The new name for your document appears in the Word window title bar as shown in Figure 2.3. Notice that the template also may fill in some information for you, such as adding your username above the return address on the envelope, and at the upper-left corner of the letter.

FIGURE 2.3

The newly named file was set up based on the downloaded template.

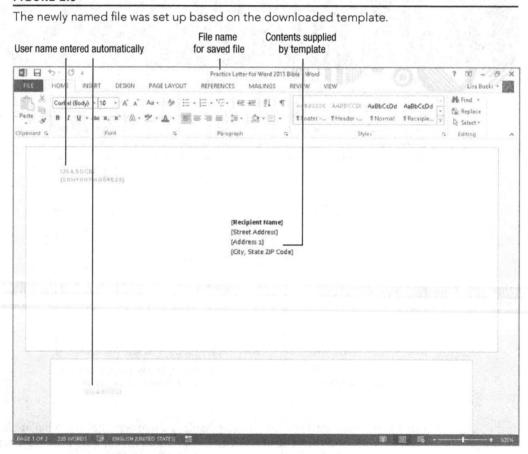

2

> **TIP**
>
> As you work on this and any other document, press Ctrl+S frequently to save your most recent changes. Like any other application, Word 2013 can crash from time to time, and the more recently you've saved your work, the less you'll have to redo when a crash happens.

Filling in the envelope

As shown in Figure 2.3, the template you selected created a page for the envelope at the top of the document. It also includes several placeholders or *content controls* enclosed in square brackets—[ ]. Examples include [COMPANY ADDRESS] at the upper left and one for each line of the addressee information in the center of the envelope. To fill in a control, simply click it and type to replace the placeholder information. Fill in the envelope content controls now.

1. **If you want to add your own custom information to the letter, you can do one of two things:**

   a. **Click each content control on the envelope page and type the desired information.**

   b. **Click each content control listed below and type the specified information:**

[COMPANY ADDRESS]	**123 N. Main St.**
	Evansville, IN 47701
[Recipient Name]	**Elaine Smith**
[Street Address]	**500 Crane Circle**
[City, State ZIP Code]	**Evansville, IN 47750**

> **NOTE**
>
> Press Enter at the end of the first line when making your entry in the [COMPANY ADDRESS] content control. Notice that the template is set up to format the text for that control with all caps.

2. **Right-click the [Address 2] content control, and click Remove Content Control in the shortcut menu.** You will also need to take this step when filling in your own information if you don't use this particular control.

3. **Press Delete to remove the blank line.**

4. **Press Ctrl+S to save your work.** The envelope text should now appear as shown in Figure 2.4.

FIGURE 2.4

Filling in the content controls on the envelope goes quickly and results in a nicely formatted envelope.

> **NOTE**
>
> Some templates use a legacy type of content placeholder called a *field*. Chapter 24, "Creating Custom Forms," explains how you can create content controls and fields and explores the differences in working with them. When working with a field code, you can press Shift+F9 to toggle between the code itself and the displayed result, so that's one way to tell the two types of placeholders apart.

Filling in the letter

Some content controls in templates offer even more automation, and the Letterhead and envelope template contains a couple of examples. At the top of the second page of the document, which holds the letter, a [Pick the date] control appears. When you click that control, a down arrow appears. Clicking it in turn displays a drop-down calendar or *date picker* that you can use to select the date. Below the date, the inside address for the letter includes content controls that are set up to retrieve information entered in other controls—in this case, the recipient information you already entered on the envelope. Even the name in the greeting or salutation line is filled in for you. The remaining controls for the body, closing, and footer work like those on the envelope page in the file.

Fill in the rest of the letter now, either using the text suggested in the steps below or your own text if you prefer.

1. **Scroll down the document so that you can see the top half or so of the second page.** To scroll, you can click the down arrow at the bottom of the vertical scroll bar at the right side of Word, or drag the scroll box on the bar down.

2. **Click the [Pick the date] content control, and then click the down arrow at its right side to display the date picker calendar.** See Figure 2.5.

FIGURE 2.5

A date picker content control shows a calendar to make date entry faster.

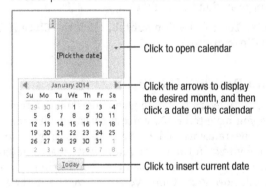

3. **Click the Today button at the bottom of the date picker calendar.** This inserts the current date. To insert another date, use the left and right arrows in the upper corners of the date picker to move to the desired month, and then click a date.

4. **Click the [Address 2] control in the inside address, and press the Delete key three times.** This deletes the control and the line it occupied.

5. **Scroll down if needed, and click the body text control under the greeting line.** This selects all the text in the control, which will be replaced by the text you type.

6. **Type the following text, pressing Enter after the first line to create a new paragraph:**

Thank you for joining the Evansville Evenings Book Club.

We have received your membership fee payment: check #152 in the amount of $20. Membership fees fund basic refreshments for our meetings, but members are free to bring additional snacks and beverages as desired.

7. **Click the closing content control ([Sincerely]), and type:**
   Welcome to the group,

8. **Scroll down to the bottom of the page until you see the light blue footer text, which includes the return address you typed for the envelope.**

9. **Double-click the [COMPANY E-MAIL] content control.** This opens the footer area for editing and selects the control.

10. **Either type an email address or press Delete three times to remove the control.**

11. **Click the [COMPANY PHONE] content control in the footer, and either type a phone number or press the Backspace key nine times.** The use of Backspace in this instance both removes the control and the two vertical pipe characters used to set off each piece of information in the footer.

12. **On the Header & Footer Tools ⇨ Design subtab, click the Close Header and Footer button in the Close group.**

Formatting, saving, and printing the letter

The predefined formatting set up in every template also makes using a template a great time-saver. That doesn't mean you have to be 100 percent satisfied with the predefined formatting. You can change the appearance as well as the content of any document based on a template. For example, the body text in the letter you've just created might look a little small to you. One quick and dirty way to change document formatting is to apply a new theme, a technique you'll try out now. From there, you can save the letter and print it. During the printing process, you'll be able to see a preview of the finished document. Go for it now.

1. **Click the Design tab on the Ribbon.**

2. **In the Document Formatting group, click Themes.**

3. **Move your mouse pointer over the Facet theme.** Live Preview displays the document body text using the appearance specified by that theme, which includes slightly larger text.

4. **Click the Facet theme to apply it to the document.**

5. **Press Ctrl+S or choose File ⇨ Save.** This saves your most recent additions to the document text, as well as the new theme setting.

6. **Choose File ⇨ Print.** A preview of the first envelope page of the document appears.

7. **Below the envelope preview, click the Next Page (right arrow) button.** The second page, which is the letter itself, appears in the preview pane, as shown in Figure 2.6.

8. **Under Printer, if you don't see the name of the printer to use, click the drop-down box, and then click the desired printer in the list.** "Ready" appears below the name of any printer that's connected to your computer and turned on.

9. **Under Settings, click in the Pages text box and type** 2. This tells Word to print only the letter page of the document. (Page 1 is the envelope.)

10. **Click Print.** Word sends the letter page to the printer.

FIGURE 2.6

The printing process enables you to preview the finished document.

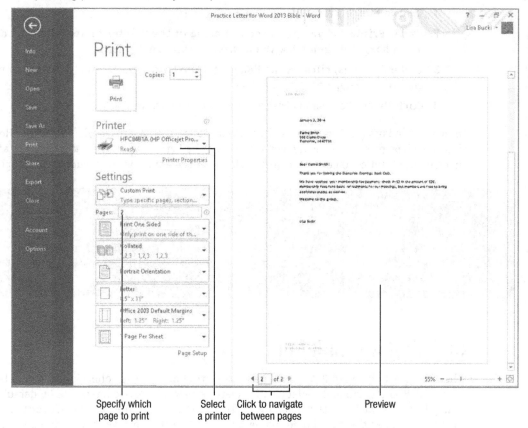

Specify which page to print   Select a printer   Click to navigate between pages   Preview

Printing the envelope

The process for printing an envelope page works just like printing a letter: give the Print command, choose which page to print, and go. The trickiest part is inserting the blank envelope correctly in your printer. Many of today's printers have sliding guides in either the manual feed or the paper tray. You slide those guides closer together so that they feed the envelope into the printer at the right spot and prevent slipping. You also need to insert the envelope itself in the right aspect for your printer: face up or face down. Look for a small icon on your printer's tray or feed that diagrams how to place the envelope, or consult the printer manual to find out how to do it correctly. Once your blank envelope is in place and the printer is turned on, you can send the envelope information for your first document to the printer.

1. **Choose File ⇨ Print.**
2. **Under Printer, if you don't see the name of the printer to use, click the drop-down box, and then click the desired printer in the list.**
3. **Under Settings, click in the Pages text box and type** 1. This tells Word to print only the envelope page of the document.
4. **Click Print.** Word sends the letter page to the printer.

For most of today's printers, you need not even change the paper size when printing. However, if the envelope prints incorrectly, you could click the Letter paper size under Settings after choosing the Print command, and then click one of the Envelope sizes, such as Envelope #10.

> **TIP**
>
> If you choose a letter template that doesn't include an envelope page, Word still gives you an easy way to create one. Select the inside address at the top of your letter, and press Ctrl+C to copy it. Choose Mailings ⇨ Create ⇨ Envelopes. The Envelopes and Labels dialog box opens with the copied address in the Delivery address text box. Enter a Return address if desired. From there you can click Print to send the envelope to the printer or click Add to Document to add it to the letter document file.

Creating a Blank File

When you start the Word 2013 app, the upper-left choice in the collection of templates that appears is Blank document. Selecting it creates a new, blank document file by default for you. (The actual name of the template applied to new, blank files is Normal.dotm.) This document file has the placeholder name *Document1* until you save it to assign a more specific name, as described later in the chapter. You can immediately start entering content into this blank document.

If you need another blank document at any time after starting Word, you can create it by following these steps:

1. **Select File ⇨ New.** The New Document dialog box appears.
2. **Click the Blank Document tile.** See Figure 2.7.

Clicking Ctrl+N also creates a new, blank file directly.

FIGURE 2.7

Click this tile or icon to create a blank file.

Typing text

When you create a new, blank document, you can begin typing text to fill the page. As you type, each character appears to the left of the blinking vertical insertion point. You can use the Backspace and Delete keys to delete text, the spacebar to enter spaces, and all the other keys that you're using for typing.

Word also enables you to start a line of text anywhere on the page using the Click and Type feature. To take advantage of Click and Type, move the mouse pointer over a blank area of the page. If you don't see formatting symbols below the I-beam mouse pointer, click once. This enables Click and Type and displays its special mouse pointer. Then, you can double-click to position the pointer on the page and type your text. Figure 2.8 shows snippets of text added to a page using Click and Type.

NOTE

Click and Type only works in the Print Layout view, so to learn more about that view, see the section called "Choosing the Right Word View for the Task at Hand" later in this chapter. Changing to another view does not remove the Click and Type text positioning, even though it might appear to n a view such as Outline view. The document will look the same when you change back to Print Layout view.

FIGURE 2.8

Double-click and type anywhere on the page.

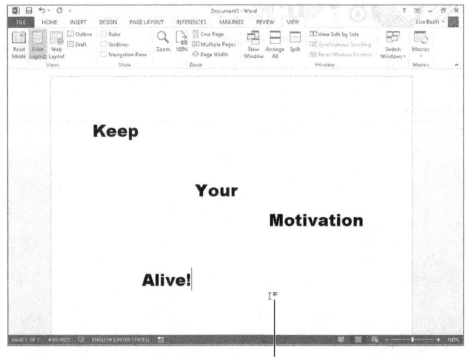

Click and Type mouse pointer

Using word wrap

By default, the margins for a blank document in Word 2013 are 1 inch on the left and the right. When you type enough text to fill each line, hitting the right margin boundary, Word automatically moves the insertion point to the next line. This automated feature is called word wrap, and it's a heck of a lot more convenient than having to make a manual carriage return at the end of each line.

If you adjust the margins for the document, word wrap always keeps your text within the new margin boundaries. Similarly, if you apply a right indent, divide the document into columns, or create a table and type in a table cell, word wrap automatically creates a new line of text at every right boundary. Just keep typing until you want or need to start a new paragraph (covered shortly). Later chapters cover changing margins and indents and working with tables and columns.

Inserting versus overtyping

Like its prior versions, Word 2013 offers two modes for entering text: Insert mode and Overtype mode. In Insert mode, the default mode, if you click within existing text and type, Word inserts the added text between the existing characters, moving text to the right of the insertion point farther right to accommodate your additions and rewrapping the line as needed. In contrast, when you switch to Overtype mode, any text you type replaces text to the right of the insertion point.

Overtyping is a fine method of data entry—when it's the mode that you want. Unfortunately, in older Word versions, the Insert key on the keyboard toggled between Insert and Overtype modes by default. Because the Insert key is often found above or right next to the Delete key on the keyboard, many a surprised user would accidentally hit the Insert key and then unhappily type right over his text.

In Word 2013, the Insert key's control of Overtype mode is turned off by default. You can use the Word Options dialog box to turn Overtype mode on and off, and also to enable the Insert key's control of Overtype mode. Select File ➪ Options, and then click Advanced in the list at the left side of the Word Options dialog box. Use the Use overtype mode check box (Figure 2.9) to toggle Overtype mode on and off, and the Use the Insert key to control overtype mode check box to toggle the Insert key's control of Overtype mode on and off. Click OK to apply your changes.

FIGURE 2.9

The Word Options dialog box enables you to turn Overtype mode on and off.

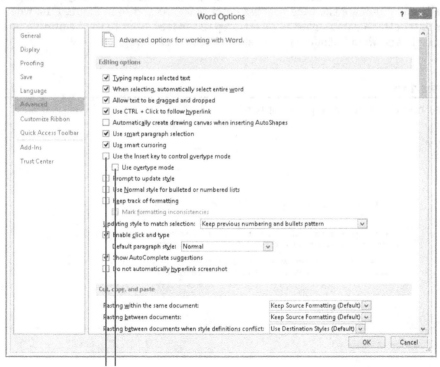

Control Overtype mode and the Insert key

Using default tabs

Every new, blank document has default tab stops already set up for you. These tabs are set at ½-inch (0.5-inch) intervals along the whole width of the document between the margins. To align text to any of these default tab stops, press the Tab key. You can press Tab multiple times if you need to allow more width between the information that you're using the tab stops to align.

TIP

To display the rulers so that you can better work with text alignment features like tabs in a document, click the View ➪ Show ➪ Ruler check box to check it.

Making a new paragraph

In legacy versions of Word, when you wanted to create a new paragraph in a blank document, you had to press the Enter key twice. That's because the default body text style didn't provide for any extra spacing after a paragraph mark, which is a hidden symbol inserted when you press Enter.

Starting with Word 2007, pressing Enter by default not only inserts the paragraph mark to create a new paragraph, but also inserts extra spacing between paragraphs to separate them visually and eliminate the need to press Enter twice. As shown in Figure 2.10, when you press Enter after a paragraph, the insertion point moves down to the beginning of a new paragraph, and Word includes spacing above the new paragraph.

FIGURE 2.10

Press Enter to create a new paragraph in Word.

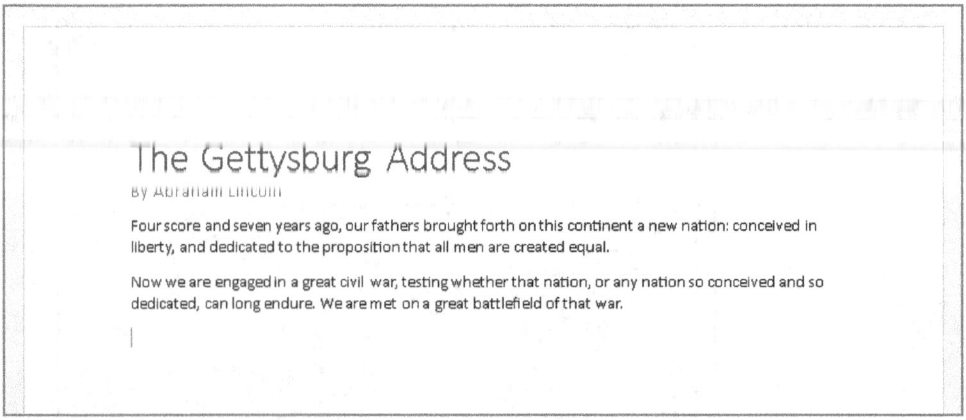

The Gettysburg Address
By Abraham Lincoln

Four score and seven years ago, our fathers brought forth on this continent a new nation: conceived in liberty, and dedicated to the proposition that all men are created equal.

Now we are engaged in a great civil war, testing whether that nation, or any nation so conceived and so dedicated, can long endure. We are met on a great battlefield of that war.

Creating a File from a Template

Every new document you create in Word 2013—even a blank document—is based on a *template* that specifies basic formatting for the document such as margin settings and default text styles. When you create a blank document, Word automatically applies the default global template, `Normal.dotm`.

While a document *theme* supplies the overall formatting for a file, a template takes that a step further. A template may not only include particular text and document formatting selections, but also has placeholders and example text as you saw when you created your first document earlier in the chapter. Templates also can contain automatic *macros* that swing into action each time you create, open, or close a document, as well as other macros you can use to perform tasks for building the document.

Using templates can dramatically reduce the amount of time you spend thinking about your document's content and formatting, because someone else has already invested the time to answer those questions. For example, a home repair company might set up a template for written estimates, job contracts, and change orders. Rather than starting every such document from scratch, the project manager could simply create a new document using the applicable template, and fill in the information pertinent to the current client.

In that type of scenario or in your business and personal life, using templates offers the following benefits:

- The documents produced will be consistent, even when they are produced by different people.

- If the templates are carefully developed and reviewed, using them ensures that your documents will be complete with all the needed information, every time.

- Setting up templates with your company logo and contact information ensures that information will appear on every document you create, which helps with branding and promoting your organization.

- For longer documents like reports or newsletters, the benefit of using a template increases, because designing all the formatting in such documents can be time consuming.

Take a look at the templates available to you via Word now.

> **NOTE**
>
> Templates can contain macros with shortcut key assignments, styles for working on particular kinds of documents, and even custom content controls like those you worked with earlier in the chapter. You'll learn about creating your own styles, macros, fields, and controls in later chapters, as well as how to save the custom features you create in your own templates.

Reviewing available document templates

When you start Word 2013 or click File ⇨ New, the right pane of the screen displays a selection of templates, shown in Figure 2.11. You can scroll down this screen to see a selection of suggested templates.

Starting Word or clicking File ⇨ New shows you Word's templates.

> **TIP**
>
> You can save a step by adding the New command to your Quick Access Toolbar. Click the Customize Quick Access Toolbar arrow at the right end of the QAT, and then click New.

Blank document and pinned templates

The Blank document template always appears among the templates. Selecting it creates a new document based on Normal.dotm. Figure 2.11 also shows the Letterhead and envelope template. If you followed the earlier example, it will appear the next time you choose File ⇨ New, because Word automatically includes recently used templates in the list. If you look carefully at Figure 2.11, you'll see that a small pushpin icon to the right of the Welcome to Word template name. That means that item is *pinned* to stay on the list of templates. To pin or unpin a template, point to its thumbnail, move the mouse pointer over the pushpin icon, and click the icon to toggle it to be pinned or unpinned.

Common templates you might want to pin to the list include:

- **Blog post:** This creates a new document based on Blog.dotx, a special template that's designed for blog entries.
- **Single spaced (blank):** This creates a new document based on the Single spaced.dotx template, with a Normal style that lacks extra spacing after paragraphs. If you choose this template, you have to press Enter twice to create paragraphs, as in older versions of Word.

To create a blank document based on Normal.dotm, you could simply press Ctrl+N, bypassing the need to choose the New command.

> **NOTE**
>
> It is possible to update the Normal.dotm template file on your system with custom content and text, but most experts don't recommend doing so. Keeping Normal.dotm clean and lean enables you to always start with a clean document slate when you need to.

Online templates

Virtually all of the templates in Word 2013 exist in the cloud rather than being installed on your computer. In addition to the suggested templates shown when you click File ⇨ New, you can scroll down to see and select additional templates. Any template that you select is downloaded to your system and stored there for future use.

If you don't see a template that suits your needs, you can search online for additional templates. You can type a search word or phrase in the Search online templates text box above the templates and press Enter to begin a search. Or you can click one of the Suggested searches links below the Search online templates text box, such as Cards. After the search runs, scroll down to view additional results, or use the Filter by list at the right (see Figure 2.12) to refine the results.

FIGURE 2.10

You can refine the Cards search by clicking the Avery (or another) category under Filter by in the right pane.

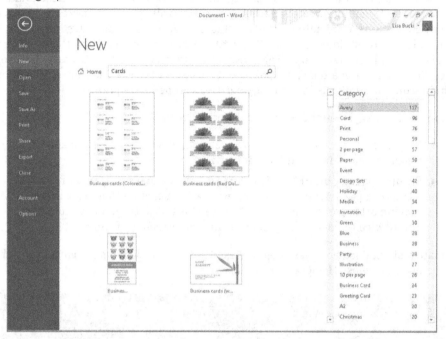

Creating the file from the template

Now that you're familiar with what templates do and where to find them, follow these steps when you want to create a new document based on a template:

1. **Select File ⇨ New.**
2. **To search for a template, type a search word or phrase in the Search online templates text box and press Enter, or click one of the Suggested searches links.** (If you don't need to search for a template, skip to Step 4.) Thumbnails or tiles and names for the matching templates appear in the middle section of the screen.
3. **To narrow the list of templates shown, click a category under Filter by in the right pane.**
4. **Click the thumbnail for the desired template.** Documents for the three direct templates discussed earlier will open immediately. For other templates, a preview for the template appears in its own window, as you saw back in Figure 2.2.

> **NOTE**
>
> As noted earlier, when you see FEATURED and PERSONAL above the template thumbnails, it means you have saved a custom template. Click PERSONAL to find and select one of your custom templates.

5. **Click the Create button to download the template and create the new file.** The window displays a message that the template is downloading, and then the new document opens onscreen, showing a page for the envelope at top, and then a page for the letter itself.

The new document appears onscreen.

NOTE

Some of the templates available via `Office.com` were created in earlier Word versions. Those documents will open in Compatibility mode, which is described later in this chapter.

Working with template content

As shown in Figure 2.13, a template might hold a variety of sample contents and placeholders.

FIGURE 2.13

Replace template placeholders with your own content.

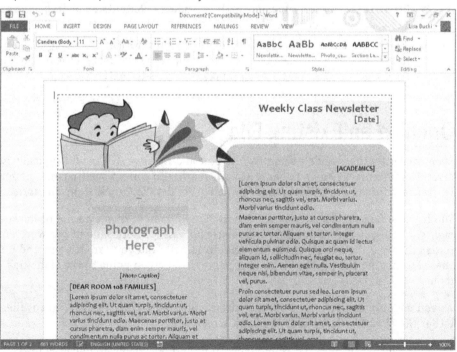

You can work with these placeholders and other contents as follows to finish your document:

- **Graphics Placeholders.** The box in Figure 2.13 that says *Photograph Here* is a placeholder for a graphic. Click the placeholder to select it, click the Insert tab on the Ribbon, and then click the Pictures or Online Pictures choice in the Illustrations group to select a replacement item. Chapter 14 provides more information about working with artwork in your Word documents.

- **Labels for Text.** Some templates include lists of items with a colon after each. Clicking to the right of the colon for any of the label item places the insertion point at a precise position, ready for you to enter the text to go with the label.

- **Bracketed or Gray Field Placeholders.** Template text that appears with square brackets and sometimes gray shading, such as the [Date], [Photo Caption], and other such fields shown in Figure 2.13, may be either content controls or text form fields. Clicking one of these placeholders selects the entire placeholder, and then any text you type replaces the placeholder contents.

- **Content Controls.** As you saw earlier in the chapter, these types of controls may feature automation such as a date picker, graphic selector, or linked entries. Click the control and make a selection or type to use it.

- **Other Text.** You can supplement the template's contents by adding your own text anywhere in the document.

- **Styles.** Templates also include predefined styles (formatting) that you can apply to text that you add. See Chapter 7, "Using Styles to Create a Great-Looking Document," to learn more about applying styles to text.

Opening an Existing File

Even the best writers revisit their work to edit and improve it. You will typically work on a given Word document any number of times, whether to correct spelling and grammar errors, rearrange information, update statistics and other details, or polish up the formatting.

You learn in Chapter 1 that you can choose File ⇨ Open to display a list of Recent documents, which you can pin or unpin for faster access. The left pane of the Word 2013 Start screen displays the list of Recent documents as well, and you can also pin and unpin files there by clicking the pushpin icon that appears when you point to the right side of the file name.

As you might guess, you can open an existing file by clicking it in the Recent files list on either the Word Start screen or the Open screen.

However, the Recent files list is dynamic, so if your document no longer appears there, you will need to navigate to it and open it from the location where you saved it. (The next section covers saving.) You can save documents to and open them from one of two overall locations from the Open screen:

■ **Computer:** Clicking Computer displays Recent Folders that have been used for storing documents, which is by default set as your user My Documents folder (part of the Documents library by default) and Desktop folder (files on the desktop). If you click either of those folders or the Browse button, the Open dialog box appears, as shown in Figure 2.14. You can use it to navigate to other locations, including shared folders on your local network.

FIGURE 2.14

You can open files stored on your computer or network.

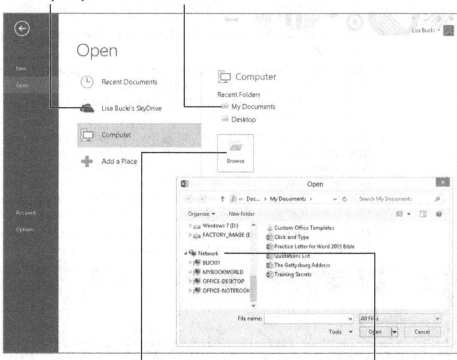

Click to use your SkyDrive   Default folders for documents

Click to use the Open dialog box to find another folder, disk, or location   Even select another location on your network

■ **SkyDrive:** Microsoft hosts SkyDrive cloud storage. When you create a Microsoft account to sign in to Windows, your account automatically includes your own SkyDrive storage. To take advantage of that storage from within Word, sign in to Word with your Microsoft account information, and click your SkyDrive in the middle list shown in Figure 2.14. If you have installed the SkyDrive for Windows client application in Windows, that process sets up SkyDrive folders on your system that automatically sync with your SkyDrive storage in the cloud, so you can access those files from another computer or device if needed. Chapter 27, "Collaborating in the Cloud with SkyDrive," will show you how to set up and use SkyDrive. You can jump ahead to that chapter if you want to use SkyDrive in the near future.

NOTE

As mentioned in Chapter 1, if you've downloaded a Word file directly from the Web, the Open list of places also includes an Other Web Locations choice. Click it to see websites from which you've downloaded files listed as Recent Folders at the right. If clicking a folder doesn't reconnect with the website as expected, right-click a choice and click Copy path to clipboard. You can then paste the path into your Web browser's address bar and press Enter to return to the site from which you downloaded the file.

For now, use these steps to open a file that's not on the Recent files list:

1. **From the Word Start screen, click Open Other Documents; within Word, select File ⇨ Open.**

2. **Under Recent Folders, click My Documents, Desktop, or the Browse button.** All three choices display the Open dialog box, the difference being that both My Documents and Browse initially show the Documents library, whereas Desktop shows your user Desktop folder.

3. **Navigate to the desired folder using the Navigation pane at the left side of the Open dialog box or by double-clicking subfolder icons in the list of files.** In the Navigation pane, double-click a higher-level location such as Computer or Network to open its tree, and then navigate down through the tree by clicking the white triangles that appear beside computer, disk, and folder names to open those locations. Click the folder or subfolder that holds the file to open when you see it in the tree.

4. **Click the name of the file to open in the main file list, and then click the Open button.** Or simply double-click the file name when you see it.

TIP

You can still directly open a Word file by double-clicking it in a File Explorer (Windows 8) or Windows Explorer (Windows 7) window on the desktop. Use the Search box in the upper-right corner of a folder window in either operating system to search for a file. In Windows 8, you also can point to a right screen corner, click the Search charm, click Files in the right pane, and then type a file to search for in the text box under Search; if the desired file name appears, click it.

Saving and File Formats

As long as you see "Document1" in Word's title bar, you run the risk of losing your investment of time and creativity if a power surge zaps your computer or Word crashes. Even for previously saved files, you should save your work often to ensure that you won't have to redo much work should something go wrong. Saving in Word works as it does in most other apps, with a few variations based on how you want to use or ultimately share the document.

Saving as a Word file

The first time you save any file, even one created from a template, you will choose the location where you want to save it, and give the file a meaningful name. Word will suggest a name that's based on the first line of text in the document, but chances are it won't provide the benefit of making the file easy to find when you need to reopen it. I always recommend establishing a consistent file-naming system, particularly when you create many similar files. Including the date and client or contact person name in the file name are two tricks. For example, Smith Systems Marketing Plan 12-01-15 is more descriptive than Smith Marketing or even Smith Marketing v1. When viewing dated file names, you can easily see which one's the latest and greatest. Word automatically adds the .docx extension to every file saved in the default format. This section and the next present more ins and outs concerning file formats.

Here's how to save a file for the first time:

1. **Choose File ⇨ Save As or press Ctrl+S.** The Save As screen appears.
2. **Click Computer in the middle pane.** As noted earlier, you could leave your SkyDrive selected, and save the file there. Chapter 27 describes that process.
3. **Under Computer, click a folder, or the Browse button.** Any choice displays the Save As dialog box, which is similar to the Open dialog box shown in Figure 2.14.
4. **Navigate to the desired folder using the Navigation pane at the left side of the Save As dialog box or by double-clicking subfolder icons in the list of files.** In the Navigation pane, double-click a higher-level location such as Computer or Network to open its tree, and then navigate down through the tree by clicking the white triangles that appear beside computer, disk, and folder names to open those locations. Click the folder or subfolder that holds the file you want to open when you see it in the tree.
5. **Drag over the contents of the File name text box to select them if needed, and then type the desired file name.**
6. **Press Enter or click the Save button.** Word saves the file and returns to it onscreen.

> **TIP**
>
> Use the New folder button above the list of files in the Save As dialog box to create a new folder within the current folder. After clicking the button, type a folder name and press Enter. You can add a folder to the Favorites list in the Navigation pane by dragging it from the file list to the Favorites section.

After you've named the file, you can press Ctrl+S or choose File ⇨ Save to save the current document.

If you want to create a copy of the file, save it, and then choose File ➪ Save As. This reopens the Save As dialog box. You can choose another save location, enter another file name, and then click Save to create the file copy. Changes you make to the copy appear only there. Save As is a quick and dirty alternative to setting up a template. The upside is that you may have less text to replace than with a template. The downside is that you may forget to update text that needs changing that otherwise would not have been in the template.

Converting to another format

Not every user immediately upgrades to the latest version of a particular program or uses the same platform as each of us. Nearly every Word user experiences a situation where they need to convert a document to another file format so someone else can open it on their computer or other device. And there may be instances where you need to save a document as a web page for addition to a website, as a PDF file that can be opened on an iPad, and so on. Word can handle other file formats for both incoming and outgoing files.

Converting a file from an earlier Word version

When you open a file in Word 2013 that was created in an earlier version of Word, [Compatibility Mode] appears in the title bar to the right of the file name. In this mode, some of the latest features in Word are disabled so that you can still use the file easily in an older Word version. In some cases, you may prefer to convert the file to the current Word format to take advantage of all Word's features. The only caution is that this can result in some layout changes to the document. If that's worth it to you, then by all means, convert the file. Even though Word 2007 and Word 2010 files use the same .docx file name extension as for Word 2013, the formats are not precisely identical, so even files from those versions may need to be converted.

1. **Choose File ➪ Info.** The Info screen appears, with options for finalizing the current document file. As shown in Figure 2.15, a Convert button appears beside Compatibility Mode in the list of choices.

FIGURE 2.15

Convert a file to the current Word format and leave Compatibility Mode

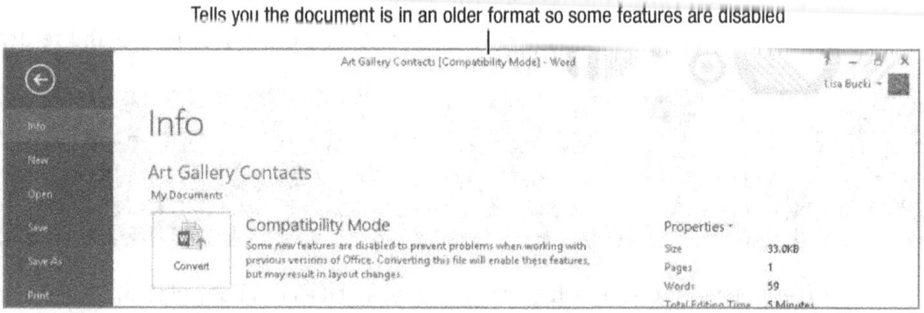

Tells you the document is in an older format so some features are disabled

2. **Click Convert.** A message box appears, telling you that the document will be upgraded to the newest file format.

3. **Click OK.** Word changes the document to the Word 2013 .docx format and removes [Compatibility Mode] from the title bar.

4. **Save the file.**

CAUTION

Once converted, the previous version of the file is gone forever. If you think you might need the file in that previous version, such as to share it with other users, make a copy of the file or save the file under a new name before clicking Convert. The Convert option renames the original file—the .doc version will be gone. The first time you convert, Word does alert you to what it's doing, but if you're like most users you won't read the fine print and you'll click "Do not ask me again about converting documents." If you do happen to click that option, in the future there will be no warning— and if you're like me, you will forget it was there the first time.

When you convert, Word converts the document currently displayed to Word 2013 .docx format. At this point you can still recover the original file by closing the file without saving the changes. Until you save, the converted file exists only in the current window.

Using Save As

The Save As dialog box includes a Save as type drop-down list directly below the File name text box. After you choose File ⇨ Save As, click Save as type to display the choices shown in Figure 2.16. Click a choice in the list, specify the file name, and then click Save. Word saves the file in the designated format, adding the file name extension for that format.

You might notice added behavior in the Save As dialog box when you select certain file types. For example, if you click Word Template, the folder specified for the save changes automatically. This is because storing your Office templates in a centralized location makes them easier to use. In an example like this, it's usually best to stick with the change suggested in the Save As dialog box and just click Save.

TIP

Most other word processing programs can open a Rich Text Format or Plain Text document. Even spreadsheet and database programs can open plain text files that are set up correctly with delimiters (characters such as commas used to separate each field or "column" of data). The OpenDocument Text format comes in handy when sharing with users of such freeware tools as OpenOffice. If you don't see the specific format requested by someone who needs your file on the Save as type list, try one of these three formats.

FIGURE 2.17

Use the Save as type drop-down to select another file format.

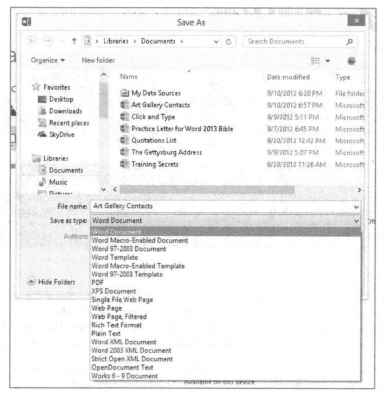

Using Export

If you need to save a file in another common format, you might choose to use the File ⇨ Export ⇨ Change File Type command instead. As shown in Figure 2.17, choosing this command opens an Export screen with a Change File Type list at the right. Word gives a small description of each of the file types there to make it easier to select the right one. Click the format to use, and then click Save As. Word opens the Save As dialog box with the specified format already selected for Save as type. From there, specify a file name and save location as usual, and click Save.

> **NOTE**
>
> Chapter 25, "Sharing and Publishing Documents," will detail even more specialized formats and methods you can use for making your Word docs available to others, including publishing to your blog and a cool new method of presenting online.

FIGURE 2.17

Learn more about and choose an alternate save format on the Export screen.

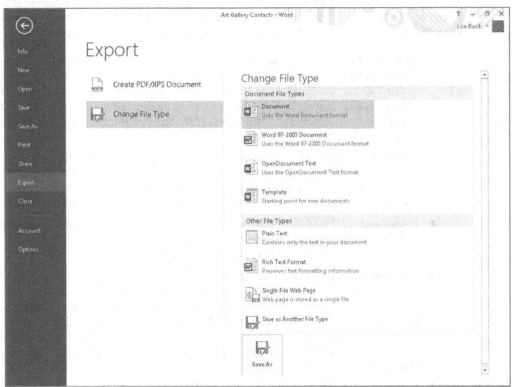

Compatibility with Previous Versions of Word

Between the 97 and 2003 versions of Word, the .doc file format remained basically unchanged. Feature enhancements such as document versioning and floating tables necessitated some modifications to the file format.

Even so, you can still open most Word 2003 files in Word 97 and the documents will look basically the same. Only if you use newer features will you see a difference, and usu-ally that just means reduced functionality rather than lost data or formatting. However, when it comes to post-2003 versions of Word, file format changes introduce meaningful differences.

Understanding .docx

Word 2013, Word 2010, Word 2007, and Word 2003 users will continue to see interoperability. However, Word 2013's, 2010's, and 2007's "native" format is radically different—and better—than the old format. The new format boasts a number of improvements over the older format:

- **Open format:** The basic file is in ZIP format, an open standard, which serves as a container for .docx and .docm files. Additionally, many (but not all) components are in XML format (Extensible Markup Language). Microsoft makes the full specifications available free, and they may be used by anyone royalty-free. In time, this should improve and expand interoperability with products from software publishers other than Microsoft.

- **Compression:** The ZIP format is compressed, resulting in files that are much smaller. Additionally, Word's "binary" format has been mostly abandoned (some components, such as VBA macros, are still written in binary format), resulting in files that ultimately resolve to plain text and that are much smaller.

- **Robustness:** ZIP and XML are industry-standard formats with precise specifications that offer fewer opportunities to introduce document corruption. Hence, the frequency of corrupted Word files should be greatly reduced.

- **Backward-compatibility:** Though Word 2013, 2010, and 2007 have slightly different formats, they still fully support the opening and saving of files in legacy formats. A user can opt to save all documents in an earlier format by default. Moreover, Microsoft makes available a *Compatibility Pack* that enables Word 2000–2003 users to open and save in the new format. In fact, Word 2000–2003 users can make the .docx format their default, providing considerable interoperability among users of the different versions.

- **Extensions:** Word 2013 has four native file formats: .docx (ordinary documents), .docm (macro-enabled documents), .dotx (templates that cannot contain macros), and .dotm (templates that are macro-enabled, such as Normal.dotm).

Calling the x-file format "XML format" actually is a bit of a misnomer. XML is at the heart of Word's x format; however, the files saved by Word are not XML files. You can verify this by trying to open one using Internet Explorer. What you see is decidedly not XML. Some of the components of Word's x files, however, *do* use XML format.

Using the Compatibility Checker

Word runs an automatic compatibility check when you attempt to save a document in a format that's different from the current one. You can, without attempting to save, run this check yourself at any time from Word 2013. To see whether features might be lost in the move from one version of Word to another, open the document in Word 2013. Choose File ➪ Info ➪ Check for Issues ➪ Check Compatibility.

For the most part Word 2013 does a good job of checking compatibility when trying to save a native .docx file in .doc format. For example, if you run the Compatibility Checker on a Word 2013 document containing advanced features, you will be alerted, as shown in Figure 2.18.

FIGURE 2.18

Using the Compatibility Checker to determine whether converting to a different Word version will cause a loss of information or features.

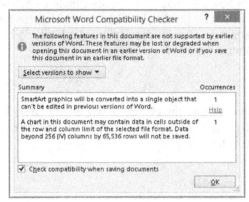

When moving in the other direction—checking a Word 2003 (or earlier) document for compatibility with Word 2013—the checker usually will inform you that "No compatibility issues were found." Note, however, that the Compatibility Checker doesn't check when you first open a document formatted for Word 2003 (or earlier). It's not until you try to save the file that it warns you about any unlikely issues.

Choosing between *.doc* and *.docx*

Word's options enable you to choose to save in the older .doc format by default. A person may opt to do this, for example, if the majority of users in his or her organization still use Word 2003 or earlier. That's certainly a plausible argument, but consider one occasional down side to Word's binary .doc format. With a proprietary binary file format, the larger and more complex the document, the greater the possibility of corruption becomes, and it's not always possible to recover data from a corrupted file.

Another issue is document size. Consider a simple Word document that contains just the phrase "Hello, Word." When saved in Word 97–2003 format, that basic file is 26 K. That is to say, to store those 11 characters it takes Word about 26,000 characters!

The same phrase stored in Word 2013's .docx format requires just 11 K. Make no mistake: that's still a lot of storage space for just those 11 characters, but it's a lot less than what's required by Word 2003. The storage savings you get won't always be that dramatically different, but over time you will notice a difference. Smaller files mean not only lower storage requirements but faster communication times as well.

Still another issue is interoperability. When a Word user gives a .doc file to a user of WordPerfect or another word processor, it's typical that something is going to get lost in translation, even though WordPerfect claims to be able to work with Word's .doc format. Such documents seldom look identical or print identically, and the larger and more complex they are, the more different they look.

With Word's adoption of an open formatting standard, it is possible for WordPerfect and other programs to more correctly interpret how any given .docx file should be displayed. Just as the same web page looks and prints nearly identically when viewed in different web browsers, a Word .docx file should look and print nearly identically regardless of which program you use to open it (assuming it supports Word's .docx format).

Persistent Save As

If, despite the advantages of using the new format, you choose to use Word's .doc format, you can do so. Choose File ➪ Options ➪ Save tab. As shown in Figure 2.19, set "Save files in this format" to "Word 97–2003 Document (*.doc)."

FIGURE 2.19

You can tell Word to save in any of a variety of formats by default.

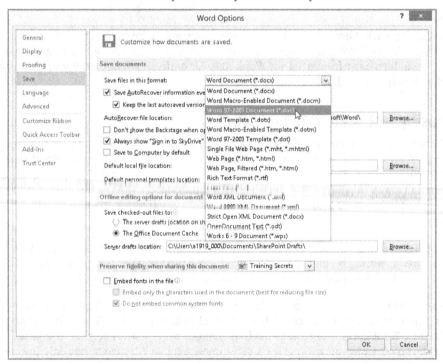

Note that even if you set `.doc` or some other format as your default you can still override that setting at any time by using Save As and saving to `.docx` or any other supported format. Setting one format as the default does not lock you out of using other formats as needed.

Microsoft Office Compatibility Pack

As of this writing, users of legacy versions of Word such as Word 2003 could open Word 2007, 2010, and 2013 files after installing a Compatibility Pack. While the Compatibility Pack was not developed specifically for Word 2013 files, in my testing, I was able to open a Word 2013 file in Word 2003 with the Compatibility Pack installed. The Compatibility Pack is a free download found at `www.microsoft.com/en-us/download/default.aspx`. Click in the Search Download Center text box at the top, type **Compatibility Pack**, and press Enter. Check the Search results for "Microsoft Office Compatibility Pack for Word, Excel, and PowerPoint File Formats," and download it. At this time, that was the latest version of the Compatibility Pack available, but it's possible an update could be released at a later time.

Converting a *.docx* file into a *.docm* file

Word 2013 uses four primary XML-based file formats:

- `.docx`: An ordinary document containing no macros
- `.docm`: A document that either contains macros or is macro-enabled
- `.dotx`: A template that does not contain macros
- `.dotm`: A template that either contains macros or is macro-enabled

It is important for some purposes for users to be able to include macros not just in document templates, but in documents as well. This makes documents that contain automation a lot more portable. Rather than having to send both document and template—or, worse, a template masquerading as a document—you can send a document that has macros enabled.

Because Word 2003 documents can contain legitimate macros, there is no outward way to know whether any given `.doc` document file contains macros. If someone sends you a `.doc` file, is opening it safe?

Though it's not clear that the new approach—distinct file extensions for documents and templates that are macro-enabled—is going to improve safety a lot, it does provide more information for the user. This is true especially in business environments, where people don't deliberately change file extensions. If you see a file with a `.docm` or `.dotm` extension, you know that it contains macros, and that it might warrant careful handling.

If you want to convert a `.docx` file so that it can contain macros, you must use Save As and choose Word Macro-Enabled Document as the file type. You can do this at any time—it doesn't have to be when the document is first created. You can also remove any macros from a `.docm` file by saving it as a Word document (*.docx).

Even so, you can create or record a macro while editing a .docx file, and even tell Word to store it in a .docx file. There will be no error message, and the macro will be available for running in the current session. However, when you first try to save the file, you will be prompted to change the target format or risk losing the VBA project. If you save the file as a .docx anyway and close the file, the macro will not be saved.

Understanding and Avoiding Macro Viruses

When Word macro viruses first started appearing, ordinary Word documents could not contain macros—only templates could. Therefore, one of the most popular ways of "packaging" macro viruses was in a .dot file that had been renamed with a .doc extension. The virus itself often was an automatic macro (typically AutoExec) that performed some combination of destruction and propagation when the rogue .dot file was first opened. A common precaution was to press Shift as you opened any Word file—.doc or .dot—to prevent automatic macros from running. In fact, even with various advances in security and antivirus software, pressing Shift when you open an unfamiliar Word document is still not being overly cautious. It's a good policy to check the Trust Center macro settings by choosing File ➪ Options ➪ Trust Center and then clicking the Trust Center Settings button. Make sure that Macro Settings is selected at the left side of the menu and that the Disable all macros with notification option is selected. With this setting enabled as it is by default, you will be prompted about whether to enable macros when you open a file that has them, as shown here.

Further exploring the .docx structure

A last look at the .docx file structure reveals clues about why it's different from the older .doc format. As indicated earlier, Word's new .docx format doesn't itself use XML format. Rather, the main body of your document is stored in XML format, but that file isn't stored directly on disk. Instead, it's stored inside a ZIP file, which gets a .docx, .docm, .dotm, or .dotx file extension.

To verify this, you could create a simple Word 2013 file, and save and close it. Next, in Windows Explorer (Windows 7) or File Explorer (Windows 8), display file name extensions and change the file's extension to .zip. Finally, the double-click the file to display the contents of that ZIP file, as shown in Figure 2.20.

Word `.docx` files can contain additional folders as well, such as one named `customXml`. This folder is used if the document contains content control features that are linked to document properties, an external database or forms server, and so forth.

The main parts of the Word document are inside the folder named `word`. (See Figure 2.20.) A typical `word` folder for a simple document is shown in Figure 2.21.

FIGURE 2.20

When viewed as ZIP files, most .docx files contain three main folders and a Content Types XML document.

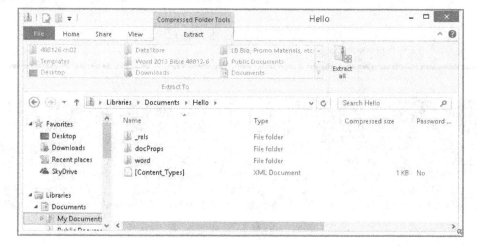

FIGURE 2.21

The Word document's main components are stored inside the .docx file in the folder named word.

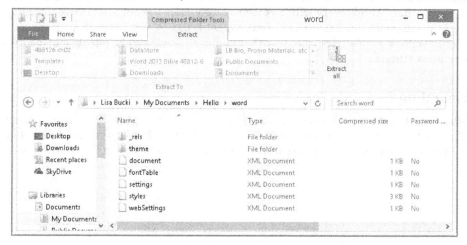

The main text of the document is stored in document.xml. Using an XML editor you could actually make changes to the text in document.xml, replace the original file with the changed one, rename the file so that it has a .docx extension instead of .zip, and open the file in Word, and those changes would appear. More complex Word files contain additional elements, such as clip art, an embedded Excel chart, several pictures, and some SmartArt, as well as custom XML links to document properties.

Quick Q & A

Q: What's an XML editor? When I double-click an XML file, it just opens Internet Explorer, which doesn't let me edit anything.

A: There are specialized XML editors. You can also use Expression Web or SharePoint Designer. You can also use anything that edits plain-text files, such as Notepad.

TIP

You can replace the images in a .docx file without editing the file in Word. Rename the .docx file so that it has a .zip extension. Extract the images stored in the word\media folder so you can see what's what. Give the replacement images the same respective names as the existing ones. Replace the contents of the word\media folder with the new images. Finally, replace the .zip extension with the original extension. This might not make ergonomic sense for just a few images, but if you have dozens it could save you a substantial amount of time.

Navigation and Selection Tips and Tricks

Bible readers already know the basics of using the Windows interface, so this book skips the stuff that I think every Windows user already knows about, and instead covers aspects of Word you might not know about. In our great hurry to get things done, ironically, we often overlook simple tricks and tips that might otherwise make our computing lives easier and more efficient.

Selecting text

When you want to make a change in Word, such as formatting text, you have to select it first. This limits the scope of the change to the selection only. Word lets you take advantage of a number of selection techniques that use the mouse or the mouse and keyboard together.

Dragging

Dragging is perhaps the most intuitive way to select text, and it works well if your selection isn't limited to a complete unit such as a word or sentence. Simply move the mouse pointer to the beginning of what you want to select, press and hold the left mouse button, move the mouse to extend the selection highlighting, and release the mouse button to complete the selection.

Triple-clicking

When you triple-click inside a paragraph, Word selects the entire paragraph. However, *where* you click makes a difference. If you triple-click in the left margin, rather than in a paragraph, and the mouse pointer's shape is the arrow shown in Figure 2.22, the entire document is selected.

FIGURE 2.22

A right-facing mouse pointer in the left margin indicates a different selection mode.

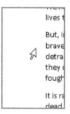

Is triple-clicking in the left margin faster and easier than pressing Ctrl+A, which also selects the whole document? Not necessarily, but it might be if your hand is already on the mouse. In addition, if you want the Mini Toolbar to appear, the mouse method will summon it, whereas Ctrl+A won't.

Ctrl+clicking

Want something faster than triple-clicking? If you just happen to have one hand on the mouse and another on the keyboard, Ctrl+click in the left margin. That also selects the entire document and displays the Mini Toolbar.

If you Ctrl+click in a paragraph, the current sentence is selected. This can be handy when you want to move, delete, or highlight a sentence. As someone who sometimes highlights as I read, I also find that this can help me focus on a particular passage when I am simply reading rather than editing.

Alt+clicking

If you Alt+click a word or a selected passage, it looks up the word or selection using Office's Research pane. This method of displaying the Research pane can just be a little faster than selecting one of the Proofing group options on the Review tab.

Alt+dragging

You can use Alt+drag to select a vertical column of text—even if the text is not column oriented. This can be useful when you are working with *monospaced* fonts (where each character has the same width) and there is a de facto columnar setup. Note that if the text uses a *proportional font* (where character widths vary), the selection may appear to be irregular, with letters cut off as shown in Figure 2.23.

FIGURE 2.23

With the Alt key pressed, you can drag to select a vertical swath of text.

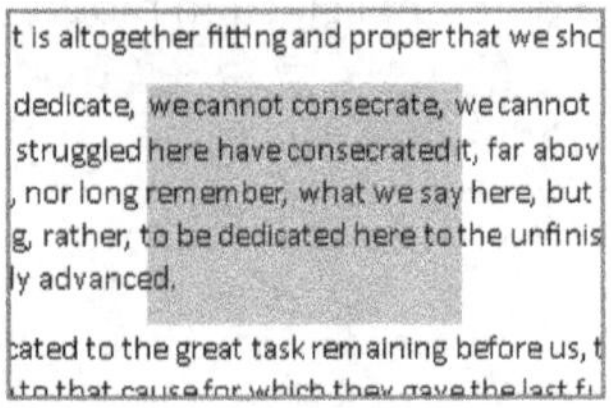

Shift+click

Click where you want a selection to start, and then Shift+click where you want it to end. You can continue Shift+clicking to expand or reduce the selection. This technique can be useful if you have difficulty dragging to highlight exactly the selection you want.

Multi-selecting

A few versions of Word ago, it became possible to make multiple noncontiguous selections in a document. While many know this, many more don't. To do it, make your first selection. Then, hold down the Ctrl key to make additional selections. Once you've made as many selections as you want, you can then apply the desired formatting to them, copy all of the selections to the clipboard, paste the contents of the clipboard over all of the selections, and so forth.

Gestures and touch navigation

The 2013 version of the Office applications now can be used effectively on touch-enabled devices in addition to desktop and laptop computers. Although your desktop or notebook computer will likely remain your primary Office 2013 platform for now, the new convenience and flexibility of using Word on a touch-enabled device like a tablet makes that platform a viable choice for road trips and extra work at home. Here's a brief introduction to the touch gestures and their basic uses in Word 2013:

- **Tap:** This is the equivalent of a mouse click. Move your finger over the desired item, and then touch and release, as when pressing a keyboard key. Tap to select buttons and other interface features and position the insertion point.

- **Tap-hold:** Move your finger over the desired item, and then touch and hold as when holding down a keyboard key. For example, tap-hold a QAT button to display the menu for customizing the QAT.

- **Double-tap:** This is the equivalent of double-clicking. Move your finger over the desired item, and touch and release twice. For example, you can double-tap to zoom in on graphics in one of Word's new views. (More on this later in the chapter.)

- **Pinch:** Drag your thumb and forefinger together on the screen. Use this action to zoom out in a document.

- **Stretch:** The opposite of pinch, in this gesture you drag your thumb and forefinger apart on the screen. Use this action to zoom in.

- **Slide:** Tap-hold, and then drag your finger. The tap-hold generally selects an object, and then dragging moves it into position.

- **Swipe:** Quickly drag your finger on screen, then lift it off. This action also can be used for scrolling and selecting.

Touch-enabled systems also give you the ability to display an onscreen keyboard for entering text. Tapping the Touch Keyboard button on the taskbar opens the keyboard. Tap its Close (X) button to close it when you've finished entering information.

> **TIP**
>
> Word Help has a topic called Office Touch Guide that provides even more specifics about navigating and working via touch.

Using the Navigation pane

You can press Page Up or Page Down to scroll a document a screen at a time, but that can become tedious for a lengthy document such as a report or book chapter. Word includes a Navigation pane that enables you to use three quick methods for navigating in a document. To display the Navigation pane, check the View ⇨ Show ⇨ Navigation Pane check box visible in Figure 2.24.

FIGURE 2.31

Use the Navigation pane to move around a long document quickly.

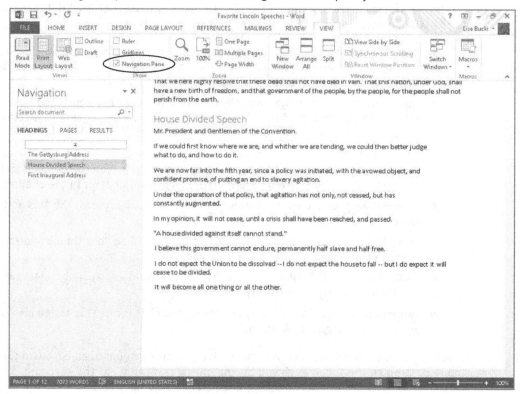

Once you've displayed the pane, here's how to use it:

- **Move between headings:** Click HEADINGS under the Search document text box, and then click the heading to jump to in the document. For example, in Figure 2.24, I've jumped to the "House Divided Speech" heading. Click the top bar to go back to the beginning of the document.

- **Move between pages:** Click PAGES to display page-by-page thumbnails of the document in the pane, scroll down the thumbnails, and then click the thumbnail for the page to go to.

- **Search and move between results:** This technique involves searching for text, displaying the RESULTS, and navigating to the found matches. Chapter 9, "Find, Replace, and Go To," provides more detail about how to navigate by searching.

Clear the Navigation Pane check box or select the pane's Close (X) button to close the Navigation pane.

Keyboard shortcuts

Word 2013 continues to offer you the option of performing many tasks via keyboard short-cuts. If you're a highly skilled typist, using keyboard shortcuts can save time over using the mouse, because you never have to lift your hands off the keyboard. For example, say you're typing and want to underline a word for emphasis. Just before typing the word, press Ctrl+U to toggle underlining on. Type the word and then press Ctrl+U again to toggle the underlining back off.

In addition to keyboard shortcuts for applying formatting, Word enables you to use keyboard shortcuts to navigate in a document, perform tasks such as inserting a hyperlink, or select commands from the Ribbon (using KeyTips, as described in Chapter 1). This section helps to round out your knowledge of keyboard shortcuts in Word 2013.

Creating a list of built-in keyboard shortcuts

Word boasts a broad array of keystrokes to make writing faster. If you've been using Word for a long time, you very likely have memorized a number of keystrokes (some of them that apply only to Word, and others not) that make your typing life easier. You'll be happy to know that most of those keystrokes still work in Word 2013.

Rather than provide a list of all of the key assignments in Word, here's how to make one yourself:

1. **Press Alt+F8.** The Macros dialog box appears.
2. **In the Macro name text box, type** listcommands.
3. **Click the Run button or press Enter.** The List Commands dialog box opens.
4. **Leave the Current keyboard settings options selected, and click OK or press Enter.** Word creates a new document with a table showing all of Word's current keyboard shortcuts.
5. **Save and name the file as desired.**

If you've reassigned any built-in keystrokes to other commands or macros, your own assignments appear in place of Word's built-in assignments. If you've redundantly assigned any keystrokes, all assignments will be shown. For example, Word assigns Alt+F8 to ToolsMacro. If you also assigned Ctrl+Shift+O to it, your commands table would include both assignments. The table also shows those assignments and commands you haven't customized.

TIP

If you want a list of Word's default built-in assignments, open Word in safe mode (hold down the Ctrl key as Word is starting and then click Yes) and run the listcommands macro again as just described.

Office 2003 menu keystrokes

One of Microsoft's aims was to assign as many legacy menu keystrokes as possible to the equivalent commands in Word 2007, 2010, and 2013, so if you're used to pressing Alt+I,B to choose Insert ⇨ Break in Word 2003, you'll be glad to know it still works. So does Alt+O,P, for Format ⇨ Paragraph.

Now try Alt+HA for Help ⇨ About. It doesn't work. In fact, none of the Help shortcuts work, because that Alt+H shortcut is reserved for the Ribbon's Home tab. Some others don't work either, but at least Microsoft tried. See Chapter 29, "Keyboard Customization," to learn more about setting up keyboard combinations that work for you.

Some key combinations can't be assigned because the corresponding commands have been eliminated. There are very few in that category. Some other legacy menu assignments haven't been made in Word 2013 because there are some conflicts between how the new and old keyboard models work. There are, for example, some problems with Alt+F because that keystroke is used to select the File tab. For now at least, Microsoft has resolved to use a different approach for the Alt+F assignments. Press Alt+I and then press Alt+F to compare the different approaches.

Custom keystrokes

You can also make your own keyboard assignments. I cover this in greater detail in Chapter 29, but to get a sneak peek, choose File ⇨ Options ⇨ Customize Ribbon, and then click the Customize button beside Keyboard shortcuts under the left-hand list.

If you prefer to highly customize the keyboard shortcuts, you can assign Alt+K (it's unassigned by default) to the ToolsCustomizeKeyboard command. Then, whenever you see something you want to assign, pressing Alt+K will save you some steps. To assign Alt+K to that command:

1. **Choose File ⇨ Options ⇨ Customize Ribbon.** The Customize Ribbon choices appear in the Word Options dialog box.
2. **Click the Customize button to the right of Keyboard shortcuts, below the left list.** The Customize Keyboard dialog box opens.
3. **Scroll down the Categories list, and click All Commands.**
4. **Click in the Commands list, and press the T key to skip to the Ts.**
5. **Scroll down and click ToolsCustomizeKeyboard.**
6. **Click in the Press new keyboard shortcut key text box, and then press Alt+K (or whatever other assignment you might find preferable or more memorable).** Make sure that the Save changes in drop-down list has Normal selected, so the keyboard shortcut change will be saved to the default document template.
7. **Click Assign, click Close, and click Cancel to dismiss the Word Options dialog box.** If you've told Word to prompt before saving changes in Normal.dotm, make sure you click Yes to saving this change (when prompted).

Choosing the Right Word View for the Task at Hand

To expand the ways of working with documents, Word offers a number of different environments you can use, called *views*. For reading and performing text edits on long documents with a minimum of UI (user interface) clutter, you can use the Read Mode view. For composing documents and reviewing text and basic text formatting, you can choose a fast-display view called Draft view.

For working with documents containing graphics, equations, and other nontext elements, where document design is a strong consideration, there's Print Layout view. If the destination of the document is online (Internet or intranet), Word's Web Layout view removes paper-oriented screen elements, enabling you to view documents as they would appear in a web browser.

For organizing and managing a document, Word's Outline view provides powerful tools that enable you to move whole sections of the document around without having to copy, cut, and paste. An extension of Outline view, Master Document view enables you to split large documents into separate components for easier management and workgroup sharing.

Change to most of the views using the Views group of the Ribbon's View tab.

Print Layout

Print Layout is Word 2013's default view, and one that many users will be comfortable sticking with. One of Word 2013's strongest features, Live Preview, works only in Print Layout and Web Layout views.

Print Layout view shows your document exactly as it will print, with graphics, headers and footers, tables, and other elements in position. It presents an accurate picture of the margin sizes and page breaks, so you will have a chance to page through the document and make design adjustments such as adding manual page breaks to balance pages or using shading and paragraph borders to set off text. Figure 2.25 shows this workhorse view.

FIGURE 2.26

Print Layout view reproduces how the printed document will look.

Ribbon Display Options button

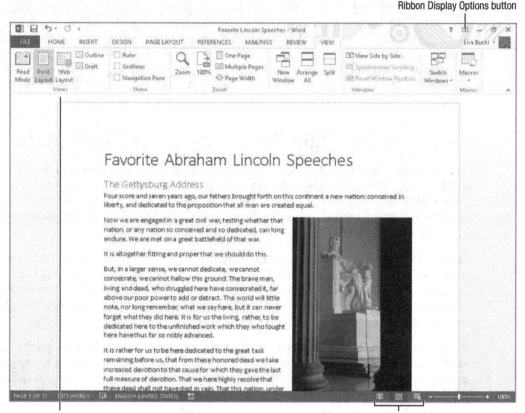

Views group with choices for changing views   Read Mode, Print Layout, and Web Layout buttons

Change back to this view at any time with View ⇨ Views ⇨ Print Layout, or click the Print Layout button on the status bar, near the zoom slider.

Draft view

When you want to focus on crafting the text of your document, you can turn to Draft view. Choose View ⇨ Views ⇨ Draft to flip your document to this view. Draft view hides all graphics and the page "edges" so that more text appears onscreen. By default, it continues to display using the styles and fonts designated in the document.

You can further customize Draft view to make the text even plainer. Choose File ⇨ Options. In Word's Options dialog box, click Advanced at the left, and then scroll down to the Show document content section. Near the bottom of the section, notice the option to Use draft font in Draft and Outline views. Check this option to enable it, and then use the accompanying Name and Size drop-downs to select the alternate text appearance. Click OK to apply the changes. For an example, Figure 2.26 shows Draft view customized to use 10 pt. Courier New font for all styles.

FIGURE 2.26

You can customize Draft view to use a plainer font.

If you plan to toggle between regular and custom Draft view fonts very often, you should know that Word has a built-in `ViewDraft` command that toggles the Use draft font in Draft and Outline views setting on and off. To make it more accessible, you might either assign it to a keyboard shortcut or put it onto the QAT for ready access. In the Word Options settings for QAT customization, it's in the All Commands list. Chapter 30, "Customizing the Quick Access Toolbar and Ribbon," explains how to customize the QAT.

Read Mode and Object Zoom

Read Mode, also new in Word 2013, displays a limited number of tools, zooms the document to a larger size, and repaginates it for reading. You can't edit document text in this view, but you can move and resize other objects such as pictures. Use the arrow buttons to the left and right of the text to page through the text. (This latter functionality seems tailor made for touch-enabled devices.) Use this mode's View menu to change some of the onscreen features. For example, as shown in Figure 2.27, you can choose another page background color to make your eyes more comfortable while reading. You also can display and hide the Navigation pane or Comments, change Column with, or change the overall Layout of the view. The Tools menu enables you to find document contents or search the web with Microsoft's Bing for a highlighted text selection.

FIGURE 2.27

Kick back and enjoy your document's contents in Read Mode.

Change viewing options for the mode on this menu

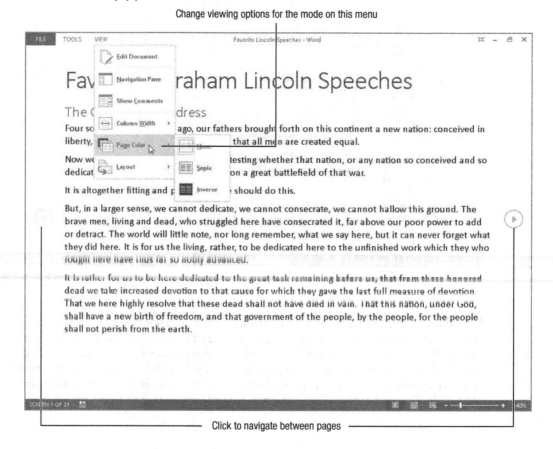

Click to navigate between pages

One great feature of the Read Mode view is that it enables you to zoom in on graphics in the document. Double-click a graphic to display the zoomed version of it, as shown in Figure 2.28. Clicking the button with the magnifying glass at the upper-right corner of the zoomed content zooms in one more time. To close the zoomed object, press Esc or click outside it on the page.

FIGURE 2.28

Double-click a graphic to zoom in on it in Read Mode.

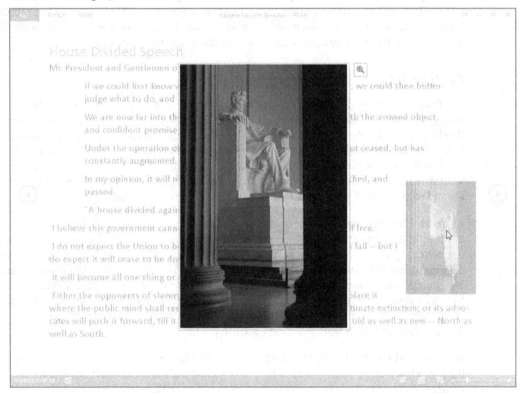

If you want, you can use the Auto-hide Reading Toolbar button at the upper-right to hide even the few menus in the view. From there, you can click the three dots near upper-right to temporarily redisplay the tools, or click Always Show Reading Toolbar to toggle them back on.

To exit Read Mode, you can click the Print Layout view button on the Status bar, or press Esc. In some cases, when Always Show Reading Toolbar is not toggled on, you may need to press Esc twice to exit Read Mode.

TIP

In addition to the arrow buttons on the screen, Read Mode offers a variety of ways to scroll the document pages: Page Down/Page Up, Space/Shift+Space, Enter/Shift+Enter, Right/Left arrow keys, Down/Up arrow keys, and the scroll wheel on your mouse.

Web Layout

Web Layout is designed for composing and reviewing documents that will be viewed online rather than printed. Hence, information such as page and section numbers is excluded from the status bar. If the document contains hyperlinks, they are displayed underlined by default. Background colors, pictures, and textures are also displayed.

Outline (Master Document tools)

The final distinct Word view is Outline (View ⇨ Views ⇨ Outline). Outlining is one of Word's most powerful and least-used tools for writing and organizing your documents. Using Word's Heading styles is one way to take advantage of this tremendous resource. Heading levels one through nine are available through styles named Heading 1 through Heading 9. You don't need to use all nine levels—most users find that the first three or four are adequate for most structured documents. If your document is organized with the built-in heading levels, then a wonderful world of document organization is at your fingertips.

As an outline manager, this view can be used on any document with heading styles that are tied to outline levels. (If you don't want to use Word's built-in Heading styles, you can use other styles and assign them to different outline levels. Additionally, you can build a document from the headings found in Outline view. You can expand and collapse text to focus on different sections of the document as you work, or to see an overview of how the topics in your document are flowing. (I cover the myriad tricks you can use for outlining in Chapter 3, "Working Smarter, Not Harder, in Word.") Click Outlining ⇨ Close ⇨ Close Outline View to finish working with outlining.

As suggested by the title of this section, Outline view has a split personality, of sorts. Outline view's other personality includes the Master Document tools. As shown in Figure 2.29, if you click Show Document in the Master Document group of the Outlining Ribbon tab, additional tools appear.

I cover the Master Document feature in detail in Chapter 18. For now, though, I'll just dish out a little description. This is an extremely powerful document control feature for users who are working on parts of the same document. Each document part can be developed as a separate file, and then combined into a single longer document. Master documents provide a way to carefully control the checking out and checking in of document parts, as well as to manage problems inherent in working with very large documents.

FIGURE 2.29

Click Show Document in the Master Document group to display the Master Document tools.

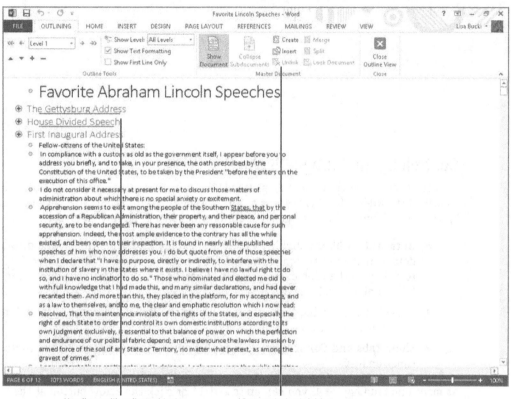

Headings with collapsed text   View controls at right

Resume Reading

Word 2013 includes a new Resume Reading feature. When you reopen a document you were previously editing, and the insertion point was on a page beyond page 1 when you closed the file, a prompt appears at the right side of the screen asking if you want to go back to the page you were last working on, as shown in Figure 2.30. Click the pop-up to go to the specified location. If you don't initially click the message, it shrinks to a smaller pop-up with a bookmark icon on it. You can move the mouse over it or click it to redisplay the message, and then click to jump to the later spot in the document. Scrolling the document makes the pop-up disappear.

FIGURE 2.00

Click the pop-up to return to the page you were last working on before you closed the document.

Welcome back!
Pick up where you left off:

House Divided Speech
A few seconds ago

Controlling the Ribbon display

You can choose whether or not to display the Ribbon in views other than Read Mode. Figure 2.25 identified the Ribbon Display Options button, visible in Print Layout, Web Layout, Outline, and Draft views. Clicking it opens a menu of options for controlling Ribbon display:

- **Auto-hide Ribbon:** Clicking this choice totally hides the Ribbon and displays three dots near the upper-right corner of the screen instead. Click the three dots button to redisplay the Ribbon temporarily. When you click back in the document, the Ribbon hides itself again.

- **Show Tabs:** Choosing this option collapses the Ribbon to a row of the tab names only. Click a tab to see its command.

- **Show Tabs and Commands:** Choose this option to return the Ribbon to its normal functionality.

As mentioned in Chapter 1, you can press Ctrl+F1 or click the arrow button at the lower-right corner of the Ribbon to collapse and expand the Ribbon. You also can double-click a Ribbon tab to collapse and re-expand it. When the Ribbon is collapsed, you can click any tab once to turn it back on temporarily. In that case, you'll see a pin button at lower-right where the arrow previously appeared. Clicking the pin button expands the Ribbon so that it stays onscreen.

Showing and hiding rulers

Another sometimes-overlooked tool is the ruler. It's useful for aligning and positioning text and other objects, which you'll learn about in later chapters. The ruler toggles on and off via the View ➪ Show ➪ Ruler check box.

Splitting the view

Choose View ➪ Window ➪ Split to divide the document window into two equal panes.

This feature comes in handy when you need to look at a table or a figure on one page of a document while you write about it on another page.

As another example, you might want to have one view of your document in one pane while using another view in the other, as shown in Figure 2.31. When viewing a document in two split panes, note that the status bar reflects the status of the currently active pane. Not only can you display different views in multiple panes, but you can display them at different zoom levels as well.

FIGURE 2.31

Split panes can display different views.

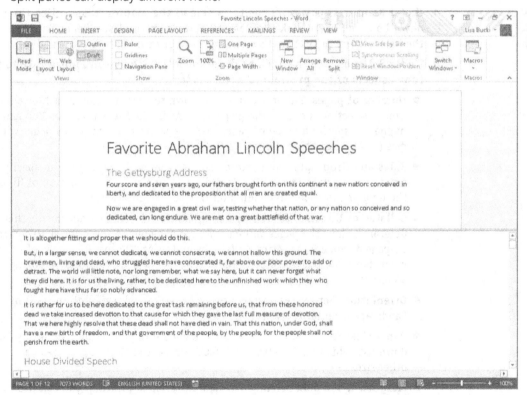

You can remove the split by dragging it up or down to the top or bottom of the screen, leaving the desired view in place, or double-clicking anywhere on the split line. Alternatively, Choose View ⇨ Window ⇨ Remove Split.

Printing a Document

You got a taste of printing a document in the project you tackled at the beginning of the chapter. Here are the steps for printing a document:

1. **Choose File ⇨ Print.** A preview of the first page of the document appears.
2. **Below the preview, use the Next Page (right arrow) and Previous Page (left arrow) buttons to preview all the document contents.** This gives you a final opportunity to check page breaks, headers and footers, and features that may be issues before you waste paper.
3. **To print more than one copy, change the Copies text box entry.**
4. **Under Printer, if you don't see the name of the printer to use, click the drop-down box, and then click the desired printer in the list.** "Ready" appears below the name of any printer that's connected to your computer and turned on.
5. **Under Settings, use the various drop-down lists shown in Figure 2.32 to fine-tune aspects of the printout.** These include:

   - **Number of pages:** Either use the drop-down to specify a range such as a section or selection, or enter the pages to print in the Pages text box. You can use a hyphen to specify a range of pages (1-3), separate noncontiguous pages with commas (5, 7), or combine the two (1-3, 5, 7).

   - **Sides and flipping:** If your printer can print on both sides, you can specify two-sided printing with the second drop-down. You also have the option of flipping on the long or short end, depending on the page orientation.

   - **Collated or Uncollated:** When printing multiple copies of a document, this determines how the pages will emerge. For example, if you printed 10 copies of a 24-page document, selecting Collated would print 10 separate copies of the document, but selecting Uncollated would print 10 page 1s, followed by 10 page 2s, and so on.

   - **Orientation:** Set up the document to print in Portrait Orientation (tall) or Landscape Orientation (wide).

   - **Paper size:** Select the size that you've loaded into your printer from this drop-down list, which reads Letter by default, or use the More Paper Sizes choice to find other sizes.

   - **Margins:** If you didn't change the margins prior to printing, you can use this drop-down to choose a different margin setting than the one initially shown.

   - **Pages per sheet:** If the selected printer is capable, use this drop-down to print up to 16 Pages Per Sheet or scale the printout.

FIGURE 2.32

Take a careful look at print settings before sending the document to the printer.

6. **Click Print.** Word sends the page to the printer.

Summary

In this chapter you've learned basic yet essential skills for creating and working with document files, using file formats, navigating a document, and more. Putting it all together, you should now have no problem doing the following:

- Creating and printing a basic document and envelope
- Creating a document using a blank template or one with predefined content
- Opening a document you've already saved
- Saving a document or copy, including choosing another format
- Navigating issues of file formats and compatibility
- Selecting text and moving between pages and headings
- Using Word's keyboard shortcuts, views, and view tools
- Sending your document to the printer with the right settings

Working Smarter, Not Harder, in Word

IN THIS CHAPTER

Using styles for consistent and professional formatting

Building well-organized documents through outlining

Making corrections automatically with AutoCorrect to save time

Viewing and changing file properties

Discovering power user techniques

L everage increases power. This chapter provides a quick introduction to three of Word's power features that you can leverage to save time and create better documents: styles, outlining, and AutoCorrect. Using these features each time you start a new document ensures you will realize their maximum benefit. This chapter provides an overview of these features, which are covered in greater detail in subsequent chapters, as well as sharing information about adding file properties and giving you some power tips you can put to work right away.

Achieving Attractive Documents with Styles

Many users type text in a document and then apply individual formatting settings to selections throughout the document. This approach not only takes a lot of time, but also can lead to inconsistencies. Suppose, for example, that in the course of applying a half dozen formatting attributes to achieve a certain "look" for a heading, you forgot an attribute here and there, or maybe set a different indentation in one instance. This gives your document an uneven and unprofessional appearance. In the case of headings, it can also make a document harder to follow, creating confusion in the reader's mind about which heading levels are equal to one another and which ones are subheadings. Consistency helps your reader distinguish among chapter titles, magazine article titles, section titles, and other organizational cues in the text.

A *style* is a collection of formatting attributes that you can apply to text in a document. A style can contain information about the font (including whether it's regular, italic, bold, or bold italic), point size, text color, shading, borders, effects (such as strikethrough, super-script, or subscript), underlining, and even language. A style also can contain additional information about spacing, indentation, line and page break behavior, numbering, and bullets.

If you routinely create documents with headings, titles, lists, and other elements that require multiple formatting changes, using styles can save you time. Rather than applying several separate formatting settings, you apply the style to make all those formatting set-tings in one fell swoop. Using styles can also improve formatting consistency, making your documents look more professional.

Styles also provide leverage when and if someone wants something changed. For example, if a client or your boss doesn't like the heading formatting in a document you prepared and you didn't use styles, you could be in for a lot of arduous work in changing the heading formatting, particularly in a long document. If you use heading styles, however, all you have to do is change the style definitions, and all text formatted with the updated styles automatically changes.

Styles versus direct formatting

Say you type a heading, select it, press Ctrl+B (bold), and then open the Font dialog box to apply the Small Caps effect and a larger point size. You might also open the Paragraph dia-log box to change the indentation and spacing.

This way of applying formatting attributes is called *direct formatting*, in contrast to *style formatting*. Direct formatting has a number of disadvantages that are discussed in Chapter 7, "Using Styles to Create a Great-Looking Document." Repeatedly applying the same sets of direct formatting to particular kinds of recurring text, such as headings, is a procedure both tedious and error-prone.

Instead of using direct formatting, you can use a style. The Normal.dotm template applied to blank documents includes a number of styles that you can work with immediately. For example, you can apply the Heading 1 style to headings at the top level of organization in your docu-ment. To apply this style to a heading, simply click in the heading and, with the Home tab of the Ribbon displayed, click Heading 1 in the Style gallery. As shown in Figure 3.1, you also can drag to select a series of headings and then apply the style to all of them.

FIGURE 3.1

To apply a style to selected text, click the style in the Style gallery.

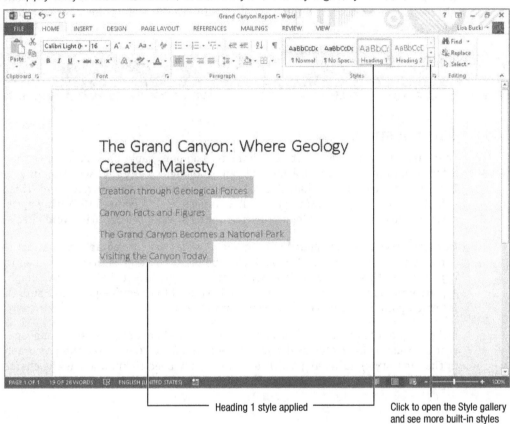

Heading 1 style applied

Click to open the Style gallery and see more built-in styles

Keyboard Shortcuts for Often-Used Styles

Word has built-in keyboard shortcuts for certain frequently used styles:

Normal	Ctrl+Shift+N
Heading 1	Ctrl+Alt+1
Heading 2	Ctrl+Alt+2
Heading 3	Ctrl+Alt+3

If the desired style does not initially appear in the Style gallery, you can scroll through the list of styles using the up and down scroll buttons at the right side of the gallery. Alternately, you can open the gallery by clicking the More drop-down arrow below the down scroll triangle.

> **NOTE**
>
> If the style you want still isn't shown, you might need to jump ahead to Chapter 7, to the section on the Style gallery.

Types of styles

There are two basic types of styles: character and paragraph. Character styles convey character-level formatting information and can be applied to any text selection in a document. If no text is selected, the character style will be applied to the current word (this is the default; to change the default, choose File ➪ Options ➪ Advanced ➪ Editing options, and clear the check beside the When selecting, automatically select entire word check box).

Paragraph styles can be applied only to one or more whole paragraphs and affect the entire paragraph (although later in the book you will learn techniques that enable you to seemingly sidestep this limitation). Because paragraph styles affect the entire paragraph, if you're applying a style to a single paragraph, you don't need to select it—just make sure that the insertion point is in the paragraph you want to style.

Although Word offers just two basic types of styles, there are three additional special cases that are sometimes treated as distinct style types: *linked* (character and paragraph together in the same style), *table*, and *list*. Even so, you only need to know about the character/paragraph distinction to begin using styles effectively.

Constructing Documents Faster with Outlining

Word's outlining capability, long one of Word's strongest features, works in concert with the built-in heading styles you just learned about. When you use Word's Heading 1 through Heading 9 styles in a document, you can use Word's Outline view to organize and reorganize your text. Note that you don't need to use all nine levels. Most documents can be better organized within just two or three heading levels. The lowest level in the outline is the Body Text level.

To display a document in Outline view, click the View tab and click Outline in the Views group. Figure 3.2 shows a document using the Heading 1 through 3 styles for the levels of organizational hierarchy that were needed. The figure shows the style area at the left side of the view so you can see what styles are applied. (You can display the style area by choosing this is the default; to change the default, choose File ➪ Options ➪ Advanced ➪ Display, enter the width for the style area in the Style area pane width in Draft and Outline views, and click OK. Entering 0 for the width hides the style area.)

FIGURE 3.2

Outlining enables you to see an overview of your document's organization. The style area at the left reveals the applied Heading styles.

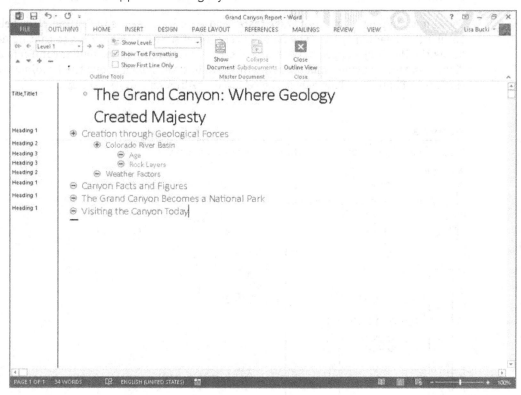

The Outline view automatically indents lower-level headings to make the organizational hierarchy visually evident. Body text (non-heading text) can be suppressed so that you view only the overall organization.

You also can start a document in Outline view. The first line you type becomes a Level 1 (Heading 1) heading. From there, you can:

- Press Tab to indent a line to the next lower outline/heading level.
- Press Shift+Tab to promote line to the next higher outline/heading level.

Organizing content via outlining

Suppose, in reviewing the document shown in Figure 3.2, your boss decides that the Canyon Facts and Figures section should be moved to the beginning of the document. Without the benefit of Word's Outline view, you would have to carefully select everything encompassed in that section, cut it to the Clipboard, and then paste it before the current first Heading 1 heading.

You can accomplish this sort of task faster and with fewer errors in Outline view. Select Level 1 (for Heading 1) from the Show Level control shown in Figure 3.3 so that no detail below the Heading 1 appears. Click anywhere in the heading to move (Canyon Facts and Figures in this example), and click the Move Up button, shown above the headings and to the left in Figure 3.3. This moves the selected heading and all its text up.

FIGURE 3.3

Outline view gives you tremendous organizational power.

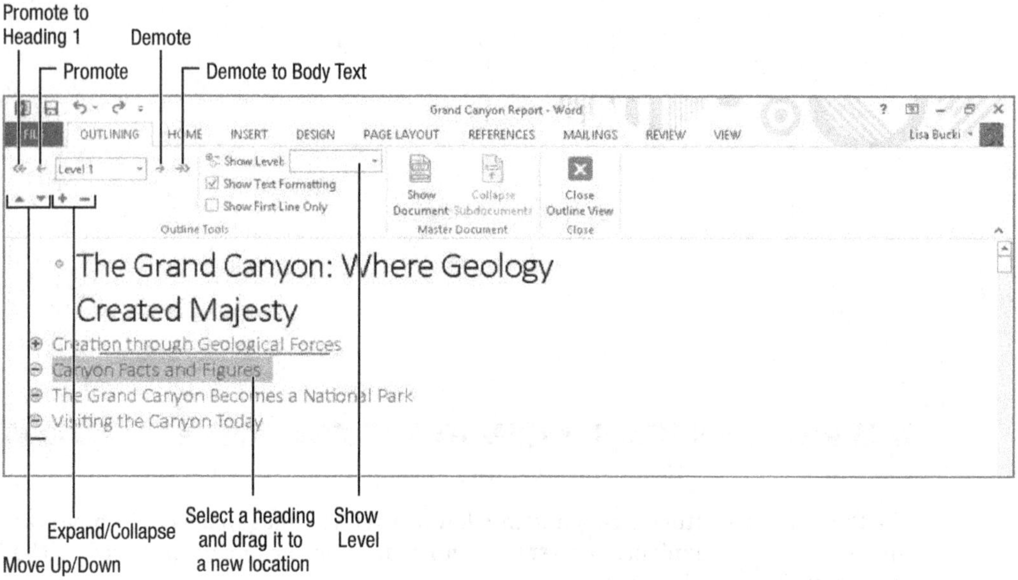

You can press Alt+Shift+Up, instead of clicking the Move Up button. Alt+Shift+Down moves the selected level down. (Note that rather than selecting a heading you can click in it to position the insertion point within it and then use a button or keyboard shortcut to move it up or down.) Finally, you can select and drag a heading to another location in the outline.

The Outlining tab also offers these tools in the Outline Tools group, identified in Figure 3.3, for rearranging and viewing your outline:

- **Promote and Demote:** Clicking the Promote button moves heading holding the insertion point up one level in the outline hierarchy, such as from Level 2 (Heading 2) to Level 1 (Heading 1). Clicking Demote moves the heading one level down. Find Promote and Demote in the Outline Tools group, at upper left.

TIP

The ScreenTips for the Promote and Demote buttons say that their shortcut key combinations are Alt+Shift+Left and Alt+Shift+Right, respectively. But as of this writing, in Word 2013 Tab and Shift+Tab still work for promoting and demoting, too.

- **Show Levels:** Click this drop-down list to open it, and then click the level to display. This action hides the levels below the selected level. For example, if your document has three heading levels, you can select Level 1 from Show Level to hide Levels 2 and 3 so that you can focus on the top-level flow of topics in the document.

- **Expand and Collapse:** Clicking the Expand button displays the next heading level contained within the selected heading or heading holding the insertion point. Click Expand multiple times to display subsequent heading levels and the body text when you reach the lowest level of your outline. For example, in Figure 3.4, I clicked in the top Level 1 heading and then clicked Expand twice to display the Level 2 and 3 headings. Clicking Collapse hides the text and headings within a selected heading. When a heading has a plus button to the left, you also can double-click that button to expand and collapse the heading.

FIGURE 3.4

Click Expand twice to see the next two heading levels under a Level 1 heading, as for the top heading in this document.

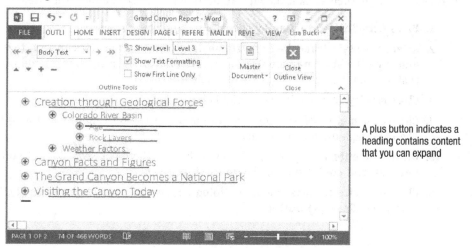

99

CAUTION

If you delete a heading that has information collapsed under it, Word deletes the heading and all of its collapsed contents. If this isn't what you want, expand the heading contents, move them elsewhere in the document as needed, then delete the heading.

NOTE

Don't confuse the different level settings. The Show Level setting affects only what you see. The Level setting on the left, however, affects actual document contents.

When you are finished working with the outline and want to close the Outlining tab from the Ribbon, click the Close Outline View button in the Close group at the right end of the tab.

Creating custom levels for non-heading styles

Sometimes it can be useful to treat certain document styles, such as document titles, captions for tables, figures, and so on, as if they were heading levels in order to make them visible in Outline view. At the same time, you usually don't want to use the same styles you use for headings (except possibly for the document title when the document is to become part of a larger document). Word enables you to associate any style with any outline level.

For example, you could associate the Caption style with outline Level 9 if you're not using the Heading 9 style in the document. After you associated the style with the outline level, Outline view would use Level 9 to display any text using the Caption style.

To associate a style such as Caption with an outline level, use the following steps:

1. **Press Ctrl+Shift+S to display the Apply Styles task pane.**
2. **Select the style from the Style Name drop-down list or click in that text box and type the style name without pressing Enter.** Pressing Enter would inadvertently assign the style to the current selection.
3. **Click Modify.** The Modify Style dialog box opens.
4. **Choose Format ⇨ Paragraph from the menu at the bottom of the dialog box.** The Paragraph dialog box opens.
5. **On the Indents and Spacing tab, open the Outline level drop-down list under General, and click Level 9, shown in Figure 3.5.**
6. **Click OK twice to close the open dialog boxes, and then click the Apply Styles task pane Close (X) button.**

FIGURE 3.5

Use the Outline level drop-down list when modifying Paragraph style settings to associate a style with the designated outline level.

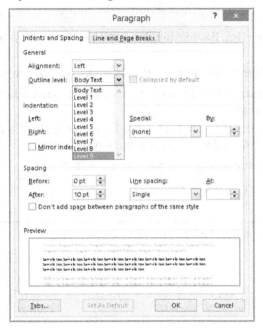

Outlining versus browsing headings in the Navigation pane

You learned in Chapter 2, "Diving Into Document Creation," that you can use the Navigation pane to move around the document. When HEADINGS is selected at the top of the pane, the document's headings appear in an indented hierarchy in the pane, similar to the way they appear in Outline view. When headings appear in the Navigation pane, you can reorganize or shuffle them around in much the same way that you can in Outline view. Click a heading in the Navigation Pane to scroll the document and move the insertion point to the beginning of that heading.

Viewing headings in the Navigation pane also provides the advantage of enabling you to see the document outline while working in Print Layout view. This means that if the body text you're writing suggests a needed outline change, you can view the outline simultaneously and decide the best way to change it.

While the Navigation pane does not *require* the use of Heading styles, viewing headings in the Navigation pane again emphasizes how useful formal headings can be in formatting, organizing, and reorganizing all kinds of documents. Without styles that contain organizational-level settings, however, hierarchical information is hard to keep track of when you're moving things around, and what you see in the Navigation pane won't necessarily indicate which headings are subordinate and which are superior.

Here's how to use the Navigation pane to work with your document outline:

1. **Click the View tab, and then click Navigation Pane in the Show group to check it.**
2. **Click HEADINGS below the Search document text box in the Navigation pane.**
3. **To collapse a heading's contents, click the black triangle; to expand a heading's contents, click the white triangle.**
4. **To move a heading, drag it until the blue horizontal line appears in the desired location as shown in Figure 3.6, and then release the mouse button.**
5. **Click the Close (X) button in the Navigation pane to close it.**

FIGURE 3.6

View and modify the document outline in the Navigation pane.

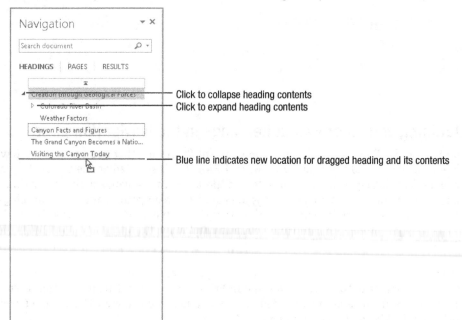

Cleaning Up Content with AutoCorrect

If you've spent some time now creating your first few Word documents, you may have noticed that Word automatically does things like capitalize the first letter of a sentence if you failed to do so, or correct typos such as changing teh to the.

This automatic feature is called *AutoCorrect*. Word has hundreds of built-in autocorrections that correct everything from abbout (about) to yoiu (you). Learn how to customize AutoCorrect to suit your needs in the rest of this section.

How AutoCorrect works

AutoCorrect by default fixes common typing and formatting errors that we all make:

- Accidentally typing two capital letters at the beginning of a sentence.
- Failing to capitalize the first letter of a sentence, table cell, or day name.
- Accidentally typing with the Caps Lock key on.
- Some words that are misspelled according to the Word spelling checker dictionary. (If AutoCorrect were able to correct every word according to the dictionary, you wouldn't need to run the Spelling & Grammar checker feature.)

In addition, AutoCorrect includes its own list of corrections. It not only can correct specific word misspellings, such as changing *adequite* to *adequate*, but also can convert certain character sequences into symbols. For example, when you type **(tm)**, AutoCorrect by default changes it to the ™ trademark symbol. It also converts several typed character combinations into smileys (emoticons) and various arrows.

You can customize the list of entries that AutoCorrect automatically replaces as well as its other default corrections in the AutoCorrect dialog box.

TIP

Anytime AutoCorrect makes an unwanted correction, you can immediately press Ctrl+Z to undo it. If you don't do so immediately, move your mouse pointer back over the word until you see a bar with a blue outline under the first letter. Point to that bar to display the AutoCorrect Options button, and then click the button. Click the desired option for undoing the correction, including telling AutoCorrect to stop making that particular fix in the future.

AutoCorrect options

You can make changes to how AutoCorrect behaves on the AutoCorrect tab of the AutoCorrect dialog box. Choose File ➪ Options ➪ Proofing tab ➪ AutoCorrect Options to display that tab in the AutoCorrect dialog box, shown in Figure 3.7.

3

FIGURE 3.7

Choose settings on this tab to cure many typo headaches.

The top check box, Show AutoCorrect Options buttons, controls whether the AutoCorrect Options button appears when you point to an AutoCorrected word, as described in the previous tip.

The next five check boxes control the five formatting typos AutoCorrect automatically fixes. You can turn these options on and off as needed. For example, if you writing a poem and you don't want to use any capital letters, even in sentences, clearing the Capitalize first letter of sentences check box before typing the poem could save some frustration.

Tip

If you find yourself frequently customizing the list of entries that AutoCorrect replaces, you can add a button for opening the AutoCorrect dialog box to the QAT. Right-click the QAT and choose Customize Quick Access Toolbar. Open the Choose commands from drop-down list and click Commands Not in the Ribbon. Scroll down the left list that appears, and click the first AutoCorrect Options... item listed. Click Add, and then click OK. Then you can use the new button on the QAT rather than going through the Word Options dialog box.

The Replace text as you type check box controls whether AutoCorrect enforces its other list of symbol and word corrections. In most cases, you will want to leave this choice checked, but you might want to uncheck it if, for example, you are a teacher creating a spelling test and you don't want your typos corrected in the document.

Removing built-in AutoCorrect entries

For many of us, the Replace text as you type option's correction list saves many hours of proofreading and correcting documents. Becoming acquainted with Word's built-in list can save you some surprises, because you'll learn what corrections you can count on it to make. Even so, this list may include some corrections you probably can't live with.

Suppose, for example, that you are writing a business plan for your new business, Fall In Cafe. You want to keep the name simple, yet AutoCorrect insists on correcting *Cafe* to *Café*. You could delete the café entry from the corrections list to stop the unwanted correction.

1. **Click File ➪ Options ➪ Proofing ➪ AutoCorrect Options.**
2. **Type the first three or four letters of the entry that you want to delete so that it displays in the list of replacements.** If needed, scroll the list further to display the entry to delete.
3. **Click the entry in the list.**
4. **Click the Delete button.**

> **TIP**
>
> Word deletes the selected correction immediately. However, the typo and correction remain visible in the Replace and With text boxes above the list. If you need to reinstate the entry, immediately click the Add button. Otherwise, you'll have to add the entry back manually as described next.

5. **Repeat Steps 2 through 4 to delete additional corrections from the list as needed.**
6. **Click OK twice to close the AutoCorrect and Word Options dialog boxes.**

Adding an AutoCorrect entry

You can customize the AutoCorrect feature by adding more corrections. You can not only add entries to correct additional typos, but also create shortcut entries that make your writing life easier. For example, you could create a shortcut for automatically entering your company name. Instead of typing **Fall In Cafe**, you could type **fic**, and AutoCorrect would automatically change the text to **Fall In Cafe**. Creating AutoCorrect entries for names and words that are long or difficult to type increases your accuracy and speed.

Note In Figure 3.8 that you have the option of inserting the replacement either as plain text or as formatted text. You can create plain-text entries directly from the dialog box. To create formatted text entries, however, you must first type, format, and select the example With text in a Word document.

FIGURE 3.8

Select the Formatted text option to include the formatting of the example text with the AutoCorrect entry.

Follow these steps to make either a formatted or unformatted custom AutoCorrect entry:

1. **For a formatted entry, type the text in the Word document, select it, and format it as desired.** Leave the text selected for the next step.
2. **Click File ⇨ Options ⇨ Proofing ⇨ AutoCorrect Options.**
3. **Under Replace text as you type, click in the Replace text box, and type the typo or shortcut entry that you want AutoCorrect to fix.** For example, Figure 3.8 shows **fic** entered here, the new shortcut for the formatted **Fall In Cafe** text shown in the With box.

4. **For an unformatted entry, click in the With text box, and type the desired correction; for a formatted entry, the text you selected in step 1 should already appear, so just click the Formatted text option button beside With to select it.** For an unformatted entry, leave the Plain text option selected as it is by default.

5. **Click the Add button.**

6. **Click OK twice to close the AutoCorrect and Word Options dialog boxes.**

TIP

To avoid AutoCorrect errors, some users like to include an asterisk or other symbol at the beginning of the Replace entry. For example, you could enter ***fic** in Step 3 above rather than just **fic**.

Adding and Reviewing Properties

Most users create a wide variety of documents or work in an environment where a number of users work together on documents. In such a case, finding the right document can be challenging at times, especially if there are many documents with similar names and subjects. That's why Word, like many other programs, enables you to add identifying *properties* or *metadata* to any file. Properties include such items as a Title, Tags (keywords), or Comments. Word 2013 actually includes three locations where you can add properties.

NOTE

Windows 8 in particular can help you find a file based on the Authors, Tags, and Title properties. In a File Explorer window, click in the Search Documents text box beside the address bar. Click the Search Tools Search tab, click Other Properties in the Refine group, click the property type to search for, type the property information, and press Enter.

Viewing properties on the Info screen

Clicking File and leaving Info selected shows basic properties along the right side of the screen in Backstage view, as shown in Figure 3.9. To add a property such as a tag, click the gray Add... choice beside it, type the property information to include, and click a blank area. You can separate multiple properties such as multiple tags by typing a comma.

FIGURE 3.9

Use File ➪ Info to view Properties at the right.

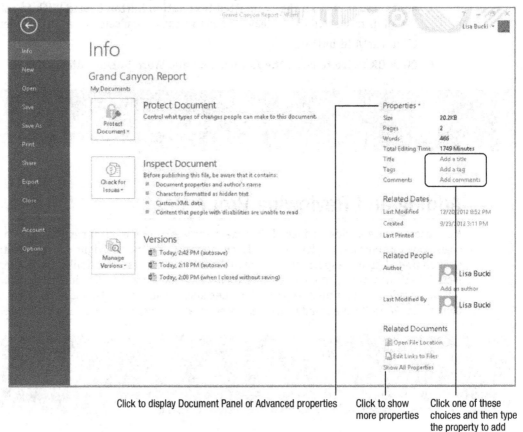

Click to display Document Panel or Advanced properties — Click to show more properties — Click one of these choices and then type the property to add

To view more properties in the Backstage, click the Show All Properties link below the displayed properties. Click Properties above the list of properties to open a menu that enables you to work with properties in two other ways, as described next.

Using the Document Panel

If you choose File ➪ Info, click the Properties choice above the properties at the right, and then click Show Document Panel, the Document Panel appears above the document, just below the Ribbon. You can type in any of the text boxes shown to make a change to a property. When you finish working with the Document Panel, click its Close (X) button to close it.

FIGURE 3.10

The Document Panel appears above the document and enables you to display a limited number of properties.

Showing advanced properties

You can open a Properties dialog box that displays all the available properties for the document, divided on different tabs, as shown in Figure 3.11. You can display this dialog box in one of two ways:

- Choose File ➪ Info, click the Properties choice above the properties at the right, and then click Advanced Properties.

- Click Document Properties in the upper-left corner of the Document Panel, and click Advanced Properties.

FIGURE 3.11

The Properties dialog box is considered advanced because it holds all the properties.

Some tabs of the Properties dialog box, such as the Statistics tab, only let you view information. On others, such as Summary, you can edit property entries in text boxes as needed. The Custom tab works a little differently. To add a custom property there, click a choice in the Name list, select one of the items on the Type drop-down list, type the property contents in the Value text box, and then click Add.

Click OK when you finish working in the Properties dialog box.

Power User Techniques

In this section I highlight some great power techniques that have stood me in good stead over the years. Some of these are mentioned elsewhere in the book but only in passing, so it's possible that they have escaped your notice.

Updating styles

Word's built-in styles change in appearance when you apply a new theme to the document. However, there's no guarantee that changing themes alone will make a particular style look the way you want it to. For example, you might want to make headings using the Heading 1 style larger or apply bold to make them more prominent. When you update the style, all text formatted with the style throughout the document is updated to match. This gives you a fast way of changing the look of your document. By default, the style updates you make only appear in the current document and do not affect other documents using the same template and styles.

To update a style, use the Styles pane.

1. **Select the styled text, and change its formatting as desired.** Leave the text selected for the next step.

2. **Click the Styles group dialog box launcher on the Home tab of the Ribbon.** The Styles task pane opens.

3. **Move the mouse over the style in the task pane, click the down arrow that appears, and click Update [Style Name] to Match Selection as shown in Figure 3.12.** (You also can right-click the style to open the menu.) Word immediately applies the style change throughout the document.

4. **Click the Styles pane's Close (X) button to close it.**

FIGURE 3.12

Updating a style with new formatting changes all text using that style throughout the document.

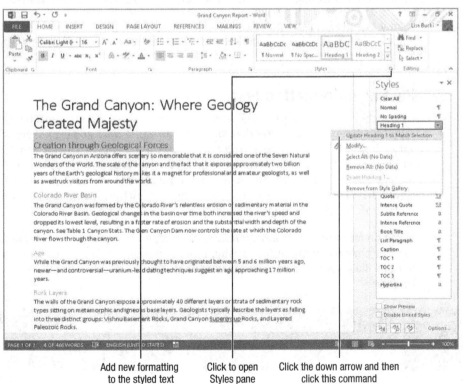

Add new formatting to the styled text

Click to open Styles pane

Click the down arrow and then click this command

Word offers a few optional shortcuts for updating a style:

- **Update the style from the Style gallery.** If the style to update appears in the Style gallery, you can right-click it there and click the Update [Style Name] to Match Selection command. This saves the trouble of displaying the Styles pane.

- **Add Redefine Style to the QAT.** If you frequently need to update styles, you can add the Redefine Style command to the QAT. Redefine Style is one of the many useful Word commands that exists behind the scenes until you add it to the QAT or Ribbon. Right-click the QAT and choose Customize Quick Access Toolbar. Open the Choose commands from drop-down list and click Commands Not in the Ribbon. Scroll down the left list that appears, and click the Redefine Style. Click Add, and then click OK. Then after you apply new formatting to some styled text, you can click the new button on the QAT to update the style rather than using the Styles pane.

GoBack

GoBack, another behind-the-scenes command that by default has the Shift+F5 shortcut key assigned to it, cycles the insertion among the current insertion point location and the last three places in which editing occurred. If multiple documents are open and editing last occurred in a document that's not onscreen, Shift+F5 will take you there.

If only one file is open, and if it was just opened, then Shift+F5 will take you to the last place in which editing occurred the last time that file was opened. This can be a good way to find where you left off.

Pasting unformatted text

One of the most frequently used features in Word is pasting unformatted text. When you copy text from a browser, another Word file, an Excel worksheet, or some other source, you very often just want the text, and not the extraneous formatting (which might include odd bits of HTML) as well. Microsoft realized that users often need to paste unformatted text, so the Paste button's drop-down menu includes the Keep Text Only button, shown in Figure 3.13. Pointing to one of the Paste Options buttons displays a Live Preview of how the pasted information will look as well.

If you prefer to use keyboard shortcuts, after copying text with Ctrl+C, you can press Alt+HVT to paste the table without formatting. In older versions of Word, you had to display the Paste Options dialog box to paste unformatted text. The keyboard shortcut was Alt+ESU, followed by Enter.

> **NOTE**
>
> Remember that with multikey KeyTip combinations, press Alt plus the first letter, and release. Then press the next letters in sequence. Another way of stating the Alt+HVT example is press Alt+H, then press V, then press T.

FIGURE 3.13

Live Preview shows how the top table would look when pasted as text.

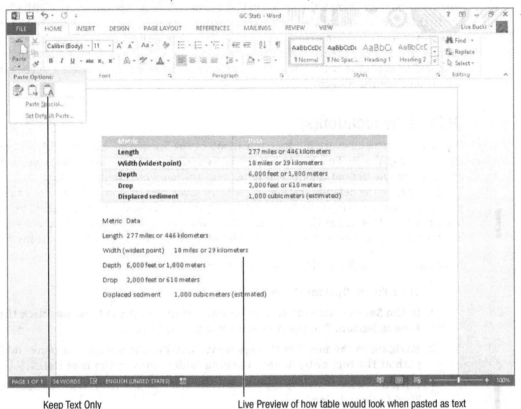

Keep Text Only   Live Preview of how table would look when pasted as text

Wrap to fit

If you don't like having to scroll horizontally in a document but keep Word zoomed above 150 percent most of the time and often create landscape oriented (wide) documents, you may want to take advantage of a couple of features that will eliminate the need to scroll horizontally.

First, use Draft view whenever possible. To use Draft view click Draft in the Views group of the View tab on the Ribbon.

Second, enable Word's ability to wrap text to fit the window onscreen. Choose File ➪ Options ➪ Advanced. Scroll down to the Show document content section, and click to enable Show text wrapped within the document window. Note that this won't work in any of the layout views, because it doesn't accurately display document layout.

Applying styles (Ctrl+Shift+S)

When you want to change the style applied to the selected text, press Ctrl+Shift+S, type the first few characters of the style name until it appears in the Style Name box (you can also press the up or down arrow to finish selecting the desired style). Press Enter to apply the selected style to the text. With this method, you never have to take your hands off the keyboard to apply the style. You'll save a few seconds every time you use a keyboard short-cut rather than the Ribbon.

Default file location(s)

If you store each and every file that you create in the Documents library (which by default places them in the My Documents folder that is part of your personal folders), you'll eventually have trouble finding the file you need, because you'll be scrolling through so many files. You can change the default location where Word saves files in Word options. For example, you might want to change the save location if your employer wants you to store project files in a network folder rather than your local hard disk. Or, you may have a second hard disk installed in your computer for your data files and want to save to a folder on it instead.

To change the default location to which files are stored in Word:

1. **Click File ⇨ Options ⇨ Save.**
2. **In the Save documents section beside Default local file location, click the Browse button.** The Modify Location dialog box opens.
3. **Navigate to the new file storage location using the Navigation pane, folder path at the top, or by double-clicking folder icons in the files list.**
4. **Click OK twice.** This applies your change and closes both the Modify Locations and Word Options dialog boxes.

> **NOTE**
>
> The Advanced tab of the Word Options dialog box enables you to change additional file locations. Scroll down to the General section, and click the File Locations button. Now use the File Locations dialog box to change other locations, such as the default location for User templates.

Playing Favorites

The Navigation pane in Word's Open and Save As dialog boxes includes a list of *favorites*—handy locations for storing files. You can customize the Favorites list to include your own favorite location:

1. **Click File ⇨ Open.**
2. **Click Computer under Open in the middle pane.**
3. **Click the Browse button under Computer in the right pane.** The Open dialog box appears.

4. **Navigate to and open the folder that you want to mark as a favorite.**

5. **In the Navigation pane, right-click Favorites, and click Add current location to Favorites.**

6. **Continue and open a file, or just click Cancel to close the dialog box and then the Back button at the upper left of the File tab to return to your prior document.**

> **NOTE**
>
> You also can drag a folder to the Favorites list. This works within the Open dialog box, so in place of Step 4 above, you could navigate to the point where you see the folder in the file/folder list at left, and then drag it into the Favorites list in the Navigation pane at the left side of the Open dialog box. Or, in a File Explorer (Windows 8) or Windows Explorer (Windows 7) window, you can likewise drag a folder from the list at the right and drop it into the Favorites in the Navigation pane.

After you've added a location to the Favorites list, click it in the list to jump directly to that folder in the Open or Save As dialog box.

Once a favorite outlives its usefulness, remove it. Right-click it in the Favorites list in either the Open or Save As dialog box, and choose Remove as shown in Figure 3.14. The original location is untouched. Only the shortcut to it is removed from the Favorites area.

FIGURE 3.14

You can remove a favorite that you no longer need.

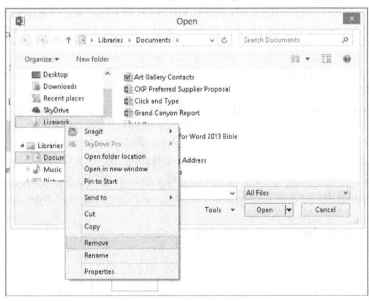

Don't like the default arrangement? Then drag the shortcuts around so that they meet your needs.

Enabling AutoRecover and backup saving

If you hate losing work (and most of us do), make sure that the AutoRecover feature is active and set to a relatively short save interval. Most users set up AutoRecover to save the necessary information every 10 minutes or less. AutoRecover is not the same thing as saving a copy of your file, however. AutoRecover attempts to recover your documents only if Word crashes or you otherwise forget to save something. It does not automatically do a normal save of your document. Saving your document is up to you.

In addition to pressing Ctrl+S often, it's a good practice to tell Word to make a backup copy each time you save your file. This feature does act as an automated way of creating another copy of your file. If somehow a crash corrupts the main document file, you can work from the backup copy instead. Depending on when you last saved, the backup copy may not have all of your most recent changes, but it will ensure you will lose less work than if your document is corrupted and you don't have a backup.

The AutoRecover feature is enabled by default, but saving a backup copy is not. Here's how to ensure that both of these features are turned on and set up as you prefer:

1. **Click File ⇨ Options ⇨ Save.** The AutoRecover settings appear in the Save documents section of the displayed tab in the Word Options dialog box.

2. **Make sure that the Save AutoRecover information every check box is checked.**

3. **If needed, change the minutes text box entry beside Save AutoRecover information every to adjust the save interval.** You can either double-click the text box entry and type a new one, or use the spinner arrow buttons. Choose an interval that reflects your work habits. If you're a fast worker you might want to set it to as little as every minute or two. For most users the default 10 minutes seems a bit too infrequent.

4. **Make sure that the Keep the last autosaved version if I close without saving check box is checked.** This ensures that Word's file versioning feature will keep at least one autosaved copy of your files available even if you forget to save.

5. **Click the Advanced tab in the Word Options dialog box.**

6. **Scroll down to the Save section, and click the Always create backup copy to check (enable) it.** Word will now begin saving a backup copy each time you save a file.

7. **Click OK to close the Word Options dialog box.**

The AutoRecover save interval feature also controls how often Word creates autosaved versions of files (`.asd` files). When you choose File ➪ Info, the Versions section lists all `.asd` (autosaved) file versions. Click one of the listed autosaved files to open it. As shown in Figure 3.15, a yellow Message Bar appears at the top and asks whether how you want to use the file. Click Compare to incorporate any changes from the autosaved version of the file as marked corrections in the current version, or click Restore to replace the current file with the autosaved version.

FIGURE 3.15

When you open an autosaved file version, you can compare it to the current file or restore it.

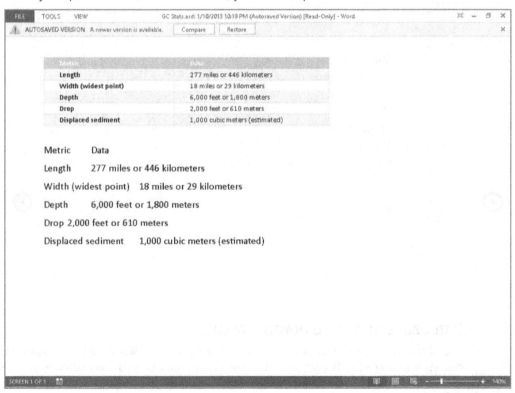

To access autosaved versions of other files from the Info choices on the File tab, click the Manage Versions button and then click Recover Unsaved Documents as shown in Figure 3.16. By default, this displays the Open dialog box and shows all .asd files in C:\Users*user name*\AppData\Local\Microsoft\Office\UnsavedFiles.

Note that this is not the same location as the AutoRecover files location set in File ⇨ Options ⇨ Advanced ⇨ File Locations. Instead, this is where Word saves versions of unsaved files left over from previous Word work sessions. (You made sure that this feature was enabled in Step 4 earlier.) According to Word's online Help, the autosaved versions will be kept in the above folder for four days after Word creates them. These autosaved file versions serve as one of several last ditch efforts to recover a document you think something you worked on is hopelessly lost.

FIGURE 3.16

You also can choose a command that opens the location where Word stores autosaved versions of other files.

Don't save only to removable media

One of the most common causes of corrupted documents in Word (and other apps, for that matter) is saving a file directly to removable media such as a USB flash (thumb) drive. Because of the way Word creates and uses temporary files, many of those working files end up in the same folder in which the original file is being edited. As you edit, temporary files are constantly being opened. In some cases they can be many times larger than the original file. This makes it exceedingly easy for removable media to fill up. Once Word runs out of space, you can kiss your file goodbye. While the idea of saving your file directly to a USB drive, SD card, CF card, or other removable media may be tempting, it's a safer practice to save your files to your computer's hard disk, and then copy the files to the removable media after saving and closing them in Word.

Another corruption scenario occurs when removable media is removed while Word still has the file open. And by "open," I mean that quite literally. Word often separates the file into different pieces to make editing more efficient from a programming standpoint. Usually Word doesn't reassemble the file until it has been fully closed. A recent Save isn't sufficient. If you remove the media before the file closes, you quite likely will corrupt the file. Even if you close the file, removing the media before you have properly ejected it from the system can damage files on the drive. (For this reason, better quality USB drives have an LED light that flashes while the drive is saving and remains on until you eject the drive.)

Something similar can happen, although this is less common, if a file being edited resides on a server and you lose connection with the server before the file is properly closed. Think of the server as you think of removable media. If you lose your server connection, you can save a copy of the file to your local computer, and then use Save As to later resave it to the server when you're able to reconnect.

So, if you shouldn't edit directly on removable media, what should you do? Use an Explorer window from the Windows desktop to copy the file to your own local hard drive. Edit it there, save it, and close it. Then use Explorer to copy the changed file back to the location or removable media where you want it.

You can further protect yourself by telling Word to copy remote files to your computer when they are stored on a server. In File ⇨ Options ⇨ Advanced, scroll down to the Save section, and click to enable the Copy remotely stored files onto your computer, and update the remove file when saving check box.

Open and Repair

Word's Open dialog box includes an Open and Repair command. It's easy to overlook this option because you have to know where in the dialog box to find it, but it is simple to access and use.

Whenever Word is unable to open a file the normal way, Open and Repair might be your best hope of recovering as much as possible to avoid losing difficult-to-redo editing. When you encounter a file that Word says it can't open, display the Open dialog box and select the file. Rather than click Open, click the drop-down arrow next to the Open button, and choose Open and Repair as shown in Figure 3.17. In recent Word versions, this has been fixing more and more documents (although it's not a miracle worker).

3

FIGURE 1.17

The Open drop-down list enables you to choose other methods for opening a file, including Open and Repair.

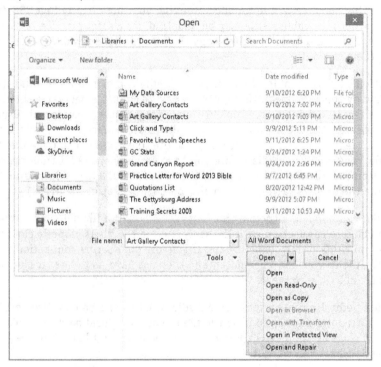

Last ditch salvage

If Open and Repair fails, your last resort might be to attempt to use Recover Text from Any File, which you access by selecting Recover Text from Any File from the File type list beside the File name text box in the Open dialog box. Note, however, that this recovery feature should not be used on files saved in any of Word's new .docx and .docm formats. That's because those files are actually compressed ZIP files, and you will not recover any useful text from them. Instead, rename the damaged file so that it has a .zip extension. Then, open the ZIP file and look for a folder named Word. Inside that folder there should be a file named document.xml (yes, document.xml is the actual filename). That file will contain the text of your document amid a lot of XML commands.

Sorting paragraphs that aren't in a table

Many Word users are familiar with sorting the rows in a table, but many don't realize that Word enables you to sort any list—even one that's not in a table. Select the items you want sorted and click the Sort button in the Paragraph group of the Home tab. This opens the Sort Text dialog box, which you can use to specify the details for the sort.

Moving paragraphs easily

If you ever have two paragraphs that you need to quickly swap, don't reach for the mouse. Instead, put the insertion point into either paragraph and use Shift+Alt+Up or Shift+Alt+Down to move the current paragraph up or down so that it changes places with the other paragraph. These are outlining keyboard shortcuts, but they work great for when you're editing text in Print Layout view as well. You can also quickly move rows around in tables using these shortcuts.

Summary

In this chapter you've learned about some of Word's most useful and important power features and tools. You should now be familiar with them and ready to start using them to enhance and simplify your work with Word documents. You can now work smarter in Word by:

- Using styles to format a document more quickly and consistently, ensuring a more professional and refined look for your documents
- Building a document from the top down by creating and organizing headings in Outline view
- Using the Navigation pane to view outline HEADINGS and rearrange them
- Understanding how AutoCorrect cleans up typos
- Removing unwanted AutoCorrect entries and adding your own automatic corrections and shortcuts to reduce tedium and improve your productivity
- Adding properties that make it easier to find files
- Taking advantage of some key Word Options and power techniques to make Word easier, faster, and more powerful for everyday word processing

3

Zapping Word's Top Annoyances

IN THIS CHAPTER

Dealing with graphics

Eliminating irritating editing issues

Making view annoyances vanish

Teaching Word to look for Help locally

Conquering the activation blues

Stopping some automated changes

With an estimated 500 million users worldwide, Microsoft Word leads the word processing pack. This means that for most of us, jobs and other organizations require that we spend a fair amount of time using and getting used to Microsoft Word. Even though Microsoft invests tremendous resources in making each version of Word better than its predecessor, many users eventually encounter a Word feature or behavior that doesn't work as they would like or that becomes downright exasperating.

This chapter details a number of annoying things that prevent many users from enjoying and using Word as the makers intended. Some of the settings and behaviors here are defaults; others get turned on by accident. Some require you to dig a little deeper to find out what makes Word tick. What the annoyances covered in this chapter have in common is that they can be tamed or turned off. If some things about Word are giving you a headache, this chapter is your aspirin.

Dealing with Graphics Annoyances

More than ever, documents tell stories through graphics such as shapes, charts, and pictures in addition to text. Word 2013's tools for incorporating graphics in documents and formatting the graphics are better than ever. Selecting a graphic displays one or more contextual tabs jam-packed with settings you can use to refine the selected item's appearance. That being said, a few aspects of working with graphics can trip up your document design process. Learn how to deal with these graphics issues now.

Dismissing the drawing canvas

Figure 4.1 shows the *drawing canvas*. In earlier versions of Word, whenever you inserted a shape, the drawing canvas would appear automatically as a container for the shape. (It also displayed *Create your drawing here* inside the canvas.) Intended to clarify to the user that drawing objects exist in a different layer than text, the drawing canvas ended up getting in the way and confusing users.

FIGURE 4.1

If you upgraded from a pre-2010 version or another user changed settings, Word 2013 might still display the drawing canvas.

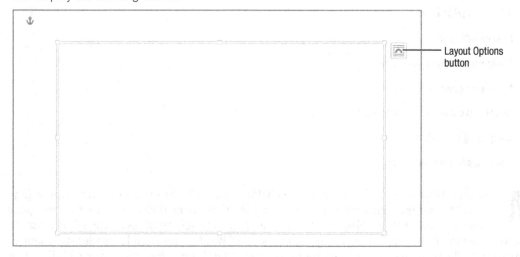

Layout Options button

In Word 2013 the drawing canvas does not appear by default, but if you're one of the few users who actually got used to it and want it back, you can have it back. On the other hand, if you prefer not to use it and it appears in Word 2013 because you upgraded from a pre-2010 version of Word, you can get rid of it.

Use another of Word's Options settings to make the drawing canvas stop appearing (or to make it appear).

1. **Click File ⇨ Options ⇨ Advanced.**
2. **Under Editing options, click the Automatically create drawing canvas when inserting AutoShapes check box.** Clearing the check box turns off the drawing canvas, while checking it turns it back on. Shapes were called AutoShapes in older Word versions, hence the appearance of that term in this option.
3. **Click OK.**

Note in Figure 4.1 that in this version of Word, a Layout Options button that is a new Word 2013 feature appears beside the upper-right corner of the drawing canvas. This button also appears when you insert graphics without the drawing canvas, so you have the same tools for working with your graphic content whether or not you use the drawing canvas. Chapters 13 through 15 provide more detail about creating and formatting various types of graphics, including using the Layout Options button and other new formatting settings buttons.

Fixing text wrapping

Working with how text behaves around a graphic is another feature of working with graphics that can prove repetitive or problematic. The Wrap Text setting available for graphics, usually found on a Format contextual tab for the selected object, controls how text positions itself or flows relative to the position of a graphic you insert. For example, you can set Wrap Text to Top and Bottom to have the text stop at the line above the graphic and restart on the line below the graphic, so that no text appears beside the graphic.

The default Wrap Text setting for inserted shapes in Word 2013 and at least a few prior versions has been In Front of Text. With this setting, the text doesn't wrap around the shape at all. Instead, the graphic appears on top of the text, obscuring the text behind it. This seems an odd choice, because there are only limited instances where most users would want to apply this setting. For example, I tend to use the Square and Tight wrap text settings most frequently. Figure 4.2 compares the default wrapping (top) versus square wrapping. As you can see, the text behind the top shape can't be read with the default wrap setting. The default Wrap Text setting for other types of graphics is In Line with Text.

FIGURE 4.2

The top square has the default In Front of Text wrapping, and the bottom one has Square wrapping.

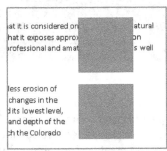

Word 2013 fortunately enables you to change the default wrap and position setting (collectively called the layout) for new pictures, charts, or SmartArt graphics you insert in documents. Here's how to select a new default layout for these graphics:

1. **Insert a picture, chart, or SmartArt graphic, and leave it selected.**

> **NOTE**
>
> A SmartArt graphic is a special type of automated diagram in Office applications. You can choose an overall SmartArt type—such as Lis, Process, Cycle, or Hierarchy—then choose a specific diagram style. From there, you add your text in the shapes in the SmartArt graphic to build its contents. The section called "Inserting SmartArt" in Chapter 13 provides more information about creating and working with SmartArt graphics.

2. **In the Arrange group of the Format contextual tab, choose the desired page position and wrap settings from the Position and Wrap Text drop-down lists.** Note that the full name of the contextual tab depends on the type of object you created and selected. It might be the Chart Tools Format, Picture Tools Format, or SmartArt Tools Format tab. You can also click More Layout Options at the bottom of the Wrap Text menu, use the Layout dialog box that appears to set more detailed wrap and position settings, and then click OK.

3. **In the same tab and group, click Wrap Text ⇨ Set as Default Layout.** Future picture, chart, and SmartArt graphics you insert will use the Position and Wrap Text settings specified by your new default.

> **NOTE**
>
> The Set as Default Layout option is unavailable for inserted shapes. However, if you've inserted a picture, chart, or SmartArt graphic, one of a few things may be wrong if it's still unavailable. For example, you may not have changed the wrap setting yet, and in some cases you also have to change a position setting to make the command available. Also, if you're working with a chart or SmartArt, make sure the overall chart or SmartArt is selected, not an element within the overall graphic.

> **NOTE**
>
> Another Wrap Text setting, Behind Text, also does not wrap but instead places the graphic on the layer behind the text. Because you can see the text, this type of wrapping can be useful for adding interesting background colors or effects to parts of the document. You'll learn more details about wrapping text around various types of objects in Part IV, "Illustrating Your Story with Graphics."

Resetting a graphic

For each type of graphic, you can change around a couple of dozen overall settings, from recoloring and cropping a picture to recoloring a SmartArt Graphic. There are so many settings that it is possible to overdo it with your choices and create a frankengraphic. In older versions of Word, you had to re-create the graphic from scratch or remove all the settings you applied; now you can simply reset the graphic to its original appearance. Word offers a Reset Graphic command for several types of graphics. For example, in Figure 4.3, the top graphic is a plain picture of a blue background fill pattern, with an added wide, dark border, cropped to a heart shape. The bottom graphic is a copy of that same formatted object that has been reset to its original plain rectangle appearance using the Reset Picture command shown in the Adjust group on the Ribbon.

FIGURE 4.3

The top picture has the added border and cropping, whereas the bottom copy was reset to its original appearance.

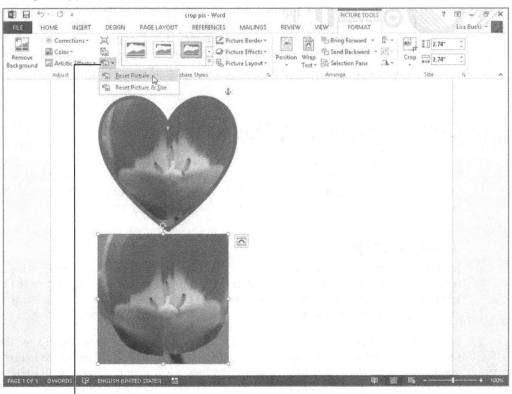

Click for choices for resetting a picture

4

The Reset Picture command is pretty handy. Figuring out where it is can be a little trickier. Here's where to find it based on the type of graphic:

- **SmartArt:** SmartArt Tools ⇨ Design contextual tab, in the Reset group at far right.
- **Pictures:** Picture Tools ⇨ Format contextual tab, Adjust group. Click the Reset Picture down arrow button if you need to choose between Reset Picture and Reset Picture & Size.
- **Charts:** Chart Tools ⇨ Format contextual tab, Current Selection group, Reset to Match Style command. This command works slightly different. It resets formatting for individual chart elements to match the overall chart style you've applied from the Chart Styles gallery in the Chart Styles group of the Chart Tools ⇨ Design contextual tab; it does not reset the chart to its initial appearance when you created it.
- **Shapes and WordArt:** Not applicable because shapes and WordArt cannot be reset.

Overcoming Editing Annoyances

Word has dozens of editing options. The typical user in the broader Word community often has a love/hate relationship when it comes to particular settings and behaviors. What some users hate, others love, and vice versa. Word's options give every use the opportunity to turn off editing features that they dislike or have difficulty using.

Insert/Overtype

In older versions of Word, pressing the Insert key toggled between Insert mode, where typing text adds characters to the left of the insertion point and moves existing text to the right, and Overtype mode, where typing replaces text to the right of the insertion point. You learned about creating text in these modes in Chapter 2, "Diving Into Document Creation."

Because on many keyboards the Insert key is right beside or below the Delete key, users often inadvertently switch to Overtype mode when trying to delete text. The result: inadvertently overtyping text. Word 2007 first removed the Insert key's control over toggling between the two text entry modes, but the way that it implemented the new method of toggling between the modes isn't obvious or intuitive to many users. Fortunately, you can easily switch between the Insert and Overtype modes:

1. **Right-click the status bar at the bottom of the Word screen and ensure that Overtype has a check mark by it as shown in Figure 4.4.** This turns on display of the INSERT/OVERTYPE indicator on the status bar.
2. **Press Esc to dismiss the Customize Status Bar menu.**

3. **Click the INSERT/OVERTYPE indicator on the status bar to change between the modes as needed.** The name displayed on the indicator tells you the current mode, so clicking INSERT changes to Overtype mode, and vice versa.

FIGURE 4.4

Turn on your ability to change between Insert and Overtype modes by customizing the status bar.

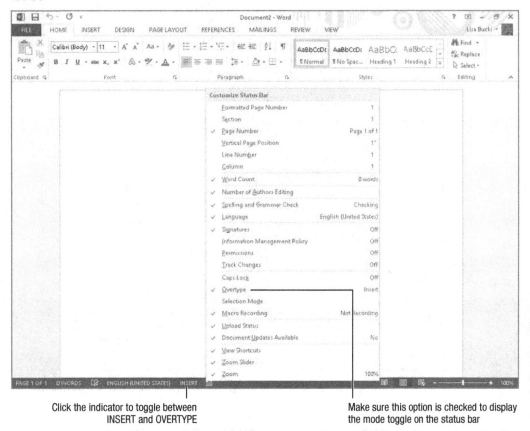

Click the indicator to toggle between
INSERT and OVERTYPE

Make sure this option is checked to display
the mode toggle on the status bar

You still can revert to the prior behavior of having the Insert key toggle between Insert and Overtype modes. Select File ➪ Options ➪ Advanced tab. Under Editing Options, click to enable the Use the insert key to control overtype mode option as shown in Figure 4.5, and then click OK. Of course, reverse this setting to turn the Insert key behavior back off.

(Before clicking OK, you also could check the Use overtype mode check box just below Use the insert key to control overtype mode to turn on Overtype mode.)

FIGURE 4.5

Control the Insert key toggle behavior in Word Options.

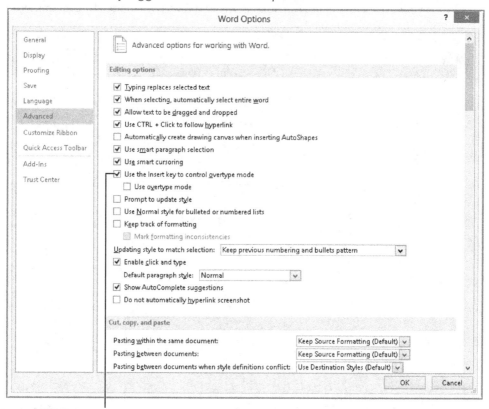

When checked, you can press the Insert key to toggle between Insert and Overtype modes.

TIP

After you choose File ⇨ Options ⇨ Advanced, scroll down to the Cut, copy, and paste section. If you click to enable the check box for Use the Insert key for paste, in the future you can press Insert to paste copied text and graphics rather than clicking the Paste button or pressing Ctrl+V. Of course, you only want to enable this option when you're not using the Insert key to toggle typing modes, or you'll end up with a whole new type of confusing behavior from Word.

Typing replaces selected text

In most Windows programs, when you select text and begin typing, the selected text is replaced by the new text you type. Note that I'm not talking about Overtype being controlled by the Insert/Overtype toggle that you can display on the status bar or assign to the Insert key.

Word has a different mode of editing that is an available option. When text is selected and you type new text, the selection isn't deleted. Instead, Word unselects it and shoves it to the right.

If you find that you often accidentally delete text you've selected, you might want to deliberately turn off the Typing replaces selected text choice in Word options. More often, however, users mistake this feature for Insert/Overtype, and turn it off assuming that they're turning Overtype off. Then, when Overtype doesn't stop, users forget the exact Options change they made, so they don't know that the simple fix is turning the Typing replaces selected text option back off.

Here's where to find this option to turn it on and off:

1. **Click File ➪ Options ➪ Advanced.**
2. **At the top under Editing options, click the Typing replaces selected text check box.** Clearing the check box turns off the behavior where Word lets you overtype the selection, while checking it ensures that new text is inserted and existing text moves right.
3. **Click OK.**

> **NOTE**
> Many users prefer to keep their hands on the keyboard and use a lot of keyboard shortcuts. With dozens of keyboard shortcuts available in Word, it takes a while to become familiar with them all. There's a shortcut for discovering the key combination for any command. See Chapter 29, "Keyboard Customization," to learn more.

4

Formatting control covers up Live Preview

Live Preview can save you a lot of time because you can point to various choices to see the impact, rather than having to repeatedly open a gallery or drop-down list and make different choices. In most cases, Live Preview works like a charm. However, in some instances, the Live Preview can cover up the text or object that you're trying to preview in the document. There are two temporary fixes for this:

- **Resize the gallery or drop-down list.** Some drop-down lists, such as the Font drop-down list in the Font group of the Home tab, have a resizing control with four dots at the bottom, as shown in Figure 4.6. Galleries such as the Style gallery may have three dots in the lower-right corner when you open them. Use the dotted control to drag up to resize the drop-down list or gallery so that you can see the Live Preview in the text. With this method, you will have to scroll the list or gallery more to preview additional choices.

FIGURE 4.6

The dots at the bottom of a drop-down list or corner of a gallery indicate you can drag up to resize it and expose more of the document for Live Preview.

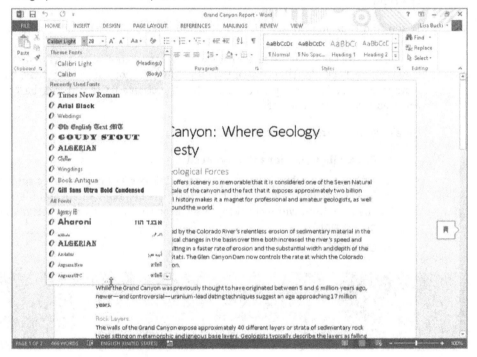

■ **Scroll the document and try again.** If the overlap between the menu or gallery is slight, press Esc to close the menu or gallery. Scroll the document text down so that the selected area where Live Preview appears is below the open menu or gallery. Of course, this method has the limitation that it doesn't work for text and images at the top of the first page of the document, because you can only scroll down to the point where the top of the first page appears.

If you don't find Live Preview helpful, you can turn it off. In File ⇨ Options ⇨ General, remove the check next to Enable Live Preview in the top section, User Interface options. If you still want to preview fonts before applying them, you can use the Font dialog box instead of the Font drop-down list. Its Preview box shows you how the selected text will appear with the highlighted font applied, as shown in Figure 4.7. Select text, and then open the Font dialog box by clicking the dialog box launcher in the Font group of the Home tab on the Ribbon.

FIGURE 4.7

Some of Word's remaining dialog boxes provide formatting previews.

Clearing formatting

The section "Updating styles" in Chapter 3, "Working Smarter, Not Harder, in Word," introduced you to the Prompt to update style option on the Advanced tab of the Word Options dialog box. When that feature is enabled and you apply direct formatting to text to which you've previously applied a style, Word opens a dialog box asking if you want to change the styles.

Direct formatting has another, perhaps unexpected, behavior with relation to styles. For example, let's say you apply the Heading 1 style to a line of text, and then you apply bold to a single word within the heading. Later, you select the line of text and change it to the Heading 2 style. If you expected that Word would remove the bold formatting and apply the style to all of the text on the selected line, you'd be wrong. The direct formatting trumps the style in most instances.

4

You have to clear direct formatting such as bold or italic to revert to the style's settings. First, select the text. If you've modified paragraph formatting, such as changing the line spacing or indention, press Ctrl+Q, which is by default assigned to the ResetPara command. If you've modified character formatting, such as applying bold or changing the font, press Ctrl+Space, which is assigned to ResetChar.

Sometimes you might want to remove all of the formatting for a paragraph altogether. If you click the dialog box launcher in the Styles group of the Home tab, the Styles pane (or Styles task pane) opens. As shown in Figure 4.8, the top choice in its list of styles is Clear All. Clicking it reverts the text to the Normal style and removes any paragraph formatting for the paragraph holding the insertion point. To also remove direct formatting, select the formatted text and then click Clear All.

FIGURE 4.8

Revert text to the Normal style with the Clear All choice.

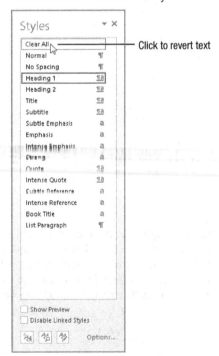

Click to revert text

On the other hand, you can set up Word to automatically update a style to include any direct character or paragraph formatting you apply:

1. **Click the dialog box launcher in the Styles group of the Home tab.** The Styles pane opens.
2. **Right-click the style to auto update, and click Modify.** The Modify Style dialog box opens.
3. **Click the Automatically update check box to check it.** See Figure 4.9.
4. **Click OK.**

FIGURE 4.9

Check the Automatically update check box to have Word automatically redefine the selected style when you make direct formatting changes.

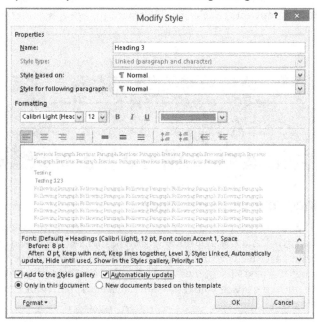

NOTE

You also can display the Modify Style dialog box via the Apply Styles pane. Press Ctrl+Shift+S, select the style from the Style Name drop-down list, and then click Modify.

CAUTION

Word will not let you automatically update the Normal style, because so many styles ultimately are based on Normal.

Mouse selection

Have you ever tried to use the mouse to select everything in a paragraph except for the paragraph mark? Perhaps you want to replace what's typed but want to keep the current paragraph formatting and style. But when you use the mouse to try to leave the paragraph mark unselected, Word jumps right past that last character and selects the paragraph mark as well.

You can make this behavior stop:

1. **Click File ⇨ Options ⇨ Advanced.**
2. **At the top under Editing options, click the Use smart paragraph selection check box to clear it.**
3. **Click OK.**

TIP

With a more precise optical mouse, common today, it is possible to omit the paragraph mark even when smart paragraph selection is turned on. Another workaround for smart paragraph selection is to press Shift+Left Arrow to nudge the selection one character to the left after selecting with the mouse. Smart paragraph selection applies only to selection using the mouse.

Cut and paste sentence and word behavior

Have you ever copied a sentence and then pasted it at the end of another sentence and ended up with no space between the period and the beginning of the pasted sentence, and too much space at the end? Smart cut and paste deals with this problem, by inserting a space between the period and the beginning of the pasted sentence automatically. However, if you're accustomed to compensating for the missing space yourself, Word's automatic behavior can be a nuisance, and you can turn it off.

1. **Click File ⇨ Options ⇨ Advanced.**
2. **Scroll down to display the Cut, copy, and paste options.**
3. **Beside the Use smart cut and paste check box, click the Settings button.** The Settings dialog box shown in Figure 4.10 opens.

FIGURE 4.10

You can fine-tune smart cut and paste behavior in this dialog box.

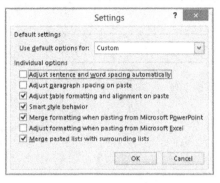

4. Click the **Adjust sentence and word spacing automatically** check box to clear it.

5. Click **OK** twice to close both the Settings and Word Options dialog boxes.

Tackling View Annoyances

Clutter or missing tools onscreen can put a crimp in how quickly you work in Word. In this section you learn how to quickly stop some of the most common view annoyances.

Nonprinting indicators/formatting marks

You can display nonprinting formatting indicators and marks onscreen to help diagnose formatting issues in a document. However, most users prefer to hide those marks when they're not needed, because they can make the document harder to read for editing. In particular, many users find the paragraph mark bothersome and distracting. The Show/Hide setting is enabled within the document. This means that if you receive and open a document created by another user, it might have the unwanted nonprinting characters displayed in it.

I like having as much visual information as possible when I'm writing, but if you want to stop this behavior, here's how: press Ctrl+Shift+8 (Show/Hide) to toggle these nonprinting marks off and on. You can also toggle them on and off by clicking the ¶ (Show/Hide) button in the Paragraph group of the Ribbon's Home tab.

If all of the marks don't go away, you'll need to examine the settings a bit more carefully. If individual marks are independently enabled, clicking the Show/Hide tool won't have any effect. Click File ⇨ Options ⇨ Display to see the settings shown in Figure 4.11. The Show/Hide toggle affects only marks that aren't independently checked. Any that are independently checked stay on regardless of the overall toggle.

4

FIGURE 4.11

If any individual marks are checked here, they can't be toggled with Ctrl+Shift+8 or the Show/Hide button.

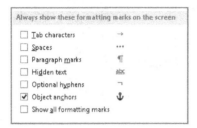

Missing Ribbon tabs

When you get into certain advanced features, you'll need to work with two Ribbon tabs that may be hidden: the Developer and Add-Ins tabs. The Developer tab is hidden by default. The Add-Ins tab will normally appear whenever you load an add-in with a tab, but if it doesn't appear, that means that it's been turned off. Here's how to display and hide these two tabs and others as needed:

1. **Click File ⇨ Options ⇨ Customize Ribbon.**
2. **In the Main Tabs list at the right side of the Word Options dialog box, click to check and uncheck tabs as needed.** When checked here, a tab appears on the Ribbon. Unchecked tabs do not appear.
3. **Click OK.**

Dealing with Online versus Local Help Content

By default, if you're online, Word's Help system assumes that you'd prefer to access Help using online services. It's nice to know that the Help system can search online as a last-ditch effort if your own local Help can't find an answer. However, it's not necessarily good that it's the first ditch and not the last. If you are on a slow wireless connection in a public location, are working somewhere where you don't have online access, or are still on a dial-up connection, Help will work more slowly than when using the installed Help information offline.

In any event, you can tell Word to use your own local offline Help. To set the source of Word Help, press F1 to display Word Help. Click the drop-down arrow beside Word Help, shown in Figure 4.12. To force Word to use only the local Word Help files, choose Word Help from your computer. If your system was somehow temporarily disconnected from the Internet and you need to reconnect Help, choose Word Help from Office.com.

FIGURE 4.12

Use Word's local offline Help files when your Internet connection is slow or limited.

Activation Blues

Are your Ribbons faded and unavailable? Are you unable to save new files? If so, then it's possible that your version of Word has not been activated. Word requires activation. If you're using a trial version, you have to pay to activate the software. Even if you're using a purchased version, you still have to activate; normally you will be prompted to activate it the first time you start the program and can just follow the prompts to do so. After a trial period, if you don't activate Word, it goes into "reduced functionality" mode.

To determine whether activation is the source of your woes:

1. **Click File ⇨ Account.** On the right side of the screen, under Product Information Office, a yellow Activation Required box will appear if Word is not activated.
2. **Click the Change Product Key link.**
3. **Type your product key, and click Install and then OK.**
4. **Follow the prompts in the Microsoft Office Activation Wizard that appears.**

If activation isn't the problem, Word may have a corrupted Normal.dotm template (or other global add-in) or corrupted registry entries. Visit http://word.mvps.org/ and search for "troubleshooting" for additional help.

> **NOTE**
>
> The Office 2013 apps are also available by subscription under the Office 365 brand. It's set up so that the system administrator can install and activate groups of users in a single operation. If you find that your work installation of Word isn't activated for some reason, contact your company's IT troubleshooter for Help.

Automatic Annoyances

Word makes certain text and formatting changes automatically by default. These automatic changes might work for you—or not. This section shows you how to reclaim your ability to create your text yourself.

Bullets, numbers, boxes, and borders

Word sometimes senses that you're typing a bulleted or a numbered list and uses its AutoFormat As You Type feature to help you. For example, if the insertion point is at the beginning of a new paragraph and you press Tab, type an asterisk (Shift+8), and press Tab again, Word converts the asterisk to a bullet and applies the List Paragraph style to the paragraph. Similarly, if you press Enter after a paragraph, type a number of underline characters, and press Enter again, Word converts your underline characters into a border line beneath the paragraph.

You can tell Word what to AutoFormat and what not to.

1. **Click File ⇨ Options ⇨ Proofing.**
2. **Click the AutoCorrect Options button.** The AutoCorrect Options dialog box appears.
3. **Click the AutoFormat As You Type tab.** See Figure 4.13. This tab controls automatic corrections. The AutoFormat tab's settings, on the other hand, apply when you display and use the AutoFormat command. For more about the differences between these two features, see "AutoFormat versus AutoFormat as You Type" and "Working with the AutoFormat Command" in Chapter 11, "Cleaning Up with AutoCorrect and AutoFormat."
4. **Click to check and uncheck features as needed.** For example, under Apply as you type, you can uncheck the Automatic bulleted lists and Automatic numbered lists check boxes to have Word stop automating those types of lists.
5. **Click OK twice to close both dialog boxes.**

FIGURE 4.13

You can enable or disable more than a dozen AutoFormat Actions.

Capitalization

Word makes some automatic corrections to capitalization that may not be what you want. For example, it assumes you want the first word in every sentence to be capitalized and caps it if you fail to do so. This might not be what you want in all circumstances, such as if you're writing poetry or typing in a list of parts or products that you want to appear in lowercase. You also can turn off this behavior in Word:

1. **Click File ⇨ Options ⇨ Proofing.**
2. **Click the AutoCorrect Options button.** The AutoCorrect Options dialog box appears.
3. **Click the AutoCorrect tab if needed.** See Figure 4.14.
4. **Click to check and uncheck the second through sixth check boxes as needed.** For example, clear the Capitalize first letter of sentences check box if you want to control sentence capitalization.
5. **Click OK twice to close both dialog boxes.**

FIGURE 1.11

You can enable or disable automatic capitalization on the AutoCorrect tab.

Summary

In this chapter you've learned how to control features and defaults that can trip up your ability to work quickly and effectively in Word. Among other things, you've learned how to do the following:

- Disable or enable the drawing canvas, change the default Wrap Text setting used for some graphic objects, and reset a graphic to its default formatting

- Overcome a number of editing annoyances, including by gaining control over the Insert key, clearing direct formatting so you can change styles, and controlling how Word pastes sentences from the Clipboard

- Control whether nonprinting characters appear and display Ribbon tabs that were turned off

- Save time and improve Help performance by using the built-in offline Help system

- Determine whether a lack of activation is the source of Word's nonperformance

- Control a number of Word's automatic formatting and capitalization behaviors

Part II

Working with Document Style and Content

P art II focuses on the baseline features that every Word user needs and employs—regardless of what types of documents you create in Word. This section covers the basics thoroughly but doesn't belabor easily mastered skills. Beyond that and more important, Part II is heavy on tips and shortcuts, pitfalls, and core techniques such as using document styles to save you time and work.

Chapter 5 begins with the basic unit of formatting—character formatting. Chapter 6 introduces and explains paragraph formatting, contrasting it with character formatting, and setting the stage for Styles. Chapter 7 combines elements of character and paragraph formatting, providing a full exposition on understanding and using Word styles and the various style tools Word offers. Chapter 8 will show you everything you need to know about the Clipboard, which is perhaps the most important time-saving word processing tool ever conceived. Finally, Chapter 9 will guide you through using Word's powerful Find and Replace tools.

IN THIS PART

Font/Character Formatting

IN THIS CHAPTER

Looking again at text formatting methods

Choosing between character styles versus direct character formatting

Applying, clearing, and copying character formatting

Using the Font dialog box and Mini Toolbar

Learning about OpenType features

Commanding character formatting keyboard shortcuts

In some early word processors, users applied text formatting by inserting formatting codes. For example, you had to add a code to turn on bold formatting, and add a second code to turn bold off later. Text between the codes was bold. This method of relying on a pair of codes often tripped up users. Accidentally delete one code in the pair, and you inadvertently changed the formatting for half the document.

Rather than letting you turn formatting on or off for a string of characters, Word uses an object-oriented formatting approach. In Word, you format objects such as letters, words, paragraphs, tables, pictures, and so on.

Another way to think about formatting is in *units*. Formatting can be applied to any unit you can select. The smallest unit that can be formatted is a single character. Discrete units larger than characters are words, sentences, paragraphs, document sections, and the whole document. Some types of formatting apply only to certain type of units. For example, you can't indent a single word; indention is a paragraph-level setting that applies to some or all of the lines in a paragraph.

Reviewing the Ways You Can Format Text in Word

Word has four levels of formatting: character/font, paragraph, section, and document. Character or font formatting includes bold, italic, points, superscript, and other attributes. You can apply character formats to a unit as small as a single character. Later chapters cover the other levels of formatting.

Font formatting might suggest for many people just changing from one font or typestyle design (for example Calibri, Times New Roman, Arial, or Tahoma) to another. The term *character formatting* used in this book more broadly encompasses all the formatting settings you can change for characters, but because Word positions all of these settings in a group called Font, as shown in Figure 5.1, font formatting and character formatting have come to be used interchangeably. It helps, however, to think in terms of character formatting, as a character is the smallest thing you can format in Word.

FIGURE 5.1

Find many character or font formatting settings in the Home tab's Font group.

NOTE

You also may see the term *text level formatting* in the Word interface; this term means the same thing as character formatting.

Note also that the Font group in the Home tab does not offer all the available character-level formatting. For example, the Font group doesn't include a tool for changing character spacing. In addition, the Font group's Change Case button (its menu has Sentence case, lowercase, and other commands) doesn't change formatting at all. Changing capitalization is distinct from applying the Small caps or All caps character-formatting settings to text.

Formatting Characters Directly or with Styles

Word includes paragraph styles and character styles. *Paragraph styles* can be applied only to a whole paragraph. *Character styles* provide formatting flexibility so that users can apply a style to characters within a paragraph. For example, you can create a style for all the article titles used within a document, or all the phone numbers, or all the web page addresses. Character styles enable you to distinguish one type of formal text from the surrounding paragraph text, and to do so consistently throughout the document.

A third type of style is a *linked style*. A linked style can behave like either a character or paragraph style, depending on the circumstances. If you have one or more entire words selected, selecting a linked style applies the style's character formatting to the selected words within the paragraph only. (Paragraph formatting such as line spacing is ignored.)

The rest of the paragraph retains its original paragraph formatting. If you select the entire paragraph or merely place the insertion point within the paragraph without selecting any words, then an applied linked style behaves like a paragraph style, formatting the text with both the character and paragraph settings of the linked style. A number of the default styles in the `Normal.dotm` default template, including the heading styles, are linked styles.

The alternative to applying a character style is applying character formatting directly. As you're typing along, it's quite easy to use the Font group choices or shortcut keys to apply bold, italic, or underlining to text. That's called *direct formatting*, and often this is the easiest and fastest way to format text, particularly within a paragraph.

Word's default document template includes dozens of built-in styles, and Word gives you clues to help identify paragraph styles versus character styles, linked styles that you can use both ways, and direct formatting applied to text. Use the Styles task pane and Style Inspector to learn more about the styles and formatting applied to the selected text and also the styles that are available.

1. **Select the text that has the formatting you want to examine.**

2. **Click the dialog box launcher in the Styles group of the Home tab.** The Styles task pane appears. As shown in Figure 5.2, a symbol appears to the right of each style name. These symbols identify the type of style:

   - **Paragraph symbol:** A paragraph style that can only be applied to whole paragraphs.

   - **Lowercase a character:** A character style that that can be applied to selected text within a paragraph without changing the entire paragraph's formatting.

   - **Both a paragraph symbol and a lowercase a character:** A linked style you can use either as a paragraph or character style. With the insertion point in the paragraph, applying the style formats the whole paragraph. With text selected in the paragraph, applying the style formats only the selected text.

3. **Click the Style Inspector (middle) icon at the bottom of the Styles task pane.** The Style Inspector, also shown in Figure 5.2, opens. As you can see in Figure 5.2, this pane identifies the styles and formatting applied to the selected text:

   - **Paragraph formatting:** Shows the applied paragraph style, Normal in this example.

   - **Text level formatting:** Shows the applied character style, if any. In this example, the Subtle Emphasis style is also applied to the selected word within the paragraph.

   - **Plus boxes:** Lists any direct character formatting applied in addition to the applied styles.

4. **Click the Close (X) button on the Style Inspector and Styles pane to close them.**

5

FIGURE 5.3

Examine the styles and formatting applied to selected text in the Styles task pane and Style Inspector.

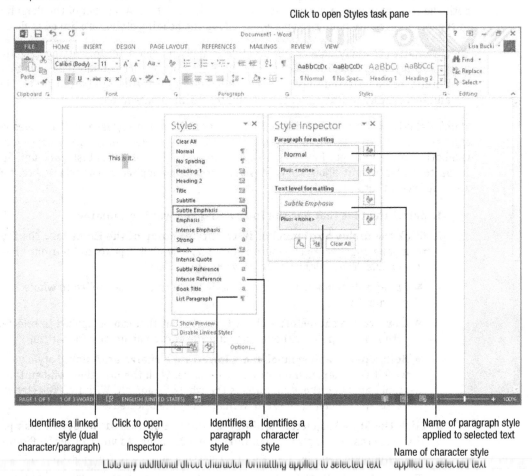

Click to open Styles task pane

Identifies a linked style (dual character/paragraph)

Click to open Style Inspector

Identifies a paragraph style

Identifies a character style

Name of paragraph style applied to selected text

Name of character style applied to selected text

Lists any additional direct character formatting applied to selected text

Given that creating and applying styles involves more thought, preparation, and work than using direct formatting, compare the pros and cons of each with regard to speed and functionality when creating and updating a document. Say you are creating a marketing document for your company's new product, and you want the product name to appear in bold throughout the document. You could apply the bold formatting directly by pressing Ctrl+B (for bold), typing the product name, and then pressing Ctrl+B again to toggle bold off each time you type the product name.

Next, your boss decides the product name should appear in bold and small caps. Because chances are you've also bolded other text in the document, you would have to manually find and reformat each instance of the product name to include the new small caps direct format.

If instead you had created a new character style named Product Name and applied it to each instance of the product name, you could simply modify the Product Name style to include the small caps formatting, and all product name instances would immediately display the new formatting.

The commandment is this: *If the formatting is something you will need to repeatedly apply to certain categories of text (such as book titles, programming commands, product names, jargon, and so on), create a character style and use it.*

If conversely the use is *ad hoc* and not something for which you'll have a recurring need, then go ahead and use direct formatting. For example, when you're writing a letter or memo, you may want to use bold or italics for emphasis. In those cases, using direct formatting fits the bill.

> **TIP**
>
> To streamline using styles, you can assign keyboard shortcuts to some of them. From Word Options (File ⊃ Options), select the Customize Ribbon tab and click the Customize button beside Keyboard shortcuts. Choose Styles in the Categories list. Click the desired style in the Styles list, click in the Press new shortcut key text box, press the desired keys (the exact combination you want to assign, such as Alt+9 or Ctrl+Shift+F7), and then click Assign. Click Close to close the Customize Keyboard dialog box, and then click OK to close the Word Options dialog box.

Applying Character Formatting

There are at least six ways of directly applying various kinds of character formatting:

- Using the Font group on the Home tab of the Ribbon
- Using the Font dialog box (Ctrl+D or Ctrl+Shift+F, or click the Font group dialog box launcher)
- Using the Mini Toolbar (hover the mouse over selected text)
- Using keyboard shortcuts (see Table 5.1 later in this chapter or the topic Keyboard shortcuts for Microsoft Word in Word Help to learn about shortcuts beyond those presented in this chapter)
- Using the Font group's tools or buttons added to the Quick Access Toolbar (QAT)
- Using the Language tool on the status bar

This section describes these methods and gives a sense of which ones to use. A lot depends on your working style, but your choice can also depend on what you happen to be doing. On any given day many users may take advantage of at least five of the six methods.

5

Formatting techniques

To apply character formatting, you have three basic options:

- **As you go method:** Apply formatting before you start typing a word or passage, and then turn it off when you're done. For example, click the Bold button in the Font group of the Home tab, type a word, and then click the Bold button again.
- **Selection method:** Select the text you want formatted and then apply the formatting.
- **Whole-word method:** Click anywhere in a word and then choose the desired formatting.

> **NOTE**
>
> The whole-word method is settings-dependent. It will work by default, but it will not work if you've turned off "When selecting, automatically select entire word" in the Editing options section of Word Options (File ➪ Options ➪ Advanced).

It would be redundant to repeat the basic steps for each and every formatting type. The techniques described here apply to all character formatting described in this chapter.

Repeating formatting (F4)

You can save a lot of time in Word by using the Repeat or Redo command keyboard shortcut, F4. Pressing F4 will repeats whatever you just did, from typing what you just typed again to repeat formatting.

Suppose for example that you're scanning a newsletter looking for people's names, which need to be made bold. You see the name John Smith, so you select it and press Ctrl+B. Thereafter, however, it might be faster to position one hand on the mouse and the other on the F4 key. From there, you can repeat the formatting on individual words or phrases. For example, if Jane Doe is the next name you find after John Smith, you could double-click on Jane, press F4, double-click on Doe, and press F4 again. Or, you could drag over Jane Doe to select both the first and last name, and then press F4. The F4 key enables you to temporarily forget about pressing Ctrl+B, right-clicking, or traveling to the top of the Word menu in search of a formatting tool.

Note that F4 and Ctrl+Y both do the same thing. Which you use is your choice. Many prefer F4 because it can be pressed with one finger. Others prefer Ctrl+Y because it doesn't involve as much of a stretch as F4.

> **TIP**
>
> F4 only repeats the last formatting applied, but not multiple formatting actions. For example, if you applied first bold and then italic to a word and then selected a new word and pressed F4, only the italic would be applied, not the bold. If you have multiple or compound character formatting to repeatedly apply to a non-style-formatted series of words or selections, use the Font dialog box instead of individual commands. When you use the Font dialog box, all changes applied when you click OK become a single formatting event to the F4 key, so F4 can now apply multiple types of character formatting all at once.

Copying formatting

If you don't want to use a character style but still need to apply numerous formatting settings to selected text, you can use one of two common methods for copying formatting: the Format Painter and the shortcut key combinations for copying and pasting formatting. Note that these tools aren't limited to direct formatting. They'll work with style formatting as well.

Format Painter

To use the Format Painter, click or drag to select the text with the formatting you want to copy. If you want to clone that formatting just once, click the Format Painter button in the Clipboard group on the Home tab, shown in Figure 5.3. If you want to apply that formatting multiple times, double-click the Format Painter. The mouse pointer changes to include a paintbrush.

FIGURE 5.3

Use the Format Painter in the Clipboard group to copy formatting.

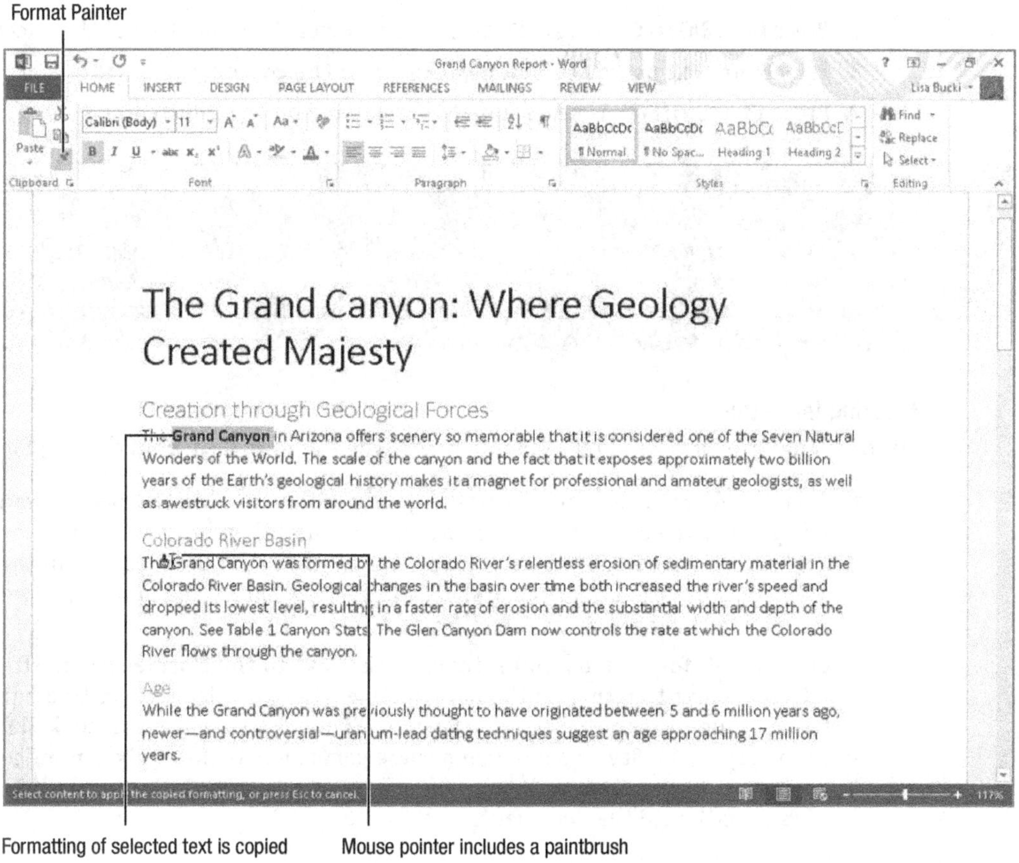

Format Painter

Formatting of selected text is copied   Mouse pointer includes a paintbrush

To copy the formatting to a single word, double-click the word. Otherwise, drag over the destination text to format. If you double-clicked the Format Painter, repeat making selections until you're done applying the copied formatting. Press Esc or click the Format Painter again to deactivate it.

> **NOTE**
>
> If you are copying character formatting to a single word with Format Painter, you often can also simply click the destination word. However, if you accidentally click on a space between words, the formatting does not copy, so I've used double-click in the above instructions. Also note that if the text formatting you have copied is actually a paragraph or linked style, clicking or double-clicking with Format Painter active reformats the whole paragraph.

Keyboard method

If you prefer to use keyboard shortcuts for your formatting work where possible, use this method to copy and paste formatting:

1. **Select the text with the formatting to copy.**
2. **Press Ctrl+Shift+C.** This keyboard shortcut copies the formatting of the selected text.
3. **Select the text on which you want to paste the copied formatting.**
4. **Press Ctrl+Shift+V.** Word pastes the formatting on the selected text.

> **NOTE**
>
> When reformatting entire paragraphs with copied character formatting, be sure that when you select the text with the formatting to copy, you select the paragraph mark. The paragraph mark stores paragraph-level formatting such as line spacing and spacing before and after paragraphs. To ensure that your selection includes the paragraph mark, triple-click the paragraph or move the mouse into the left margin until the arrow pointer tilts right and double-click.

Clearing formatting

Clearing formatting removes formatting from text. There are two degrees of clearing formatting:

- **Clearing direct character formatting only and returning the text to its underlying style.** To clear text in this way, select it and then press Ctrl+Spacebar on the keyboard. Alternately, you can reapply the style via the Style gallery in the Styles group of the Home tab or the Styles pane you saw earlier in Figure 5.2. By default, reapplying the style clears direct formatting.
- **Clearing all formatting and returning the text to the Normal style.** After you select the text to return to the Normal style, click the Clear Formatting button in the Font group of the Home tab, shown in Figure 5.4. You also can click Clear All at the top of the Styles pane. Using these commands is the equivalent of copying a selection to the Clipboard and then using Paste Special ⇨ Unformatted Text to paste it back into the document.

FIGURE 5.4

The Clear Formatting tool removes not only direct formatting, but also paragraph and style formatting.

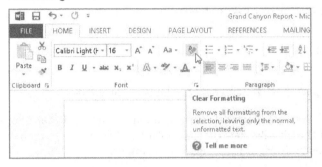

Using the Font group on the Home tab

Figure 5.5 shows you the Font group of the Home tab. It includes more than a dozen direct formatting tools on two rows. Figure 5.5 identifies some of the tools in the group that offer formatting options you may not have considered previously, beyond the typical bold, italics, and underlining.

FIGURE 5.5

The Font group puts character formatting choices a mouse click away.

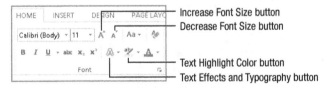

The pictures on some of the buttons in the Font group—such as Bold, Italic, and Underline—make their purpose obvious. The other buttons might call for more clarification. Hover the mouse pointer over each of the controls to see what it does. Notice that for many of the controls, keyboard shortcuts are indicated in the ScreenTip. Some tools, for whatever reason, might not show shortcuts. Jump ahead to the "Character formatting keyboard shortcuts" section later in this chapter if you're just dying to know what's assigned to what.

5

A number of the Font tools offer a Live Preview to help you make the best formatting selection:

- Font (the overall type design, such as Calibri)
- Font Size
- Text Highlight Color
- Font color
- Text Effects and Typography (which you'll see later in the chapter)

As shown in Figure 5.6, Live Preview shows you the results of the selected (but not yet applied) formatting. Two of the Live Preview controls—Font and Font Size—can be rolled up and out of the way, as shown in Figure 5.6. The others cannot.

FIGURE 5.6

Live Preview shows how the selected font would look when applied.

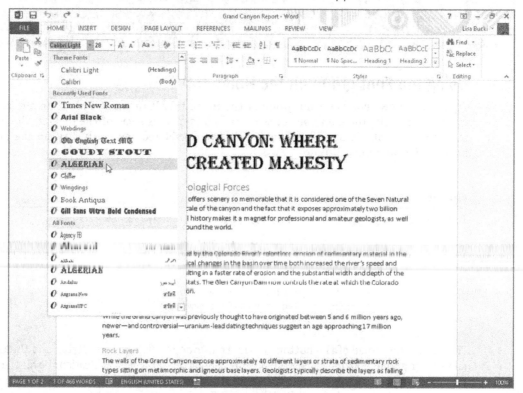

As shown in Figure 5.5, there's also the Font dialog box launcher, in the lower-right corner of the font group. Clicking it opens the Font dialog box, which you'll learn more about later in the chapter.

Font

As noted earlier, the font defines the overall appearance or style of text lettering. The fonts you apply are key to a document's appearance, formality, and readability. Windows includes dozens of built-in fonts you can apply in your documents, and you can find literally thousands more online that you can buy and install.

Use the Font drop-down list at the left end of the top row of the Font group of the Home tab to apply another font to selected text. Click the control's down arrow, scroll to display the available fonts, point to a font to see a Live Preview (refer to Figure 5.6), and then click the font to apply.

> **TIP**
>
> Limit the number of fonts used in a document to two or three to achieve a consistent look. Generally speaking, use one font for headings, one for body text, and one for special elements that you might want to emphasize, such as quotes or sidebars.

> **NOTE**
>
> If you have purchased or otherwise acquired unique fonts and installed them on your system, keep in mind that other users with whom you share documents may not have those fonts. When a document uses such a font, the text formatted with that font may not display or print correctly on other users' systems. To help avoid such problems, you can embed the fonts used in a document when saving. To turn on font embedding, choose File ➪ Options ➪ Save. Under Preserve fidelity when sharing this document, click the Embed fonts in the file check box to check it. To embed only needed characters, also check Embed only the characters used in the document (best for reducing file size). You also can leave Do not embed common system fonts checked. Click OK to apply the settings change.

Font Size

Font or Point Size controls the height of the font, generally measured in points. A point is $1/72$ of an inch, so 12 points would be $12/72$ (or $1/6$) of an inch. For Word, a font set's point size is the vertical distance from the top of the highest ascending character to the bottom of the lowest descending character.

Use the Font Size drop-down list just to the right of the Font control in the Font group of the Ribbon to choose a size for selected text. You aren't limited to the range of sizes you see in the Font Size drop-down list. Word can go as low as one point and as high as 1,638 points.

5

Plus, you can set the height in increments of half a point. Hence, a point size of 1637.5 is perfectly valid. To apply a size not included in the drop-down list, select the number shown in the Font Size control, type a new size, and press Enter.

> **NOTE**
>
> The ScreenTips for the Font and Font Size controls give shortcut key combinations of Ctrl+Shift+F and Ctrl+Shift+P, respectively, for the tools. These shortcut key combos do not activate the tools on the Ribbon. Instead, the shortcuts open the Font dialog box and select the applicable formatting setting there.

Increase Font Size and Decrease Font Size

You also can change text size with the Increase Font Size and Decrease Font Size tools (which are the two A buttons immediately to the right of the Font and Font Size tools in Figure 5.5). If you hover the mouse pointer over these you'll also learn that they both have shortcuts, Ctrl+Shift+. (the period character) and Ctrl+Shift+, (the comma character), respectively.

> **NOTE**
>
> The ScreenTips actually identify the shortcut key combinations as Ctrl+> and Ctrl+<, and technically that's right because > and < are a shifted period and comma, respectively. Presenting them both ways here will help you know exactly what keys to press.

If you click the drop-down arrow next to the Font Size tool, you'll notice that the font sizes listed do not consistently increase by twos. Instead, they go from 8 to 12 in increments of one, then from 12 to 28 in increments of two, and then leap to 36, 48, and 72. The Increase and Decrease Font Size tools follow the listed increments.

If you want a finer degree of control (for example, when you're trying to make text as large as possible without spilling onto an additional page), you should know about two additional default shortcut keys: Ctrl+[and Ctrl+]. These two commands shrink or enlarge the selected characters by one point. The extra granularity often is just what you need to find the largest possible font you can fit inside a given space, such as a page, table, or text box.

Working with text color

Word has three color settings that you can apply at the character level:

- **Font Color:** The color of the characters themselves
- **Shading:** The color of the background immediately behind the text
- **Text Highlight Color:** The electronic equivalent of those neon-colored felt markers you use to focus your attention on key points buried within text

Font Color

The Font Color setting determines the colors of the lettering for the selected text. Click the Text Color drop-down arrow in the Font group of the Home tab to open a palette or gallery of colors, as shown in Figure 5.7.

FIGURE 5.7

Changing text color

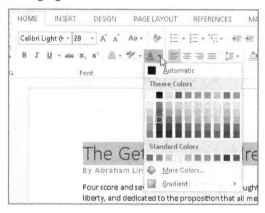

The theme applied to the document determines the available colors shown under Theme Colors in the gallery. The Automatic choice at the top can be black or white, and is based on the shading applied to the text. If the shading is so dark that black text can't be read without difficulty, Word automatically switches the Automatic color to white. The Standard Colors choices are the same no matter what theme is applied. You can click one of the colors under Theme Colors or Standard Colors to apply it to the selected text, or you can use the More Colors or Gradient choices to apply custom colors of blends of colors to the text.

Shading

Given that the Shading tool appears in the Paragraph group of the Ribbon, you might be tempted to believe that shading is paragraph-level formatting. Indeed, with nothing selected, your Shading choice applies to the entire current paragraph holding the insertion point.

However, if you select a single word or character, Shading suddenly acts like a character-formatting attribute. In reality, that's what it is. Because people seldom vary the shading within any given paragraph, Word includes it with the other paragraph formatting settings. And yet, just like font, font/point size, bold, and italic, shading is a character attribute.

5

As shown in Figure 5.8, the combination of the Shading and Font Color settings both contribute to the readability of the text. There needs to be adequate contrast between the two in order for the document to remain readable.

FIGURE 5.8

Despite its position in the Paragraph group of the Home tab, shading can be applied to a selection of characters.

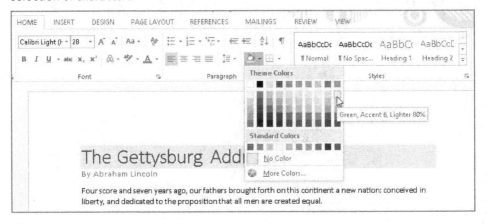

Text Highlight Color

The Text Highlight Color control—more generally known as the *highlighter*—is shown just to the left of the Font Color control in Figure 5.7. It actually has four modes of operation. Most people are aware of one mode or another, but not all four.

One method is to select text and then click the Text Highlight Color button in the Font group. This method, which directly applies the currently selected highlight color to the selected text, is the one that most users know and use. To change the highlight color, click the drop-down arrow and click a color in the gallery.

> **TIP**
>
> If you use this first highlight method, Word undoes the selection after you apply highlighting. This can be irritating if you use the wrong color, but if you immediately press Ctrl+Z or click Undo, Word not only undoes the highlighting, it also reselects that section of text so you can take another stab at highlighting it.

A second method is to turn the highlighter on by double-clicking the Text Highlight Color button, and then to use the mouse to select areas you want highlighted. The highlighter mouse pointer stays active until you click the Text Highlight Color button again, or until you press the Esc key.

A third method can be used to apply highlighting to all occurrences of a given word or phrase in a document, using the most recently applied highlighting color:

1. **Click the arrow for the Find button in the Editing group of the Home tab, and click Advanced Find.** The Find dialog box opens.

2. **Type the word or phrase to highlight in the Find what text box.**

3. **Click Reading Highlight ⇨ Highlight All, as shown in Figure 5.9.** The figure also illustrates the result of applying the reading highlight to the specified word, nation. Several instances of the word are highlighted throughout the document. Note that you can use the Clear Highlighting choice on the Reading Highlight dropdown to remove the highlighting from the specified word or phrase.

4. **Click Close.** The Find and Replace dialog box closes.

FIGURE 5.9

Use Find to apply a reading highlight to every occurrence of a word or phrase in your document.

A fourth highlighting method might be even more useful than the Reading Highlight feature. It works from the Replace dialog box. Press Ctrl+H (Replace). In the Find what text box, type the word or phrase you want to highlight. Clear the contents of the Replace with text box, but make sure that the insertion point remains in the text box. Click the More >> button, and in the lower-left corner choose Format ⇨ Highlight. Click Replace All to apply highlighting to all occurrences of the word or phrase in the Find what text box. Click the Close button to close the dialog box. Highlighting applied this way is more robust than highlighting inserted via the Reading Highlight feature and will not disappear if you choose to manually manipulate highlighting.

Note that when the Replace with text box is blank but has associated formatting, the formatting is applied to text that matches the Find what text box. If both formatting and Replace with text are absent, Replace deletes all occurrences of the matching text.

By default, highlight formatting appears when you print the document. You can choose not to print highlighting, giving you the best of both worlds. You can mark up a document for your own benefit, and then—if you wish—print it out without the highlighting. Not only is this good for keeping internal guides private, it also saves money on yellow ink. To prevent the printing (or displaying) of highlighting, choose File ⇨ Options, select the Display tab, and remove the check next to Show highlighter marks. If you hover over the information while you're here, the tip informs you that this controls both display and printing. Click OK when you're done. Of course, you'll need to repeat this process and check Show highlighter marks after printing to redisplay the highlighting onscreen.

> **NOTE**
>
> You may be wondering what the difference between text shading and highlight coloring is, as the two look very similar, and you use similar methods for applying them. The key difference is that the colors for the Text Highlight Color tool work the same as the Standard color choices or any custom colors you apply using another color gallery or palette: The applied text highlight color doesn't change when you change the document theme. In contrast, if you use one of the Theme Colors choices in the Shading gallery in the Paragraph group, the shading color does update when you change the document theme.

Change Case

The Change Case button doesn't really fit in the Font group, but that's precisely why I'm including it. Case is not formatting. Case is a choice of what capitalization to use—uppercase, lowercase, or some combination thereof. Why does Microsoft put it in the Font group? Probably because it can affect groups of characters, so it makes more sense here than anywhere else. And the Change Case setting for text is not saved as part of any style you create or update. The case options you can apply to selected text via the Change Case button in the Font group are:

- **Sentence case:** Capitalizes the first word in the selected text.
- **lowercase:** Removes all capitalization from the selection.

- **UPPERCASE:** Converts all letters of the selected text to uppercase.
- **Capitalize Each Word:** Capitalizes the first letter of each word.
- **tOGGLE cASE:** Reverses the case of each letter in the selection.

> **TIP**
>
> The formal method of capitalizing documents and section headings is called *title case*. You can easily achieve title case in your documents by applying the Capitalize Each Word setting and then converting prepositions, articles, and conjunctions back to lowercase, leaving only the major words capitalized.

> **TIP**
>
> When you need to distinguish between an uppercase i (I), a lowercase L (l), the number one (1), and the vertical line segment (|, usually typed with Shift+\ on most U.S. keyboards), one font that makes the distinction clearest is Comic Sans. It's also a very comfortable and readable font, its nonprofessional-sounding name notwithstanding. If after applying Comic Sans you're still uncertain as to what's what, try toggling the case. Properly distinguishing among these characters, as well as between 0 (zero) and O (capital o), can make a world of difference when you are trying to convey part numbers, serial numbers, usernames, and passwords.

Language

By default, Word is set up to edit and perform spelling and grammar checks in a single language. To work with editing and formatting choices for a second language, you have to install the language in the Word Options dialog box. Choose File ➪ Options, and select the Language tab. Under Choose Editing Languages, open the [Add additional editing languages] drop-down list, click the language to add, and click Add. Click OK, and then restart Word when prompted so that the new editing language will take effect.

Even after that, language settings do not appear in the Home tab's Font group nor the Font dialog box, which you'll see shortly. So how do you know language is a character-formatting attribute? Two reasons: it can be applied to a single character in a document, and it can be included in a character-style definition, as shown in Figure 5.10.

In many cases, Word correctly recognizes text from an installed language and formats it as such, but if not, you can set the language for selected text using the Language tool on the status bar. If you don't see the tool on the status bar, then right-click the status bar, click to enable Language, and then press Esc.

To open the Language dialog box to change settings for the selected text, click the language displayed on the status bar. Among the Language tool's more useful features is the Do not check spelling or grammar setting (see Figure 5.11), which you can apply to text. This can be handy for technical jargon and programming keywords that you might not want checked.

5

FIGURE 5.10

Language is included among the attributes associated with a character style.

Conversely, the Detect language automatically check box can be a real troublemaker. With that setting turned on, it's possible for text to unintentionally be tagged as some other language, resulting in large sections of text being flagged as misspelled. If the corresponding proofing tools are not installed, the text is not checked at all. This can leave large sections of text unintentionally unchecked. You should turn that setting off unless you actually need it. It is enabled by default!

To set the default for all documents based on the current template, choose the desired language as well as the desired settings for the last two options, and then click Set As Default. Confirm the settings by clicking Yes. Note that even though the confirmation box doesn't mention the latter two settings, they are included in the changes made to the underlying template.

FIGURE 5.11

The Do not check spelling or grammar setting can be useful for technical writers. Detect language automatically can cause problems for chronically bad spellers.

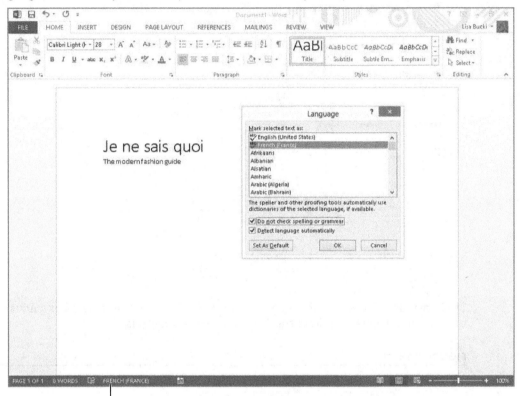

Shows the language applied to selected text; click to open the Language dialog box

Formatting via the Font dialog box

The Font tab of the Font dialog box, shown in Figure 5.12, can be a useful tool when you're applying multiple character format changes at the same time. Note, however, that the Font dialog box and the Font group on the Ribbon do not provide identical capabilities. The Font dialog doesn't provide a full Live Preview and instead has a smaller preview area. On the other hand, it offers settings not available in the Font group, such as Underline color, Double strikethrough, Small caps, All caps, and Hidden. It also enables you to access detailed Text Effects settings.

5

FIGURE 5.12

The Font tab of the Font dialog box offers additional formatting choices beyond the Home tab's Font group.

The Home tab's Font group offers none of the controls in the Font dialog box's Advanced tab, shown in Figure 5.13. Note the Scale and Spacing controls.

FIGURE 5.13

The Advanced tab of the Font dialog box enables you to scale and space characters.

Use the Scale setting to stretch or compress the selected characters. You may want to do this to make text fill a particular amount of space in the document to create balance or to add emphasis or a modern appearance. The Spacing setting expands or condenses only the spacing between characters. Scaling and spacing expansion are demonstrated on the text shown in Figure 5.14. The bottom copy of the text was scaled to 150% and its Spacing set to Expanded By 2.8 pt. (That means an additional 2.8 points of spacing was inserted between each character.) In this example, the applied settings cause the bottom sample to span the width of the page.

FIGURE 5.14

Scaling and horizontal spacing can give text with the same basic font settings very different appearances.

The Gettysburg Address
The Gettysburg Address

The Position setting raises or lowers the selected characters by a specified number of points. Unlike spacing, which can vary by as little as .1 points, position's smallest gradation is .5 points. This tool is sometimes used to adjust subscripts and superscripts if the built-in versions don't accomplish the desired effect, or you need the subscripts and superscripts to be the same size as the surrounding text.

Kerning is an advanced typography control that adjusts the space between certain letter pairs when they appear together and are formatted in a proportional font (with varying letter widths). For example, in the letter pair *Wa*, kerning removes a little bit of space so that the *a* tucks in under the right side of the *W*, yielding a more attractive and readable appearance. Overall, kerning visually balances out the spaces between various letter combinations. Kerning is turned on by default for font sizes above 14 points, as the effects of kerning are more obvious the larger the font size. You can turn kerning off by clearing the Kerning for fonts check box on the Advanced tab of the Font dialog box, or you can change the accompanying font size to determine when kerning takes effect.

TIP

If you have a chronic need to adjust subscripts and superscripts, you might consider creating a character style that gives you the desired formatting.

5

Understanding OpenType features

Figure 5.13 also shows the OpenType Features settings on the Advanced tab. Developed largely by Microsoft, OpenType is the successor to TrueType fonts, which helped in making fonts scalable. OpenType adds additional features that allow you to manipulate some of the more intricate aspects of fonts and number spacing. For example, if you have problems aligning numbers in numbered lists, you might try a different Number spacing choice under OpenType features.

Many OpenType fonts include *ligatures* at certain sizes. When a ligature occurs, similar stroke components of adjoining characters are joined, so that the characters form a new *glyph*, or typographic character. This happens frequently for the lowercase letter f, as shown in Figure 5.15. You can turn ligatures off by choosing None from the Ligatures drop-down list of the Font dialog box, or use one of the other choices beside it and Standard Only to increase the number of ligatures that Word automatically applies. You also can change settings for OpenType Number forms and Stylistic sets.

FIGURE 5.15

The f and t are joined in the top two examples, but not the bottom one.

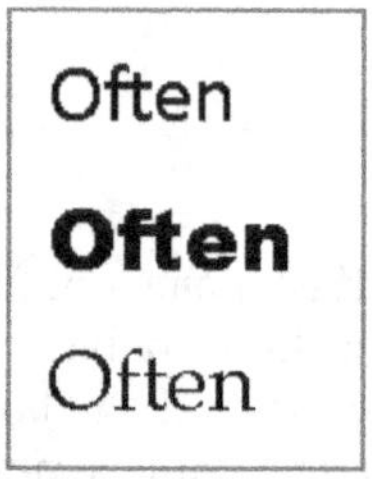

Often

Often

Often

The Mini Toolbar

Yet another tool for applying formatting is the Mini Toolbar. This feature is fully explained in Chapter 1, "Taking Your First Steps with Word." Shown in Figure 5.16, the Mini Toolbar has a sampling of character-formatting tools from the Font group of the Home tab.

FIGURE 5.16

The Mini Toolbar has a sampling of character-formatting tools from the Font group of the Home tab.

The Mini Toolbar's singular but important claim to fame for many users will be its ergonomic utility. When you need something on it, it's right there, close to the text. Many of its tools are easily accessible via direct keystrokes, as you'll see in the next section in this chapter.

Text Effects and Typography

Even though the Text Effects and Typography gallery is in the Font group of the Home tab and it does apply character formatting, its settings are so many and varied that it war-rants separate discussion. You can use the tools found on this gallery to apply formatting that makes regular text look like a WordArt object. (For a detailed discussion of WordArt objects, see Chapter 14, "Adding Pictures and WordArt to Highlight Information.") As in the example shown in Figure 5.17, you can use one of the choices at the top of the gallery to apply a WordArt-like overall appearance to selected text.

FIGURE 5.17

The Text Effects and Typography gallery in the Font group of the Home tab enables you to apply WordArt-like formatting and effects to regular text.

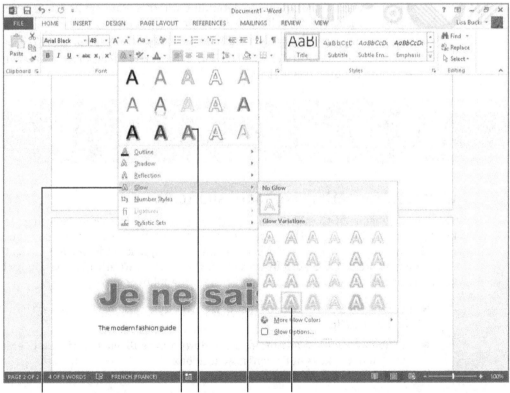

Click one of the listed effects to see a subgallery

Choose an overall look for text

Live Preview of an effect, in this case a glow

In addition, you can reopen the gallery and click any of the effects listed at the bottom of the gallery to see a subgallery of specific effects choices, as in the example in Figure 5.17. In most cases, the selected text will display a Live Preview of any effect you move the mouse pointer over. The available effects are:

- **Outline:** Displays a gallery where you can apply a theme or standard color for the text outline, as well as Weight and Dashes choices you can use to alter the outline style.

- **Shadow:** Make a choice from the Outer, Inner, or Perspective categories to add a text shadow, or click the choice under No Shadow to remove any existing shadow.

- **Reflection:** Use a choice to add a text reflection, which is a partial mirror image of the text.

- **Glow:** Click one of the Glow Variations choices (see Figure 5.17) to surround the selected text with a colored glow.

- **Number Styles:** If your text includes numbers, select a formatting variation here. The subgallery includes a description of each choice.

- **Ligatures:** When the text includes letter pairs that can be optionally joined with a ligature, make a choice here to determine whether Word applies some or all of the ligature types. The subgallery includes a description of each choice.

- **Stylistic Sets:** Click a choice here to add interest to the letter appearance. For example, one of the styles may size lowercase letters the same height as uppercase without changing letter shape.

> **TIP**
>
> As with other types of document formatting, resist the temptation to apply too many effects to document text. Doing so can reduce readability and even look a bit too gaudy.

Character formatting keyboard shortcuts

You can apply many of the character formatting settings discussed in this chapter via built-in keyboard shortcuts. Longtime Word users typically have many of these shortcuts committed to memory. Newcomers, however, might need a quick guide. As you navigate your way through Word 2013, keep your eyes open. Quite often, Word will show you its built-in key assignments. To make sure this happens, do the following:

- In File ⇨ Options ⇨ General, set ScreenTip Style to something other than Don't show ScreenTips.

- In File ⇨ Options ⇨ Advanced, scroll down to the Display section, and enable the Show shortcut keys in ScreenTips check box.

Table 5.1 provides a quick reference of keyboard shortcuts related to character formatting. This list might not be exhaustive.

TABLE 5.1   Default Character Formatting Keyboard Shortcuts

Command	Keystroke
All Caps	Ctrl+Shift+A
Bold	Ctrl+B, Ctrl+Shift+B
Copy formatting	Ctrl+Shift+C
Font dialog box	Ctrl+D, Ctrl+Shift+F
Highlighting	Alt+Ctrl+H
Hyperlink	Ctrl+K
Italics	Ctrl+I
Paste formatting	Ctrl+Shift+V
Font/Point size	Ctrl+Shift+P
Font/Point size: decrease by one point	Ctrl+[
Font/Point size: decrease to next preset	Ctrl+ < (Ctrl+Shift+,)
Font/Point size: increase by one point	Ctrl+]
Font/Point size: increase to next preset	Ctrl+ > (Ctrl+Shift+.)
Remove non-style character formatting	Ctrl+Space
Small caps	Ctrl+Shift+K
Subscript	Ctrl+=
Superscript	Ctrl+Shift+=
Symbol font	Ctrl+Shift+Q
Toggle case of selected text	Shift+F3
Underline	Ctrl+U
Word underline	Ctrl+W

5

Summary

For most of us, our words form the most important thing about the documents we create. Judiciously used character formatting can help our words convey greater meaning by highlighting important words and phrases in a document. In this chapter you've seen the variety of formatting changes you can make on words and characters. You should now be able to:

- Apply character formatting to a text selection of any size, from a single character up to a complete document
- Choose whether to apply formatting directly or to use a character style
- Distinguish between character formatting and characters
- Decide, from among the variety of formatting tools, which one to use in any given formatting situation
- Remove unwanted character formatting
- Explore advanced character formatting settings such as the use of OpenType ligatures and WordArt-like effects
- Save time by using keyboard shortcuts and shortcut techniques

Paragraph Formatting

IN THIS CHAPTER

Working with paragraph styles or direct formatting

Finding and applying paragraph formatting tools

Indenting and aligning paragraphs

Adding spacing around and within paragraphs

Lining up text with tabs

Applying numbering, bullets, shading, and borders to emphasize paragraphs

Everything you type in Word exists in paragraphs. Even if you type nothing at all, every Word document—even one that you believe is completely empty—contains at least one blank paragraph that already has formatting settings assigned to it. You can think of each paragraph as another type of formatting unit.

This chapter goes into detail about the numerous paragraph formatting choices available in Word, including indentation, alignment, spacing, list formats, shading, and borders. You'll also learn about the interaction between selected Word options and the nuances of paragraph formatting.

Choosing Between Styles and Paragraph Formatting

When it comes to document design and formatting, you can often achieve a similar look using totally different tools in Word 2013. For any given paragraph, however, only one way is the most efficient. After you learn about the various ways to format paragraphs, developing the habit of using the most efficient tools will serve you well, especially when much of your workday involves creating documents.

As with character formatting, when you are formatting paragraphs, you have to choose between applying direct formatting and using paragraph styles. Many users simply ignore the existence of styles and use all direct formatting. But whether they realize it or not, every blank document created using the default `Normal.dotm` template contains a single paragraph style, called Normal, and a single character style, called Default Paragraph Font.

Generally speaking, paragraph styles can save a lot of time, because you can apply several new formatting settings to a paragraph in only a couple of mouse clicks. And when you update any style, either character or paragraph, Word updates all the text in the document with the new style settings.

Despite the obvious advantages of using paragraph styles, such as the ability to find and replace styles, which you'll learn more about in Chapter 9, "Find, Replace, and Go To," you may not find a style that includes all the formatting that you want to apply to a given paragraph. In such a case, you will need to apply direct formatting. That's the reason why this chapter takes the time to highlight the various direct paragraph formatting settings.

For a one-time ad hoc need, direct paragraph formatting is entirely appropriate. For example, if you're creating a centered title on a one-page flyer you're going to tack to a bulletin board, feel free to simply press Ctrl+E or click the Center button in the Paragraph group to align the text.

On the other hand, if it's formatting that you're going to need again and again, then use a paragraph style, even if you have to modify an existing style or create a brand-new style. For example, if you are formatting a number of headings in a newsletter you will be writing monthly for the next five years, either adapt and start applying the built-in heading styles (Heading 1, Heading 2, and so on), or create and use your own custom heading styles. The more work styles can do for you, the less time you're going to have to spend applying and reapplying direct paragraph formatting.

Finding Paragraph Formatting Tools

Word stores each paragraph's formatting in its paragraph mark. Say you have two paragraphs with different line spacing settings applied. If you click at the beginning of the second paragraph and press Backspace to combine the paragraphs, suddenly the combined paragraphs use the same line spacing. (They use the spacing of the top paragraph, which is a little counterintuitive.)

Similarly, say you create a double-spaced paragraph and then press Enter to start a new paragraph, creating a paragraph mark on a line by itself. Then, you cut a few sentences from a single-spaced paragraph elsewhere in the document and paste them just to the left of the new paragraph mark. Word reformats the pasted single space text with the double-spaced formatting setting stored in the paragraph mark.

That's just two examples of why you may need to see the paragraph marks when formatting and editing a document, especially when you're cutting or copying and pasting text. Pressing Ctrl+Shift+8 or clicking the Show/Hide button in the Paragraph group of the Home tab toggles the paragraph marks and other nonprinting characters on and off as needed.

6

In Figure 6.1, all of numbered item 1 is a single paragraph. The character that you see after "Train yourself, too." is called a *manual line break*, which is the type of line return you create when you press Shift+Enter. Because a manual line break does not create a paragraph mark, text before and after a manual line break is within the same paragraph, as you see in the numbered item in Figure 6.1. To Word, the only thing that distinguishes one paragraph from another is the paragraph mark. A single sentence or short phrase with a paragraph mark after it, as for a list of items, is considered to be a complete paragraph. Similarly, a paragraph mark that contains no associated text at all is also considered to be a paragraph.

FIGURE 6.1

A paragraph is everything between two paragraph marks.

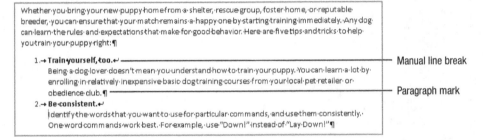

Many new Word users find the display of nonprinting characters (such as paragraph marks, manual line breaks, spaces, and tabs) distracting. However, displaying them can give you essential clues about what's going on in a document.

Sometimes it's useful to use a manual line break within a paragraph while still keeping it as a single paragraph. This most often is done within numbered or bulleted paragraphs, as shown in Figure 6.1. That way any paragraph formatting you do to any part of the paragraph is done to the entire paragraph (such as the main indentation and numbering). If the paragraphs are numbered or bulleted, a manual line break prevents a new number or bullet from being assigned while keeping all the text pertaining to that topic or item together as a single paragraph.

You also can use the Reveal Formatting pane shown in Figure 6.2 as a formatting diagnostic aid. You display it by pressing Shift+F1. It shows all the formatting that's applied to the selected text or the word holding the insertion point. It has four segments: Font (character formatting), Paragraph, Bullets and Numbering, and Section. It also displays the selected text, if any, using the current common formatting. If the insertion point is beside a paragraph mark without any text, the Reveal Formatting pane displays the words "Sample Text" using common current formatting.

FIGURE 6.2

Press Shift+F1 to open the Reveal Formatting pane. It shows all the formatting in effect for the selection.

Why do I say that it displays the common formatting? That's because the selected text might not be formatted homogeneously. Say the selected sentence was "It was a **dark** and *stormy* night." Because some formatting (bold and italic in this case) might not be common to the entire selection, you have to bear in mind that Reveal Formatting may not list all the formatting applied in a given selection.

You can use the triangles beside the section names in the Reveal Formatting pane to expand and collapse the formatting information. Clicking a black triangle collapses the formatting details, whereas clicking a white triangle expands and reveals formatting details. When you finish using the pane, click its Close (X) button to close it.

> **TIP**
>
> The Reveal Formatting command does not appear on the Ribbon. If you can't remember the Shift+F1 shortcut for displaying it, you can add a button for it to the Quick Access Toolbar or the Ribbon. Reveal Formatting is listed with the Commands Not in the Ribbon. See Chapter 30, "Customizing the Quick Access Toolbar and Ribbon" to learn how to add the button in the desired location.

Paragraph formatting attributes

You can apply paragraph formatting using a wide variety of paragraph attribute buttons and tools. Many of those attribute controls, but not all, can be found in the Paragraph group in the Home tab, shown in Figure 6.3. Indent and Spacing, both of which are paragraph attributes, are located on the Paragraph group in the Page Layout tab, also shown in Figure 6.3. A number of attributes missing from the Ribbon are on the horizontal rulers: left and right indent, hanging and paragraph indent, and tab settings.

FIGURE 6.3

The Paragraph sections in the Home and Page Layout tabs contain a number of paragraph-formatting controls.

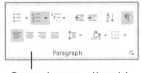
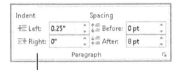

Paragraph group on Home tab   Paragraph group on Page Layout tab

Many paragraph attributes—but again, not all—are also found in the Paragraph dialog box, shown in Figure 6.4. You can display the Paragraph dialog box by clicking the dialog box launcher in the lower-right corner of either Paragraph group, by double-clicking any of the indent controls on the horizontal ruler, or by pressing the legacy keystrokes Alt+O and Alt+P.

FIGURE 6.4

The Paragraph dialog box contains controls for most, but not all, of Word's direct paragraph-formatting attributes.

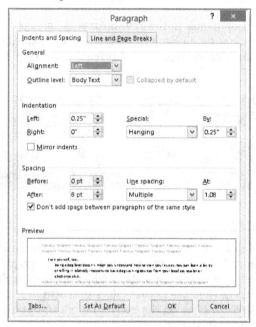
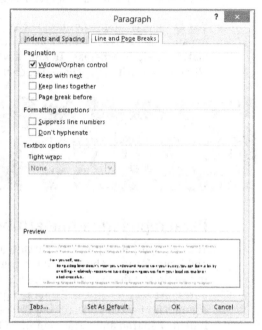

You have to open other dialog boxes to find additional paragraph-formatting settings. For example, click the Tabs button in the lower-left corner of the Paragraph dialog box to open the Tabs dialog box. To find border and shading formatting choices, click Borders and Shading in the bottom of the Border tool's list of settings (on the Home tab), shown in Figure 6.5.

You might be wondering from all this how to determine whether a setting is a paragraph formatting attribute. One way is to see whether the attribute can be applied to a paragraph without the whole paragraph's being selected. For example, if you click anywhere inside a paragraph and click the Center button in the Paragraph group of the Home tab, Word centers the whole paragraph. The same anywhere-in-the-paragraph rule is true for each of the other alignment options. The same applies to borders, shading, indentation, bullets, numbering, and line spacing.

Note, however, that two "paragraph-formatting" attributes behave according to the *if nothing is selected, format the whole paragraph* rule, but behave differently if part (but not all) of a paragraph is selected. These two are shading and borders. While they generally are considered paragraph formatting, they also can be character formatting.

FIGURE 6.5

Open the Borders and Shading dialog box by clicking Borders and Shading at the bottom of the Borders menu in the Paragraph group of the Home tab.

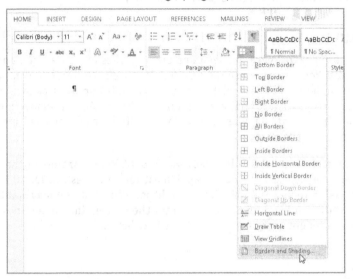

Paragraph formatting techniques

You can use either of two techniques to apply paragraph-formatting attributes. As noted, you can simply place the insertion point in the paragraph you want and then choose the attribute (using the Ribbon, a dialog box, a keystroke, the shortcut menu, or the Mini Toolbar).

The other technique is to select a range of paragraphs (up to and including the entire document), and then apply the formatting. Note that even though shading and border formatting can apply to a selection of characters/words, if the selection includes or spans a paragraph mark, the formatting is applied to the entirety of all the paragraphs in the selection, even those that aren't fully selected.

Structuring Text with Paragraph Formatting

You can think of Word's paragraph formatting choices as encompassing two approaches:

- **Structural formatting:** Attributes that affect the overall structure of the text, such as alignment, indentation, tabs, and so on
- **Decorative formatting:** Attributes that add other elements to affect the interior appearance of the text, such as shading, borders, numbering, and bullets

Used properly, both structural and decorative formatting can help the reader navigate the document more easily or find important information. This section deals with structural formatting. The subsequent section covers decorative formatting.

Adding indentation

Indentation refers to adding extra space between one or more lines of a paragraph and the left and/or right margins. You typically use indentation for automatically indenting the first line of paragraphs, indenting quotes relative to both the left and right page margins, and setting up hanging indentation for bulleted or numbered text. Add or remove indentation in preset, half-inch increments by clicking the Decrease Indent or Increase Indent button in the Paragraph group of the Home tab.

You can also add indentation using the Indent Left and Indent Right controls in the Paragraph group of the Page Layout tab. For example, most report styles call for all lines in quotations to be indented .5 inches from the left or right margins, but you may want to use .75 inches instead. As shown in Figure 6.6, you can enter the desired indent settings for the selected paragraph in the Indent Left and Indent Right text boxes.

FIGURE 6.6

Set custom left and right paragraph indentation in the Paragraph group of the Page Layout tab.

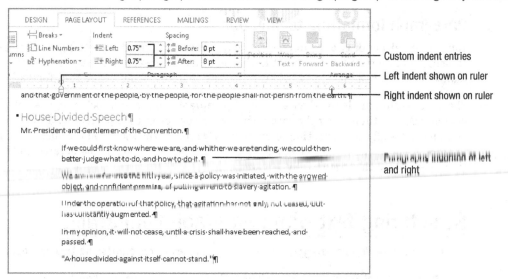

Indenting with the Ruler

The horizontal Ruler provides a mouse-based way to create indents and is especially easy for creating first line and hanging indents. A *first line indent* indents only the first line of a

6

paragraph. A *hanging indent* indents all lines except the first line, as for the numbered and bulleted lists you see throughout this book.

This method also enables you to see how the text will change as you drag, so that you can judge as you go how much indentation to apply.

1. **To display the ruler if needed, click the View tab and click Ruler in the Show group.** The Ruler check box controls the display of the ruler within the current document only, so you may need to turn it on and off frequently.

2. **Select the paragraphs to indent.**

3. **Drag the indent symbols on the ruler as needed to apply the desired indentation.** Refer to Figure 6.7 to see what each of these symbols looks like:

   ■ **First Line Indent:** Drag to the right to indent the first line or to the left to reduce or remove indentation.

   ■ **Hanging Indent:** Drag to the right to indicate the amount of indentation to apply to all but the first line of the paragraph.

   ■ **Left Indent:** Drag right or left to add or remove indentation for all lines of the paragraph relative to the left margin.

   ■ **Right Indent:** Drag left or right to add or remove indentation for all lines of the paragraph relative to the right margin.

4. **Repeat Steps 2 and 3 to apply different indentation settings to other paragraphs as needed.**

5. **To hide the ruler if needed, click the View tab and click Ruler in the Show group.**

FIGURE 6.7

Use the mouse to drag indentation controls on the ruler provides.

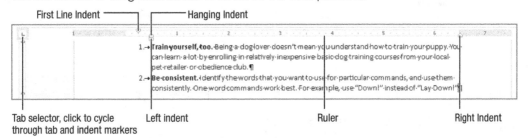

TIP

If you have trouble dragging the ruler's tiny indent controls with the mouse, you can use the tab selector control at the left end of the horizontal ruler. Click the (usually) L-shaped control to cycle through the different tabs and indents and stop at the either the First Line Indent or Hanging Indent marker. With that control displayed, you can now set a first-line or hanging indent by clicking the desired position on the ruler.

It you press the Alt key while dragging the indent controls on the ruler, Word displays the measurement as shown in Figure 6.8, allowing for more informed positioning.

FIGURE 6.8

Press Alt while dragging indent controls on the ruler to see precise measurements.

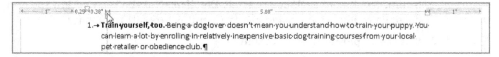

Custom and mirror indents

Many users still prefer to set indents in the Indentation section of the Indents and Spacing tab of the Paragraph dialog box, shown in Figure 6.9. For example, clicking the up and down arrow buttons for Left or Right increments those settings by .1 inch. You can choose either First Line or Hanging from the Special list to immediately set up either of those types of indents, or click the Mirror indents check box so that you can create indents to accommodate book style printing. When Mirror indents is enabled, the Left and Right text boxes become Inside and Outside, as shown in Figure 6.9.

FIGURE 6.9

Use the Paragraph dialog box to enter precise indent settings or add mirror indents.

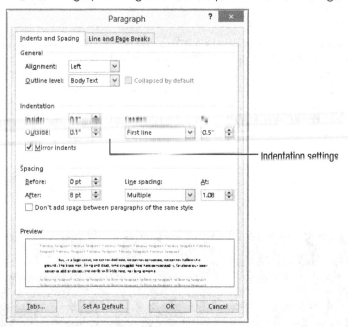

> **NOTE**
>
> Mirror indents are different from Mirror Margins, which is a Page Setup setting discussed in Chapter 16, "Setting Up the Document with Sections, Headers/Footers, and Columns."

Changing text alignment

Horizontal alignment determines how any given paragraph is oriented between the left and right margins. The Paragraph group of the Home tab includes four alignment buttons. Click a button or use its shortcut key to apply the specified alignment to the selected paragraph(s):

- **Align Left (Ctrl+L):** Starts the left side of each line of text at the left margin, leaving a ragged right paragraph edge.
- **Center (Ctrl+E):** Centers each line in a paragraph between the left and right margins, giving both sides of the paragraph a ragged appearance.
- **Align Right (Ctrl+R):** Moves each line of the paragraph over to the right, so the right side aligns at the right margin, leaving a ragged left edge.
- **Justified (Ctrl+J):** Adds additional spacing between letters to align the left and right side of each line of text to its respective margin, giving straight left and right paragraph edges.

> **CAUTION**
>
> Justified alignment can cause an unpleasant appearance when used in combination with a font size that's too large. With a large font size, fewer words fit on each line, and Word therefore might have to add large amounts of white space to justify the text, creating a distracting amount of white area within the text. If you notice this effect when using justified alignment, experiment with applying a smaller font size to fix the problem.

Changing spacing

You also may need to change the paragraph spacing settings for various documents to improve readability or conform with document-formatting styles and requirements. For example, most academic reports require double-spaced formatting, whereas most business letters use single-spaced or a limited amount of space between lines.

By default, the Normal paragraph style includes extra spacing after the paragraph. Pressing Enter once at the end of a paragraph automatically includes the needed spacing between the current paragraph and the next paragraph.

Use the Line and Paragraph Spacing drop-down list in the Paragraph group of the Home tab to change paragraph spacing.

Between lines

By default, the Normal paragraph style is set to 1.15 line spacing. To change to another line spacing setting:

1. **Select the paragraphs to change.**
2. **Click the Paragraph and Line Spacing button in the Paragraph group of the Home tab.** A menu with preset spacing settings and other commands appears.
3. **Move the mouse pointer over one of the spacing choices.** A Live Preview of the spacing appears in the document, as shown in Figure 6.10.
4. **Click the spacing to apply.**

FIGURE 6.10

Changing line spacing within the second paragraph of the document

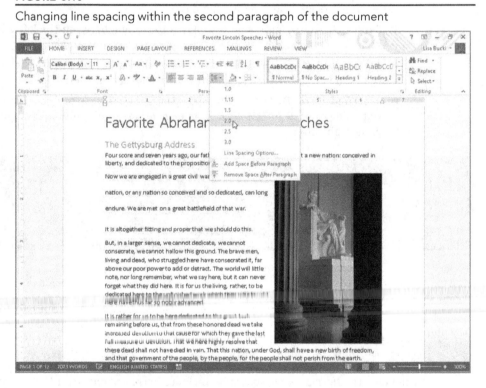

If you click Line Spacing Options in the menu in Figure 6.10, Word opens the Paragraph dialog box, with its Indents and Spacing tab displayed. You can use the Line Spacing choice there to apply Single, 1.5 lines, or Double spacing. You also can use the At least, Exactly, or Multiple choices and make an entry in the At text box to set line spacing by smaller increments such as the 1.08 default for Word 2013's Normal paragraph style.

6

Before and after paragraphs

The Normal paragraph style also includes 8 pt of extra spacing after each paragraph. You can add spacing both before and after paragraphs to set them apart and make your document more readable. For example, the built-in Heading 1 style includes 12 pt of spacing before the paragraph. This creates a larger gap between the preceding text and a heading, visually cueing the reader that one major topic is ending and another beginning.

To adjust spacing before and after paragraphs:

1. **Select the paragraphs to change.**
2. **Click the dialog box launcher in the Paragraph group of the Home tab.** The Paragraph dialog box opens with its Indents and Spacing tab selected.
3. **Under Spacing, change the values in the Before and After text boxes as desired.** Clicking one of the up and down arrow buttons increments the setting by 6 pt. If that's too large a change, drag over the entry of one of the text boxes and type the desired size.
4. **Click OK to apply the new spacing.**

Setting and using tabs

Computer users increasingly have been using tables rather than tabs for aligning lists of text within a document. Although both formatting methods can give similar results and derive from the same root word, tabulation, tables give better control, more flexibility, and more formatting options than tabs. Still, there are many instances where using tabs on the fly provides a faster document-formatting solution.

By default, a new document includes default preset tabs every .5". When you set your own tab, all the built-in preset tabs to the left of the one you set are removed, leaving the manually inserted tab and all remaining preset tabs to the right.

Tabs versus tables

If you can use tabs, and you can use tables, when should you use which? There are times when tabs give you precisely what you want, and in a way that a table either can't or can't without your jumping through hoops. For example, if you want lines connecting two tabbed items, while there are other ways to accomplish the same effect, it's almost always faster and easier to use tab leaders.

If you need to create an underscored area for a signature or other fill-in information on a paper form, the solid tab leader line is definitely the way to go, even though you could draw lines where you want them instead, using Insert ⇨ Illustrations ⇨ Shapes ⇨ Line (holding down the Shift key as you draw to keep the line perfectly horizontal, of course). However, graphical lines have a way of not always staying where you put them, so you'll usually find that it's much more efficient and predictable to just use a leader line, as described shortly under "Working with tab leaders."

> **TIP**
>
> Word includes a new feature for creating a formal document signature line rather than a basic fill-in area. For more, see "Adding a signature line" in Chapter 26 , "Managing Document Security, Comments, and Tracked Changes."

Another situation in which tabs give you what you want is with simple document headers. The default header for Word 2013 documents contains a center tab and a right tab. This enables you to easily create a header with text to the left, centered text, and right-aligned text, simply by separating those three components with tabs. Tabs also can be useful inside actual tables for aligning numbers at the decimal point. (To insert a tab inside a table, press Ctrl+Tab.)

However, for more complex presentations of information, particularly when you might need organizational control (copying and moving rows and columns), you'll save time and work by creating a table. Chapter 13, "Building Tables, Charts, and SmartArt to Show Data and Process," covers how you can quickly build and format tables in a document.

Setting tabs in a dialog box

If you prefer the precision of typing in the tab measurements you want or if you need to include a leader, use the Tabs dialog box shown in Figure 6.11 to create your tabs. With the Tabs dialog box, you also can specify a tab alignment. Figure 6.12 shows examples of the various alignments.

1. **Select the paragraphs to change.**
2. **Click the dialog box launcher in the Paragraph group of the Home tab.** The Paragraph dialog box opens with its Indents and Spacing tab selected.

FIGURE 6.11

Use the Tabs dialog box to set and clear tabs, set the default tab stop interval, and set a tab leader.

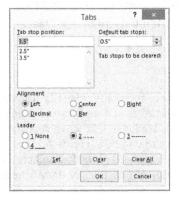

FIGURE 6.12

The first three lines show left, center, and right tabs; the number lines show a decimal tab; and the final lines show a bar tab.

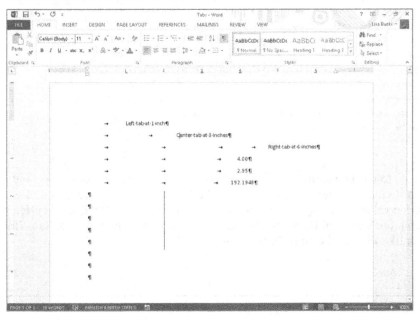

3. **Click the Tabs button in the lower-left corner.** The Tabs dialog box appears.

4. **To set a tab, click in the Tab stop position text box, type the tab measurement, click the desired choices under Alignment and Leader, and click Set.**

5. **To remove a tab, click it in the Tab stop position list, and click Clear.**

6. **Click OK to close the dialog box.**

Working with tab leaders

Tab leaders are dashed or solid lines typically used to help the reader visually line up information separated by tabs. Tab leaders often are used in tables of contents and indexes, such as the one shown in Figure 6.13. You choose the type of leader to add when setting the tab, as noted in Step 4 above. The Leader section of the Tabs dialog box (Figure 6.11) offers four leader settings. The first removes any previously-applied leader for the tab selected in the Tab stop position list. The next three choices create a dotted, dashed, or underline leader, respectively, for a new or existing tab.

FIGURE 6.13

Tab leaders are visual aids that help the reader better track content separated by tabs.

Contents
Creation through Geological Forces..1
   Colorado River Basin 1
      Age...1
      Rock Layers...1
   Weather Factors..2
Canyon Facts and Figures..2
The Grand Canyon Becomes a National Park...2
Visiting the Canyon Today..2

For example, to create a signature or other fill-in area for a printed form, type and format the prompt (Name: Phone, and so on). Open the Tabs dialog box, enter the desired Tab stop position value, click Right under alignment, and then click the Leader option 4 (solid underscore). Click OK, and then click to the right of your prompt and press Tab. This creates something like what is shown in Figure 6.14.

FIGURE 6.14

Tab leader lines are ideal for creating underscored fill-in areas for paper forms.

Name: _____ ¶

> **NOTE**
>
> To change a tab leader, click the tab in the Tab stop position list of the Tabs dialog box, click the desired style under Leader, and then click Set. Similarly, you can click a tab in the Tab stop position list, and then click Clear to remove the tab stop. When you finish working with Tabs, click OK to close the Tabs dialog box.

Setting tabs with the ruler

You can set tabs using the horizontal ruler as well. First, display the ruler if needed by checking Ruler in the Show group of the View tab. Then determine the tab type by clicking the tab selector control at the left end of the ruler. (Refer to Figure 6.7 for its location.) As indicated earlier, this control cycles among Word's five built-in tab types, as well as First Line Indent and Hanging Indent controls. Figure 6.15 shows the markers or buttons for the five built-in tab types. When the desired tab type appears on the control, click the lower portion of the ruler (below the eighth-inch hash marks) to set the desired tabs. Drag a tab marker along the ruler to correct its placement; holding the Alt key while dragging shows you the exact location.

FIGURE 6.15

Choose a tab type using the control at the left side of the ruler, and then click the ruler to set the tab.

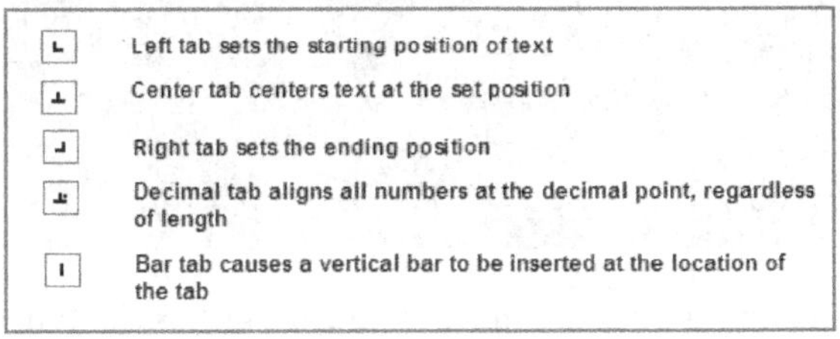

L	Left tab sets the starting position of text
上	Center tab centers text at the set position
⌐	Right tab sets the ending position
⬭	Decimal tab aligns all numbers at the decimal point, regardless of length
I	Bar tab causes a vertical bar to be inserted at the location of the tab

To remove a tab from the ruler, simply drag the tab marker down and away from the ruler until the mouse pointer is no longer in the ruler area.

Setting Off Text with Paragraph Decoration

A second overall kind of paragraph formatting is something that might be termed *paragraph decoration*. This includes shading, boxes, bullets, and other semi-graphical elements that help the writer call attention to particular paragraphs, or that help the reader better understand the text.

Numbering or bulleting lists of text

Automatic numbering and bulleting helps clarify the nature of the lists in your document, as well as saving you the trouble of having to insert numbers and bullets manually, set tab stops and a hanging indent, adjust the spacing between paragraphs, and apply all the other paragraph-formatting settings needed for a list. Another benefit of using Word's numbered list tool is that if you need to change the order of the items in the list, all you have to do is drag or cut and paste them. The list then automatically renumbers itself.

Traditionally, you create a numbered list to show steps in a process and a bulleted list for a nonchronological list of items. Numbered lists are also useful when you want to count the items in a list, such as when you are providing a "Top 10" list.

You can apply numbering or bullets to selected paragraphs by clicking the Numbering or Bullets button in the Paragraph group of the Home tab. Each paragraph in the list becomes a separate numbered or bulleted item.

You also can click the Numbering or Bullets tool and just start typing a brand-new list. When you're done with your list, simply press Enter twice to stop the numbering or bulleting. If you create additional indent levels in the list by pressing the Tab key, Word automatically uses different and appropriate numbering or bullet schemes for each level.

NOTE

If Automatic bulleted lists or Automatic numbered lists are enabled, then you don't even need to click the Numbering or Bullets tool. To begin a numbered list, simply type 1. (1 followed by a period) and press the spacebar, and Word automatically replaces what you type with automatic number formatting. Other variations work, too, such as 1<tab>. To begin a bulleted list, simply type * and press the spacebar. When you want to end either kind of list, press Enter twice.

You can change the number or bullet style by clicking the arrow for either the Numbering or Bullets tool. As shown in Figure 6.16, when you move the mouse pointer over a new bullet or numbering style, a Live Preview appears in the selected list. Click the desired format in the gallery to apply it to the list.

The Multilevel list button to the right of the Numbering button in the Paragraph group of the Home tab enables you to create an outline-style multilevel list. Its default format uses 1. (level 1), a. (level 2), i. (level 3) style academic formatting, but it, too offers a gallery of other formal and informal styles. Use Tab or Shift+Tab at the beginnings of lines to build the multilevel outline.

FIGURE 6.16

Live Preview shows the new numbering or bullet style.

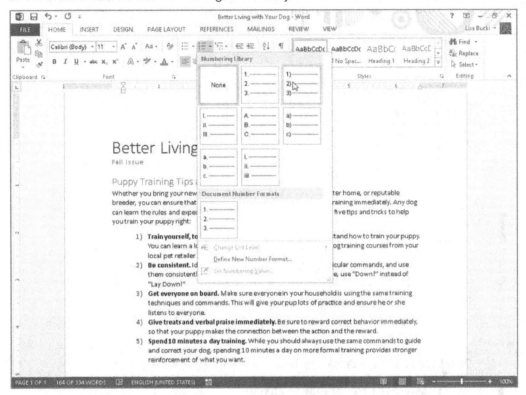

Line and page break controls

Figure 6.17 shows the Line and Page Breaks tab of the Paragraph dialog box, which offers additional paragraph-level formatting controls. Some of the settings found here are particularly useful for long documents with abundant headings, because they enable you to control what text stays together without the need for you to insert manual page breaks that you'd have to remove or move later if you edit the document.

FIGURE 6.17

Control how paragraphs behave around page breaks and with special formatting here.

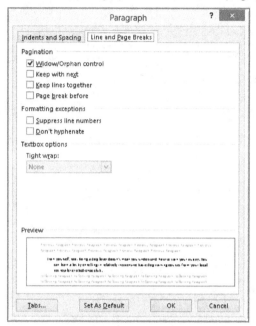

To set Line and Page Breaks options:

1. **Select the paragraphs to change.**

2. **Click the dialog box launcher in the Paragraph group of the Home tab.** The Paragraph dialog box opens with its Indents and Spacing tab selected.

3. **Click the Line and Page Breaks tab.**

4. **Click to check (enable) or uncheck (disable) the desired options under Pagination:**

   - **Widow/Orphan control:** Prevents a solitary paragraph line from being "stranded" on a page by itself without the rest of the paragraph. Widows precede the main portion of the paragraph and thus appear alone at the bottom of a page above the page break, whereas orphans follow the rest of the paragraph and appear alone at the top of the page below the page break).

   - **Keep with next:** Forces a paragraph to appear with the paragraph that follows. Use this setting to keep headings together with at least the first few lines of the first paragraph under that heading. You can also enable this setting to keep captions and pictures, figures, tables, and so on, on the same page.

- **Keep lines together:** Prevents a paragraph from breaking across two pages.
- **Page break before:** Forces an automatic page break before the paragraph. For example, you could enable this check box to force each chapter to begin on a new page.

5. **Click to check (enable) or uncheck (disable) the desired options under Formatting exceptions:**

- **Suppress line numbers:** Enable this check box to temporarily hide line numbers that you've previously set up. (You will learn to do this in Chapter 16.) Hiding the line numbers is faster than removing and reapplying them.

- **Don't hyphenate:** Instructs Word not to perform hyphenation in the selected paragraphs. This often is done by those trying to reproduce a quote and maintain its integrity with respect to the words and position of the original being quoted.

6. **Click OK to close the dialog box.**

What's That Dot?

As you are working with various paragraph formatting choices you may notice a square dot appear at times to the left of some paragraphs. The square dot appears to the left of a paragraph when any of these attributes are assigned to that paragraph:

- Keep with next
- Keep lines together
- Page break before
- Suppress line numbers

The dot will not print, but provides a visual reminder that you have applied special line and page break formatting.

Shading paragraphs

You can shade paragraphs as well as individual words with the Shading drop-down in the Paragraph group of the Home tab. As shown in Figure 6.18, after you open the control, point to a color to see a Live Preview on the selected text. Or, if no text is selected within a paragraph, Word applies the shading to the entire paragraph holding the insertion point. When you find the color you want, click it to apply it.

FIGURE 6.18

Word applies the shading to selected text or the whole paragraph holding the insertion point.

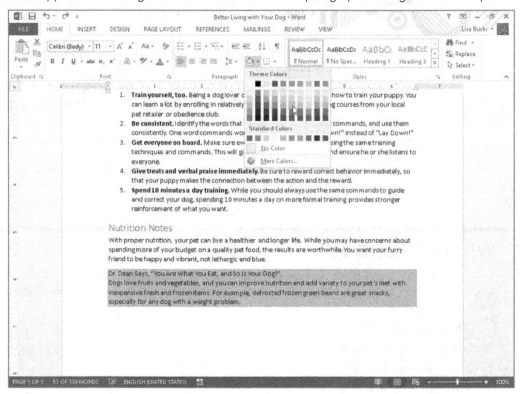

The Shading tab of the Borders and Shading dialog box offers additional shading options. To display the Borders and Shading dialog box, click the drop-down arrow next to the Border tool in the Paragraph group of the Home tab, and click Borders and Shading (at the bottom of the list). As shown in Figure 6.19, open the Style drop-down list under Patterns, and scroll down to view the various opacity and pattern settings that can be applied to the shading. Click the one you want, check its appearance in the Preview area at right, and then click OK to apply the change. Patterns often are more useful when you're preparing documents for grayscale printing in which shading variations might be too subtle.

FIGURE 6.19

Change opacity or apply a pattern to a shaded selection.

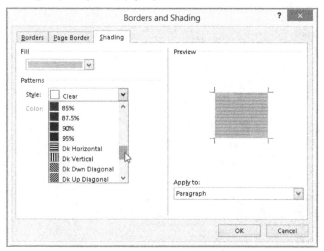

Borders and boxes

You can apply borders above and below or beside selected paragraphs for emphasis, or to set off one or more paragraphs from the rest of the text by boxing it. The Borders gallery in the Paragraph group of the Home tab offers several preset border types that you can preview with Live Preview. For example, as shown in Figure 6.20, after you click the Borders drop-down list arrow, pointing to Inside Borders displays lines between the paragraphs in the selected numbered list. Click a preset in the menu to apply it. Using Live Preview helps in this instance because the resulting box or border applied depends on how many paragraphs you've selected and how they're otherwise formatted.

Click the Borders and Shading command at the bottom of the drop-down list shown in Figure 6.20 to open the Borders and Shading the dialog box with the Borders tab selected, as shown in Figure 6.21. To use the dialog box to apply a border:

1. **Click the Border drop-down arrow in the Paragraph group of the Home tab, and then click Borders and Shading.**
2. **Make a selection from the Style list.**
3. **Click the Color box and click the border color to use.**

FIGURE 6.20

Preview and apply a border or box preset

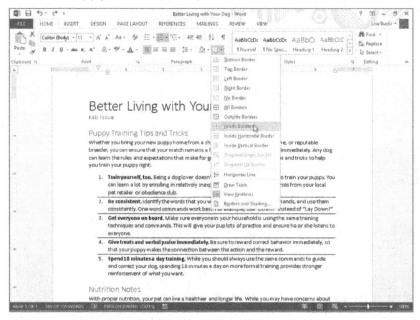

FIGURE 6.21

The Borders and Shading dialog box provides complete control over a paragraph's border.

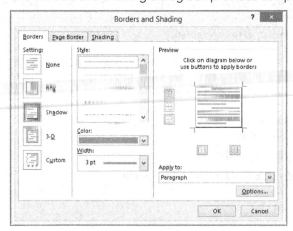

4. **Open the Width drop-down and click a width.**

5. **Then, either click one of the presets under Setting to apply that style of box to the selected paragraph (Figure 6.20 shows the Shadow style of box selected), or click the four sides of the Preview box at right as needed to apply or remove the border on the specified side.**

6. **Make sure Paragraph is selected from the Apply To drop-down.**

7. **Click OK.**

Additionally, you can adjust the distance between the border and paragraph text by clicking Options in the lower-right corner of the dialog box. You can individually adjust the distance for any of the four sides.

> **CAUTION**
>
> Note that the Border button in the Paragraph group of the Home tab changes to the last border preset that you applied. This does not apply if the last option you picked was Borders and Shading.

Caveats for printing and viewing

With formatting tools that are so easy to use, it's always tempting to think that more is better. Sometimes more is just more. And sometimes more can create issues for readers of your documents, whether they are printing them or viewing them onscreen. Before you wrap up that document and send it to the printer or email it to another user, review your document for these potential problems:

- **Lack of spacing between paragraphs:** Applying bold and italic character formatting to create "headings" often doesn't break up the text enough. Use paragraph styles or insert spacing above and below heading paragraphs to give your reader's eyes a break. Adding a border below every heading also helps.

- **Lack of spacing between lines:** Make sure you understand the intended purpose of a document, and set line spacing accordingly. If your instructor or boss wants you to double-space the text in your report, make sure that you've done so.

- **Shading that's too dark for printing:** If you apply navy shading behind black text, chances are it won't be readable when printed, especially if your color printer does a poor job rendering color or you are printing to a black and white printer. Choosing the Lighter 60% or Lighter 80% variations of the right six accent colors under Theme Colors in the Shading pallet usually is safer than choosing one of the deeper variations on the rows below.

- **Shading that's not optimized for onscreen viewing:** If you believe most users will be reading your document online or if you plan to convert it to a PDF, keep in mind that it's sometimes easier to read light text on a dark background onscreen. This means that you might consider changing to a white text fill and dark shading for paragraphs you want to emphasize.

Summary

In this chapter we've explored the ins and outs of direct paragraph formatting. You should have also started to develop a better sense of when to use direct paragraph formatting, and when to take it to the next level and create your own style, one of the skills you'll learn in Chapter 7. You should now be able to do the following:

- Decide when to use direct formatting, and when to use a style
- Distinguish between paragraph-formatting attributes and other kinds of attributes
- Properly indent and align any paragraph, as well as determine how to find and use the appropriate tools
- Adjust line spacing in a paragraph and spacing before and after paragraphs
- Decide when to use tabs versus when to use a table
- Apply and remove bullets and numbering
- Use shading and boxes to highlight paragraphs

Using Styles to Create a Great Looking Document

S tyles combine power and flexibility to serve as Word's most important formatting method. Some users hesitate to take advantage of styles because they can seem like an intimidating "advanced" feature with a dizzying array of options.

This chapter gives you a handle on which style tools to use for what in Word 2013 so that you can format new documents and update the look of older ones with ease. You will learn various ways to apply, clear, create, and modify styles. The chapter also introduces Style Sets, the Style Inspector, and methods for managing styles.

Using the Styles Group to Apply Styles

It's hard to overstate the value that styles deliver when creating and formatting a document. Not only do styles help a document look more lively and consistent, they give the reader a road map to understanding the relative priority of the text. Applying heading styles helps your readers identify major topics and their subtopics, and you can use other styles to emphasize special content such as quotations and sidebars. Figure 7.1 compares a basic document that uses the default Normal style for all text to an improved version with title and heading styles applied.

FIGURE 7.1

Styles not only enhance the look of a document but also improve document readability.

The Styles group on the Home tab of the Ribbon contains the primary set of commands and choices for applying and working with styles. On its face are three controls, shown in Figure 7.2: the Style gallery, the More button for expanding the gallery, and the Styles pane launcher. Note that in the gallery, a highlight appears around the name of the style applied to the paragraph holding the insertion point.

FIGURE 7.2

The Styles group is the command and control center for styles.

The number of styles that initially appear in the gallery depends on your screen resolution. As Figure 7.2 illustrates, at a very low screen resolution, the Style gallery might only display a handful of styles. To see all the available styles, click the More button to open the full gallery, as shown in Figure 7.3. If there are still more styles in the gallery, you can access them using the vertical scroll bar or by dragging the lower-right corner control to expand or shrink the size of the gallery.

FIGURE 7.3

Click the More button to open the Style gallery and see all the available styles.

NOTE

Word 2007 and 2010 sometimes called text formatting styles "Quick Styles" and the Style gallery the "Quick Styles gallery." This confusing terminology appears to have been eliminated when it comes to text formatting, but you might notice the term "Quick Style" applied to the galleries for formatting other types of objects, such as WordArt or SmartArt.

Notice also the Colors and Fonts controls. These tools work with themes, which aren't the same thing as styles. You can change the theme applied to the document to dramatically update its appearance. Unlike styles, however, themes are tied to the use of theme elements such as theme colors and effects applied to objects in your document. One way to think about themes is as design elements that affect the aesthetic appearance of a document. Styles, on the other hand, are geared more to the formatting of text and paragraphs. Chapter 18, "Saving Time with Templates, Themes, and Master Documents," explores themes.

In a moment you'll learn how to use the gallery and other mouse-oriented methods for applying styles. Word includes built-in shortcut keys for applying the most commonly-used styles. Using only the keyboard shortcuts listed in Table 7.1, you can accomplish a significant amount of style formatting in a typical report or similar document. Move the insertion point into the paragraph to format, and press the keyboard shortcut for the desired style.

TABLE 7.1   Keyboard Shortcuts for Applying Built-in Styles

Press This Keyboard Shortcut	To Apply This Style
Ctrl+Shift+N	Normal
Alt+Ctrl+1	Heading 1
Alt+Ctrl+2	Heading 2
Alt+Ctrl+3	Heading 3

Applying styles from the Style gallery

When you first start typing in any new Word document, Word automatically applies the default Normal style to the text. As you create different types of content in the document, you should consider applying an appropriate style. For example, if you type a heading, consider applying a heading style to it, such as Heading 1, 2, or 3. The Normal.dotm template also includes built-in styles for the titles, subtitles, quotes, sidebars, emphasizing text, and more. To apply a style:

1. **Click in the paragraph to format, or select the text to format.** Whether you need to select the text depends on whether the style is a paragraph style, character style, or linked style. This is explained further in Step 3. (The section called "Formatting Characters Directly or with Styles" in Chapter 5, "Font/Character Formatting," explained what paragraph, character, and linked styles are and the differences in how they work.)

2. **If needed, click the More button to open the Style gallery.**

3. **Move the mouse button over a style to display a Live Preview of how the selected text would look with the style applied.** See Figure 7.4. If you've just moved the insertion point to the paragraph rather than selecting text, Live Preview shows

the style you've pointed to applied to the entire paragraph when it's a paragraph or linked style. For a character-only style, the style preview appears for only the word holding the insertion point. If you find that you need to apply a character style to more than just the current word, move the mouse pointer off the gallery and click in a blank area of the document. Then select the text and start over.

4. **Click the style in the gallery to apply it and close the gallery.**

FIGURE 7.4

Point to a style in the Style gallery to see a Live Preview in the current paragraph or selection.

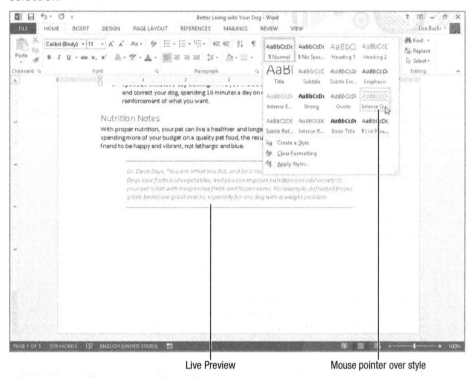

Live Preview   Mouse pointer over style

NOTE

`Normal.dotm` contains many different styles, and one of them happens to be named Normal. In fact, every Word template contains a style named Normal, so the actual formatting of this style will vary depending on whether you used an alternate template to create the document. You can think of the Normal style as the base or body style, other traditional terms for the body text in a document.

Applying styles using the Styles pane

Word 2013 continues to offer the Styles pane (or task pane), which you can use to view even more styles than appear in the Style gallery, and which offers additional commands for working with styles. You can either click the launcher in the lower-right corner of the Styles group of the Home tab or press Alt+Ctrl+Shift+S to open the Styles pane, shown in Figure 7.5. The pane by default lists only Recommended styles, and the style applied to the text holding the insertion point has a rectangular selection box around it (the Intense Quote style in Figure 7.5). See the "Recommended styles" section later in the chapter to learn more about what they are and how to work with them.

FIGURE 7.5

Click the Styles group launcher or press Alt+Ctrl+Shift+S to open the Styles pane.

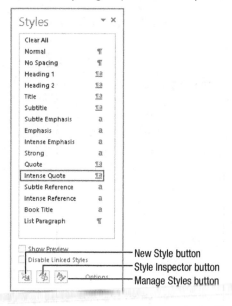

The basic method for applying a style from the Styles pane is similar to that for the Style gallery:

1. **Click in the paragraph to format, or select the text to format.** Whether you need to select the text depends on whether the style is a paragraph, linked, or character style.

2. **Click the style in the Style pane to apply it.**

This method doesn't enable you to get a Live Preview of the style before you apply it, but you can get information about a style prior to applying it in the Styles pane. You can do either of the following:

- Move the mouse pointer over the style to display a ScreenTip with information about the style's Font formatting settings, Paragraph formatting settings, and Style-related settings.
- Click the Show Preview check box below the list of styles in the pane. As shown in Figure 7.6, the styles listed in the pane preview their formatting settings. Also notice that this may make the basic list of styles too long to display in the pane, depending on your system's screen resolution. When that's the case and you move the mouse pointer over the list of styles, a scroll bar appears, and you can use it to scroll to the style choices you want.

FIGURE 7.6

Check Show Preview to see how each style looks in the Styles pane.

Select some text holding a particular style in the document, and then move the mouse pointer over that style in the Styles pane, and a drop-down list arrow appears to the right of it. Click the arrow to open a menu of commands for working with the style, as shown in Figure 7.7. (You also can right-click the style in the Styles gallery of the Styles group of the Home tab to see the same menu.) The commands available on the menu vary depending on the type of style and whether you've selected any text in the document. The two most useful ones for working with the style formatting are:

- **Select All/Select All # Instance(s):** Click Select All to select all instances of the style in the document if it's the first time you're selecting the style during the current work session; after that the command changes to Select All # Instance(s). You can then reopen the drop-down list see the number of locations in the document where you've applied the selected style. You can then select another style to apply to all the selected areas of text, quickly changing from one style to another throughout the document. If you've previously selected and then deselected all instances of the style, you can reopen the menu and choose Select All # Instance(s) to reselect them.

- **Remove All/Clear Formatting of # Instance(s):** Click this option to clean up a document's extraneous formatting. If you have not selected instances of the style in the current Word work session, the command that appears is Remove All. That command changes to Clear Formatting of # instances after you've selected all the instances of the style using one of the options noted in the prior bullet. Remove All/Clear Formatting of # Instance(s) does not delete the text in question. Instead, it removes the style wherever it is used, and resets the formatting of those occurrences to the default style for the current document, usually Normal.

FIGURE 7.7

Open the style's menu to access helpful commands.

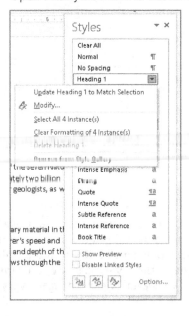

> **NOTE**
>
> In Figure 7.7, shown earlier, the drop-down menu for the Heading 1 style has its Delete option grayed out (dimmed). You cannot delete a built-in style. You can hide it using the Remove from Style Gallery choice, but you can't delete it from the template.

Applying Styles with the Apply Styles Pane

You can also display the Apply Styles pane (shown here) by pressing Ctrl+Shift+S. It has some of the same tools as the Styles pane. You can select a style to apply from its scrollable Style Name drop-down list, or use its Reapply and Modify buttons to work with style settings. It's just a matter of preference whether you want to use the Styles pane or the Apply Styles pane.

> **TIP**
>
> To close any task pane when you've finished using it, click its Close (X) button.

Reapplying or resetting a style

After you apply a style, you can apply direct formatting such as bold, italic, paragraph spacing changes, and so on. If you later decide to remove the added formatting, you don't have to backtrack setting by setting. Instead, you can reapply the style or reset the text to the style to remove the extra formatting settings all at once. Use any of these three methods to get the job done after selecting the text to reset:

- Click the style again in the Styles pane.
- Click Reapply in the Apply Styles pane.
- Press Ctrl+Spacebar.

> **NOTE**
>
> A Disable Linked Styles check box appears at the bottom of the Styles pane. When you check this feature, linked styles can only behave like paragraph styles. This means that you can't apply a linked style's formatting to a selection within a paragraph, you can only apply it to an entire paragraph.

Clearing all styles from selected text

You can clear all style formatting from selected text, which returns the text to the default Normal style. As for some of the other aspects of dealing with styles, Word 2013 provides many ways to handle this task in addition to using the Clear Formatting of # Instance(s) command in the Styles task pane as described earlier:

- Click the Style gallery More button, and then click Clear Formatting at the bottom. (Refer to Figure 7.4.)

- In the Styles task pane, click the Clear All choice at the top.

- On the Home tab of the Ribbon, click the Clear Formatting button in the upper-right corner of the Font group.

Modifying and Creating Styles

Despite the variety of styles available in most document templates, you may not find the exact style to give your document the appearance you want. The font or point size might be wrong, or the spacing might be off. No problem. Change it. Or, if you still need the existing style but want a slightly different version for another purpose, create a new style.

CAUTION

When experimenting with styles, make a copy of the document and/or template in question, and work with the copy. That way, you can fall back to the previous copy of the document if you either change your mind or make a colossal formatting mistake.

Modifying an existing style

When you've already applied a style throughout a document, you might want to modify that existing style to adjust the look of the already formatted text rather than applying a different style. You might need to make only a slight change to the style, such as adjusting its font size or spacing. To change an existing style:

1. **Right-click the style in the Style gallery or open the style's menu in the Styles pane, and click Modify; you also can select the style and click the Modify button in the Apply Styles pane.** Any of the methods opens the Modify Style dialog box shown in Figure 7.8.

2. **Make the desired formatting changes to the style.** The Formatting section of the dialog box includes a number of the settings found in the Font and Paragraph groups on the Home tab of the Ribbon. If the formatting you need to change isn't shown, click the Format button in the lower-left corner and click one of the choices

there, such as Numbering or Text Effects, to open a dialog box with additional formatting settings. Click Close or OK to finish working in that additional dialog box.

3. **Click OK to close the Modify Style dialog box.** Word updates the formatting for all text with the style applied in the document.

FIGURE 7.8

Use the Modify Style dialog box to make changes to a style.

CAUTION

Keep Automatically update in the Modify Style dialog box turned off unless you absolutely need it. When that check box is enabled, each time you make changes to text using a specific style, those changes are automatically incorporated into the style's definition. All other text in the document formatted with that style will automatically change to reflect the changes in the style's definition. That might be just what you want if you've used the style in just one way in the document. On the other hand, if you've used the style in various ways (for example, say you have used Heading 3 for headings, table titles, sidebar titles, and so on) you might want formatting changes to apply in some of those instances but not others. In such a case, having Automatically update checked would work against you, because it would likely update text that you wanted to remain as is. Note that for this reason, there is no Automatically update option when you select the Normal style and open the Modify Style dialog box. You are so likely to apply other formatting to Normal text that any automatic updating would create an endless loop of updates to the Normal style.

A second way to update a style is to use the controls in the Font and Paragraph groups in the Home tab of the Ribbon to reformat some text to which you previously applied the style. When the text looks the way you want, click the style's drop-down arrow in the Styles pane, and then click Update *Style Name* to Match Selection.

If you find you frequently update style formatting, remember that you can enable Prompt to update style in Word's Advanced options. Then, any time you make formatting changes to styled text (except for the Normal style, which can't be automatically updated by any method) and then click the style's name in the Styles pane, Word displays the prompt dialog box shown in Figure 7.9. The Update the style to reflect recent changes option will add the new formatting to the style's definition, whereas the Reapply the formatting of the style to the selection option will revert the style. Leave the former option selected and then click OK to finish changing the style. To enable Prompt to update style, choose File ⇨ Options ⇨ Advanced, and in the Editing options section, click to check Prompt to update style. Click OK.

FIGURE 7.9

If you've enabled Prompt to update style, Word asks you to confirm whether you want to update or reapply the style.

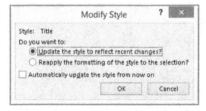

> **TIP**
>
> The Redefine Style command covered in Chapter 3, "Working Smarter, Not Harder, in Word," does work for the Normal style. Even though adding this command to the QAT and using it isn't automatic, it does give you a faster way to work with the Normal style if you're someone who likes to experiment often with the look of document body text.

Creating a style from scratch

There are a couple of different ways you can create a new style. In general, every new style you create will be based on an existing style. So you will want to start from a style that's similar to the type of style you need to create. For example, if you want to create a Body Text style, start by reformatting some Normal text. Or, if you want to create a new heading style, start from the existing heading style that's closest to the look you want.

Here's how to use the Create New Style from Formatting dialog box to save a new style:

1. **Select some text that uses a style similar to the one you want to create, and apply desired formatting.** Leave the text selected.

2. **Click the New Style button in the lower-left corner of the Styles pane.** The Create New Style from Formatting dialog box shown in Figure 7.10 appears.

3. **Type a name for the style in the Name text box.**

4. **Make further adjustments to the style settings as needed.** For example, use the Style type drop-down list to indicate whether the style is a Paragraph, Character, Linked (paragraph and character), or another type of style. If you leave Paragraph selected as the style, use the Style for following paragraph drop-down to choose which style Word automatically applies to any new paragraph you create by pressing Enter. For a heading style, you would want this to be a Normal or body text style in many cases. Also apply any additional formatting changes as needed.

5. **Leave Add to the Styles gallery checked to provide access to the style via that control on the Home tab of the Ribbon.**

6. **Click OK to finish creating the style.**

FIGURE 7.10

Set up a completely new style in this dialog box.

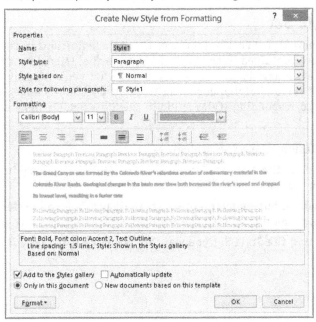

You also can also use the Modify Style dialog box to create a new style. Just change the entry in the Name text box in addition to making any formatting changes, and when you click OK Word creates the new style.

Changing the Whole Document via Style Sets

Word 2013 offers an improved version of the Quick Style Sets feature offered in prior Word versions. You can find them, now called Style Sets, in a gallery on the Design tab, in the Document Formatting group. Applying a different Style Set updates all the style formatting throughout the document to use different paragraph and character style formatting.

I emphasize *style formatting* because if paragraphs have direct formatting applied, applying a Style Set does not override that formatting. For example, if you manually change the alignment of a series of paragraphs from left aligned to centered, any alignment formatting in a Style Set you apply will be ignored.

The impact of applying a particular Style Set—indeed, seeing any effect at all—depends on your having used styles in your document. If you simply left all the text formatted with the Normal style, then at most applying a new Style Set will change the font. For maximum benefit from Word's style features, you need to lay the proper foundation, which means using styles to differentiate different kinds of text (headings, body, captions, and so on).

Applying a Style Set

When you apply a new Style Set, Word replaces the style definitions in the current document with those contained in the Style Set's .dotx file. (More about this shortly.) It effectively overlays a new document template over what you're already using (even though the name of the underlying document template does not change), updating all text that uses any corresponding styles found in the Style Set. To apply a new Style Set to the document:

1. **Click the Design tab on the Ribbon.**
2. **If needed, click the More button to open the Style Set gallery in the Document Formatting group.**
3. **Move the mouse button over a Style Set to display a Live Preview of how the selected text would look with the style applied.** See Figure 7.11.
4. **When you find the Style Set you want to use, click it to apply it to the document.**

FIGURE 7.11

Point to a Style Set in the gallery to see a Live Preview of the potential new document styles.

Creating and deleting Style Sets

You create your own Style Sets to give yourself even more power and flexibility to format your documents with just the styles you want. Word stores each Style Set in a .dotx (not macro-enabled) template. When you create a Style Set, Word automatically suggests saving it in C:\Users*user name*\AppData\Roaming\Microsoft\QuickStyles folder. Leave this folder selected so that your custom Style Set will be automatically included in the Style Set gallery. Follow this process to create and save a Style Set:

1. **Apply a Style Set, if needed, and modify the document styles as desired.** The modified document styles will be stored in the new Style Set.

2. **Click the Design tab, click the More button in the Document Formatting group to open the Style Set gallery, and then click Save as a New Style Set.** The Save as a New Style Set dialog box shown in Figure 7.12 appears.

3. **Type a name for the Style Set file in the File name text box.**

4. **Click Save.**

FIGURE 7.12

Word automatically suggests a specific folder to hold your new Style Set file.

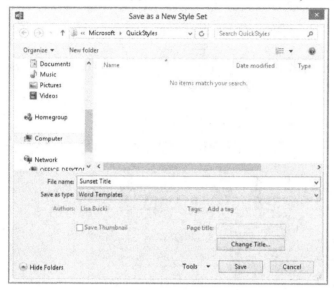

When you display the Style Set gallery after creating at least one custom Style Set, the gallery includes your Style Set in the new Custom category. If you want to delete a custom Style Set, right-click it in the gallery as shown in Figure 7.13, and click Delete. Click Yes in the dialog box that prompts you to confirm the deletion.

FIGURE 7.13

Right-click a Custom Style Set in the gallery and then click Delete to remove the Style Set.

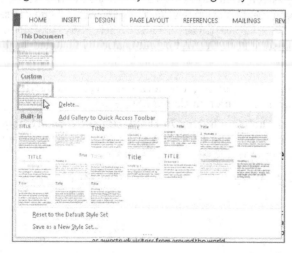

Word stores each of its default Style Set files in the `C:\Program Files (x86)\Microsoft Office\office15\1033\QuickStyles` (32-bit version) or `C:\Program Files\Microsoft Office\office15\1033\QuickStyles` (64-bit version) folder, as shown in Figure 7.14. The default Style Sets are stored as Word template (`.dotx`) files. In theory, you can apply one of the Style Sets to a blank document, modify the styles, and then use the Save as a New Style dialog box to navigate to the folder holding the default Style Set files, and enter the name of one of those files to save over it, thus modifying it. In practice, though, leaving the default Style Set files undisturbed and creating your own Style Set files gives you the choice to continue using the default styles in the future along with your custom sets.

FIGURE 7.14

The default Style Sets are stored as Word template files.

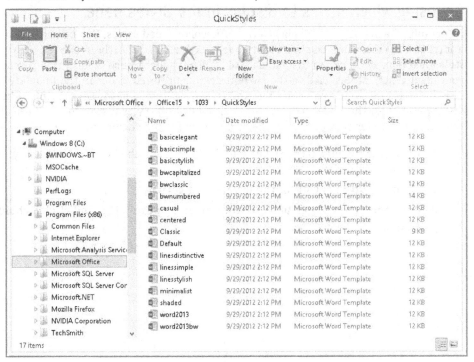

> **NOTE**
>
> The default .dotx files contain no text or other formatting, but only style information for dozens of built-in styles. To see a list of these styles, double-click one of the .dotx files in a folder window to open a blank document based on it in Word. Display the Styles pane, and then display all styles as described later in this chapter.

Changing your mind

If you've been experimenting with Style Sets but now want to revert to the styles of the document's underlying template, in most cases you can. Click the Design tab, and in the Document Formatting group, click the More button to open the Style Set gallery. Click Reset to Default Style Set near the bottom of the gallery to reset the styles immediately.

Managing Styles

You have control over numerous other aspects of how and where styles appear and behave in Word. Cleaning up or expanding the style listings can make you much more efficient when you're taking on the task of formatting your document. This section covers the most important style management features you need to know about.

Choosing which styles to display in the Styles pane

By default, the Styles pane displays a list of Recommended styles. You can change and prioritize the recommended styles that appear as described shortly in the "Recommended styles" section. But you can instead choose to display just in use styles (used throughout your documents), styles used in the current document, or all styles in the template. The last choice is great when you can't find the type of style you need. For example, when you display all styles, the Styles pane includes nine heading styles instead of the normal three. To choose the styles that appear in the Styles pane for the current document:

1. **Display the Styles pane if needed.** To do so, click the launcher in the Styles group or press Alt+Ctrl+Shift+S.
2. **Click the Options link in the lower-right corner.**
3. **Open the Select styles to show drop-down (Figure 7.15), and click a choice.**
4. **Click OK.**

FIGURE 7.15

Choose how many styles Word lists in the Styles task pane.

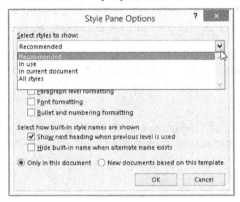

Removing a style from the gallery

Depending on how avidly you create and use your own styles, your Style gallery could rapidly fill with styles, making it more cumbersome to use than it otherwise would be. You might want to trim the styles that appear in the gallery for certain documents, so you can more readily work with the styles you prefer. Removing a style from the Style gallery does not remove the style from the document; it only removes it from the gallery listing.

Use the Styles pane to control a style's inclusion in the Style gallery. Click the style's drop-down arrow, and then click Remove from Style Gallery to remove it. To reinstate the style in the gallery, display its menu again, and then click Add to Style Gallery.

You also can remove a style from the Style gallery by right-clicking the style and clicking Remove from Gallery.

Recommended styles

Word includes a Manage Styles dialog box that enables you to perform advanced style management operations. Though there's not room to cover all the options exhaustively, you can get familiar with some key options here. To open the dialog box, click the Manage Styles button at the bottom of the Styles task pane.

The Recommend tab, shown in Figure 7.16, controls which styles show up on the list of recommended styles. A *recommended style* shows up in each of the style-related task panes and the Style gallery. Click a style in the list at the top, and then click the desired button under Set whether style shows when viewing recommended styles. Clicking Show ensures the style will be displayed, or you can select Hide until used or Hide. It's a great way to focus the options when you want to exercise strong control over document formatting.

In the list of styles at the top of the dialog box, you can apply your changes one at a time or by using standard Windows selection techniques to select multiple styles. Note the Select All and Select Built-in buttons, too, which enable you to quickly distinguish between Word's standard styles and user-created styles.

Use the Move Up/Move Down/Make Last/Assign Value tools to determine the recommended order. You can even alphabetize them, if that makes more sense to you. Click OK to apply your changes when finished.

FIGURE 7.16

Use the Recommend tab to control what styles show up when you restrict style controls to displaying recommended styles.

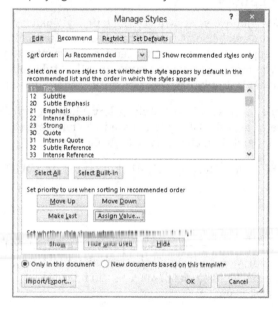

Restricted styles

For even stronger style enforcement, the Restrict tab of the Manage Styles dialog box enables you to limit which styles can be used. This is a good tool for designing templates and forms in which you want extremely tight control over the content formatting. It's also useful in setting up training classes for Word, when you might want to tame the options a bit to avoid overwhelming the novice user.

Additionally, if you want to enforce the use of only styles—and not direct formatting—the restricted styles capability provides a way to do it. Check Limit formatting to permitted styles, shown near the bottom of Figure 7.17, to accomplish this feat.

By restricting formatting only to styles, you effectively prevent the use of direct formatting tools. As shown in Figure 7.18, when formatting is restricted to Normal and Heading 1 through Heading 5, most of the Ribbon Font and Paragraph controls are grayed out (dimmed) as unavailable.

FIGURE 7.17

The Restrict tab enables you to make direct formatting off-limits.

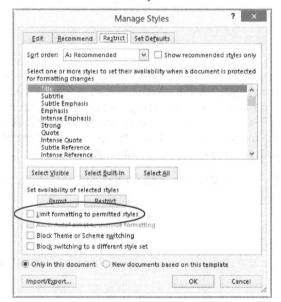

FIGURE 7.18

Limiting formatting to the use of styles turns off many of the direct formatting tools on the Home tab of the Ribbon.

To control the availability of a particular style, click it in the list on the Restrict tab, and then click either Permit or Restrict under Set availability of selected styles. Note that not only can you limit formatting only to permitted styles; you can also enable Block Theme or Scheme switching. If you want to tame "artistic" tendencies of users whose mission statement apparently includes using up all the colored ink or toner in the company printer, this provides an avenue of attack.

When you finish making your choices, click OK. A Start Enforcing Protection dialog box prompts you to enter and confirm a password. Do so, and then click OK.

Deleting a style

You can delete a style from the Styles pane. As mentioned earlier, Word won't let you delete certain built-in styles such as Normal. However, you can delete any custom style you create if you decide not to use it. Point to the style in the task pane, click its down arrow, and then click Delete *Style Name*. At the confirmation prompt, click Yes.

Style Inspector

The Style Inspector enables you to quickly determine whether the formatting for selected text consists of a style alone, or a style and direct formatting. In Figure 7.19, notice that under the Paragraph formatting and Text level formatting (character), the first box identifies the applied style, and the second box has the word Plus:. The text to the right of the Plus: identifies any potential direct formatting applied over the style.

To use the Style Inspector, select the text to diagnose, and then click the Style Inspector button at the bottom of the Styles pane.

FIGURE 7.19

The Style Inspector can help you diagnose where direct formatting has been applied to styled text.

Summary

In this chapter you explored a variety of features that can help you format a document faster and more consistently through styles. You should also be able to do the following:

- Use the Style gallery, Styles pane, and other methods to apply, create, and modify styles
- Use the Styles pane to quickly select all occurrences of any given style
- Reapply a style's formatting
- Update the look of the whole document by applying a Style Set
- Create and delete a custom Style Set
- Control which styles appear in the Styles pane and the Style gallery
- Use the Manage Styles dialog box to hide and restrict styles and direct formatting
- Use the Style Inspector to solve formatting mysteries

7

Cutting, Copying, and Pasting Using the Clipboard

IN THIS CHAPTER

Understanding the Windows Clipboard versus the Office Clipboard

Learning the various ways to move and copy document content

Copying and moving sections with collapsible headings

Taking advantage of pasting options

Setting the default paste option and using Paste Special

Managing Clipboard pane items

Working with the Office Clipboard and pasting options

O nly very rare individuals can compose a document and get all their thoughts in the right order on the first take. Most of us work with more of a stream-of-consciousness style, jumping back and forth between topics while we try to capture our thoughts. Luckily for us, Word enables us to rearrange the content in any document as much as needed to create a more cohesive flow and enhance clarity.

You can pick words up either alone or in groups and move them around in the document. If you create a line you like, you can repeat it and tweak it.

Word's Cut, Copy, and Paste commands work in conjunction with the Office Clipboard, a multifunction center for rearranging document content. In this chapter, you'll learn the various ways you can use these tools and customize how they work for you.

Understanding the Office Clipboard

A *clipboard* is a temporary storage area you can use to transfer text, files, pictures, and other objects between different programs or different parts of a single program. You copy or cut text from one location, and then paste it in the destination location.

Windows has long had a clipboard that you can use in just about any Windows program. You can use Windows' Clipboard to transfer files, pictures, text, and so on between different documents in different programs. The Windows Clipboard stores only a single item at a time.

The Office Clipboard in Office 2013 can store up to 24 items. Each time you copy or cut a new selection, Office adds it to the top of the list in the Office Clipboard. When the Clipboard reaches 24 items, adding another item causes the oldest item to disappear.

All of this happens behind the scenes, because the Clipboard pane for the Office Clipboard remains hidden until you want to work with more of the items it holds. An ordinary paste command pastes the most recent item from the top of the list. The "Using the Clipboard Pane" section later in this chapter explains how to use the Office Clipboard in more detail.

NOTE

For the Office Clipboard to collect up to 24 items, either the Clipboard pane must be displayed or the Collect Without Showing Office Clipboard option must be enabled in the pane. The "Using the Clipboard Pane" section also covers how to turn on this setting.

Adding and Moving Document Content with Cut, Copy, and Paste

Word offers a number of ways to accomplish a copy or move operation. The first two copy or move methods require you to complete two separate actions:

- When you copy a selection, use the Copy command so Word places a duplicate of it on the Office Clipboard. You then must select a destination for the duplicate by positioning the insertion point, and use Paste to place the duplicate in position.

- When you move a selection, use the Cut command so Word removes the text from its current location and places the text on the Office Clipboard. From there, you again move the insertion point to the desired destination and choose Paste to place the moved selection in position.

NOTE

Even if you don't open the Office Clipboard, you can paste the most recently cut or copied selection into multiple destination locations. For example, say the creator of the document typed the full name "Sara Smith" the first time in the document, but only typed "Smith" in three subsequent locations. You could copy Sara and paste it beside the three locations of "Smith" to include the full name.

What concerns you up front is the commands and techniques you use to copy or move any selected text. Word gives you a number of methods for doing this.

Keep in mind that in some instances when you move or copy text, you may have to do some cleanup afterward depending on how the document is formatted and how well you made your selection. For example, you may need to click at the end of a pasted paragraph and press Enter to add a new paragraph break, or you might need to click at the end of a sentence and press the Spacebar to make sure sentences don't run together.

CAUTION

If you're moving an entire paragraph and want to make sure that its formatting remains intact, you have to be sure the selection includes the paragraph mark. Either move the mouse pointer to the left margin until it tilts right and then double-click. Or, click Show/Hide in the Paragraph group of the Home tab so that you can see the paragraph mark and be sure to drag all the way over it when you make your selection.

You can use the Clipboard in a variety of ways, and other copy and move methods skip the Clipboard altogether. The following sections present all of the copy and move methods to you.

Using the Ribbon

The Clipboard group at the far left end of the Ribbon holds the tools that give you one way to accomplish copying or moving text with the mouse. Here's how to do it:

1. **Select the text to copy or move.**

2. **In the Clipboard group of the Home tab, click the Copy button to duplicate the selection, or the Cut button to remove it.** Refer to Figure 8.1. The Paste button isn't available until you cut or copy at least one selection.

FIGURE 8.1

The Clipboard group enables you to copy, cut, and paste text with the mouse.

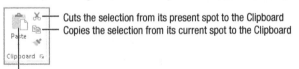

— Cuts the selection from its present spot to the Clipboard
— Copies the selection from its current spot to the Clipboard

Pastes the cut or copied selection at the insertion point

3. **Use the method of your choice to move the insertion point to the destination location where you'd like to place the copied or cut text.** Keep in mind that this destination location can be another Word file, another Office file, or a file or location in another program that accepts pasted content. If you need to, use the taskbar to switch between documents and apps to go to the paste destination.

4. **In the Clipboard group of the Home tab, click the Paste button.** The text appears at the insertion point, and a Paste Options button appears at the bottom right, as shown in Figure 8.2. You can ignore the button or choose an option from it. The "Using Paste Options" later in this chapter explains what paste options are available and how they work.

FIGURE 8.2

The pasted text appears at the new location.

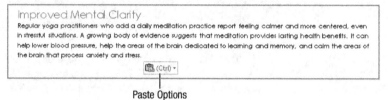

Paste Options

> **NOTE**
>
> Cut works only in editable windows. If you try to cut text from a normal Internet Explorer window, for example, it won't work. You can't cut that 105° from the Weather Channel's forecast (but you can copy it). If it's an editing window, such as a filled-in text area or a blogging composition window, then you likely can cut text for use elsewhere.

Using the keyboard

Keyboard shortcuts provide perhaps the most familiar method for copying, cutting, and pasting. Word uses the keyboard shortcuts for these actions, which have been available in Windows and Windows apps for well beyond a decade. When you use the keyboard shortcuts to copy or move selected text, follow the same process just outlined for the Ribbon, but use these keystrokes instead of the commands:

- **Copy:** Ctrl+C
- **Cut:** Ctrl+X
- **Paste:** Ctrl+V

> **NOTE**
>
> You can use the same overall process to copy and move objects other than text within and between documents. Pasting objects such as tables, pictures, or WordArt comes with a few special issues, such as how to deal with text wrapping. Later chapters—such as Chapter 14, "Adding Pictures and WordArt to Highlight Information," and Chapter 15, "Adding Drop Caps, Text Boxes, Shapes, Symbols, and Equations"—touch on the ins and outs of pasting non-text selections.

Using non-Clipboard methods

Suppose you have carefully assembled 24 items on the Office Clipboard that you still need to paste in various locations, but you encounter another text selection, graphic, or other object you need to copy or move. These next few methods—dragging and dropping, F2, and the Spike—enable you to copy and move selections without using the Clipboard.

Dragging and dropping

You probably already knew about drag-and-drop, but you might not have realized that it doesn't involve the Clipboard. Select what you want copied (text, graphics, whatever) or moved. Then, to *move* the selection elsewhere, simply drag it to the desired location.

To *copy* the selection to a second location, press and hold the Ctrl key while dragging it to the desired spot. As shown in Figure 8.3, a plus sign appears with the mouse pointer, signifying that the action will copy rather than move the selection.

FIGURE 8.3

Press and hold Ctrl while dragging a selection to copy rather than move the text, as indicated by the + beside the mouse pointer.

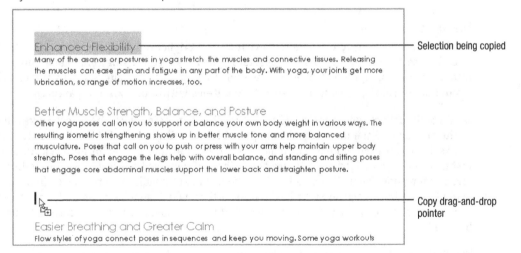

Selection being copied

Copy drag-and-drop pointer

Note that when you're dragging text from Word to another program, such as Internet Explorer, Word automatically copies, rather than moves, the text. For example, you can copy a phrase or a name from Word into the Google (or other) Search text field in Internet Explorer, Firefox, Chrome, or another browser. You do not need to press Ctrl in this case.

The F2 factor

Another unfamiliar copy and move method dates back to Word for DOS. Using the mouse or keyboard, select the text or other items you want moved or copied. To move the selection elsewhere, press F2. To copy it, press Shift+F2. The left end of the status bar now prompts, "Move to where?" or "Copy to where?" as shown in Figure 8.4.

FIGURE 8.4

Select text and press F2 or Shift+F2, and Word prompts you for a destination for the selection.

Next, using any method you choose, move the insertion point to where you want to place the selection (or select the text or other items you want the current selection to replace). Then press Enter.

The Spike

Word offers another way to move text without the Clipboard called the *Spike*. Use the Spike to collect selections of text using a special keyboard shortcut. Word puts each Spiked item into a separate paragraph. This can be useful if you plan to use the Spike to create a list. It's not so useful if you want to insert Spiked items within an existing paragraph.

Word's Spike collects deletions in FIFO (first in, first out) order, with the oldest Spiked deletion at the bottom and the most recent deletion at the top. Unlike the Office Clipboard, however, Word's Spike won't let you paste or remove one item at a time—it's all or nothing. An example instance when you might want to use the Spike is if you need to create a summary list at the end of a long document. You could add all the document headings to the Spike (immediately using Undo after using the Spike keyboard shortcut, which also happens to delete the selection), empty them from the Spike at the end of the document, and then reformat them as a bulleted list.

The Spike is actually a special AutoText entry that Word creates for you on demand. (An *AutoText entry* is a stored text item that you save so that you can insert it wherever needed; Chapter 12, "Getting Smart with Text: Building Blocks, Quick Parts, Actions (Tags), and More" covers working with AutoText entries.) To use it, select the text you want to collect and press Ctrl+F3; this deletes the text, copying it to an AutoText entry named Spike. If you want to copy text rather than move it, immediately press Ctrl+Z (Undo). This restores the deleted text, but does not affect the copy of it already stored in the Spike. Continue collecting selections in this way.

When you're ready to use the contents of the Spike, move to the destination location, and then:

- To insert the contents of the Spike and empty (delete) it at the same time, press Ctrl+Shift+F3.
- To simply use the Spike contents, type **Spike** as shown in Figure 8.5 and press Enter or F3.

FIGURE 8.5

When you use the Spike AutoText entry, the initial entries in the list of items stored in the Spike appear in a ScreenTip.

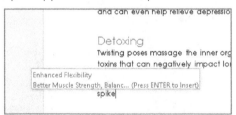

Recall that all but the topmost of the Office Clipboard's items are lost when Office is closed. The Spike, because it is an AutoText entry, resides with your Building Blocks, another type of saved text that you can insert where needed. (Chapter 12 also provides more detail about using Building Blocks.) As long as you don't use the Ctrl+Shift+F3 insertion method, the Spike continues to live on when you close Word, reboot Windows, and so on. Long live the Spike!

8

TIP

You may have guessed that the Spike isn't the only AutoText or Building Block you can use to store text that can be retained between Office sessions. You can also use AutoCorrect. AutoText, Building Block, and AutoCorrect items can be deleted when no longer needed, so they provide great ways for you to create your own data entry shortcuts.

Working with heading styles and document organization

Word 2013 includes a feature where you can work with the document outline within Print Layout, Web Layout, and Read Mode views as long as you've applied the built-in heading styles in the document. As shown in Figure 8.6, when you click within a styled heading paragraph, a triangle appears to the left of the heading name. Click a gray down-pointing triangle to collapse the heading's text. Click a white right-pointing triangle to expand the heading's text.

FIGURE 8.6

Expand and collapse document text below heading paragraphs in Print Layout view.

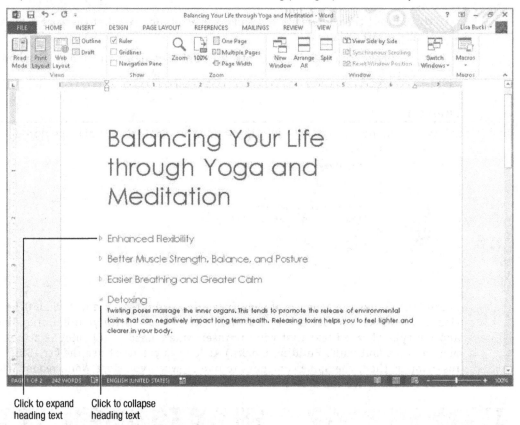

Click to expand   Click to collapse
heading text   heading text

Collapsing the heading text makes it easier to reorganize the document via the various copy and move methods. For example, you can cut and paste a heading to move it and all the text collapsed under it. When you paste the heading into a new position, the Paste Options button appears as shown in Figure 8.7 so that you can decide how to handle the formatting of the pasted text. You can later click the white triangle to redisplay the collapsed text under the heading. If you drag and drop the heading, its text expands below the heading, along with the Paste Options button.

FIGURE 8.7

The collapsed text travels along with the heading you copy or move.

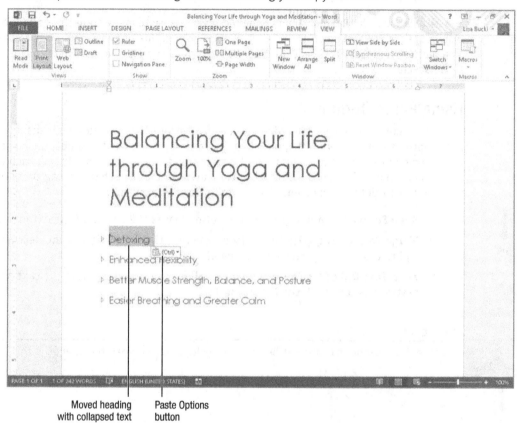

Moved heading
with collapsed text

Paste Options
button

Managing Pasting Options

You've so far seen a couple of instances of the Paste Options button appearing when you paste a selection you've cut or copied. You can either choose Paste Options after completing a paste using that button, or you can choose Paste Options during the process of pasting. If you have a favorite Paste Options choice, you can set it as the default method rather than having to specify what you want each time.

You also can use the Paste Special command from the Paste menu to paste a selection with other types of formatting not offered in Paste Options. One of those choices is to paste text as a picture, a process this section illustrates for you. You learn about Paste Options and Paste Special next.

Using Paste Options

You've already seen how pasting displays a Paste Options button. Clicking it displays the Paste Options menu shown in Figure 8.8. You can click one of the three buttons on the Paste Options menu to control how Word handles the formatting of the pasted text. Each of these buttons also has a shortcut key, listed in the button ScreenTip, that you can press to select it. From left to right on the menu, the Paste Options buttons are:

- **Keep Source Formatting (K):** This option leaves the original formatting applied.
- **Merge Formatting (M):** This option examines the formatting in the destination and reformats the pasted text to match.
- **Keep Text Only (T):** This option strips all extra formatting from the text and pastes it as text with the Normal style.

FIGURE 8.8

Click the Paste Options button after pasting a selection to reveal the choices in this menu.

If the selection you are pasting came from another file or application or is an object other than text, you may see additional Paste Options, such as Use Destination Styles (S) or Use Destination Theme (H). Paste Options works with Live Preview, so if you'd like to see the impact of a certain Paste Options choice, move the mouse pointer over it to see a preview of how the pasted text or object would look with that choice applied. Then click the choice that looks the way you want.

The other way you can apply a Paste Options choice is to do it directly while pasting to the destination location at the insertion point. The bottom of the Paste button in the Clipboard group of the Home tab has a down arrow you can click to open a menu. That menu, shown in Figure 8.9, includes the same choices you saw in the Paste Options button menu in Figure 8.8. As for the Paste Options button, the choices on this menu work with Live Preview, so you can move the mouse pointer over the various buttons to preview the paste material's appearance before clicking to finish the paste.

FIGURE 8.9

Click the Paste button down arrow and then click a Paste Option to paste and format text in one step.

Setting the default paste method

In Figure 8.8, the left Paste Options button, Keep Source Formatting, is selected. That is the default Paste Option in Word 2013. You can change the default paste method. If you click Set Default Paste in the menus shown in Figure 8.8 or Figure 8.9, Word opens File ⇨ Options ⇨ Advanced; from there you can scroll down to the Cut, copy, and paste section shown in Figure 8.10. You can set the default for Pasting within the same document or Pasting between documents to Keep Source Formatting (Default), Merge Formatting, or Keep Text Only. If needed, you also can change the defaults if there's a style conflict or if you're pasting from another program. After making your choices, click OK.

FIGURE 8.10

Set default Paste Options for pasting within and between documents.

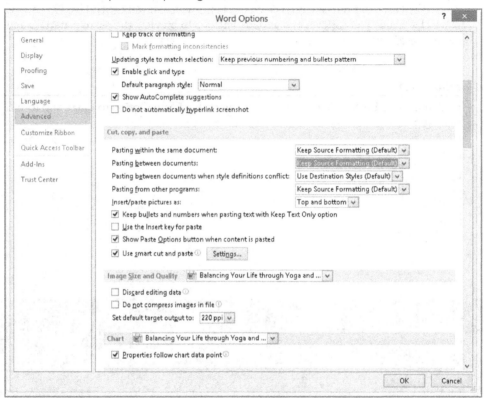

Paste Special

The Paste button drop-down menu also includes a Paste Special option, shown in Figure 8.4. Clicking Paste Special opens the Paste Special dialog box with options for converting the format of the Pasted Item, as shown in Figure 8.11.

> **NOTE**
>
> You can open the Paste Special dialog box using the legacy keystrokes Alt+E, S. (This keystroke dates back to Word 2003, where it accessed Edit ➪ Paste Special in the menu.) Pressing Alt+Ctrl+V, which you might find easier and more direct, also opens the dialog box.

FIGURE 8.11

Use Paste Special to determine whether to convert the format of the pasted item.

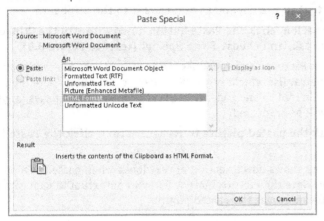

In the As list, click the format you want to use to paste the selection at the insertion point. The Paste link option to the left of the As list, when available, creates an OLE bookmark around the selected text or object and inserts a LINK field code with a reference to the document name and bookmark where the source is located. You'll learn more about the LINK field in Chapter 23, "Automating Document Content with Fields." Bookmarks are covered in Chapter 19, "Enhancing Navigation with Bookmarks, Hyperlinks, and Cross References."

If the source is ever deleted or otherwise unavailable when the document that contains the link is updated, Word will indicate that the source cannot be found, and the update will fail. This, of course, is a lot better than replacing the displayed item with an error message.

CAUTION

If you notice stray bookmarks with names like OLE_LINK3 in your document, don't delete them without considering the possible consequences. If you know where the one in question came from and still want to delete it, that's fine. If you're unsure of its origin, leave it alone, as something else in that document or another document probably depends on its presence there.

Copying and pasting a picture of text

While the Clipboard won't perform OCR (optical character recognition) for you, it will let you do the opposite—paste a picture of your text. This can be useful for a variety of reasons, such as when you want something that looks like text but can be manipulated as a graphic.

To paste a "snapshot" of text (which can include graphics, by the way), follow these steps:

1. **Select the target text in the document and copy it to the Clipboard.**

2. **Move to the destination, click the Paste button down arrow in the Clipboard group of the Home tab, and choose Paste Special (refer to Figure 8.9).**

3. **In the As list, click Picture (Enhanced Metafile).** Sometimes one works but not the other, or vice versa. Use whichever result works or looks best. Note, however, that the picture is limited to one page. If the text spans multiple pages, anything beyond one page will be truncated.

4. **If you want to link the pasted picture to its source text, click the Paste link option.**

5. **Click OK.** Figure 8.12 shows how a section of text looks when pasted as a picture in a new document. Note the Picture Tools ⇨ Format contextual tab appears on the Ribbon so that you can format the pasted picture.

FIGURE 8.12

When you paste a text selection as a picture, you can use Picture Tools to format it.

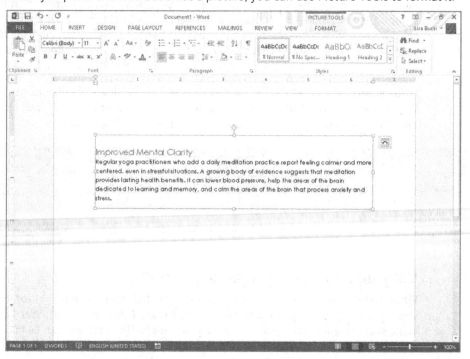

Using the Clipboard Pane

The Office Clipboard remains effectively dormant unless you display the Clipboard pane or turn on the Collect Without Showing Office Clipboard option. To open the Clipboard pane, click the dialog box launcher in the Clipboard group of the Home tab. If you want to have the Clipboard pane store multiple items even when it's not displayed, click the Options button at the bottom of the pane, and then click to check Collect Without Showing Office Clipboard, shown in Figure 8.13; from that point, you can close the Clipboard pane, and it (the Office Clipboard) will store multiple copied or cut items.

FIGURE 8.13

You can set up the Office Clipboard to gather copied and cut selections without appearing onscreen.

The complete Options settings for the Office Clipboard and its Clipboard pane are:

- **Show Office Clipboard Automatically:** Automatically displays the Office Clipboard when you copy items using the mouse, keyboard, or Ribbon tools.

- **Show Office Clipboard When Ctrl+C Pressed Twice:** Automatically displays the Office Clipboard when Ctrl+C is pressed twice (and sometimes just once) while a copyable item is selected.

- **Collect Without Showing Office Clipboard:** Automatically adds items to the Office Clipboard even if the Clipboard is not displayed.

- **Show Office Clipboard Icon on Taskbar:** Shows the Office Clipboard icon in the notification area of the Windows taskbar when the Office Clipboard is active; the icon may be hidden, so to display it, use the taskbar's Show hidden icons button.

- **Show Status Near Taskbar When Copying:** Displays a message near the Windows notification area when you copy or cut items to the Office Clipboard.

While the second option indicates that two presses of Ctrl+C causes the Clipboard pane to appear, that's not always the case. If no text is selected, the Clipboard won't appear. If text is selected, sometimes just a single press of Ctrl+C will cause the Clipboard to show.

Pasting from the Clipboard pane

When the Clipboard pane is open, you can paste any of its (up to 24) items into the current document. The Office Clipboard can hold all kinds of cut or copied objects—graphics, text, spreadsheet cells or ranges, PowerPoint slides, Word documents, sounds, and more. The only limit on the size of any given item you can store on the Clipboard are your computer's RAM and other resources.

To paste the entire contents of the Clipboard pane, move the insertion point to or select where you want the pasted item(s) to go, and choose Paste All at the top of the task pane (Figure 8.14).

To paste a single item from the Clipboard pane:

1. **Move the insertion point to the destination location where you want the pasted item(s) to go.**

2. **Click the item to paste in the Clipboard pane.** You can paste from any location in the queue. Unlike with Ctrl+V or the Paste tool, you are not limited to the item at the top of the list.

Keep in mind that the Office Clipboard is not fully integrated into Windows itself. Each new copy or cut is added to the Office Clipboard, regardless of the program in which the copy or cut is performed. You can only paste from the Office Clipboard in Office programs (and not all of those). As indicated, non-Office programs such as Notepad and Internet Explorer, for example, can access only the "top" item.

FIGURE 8.14

Click Paste All to paste all of the Clipboard pane items at the insertion point, or click an individual item to paste it alone.

Removing items from the Clipboard pane

Pasting from the Clipboard pane does not affect the queue itself. Copying or cutting more selections will cause items to scroll off the list. If you want to remove an unwanted item from the Clipboard pane, right-click the item and choose Delete. Any items below that one in the list move up. If the most recent Copy or Cut caused a former 24th item to be removed from the list, deleting one above it will not restore that item. The Clipboard's limit really is 24 items—there is no invisible storage location for items 25 and beyond.

To empty the Clipboard pane, click Clear All at the top of the pane. (Refer to Figure 8.14.) Another way to empty the Clipboard is to close all Office programs. Office 2013 will not remember the Clipboard's items, except for the top one, after all Office programs are closed. The good news, at least for any individual Windows session, is that as long as at least one Office 2013 program remains running (such as Outlook, which many users keep open so they can receive email and calendar alerts), the Clipboard pane's contents remain intact. After all Office programs are closed, however, the Office Clipboard's contents are lost.

System tray icon and notification

The Show Office Clipboard Icon on Taskbar option shown in Figure 8.13 enables you to know that the Office Clipboard is active, even when it's not displayed. When this option is checked, you can click the Show hidden icons button in the Windows notifications area at the right end of the taskbar to see the menu shown in Figure 8.15.

FIGURE 8.15

Point to the Office Clipboard icon to see how many items are on the Clipboard or right-click for options.

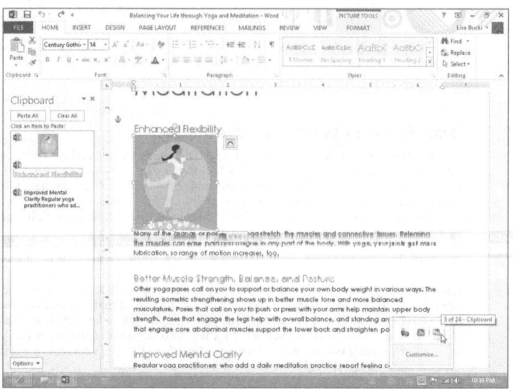

Right-click the notification icon to see three self-explanatory commands: Show Office Clipboard, Clear All, and Stop Collecting. Pointing to Options at the bottom of the shortcut menu displays the same choices described in the list at the beginning of the "Using the Clipboard Pane" section.

Summary

In this chapter you've learned about the relationship between the Windows Clipboard and the Office Clipboard. You've learned how to control when the Clipboard appears, as well as how to prevent it from appearing at all. You should now know how to do the following:

- Copy or move text with the tools in the Clipboard group of the Home tab or short-cut keys
- Use methods that bypass the Office Clipboard, including drag-and-drop, F2, and the Spike
- Collapse headings with heading styles applied to rearrange sections of the document more quickly
- Use the Paste Options to control the formatting of pasted text, or use Paste Special to convert the pasted object
- Accumulate items on the Office Clipboard without its being visible
- Paste individual items from the Office Clipboard, or paste its entire contents in one fell swoop
- Use the Office Clipboard notification icon

8

Find, Replace, and Go To

IN THIS CHAPTER

Throughout the years, for many, Word's fabulously powerful array of Find and Replace tools stands out as a great strength. You can accomplish some pretty amazing and sophisticated techniques with these tools, replacing hours of tedious editing and reformatting with a few short techniques. This chapter helps you learn all of the ways that you can make Find and Replace work for you, giving you the skills and knowledge to dazzle your colleagues and friends.

Searching with the Navigation Pane

Word 2013 provides two ways to find a word or phrase used throughout the document. You can use the traditional Find and Replace dialog box like the one found in many different applications, or you can use the Navigation pane. Both methods are useful for finding instances of text that you may want to edit. The benefit of using the Navigation pane is that it lists the found results within the context of the heading or sentence where it appears. You can quickly scroll down the pane and select the instance that you want to edit, rather than repeatedly clicking Find Next to move to and review the next matching instance. This makes the Navigation pane a good option for performing a find in a long document.

The Navigation pane also solves the issue of the legacy Find and Replace dialog box sometimes covering the text you're trying to review. While the prior version of Word offered a Browse Object feature on the scroll bar that you could use to find the next instances of a search term, Word 2013 has eliminated that feature in favor of the Navigation pane.

Both the Navigation pane's Search document text box and the legacy Find what field can contain up to 255 characters. This makes it possible to search for long and complicated phrases—and not just text. Those 255 characters can contain a variety of wildcards to search for patterns of text as well. You'll learn how to use wildcards later in the chapter.

To search for text in a document with the Navigation pane:

1. **Click Find in the Editing Group of the Home tab or press Ctrl+F.** Or, you also can check Navigation Pane in the Show group of the View tab. The Navigation pane appears to the left of the document.

2. **Make sure RESULTS is selected under the Search document text box.** This tells Word to list the matching instances of text in the pane in addition to highlighting them in the document.

3. **Click in the Search document text box, and start typing the word or phrase to find.** By default, as you type, Word finds and highlights all matching text—incrementally. So if you type **g**, Word highlights every *g* in the document. Add an **r** and Word highlights every instance of *gr*. Keep on typing and Word narrows the list of matches. As shown in Figure 9.1, the Navigation pane displays every match in context, so you can quickly determine whether the matching text is the instance you seek. In the document, by default, Word highlights all the matches. See the next section, "Navigating Find results in the pane," for more information on reviewing the find results.

FIGURE 9.1

The Navigation pane provides an interactive approach to searching.

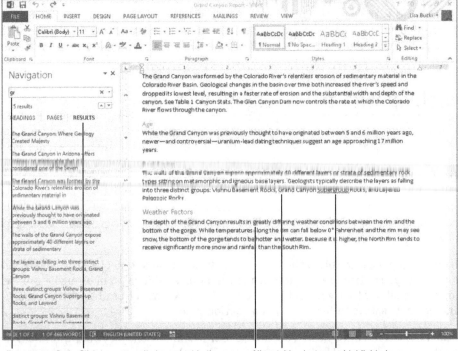

Enter text to find   Click to see results in context in the pane   All matching instances highlighted

TIP

While the Navigation pane doesn't provide access to Replace, it provides a good way to quickly look at all of the potential matches when you're getting ready to do a large-scale Replace. This is a good way to make sure that you won't be applying a change to an unintended match.

Navigating Find results in the pane

After you finish the Find in the Navigation pane, it shows you how many matching results it found. You can review the results within the pane by using the scroll bar that appears at the right side of the pane when you move the mouse pointer over it. From there, you can use one of two methods to select a result in the pane and see the corresponding instance in the document:

■ Use the scroll bar to scroll down the results, and then click any result in the list to see it in the text, as shown in Figure 9.2.

■ To find each successive match, you can click the Next Search Result or Previous Search Result button in the pane, also shown in Figure 9.2.

FIGURE 9.2

Use the Next Search Result button to display the next match in the document window or scroll and click a result.

Click to clear search   Previous Search Result   Next Search Result

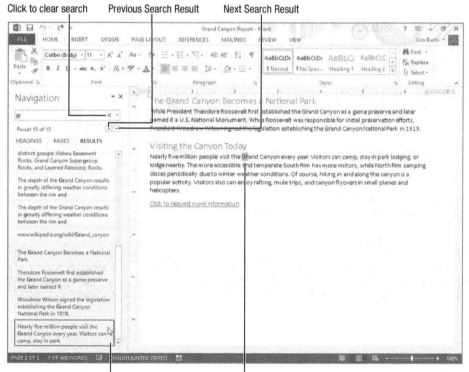

Selected match Is double-highlighted in text

243

No matter which method you use to select a search result, Word scrolls to it and double-highlights it—overlaying the yellow with light gray—so that you can identify the instance and decide whether to change it.

To clear the search results, click the X button to the right of the search term. You can then start a new search or click the Navigation pane Close (X) button to close the pane.

> **NOTE**
>
> Both the Navigation pane and the Find and Replace dialog box with Find, Replace, and Go To tabs are *non-modal*. This means that you can click in the text and edit the document while the pane or dialog box is still onscreen, which is more handy than repeatedly closing and reopening either the pane or the dialog box.

Searching for selected text

Whether you search in the Navigation pane or the Find and Replace dialog box, Word can automatically fill in the Search document or Find what text boxes, assuming the text box is empty. Select text to find in the document. When you press Ctrl+F or open the Find and Replace dialog box, Word copies the selected text to the applicable text box. The selected text has to be within a paragraph and can't contain any line, paragraph, or section separators or breaks. If the selection contains more than 255 characters, it will be truncated.

Finding something other than text

The drop-down arrow at the far-right end of the Navigation pane Search document text box is the Search for more things button. This button enables you to quickly find graphics, tables, equations, footnotes, endnotes, and comments throughout the document. Note that the Graphics search will find pictures that are in the drawing layer (that is, ones that are not in line with text), unlike the ^g special search code covered later, which matches only inline graphics.

For example, clicking Search for more things and then clicking Tables as shown in Figure 9.3 finds the first table in the document, which is highlighted at the right beside the Search for more things menu. If more tables were in this particular document, the search results would list them so that you could select the one to review using the techniques already described for matching text selections.

> **TIP**
>
> Clicking Find, Replace, or Go To in the Search for more things menu displays the legacy Find and Replace dialog box with the corresponding tab showing.

FIGURE 9.3

Use the Search for more things button to find non-text objects.

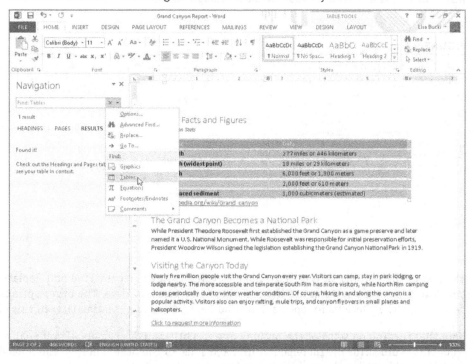

9

Navigation pane search options

If you click on Options, shown in Figure 9.3, Word displays options available for searching within the Navigation pane. The Find Options dialog box, shown in Figure 9.4, includes a number of options you might be familiar with from the legacy Find dialog box. The Incremental find choice pertains to the Navigation pane only. When checked, this option tells Word to search immediately as you type the search text, and to narrow the search as you type more search. Highlight all determines whether Word highlights all the matches or just does so one at a time as you navigate through them.

FIGURE 9.4

The Navigation pane's Find Options are mostly identical to legacy Find dialog box search options.

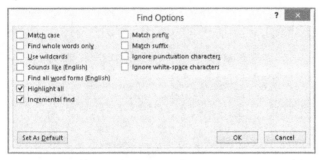

The rest of the options shown here also are available in the legacy Find and Replace dialog box. The two search systems are linked, which can save you time. The other options are described in the "Options for Special Find and Replace Actions" section later in this chapter.

Note that turning on some of the options disables others. For example, if you enable Use wildcards, Word turns off Incremental find and some of the other choices. You'll need to practice working with the options to see how they all interact.

Starting an Advanced Find from the Ribbon

If you're a longtime Word user and want to stick with the Find and Replace dialog box, you can. For example, you might want to take advantage of the choices for finding special characters in the dialog box if you don't want to remember the codes for these special characters. The trick is you have to select the Advanced Find command to use the dialog box now:

1. **Press Ctrl+Home to move the insertion point to the top of the document.** This step isn't essential, but it ensures you will search your entire document when needed.

2. **Click the Find arrow in the Editing Group of the Home tab and then click Advanced Find in the menu that appears.** The Find and Replace dialog box opens with the Find tab selected.

3. **Type the search text in the Find what text box.** Figure 9.5 shows an example of search text entered there.

FIGURE 9.5

You can still search using the Find dialog box.

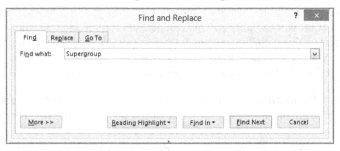

4. **Click Find Next to find the first matching instance of the search text.** Word scrolls the document and highlights the match in gray. If you need to, drag the Find and Replace dialog box out of the way to see the match. You also can click in the document to edit the text if needed, and then click back in the dialog box to resume the search.

5. **Click Find Next to review matches until the message box appears that tells you the search is complete, and then click OK.**

The Find and Replace dialog box Find what text box includes a drop-down list of recent searches. Open it to see up to seven recent searches (refer to Figure 9.6), and click a search term in the list to re-enter it in the text box. Note that Word does not retain these searches after being closed and reopened. However, if you are repeating a complicated search, it pays to use the legacy Find instead of the Navigation pane.

FIGURE 9.6

Word remembers the seven most recent searches from the current session.

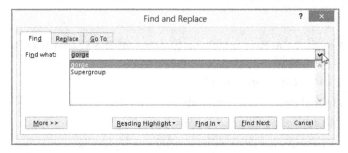

9

Replacing Text via the Ribbon

The Replace tab of the Find and Replace dialog box enables you to find a word or phrase and replace it with another word or phrase. This can be used for editing reasons, such as to replace a proper name that you've globally mistyped. Or, you can use it as a shortcut tool to save typing. For example, you could type **S Rim** where needed in the document and later replace it with the full term, **South Rim**. Replacing works much like using the legacy Find tab:

1. **Press Ctrl+Home to move the insertion point to the top of the document.** This step isn't essential, but it ensures you will search your entire document when needed.

2. **Press Ctrl+H or click Replace in the Editing Group of the Home tab.** The Find and Replace dialog box opens with the Replace tab selected.

3. **Type the search text in the Find what text box.**

4. **Type the replacement text in the Replace with text box.** Figure 9.7 shows an example of search and replacement text entered.

FIGURE 9.7

Specify both find and replace terms to make selected or global updates.

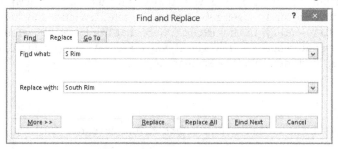

5. **Click Find Next to find the first matching instance of the search text.** Word scrolls the document and highlights the match in gray.

6. **Choose how to handle the found match:**
   - Click Replace to replace the first found instance and find the next.
   - Click Replace All to replace all matching instances.
   - Click Find Next to skip the match without making a replacement and find the next match.

7. **In the message box that tells you the search is complete, click OK.** If you used Replace All, the message box includes a count of the number of replacements made.

Using Search Codes

In addition to entering text in the Navigation pane's Search document text box, and the Find what and Replace with text boxes in the Find and Replace dialog box (on both the Find and Replace tabs), you also can type certain codes that enable you to match special characters such as the paragraph mark, tabs, line breaks, page breaks, and a variety of other characters or patterns that a plain search text won't. For example, if you have an old document where the writer pressed Enter twice after every paragraph, you can replace the double paragraphs by entering **^p^p** in the Find what text box and a single code for one paragraph, **^p**, in Replace with.

These *search codes* sometimes are mistakenly called *wildcards*. In Word, wildcards are a different type of shortcut. You'll read about wildcards a little later in this chapter. They are extremely powerful and versatile, but can be a bit difficult to grasp. Search codes, on the other hand, are somewhat more accessible and easier to understand and use. Where it makes sense, you'll find examples showing how these search codes might be useful.

In the sections that follow, I've tried to be as specific as possible about what codes you can use where. Search code usage is not always the same in both the Find what and Replace with text boxes. In addition, in some cases, a code won't work when the Use wildcards search option is enabled. The heading for each section indicates whether the codes there work with wildcards.

9

Find what and Replace with codes (Use wildcards on or off)

The codes in Table 9.1 can be used in either the Find what or Replace with text boxes, and the Use wildcards option can be on or off.

TABLE 9.1 Codes That Work in Find What and Replace With (Use Wildcards On or Off)

Character	Code	Example
Tab	^t or ^9	^t^t finds two tabs with no intervening text (which often indicates an extraneous formatting mistake or a missing column entry).
ASCII character	^nnn, where nnn is the ASCII character code	^174 matches the ASCII character «. It is often used when the exact symbol match is otherwise uncertain or when all you know is the character code.
ANSI character	^0nnn, where 0 is zero and nnn is the character code	^0171 matches the ANSI character «. (This is the same character as ASCII ^174.)
Em dash (—)	^+ or paste the em-dash character into the text box	Enter ^+ into the Find what text box and -- (two hyphens) into the Replace with text box to prepare a document for a graphic designer who doesn't like Word's em-dash character.
En dash (–)	^= or paste the en-dash character into the text box	^= finds and replaces regular hyphens (-, between the 0 and = keys) with en dashes.
Caret character (^)	^^	Use ^^^^ to search for ^^.
Manual line break (Shift+Enter)	^l (lowercase l) or ^11	When pasting text from other word processors or the Web, you often see manual line breaks instead of paragraph marks: find ^l and replace with ^p to restore proper paragraphs.
Manual column break	^n or ^14	Find ^n and replace with nothing (an empty Replace with text box) to remove manual column breaks.
Page or section break	^12	Find ^12 and replace with ^p to replace extraneous page breaks with paragraph marks; follow up by finding ^p^p and replacing with ^p to remove extraneous paragraph marks.

Character	Code	Example
Manual page break	^m matches both manual page breaks and section breaks (Use wildcards enabled); ^m, matches and inserts only manual page breaks (Use wildcards disabled)	With Use wildcards turned off, find ^m and replace with ^12 when major changes have been made to a previously carefully paginated document that has undergone major editing that renders leftover manual page breaks obsolete.
Nonbreaking space (Ctrl+Shift+Space)	^s	Find ^s and replace with a plain space to prevent odd line-break behavior.
Nonbreaking hyphen	^~	Find ^~ and replace with a plain hyphen to prevent odd line-break behavior.
Optional hyphen (Ctrl+-)	^-	Find ^- and replace with nothing (an empty Replace with text box) to strip out optional hyphens.

Find what and Replace with (Use wildcards off): paragraph mark

The code for paragraph marks is ^p. This code is typically used to find the beginning or end of paragraphs, as well as to "clean" text that contains extraneous empty paragraphs.

Example: ^pt would match paragraphs that begin with the letter *t*. Or find ^p^p and replace with ^p to remove extraneous empty paragraphs. An alternate code for the paragraph is ^13.

Find what field only (Use wildcards off)

The following codes work only in the Find what text box because they mean "any _____"— such as any character, any footnote, or any graphic. Table 9.2 lists these types of codes.

TABLE 9.2   Codes That Work in Find What Only (Use Wildcards Off)

Character	Code	Example
Picture or other graphic (inline only)	^g	Suppose you have a number of graphics using In line with text wrapping, but now want them to be formatted so that text wraps around them. Use ^g to find the first instance, close the dialog box, and change the wrapping. Repeat as needed.
Footnote or endnote	^2	Run a find with ^2 to locate footnote and endnote reference marks—whether in the body text or in the notes areas.

Continues

TABLE 9.2   *(continued)*

Character	Code	Example
Footnote mark	^f	Find what ^f and replace with red font color to make footnote reference marks easier to spot.
Endnote mark	^e	Find what ^e and replace with red font color to make footnote reference marks easier to spot.
Any character	^?	Find what **unioni^?e** to match *unionize* and *union-ise* (as well as *unionite* and *unionixe*).
Any digit (0 through 9)	^#	Find what **(^#^#^#) ^#^#^#–^#^#^#^#** to match a common US telephone number pattern.
Any letter (accented or unaccented)	^$	Find what **^$^$^#^#^#** to match two letters followed by three numbers; the pattern ^$^#^$ ^#^$^# matches any Canadian postal code.
Unicode character	^unnnn	Find what **^u0065** to find the letter *a*.
Field (when field codes, rather than field code results appear; Alt+F9 toggle)	^d	Find what **^d** and find the first field; press Ctrl+Shift+F9 to convert the field code to hard text if desired.
Opening and closing field braces (when field codes are visible)	^19 (left) and ^21 (right)	Find what ^21. (include the period in the search text) finds any field that occurs at the end of a sentence; find what before^19 would find the word *before* followed by a space and any field code.
Comment	^a or ^5	Find what **^a** and Replace with nothing (an empty Replace with text box) to quickly remove all comments from a document.
Section or page break	^b	Use in place of Table 9.1 codes when Use wildcards is disabled.
White space	^w	Find what **^#^#^#^w^#^#^#** to match two three-digit groups of numbers separated by any amount of white space; or use **John^wSmith** to find any occurrences of John and Smith that are separated only by white space.

Codes that work only in the Replace with box (Use wildcards on or off)

Two of the most useful codes can be used only in the Replace with box, but they can be used regardless of whether Use Wildcards is enabled. These two allow for some of the most powerful find/replace editing you can do with Word.

Clipboard contents

The code for Clipboard contents is ^c. The Clipboard, as you know, can hold a tremendous amount of text, graphics, and formatting. One possible use of this facility is to include an arbitrary replacement symbol or token for text and/or graphics that will be provided later. This can be especially useful when you will need to include the item in more than one place in a document. When the material is ready, simply copy it to the Clipboard. Then put the token into Find what and **^c** into the Replace with field. Note that "clipboard" in this case refers only to the top item in the Office Clipboard, the item that was most recently copied or cut. However, the contents can come from anywhere in Windows.

Find what matching text

You can think of ^& as the "ditto" code. Regardless of how complex the Find what pattern is, ^& will contain the text that actually matched it. For example, if you were searching for ^$^#^#^#^#, i.e., any letter followed by any four numbers, then ^& becomes the actual text that matches that. On successive hits it might be S4122, T4523, a6678, and so on. You can then use ^& in the Replace with box along with other characters.

Suppose you're trying to place brackets around every part number in a large document. Set Find what to a pattern that matches the part number pattern (for example, **^#^#^#^-** **^#^#^#^#** for numbers like 908-5534 and 324-8776), and put **[^&]** in the Replace with box. Whatever number matches the pattern will be replaced by the same number enclosed in brackets.

Options for Special Find and Replace Actions

The options in the Find and Replace dialog box and the Find Options dialog box for the Navigation pane provide a number of options that greatly expand find and replace functionality, utility, and power. Some of these options are explicitly designated using check boxes. Others are implicit, based on the "environment" in which you are searching, such as whether text is selected, as well as the nature of the selection.

> **NOTE**
>
> The Highlight all and Incremental find options of the Find Options dialog box were discussed earlier in the "Navigation pane search options" section.

Search within selected text (Find in)

You've already seen what happens when a word is selected when you press Ctrl+F and the Search document text box is empty. The same applies when you press Ctrl+H or start Advanced Find. However, you can use the Find and Replace dialog box to perform a find or replace only *within* a preselected area of text in the document. This doesn't work with the Navigation pane.

Select the text to search, and then start a find or replace using the Find and Replace dialog box. Click the Find in button, and then click Current Selection as shown in Figure 9.8. Word initially shows a gray highlight behind all matches in the selected area. You can then run the find or replace operation as normal.

FIGURE 9.8

You can make a selection and search only within it.

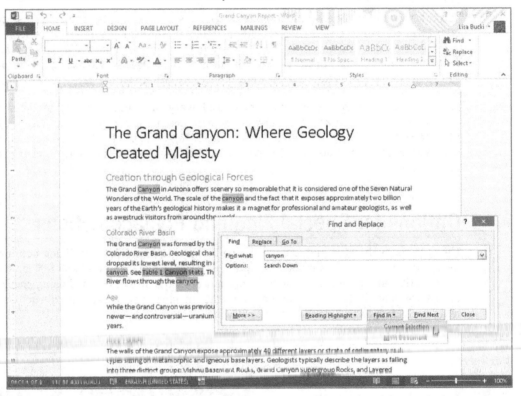

Reading Highlight

Click Reading Highlight and then Highlight All to apply temporary highlighting to all parts of the document that match the Find what text or pattern. It's "temporary" because the next time you use the highlighting tool directly, the Reading Highlight goes away. You can also clear the highlighting by reopening the Find and Replace dialog box if needed and choosing Reading Highlight ⇨ Clear Highlighting.

More or Less

Figure 9.8 shows the Find and Replace dialog box in its minimalist state. In many, if not most, instances, this is all you'll need to see. If you don't see what you want, click the More button. Figure 9.9 shows how the dialog box expands. Clicking the Less button returns the dialog box to its prior smaller size. The sections that follow explain each of the options that appear.

FIGURE 9.9

Click the More button to reveal the Find and Replace options.

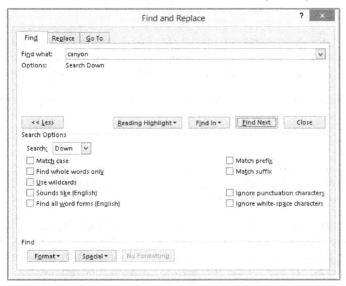

Search direction

You use the Search drop-down list to control the search direction. If no text is selected it defaults to All, which means that Word will search from the insertion point forward, wrap back to the beginning, and stop at the insertion point. Down searches from the insertion point to the end of the document, and Up searches from the insertion point toward the beginning.

Match case

This option tells Word to match the exact capitalization specified in the Find what box. For example, by default, setting Find what to **the** will match "the" no matter how it appears in a document: *The*, *THe*, *Thee*, *these*, *THEATRE*, *the*, *other*, and *narthex*. With "Match case" enabled, the same "the" would match only *these*, *the*, *other*, and *narthex*. An additional option enables you to narrow the focus to whole words only.

Find whole words only

Use this option to find whole words. From the preceding example, with this option enabled, "the" now matches only the word *the*. You could combine the Whole Words option with Match case to try to locate only the word *The* (for example). For maximum utility, you might combine the Whole Word option with other search terms if you want to find the word *The* when it's not at the beginning of a sentence.

Use wildcards

The Use wildcards option enables the use of a special set of operators to enhance your searches. When Use wildcards is enabled, different rules and different codes apply, although, as indicated earlier in this chapter, some codes work regardless of the Use wildcards setting.

For Find what and Replace with, note that the Special drop-down list changes depending on which text box is selected. We'll look at each in turn.

Find what codes

To see a list of the special codes allowed in the Find what box when Use wildcards is enabled, click More if necessary, click in the Find what field, and then click Special at the bottom of the expanded Find dialog, as shown in Figure 9.10.

There is one very important thing you need to know about Find What when using wildcards: Every actual search character specified in the Find what box is case-specific. For example, if you type an *m*, Word will match only *m*, and not *M*. Remember this. I will explain later why some searches don't work and need to be made smarter.

Of the Find what Special codes shown, only the top listed are actually wildcard operators, because the others match the specific characters indicated. When "Use wildcards" is selected, use the Special list to insert characters for searching (at least until you become familiar with them), as some of them are different from what you use to search when "Use wildcards" is not enabled.

The search operators are used to search for a wide and flexible variety of text patterns. Most of them can be used in combination to achieve even more powerful searching capabilities.

> **TIP**
>
> Note that a number of characters act as operators for wildcard searches, such as @, [,], {, }, *, ?, and even \ itself. If you need to search for any of those characters while wildcard search is enabled, precede the character with \. For example, to find a \ character, use \\. To find [, use \[, and so on.

FIGURE 9.10

Click Special to see a list of codes that are allowed in Find what when Use wildcards is enabled.

Any Character: ?

In a non-wildcard search, the code for any character is ^?. For wildcard searches, omit the caret (^). For example, to match all five-letter words beginning with *m* and ending with *h*, specify the Find what as **m???h.**

However, is that really correct? No, it's not. That's because ? can be *any* character, not simply a letter. Hence m???h would match not only *mitch* and *motch*, but also *m123h*. On the other hand, because the wildcard-enabled Find what box is case-specific, the pattern shown won't match *Mitch*, *Match*, or *Motch*. To build the correct search, use the range [a-z] feature, explained below.

Character in Range: [-]

There is an inherent order to the characters you use on your computer. To see that order, choose Insert ➪ Symbols ➪ Symbol ➪ More Symbols ➪ Symbols tab, then choose (normal text) from the Font drop-down list (see Figure 9.11). Note that A is selected. Near the bottom, the from field is set to ASCII (decimal), and the Character code text box displays 65. If you click the letter B, the code becomes 66. The code for a lowercase *a* is 97, *b* is 98, and so on.

FIGURE 9.11

Use the Symbol table to determine what characters are in specific ranges.

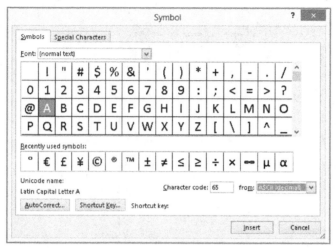

For example, if you try to specify a range of [G-A], that's not a valid range, and Word displays an error message saying so. However, [A-G] *is* a valid range, and would match any character from *A* to *G*.

In non-wildcard searches you can specify ^$ to match any letter. To succinctly specify "any letter" in a wildcard search, you might try [A-z]. However, that will also match the characters [, \,], ^, _, and '.

What you're really looking for is [A-Z] and [a-z]. You can specify that using [A-Za-z]. Another interesting thing about ranges is that they're a bit more powerful and embracing than sets. For example, recall that [aeiou] doesn't match any accented vowels. Well, the range [a-z] does match the accented lowercase vowels, but it also matches many more characters.

Beginning of Word: <

The < operator is used to match the beginning of a word. For example, <ton would match *ton, tongue, tone, tonor,* and so on. This can be useful when you're trying to locate words in which *ton* doesn't occur in the interior of a word, such as *Newton, stone,* and *Estonia.*

End of Word: >

The > operator is used in the same way as the < operator, but to find letters or patterns that occur at the end of words. For example, [uU]> would match only words that end in the letter *u*, regardless of case.

A common use for < and > is to use them together to find whole words. This can be especially useful because, as noted previously, when wildcards are used, the Find whole words only option is unavailable. Moreover, < and > let you carefully target which whole word you're looking for. For example, entering ing a <car> in Find what would let you match the trailing portion of *driving a car*, while not matching *Seeing a careless plan*.

Expression: ( )

Recall the ^& search operator, which inserts the matching text into the Replace with box. The () operators enable you to divide the Find what matching text into distinct components so you can rearrange them. The () operators are used in conjunction with the **\n** Replace with operator. Use **\n**, replacing the n with a number, to refer to each component between () operators in the Find what text box; for example, if you enclose three items in () in Find what, you can refer to them as **\1**, **\2**, and **\3** respectively in the Replace with text box. This can be especially useful when you're working with lists that aren't in tables, when you need to swap the order of the components, or when you have to insert a required component.

For example, suppose you work for a firm named "White Williams and Robinson." The partners have reached a new agreement to list their names alphabetically in the company name, making the new name "Robinson White and Williams."

To make this replacement throughout a document, you could set Find what to **(White) (Williams) (and) (Robinson)**. This breaks the name into four expressions, which you can now refer to as \1, \2, \3, and \4, with each numbered code representing its expression's respective order from left to right.

So, to change "White Williams and Robinson" (**\1 \2 \3 \4**) to "Robinson White and Williams," you would then enter **\4 \1 \3 \2** in the Replace with text box, and then use Find Next and Replace to make each replacements.

If you include other wildcards in the expressions and other text and punctuation in the Replace with string, this creates an almost endless array of possibilities when you're using Find and Replace to perform complex editing chores. Keep in mind, however, that it sometimes takes a bit of experimenting to get it just right, and that Replace All might give you results you aren't expecting. Always check your results by using Replace, rather than Replace All, at least until you're positive you'll get the results you want.

9

NOTE

Although the opportunities to be clever with such expressions are tempting, in any given situation you need to weigh the time involved in solving such problems against using simpler methods. In the current instance, if you can't work out a pattern-matching method quickly, it might be faster to simply use the non-wildcard method outlined at the beginning of this section, using visual inspection to decide when to insert the comma. Or simply turn on the grammar checker's "Comma required before last list item" option. On the other hand, sometimes a considered use of wildcards can save you hours of tedious editing. Just make sure you don't spend even more hours trying to work out a clever solution.

Not: [!]

Use the ! operator inside brackets to tell Find not to match a given character or range. For example, the Find what expression [!0-9] [0-9] [0-9] [0-9] [!0-9] can be used to match only three-digit numbers. Without the leading and trailing [!0-9] expressions, you would match three digits wherever they occur, including multiple locations within any number with four or more digits.

Another inventive use might be to look for the use of the letter *q* where it's *not* followed by a *u*. For this, specify the Find what expression as **[Q] [!Uu]**. If you were writing a treatise on the Middle East, this might enable you to quickly focus on transliterated proper names so you could scrutinize their spelling more carefully.

Num Occurrences: { , }

This special search item can be used expression is used to shorten Find what expressions by letting you specify the number of times the character or expression preceding it occurs. Naturally, it would be silly to use e{2} to search for two *es*. Simply use ee. However, if you needed to search for exactly 25 consecutive *es*, then e{25} is more efficient. Practically speaking, you may use this more often to search for repeated numbers or other non-letter characters. You can include the comma and another number after it as needed, resulting in three different ways to use special search code; for example, if you are searching for repeated 0 characters (zeros), you could make the following Find what entries:

0{3} finds exactly three consecutive zeros, as in 000.

0{3,} finds three or more consecutive zeros.

0{3,5} finds instances of between three and five consecutive zeros.

> **NOTE**
>
> This method is not precise. For example, when you search for three occurrences of a single character, it will also match subsets of three of the matching character within longer strings (when there are four or more instances of the character).

0 or More Characters: *

The * wildcard is extremely useful in looking for larger patterns. For example, suppose you want to embolden the word *When* anytime it occurs at the beginning of a paragraph. The expression ^13When*^13 will match and select any paragraph that begins with the word *When*, along with the paragraph mark that precedes it. If you omit the opening ^13, however, then *^13 matches any occurrence of *When* up to the first paragraph mark that follows it, even if *When* isn't at the beginning of a paragraph.

If it matches the preceding paragraph mark, how would you separate out the target paragraph and the extraneous paragraph mark? You would use the grouping and rearranging operators, () and \. For example, if you specify (^13)(When*^13), then \1 is the extraneous paragraph mark, and \2 is the target paragraph that begins with *When*.

We're still left with the question of how to apply bold just to the word *When*. Now is when you have to get creative and combine the different techniques. Remember that ^c places the Clipboard contents into the Replace with box. First, copy a bold occurrence of *When* to the Clipboard. Next, rephrase the Find what expression so that you isolate the word *When* as a grouping expression. Do this with **(^13(When)(*^13)**. Finally, specify Replace with as **\1^c\3**, as shown in Figure 9.12.

FIGURE 9.12

Creative use of wildcard operators can save editing time.

Replace with codes

The preceding section focuses on the Find what codes. Codes that work in the Replace with field with wildcards enabled are shown in Figure 9.13.

FIGURE 9.13

The available Special codes that can be used in the Replace with field change when Use wildcards is enabled.

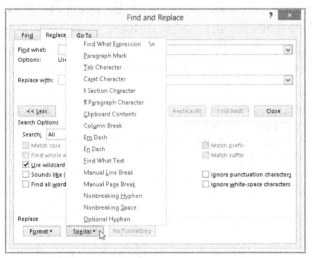

These of these are especially useful in wildcard searches and were already explained earlier in this chapter: \n, Clipboard contents (^c), and Find what text (^&). For a detailed explanation of each of these, see the "Expression: ( )," "Clipboard contents," and "Find what matching text" sections, respectively.

Sounds like (English)

The Sounds like (English) option matches homonyms and phonetically "correct" inventive spellings. It works fairly well, but not perfectly. While surfboard matches *surphbored*, surfbored doesn't.

> **NOTE**
>
> Of course, if you've set up Word to use another language, then the Find and Replace dialog box will indicate that and will be able to work in that language.

Find all word forms (English)

This option is designed to find all forms of words that have the same root as the search text. For example, in theory, react would match *reacted*, *reacts*, *reacting*, *reaction*, and *reactionary*, but it doesn't match the latter two. In general it tends to match verb forms fairly well, but doesn't do very well with nouns, adjectives, and adverbs.

Match prefix and Match suffix

These two options effectively enable you to target words beginning or ending with specific patterns, without having to use more complicated search specifications. With Match prefix enabled, a Find what entry of dis matches all words that begin with *dis*, while at the same time preventing matches when *dis* occurs elsewhere in the word. For example, it would match *disappointing*, *disillusionment*, and *dissection*, but would not match *TARDIS*, *indistinguishable*, or *antidisestablishmentarianism*.

The Match suffix option works for suffixes. For example, in a philosophical work, it might be useful for finding all words ending with *ism*. Just don't mistake *prism* or *isomorphism* for *communism* and *totalitarianism*.

When you're using the Use wildcards option, Sounds like, and Find all word forms (English), both Match prefix and Match suffix are disabled. You can use Match prefix and Match suffix at the same time. You will quickly discover, however, that you will never match anything at all—not even *ionization*. This is called a bug.

Ignore punctuation characters

This option tells Word to ignore punctuation characters that intervene in a word's spelling. For example, suppose a document uses things like *char(act)er* or *dis"appoint"ment* to make a point or stress something about a word. Ordinary searching for **character** or **disappointment** would find neither. By enabling Ignore punctuation characters, you tell Word to find *dis"appoint"ment*. However, it can't find *char(act)er*. That's because "(" and ")" aren't considered punctuation characters for this purpose.

Punctuation characters that are ignored include the following: commas, semicolons, periods, question marks, exclamation marks, forward slashes (/), quotes (single and double, smart and dumb), and the hyphen (simple –, but not the em dash or en dash).

Ignore white-space characters

Use this option to find words that might be broken up by spaces, optional hyphens, or tabs. For example, with this option enabled, a search for `direction` would match *direct[space] ion* and *direc[tab]tion*. This can be useful in searches for specific words in imported or converted text that might not be perfectly formed, or that might have irregular spacing because of the way it was presented in another word processor or on the Web. This option does not ignore nonbreaking spaces, nonbreaking hyphens, em spaces, or en spaces, however.

Ignore white-space characters and Ignore punctuation characters can be combined for even more useful searching. When you're looking for a word or a name in a long article, for example, you might paste the article into Word just so you can use this feature to bypass "garbage" that sometimes prevents an ordinary search from finding something you know is there.

Finding and Replacing Formatting

One of Word's greatest strengths is its ability to both search for formatting in the Find what box and apply formatting using the Replace with box. To use formatting in find/replace operations, click the More button to expose the full dialog box, click in either Find what or Replace with, and then click the Format button in the bottom-left corner, shown in Figure 9.14.

FIGURE 9.14

Use the Format button in the Find and Replace dialog box to specify formatting to search for or apply.

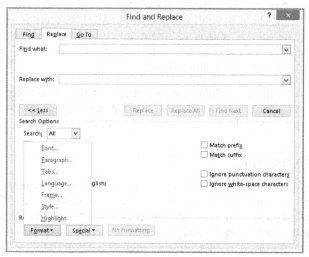

For example, to search for text that has been highlighted, click in the Find what box and type the text you're looking for. Choose Format ➪ Highlight. As shown in Figure 9.15, the formatting to be included in the search appears under the Find what box.

FIGURE 9.15

When formatting is included in a search, the Format indicator appears under Find what and/or Replace with.

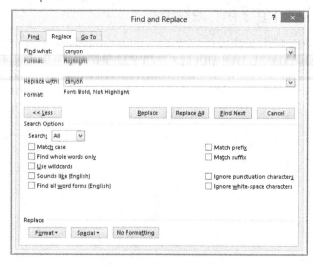

TIP

If you want to find and replace just formatting (that is, particular formatting settings applied to any text in the document), click in the Find what or Replace with text box, do not type anything, and select the formatting settings you want from the Format menu.

Suppose you also want to remove highlighting. Click in the Replace with field, type the text, and choose Format ⇨ Highlight twice. The first time displays Highlight in the Replace with box's Format area; the second time adds the word "Not."

At the same time, you can not only remove the highlighting, but also make all the matching text that was highlighted bold. To do that, choose Format ⇨ Font, and use the Font dialog box to select Bold from the Font style list, then click OK; or you could instead press Ctrl+B. You can add some attributes to the Find what and Replace with boxes using keyboard shortcuts instead of having to use the Format option. This can save time, as well as screen real estate, because you don't need to click More for such attributes.

Unfortunately, highlighting's normal shortcut (Alt+Ctrl+H) does not work in the Find and Replace dialog box. Several keyboard shortcuts do work in the Find and Replace dialog box, however. They are shown in Table 9.3.

NOTE

Two handy shortcuts are Ctrl+Spacebar and Ctrl+Q. These clear character and paragraph formatting, respectively, from the Find what and Replace with text boxes. Because Alt+T is redundantly assigned in the Find and Replace dialog box, you can't count on being able to press Alt+T to remove the formatting from the boxes. Quickly pressing Ctrl+Space and Ctrl+Q might be faster than trying to figure out later not only why formatting is still on, but how "Match suffix" was enabled too.

TABLE 9.3   Formatting Keyboard Shortcuts That Work in Find and Replace

Action/Command	Shortcut key
Clear all character formatting	Ctrl+Spacebar
Subscript	Ctrl+=
Superscript	Ctrl+Shift+=
Single space	Ctrl+1
One and a half space	Ctrl+5
Double space	Ctrl+2
Bold	Ctl+B
Double underline	Ctrl+Shift+D

Continues

TABLE 9.3 (continued)

Action/Command	Shortcut key
Centered	Ctrl+E
Hidden text	Ctrl+Shift+H
Italic	Ctrl+I
Justified	Ctrl+J
Small caps	Ctrl+Shift+K
Left aligned	Ctrl+L
Clear paragraph formatting	Ctrl+Q
Right aligned	Ctrl+R
Underline	Ctrl+U
Word underline	Ctrl+W

Jumping to a Document Location with Go To (Ctrl+G)

The third tab in the Find and Replace dialog box houses the Go To functions. Go To enables you to easily find locations or objects in the document that you can't find with the Navigation pane or Find and Replace. The shortcut key for Go To is Ctrl+G or F5. Like the Find and Replace dialog box's other states, the Go To tab is also non-modal, meaning you can edit your document without dismissing the dialog box.

Shown in Figure 9.16, the Go to what list is home to a variety of different document elements to which you can go. As you scroll through them, notice that some have additional options that are specific to certain kinds of go-to-able parts of a Word document.

FIGURE 9.16

Most of the Go to what choices enable you to move relative to the current location. Entering 15 here would cause you to jump ahead five pages.

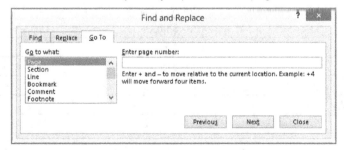

The Go to what list can be set to any of several possible items. Not all of these features are uniquely addressable in this dialog box. You will see some of the alternatives in the following sections so you can get an idea of whether the Go To tab is the best form of transportation for your particular journey.

Another thing to be aware of is that what you see isn't always what you get. Some of the Go Tos offer additional options beyond what the "Enter + and –" instructions tell you.

Page

Go To Page lets you jump to any page in the current document. As with many of the Go To items, you can specify page numbers absolutely or relatively. For example, +25 would cause you to jump ahead 25 pages, while 25 would cause you to jump to page 25.

Note, however, that you can have different numbering systems in control in different sections within the same document. Suppose that your document has front matter in Section 1 numbered as i through v, a body in Section 2 numbered as 1 through 12, and back matter in Section 3 numbered as a through c. Page 2 might refer to ii, 2, or b. Go To 2 will take you to page 2 of Section 2 if you specify nothing else, just as using ii or b in the Enter page number field will take you to Section 1 or 3, respectively.

In addition to specifying pages in the way shown, you can specify the section number as shown in Figure 9.17. For example, p2s1 would take you to page 2 of Section 1 (as would s1p2). Entering the word top takes you to the top of the current page, whereas bottom takes you, well, nowhere at all. For some reason Word knows about top, but it doesn't know about bottom (or end either, for that matter).

FIGURE 9.17

You can include a section number along with the page number you specify.

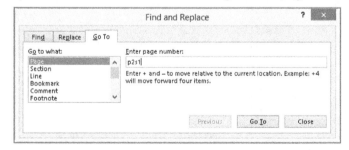

Section

While the Enter page number text box shown in Figure 9.17 is rather liberal in what it can accept, the Section counterpart isn't. Stick with actual and relative section numbers.

Line

Line numbers can be a bit confusing. Most of us don't even think in terms of line numbers, so the fact that something occurs on line 211 in the document isn't even interesting, let alone relevant. However, folks working with legal documents and some others do in fact need to know the answer to "What's the line number?"

Go To Line, however, uses the entire document as its source of line numbers, so if you tell it line 1, then it takes you to the beginning of the document. It doesn't help to tell it p1911 or 11p19. It throws away everything except for the last number (and any + or − that might be there with it), and takes you to that line number. Hence, p1911 takes you to line 1, while 11p19 takes you to line 19. Note that the status bar won't tell you the absolute line number in the document. It will tell you only the line number on the current page.

If your document skips lines by using double spacing or Before/After paragraph Spacing, that is not factored in. Word does count extra lines you create by pressing enter or Shift+Enter, page breaks, and section breaks, though.

Bookmark

If you select Bookmark from the Go to what list of the Go To tab of the Find and Replace dialog box, you can select a bookmark from the Enter bookmark name list, and then click Go To to jump to it. Bookmarks are one of the items for which there is another transportation medium: the Bookmark dialog box, shown in Figure 9.18. Unlike the Go To tab's dialog box, the Bookmark dialog box is not non-modal. You cannot type or edit in the document window while the Bookmark dialog box is onscreen.

FIGURE 9.18

The Bookmark dialog box offers additional options for locating, sorting, and displaying bookmarks.

On the other hand, the Bookmark dialog box does let you choose how to sort the bookmarks, as well as whether to display hidden bookmarks (more about those later). The Bookmark dialog box shows you the top dozen bookmarks, perhaps saving you from scrolling, but certainly saving you from clicking a drop-down arrow. You can also add and delete bookmarks from this dialog. Chapter 19, "Enhancing Navigation with Bookmarks, Hyperlinks, and Cross References," goes into more detail about creating and working with bookmarks.

Comment

Go To Comment is another item for which Go To is not the only or best means of navigation. In the Review tab of the Ribbon, you have the option of navigating either via the Reviewing pane or by using the Next and Previous buttons in the Comments group of the Review tab. You also can open the Navigation pane, click the down arrow button at the right end of the Search document text box at the top, point to comments, and click All Reviewers. Those provide more informed navigation as well. Chapter 26, "Managing Document Security, Comments, and Tracked Changes," provides more information about working with comments.

Footnote and Endnote

Like comments, footnotes and endnotes also have alternative and better-informed means of navigation. Moreover, if the document is onscreen, you can click on a footnote or endnote reference mark to jump to it, or hover over the mark to read the note as a ScreenTip. The Go To approach can be useful, however, if someone sends you a note asking what you meant in Footnote 1546, because Go To gets you there very quickly. On the other hand, if your document contains over 1,500 footnotes, you have bigger troubles than Go To can solve.

Field

The Go To Field feature is actually pretty neat. Unlike with some of the other Go To features discussed so far, fields do not have other good means of navigation. What makes Go To Field special, as shown in Figure 9.19, however, is that you can filter by field type. For example, if you wanted to examine SEQ fields, REF fields, or whatever, you could limit your focus to just those.

FIGURE 9.19

Using Go To and specifying a field enables you to systematically examine fields of any particular type.

Table, Graphic, and Equation

As with fields, there are no other built-in navigation systems for tables, graphics, and equations, except for the Browse Object buttons (and only for tables and graphics). Because it's non-modal, Go To can be very useful in examining tables, graphics, and equations in reports, letting you quickly survey them for formatting and structural consistency, as well as completeness.

Object

The drop-down list that appears when you select Object in the Go to what list in the Go To tab of the Find and Replace dialog box offers a similar kind of functionality as that offered for fields (see Figure 9.20). It enables you to navigate by object type. For example, if you need to see each embedded Excel worksheet, click that choice and then use the Previous and Next buttons to move between worksheets.

FIGURE 9.20

When Go to what is set to Object, you can choose the kind of object to focus on.

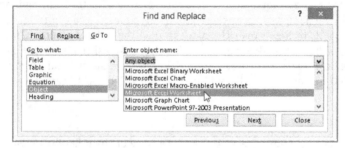

Heading

Like several other Go to what choices, the Heading choice offers less navigational flexibility and functionality than options offered by other Word features, such as Outline view and the Navigation pane.

Summary

In this chapter you've seen the ins and outs of finding, replacing, and going to specific kinds of items contained in Word documents. You've learned how to search using special options and operators, as well as how to use wildcards to customize your own searches. You should now be able to do the following:

- Search for text using the Navigation pane
- Find other types of objects with the Navigation pane
- Set Navigation pane search options
- Start an "advanced" find using the Find and Replace dialog box
- Replace text using the Replace tab in the Find and Replace dialog box
- Find and replace formatting in text
- Use keyboard shortcuts to apply selected kinds of formatting in the Find and Replace dialog box, as well as quickly clear formatting for the next search
- Decide when to use Go To versus other more focused navigational tools for reviewing comments, tables, and other kinds of document elements

9

Part III

Improving Document Content and Consistency

So far, you've read a lot in this book about working with the appearance of text. Part III of *Microsoft Word 2013 Bible* moves the focus to the quality of the document content. Word includes a number of features to help you improve the quality of your writing, eliminate mistakes as you go, and quickly add or preserve specific types of document content.

Chapter 10 begins with Word's different language tools—spell checking, grammar checking, and the thesaurus. Chapter 11 shows you how to use and control AutoCorrect, a feature that can save you work by automatically fixing your mistakes as well as letting you use shorthand for difficult words and phrases; the chapter also covers AutoFormat, which can perform such neat tricks as creating lists for you automatically. Chapter 12 introduces Building Blocks and Quick Parts, and shows you their relationship to AutoText, as well as actions and other time-savers.

Reviewing a Document with Language Tools

IN THIS CHAPTER

Specifying the language used by language features

Checking spelling and grammar

Getting a dictionary and defining words

Finding synonyms with the Thesaurus

Researching a topic with the Research pane

Translating and counting words

Word provides a variety of proofing tools, including a spelling and grammar checker, and a the-saurus. If you add a dictionary for definitions, you also can get definitions for words within documents. When you need to find facts to beef up a document, you can use Word's built-in research tools. You can even translate a selection of text to another language or count words in this document. Forge ahead to examine each of these tools on the Review tab now.

Choosing a Language

When you install Word or Office, it installs with one language selected as its default. This serves the needs of many users, but others have more specialized needs. You might correspond with relatives in a second language, write or translate documents for use in another country, or prepare informa-tion for an overseas customer. In such cases, you can install another editing language for use with Word's language features such as spelling and grammar checking. When you have multiple languages installed, you can then specify which one Word uses by default, switching between languages as needed.

Install another editing language in Word Options:

1. **Click the File tab, and then click Options.**
2. **Click the Language tab at the left side of the Word Options dialog box.**

TIP

As an alternative to Steps 1 and 2 above, you can click the Review tab, click Language in the Language group, and click Language Preferences.

3. **Open the [Add additional editing languages] drop-down list under Choose Editing Languages, scroll down if needed, and click a language to add.**

4. **Click the Add button.** As shown in Figure 10.1, the new language appears in the list of editing languages. If desired, at this point you can click a language in the list and click Set as Default to make it the default language used for editing. Or you can set the default later, as described after these steps.

5. **Click OK, and then click OK again at the message that tells you to restart Office.**

6. **Exit and restart Word.**

FIGURE 10.1

Add alternate editing languages in Word Options.

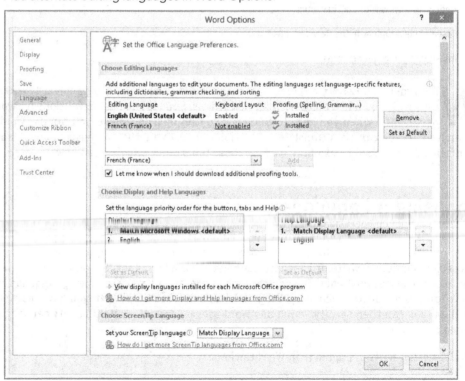

Once the alternate language has been added, you can determine which language to use as the default, if you didn't do so in the Word Options dialog box. You can instead click the Review tab, click the Language button in the Language group, and click Set Proofing Language. The Language dialog box shown in Figure 10.2 appears. Click the language to use in the Mark selected text as list, click the Set As Default button, and click OK. If you see a prompt about how the change will affect new documents based on the NORMAL template, click Yes.

FIGURE 10.2

You can choose the default editing language at any time in the Language dialog box.

TIP

When more than one language is installed, you also can click the Language displayed on the status bar to open the Language dialog box.

You also may encounter times when two different languages might be used in a document. For example, a product manual might include setup or installation instructions in several different languages. In such a case, you can select text and use the Language dialog box to specify what language to use when checking the selection. Just open the dialog box and click the desired language in the Mark selected text list—be sure to choose one of the installed languages above the heavy border. Then click OK. When you make this change, you may see wavy underlines for spelling and grammar errors appear or disappear, after Word automatically checks for errors using the new language. See Figure 10.3.

TIP

You also can install a language pack to change the Word interface, such as Ribbon commands, to a foreign language. See the language pack FAQ in Word help to learn more.

10

FIGURE 10.3

Word checks spelling based on the specified language for checking a selection.

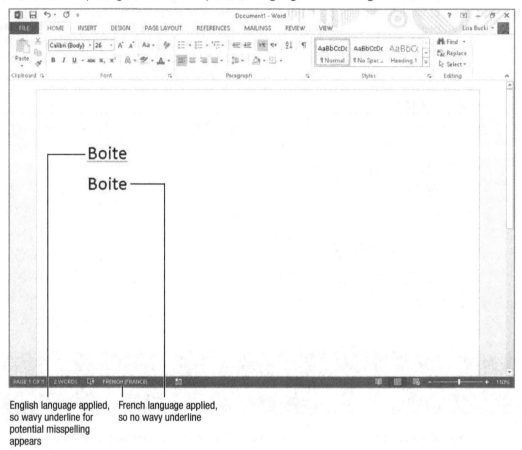

English language applied, so wavy underline for potential misspelling appears

French language applied, so no wavy underline

Checking Spelling and Grammar

Word can check the spelling and grammar of a word, a selection, or a whole document. By default, Word checks both spelling and grammar. For the spelling part of the check, Word can include not only the main built-in dictionary, but also custom word lists you create. It can also use third-party lists such as medical, legal, and technical dictionaries. The grammar check compares phrases and sentences against specified options or rules, and you can choose whether you agree with its suggestions. It's flexible enough that you can turn off specific rules to streamline checks.

Correcting flagged items

By default, Word displays wavy underlines under misspellings and grammar errors when it automatically checks grammar and spelling. It marks potential spelling errors with a wavy red underline and potential grammar errors with a wavy blue underline. One option for cleaning up a document is to right-click a wavy underline, and then click a correction in the shortcut menu that appears, as shown in Figure 10.4. You also can click Ignore, if for example the flagged item is a proper name and needs no correction. This method works well for shorter documents, where you might have fewer corrections or only a couple of pages of text to work through. However, for a lengthier document you can usually save time by running a full-fledged spelling and grammar check, as described next.

FIGURE 10.4

Right-click any wavy underline to see a shortcut menu with potential corrections.

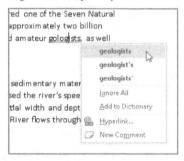

Starting the spelling and grammar check and handling corrections

When you want to check the spelling and grammar in a longer document or simply want to make sure that you don't overlook any wavy underlines, you can start a full spelling and grammar check. Here's how the process works:

1. **Press Ctrl+Home to move the insertion point to the beginning of the document.** Starting from the beginning helps ensure the check catches all errors.

2. **Press F7 or in the Review tab of the Ribbon, click Spelling & Grammar in the Proofing group (shown in Figure 10.5).** At this point, if the document doesn't contain any errors, the Spelling and grammar check completed dialog box appears and you can jump to Step 4. Otherwise, the Spelling pane (Figure 10.6) opens at the right side of Word. (Note that the name of the pane changes to Grammar when it stops on a grammar error.)

TIP

If the book icon on the status bar has an x in it, that means that proofing errors were found. You can also click this icon to open the Spelling pane. If the icon doesn't appear on the status bar, right-click the status bar, click to check Spelling and Grammar Check, and then press Esc.

10

FIGURE 10 5

Click Spelling & Grammar at the left end of the Review tab of the Ribbon to display the Spelling pane.

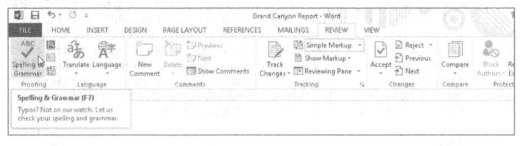

FIGURE 10.6

The Spelling pane flags any spelling or grammar errors and gives correction options.

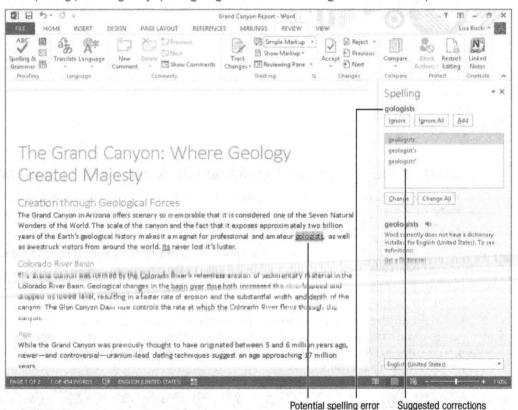

Potential spelling error   Suggested corrections

3a. **If needed, click a suggested correction in the list of corrections, and then use one of the command buttons in the pane to specify how to handle the correction.** Table 10.1 details the selections.

TABLE 10.1 **Spelling Pane Choices**

Ignore	Skips to the next questionable spelling or grammar error. Select this option if the word is acceptable to you in this context but you still want to see future occurrences.
Ignore All	Ignores this spelling for the rest of this spell check. Select this option if the spelling used is correct in all contexts in this document.
Add	Adds the spelling highlighted in red in the Not in Dictionary box to the default user spelling dictionary
Change	Changes the spelling of the flagged word or grammar error to the suggested correction or rule selected in the list of suggestions. Use this option if the suggestion is correct this time but might not be correct for future instances.
Change All	Changes the spelling of the flagged word to the selected suggestion throughout the current document. Use this option if you've reluctantly decided that Word is right, and you want to be spared any additional humiliation and embarrassment.
Dictionary Language	If the selected language is incorrect for the flagged word, use the drop-down arrow to select the correct proofing set.

NOTE

If you make a mistake and click the wrong option (or instantly regret a choice), click in the document and press Ctrl+Z to undo it. In the case of the Ignore, Ignore All, Change, and Change All options, Ctrl+Z gets you back to where you were just prior to that last button click. If you mistakenly add the item to the dictionary, however, then you will need to correct the personal spelling dictionary in order to completely revert.

3b. **If none of the suggestions is correct, click to place the focus in the document and drag over the item to correct in the document, type the correction, and then click Resume in the Spelling pane.**

4. **Repeat the processes outlined in Step 3, until you see the dialog box shown in Figure 10.7.**

5. **Click OK.**

10

FIGURE 10.7

Click OK when the Spelling and grammar check complete dialog box appears.

Setting spelling and grammar options

Word provides a variety of options to control proofing/spelling behavior not only in Word, but in other Office 2013 programs as well. Choose File ➪ Options ➪ Proofing tab to display the full set of options. Here we'll look only at the options in the When correcting spelling in Microsoft Office Programs, When correcting spelling and grammar in Word, and Exceptions for sections of the Word Options dialog box's Proofing tab, shown in Figure 10.8.

Correcting spelling in Office programs

Many of the settings are self-explanatory, but sometimes a reminder of how they work helps ensure that you select the correct ones. The first group of spelling options, When correcting spelling in Microsoft Office programs, has settings that apply throughout Office. Of special use and interest to technical writers are the first three options: Ignore words in UPPERCASE (which handles many acronyms), Ignore words that contain numbers (which handles hexadecimal numbers and many variable names), and Ignore Internet and file addresses. The latter includes not only URLs and UNC computer/disk/folder/file names, but also email addresses.

The fourth option is Flag repeated words—if your name is Dee Dee, you're probably very tired of seeing your name flagged. However, it's very common to double-type words such as *a* and *the*, so it is generally better to leave this option enabled.

The fifth option—Enforce accented uppercase in French—does just that. If you type **Eclair**, Word will suggest that you really meant **Éclair**.

FIGURE 10.8

Set detailed spelling and grammar options on the Proofing tab.

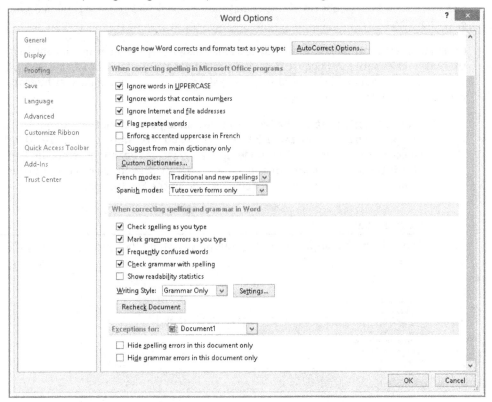

Custom dictionaries

The last check box in the section, Suggest from main dictionary only, might require a bit of explanation if you have only one custom dictionary, and you didn't even know about that one. You can have multiple custom dictionaries. Technical writers often have different "dictionaries" for different purposes and projects. While it might be OK generally to ignore words in uppercase or that contain numbers, it sometimes isn't. Therefore, you might want to create lists of the correct acronyms or variable names, and so forth, so that if you type one that the list doesn't "know" about, it will alert you.

> **NOTE**
>
> "Dictionaries" is in quotes because these really aren't dictionaries. Dictionaries tell you how to pronounce words and what they mean. Word's `.dic` files aren't what we traditionally think of as *dictionaries*; they're word spelling lists that are used for comparison.

10

For users who have multiple dictionaries (word lists), the *main dictionary* refers to the one that comes with Word. That's the one that's used all the time. If you want to restrict language features to use only Word's main dictionary, check the Suggest from main dictionary only check box.

Optionally, Word can populate the Suggestions box with spellings from multiple lists. In this case, make sure the Suggest from main dictionary only check box is cleared. Then, if you have mistakenly added a word to your custom dictionary during a spelling correction, you can remove it:

1. **On the Proofing tab of the Word Options dialog box, click the Custom Dictionaries button to open the Custom Dictionaries dialog box, shown in Figure 10.9.** The top choice in the Dictionary List, under All Languages, is RoamingCustom.dic (Default). This is the default custom dictionary associated with your user account and is where Word places found words when you click Add in the Spelling pane.

FIGURE 10.9

The default RoamingCustom.dic dictionary is where the words you add go by default.

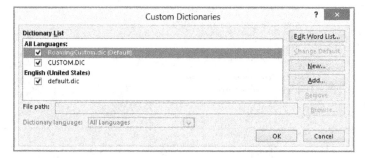

2. **Make sure that RoamingCustom.dic (Default) is selected under All Languages in the Dictionary list, and click Edit Word List.** A dialog box for the dictionary opens, as shown in Figure 10.10.

> **TIP**
>
> To choose a different default dictionary, click the desired dictionary under All Languages in the Dictionary List, and then click Change Default.

3. **In the Dictionary list, click the word you want to delete.**
4. **Click Delete.**

5. **Click OK.**

6. **Click OK to close the Custom Dictionaries dialog box.**

FIGURE 10.10

Add and delete words in the custom dictionary using this dialog box.

CAUTION

Be careful not to click Delete all. That choice deletes all the words from the custom dictionary, and Ctrl+Z won't fix it.

You can add words in the dialog box for the custom dictionary as well. Type the new entry in the Word(s) text box; click Add, and then click OK twice.

Note that you can't remove words from the main dictionary this way. Instead, you would need to create an exception list. See "Exception lists (exclude dictionaries)" later in this chapter, for more on that fascinating topic!

Creating custom dictionaries

Note the New button in Figure 10.9. If you need a specialized word list, click New, type a name for the list in the File name text box of the Create Custom Dictionary dialog box, and then click Save. Back in the Custom Dictionaries list, select the new list you just created, and click Edit Word List. Initially it will be empty. Type each new entry into the Word(s) text box, and click Add. Click OK twice to finish.

Note that Word's .dic files are plain text files. Therefore, you don't need to use Word to open them and edit them. Instead, you can use Notepad or any other plain-text editor. If you already have a word list, rename it, giving it a .dic extension, and tell Word to use it by opening the Custom Dictionaries dialog box from the Proofing tab of Word Options, clicking Add, navigating to the file location in the Add Custom dictionary dialog box, selecting the file, and clicking Open. Then you can click OK twice.

10

> **TIP**
>
> If you have a document that is loaded with unrecognized technical words, you can use it to create a custom `.dic` file. Open the file using Word. Next, in File ⇨ Options ⇨ Proofing, click Custom Dictionaries. Create a new dictionary, if needed, and set it as the default by clicking it under All Languages in the Dictionary list, and then clicking Change Default. Click OK twice.
>
> Back in the document, press F7 to begin a spell check. At each technical word you want to add to the new default dictionary, click Add in the Spelling pane. Otherwise, click Ignore All to proceed to the next word. Then you can use the new dictionary to run a spelling and grammar check on other documents. When you're done, reopen Word Options and reset your default custom dictionary to what it was previously.

Modes

Referring back to Figure 10.8, the last two options under When correcting spelling in Microsoft Office programs are French modes and Spanish modes. Depending on what language packs you have installed, you might also see Portuguese or other modes. From the mode drop-down list for whichever language you want to check, choose the setting appropriate for whatever you're writing.

Correcting spelling and grammar in Word

The next section of options shown in Figure 10.8, When correcting spelling and grammar in Word, includes settings applicable in Word only.

The first two options, Check spelling as you type and Mark grammar errors as you type, govern whether Word marks your documents with red and blue zigzags each time you make a mistake. Turn these options off if you never make mistakes and don't like it when Word second-guesses you. You can also turn it off if you like to check your spelling and grammar in one fell swoop in the Spelling pane after you've written your ideas.

The Frequently confused words setting is a renamed version of the Use contextual spelling setting from Word 2010. When enabled, this option will use the blue underline to flag any instances of words that are frequently confused, such as if you type *He was over their* rather than *He was over there*.

Clearing the check box beside Check grammar with spelling turns off grammar checking. When Show readability statistics is checked, at the end of the spelling and grammar check, Word displays a Readability Statistics dialog box rather than the dialog box informing you that the spelling and grammar check is complete. Click OK to close it after reading the statistics.

Writing Style and Settings

You can use the Writing Style drop-down list to determine whether Word checks Grammar Only or Grammar & Style. Then, click the Settings button beside the drop-down list to open the Grammar Settings dialog box shown in Figure 10.11.

The dialog box offers many settings that you can use to fine-tune what grammar errors Word checks for. These settings appear in the Grammar and style options list, and are grouped by Require, Grammar, and Style. (The Style settings only apply when you've selected Grammar & Style from the Writing Style drop-down list.) For example, by default, Fragments and Run-ons under Grammar is not checked. If you have a tendency to type incomplete sentences, checking this option could help you catch and correct such mistakes more frequently.

FIGURE 10.11

The Grammar Settings dialog box has many Grammar and Style settings.

The Style settings enable the grammar check to flag such formalities as Contractions or Passive sentences. You can experiment with the settings in the dialog box, or search for the topic Select grammar and writing style options in the Word Help window to read a description of each option. The Grammar Settings dialog box also includes a Reset All button at the bottom left that you can use to clear any changes you've made to the settings. Click the OK button when you finish to return to the Proofing settings in Word Options, and then click OK again to finish changing options.

Recheck Document

Recheck Document is active only after you've finished checking spelling in a document. Clicking this button resets all Ignore decisions for spelling and grammar. If you previously clicked Ignore or Ignore All, those decisions are all reset as if they hadn't occurred. Choose Recheck Document when you inadvertently tell Word to ignore or otherwise bypass something it questioned. The dialog box shown in Figure 10.12 appears.

10

FIGURE 10.12

Choose File ➪ Options ➪ Proofing ➪ Recheck Document to undo any decisions to ignore word misspellings and grammar rules.

Exceptions for current document

Sometimes, for whatever reason, you might choose to hide all the spelling and/or grammar errors in a particular document, while continuing to monitor spelling and grammar in other open documents. Or you might generally have errors hidden, but choose to display them at other times. The Exceptions for settings, shown in Figure 10.13, give you independent control over the display of grammar and spelling errors on a document-by-document basis. Scroll down to the bottom of the Proofing tab to see the settings, if needed. You can leave the current document selected from the drop-down list to change settings for it only, or open the drop-down list and choose All New Documents. Then check the Hide spelling errors in this document only and/or Hide grammar errors in this document only.

FIGURE 10.13

If you usually hide spelling and grammar errors, you can selectively choose to display them for individual documents.

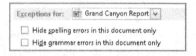

Exception lists (exclude dictionaries)

Earlier I noted that you cannot remove words from the main spelling dictionary that comes with Word. However, you can create an *exception list*, sometimes called an *exclude dictionary*. You place into that list words that Word considers correct, but that you want flagged as possible misspellings. When Word is opened, it checks whether there are entries in the exception list. If there are, then Word will flag those words as if they were misspelled, even if they aren't.

During installation Microsoft creates an empty file named `ExcludeDictionaryEN0409.lex` (for English U.S.) in a folder named `C:\Users\`*user name*`\AppData\Roaming\Microsoft\UProof`.

You can edit this plain-text file in Notepad or any other plain-text editor. You also can \.edit this file using Word, but you need to remember to save it as plain text in order for it to work.

If you have an existing exception list from previous versions of Word, you can either copy existing exceptions into the new file or simply rename your existing `.EXC` list. Once you're finished, save the file to the folder indicated above. The file will be incorporated into Word's spelling function the next time you start Word.

If you installed additional sets of proofing tools with Word 2013, there will be one `.lex` file in the `UProof` folder for each language. For French (France) and Spanish (Spain), the files are as follows (with variations for different versions of Spanish):

```
ExcludeDictionaryES0c0a.lex

ExcludeDictionaryFR040c.lex
```

As with the English exception lists, you can edit either of the above files to add entries. Then close and restart Word for the changes to take effect.

Finding Definitions

A document's purpose defines the writing style you should use. If you're writing a quick note to a friend, your language can be loose, and word choice may not be all that important. If you're writing a moody work of fiction or a scientific paper, on the other hand, you need to choose words that are adequately vivid or precise. The Define tool available on the Review tab can assist you with word choice. If you're not sure whether the word you've typed conveys your intended meaning, you can select the word and then use Define to find out.

Obtaining a definitions dictionary from the Office Store

By default, Word does not include an installed dictionary for the Define tool. It prompts you to download one:

1. **Double-click a word you might want to define to select it.**
2. **Click Define in the Proofing group of the Review tab, or press Ctrl+F7.** The Dictionaries pane opens at the right, as shown in Figure 10.14.
3. **Click the Download button below the dictionary you want to download.**

10

FIGURE 10.11

Add a free dictionary for the Define tool.

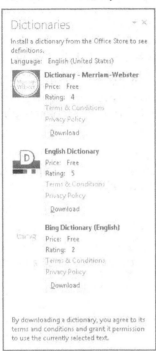

The dictionary ratings are based on actual customer reviews. You can get more information about a particular definitions dictionary by using another method to download a dictionary. This also happens to be the method you can use when you've already installed one dictionary and want to install another:

1. **Click the Insert tab, and in the Apps group, click the down arrow on the Apps for Office button.**

2. **Click See All in the menu that appears.** The Apps for Office window shown in Figure 10.15 appears.

3. **Click the Find more apps at the Office Store link at the bottom of the window.** Your web browser launches and displays available Apps for Word 2013.

4. **Scroll down to until you see another dictionary to add, as shown in the example in Figure 10.16.**

FIGURE 10.15

Use the Apps for Office window to add a dictionary for definitions.

FIGURE 10.16

Add another dictionary, such as the one from Merriam-Webster.

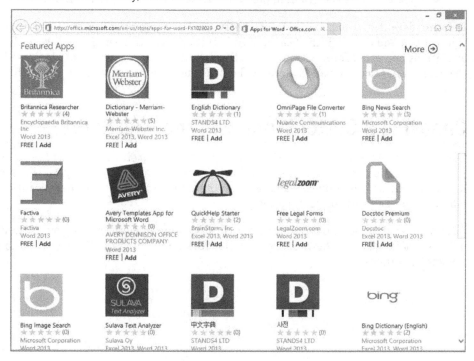

5. **Click Add.** A description page for the app appears. At this point, if you wanted more information about the app rating reviews, you could click the number in parentheses, if any, to the right of the Average Rating stars.

6. **Click Add again.**

7. **Click Continue to confirm the download.** The dictionary downloads from the Office Store and installs, becoming the new primary dictionary. (You may see a prompt to insert the dictionary using the Apps for Office button. That may or may not be necessary, depending on the nature of the app.)

> **NOTE**
>
> To turn off the use of any of your Apps for Office, such as an installed definitions dictionary, click Manage My Apps in the Apps for Office window. In the My Apps for Office and SharePoint web page that opens in your browser, click Hide beside the dictionary or app that you want to stop using.

Defining a term

Once you have a dictionary installed, you can select a word and use one of two methods to define it:

- Right-click, and click Define in the shortcut menu.
- Click Define in the Proofing group of the Review tab, or press Ctrl+F7.

The word definition appears in the Dictionary pane at right, as shown in the example in Figure 10.17. You can click the See more link, if it appears, to open a web page with further definitions and other information. To see the definition for another word, double-click it in the document. Click the pane's Close (X) button when you finish working with definitions.

Choosing a Better Word with the Thesaurus

Word's proofing tools also include the thesaurus, which is useful for finding the right word to use in a particular sentence. Use the thesaurus to find and use synonyms, which can help your writing sound livelier and less repetitive (unless you intentionally want to use repetition for emphasis or poetic effect).

One way to engage the thesaurus is to right-click the word in question and point to Synonyms in the shortcut menu, as shown in Figure 10.18. Click any word in the Synonyms list to replace the word you right-clicked.

FIGURE 10.17

The Dictionary pane shows the definition for the selected word.

FIGURE 10.18

Use the shortcut menu Synonyms list to find a better or different word.

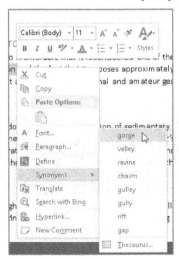

10

If you want to browse more word choices for a selected word, click Thesaurus at the bottom of the shortcut menu, click Thesaurus in the Proofing group of the Review tab, or press Shift+F7. The Thesaurus pane shown in Figure 10.19 appears at the right. You can click any synonym it lists to see synonyms for that word instead. The Thesaurus pane also sometime lists antonyms. When you see the replacement word you want, move your mouse pointer over it, click the drop-down arrow that appears to the right of it, and click Insert. Click the pane's Close (X) button when you finish using it.

FIGURE 10.19

Use the Thesaurus pane to find a better or different word.

NOTE

Word's legacy Thesaurus dialog box is still available. To access it, you'll need to assign the Thesaurus Dialog command from the Commands Not in the Ribbon choices for customizing the QAT in Word Options, as described previously in the "Starting the spelling and grammar check and handling corrections" section.

Using the Research Pane

Word's Research feature can look up a wide variety of concepts using a variety of different research resources. You can look up something that's in your document, or you can open the Research task pane and use it as you would a small information browser.

Using the Research Task Pane

To look up something that's in your document, select it and Alt+click on it. The selection can be a word, phrase, or name. You might use it, for example, if you come across an unfamiliar name and want to see if it's someone you should know about. It's also useful for looking up unfamiliar places. Figure 10.20 shows the Research pane that appears at the right after you Alt+click. The term(s) you selected and Alt+clicked appears in the first text box under Search for. To search for something else, type it in the top text box under Search for, and click the Start searching right arrow button to the right of the text box. After you perform a second search, the Back and Forward buttons in the Research pane become active, so you can browse between the topics you've looked up.

FIGURE 10.20

The Research task pane puts numerous free and paid research services at your beck and call.

To change the Research resource, click the drop-down arrow for the second text box below Search for, and in the list that appears click the Research resource that is likely to provide the kind of information you want to find. Then edit the Search for word or phrase and click the Start searching button. If you scroll to the bottom of the search results shown in the Research pane, you'll see that All Reference Books and All Research Sites are additional options for showing more results, but a specific resource often provides better targeted results. Note also that some of the Research Sites sources—such as Factiva iWorks™ and HighBeam™ Research—are paid services, while Bing is free.

As with other panes in Word, click the Research pane Close (X) button to close it when you finish performing your research.

Choosing Research options

To set your overall research strategy, click Research options at the bottom of the Research pane. This opens the Research Options dialog box, shown in Figure 10.21.

FIGURE 10.21

Use Research Options to add and remove services, as well as to exercise Parental Control over what research services can be accessed.

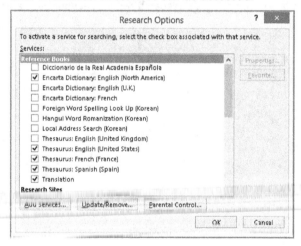

Use Add Services to add a new research service. You can specify the URL of any you know about. Additionally, over time, the list of advertised services will be populated by research providers—*maybe*. At this writing, however, the Add Services list says only "No advertised services are currently available." Use Update/Remove to get the latest updates from specific servers or groups of servers, as well as to remove certain services. Note that a number of the built-in services cannot be removed, such as Translation (Installed Dictionaries).

The Parental Control option is described next. After making your choices in the Research Options dialog box, of course click OK to close the dialog box and return to using the Research pane.

Setting Parental Controls

Clicking Parental Control in the Research Options dialog box shown in Figure 10.21 enables you to limit the Research pane to just those services that (claim to) block "offensive content." Note that you must start Word using the Run as administrator option in order to be able to use the Parental Control settings. To do this, open a folder window from the desktop and navigate to the folder holding the Word startup command (usually `C:\Program Files (x86)\Microsoft Office\Office15\` for the 32-bit version or `C:\Program Files\Microsoft Office\Office15\`), right-click the `WINWORD.exe` startup command, and click Run as administrator.

As shown in Figure 10.22, there are two levels of Parental Control. The first, Turn on content filtering to make services block offensive results, is supposed to instruct all services to block offensive results (whether they claim to be able to or not). You must check this option to enable it in order for the next option to become active. The second, Allow users to search only the services that can block offensive results, limits services to those that claim to be able to block offensive results. Using Parental Control requires that you set a password, so type the desired password in the Specify a password for the Parental Control settings text box before clicking OK to return to the Research Options dialog box.

FIGURE 10.22

If you forget or lose your password, it cannot be recovered, and you'll be stuck with Parental Control!

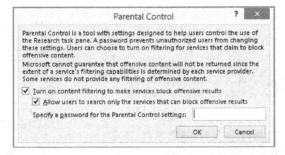

CAUTION

If you use this feature, set a simple password that you can remember but that your children are unlikely to be able to guess. If you lose or forget the password, there is no guarantee that it can be recovered, unless your kids are prescient.

10

If both levels are set, noncompliant services will be grayed out in the list of resources.

Translating Text

Do you have a complete report, letter, or other document you need to have translated? Word can translate all or part of it.

Select text in the document, and then click Translate in the Language group of the Review tab. Click Translate Selected Text. In the Research pane that appears, change the From and To languages, and then click the Start searching button above, beside the Search for text box. Figure 10.23 shows selected text in a report document translated from English to French. In addition to Spanish or French, you can translate to a number of other languages, including Russian, Hebrew, Polish, Swedish, German, Italian, Japanese, Korean, Chinese (PRC and Taiwan), Dutch, Greek, and Portuguese.

FIGURE 10.23

Word can translate whole sentences and paragraphs in the Research pane.

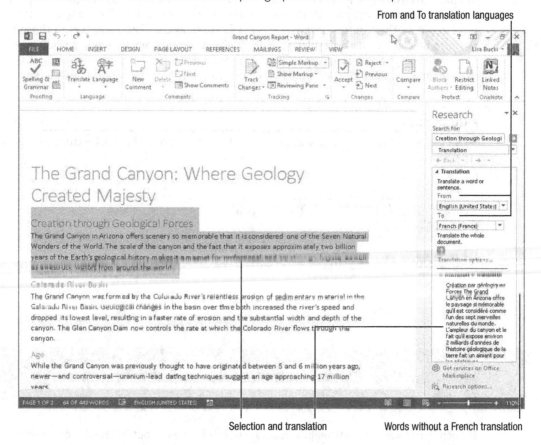

From and To translation languages

Selection and translation

Words without a French translation

> **TIP**
>
> You also can right-click a text selection and click Translate to translate text.

Word uses the Microsoft Translator service to perform its translation. As with any language translation, it can't translate proper names (such as The Grand Canyon, as shown in Figure 10.23), certain words, or idiomatic phrases (phrases that are unique to the original language). To insert the translation into the document, scroll down in the Research pane, if needed, and to display the Insert button that appears below the translated text, and then click it to insert the translation. Alternately, you can click the Insert button's down arrow, and then click Copy, so that you can paste the translation to another location in the current document or another document.

If you want the full document translated, just click the button under Translate the whole document in the Research pane. In the Translate Whole Document confirmation dialog box, click Send. Or, if the Research pane isn't already open and you want to translate the whole document, click Translate in the Language group of the Review tab, and then click Translate Document. In the Translation Language Options dialog box, choose Translate from and Translate to languages, and then click OK. Then at the Translate the Whole Document confirmation dialog box, click Send. Word sends the current document to the Microsoft Translator service, and the translation quickly (depending on your connection speed) appears in your default web browser, as shown in Figure 10.24.

FIGURE 10.24

To translate an entire document, Word uses the web-based Microsoft Translator service.

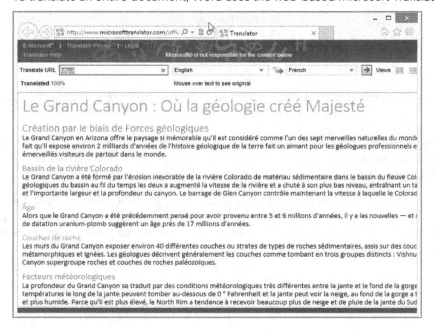

10

A quick machine translation likely may not be as perfect or as good as a competent professional translation service. However, it's certainly a leap beyond other available free tools.

Translating on the fly

To translate, select the text you want translated, right-click the selection and choose Translate. Word begins a search using the default language pair (usually from English to French). To change languages, use the drop-down arrows to change the From and To languages in the Research pane that appears, and then click the Start searching button beside the top text box under Search for. You can also type the text to be translated directly into the Search for: box.

For simple words and phrases translated among French, English, and Spanish, Word uses its own built-in Bilingual Dictionaries. For other Western languages that use the standard Latin character set, Word uses its Online Bilingual Dictionaries.

Using the Mini Translator

Word can also translate using ScreenTips, as shown in Figure 10.25.

FIGURE 10.25

When the Mini Translator is enabled, Word translates the selected word using a ScreenTip.

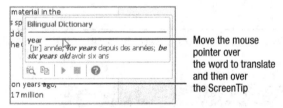

Move the mouse pointer over the word to translate and then over the ScreenTip

Before enabling the Mini Translator, you have to choose the correct To language. To do so, on the Review tab in the Language group, click Translate ➪ Choose Translation Language. The Translation Language Options dialog box shown in Figure 10.26 appears. Under Choose Mini Translator language, open the Translate to drop-down list, and click the desired language. (If you're typing in English and set the language to English (United States), the Mini Translator doesn't work. Click OK to apply the language setting.

To toggle the Mini Translator on, in the Language group of the Review tab click Translate ➪ Mini Translator. From there, when you hover the mouse pointer over any word, the semi-transparent Mini Translator ScreenTip appears. Move the mouse pointer over the ScreenTip to make the translation fully visible.

FIGURE 10.26

First set the Translate to language to enable the Mini Translator.

Taking a Word Count

Getting a count of the number of words in a document seems like a relatively simple feature, but it could be crucial in situations such as when you need to meet a minimum word count for a research paper, or when you need to ensure the text is under a maximum word count for an online advertisement or product listing. To count the words and compile other statistics in a document, click the Word Count button in the Proofing group of the Review tab. The Word Count dialog box shown in Figure 10.27 appears. Click Close when you are finished viewing its statistics.

FIGURE 10.27

The Word Count dialog box gives you critical document statistics, such as the number of words and pages.

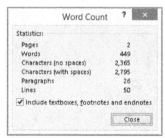

10

301

Summary

Word's language tools provide a number of resources for writers and editors. In this chapter you've seen that Word includes strong tools for checking spelling, grammar, contextual spelling and grammar, and even achieving useful translations. You should now be able to do the following:

- Check spelling and grammar, as well as optimize options for the way you work
- Create customized word lists for technical writing, and exception lists to flag selected "correct" words as wrong
- Use Word's thesaurus to find the perfect word
- Look up important terminology using Word's Research pane
- Translate words, phrases, and even whole documents
- Count words, characters, and more in a document

Cleaning Up with AutoCorrect and AutoFormat

IN THIS CHAPTER

Word's automated correction and formatting features can save you a lot of document cleanup work you'd otherwise have to do, including eliminating typos and formatting certain characters such as quotation marks and fractions. AutoCorrect actually refers to a collection of correction features. Word can correct typos just as quickly as you can type them. If you type **recieve** and press the spacebar or add a period or other punctuation, practically before you can blink, Word changes it into *receive*. Similarly, the AutoFormat feature automatically converts some things that you type into their formatted counterparts, converting lone lines into headings, asterisks into bullets, numbers into formatted numbering, straight quotes into curly "smart quotes," and so on.

This chapter's mission is to show you how to take advantage of the options for AutoCorrect and AutoFormat that you do like, turn off the options you don't care for, and even create your own custom corrections. And as a bonus, you'll learn a little more about working with automatic and manual hyphenation.

Revisiting AutoCorrect

As you first saw in Chapter 3, "Working Smarter, Not Harder, in Word," Word comes with a host of built-in AutoCorrect pairs—common misspellings and their corrected counterparts. By default, Word uses them to correct your mistakes. For example, if you type **abscence**, Word corrects it to *absence*. This is different from spell checking—which highlights a suspected misspelling but does not automatically correct it. This section of the chapter helps you delve more deeply into how you can exploit AutoCorrect's ability to clean up your typos.

> **NOTE**
>
> AutoCorrect and spell checking sometimes converge, in that you frequently have an opportunity to automatically add a flagged misspelling and suggested correction as an AutoCorrect pair. This is discussed later in this chapter.

Capping corrections

Most of us manage to not quite press the Shift key and thus fail to capitalize letters as needed on a regular basis. As shown near the top of Figure 11.1, AutoCorrect fixes several capitalization errors. To display this dialog box, choose File ⇨ Options ⇨ Proofing ⇨ AutoCorrect Options. AutoCorrect makes fixes when you:

- Accidentally type two capital letters at the beginning of a sentence
- Fail to capitalize the first letter of a sentence, table cell, or day name
- Accidentally type with the Caps Lock key on

Controlling the AutoCorrect Options button

The meaning of the Show AutoCorrect Options buttons check box at the top of Figure 11.1 might not be perfectly obvious. After an AutoCorrect occurs, if you hover the mouse pointer over the correction, an AutoCorrect button appears at the left edge of the corrected word. It's a thin blue rectangle. Microsoft's aim was to make it unobtrusive. For some users it's so unobtrusive that they hardly ever even notice it. If you drag the mouse pointer down slightly from the rectangle, a button with a lightning bolt appears, and you may also see a tooltip that says AutoCorrect Options. If you click the AutoCorrect Options button, you see options similar to those shown in Figure 11.2.

When Show AutoCorrect Options buttons is enabled on the AutoCorrect tab of the AutoCorrect dialog box, Word remembers the locations in the current paragraph where AutoCorrect actions occurred. You can display and click the AutoCorrect Options button for any of them to undo a correction, to suppress a rule, or to open the AutoCorrect dialog box to change options (using the Control AutoCorrect Options command in the bottom of the shortcut menu shown in Figure 11.2). If AutoCorrect made multiple corrections at the same time (as shown in Figure 11.2), the top option, Undo Automatic Corrections, enables you to undo all of the corrections in one step.

FIGURE 11.1

AutoCorrect corrects several types of errors, as well as correcting listed typos and inserting symbols.

FIGURE 11.2

The AutoCorrect Options button gives you the opportunity to undo or stop listed corrections.

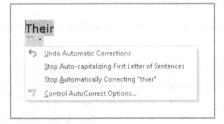

> **TIP**
>
> You also can immediately press Ctrl+Z to undo the most recent automatic correction. However, if you kept typing after the correction occurred you will have to press Ctrl+Z several times, as you will have to undo the subsequent typing before you can undo the AutoCorrect changes. You'll have to decide how much retyping you're willing to do.

Replacing text as you typo

The Replace text as you type check box on the AutoCorrect options tab controls the most powerful and flexible part of AutoCorrect. When enabled, this feature uses hundreds of built-in AutoCorrect pairs, automatically replacing misspelled words with their correct counterparts. Common default AutoCorrect Replace/With pairs include accross/across, realyl/really, questioms/questions, and teh/the. It also can replace short typed entries with corresponding symbols, such as replacing (c) with ©, or (tm) with ™. Scroll through the top of the list under Replace text as you type to see exactly which symbols AutoCorrect can insert by default.

Word's built-in list of AutoCorrect pairs is by no means exhaustive, though, so many misspelling are not automatically corrected—particularly when there are competing possibilities about what the intended word might be. For example, if I type *intented*, Word will flag it as a misspelling. But because I could have meant indented, intended, or invented—to name a few—Word does not automatically correct it.

Many Word power-users capitalize on this feature to create shorthands for longer words and phrases that are tedious to type and retype. If you're a lawyer, you might have encountered such memorable phrases as "party of the first part" and "party of the second part." You could create AutoCorrect entries that automatically replace p1, p2, and p3 with "party of the first part," "party of the second part," and "party of the third part," respectively. Then when you need to insert one of those phrases, simply type the appropriate shorthand and press the Spacebar.

To add a Replace/With pair to AutoCorrect:

1. **Choose File ⇨ Options ⇨ Proofing ⇨ AutoCorrect Options.** The AutoCorrect dialog box opens with the AutoCorrect tab selected.

2. **In the Replace text box, type the incorrect version or shorthand you want to replace.**

> **TIP**
>
> Some users like to include an asterisk or other symbol at the beginning of the Replace entry as a best practice. This helps avoid unwanted AutoCorrect changes.

3. **In the With box, type the replacement text AutoCorrect should insert.** The With text can be up to 255 characters, including spaces. Figure 11.3 shows example Replace/With entries.

4. **Click Add.**

5. **Repeat Steps 2–4 to create additional list entries as desired.**

6. **Click OK twice.**

FIGURE 11.3

Make Replace and With entries to create a new automatic correction.

11

Note that you also can delete Replace/With pairs in the AutoCorrect tab. Just select the entry to delete in the list of pairs and click Delete. You will not see a warning when making a deletion, so tread carefully. You will learn how to back up your AutoCorrect entries shortly.

Creating formatted corrections

When you enter new Replace/With pairs on the AutoCorrect tab of the AutoCorrect dialog box, by default the Plain text option button is selected to the right, above the With text box. With that option, the With replacement text takes on the formatting of the surrounding text after an automatic correction.

Sometimes, however, you might want formatted text. You might even want something other than pure text, such as a table or a picture. Or perhaps you do want plain text, but have a With item that exceeds 255 characters. For these, you need to use the Formatted text option button instead. For example, let's say you're a math teacher, and when preparing handouts and quizzes for students, you like to include a table of common length conversions for students to use with word problems. You could create an AutoCorrect Replace/With entry so that you can insert that table whenever needed, rather than retyping it in multiple documents.

To create a formatted Replace/With AutoCorrect pair (only the With item is formatted):

1. **Create, format, and select the text, table, picture, or other item you want to use as the With item.**

2. **Open the AutoCorrect dialog box (File ⇨ Options ⇨ Proofing ⇨ AutoCorrect Options), and click the AutoCorrect tab if needed.** As shown in Figure 11.4, Word attempts to preview the With item, in this example the first row of a table. If the selected item is a picture or other graphic, the preview will be empty.

FIGURE 11.4

Word tries to preview the selected formatted item.

3. **In the Replace box, type a name for the item. It can be up to 31 characters.**
   Keep in mind that this name will automatically expand into the With item when you type it into a document, so don't make it so complicated that you can't remember it, but don't use existing words or common abbreviations or acronyms that you ordinarily use either. If you want to use a common word or abbreviation, add a number to it.

4. **Click Add.**

5. **Click OK twice.**

AutoCorrect limits

Word 2013 does not have any arbitrary limits on how many AutoCorrect entries you can create. Nor are there arbitrary limits on how large a formatted With entry can be. You are limited only by the amount of available memory and disk space. If Word runs out of either, it will tell you. However, few users run into limits, even when they include entire large documents as AutoCorrect entries.

On the other end of the spectrum, for plain-text entries, as noted earlier, the size of the With item cannot exceed 255 characters. That is the usual limit on text box entries in Windows applications.

For both formatted and plain-text entries, the Replace entry cannot exceed 31 characters. As a practical matter, it's hard to imagine why you'd ever want it to get anywhere near that large. Most AutoCorrect aficionados tend to prefer terse letter-and-number combinations that give some idea about the nature of the item as an aid to memory. Keep in mind that unlike with Building Blocks there is no dialog box or gallery mechanism for inserting AutoCorrect items, so keep your Replace entries short enough to type easily.

Backing up AutoCorrect entries

Your Office 2013 AutoCorrect entries are stored in an .acl (AutoCorrect list) file. You do not have distinct lists for each Office 2013 application, nor for each Word template. Instead, there is a separate list for each language you use with Office. Word doesn't have a mechanism for automatically backing up your .acl files, so you need to make a copy of the file in Windows and place the copy in the location where you store various types of backup files.

Your .acl files are stored in C:\Users*user name*\AppData\Roaming\Microsoft\Office. The English (U.S.) AutoCorrect entries are stored in MSO1033.acl, so back up that file. For another language, replace the number in the file name with the appropriate Windows locale code to identify which file holds the entries for that language. Other common locale codes are 1034 for Spanish (Traditional Sort) and 1036 for French (France). Additional locale codes can be found on several Microsoft operated services, including MSDN:

    http://msdn.microsoft.com/en-us/goglobal/bb964664.aspx

Sharing AutoCorrect entries

Unfortunately, Word does not provide a built-in way to selectively copy AutoCorrect entries from one computer to another. You can, of course, copy your entire .acl list, but the entries in the replaced list will be lost.

A better alternative, if you have access to the macros that came with Word 2003, is to use the AutoCorrect Backup macro. It still works with Word 2013, and the procedure is described here:

```
http://support.microsoft.com/kb/826147
```

Using Math AutoCorrect

Math AutoCorrect works the same way that regular AutoCorrect does, but can be enabled or disabled independently. This feature provides more intuitive access to math symbols than other ways in Word and interfaces directly with Word's equation tools.

To view Math AutoCorrect options and Replace/With entries, choose File ⇨ Options ⇨ Proofing ⇨ AutoCorrect Options, and choose the Math AutoCorrect tab. Shown in Figure 11.5, Math AutoCorrect provides AutoCorrect access to over 200 commonly used math symbols (well, commonly used by some folks). Just go to this tab and scroll down the list to find the symbol you are looking for in the With list. Then you can type the corresponding Replace entry any time you want to insert the applicable symbol.

In the Math AutoCorrect dialog box, enable both Use Math AutoCorrect rules outside of math regions and Replace text as you type, and click OK. A math region is another name for the content control that appears when you choose Insert ⇨ Symbols ⇨ Equation ⇨ Insert New Equation. An area "outside of math regions" therefore means in the body of your document, so enabling the top check box is important.

After enabling the Math AutoCorrect options just mentioned, you can then click in the body of your document, type one of the Replace entries, and press the Spacebar. For example, type \theta to insert the theta symbol.

Alternately, choose Insert ⇨ Symbols ⇨ Symbol ⇨ More Symbols. In the Symbols tab, set Font to Symbol. Theta is in the fourth row, second column from the left. Double-click it, or select it and click Insert.

For most, typing \theta is a lot faster. There are over 200 Replace/With pairs in the Math AutoCorrect list, and learning them all might be a bit of a chore. However, if you already speak math, then many of them will occur to you quite readily. If the built-in names aren't intuitive to you, you can change them to something that is more intuitive.

FIGURE 11.5

Math AutoCorrect can work in math regions or in regular text.

Recognized functions

In Word's equation tools, variables such as x, y, z, a, b, and c are italicized. However, functions, such as sin, cos, sec, tan, and other expressions that don't represent variables are not italicized. When you're using Math AutoCorrect inside a math region (that is, when you're editing an equation), Word maintains a list of expressions and functions that are not italicized, shown in Figure 11.6. You open the Recognized Math Functions dialog box by clicking the Recognized Functions button on the Math AutoCorrect tab of the AutoCorrect dialog box, shown in Figure 11.5.

FIGURE 11.6

You can add or delete expressions you don't want italicized when you're editing in a math content control.

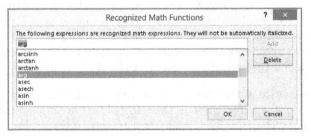

For example, suppose for some reason you suddenly want arg to be italicized in the math expressions you create. To remove arg from the do not italicize list, open the Recognized Math Functions dialog box. Scroll down to and select arg, and then click Delete.

You can also add items to the Recognized Math Functions list. Type the expression you want to add in the text box above the list and click Add. Once done, click OK, and then click OK twice more to close the AutoCorrect and Word Options dialog boxes.

Backing up the Math AutoCorrect list

As for text AutoCorrect entries, Math AutoCorrect entries are also stored in an .acl file in the C:\Users*user name*\AppData\Roaming\Microsoft\Office folder. The Math AutoCorrect list file is named MSO0127.acl. If you modify the built-in list, you should make a backup copy of that file in another location periodically.

AutoFormat versus AutoFormat As You Type

Word's AutoFormat feature makes automatic formatting changes such as applying heading styles, creating bulleted and numbered lists, and formatting special characters such as replacing straight quotation marks with curly ones (smart quotes) or converting typed in fractions to fraction symbols. AutoFormat comes in two flavors: AutoFormat and AutoFormat As You Type. The first, the AutoFormat command, works on demand. When you run AutoFormat in the current document, AutoFormat examines the text and automatically formats elements in it.

The other version, AutoFormat As You Type, works like AutoCorrect. It automatically converts certain things that you type or applies various kinds of formatting. It shares some of the same converting elements as the AutoFormat command, but offers additional options.

To set the record straight here and now, AutoFormat As You Type settings affect what happens as you type. AutoFormat settings affect what happens when the AutoFormat command is applied to existing text.

Working with AutoFormat

When might you use AutoFormat? You could format a plain-text document that has never previously been formatted and uses various text conventions to simulate formatting. You might also use AutoFormat to "clean up" a Word document that has never been formatted properly. You might in addition consider using the AutoFormat command to try to reformat a document converted from another word processor, particularly one that doesn't use styles, or, in any case, a document that manifests no indication of styles having been used.

You can use AutoFormat on the current document in its entirety, or you can apply AutoFormat to selected text. Word searches through the selected text or through the document for formatting patterns and changes. By default, Word applies automatic formatting only to text styled as Normal, leaving alone styles applied by you. Therefore, for a true test of AutoFormat, the starting document should have just a single style, Normal, with all changes made via direct formatting.

If AutoFormat encounters a standout line with bold text that's larger than the surrounding text, Word formats it as Heading 1. If AutoFormat finds smaller text but with characteristics similar in other respects, it applies Heading 2. If AutoFormat trips over a bunch of one-line text entries all together, Word will assume that's a list. If that list has numbers or bullets... well, you get the point.

Preparing to run AutoFormat

Before you run AutoFormat, you should check AutoFormat options to ensure it will make the corrections you want. Changing AutoFormat options works much like working with AutoCorrect settings, as follows:

1. **Open the document that you want to AutoFormat.**

2. **Open the AutoCorrect dialog box (File ⇨ Options ⇨ Proofing ⇨ AutoCorrect Options), and click the AutoFormat tab.** As shown in Figure 11.7, the tab lists all the corrections that running the feature will make.

3. **Check or clear options as needed under Apply and Replace.**

4. **(Optional) Clear the Styles check box under Preserve or the Plain text e-mail documents under Always AutoFormat if you want to turn off those functions.**

5. **Click OK twice.**

FIGURE 11.7

Check AutoFormat options before running AutoFormat in a document.

Unfortunately, AutoFormat is not included in the Ribbon or QAT by default, so if you want to run it, you'll need to add a shortcut key combo for it (refer to Chapter 29) or add it to the Ribbon or QAT. Here's a quick look at how to add it to the QAT:

1. **Right-click the QAT (Quick Access Toolbar) and click Customize Quick Access Toolbar.**
2. **Open the Choose commands from drop-down list, and click All Commands.**
3. **In the left list, scroll down to and click AutoFormat.**
4. **Click Add.** The AutoFormat command appears in the right list, as shown in Figure 11.8.
5. **Click OK.**

FIGURE 11.8

The AutoFormat command is not present in the Ribbon, but you can add it to the QAT or Ribbon.

AutoFormat button on QAT   All Commands   AutoFormat   Click Add

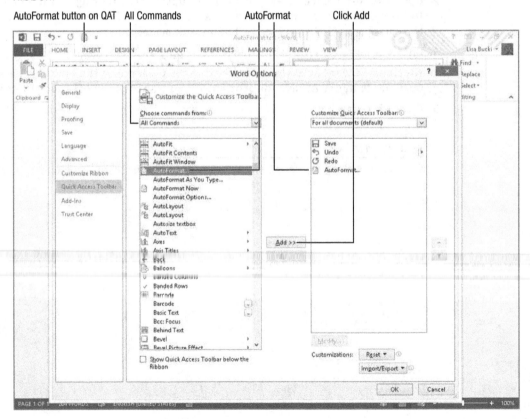

> **NOTE**
>
> There are four AutoFormat commands from which to choose. To make this chapter easier to navigate, you might consider temporarily (at least) putting three of these onto the QAT. You can always remove them later (right-click the tool and choose Remove from Quick Access Toolbar). To save time, we'll assume for the purposes of this chapter that you've followed this advice.
>
> The three I am suggesting you add to the QAT are:
>
> · AutoFormat: This command launches the AutoFormat process, opening the AutoFormat dialog box shown in the next section so you can better control that process.
>
> · AutoFormat Now: This command runs AutoFormat immediately using the current defaults.
>
> · AutoFormat As You Type: This command displays the AutoFormat As You Type dialog box. You'll learn more about this a little later in this chapter.

Running AutoFormat

Now that you're set up to run AutoFormat, open a document that's in need of formatting, or paste text from the Internet or some other source. If you want to format only part of the document, select only what you want AutoFormatted. Then click the AutoFormat command on the QAT (or use any Ribbon button or shortcut key you've created). The dialog box shown in Figure 11.9 appears. Open the drop-down list under Please select a document type to help improve the formatting process, and click General document, Letter, or Email as applicable.

FIGURE 11.9

The AutoFormat command enables you to AutoFormat in one fell swoop (AutoFormat Now) or to review each proposed change.

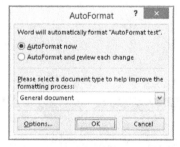

If you're satisfied with the options settings you previously made (Figure 11.7), leave AutoFormat now selected and click OK. Word AutoFormats the entire document. If you want more control over how the formatting proceeds, click the AutoFormat and review each change option button, and then click OK. Word performs the AutoFormat in one full swoop, and then presents you with the dialog box shown in Figure 11.10. Click Accept All to accept all the changes, or Reject All to reject the changes. The example in Figure 11.10 shows some repeated text. The selected text is a copy of the text above that has been AutoFormatted. You can see that AutoFormat has applied heading styles, converted a fraction at the end of the first full paragraph, and applied real bullet list formatting to the final two lines.

FIGURE 11.10

The selected text in this example is an AutoFormatted copy of the text above it.

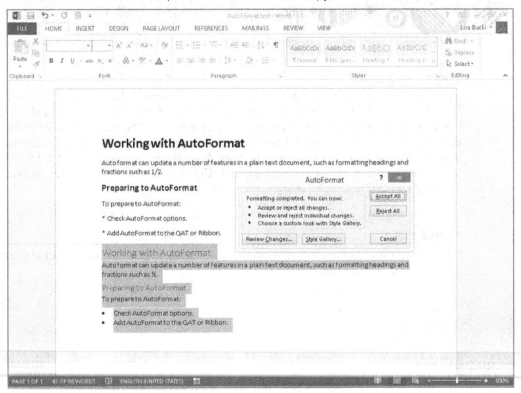

AutoCorrect turns on Track Changes behind the scenes when it formats. If you click Review Changes, the Review AutoFormat Changes dialog box adjusts to enable you to accept or reject changes, as shown in Figure 11.11.

FIGURE 11.11

You can review and accept or reject individual changes.

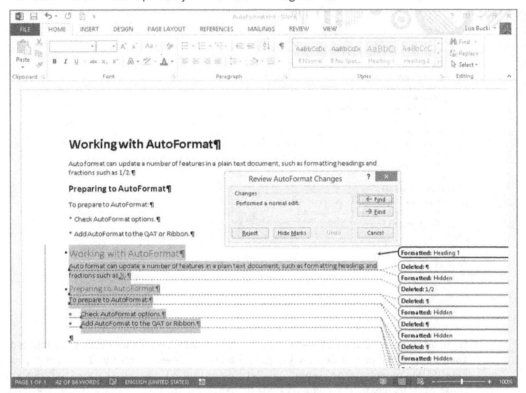

Proceed through the review as you like using the Find previous (with the left arrow) and Find next (with the right arrow) buttons. The dialog box updates with a description of the current change. Choose Hide Marks (which switches to Show Marks) to toggle the revision marks off and on. If you see a change you don't want, click Reject. When you finish here, clicking Cancel will remove any changes you rejected, while everything else will be left intact. This takes you back to the dialog box shown in Figure 11.10.

Back in the AutoFormat dialog box, click Cancel when you've finished working with changes.

AutoFormat As You Type

Word 2013 offers several AutoFormat As You Type options that it can perform to make your word processing life easier.

All but three of the AutoFormat As You Type settings are enabled by default, as shown in Figure 11.12. Open the AutoCorrect dialog box (File ⇨ Options ⇨ Proofing ⇨ AutoCorrect Options), and click the AutoFormat As You Type tab.

FIGURE 11.12

All but three of Word's AutoFormat As You Type settings are enabled by default.

Some additional options appear if support for certain Eastern languages is installed, so don't be alarmed or feel deprived if your dialog box doesn't exactly match what you see here. If you're using those languages, let's go out on a limb and assume that you know what those options mean. The common ones present for a normal US installation are shown in Figure 11.12 and in Table 11.1.

TABLE 11.1 AutoFormat As You Type Options

Replace As You Type	
"Straight quotes" with "smart quotes"	Replaces " and ' with the appropriate directional quotes
Ordinals (1st) with superscript	Replaces 1st with 1st, 2nd with 2nd, etc.
Fractions (1/2) with fraction character ()	Replaces 1/2 with ½, 1/4 with ¼, and 3/4 with ¾
Hyphens (--) with dash (—)	Replaces two hyphens with an em dash (—) whether it's truly appropriate or not
Bold and _italic_ with real formatting	Text enclosed in asterisks or underscores is automatically emboldened or italicized.

Replace As You Type *(continued)*	
Internet and network paths with hyperlinks	Common Internet URLs and e-mail addresses (e.g., www .wiley.com, or johnsmith@virginiacolony.org) are replaced with the corresponding links. URLs have http:// added, and e-mail addresses have mailto: added.

Apply As You Type	
Automatic bulleted lists	When you begin a line with an asterisk (*) followed by a space or tab, bullets formatting is applied. Oddly enough, if you use an actual bullet character, you must use a tab to force the AutoFormat.
Automatic numbered lists	When you begin a line with 1.\<space>, 1.\<tab> or 1\<tab>, Word replaces the numbers and other punctuation with numbering formatting.
Border lines	Typing a series of dashes or underscores causes Word to replace them with border formatting.
Tables	If you type a pattern of +-+, +_+, or +=+, Word assumes that you're trying to create a table. You get one column for each hyphen, underscore, or equals sign enclosed by plus signs. So +-+ yields one column, +-+-+ yields two, and so on. If you've ever seen old computer printouts from the 1970s, this makes perfect sense to you.
Built-in Heading styles	Word automatically applies heading styles (Heading 1, Heading 2, etc.) to text you type, based on the formatting. Apparently I don't think like Word, because I've never been able to get this to work at all.

Automatically As You Type	
Format beginning of list item like the one before it	When you're typing a list (formatted with one of Word's built-in list styles), Word observes how you format the beginning of the list, and then applies the same formatting to the beginning of each item that follows. For example, if each list item begins with a bold word and a period (or some other punctuation), Word will embolden the front end of each list item that follows. It doesn't work without punctuation, though.
Set left- and first-indent with tabs and backspaces	Pressing tab at the beginning of a line causes Word to indent that line. Each press indents further. Pressing Backspace removes indents. See the section "Adding indentation" in Chapter 6, "Paragraph Formatting," for a complete discussion of how this works.
Define styles based on your formatting	This IntelliSense feature is supposed to notice what you're doing and apply styles accordingly. Except for numbered and bulleted lists, I've never gotten this feature to work.

Auto tips and techniques

Sometimes AutoFormat As You Type fills a void. Sometimes, to paraphrase an old left-handed compliment, it fills a much-needed void. There are a few tips and tricks that having AutoFormat As You Type turned on makes possible (or necessary), or that remind you that other gaps are much in need of filling.

Tricks with quotes

What would you do if your editor suddenly told you that all your directional quotes needed to be removed? Or that all the straight quotes needed to be curved?

Either way, there's an easy solution. In the AutoFormat As You Type options, change the "straight quotes" with "smart quotes" option to reflect what you actually want in the document. If you want straight quotes, disable the option. If you want curly quotes, enable it.

Press Ctrl+H to open the Replace dialog box (or click Replace in the Editing group of the Home tab of the Ribbon). Make sure that no formatting is applied to the Find What and Replace With boxes, and click More to ensure that Use Wildcards and other options are all unchecked.

In both the Find What and Replace With boxes, type a single plain straight double quote ("). Note that when you type it the quote won't look curly, regardless of your settings. Click Replace All. That's it!

Use the same technique to fix the single-quote (') character throughout the document. Put a single straight quote into both the Find What and Replace With boxes and again click Replace All.

What about the other fractions?

You might have noticed that the only fractions that are automatically replaced are 1/2, 1/4, and 3/4. What about the others, such as 1/3, 2/3, 1/5, and 1/8?

Well, you can have those too, but you'll have to DIY (do it yourself). Plus, to make it easy, it helps if you have the right fonts installed on your computer. There are two methods for changing typed fractions to the appropriate fraction symbols.

Assigning fractions using symbols and AutoCorrect

To use this method, you insert a symbol for the fraction into the document, select it, and make an AutoCorrect entry for it. To begin:

1. **With a blank document using the Normal template, choose Insert and then click Symbol in the Symbols group.**
2. **On the Symbols tab, make sure that the Font selection is set to (normal text), and at the lower right change the from drop-down list setting to Unicode (hex).**
3. **Scroll down in the table of symbols until you see the fractions, and then click the one you want as shown in Figure 11.13.**

FIGURE 11.13

Insert a fraction symbol and then create an AutoCorrect entry for it.

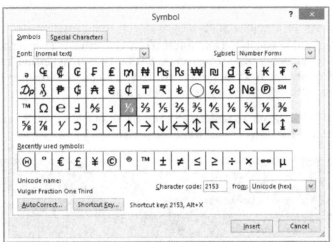

4. **Click Insert, and then Close.**
5. **Select the inserted symbol in the document.**
6. **Open the AutoCorrect dialog box (File ⇨ Options ⇨ Proofing ⇨ AutoCorrect Options), and click the AutoCorrect tab if needed.** The selected symbol should appear in the With text box.
7. **In the Replace box, type the fraction as you normally would.**
8. **Click Add.**
9. **Click OK twice.**

TIP

The MS Reference Specialty font and some other fonts contain many fraction symbols, as do some other fonts. If you don't see the fraction you need, change the Font list selection on the Symbols tab in Figure 11.13. Although this font's fractions use a horizontal divisor line versus the diagonal ones used by other font fraction symbols, they still may be a closer match than regular typed fractions.

You might be worried that if you ever change the font of an entire document, without regard to styles and the presence of the fraction symbols, the fractions will be wiped out. But Word usually notes that such characters are symbols, and they are protected in the application of different fonts. You will, naturally, want to test for robustness any AutoCorrect replacements you create. One way to do that is to insert the character, select it, and then click the Clear Formatting button in the Font group of the Home tab on the Ribbon. If it survives, it likely will work in Word documents you create. Note that characters created this way naturally scale up and down when you change font sizes, which is another advantage of this method.

Assigning fractions using equations and AutoCorrect

Assigning fractions using equations and AutoCorrect is a bit more complicated than assigning fractions using symbols and AutoCorrect, and it involves using either an EQ field or the equation tools to create the fractions you need. Then, assign an AutoCorrect entry to convert what you type into the necessary field or equation.

Using the EQ field is just about as tedious an exercise as anything you'll ever experience. The field exists only for reasons of backward compatibility.

> **NOTE**
>
> In Step 1, your insertion point should be at a normal place in the text, i.e., where you might normally type 1/3. If the insertion point is on a line all by itself, the resulting "equation" will be centered alone on a line, which presumably isn't satisfactory.

Follow these steps to assign fractions using equations:

1. **Click Insert and click Equation in the Symbols group.** Word inserts a math content control, as shown in Figure 11.14, inviting you to type the equation.

   FIGURE 11.14

   Use a math content control to build your own fractions.

2. **Type 1/3 (for example) into the space provided.**
3. **Press the Spacebar to finish the conversion.**
4. **Select the inserted symbol in the document.**
5. **Open the AutoCorrect dialog box (File ⇨ Options ⇨ Proofing ⇨ AutoCorrect Options), and click the AutoCorrect tab if needed.** The selected symbol should appear in the With text box.
6. **In the Replace box, type the fraction as you normally would.**
7. **Click Add.**
8. **Click OK twice.**

That's all there is to it.

Handling Hyphenation

Hyphenation enables Word to fill each line of text more completely. Rather than moving an entire word to the next line via word wrap, Word can insert a hyphen between syllables and wrap only part of the word to the next line. In particular, enabling hyphenation with justified text can help Word fill each line more effectively. Or, turning on hyphenation can help more text fit on a single page with left-aligned text.

On the other hand, some editors and publishers frown on hyphenation, so you should always check to see if hyphenation is acceptable to your readers or clients before using this feature. Word can hyphenate text automatically or manually, and you can insert your own manual hyphens, as well.

Turning on automatic hyphenation

You can turn on automatic hyphenation for the entire document, or selected text. Optionally, you also can change the width of the *hyphenation zone*—the area between the word and the right margin (in left aligned text) that can be blank. When a word is long enough to place it within the hyphenation zone, automatic hyphenation inserts a hyphen in the word. The default hyphenation zone width is .25″. Changing the hyphenation zone width involves a tradeoff. The wider the zone, the more ragged the text and fewer the hyphens. A narrower zone results in neater text, but more hyphens, which may affect readability or result in multiple contiguous hyphenated lines, an effect frowned upon in design circles. To change hyphenation settings:

1. **Click the Page Layout tab, and then click Hyphenation in the Page Setup group.**

2. **Click Hyphenation Options.** The Hyphenation dialog box shown in Figure 11.15 appears.

FIGURE 11.15

Adjust settings before applying hyphenation.

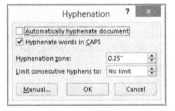

3. **Change the Hyphenate words in CAPS, Hyphenation zone, and Limit consecutive hyphens to settings as desired.** Checking Automatically hyphenate document would apply the hyphenation when you closed the dialog box. That would save you

the trouble of enabling the hyphenation separately, but it hyphenates the whole document, so you should not choose it if you want to hyphenate a selection.

4. **Click OK.**

After you've changed settings as desired, you can apply the automatic hyphenation:

1. **Select the text to hyphenate; or, to hyphenate the whole document, make sure that no text is selected.**

2. **Click the Page Layout tab, and then click Hyphenation in the Page Setup group.**

3. **Click Automatic.** Word applies the hyphenation immediately.

CAUTION

The hyphenation also will be applied to headings, which is usually not desireable. To remove unwanted hyphenation in a heading, select it, and then choose Page Layout ⇨ Page Setup ⇨ Hyphenation ⇨ None.

Using manual hyphenation

When you want to hyphenate a selection or document but want to approve each hyphen before Word inserts it, use the manual hyphenation process. This method takes a little more time, but helps ensure your document won't include any unwanted hyphens. To use manual hyphenation:

1. **Adjust hyphenation settings as described earlier, if desired.**

2. **Select the text to hyphenate; or, to hyphenate the whole document, make sure that no text is selected.**

3. **Click the Page Layout tab, and then click Hyphenation in the Page Setup group.**

4. **Click Manual.** If the selection or document has a word that could be hyphenated, the Manual Hyphenation dialog box appears with a suggested hyphenation, as shown in Figure 11.16.

FIGURE 11.16

Choose where to place hyphens when using manual hyphenation.

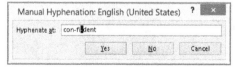

5. Click on the hyphenation location to us in the **Hyphenate at** text box, and then click **Yes;** or click **No** to reject the hyphenation and move on to the next potential hyphen location.

6. Review all potential hyphenations, and then in the **Hyphenation is complete** message box, click **OK**.

11

Adding a manual or nonbreaking hyphen

You can insert your own hyphen at a select location with a keyboard shortcut. And you can use another keyboard shortcut to insert a *nonbreaking hyphen*. This type of hyphen needs to appear within a phrase such as "laissez-faire" or a hyphenated number such as a phone number, but you typically want all parts of the phrase or number to stay together on one line rather than breaking between lines as in normal hyphenation. For example, for a phone number, you wouldn't want "555-" appearing on one line and "0101" appearing at the beginning of the next line. To insert each of these types of hyphens:

- **Manual hyphen:** Click within the word at the location where you want to insert the hyphen, and press Ctrl+– (the hyphen key) to the right of the 0 (zero) along the top of the keyboard. Note that using this feature is a little counter-intuitive. For the text to rewrap, you have to insert the hyphen in the word at the *beginning* of the line where you want the hyphen to appear. After you insert the hyphen, it and the text to its left will wrap up to the end of the line above.

- **Nonbreaking hyphen:** Click where you want the hyphen to appear and press Ctrl+Shift+– (the hyphen key); be sure to delete any unneeded spaces before or after the hyphen. Or, you type the first part of the phrase or number, press Ctrl+Shift+–, and then type the rest of the phrase or number.

NOTE

To remove a manual or nonbreaking hyphen, you have to use the Replace dialog box. Click Replace in the Editing group of the Home tab, or press Ctrl+H. Click the More button, click the Special button and then click either Nonbreaking Hyphen or Optional Hyphen (for manual hyphens). Word places the code representing the specified hyphen type in the Find what text box. You can then use the Find Next and Replace buttons to check and make each replacement, or Replace All.

Summary

In this chapter you've seen how to use and create AutoCorrect Replace/With pairs to work more efficiently. You've also learned the limits of text-only AutoCorrect entries and how to get around those limits. You've learned to exploit AutoFormat and AutoFormat As You Type to clean up document formatting. This chapter has shown you how to do the following:

- Store formatted text and graphics as AutoCorrect entries
- Back up your AutoCorrect entries to safeguard your investment of time, as well as for copying to another computer
- Enable and use Math AutoCorrect
- Suppress automatic italicization of math functions
- Back up Math AutoCorrect entries
- Turn off any AutoFormat As You Type feature you don't need
- Selectively use the AutoFormat command to convert pasted text from a series of one-line paragraphs into word-wrapped text
- Change curly quotes to straight quotes, and vice versa
- Create your own fraction AutoCorrections
- Control text hyphenation

Getting Smart with Text: Building Blocks, Quick Parts, Actions (Tags), and More

IN THIS CHAPTER

Creating a document faster with Building Blocks and Quick Parts

Creating and inserting AutoText entries

Backing up and sharing Building Blocks

Using, removing, and restoring Actions

Understanding objects and linking versus embedding

Inserting text from a file

Pasting, dragging, and dropping text and other content

Printing envelopes on the fly

Saving envelopes as part of a letter

Creating mailing labels

C ertain types of written communication—such as legal passages, product warnings or disclaimers, or a company description—can or should be repeated almost verbatim whenever used. Rather than forcing you to retype such boilerplate text, Word offers you tools for storing and inserting commonly used text, as well as tools for recycling text from other sources.

Building Blocks and Quick Parts provide a gallery-like approach to creating and inserting boilerplate content. You can take advantage of a menu of ready-to-use document parts that you can use to quickly develop a finished document. You can create your own Quick Parts, as well as AutoText entries that you may need to insert frequently in various documents. You also can insert a predesigned cover page to give a report a more polished start.

Enabling *Actions*—links that identify potential special text such as an address you might want to save to your contacts—similarly enables you to capture and reuse document information. And rather than creating document content, you can link, embed, or insert information from other files, as well as copy between documents. Finally, Word includes automated ways to create specialized documents for mailings—envelopes and labels.

This chapter shows you how to use all of these features so you can avoid reinventing the wheel.

Using Quick Parts and Building Blocks

Quick Parts and Building Blocks enable you to insert formatted text into a document with a single command. Word includes a number of predefined Building Blocks, including such features as preformatted page numbers, text boxes, and watermarks. Other chapters discuss the various ways to insert these items into a document, and in this chapter, you will see how to use the Building Blocks Organizer to do so as well. Quick Parts are essentially your own custom Building Blocks that you create and format for reuse in a document. They appear directly on a Quick Parts gallery so that they are easy to insert. This section delves into how to use both Quick Parts and Building Blocks.

Building Blocks versus Quick Parts

The distinction between Quick Parts and Building Blocks can be confusing. Quick Parts are a special subset of Building Blocks. If a Building Block belongs to the Quick Parts gallery, it will appear in the drop-down menu when you click Quick Parts in the Text group of the Insert tab, as shown in Figure 12.1. Items assigned to other galleries (tables, equations, headers, and so on) must be accessed through the full Building Blocks Organizer or the individual galleries for the respective document part type.

How do you decide what to place in the Quick Parts gallery? It's entirely up to you into which gallery you put something. However, you probably want to limit the Quick Parts gallery to items you need more frequently, as there is limited room in the gallery.

> **CAUTION**
>
> If you work in compatibility mode, Building Block features work in the current document only as long as it is open. If you attempt to save Building Block items to a legacy .dot file, however, the file will revert to an AutoText entry and will not appear in the Quick Parts gallery the next time that document is opened. This might look like a bug, but it's not. Legacy .dot files do not have the means to store and use gallery information, as those features do not exist in the .dot file specification.

FIGURE 12.1

Click Quick Parts in the Text group to open the Quick Parts gallery.

Using the Building Blocks Organizer

If what you want isn't in the Quick Parts gallery, click Quick Parts in the Text group of the Insert tab, and then click Building Blocks Organizer to open the Building Blocks Organizer dialog box shown in Figure 12.2. Click any of the items in the Building blocks list at the left to see a preview of it at the right. Click any of the headers—Name, Gallery, Category, or Template—to sort the list. Note that your default list of Building Blocks may include slightly differing items, and may be sorted differently.

Click the item you want to insert and then click Insert. Word inserts the item in the way that was specified when it was created or added to the Building Blocks Organizer (content only, content in its own paragraph, or content in its own page).

> **NOTE**
>
> Note that some Building Blocks are automatically inserted into headers or footers (as page numbers, for example), whereas others are inserted at the insertion point. For Building Blocks supplied with Word, the Gallery column name tells you where the item will be inserted. For example, three items are named Accent Bar 1, and each is in a different gallery: Page Numbers (Bottom of Page), Page Numbers (Top of Page), and Page Numbers. There are two additional items with similar names: Accent Bar, Left and Accent Bar, Right. Those two are in the Page Numbers (Margins) Gallery.

FIGURE 12.2

Use the Building Blocks Organizer to change, delete, and insert Quick Parts.

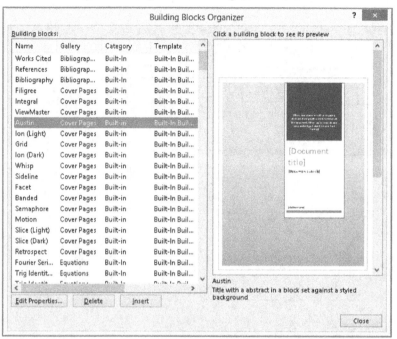

TIP

You can drag the right border of the Gallery column in the Building Blocks Organizer window to the right so that you can see more of each gallery name to assist you in making a selection.

Adding a new Building Block or Quick Part

If none of the prefabricated Building Blocks suits your needs, you can modify them or design your own from scratch. The Building Blocks feature enables you to save your work investment quickly and easily by adding it to the Building Blocks Organizer. The Building Blocks feature also enables you to name and categorize the parts you create, as well as place them into any of a number of galleries.

Adding a new Quick Part or Building Block is easy. If you have text, URLs, structures (tables, pictures, charts, content controls, etc.), and so on that you frequently reuse in different documents, you can save time and effort by saving them as distinct Building Blocks or Quick Parts.

Moreover, creating and using custom Building Blocks can help prevent mistakes and embarrassment. Have you ever inadvertently transposed two letters in your own company's URL? Have you ever mistyped a contract clause, leasing a building for ten years instead of one? By using Quick Parts and Building Blocks, you help avoid random careless errors. Of course, it is important to carefully proofread what you save as a Quick Part or Building Block.

Here's how to create you own Quick Part or Building Block:

1. **Create and format the text or object you want to save as a gallery item, and then select it.**

2. **Click the Insert tab, and in the Text group, choose Quick Parts ⇨ Save Selection to Quick Part Gallery.** This opens the Create New Building Block dialog box shown in Figure 12.3. If you are using a low screen resolution, you may not see Quick Parts on the button name and your button will look like the one shown in Figure 12.1. The ScreenTip for the correct button is Explore Quick Parts.

FIGURE 12.3

Organize your Building Blocks during the creation process to make them easier to find and use later.

3. **In the Name text box, type a name to use for the Building Block.** As indicated earlier, if you have a series of items you intend to call Item 1, Item 2, and Item 3, it's better planning to call them 1Item, 2Item, and 3Item. This will enable you to use F3 shortcuts more efficiently, a topic you'll learn more about later in the chapter. Note that omitting the space in the name increases the chances of creating unique and unambiguous names for quick insertion using the F3 shortcut.

4. **Open the Gallery drop-down list and click the desired gallery name.** To have the item appear in the gallery portion of the Quick Parts menu, add it to the Quick Parts gallery. Add only items you need frequently and for which you need insertion flexibility to the Quick Parts gallery. Choosing the AutoText gallery enables you to insert the selection by typing the Building Block name, as described later. In choosing which gallery to use, make sure that you don't add items intended for a specific document area to the wrong gallery (for example, don't put a header item into the Footers gallery). You also should be consistent in order to make it easier to find things later. Note that you cannot create new gallery names. It's not a bad idea, however, to put things that are purely text into AutoText, and actual structures into the appropriate gallery (Tables, Text Boxes, Headers, Footers, and so on). Note that all Building Block items can be inserted with most AutoText methods, even if they aren't in the AutoText gallery. One exception, however, is that only items in the AutoText gallery can be inserted with the AutoComplete feature. More on this shortly.

5. **Open the Category drop-down list and click the desired category.** You can select General for your first few user-created Building Blocks. Choose Create New Category to make your own custom categories. In the Create New Category dialog box shown in Figure 12.4, type a descriptive name that will help you stay organized, and click OK. Placing too many Building Blocks in the General category can become a little unwieldy. As you create more Building Blocks, it will be important for you to create categories to organize them.

FIGURE 12.4

Categories can help you find Building Blocks more quickly later.

6. **In the Description text box, type a little about what the Building Block is and where you'd use it.** If the Building Block consists of text, before you open the Create New Building Block dialog box, you could copy all or the beginning of the text into the Clipboard, and then paste it into the Description box by pressing Ctrl+V. The text itself can serve as an excellent description.

7. **Choose a save location from the Save in drop-down list.** The default setting usually will be Building Blocks, which refers to the `Building Blocks.dotx` template file. This file usually is located in `C:\Users\`*user name*`\AppData\Roaming\Microsoft\Document Building Blocks\1033` (or its `\15` subfolder). However, you can instead choose to store Building Blocks in the template on which the current document is based, `Normal.dotm`, in any other currently loaded global template, or in a new `.dotx` file you create just for this purpose.

8. **Open the Options drop-down list and choose a default insertion method for the Building Block you're adding.** Insert content only inserts the Building Block at the insertion point. You can also choose Insert content in its own paragraph or Insert content in its own page. Figure 12.5 shows the settings for a new Building Block holding the formatted and hyperlinked URL shown to the left of the dialog box.

9. **Click OK.**

FIGURE 12.5

Your entries for a new Building Block can include a custom Category and Save in location.

Inserting a Quick Part

As you saw earlier, to insert a Quick Part into your document you can click Quick Parts in the Text group of the Insert tab. The Quick Parts you have added appear in a gallery in the top of the menu.

Click a listed Quick Part to insert it into the current document at the insertion point. Or, for more precise control over how it's inserted, right-click the item for the list of options shown in Figure 12.6. Click one of the options at the top of the shortcut menu, such as Insert at End of Document, to choose the location for the inserted item. Note also that the shortcut menu includes the Edit Properties, and Organize and Delete commands that you can use to manage the Quick Part's settings.

FIGURE 12.6

Right-click a Quick Part in the gallery to see commands for inserting and managing it.

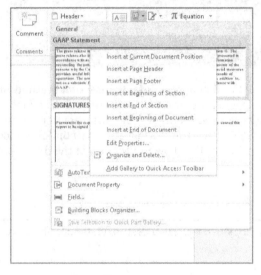

Inserting a Building Block

Given that many Building Blocks are not found on the Quick Parts gallery, you have to use other methods to insert them. You can use one of the following methods to insert a Building Block:

- **Select the Building Block from its "home" gallery.** For example, Footer Building Blocks appear in the Footer gallery that appears when you click Footer in the Header & Footer group of the Insert tab. See Chapter 16, "Setting Up the Document with Sections, Headers/Footers, and Columns," to learn more about inserting headers and footers. If you saved the Building Block to the Quick Parts gallery, it will appear when you click the Quick Parts button in the Text group of the Insert tab.

- **Click the Insert tab, click Quick Parts in the Text group, and then click Building Blocks Organizer.** Select the desired Building Block in the Building blocks list at the left side of the Building Blocks Organizer, and then click Insert.

TIP

In deciding whether you store document parts as AutoCorrect or Building Blocks (which include AutoText and Quick Parts), you should limit your AutoCorrect entries to corrections and shortcuts that you use in routine typing, and you should reserve Building Blocks for longer and more elaborate excerpts, such as tables, lists, graphics, and boiler-plate document sections.

Using AutoComplete with AutoText Gallery Entries

Word 2003 and earlier versions included an AutoComplete feature that made it easy to save and reinsert frequently used text entries. You could start typing the entry, and then press Enter (see Figure 12.7) or F3 to insert the text. This functionality was removed from Word 2007 and then reinstated in Word 2010. The AutoComplete insertion techniques work for Building Blocks that you've saved to the AutoText gallery, as described earlier.

FIGURE 12.7

If you save a Building Block in the AutoText category, you can insert it by starting to type its name and then pressing Enter when the tooltip appears.

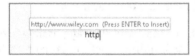

To use this feature, click in the location where you want to insert the AutoText, and start typing the name you assigned to the Building Block in the Name text box of the Create New Building Block dialog box. When the tooltip with the name appears as shown in the example in Figure 12.7, press Enter or F3. (This feature is known as AutoComplete.)

One key to remember is that you have to type the Name text box entry you entered for the AutoText Building Block in the Create New Building Block dialog box (refer to Figure 12.5), *not* the text of the entry itself (unless they are the same). You can refresh your memory about AutoText gallery names by clicking Quick Parts in the Text group of the Insert tab, and then point to AutoText; the name for each AutoText Building Block appears above the preview of its contents in the AutoText gallery. Similarly, you can open the Building Blocks Organizer to review the name for other Building Blocks assigned to the AutoText gallery you might want to insert with Enter or F3. You also can insert an AutoText entry using the gallery itself. Click the Insert tab, click Quick Parts in the Text group, point to AutoText, and click the desired entry.

TIP

If pressing F3 doesn't insert the item, type a little more of it. If you have two items named Calendar 1 and Calendar 2, you'll need to type the full name of either. If one is named 1Calendar and the other is named 2Calendar, however, you can save yourself some typing by entering only **1c** or **2c** (unless you have other gallery items that begin with those characters).

TIP

If the AutoComplete feature does not work for you, there are two things to check. First, in File ⟶ Options ⟶ Advanced ⟶ Editing options, Show AutoComplete suggestions must be enabled. Second, because of a longstanding bug in Word, AutoComplete will not work if the window and/or text is sized such that the horizontal scroll bar appears. If neither of these two conditions is the problem and AutoComplete still doesn't work, verify that File ⟶ Options ⟶ Advanced ⟶ Display ⟶ Show horizontal scroll bar is enabled.

Clearing Building Block Formatting

Word does not provide a way to store or insert Quick Parts or Building Block entries as plain text or unformatted text if you included added formatting such as character formatting when creating them. If you have a Building Block item that you want to insert but need it inserted without the formatting, you will have to use other means.

If you want Building Block items to be inserted in the most vanilla way possible, clear all formatting from the selection before adding it to the Building Blocks organizer. Or, on an ad hoc basis, you can selectively remove the formatting after inserting the item. Select the inserted text, and then click Clear All Formatting in the Font group of the Home tab.

Building Blocks: Need to Know

Working with Building Blocks can make you more productive. Initially setting things up might take a few extra minutes of thought and care, but ultimately the extra organization will yield dividends. Of course, if you're going to invest the time to create and enhance a resource, you're going to want to know how to protect that investment, as well as how to share the resource with others.

Backing up Building Blocks

As noted earlier, Building Blocks can be stored in any template that is accessible in the current document window. A template is currently accessible for any of five reasons:

- It is a Building Blocks template located in your Building Blocks folder. This folder usually is named `C:\Users\`*user name*`\AppData\Roaming\Microsoft\ Document Building Blocks\1033\15`. The default storage file is named

> Built-In Building Blocks.dotx, although if you upgraded from an earlier version, it may be named just Building Blocks.dotx.

- It is Normal.dotm (stored in the location specified in File ⇨ Options ⇨ Advanced ⇨ General section ⇨ File Locations ⇨ "User templates," usually C:\Users*user name*\AppData\Roaming\Microsoft\Templates).

- It is attached to the current document and is a template other than Normal.dotm.

- It is a global template located in your startup folder. You can choose the location of the startup folder by choosing File ⇨ Options ⇨ Advanced ⇨ General ⇨ File Locations ⇨ Startup. The default location usually is C:\Users*user name*\AppData\Roaming\Microsoft\Word\STARTUP.

- The template file itself is open in the current document window.

To find out where all the currently available Building Blocks are stored, in the Insert tab choose Quick Parts ⇨ Building Blocks Organizer. Drag the header borders as necessary so that you can see the complete template names, as shown in Figure 12.8. Note that if you did not upgrade from an earlier version of Word, the number of AutoText items from Normal.dotm might be considerably smaller.

FIGURE 12.8

The Building Blocks Organizer shows the template locations where all currently available Building Blocks are stored.

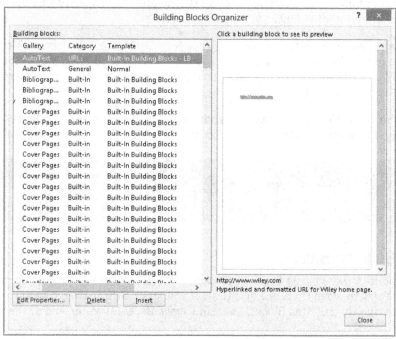

To back up your Building Blocks, back up all the templates where they are stored. Note that files cannot be backed up while they are in use, so once you determine the name and location of the templates you need to back up, you need to close Word, use File Explorer in Windows 8 (Windows Explorer in Windows 7) to navigate to the locations of the template files, and copy them elsewhere (tape, backup drive, network backup location, CD, DVD, or another target).

> **CAUTION**
>
> If Always Create Backup Copy is enabled (File ⇨ Options ⇨ Advanced ⇨ Save), Word will create a backup version of your Building Blocks.dotx file. Note that this is automatic, however, and occurs each time a change is made to your Building Blocks collection.

Sharing Building Blocks

When you start developing Building Blocks, particularly ones you plan to share with others, it can be useful to deliberately create a new .dotx file to store your Building Blocks. To share a Building Block template file, give it a name other than the default Building Blocks.dotx. It's not a bad idea to date it too, so that someone to whom you give it will have a reference point with respect to earlier Building Block template files. For example, I might give one the name Lisa Bucki Building Blocks 2013.dotx.

To create such a file, create a new blank document and save it in .dotx format—preferably in the default storage location for user Building Blocks files as noted in the "Adding a new Building Block or Quick Part" section earlier in the chapter. Then specify this file as the Save in location for Building Blocks you wish to share.

You can then copy this file across a network, copy it to CD/DVD or other removable media, or email it to others. To use it, they should copy it to their own Building Blocks folder. This typically is C:\Users*user name*\AppData\Roaming\Microsoft\Document Building Blocks\1033\15.

In sharing this file with others, make sure that they copy it to the Building Blocks folder and that they do not replace their own local copy of Building Blocks.dotx with it.

> **NOTE**
>
> In the preceding file path, 1033 is the default location for English (U.S.) files. For Spanish, French, and other languages the number will be different.

Copying Building Blocks

There is no built-in way to copy Building Blocks from one template to another en masse, but there is a way to move them one at a time. If you make a throwaway copy of the source file before moving the Building Blocks, you can simply discard it at the end of the process.

First, make a backup copy of both the source and destination templates. The destination template can be a new blank `.dotx` file stored in the default Building Blocks folder (see the previous section). In the case of the source, this is not a mere precaution, because the process actually removes Building Blocks from the source file. Make a throwaway copy of the source that you will use for this process, and maybe even name it `throwaway-copy-source.dotx`.

Second, make sure that both the destination template and the throwaway copy of the source are available. You can do this by putting both into the Document Building Blocks folder (`C:\Users\`*user name*`\AppData\Roaming\Microsoft\Document Building Blocks\1033\15`).

Third, open the source template file (not a document based on it) to make sure its Building Blocks will be available, and leave it as the current or active document.

Fourth, choose Insert ⇨ Text ⇨ Quick Parts ⇨ Building Blocks Organizer. Sort by template so you can focus your efforts only on the throwaway copy of the source file. Remember that any entry you change here will actually move the Building Block entry, not merely copy it.

Select an entry you want to move in the Building blocks list, and click Edit Properties. In the Modify Building Block dialog box, open the Save in drop-down list of available template locations, and then click the destination template to which you want the entry moved. Click OK. Repeat the process to move other Building Blocks, and then click Close to close the Building Blocks Organizer.

Deleting or changing a Building Block

You also can use the Building Blocks Organizer to delete or make changes to a Building Block. Open it by clicking the Quick Parts button in the Text group of the Insert tab. Click the item to delete in the Building Blocks list, and then click the Delete button. In the message box that asks you to confirm the deletion, click Yes.

If you want to make changes to the selected Building Block, click the Edit Properties button. The Modify Building Block dialog box with settings identical to those in the Create New Building Block dialog box show in Figure 12.5 appears. Make changes as desired, such as using the Gallery drop-down list to move it to another gallery. For example, you could click AutoText to transform the Building Block into one of the AutoText Gallery choices. Then click OK.

Using Building Blocks with the AutoText Field

Although they've renamed the feature from AutoText to Building Blocks, Word's basic infrastructure still treats Building Block entries the same way that Word 2003 and earlier treated AutoText entries.

12

This means that in addition to inserting Building Blocks into your documents in the manner indicated in this chapter, you can also insert them using the AutoText field—not just items in the AutoText Gallery, but *all* Building Blocks. Suppose that you have a series of templates in which the identical Building Block name is used for a variety of formulations of the same concept. For example, you might have a Building Block entry named Exposure Quote. In one template it might say one thing, in another something else, and in a third template still something else.

In place of an actual exposure quote in a document, however, you could instead use an AutoText field to refer to the Exposure Quote Building Block. That way, whenever the Building Block for the underlying template changes, the Exposure Quote in all documents based on that template changes as well, simply by your updating the field in the document.

To use a field rather than insert the actual Building Block itself, choose Insert ⇨ Text ⇨ Quick Parts ⇨ Field. The dialog box shown in Figure 12.9 will appear. With Categories set to All, click on AutoText in the Field names list. In the AutoText name list, at center, click the Building Block you want to insert, and click OK.

FIGURE 12.9

AutoText entries can be inserted by reference with a field.

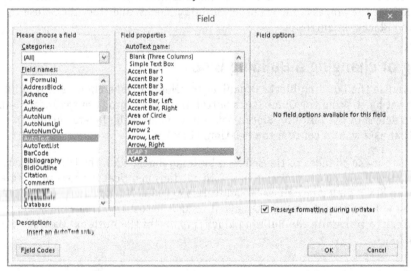

Note that even though the field name is AutoText, this method works for all Building Blocks. Fields are discussed in detail in Chapter 23, "Automating Document Content with Fields."

Inserting a Cover Page

Many formal report documents require a cover page that includes not only the document's title, but information about its author and when it was written. Although you can insert a cover page from the Building Blocks Organizer, the Insert tab also has a separate gallery just for cover pages.

1. **Open or create the document for which you want to add a cover page.**
2. **Click the Insert tab, and then click Cover Page in the Pages group.** The Cover Page gallery opens.
3. **Scroll down to view the available cover pages (Figure 12.10), and then click the one to insert.**

FIGURE 12.10

Select a cover page to insert from the gallery.

4. **Fill in the placeholders on the cover page.** For example, click the [Document title] placeholder and type a title. To remove an unneeded control placeholder, right-click it and click Remove Content Control.

Understanding Actions

Action options are special kinds of links that are associated with names, places, addresses, telephone numbers, and financial symbols, to name a few. When enabled, an Additional Actions choice appears when you right-click an item that has associated Actions, as shown in Figure 12.11.

FIGURE 12.11

Additional Actions options enable you to perform special commands for a limited selection of associated items.

If you click the Add to Contacts choice in the Additional Actions submenu shown in Figure 12.11, the new Contact window shown in Figure 12.12 opens. Notice the phone number that is right-clicked on in Figure 12.11 already appears as the Business phone number entry in Figure 12.12. In this instance, you could add additional information about the contact and then save the contact.

The choices in the Additional Actions submenu will vary depending on the nature of the text you right-click and what the associated action does. For example, say a colleague sends you a document with meeting minutes that includes the date for the next meeting. If you right-click that meeting date and click Additional Actions, you can then click either Schedule a Meeting or Show My Calendar. This example illustrates how Actions can help you better manage your schedule, contact information, and more.

FIGURE 12.12

Additional Actions include creating a new contact based on a phone number in a document.

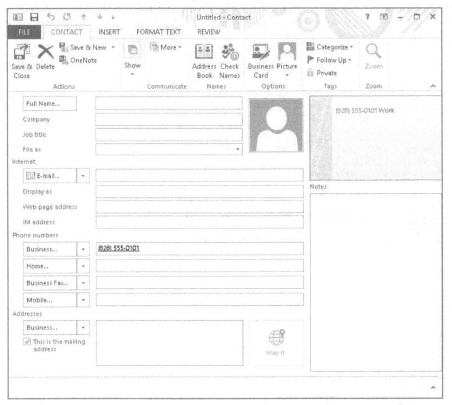

Enabling Actions

Actions are not enabled in Word by default. In order for the Additional Actions choice to appear in the shortcut menu, you have to enable Actions. Choose File ⇨ Options ⇨ Proofing ⇨ AutoCorrect Options ⇨ Actions tab. At the top of the tab, click to check the

Enable additional Actions in the right-click menu option, as shown in Figure 12.13. Figure 12.13 shows which specific Actions are checked by default when you initially enable Actions. You can check any or all of the other three Actions to enable them as well. After changing Action settings, click OK twice to close the AutoCorrect and Word Options dialog boxes and apply your changes.

FIGURE 12.13

You can enable eight different Actions in Word.

More Actions and properties

When you click some of the Actions in the Available Actions list of the Actions tab, the Properties button beside the list becomes enabled. Clicking the button launches your system's web browser and displays an article about properties for Actions. Clicking the More actions button, shown in Figure 12.13, takes you to a website where you can download additional Action add-ins. One of them—the ActiveDocs Action—even enables you to create your own custom Actions.

Inserting Objects and Files

Using a technology known as *object linking and embedding* (OLE), you can create multimedia and multidimensional documents that incorporate components from a variety of programs—and not just Office applications. A single document, for example, might contain text from Word, data and charts from Excel, and sounds or video clips from some other program.

Think of an object as a unit of information that comes from a specific program. For example, a text selection in Word might be considered an object by Excel or some other program, or even by Word itself under different circumstances. Word tables or WordArt creations can be objects as well, as can Word equations, or even whole Word documents. All or part of an Excel worksheet might be an object, as might a PDF file from Adobe, a MIDI file from a music program, an MP3 or WMA song file from a media player, and so on.

Each different object has associated with it an *owner* or *client* program. That's the program that provides the muscle needed to create, edit, or display/play the object in its original form. To see the kinds of objects that you can insert in a Word document and make the insertion:

1. **In the Text group of the Insert tab of the Ribbon, click the Object drop-down arrow, and then click Object, as shown in Figure 12.14.** You also could just click the Object button without clicking the drop-down.

FIGURE 12.14

To insert an object, click the Object tool on the Insert tab.

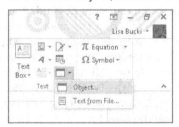

Word displays the Create New tab in the Object dialog box, shown in Figure 12.15. The contents of the Object type list depends entirely on the programs installed on your computer. The more programs installed, the longer the list of OLE-compatible objects Word displays. Many of them you probably won't recognize, and you might wonder where they came from. Creating a new object this way and exploring the options available is one approach to finding out more about the object in question.

FIGURE 12.15

The more programs you have installed on your computer, the more likely you are to have a lot of different object types listed in the Object dialog box.

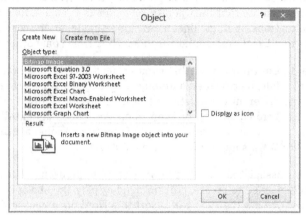

2. **Click the desired kind of object in the Object type list.**
3. **Click OK.**
4. **Create the object in its owner program, and then save and close it.**

Linking versus embedding objects in Word

When it comes to using bits and pieces of other programs' data in Word, you have two options: linking or embedding. The method you just used in the prior steps is an example of embedding. The inserted object exists only within the Word document where you created it, and does not exist as a separate file. If you refer again to Figure 12.15, you'll see that the Object dialog box includes a Create from File tab. Click that tab to see the choices shown in Figure 12.16. Use the Browse button to open the Browse dialog box, navigate to and select the file to insert, and then click Open. On the Create from File tab, click the Link to file check box as shown in Figure 12.16 to link the inserted object to its original source file. (If you do not click this check box, the object will be embedded instead.) Then click OK to finish inserting the object.

When you link an object, you store that object's location in Word. Later, when you or someone else chooses to "view" the object, Word checks the operating system to determine which program "owns" that type of file. It then uses that program to open the file. For some kinds of objects, particularly those owned by other Office programs, Word can display the object's content in place, as part of the Word document. For others, the program opens and the object is displayed in the owner program.

FIGURE 12.16

You also can insert an existing file into a document, and use the Link to file option to link rather than embed it.

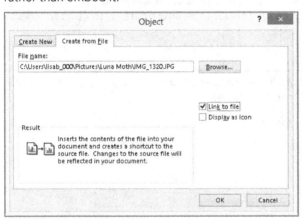

When you embed an object, a copy of the object is stored within the Word document. Depending on the size of the object, this can add greatly to the Word document size and can make Word files unwieldy. Embedding is a way to guarantee that the object is available when using the Word document, though.

As with pictures, the decision to embed versus link is driven by considerations of size, maintenance/updates, and availability. All other factors aside, an embedded object will result in a larger file than an object that is linked. This can create difficulties in emailing the Word document, transporting it on small removable media (SD card, USB flash drive, and so on), or even storing it. However, assuming these issues are not insurmountable—and they are increasingly less so, given the falling cost of storage and the increasing availability of high-speed Internet access—embedding provides assurance that the object's data will be present when needed.

In contrast, a linked-only object will work only if the original object file remains in the same storage location and hasn't been renamed. For example, if the object originally was in the same folder as the file that contains it, location should not be an issue. However, if the object originally was in a folder named Lisa Media but is now in a folder named Karen Media, the linked item will not display correctly.

On the other hand, if you have updated the contents of the source file but kept the identical name and folder, a link to it will reflect the changes, displaying the new contents in place of the old when you open the document and update the link.

For example, suppose you need to share some Excel data with a colleague within a Word document stored on your organization's network. You insert the Excel file into the

Word document with the Link to file check box checked. Later, you edit the data in the Excel file, which is also stored on the network. When your colleague subsequently opens the Word document from the network, the message about updating links shown in Figure 12.17 appears. Clicking Yes at this message includes the latest data in the linked object.

FIGURE 12.17

When you open a document with linked content, Word asks you whether to update the document with the changes in the linked information.

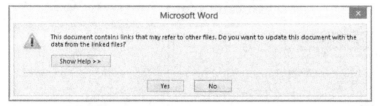

> **NOTE**
>
> When you insert a multipage document as an object into the current file, only the first page will be displayed, which can be handy if this is exactly what you want. If you want the entire multipage document to display with its original formatting, you need to use a different approach. One way would be to break up the document into separate documents—one for each page.

Displaying as icons versus content

When you insert an object into the current file, you have the option to display the content or display only an icon. If you choose the Display as icon option, shown unchecked in Figures 12.15 and 12.16, the object will still have functionality—you will be able to double-click it to open the owner application—but you will not be able to see the content inside the Word document.

Figure 12.18 shows three icons for inserted content. The one on the left represents Excel content. You can't see the content itself, but the icon clearly shows you that it represents spreadsheet information. In most cases, you probably will not want to insert visual content from other Office applications as an icon, because the point is usually to see the content itself. The next two icons represent inserted WMA song files. Word doesn't have the capability to properly display song content inside the Word window, so the file appears as an icon regardless of whether you specify that option. The middle icon was inserted with Display as icon unchecked, and so you can see its picture shows the Windows 8 Music app, the program that the song will play in when you double-click the icon. Display as icon was checked when the third icon was inserted, and Word gave it a generic package icon that provides no clue about what would happen if you double-clicked the icon. The content type and your needs will determine whether you want to display inserted files as icons.

FIGURE 12.18

Some objects, such as music files, always insert as icons; you simply control how the icon looks.

Inserting Text from Files

The other option available when you click the Object drop-down arrow in the Text group of the Insert tab, as shown in Figure 12.14, is Text from File. This command can be useful when you are pulling together a large document using content from a variety of other source documents. In some cases those other documents might have been written or might be in the process of being written by others. Or you might be working from a PDF from another source that contains content you need to update, such as information from a corporate annual report or data from a colleague's study that you need to cite in the current document. Or you might be creating a contract and need similar content from prior contracts you've written. Inserting an existing file saves work and ensures accuracy and consistency between documents.

Inserting the file

The file you want to insert need not be open when you add it into the current document. To insert a file into the current document:

1. **Position the insertion point at the location where you'd like to insert the file in the current document.**
2. **In the Text group of the Insert tab on the Ribbon, click the Object drop-down arrow, and then click Text from File.** The Insert File dialog box appears.
3. **Navigate to the target file and select it.**
4. **Use the Insert button to determine how to insert the file.** You can click the Insert button itself to insert the file, or you can click the Insert button drop-down arrow and then click Insert as Link to insert a linked copy of the file's contents, as shown in Figure 12.19.

FIGURE 12.19

You can insert a file directly or insert a link to it.

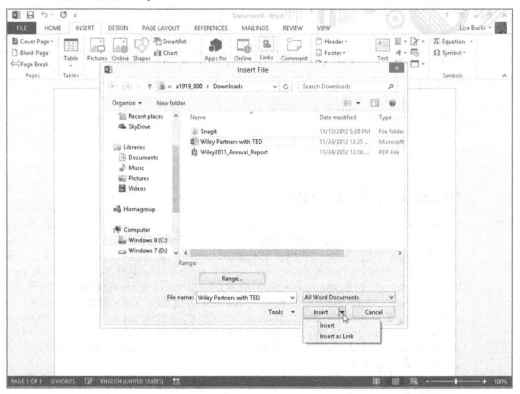

If the source file is being maintained separately, and might change, then choose Insert as Link so you can update the material in the current document when the source changes. If the source is a finished document and you simply want to incorporate the contents, choose Insert.

Note the additional option button in Figure 12.19, Range. If the source file contains bookmarks or named ranges (as used in Excel), use Range to specify the exact location of the source material.

If you choose Insert as Link, an INCLUDETEXT field code is inserted, rather than the file's text. However, that might be what you want, particularly if the file's contents aren't straightforward. If the source document contains field codes, for example, you likely will want to control exactly what happens when it is inserted into the current file. Therefore, immediately after inserting the link, right-click and choose Edit Field. As shown in Figure 12.20, you can now adjust the field code options so that the included text behaves as you think it should. See Chapter 23 for additional information about fields.

FIGURE 12.20

After inserting a link to a file, right-click the link and choose Edit Field to choose how you want the inserted file's contents handled.

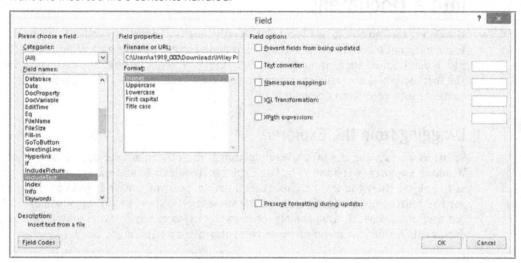

Handling formatting issues

When you insert the contents of a file using the Text from File option—whether you insert the actual contents or a link—the styles of the current document are applied to the incoming file. This may change the formatting of the inserted text, or it may not, depending on whether the inserted text relies on styles or has a lot of direct character and paragraph formatting applied. If the latter is the case, the inserted document's appearance probably won't change much.

For example, it's possible for a document template to contain additional formatting information, such as information about paper size, orientation, margins, and other Page Layout settings that are not incorporated in a document's styles. When you insert that document, all of the Page Layout settings will be discarded, and the Page Layout settings for the file where you inserted the text will take precedence.

If the file holding the text to be inserted was based on a particular template and you want to retain the same formatting settings supplied by the template, you need to create a new document based on that same template. Then use the Text from File command to deposit the contents of an existing document into the new document. This way, all the desired document formatting will remain in place.

Pasting, Dragging, and Dropping Content into a Document

The Object tool on the Insert tab isn't the only means of depositing objects into a document. Two additional tools at your disposal are dragging and dropping, and using the Clipboard, which you learned about in Chapter 8, "Cutting, Copying, and Pasting Using the Clipboard." The method you'll use will depend on whether you need to insert all or part of a document's contents into your Word document.

Dragging from the Explorer

To insert an existing file into a Word document directly from your operating system, open Windows Explorer (Windows 7) or File Explorer (Windows 8) and navigate to the location of the object (file) you want to insert. If possible, position both windows so that you can see the source and the destination at the same time. Using the right mouse button (you'll see why in a moment), drag the object from the Explorer window and drop it into the Word document. A shortcut menu presents the options shown in Figure 12.21.

FIGURE 12.21

When you use the right mouse button to drag and drop an object, Word lets you choose a Drop option.

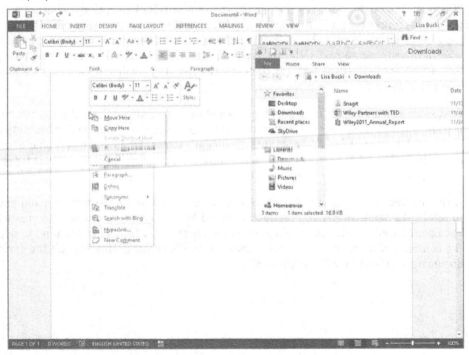

Note that Move Here is a little misleading when you're dragging objects from a folder window into Word. If you choose Move, Word actually copies. In other words, the only real options are Copy Here, which inserts the file's contents into the document at the insertion point, and Create Hyperlink Here. If you choose the latter, Word creates a standard hyperlink to the object. When you Ctrl+click on the hyperlink from Word, the default program associated with the file type is opened to display, play, edit, or otherwise handle the file.

Dragging from another open program

If you don't want to insert an entire document into the current document, you can drag a selection from another open document. What happens when you drop the content into Word depends on what is selected and being dragged, and what the source application is—Word or another Office application such as PowerPoint or Excel.

Dragging text

If you drag a text selection between two open Office documents, the default behavior in most cases is for the selection to be *moved* to the target location. Therefore, I strongly suggest that you make dragging with the right mouse button your standard default dragging behavior. Even if you *do* want to move the text, it's best to be informed about exactly what will happen.

When right-dragging from one Word document to another, you often will be presented with an additional option or two, as shown in Figure 12.22. Here, notice the two competing options: Shortcut versus Hyperlink.

FIGURE 12.22

Right-dragging text may make additional options available: Link Here and Create Shortcut Here.

If you choose Create Shortcut Here, Word inserts an OLE_LINK to the source document, and includes a reference to the file name and the exact location in a LINK object that it creates in the target document. The result in the target document is a Word object (using the Word icon), which you can double-click to open the source location.

Choosing Link Here hyperlinks the text in the source document and again inserts an OLE_LINK in the target document. In this case, the linked text appears in the document. In the target document, you can right-click the linked content, point to Linked Document Object in the shortcut menu, and then click Open Link to display the source.

The results are similar, but the utility in the target document is a little different. Which method you use should be determined by which one offers you the desired utility and effect.

Dragging other objects

What happens when you drag other objects depends a lot on the program and the extent to which that program supports dragging and dropping. You can't just assume that what you want to happen will actually happen—even if the source program is another Office 2013 program.

For example, if you try to drag a graphic from PowerPoint into Word, the result will probably surprise you. PowerPoint will not let you drag a graphic or chart outside of its own window. You will have to experiment to see whether dragging and dropping works between particular programs.

The Paste alternative

When dragging and dropping doesn't work, you can fall back to copy and paste, which was covered in depth in Chapter 8. With some programs that do not support dragging, such as the PowerPoint example just described, copying and pasting is the *only* option. Similarly, use copy and paste when you want to grab information from non-Office programs, such as Internet Explorer.

Use the source program's supported features to select the desired item, right-click the selection, and choose Copy or press Ctrl+C to copy the item to the Clipboard. Move to the Word document and click where you want to deposit the Clipboard's contents. If you're positive about the result you'll get, click Paste (in the Home tab's Clipboard group) or press Ctrl+V. If you're unsure about your options, click the Paste button arrow in the Home tab's Clipboard group and choose Paste Special.

The options that appear vary greatly depending on the nature of the item and the source program. Increasingly, the default Action is HTML Format, as shown in Figure 12.23. Note the top option listed: Microsoft Word Document Object. While it's not clear that that option would be the most useful one, it's equally unclear that HTML Format would be. Click a choice in the list, and click OK. If the results don't have the destination you need, press Ctrl+Z to unto the paste, and try another Paste Special alternative.

FIGURE 12.23

Many Clipboard items default to being pasted as HTML.

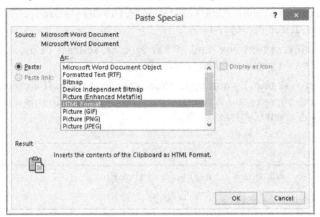

Printing Envelopes and Labels Automatically

Other tools that Word provides to save you time and prevent the need to create certain types of document content from scratch include the tools for printing envelopes and labels. Creating either can be as simple as clicking just a few tools, typing an address, and clicking Print. Word can send envelopes or labels directly to your printer, or it can add an envelope to a letter document so that you can print new envelopes as needed (for example, when you have recurring correspondence with a recipient). Similarly, you can print directly to labels using Word's tools, or you can save the labels to a file. This can be useful when you have recurring needs—such as sending mail to a membership or employee roster—especially when the underlying database doesn't change often.

Printing an Envelope

Use the Envelopes choice in the Create group of the Mailings tab on the Ribbon to start the process for creating an envelope. Here's an overview of the steps in the process; the rest of this section goes into more detail about some of the settings:

1. **Turn on your printer and insert a blank envelope in the appropriate tray with the appropriate orientation.** Most printers have an icon on the tray that indicates how to insert an envelope.

2. **If the recipient's address appears in the current document, select it and press Ctrl+C to copy it.** This will save you a bit of retyping later.

3. **Click the Mailings tab, and then click Envelopes in the Create group.** The Envelopes and Labels dialog box opens.

4. **Click the Delivery address text box, and either type an address or press Ctrl+V to paste any address you previously copied.**

5. **Click the Return address text by and type your return address.** If a previously entered return address appears and it remains correct, you can skip this step. Your finished entries might resemble those in Figure 12.24.

FIGURE 12.24

Enter envelope delivery and return addresses, and click Print.

6. **Click Print to send the document to your printer.**

Specifying the delivery address

With an address selected, when you click the Envelope tool, Word usually copies the selection into the Delivery address field. If nothing is selected, Word will try to guess where the address is, and often gets it right. The more complex the document (usually a letter), however, the worse Word's guesses are. For best results, pre-select the address and copy it to the Clipboard. You can then paste the contents of the Clipboard into the Delivery address field as shown in the example in Figure 12.24.

If you don't already have the address in the document you're writing but it is in your Outlook contacts list, you can insert an address from your contacts list using the Insert Address button above the Delivery address field. Clicking it opens the Select Name dialog box, shown in Figure 12.25. Click the address you want, and then click OK to copy it to the Delivery address field.

FIGURE 12.25

You can use addresses from your Outlook Address Book.

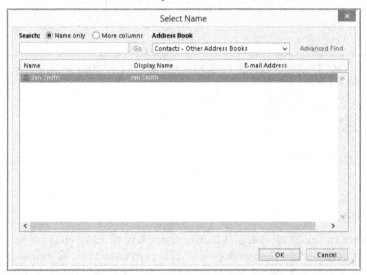

Notice in Figure 12.24 that the delivery and return addresses appear in all capital letters, no punctuation, and with two spaces between the state and ZIP code. The addresses are formatted this way to comply with USPS addressing standards. While the Post Office will deliver your mail even when you don't follow the mailing standards, it's best to get in the habit of following them for envelopes and labels to ensure the most prompt delivery of your items. After entering a Delivery address (or inserting it from your address book) or Return address, select all of the text in the Envelopes and Labels dialog box, right-click it, and click Font. Click to check the All caps check box in the Font dialog box, and then click OK. You can then edit the entry to eliminate punctuation as needed.

Spooifying the return address

By default, for the return address, Word uses the address provided in File ⇨ Options ⇨ Advanced tab ⇨ General ⇨ Mailing address. If you plan to print a lot of envelopes from Word, you can save time in the long run by filling in your complete address there.

Alternatively, you can use an address from your Outlook address book using the button above the field, as described in the "Specifying the delivery address" section. Or you can type an address or paste one in from the Clipboard. If you modify the Return address field in any way (that is, from the way it's supplied from the Advanced tab's Mailing address field) before clicking Print, Word prompts you about whether to make it the default as shown in Figure 12.26. Although Word doesn't indicate this, clicking Yes to the prompt automatically copies this address to the Mailing address field in Word Options, so don't say yes if you're printing an envelope for somebody else who just happens to be visiting.

FIGURE 12.26

If you select Yes here, Word transfers this address to the Mailing address field in the Advanced tab in Word Options.

Choosing options

Use the Options button in the Envelopes and Labels dialog box to make changes to the way Word formats and positions text on the envelope (including envelope size), as well as how Word prints the envelope. Clicking the button opens the Envelope Options dialog box, before you print the envelope.

Envelope options

Use the Envelope Options tab, shown in Figure 12.27, to set the envelope size and to adjust the Delivery and Return address fonts and positions on the envelope. Word provides more than two dozen preset standard envelope sizes. However, if you have something non-standard, set Envelope size to Custom size, enter new Width and Height settings in the Envelope Size dialog box that appears, and click OK.

To change the fonts used for the Delivery or Return addresses for *this envelope only*, click either of the Font buttons and make your changes. You can also change the position of both of the addresses by specifying the distance from the left and top. Choosing Auto leaves everything up to Word, which has preset distances based on the envelope size selected.

FIGURE 12.27

Word offers dozens of built-in envelope sizes, and you can control address appearance and positioning.

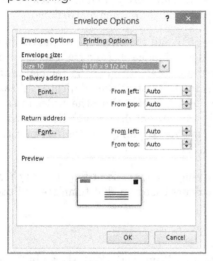

Changing the default envelope formatting

Though Word doesn't let you change the default fonts for the Delivery and Return addresses using the font options shown previously, you can change them by modifying two styles. The methods for fully changing the Return address and Delivery address styles are different, however.

To modify the Return address style, follow the instructions in the "Adding the envelope to the current document" section later in this chapter to add the envelope to the current document. Strictly speaking, this isn't essential, but it makes gaining access to the address style straightforward. You can delete the envelope from the document once you've modified the style.

After the envelope has been added to the document, click in the Return address and press Ctrl+Shift+S to activate the Apply Styles task pane, and note that the Envelope Return style displays under Style Name. In the Apply Styles task pane, click Modify. In the Modify Style dialog box, use the settings provided to change the Return address style as needed. When you're done, enable the New documents based on this template check box, and click OK.

If you want to change just the font or other formatting of the delivery address itself, the process just described will work. However, it will not let you save changes to the position of the delivery address. Did you notice that the delivery address is inside a frame, and that the frame can be used to position the delivery address? Thanks to this clever device, if you want to change the default position of the delivery address, a different method is needed.

Display the Envelopes tab in the Envelopes and Labels dialog box, and ensure that an address is contained inside the Delivery address box. Click Options. Using the Delivery Address Font control, change the font settings as desired. Use the From left and From top text boxes to set the position to the desired location on the envelope. Click OK when you're done.

Back in the Envelopes tab, click Add to Document to add the envelope to the top of the document. Choose File ⇨ Options ⇨ Add Ins. Choose Templates from the Manage drop-down list, and then click Go. Click the Organizer button at the bottom of the Templates and Add-ins dialog box. In the Organizer's Styles tab, in the left list, it should display at least some of the styles in the current document. On the right, it should show the styles in the current document's template. Click Envelope Address in the current document's listing of styles, and then click Copy to copy that style to the template. If prompted, confirm that this is what you want to do, and then click Close.

If prompted later to save changes to the underlying template, don't forget to say Yes. Now any envelopes you create in the future in documents based on that template will use your new Delivery address settings.

Printing options

The other tab in the Envelope Options dialog box is for Printing Options, shown in Figure 12.28. Note that you can also get to the Printing Options tab by double-clicking Feed in the main Envelopes tab of the Envelopes and Labels dialog box. Choose the options you need, set the Feed from source, and click OK.

FIGURE 12.28

Word provides a wide range of positioning options for printing envelopes.

Adding electronic postage and e-postage properties

If you installed electronic postage software, you can add electronic postage by clicking the Add electronic postage option, and adjust your options using E-postage Properties. Different software packages feature different options. If you don't have electronic postage software, you'll see the message box shown in Figure 12.29.

FIGURE 12.29

Word knows whether or not you've installed electronic postage software!

Adding the envelope to the current document

After you enter all the addressing information and set options in the Envelopes and Labels dialog box, you can use the Add to Document option if you want to save an envelope with a letter or other document, rather than clicking Print to send the envelope directly to the printer. For example, suppose you routinely send an invoice once a month, and you're in the habit of using last month's invoice as a template for this month's. If you add the envelope the first time, you won't have to go through the envelope-creation process each time. If your printer trays are flexible, in fact, you can save additional work by having the envelope and letter print to different trays.

The Add to Document option is also useful if you want to change the default formatting (as shown earlier in the "Changing the default envelope formatting" section), or even if you simply want to preview the envelope before committing it to paper.

Creating Labels

Word offers a wide variety of label options that work with hundreds of labels from a number of manufacturers. If you found the box of labels in the office supply store, there's an excellent chance that Word's vast label repertoire can handle it. In those rare cases when you need a label Word has never heard of, there's an excellent chance that it has one that matches the dimensions. Even when that high probability isn't met, you can still use the custom label feature to create one that works.

The label creation process works similar to creating and printing an envelope. To begin, click Labels in the create group of the Mailings tab on the Ribbon to display the Labels tab of the Envelopes and Labels dialog box, shown in Figure 12.30. If the current document contains something that Word thinks is an address, it will use that address in the Address field. Type or paste the address in the Address field as needed. Or if you're creating return address labels, click to enable Use return address to insert your address from the Mailing address field in the Advanced tab in Word Options.

FIGURE 12.30

Print a single label or a full sheet.

Choosing a label type

To select the label type that matches the printable labels you purchased, click the label preview in the Label section, or click the Options button. Both display the Label Options dialog box shown in Figure 12.31. Under Printer information, select the type of printer you have. Though you might not have seen a tractor feed or continuous feed impact printer or matrix printer in the past 10 years or so, they do still exist. Many shipping companies still use them precisely because they are an efficient way of having thousands of labels at the ready. Chances are good that most Bible readers, however, have single sheet–oriented printers (which covers most laser and inkjet printers), so you can likely just leave the Page printers option button selected.

Under Label information, choose the maker of the labels you purchased from the Label vendors drop-down list, and then select the Product number for the labels you are printing. Note that the size information is shown under Label information.

FIGURE 12.31

In Label Options, you can select any of literally hundreds of different labels.

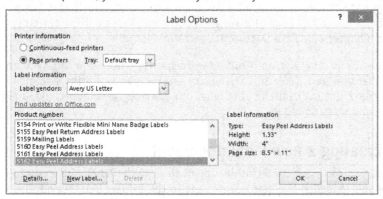

For additional information, as well as to modify the label if the default settings don't meet your needs, click the Details button to display the dialog box shown in Figure 12.32. Notice that when you change any of the settings, the Label name, which begins as grayed out, suddenly becomes available for editing. Type a new name. If you're using a given label, it's not a bad idea to make the new name a variation of the built-in name. If you know from the outset that you're going to create a custom label, you can use the New Label button instead of Details. Either way, click OK when you finish creating the new label format.

FIGURE 12.32

It's easy to modify a label's settings.

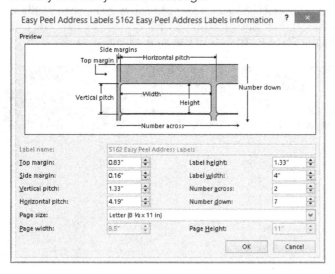

Choosing how many to print

As shown in Figure 12.30, Word can print a full page of the same label, or it can print a single label. What about a full page of different addresses? That's a different story and one that gets told in Chapter 22, "Data Documents and Mail Merge."

If you choose the Single label option, Word lets you specify which Row and Column on the sheet of labels that you want to print to. If you're careful, you can print a single label from a sheet, use the next slot over for the next label (for example, at a later time), and so on. This helps you avoid wasting labels.

Printing or creating a new label document

As for envelopes, you can click the Print document to send the label(s) directly to the printer. Be sure you've loaded the blank label page in the printer beforehand. Use the New Document button to create a new document containing the label(s). In the new document, you'll see that the label feature relies heavily upon Word's table formatting, as shown in Figure 12.33. To make it perfectly obvious that this is a table, it might be necessary to turn on gridline display as well as nonprinting formatting marks. To turn on gridlines, in the Table Tools Layout tab, click View Gridlines in the Table group. To turn on nonprinting formatting marks, press Ctrl+Shift+8. Now both gridlines and cell markers should be visible.

> **NOTE**
>
> When Single label is selected on the Labels tab of the Envelopes and Labels dialog box, the New Document option is grayed out as unavailable. That's because the option doesn't make sense for a single label.

If you want to use multiple addresses on a sheet, this is the first step. You can, of course, type the addresses into the table cells shown. Or you can convert the current file into a data document (a la mail merge), associate a data file with it, and populate the cells with Word merge fields. See Chapter 22 to learn how to use mail merge.

> **TIP**
>
> Rather than go through the steps of creating a new sheet of labels each time you need to print some, you can either save a labels document as a template or save the label table as a Quick Part or a Building Block.

FIGURE 12.33

When you insert a page of labels, the Table Tools contextual tabs appear.

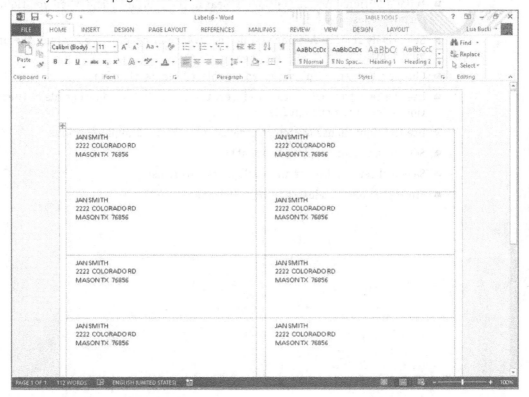

Summary

In this chapter you've learned about a number of automated features in Word 2013 that help you build particular types of document content or reuse content that you've already created. Among other things, now you know how to:

- Create your own Building Blocks
- Make some Building Blocks appear in the Quick Parts gallery
- Back up and share your Building Blocks

- Use AutoComplete to insert Building Block content
- Make Additional Actions options appear in the shortcut menu when you right-click certain types of text
- Selectively remove Actions you neither want nor need, while keeping the ones you want
- Choose whether to link or embed an object from another file
- Use the Text from File option to insert the contents from another file at the insertion point in the current file
- Use the right mouse button strategically to control dropping options
- Set up and print envelopes and labels
- Save a sheet of labels or an envelope for future use
- Store your return address in Word Options

Part IV

Illustrating Your Story with Graphics

I f you've ever prepared a corporate annual report, you're familiar with why various graphical features go a long way in enhancing communication. Financial results that take pages to describe offer can be succinctly summarized in a half-page chart or spreadsheet-like table. In other cases, visual elements can be purely decorative, as is often the case with drop caps and symbols. Or elements such as WordArt and text boxes containing pull quotes can be used to set off or highlight information. Part IV explores graphical features beyond mere words, showing you how you can use tables, charts, SmartArt, pictures, WordArt, drop caps, text boxes, shapes, symbols, and equations to illustrate and illuminate the message in any document.

Chapter 13 explores the intricacies and nuances of tables, charts, and SmartArt, all of which can be used to summarize or illustrate data. Chapter 14 shows you how to add pictures and WordArt to show as well as tell your story. Chapter 15 shows you how to insert symbols and equations, as well as adding shapes, drop caps, and text boxes to set off or emphasize information.

IN THIS PART

Chapter 13
Building Tables, Charts, and SmartArt to Show Data and Process

Chapter 14
Adding Pictures and WordArt to Highlight Information

Chapter 15
Adding Drop Caps, Text Boxes, Shapes, Symbols, and Equations

Building Tables, Charts, and SmartArt to Show Data and Process

T
ables, SmartArt, and charts enable you to illustrate data and processes in documents. They're extremely flexible and easy to create and manipulate. Thanks to numerous galleries, it's easy to create professional-looking tables and SmartArt or chart graphics quickly and with minimal effort. Live Preview also comes into play when you work with tables. This chapter teaches you about these features in Word.

Getting a Quick Start with Quick Tables

The quickest way to create a table in Word is to use one that already exists. It might not be exactly what you want, but it often will be closer to what you want and save you a lot of formatting and setup versus creating a table from scratch. It helps if you can see a picture, of course, and Word 2013 includes a Quick Tables gallery from which you can select a predefined table to insert in the current document. After you click to position the insertion point at the location where you want to insert the table, click the Insert tab. Click the Table button in the Tables group of the Insert tab, and then point to Quick Tables. The gallery shown in Figure 13.1 appears.

FIGURE 13.1

The Quick Tables gallery offers a number of preformatted tables.

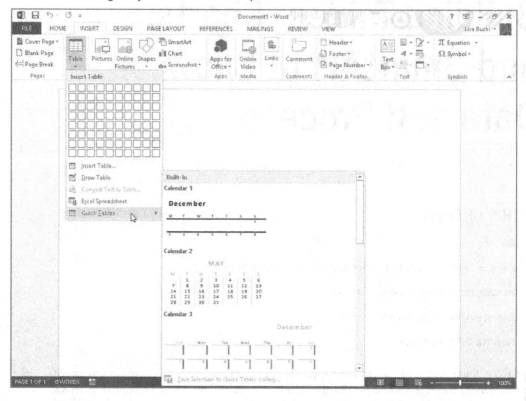

Scroll through the gallery to see if there's a table design you like—something that compares favorably with the table you envision. If there is, click on it. If it has too many rows, you can delete the ones you don't need. If it has too few columns, you can add a few more. If the proportions and other attributes aren't quite right, you can use Word's table tools to make them right. The point is that you hit the ground running

Table Basics

One way to think about a table is as a container for information. The container consists of horizontal rows and vertical columns. If someone speaks of a five-by-four (5 × 4) table, by convention and agreement this refers to a table that's five columns high and four rows wide.

If the terminology is foreign to you, think of rows as you would the windows across each floor of a skyscraper. Think of columns as the vertical columns of windows on the same skyscraper building. Rows go across, and columns go up and down.

Inserting a table from scratch

There are three basic methods for creating a table from scratch. One is to use the Table tool to select the numbers of rows and columns you want. On the Insert tab, click Table in the Tables group. Drag the mouse pointer down through the Insert Table grid. As you move the mouse, the selected table dimensions change, and Word shows a Live Preview in the document window, as shown in Figure 13.2. Click the mouse when the table has the number of rows and columns you want.

FIGURE 13.2

When a 6 × 4 table is selected in the Insert Table grid, a 6 × 4 Live Preview appears in the document window.

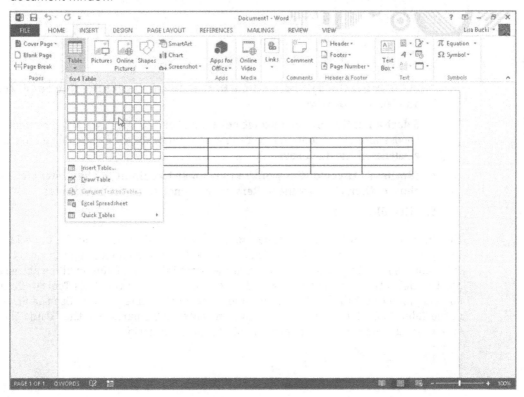

A second method for creating a table from scratch is by using the Insert Table dialog box, as follows:

1. **On the Insert tab, click Table in the Tables group, and click Insert Table.** The Insert Table dialog box shown in Figure 13.3 appears.

FIGURE 13.3

The Insert Table dialog box enables you to choose the number of columns and rows and specify additional settings when creating a table.

2. **Enter or use the spinner buttons to specify entries for the Number of columns and Number of rows.**

3. **Select an option under AutoFit behavior.** You can specify a Fixed column width or choose AutoFit to contents or AutoFit to window to make the table adjust to other elements of the document.

4. **(Optional) If you'd like Word to remember to default to the dimensions you choose, then click to check Remember dimensions for new tables.**

5. **Click OK.**

The third method for inserting a table from scratch is to draw it using the Draw Table tool. To begin, choose Insert ➪ Tables ➪ Table ➪ Draw Table. Drag a rectangle to establish the outer boundary of the table, and then use the Draw Table tool (which will be active at that point by default) to draw out the desired cells. Use the tools in the Table Tools ➪ Design tab's Borders group to set line style, weight, and color for the table borders. Use the Eraser tool in the Table Tools ➪ Layout tab to remove unwanted table parts. See the "Using the table eraser" section later in this chapter for additional information.

Cell markers and gridlines

When nonprinting formatting marks are displayed (Ctrl+Shift+8 or Home tab ⇨ Paragraph ⇨ Show/Hide), cell markers display in each cell, showing where the cells are, as indicated in Figure 13.4. You might wonder why cell markers are needed if the table borders show the location of cells. That's because not every table has borders. If a borderless table's gridlines aren't displayed, you might not even know a table is there. Toggling the nonprinting cell markers provide visibility for the table cells. Cell markers, incidentally, display whenever paragraph marks do.

When a table has no borders, it's a good idea to display table gridlines. These are non-printing marks that show the cell's dimensions. To display gridlines, click the View Gridlines choice in the Table group at the left end of the Table Tools Layout tab. See Figure 13.4.

FIGURE 13.4

Show hidden characters to display cell markers.

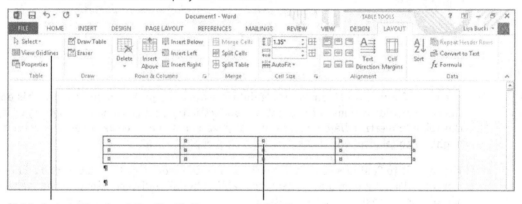

Click to display gridlines for a table without borders   Cell marker

Managing AutoFit behavior

Notice the AutoFit behavior options shown in the Insert Table dialog box in Figure 13.3. These same AutoFit options are also available when you move the mouse pointer over the table, right-click the table move handle that appears at the upper left, and then point to AutoFit, as shown in Figure 13.5. The AutoFit settings enable you to size the table and its columns automatically.

FIGURE 13.5

Right-click the table move handle to display a shortcut menu with table options, including AutoFit.

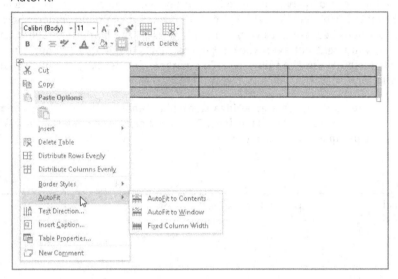

The Fixed Column Width option is straightforward enough. When you choose this option, the column widths remain fixed unless you explicitly change them by dragging or by using the Table Properties dialog box. Note that *fixed* is not the same as *equal*. The column widths might be equal also, but that's a different concept.

The AutoFit to Contents command causes a table to automatically resize as you add or remove material. It's not a temporary setting, so table columns widths continue to change when you add or remove text in existing cells.

Think of the AutoFit to Window command as "AutoFit to left and right margins." This option means that the table will remain as wide as the document text itself. If you add text disproportionately to any given column, that column will automatically resize, making the other columns correspondingly narrower. But the table itself will maintain the width of the document text.

Inserting a table based on existing content

As suggested earlier in this book, there is a correspondence between the word *tab* and the word *table*. Although the proportion of the word processing population that was raised on typewriters is rapidly dwindling, those who took typing classes learned how to fashion tables using the tab stops and the Tab key. Tab stops are metal hardware on a typewriter that literally stop the carriage when you press the Tab key.

Microsoft knows that *tab* and *table* both have the same root. As a result, Word can readily convert your tab-delineated tables into real tables, and it even can convert information delimited with other characters such as commas. If for some reason you want to convert a table back to text, Word can perform that transformation, too.

Converting text to a table

If the text is set up with tabs between the "columns," you can use the Insert Table command to convert to a table immediately. Select the text, and then in the Tables group of the Insert tab click Table ⇨ Insert Table. Word instantly determines how many rows and columns there are and presents your data in a table. Figure 13.6 shows some selected tabbed text, and a copy of that text below converted to a table with the Insert Table command. Word automatically AutoFits the new table to the width of the document, so you might need to resize columns.

FIGURE 13.6

Word easily converts a tabbed "table" into an actual Word table.

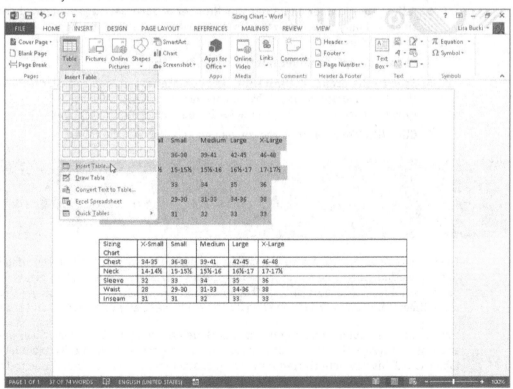

If you want control over the number of rows or columns or have text that's delimited by something other than tabs, you can use the Convert Text to Table dialog box to perform the conversion. For example, you might have a document exported from a spreadsheet or database program as a .csv (comma-separated values) or .txt (plain text) file using delimiters. Or someone may have manually delimited a list with another character, such as an asterisk. Here's how to make sure Word cleanly converts this type of content to a table:

1. **Select the list of text or data to be converted.** You can usually open a comma-separated values file or plain text file directly in Word, but you may have to import other types of files.

2. **Click Insert ➪ Tables ➪ Table ➪ Convert Text to Table.** This displays the Convert Text to Table dialog box, shown in Figure 13.7.

3. **Adjust the Number of columns or Number of rows settings as needed.** These settings will only be active when Word evaluates that there may be more than one way to divide the data.

4. **Choose an option under AutoFit behavior.**

5. **Specify the proper delimiter under Separate text at.** You can choose Paragraphs (for the paragraph mark), Tabs, or Commas; or you can click the Other option and type the custom delimiter character in the accompanying text box.

6. **Click OK.** Word performs the conversion and displays the table.

The Convert Text to Table dialog box can be a useful diagnostic tool when the simple text to table method presented earlier (Insert ➪ Tables ➪ Table ➪ Insert Table) yields unexpected results, such as more or fewer columns than you expected. When you get the wrong table dimensions, press Ctrl+Z, investigate the data, make any corrections, and try again.

You can get the wrong number of columns if there are too many tabs (sometimes obscured as a result of formatting issues) or if some rows use spaces instead of tabs to achieve the table "look." Display nonprinting formatting characters by clicking Show/Hide in the

Paragraph group of the Home tab. You might, for example, find instances where multiple tabs were typed between columns. This confuses Word, which assumes there are more columns than needed. When this happens dismiss the dialog box, find and remove the extra tabs, and try again. Don't worry about setting a properly aligned tab, because you're converting the tabbed data into a table anyway; the table will handle the alignment for you.

FIGURE 13.7

The Convert Text to Table dialog box guesses how many rows and columns you want to create.

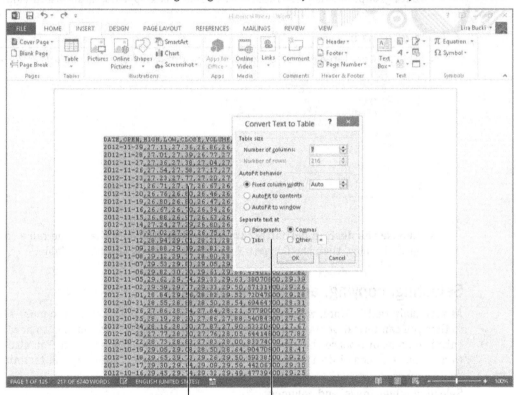

Selected comma-delimited text   Select or specify the delimiter here

Converting tables to text

Sometimes it's necessary or useful to convert an existing table to text. You might want to do this if the data needs to be provided to someone else in a different form. Some statistical programs will accept .csv data, but not Word tables. Or you might simply find it easier to manipulate the data in text form, and then transform it back into a table. Whatever the reason, it's easy:

1. **Save your document.**

2. **Move the mouse pointer over the table you want to convert, and then click the table move handle when it appears.** Word selects the entire table and the Table Tools contextual tabs appear.

3. **Click the Table Tools ⇨ Layout contextual tab, and click Convert to Text in the Data group.** The Convert Table to Text dialog box appears, as shown in Figure 13.8.

FIGURE 13.8

The Convert Table to Text dialog box prompts you to specify a delimiter for text.

4. **Choose the desired delimiter, and then click OK.** Note that if the table contains nested tables, then the Convert Nested Tables option will be available.

Selecting, copying, and moving in tables

As with plain text in Word, when working with a table you need to be able to make selections so that you can format or manipulate the contents. With a table, it's common to need to select entire columns or rows so that you can apply uniform formatting to them. You also might want to move or copy information in the table which requires a few special techniques.

Selecting tables, rows, and columns

Word offers multiple techniques for making selections in tables. For example, when you want to select an entire table, you can use one of these quick methods:

- Move the mouse pointer over the table to display the table move handle, and then click it.

- Click anywhere in the table to reveal the Table Tools contextual tabs, shown in Figure 13.9. Click the Layout tab, and then click Select ⇨ Select Table in the Tables group.

FIGURE 13.9

Use the Layout contextual tab to access a number of table selection and manipulation tools.

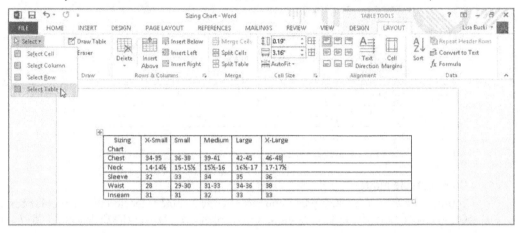

There is also a keyboard method for selecting tables, but it's a nuisance to remember and to use. With the insertion point anywhere in the table, and Num Lock engaged, press Alt+Shift+5 on the number pad. If Num Lock isn't engaged, press Shift+5 on the number pad instead. You also can click in the table and use KeyTips: press Alt, and then press JLKT, one key at a time. Another method is to use the arrow keys to move the insertion point to the upper-left cell. Press and hold Shift, and use the Down Arrow and Right Arrow keys to extend the selection highlight over all table cells.

Another table selection method involves dragging from outside the table after clicking in the table. Dragging from a location diagonally above and to the left of the table move handle down over the lower-right cell selects the entire table. Or, you can drag from outside the lower-right corner to the upper-left cell until all cells are highlighted.

To select a row without using the Ribbon, move the mouse pointer into the margin to the left of the row until it changes to a right-tilting arrow as shown in Figure 13.10, and click. Drag to expand the selection to include contiguous rows, or Ctrl+click using the Select Row pointer to select additional noncontiguous rows.

To select a column without using the Ribbon, move the mouse pointer just above the column so that it turns into a down-pointing black arrow, and click. Again, drag to expand the selection to include additional contiguous columns, or Ctrl+click to select additional discrete/noncontiguous columns.

You also can use the Select drop-down list in the Table Group of the Table Tools ⇨ Layout contextual tab. As shown in Figure 13.9, the menu includes Select Column and Select Row commands that you can choose to select the table column or row that currently holds the insertion point.

FIGURE 13.10

Word's mouse pointer changes shape to indicate what action a click will perform.

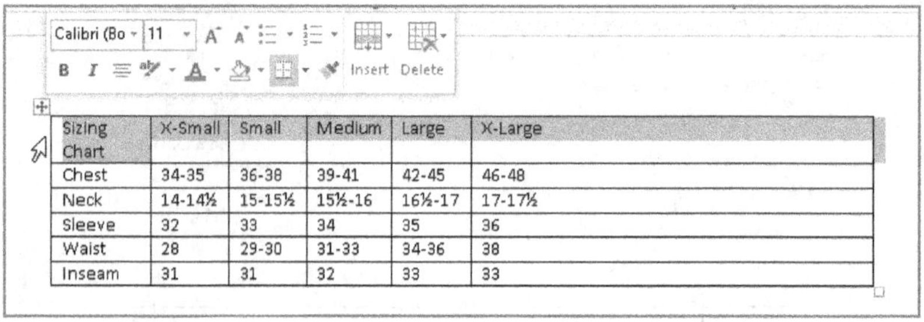

Sizing Chart	X-Small	Small	Medium	Large	X-Large
Chest	34-35	36-38	39-41	42-45	46-48
Neck	14-14½	15-15½	15½-16	16½-17	17-17½
Sleeve	32	33	34	35	36
Waist	28	29-30	31-33	34-36	38
Inseam	31	31	32	33	33

Copying table matter

You use the same copy and paste choices to copy a table selection as for regular text. Use Copy and Paste in the Clipboard group of the Home tab, or use the Ctrl+C and Ctrl+V shortcuts.

When copying all or part of a table from one table to another, you need to consider the dimensions of the source and the target. Sometimes when you paste into the new table the whole table is pasted into a single cell rather than individual rows or columns.

As a general rule, when you're pasting table matter the receiving table dimensions should match the source dimensions. If you're trying to paste a 4 × 5 set of cells into a table whose dimensions are 6 × 8, copy the 4 × 5 source to the Clipboard, select the desired 4 × 5 location in the receiving table, and then paste. Pasting without first selecting sometimes works, but sometimes it doesn't. The situation can get even weirder when you're pasting between Word and Excel, so have that Ctrl+Z (Undo) command standing by.

To control what happens with respect to formatting, see the File ➪ Options ➪ Advanced ➪ Cut, copy, and paste section. Use the top four pasting options to specify what happens when you paste under a variety of circumstances. If necessary, temporarily enable the desired behavior, perform the paste, and then go back to reset the defaults.

Moving and copying columns

To move one or more adjacent columns within a table, select them and then drag to the desired column. Release the mouse button anywhere in the destination column. The selected column(s) will move to the position of the destination column, which will scoot to the right. To move one or more selected columns to the right of the rightmost column, drop the selection at what appears to be outside the right edge of the table. As shown in Figure 13.11, when you have nonprinting characters displayed, cell markers also appear to the right of the table's right boundary. When moving columns to the right side of the table, drop them on those exterior markers.

FIGURE 13.11

Drag to the right of the cell markers outside the table to move a column there.

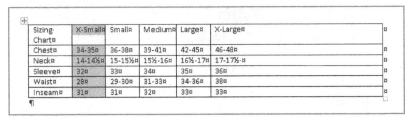

To copy one or more columns, hold the Ctrl key as you drop. The selection will be inserted at the drop point, using the same location rules that apply when you're moving columns.

When moving a column between tables, it's probably easier to use the Cut and Paste commands in the Clipboard group of the Home tab (or use Ctrl+X and Ctrl+V).

Moving and copying rows

You can move and copy rows in the same way as columns, except with respect to the last row. The last row does not have exterior cell markers. If you drop a selection of one or more rows onto the last row of a table, the selection will be placed above the last row. If you drop it after the last row, the selection will be appended to the table, but the formatting will often change.

Instead, when you want to move rows after the last current row, drop them on the last row. Then put the insertion point anywhere in the last row and press Alt+Shift+Up Arrow to move the stubborn last row up to where you want it.

> **TIP**
>
> Any time you want to move table rows around, Alt+Shift+Up Arrow and Alt+Shift+Down Arrow can be used to push the current row up or down in the table. If you're moving a single row you don't need to select anything. If you're moving multiple contiguous rows, select them first.

Changing table properties

If you need to set precise table settings, click Properties in the Table group of the Table Tools ⇨ Layout contextual tab, or right-click a table and choose Table Properties to display the dialog box shown in Figure 13.12. Use the Table tab to control overall layout and behavior; use the other tabs or the mouse to control row, column, and cell characteristics.

13

FIGURE 13.12

Use Table Properties to control overall alignment, indentation, and positioning of tables.

Preferred width

Check Preferred width and enter a measurement in the accompanying text box to set a target width for the table. The preferred width can't be absolute, however, because tables contain text and data, and are further constrained by paper and margin settings. Note that AutoFit settings override the Preferred width.

Alignment

Table alignment affects the entire table with respect to the current left and right margins. If the table extends from the left margin to the right margin, which is the default for tables inserted in Word, then the alignment controls seemingly will have no effect. This makes it easy not to notice if they're changed. If you later narrow the table, its placement on the page might suddenly seem askew. You can be sure you're centering a table by choosing Center under Alignment on the Table tab of the Table Properties dialog box.

The Indent from left setting on the tab controls how far the table is from the left margin. There is no Ribbon control for this setting, and it cannot be set with the ruler line.

Note that Indent from left is available only when Text wrapping is set to None and Alignment is set to Left. When Around text wrapping is enabled, use Positioning to set the distance from the left, as shown in the section that follows.

Text wrapping and moving a table

You can insert a table inline with other text, or if it is smaller than the full document width, you can move or drag it into position so that text outside the table wraps around it, as shown in Figure 13.13. To have this flexibility, change the Text wrapping setting in the Table tab of the Table Properties dialog box to Around. Dragging a table into a new position using the table move handle automatically changes the Text wrapping setting from None to Around.

FIGURE 13.13

Wrap text around tables for a more integrated appearance.

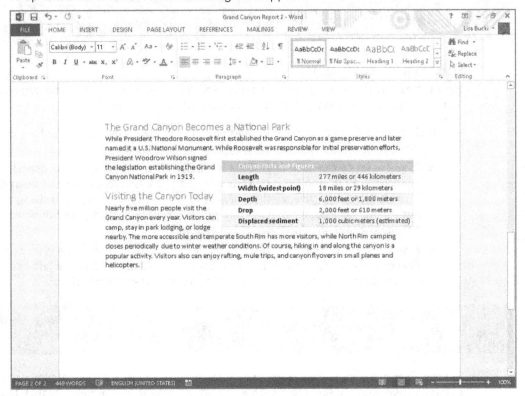

Clicking the Positioning button opens a Table Positioning dialog box. You can choose Horizontal and Vertical Position settings, and set the Distance from surrounding text for each side of the table. The Move with Text option controls whether the table's vertical position is governed by the paragraph to which it is anchored. If Move with Text is enabled, the vertical position can be relative to only paragraph. Use this setting if the paragraph's content and the table's content are interrelated so that the table would not make sense except when near that paragraph. This often is the setting you want for research reports.

Turn off Move with Text if the location of the table is not logically tied to a particular paragraph. This setting might be more in keeping with the design of a brochure or a newsletter in which the table's contents are relevant to the entire document and should appear in a particular location for aesthetic reasons.

> **TIP**
>
> When you paste a table with Ctrl+V or the Paste button in the Clipboard group of the Home tab, you can click the Paste Options button and choose a format for the pasted table.

Sizing a table, row, or column

Word tables feature several kinds of handles and mouse pointers that enable you to manipulate and select cells, rows, columns, and entire tables, for example:

- If you point to the lower-right corner of a table, the mouse pointer changes to a two-headed diagonal arrow. Drag it to resize the table.

- If you point to the bottom gridline or border for a table row, the mouse pointer changes to a resizing pointer, with a double black horizontal bar and up and down arrows. Drag when you see that pointer to resize the row height. Resizing rows is not usually necessary, because they will automatically change height when you change the font size for the text in the row.

- If you point to the right gridline or border for a table column, the mouse pointer changes to a resizing pointer, with a double black vertical bar and left and right arrows. Drag when you see that pointer to resize the column width.

> **TIP**
>
> Double-click the right column border with the resizing pointer to automatically fit the column width to its contents.

In other instances, you might need to be more precise about row and column sizes. For example, if you have a document such as an annual report or a product quality testing report, it's desirable to make column widths fairly consistent to make the report look more orderly. When that's the case, you can use the Row and Column tabs in the Table Properties dialog box to change the size for the selected row or column:

- **Row tab:** Leave Specify height checked, and enter a size in the accompanying text box. If you want to make the size more permanent, change the Row height is setting from At least to Exactly. Use the Previous Row and Next Row buttons to move to other rows to format, and click OK when done.

- **Column tab:** Leave Preferred width checked and enter a specific width (Figure 13.14). Use the Previous Column and Next Column buttons to choose the settings for other columns as desired, and click OK when finished.

FIGURE 13.14

Enter precise row and column heights on the Row and Column tabs.

Working with Table Layout and Design

Word 2013's Table Tools ⇨ Design and Layout contextual tabs provide you with most of what you need to create tables that are both aesthetically appealing and functional. The Design tab tools enable you to improve the table's appearance. The tools on the Layout tab help you ensure that the table presents information in a logical way that is meaningful to the reader.

So far we've looked at a number of basic tools that help you achieve the right structure for your tables. In this section we're going to look at how to mold tables into shape and then polish them for your audience.

NOTE

Many of the Ribbon commands described in this section are also available in the right-click shortcut menu.

Modifying table layout

We all know that situations, ideas, and data change. Let's look at how to cope with changes that impact the structure of data in a table.

All references to the Layout tab in this section refer to the Table Tools ➪ Layout contextual tab to keep the descriptions brief. None of the Layout tab tools provide Live Preview, so carefully review the impact of any layout change and use Ctrl+Z to undo a change immediately if it doesn't have the desired impact.

Deleting table, row, column, and cell contents

Sometimes you need to trim your tables by deleting rows or columns. Sometimes you have to delete the entire table, which is one of Word's less intuitive processes. If you select a table and press the Delete key, the data inside the table is deleted, but the table rows and columns remain. The same thing sometimes happens when you try to delete a cell, a row, or a column.

> **TIP**
>
> If the table is part of a larger selection of text with text both above and below the table selected, then pressing Delete does remove the table as well as the additionally selected text.

Rather than say this a half dozen times, let's just say it once. If you want to remove the contents of a cell, row, column, or table, select what you want to remove and press the Delete key. In the sections that follow we'll be looking at table structure, not contents.

Deleting a table

You can use any of the following methods to delete an entire table:

- Click anywhere in the table and in the Layout tab click Delete in the Rows & Columns group and click Delete Table, as shown in Figure 13.15. Word deletes the table immediately.

FIGURE 13.15

Delete the current cell, column, row, or table using the Layout tab's Delete menu.

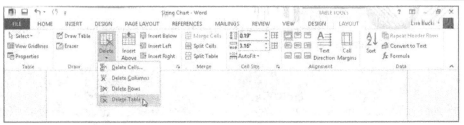

- Move the mouse pointer over the table, right-click the table move handle, and then click Cut.
- Select the table using the method of your choice, and then press Backspace.

Deleting rows, columns, and cells

To delete the current row or column, use techniques similar to deleting the table. Select the row(s), column(s), or cell(s) and press Backspace, or choose Layout ⇨ Delete ⇨ Delete Rows; Layout ⇨ Delete ⇨ Columns; or Layout ⇨ Delete ⇨ Cells.

When deleting cells, Word needs a little more information. The Delete Cells dialog box shown in Figure 13.16 prompts you to specify how to shift remaining cells, or whether you in fact really mean to delete the row or column. Make your selection and click OK.

FIGURE 13.16

Word prompts to find out how to handle the rest of the column or row when you delete a single cell.

Inserting rows, columns, and cells

To insert a row or column into a table, click in the row or column adjacent to where you want to insert, and then click Insert Above, Insert Below, Insert Left, or Insert Right in the Rows & Columns group of the Layout tab (refer to Figure 13.15), depending on where you want the new row or column to appear.

> **TIP**
>
> To add a new row to the end of an existing table, place the insertion point at the end of the entry in the bottom-right cell and press the Tab key. To add a new interior row, click outside the right side of the table above where you want the new row to appear, and press Enter.

To insert multiple rows or columns you have a couple of options. Select the number of rows or columns you want to insert, and then click the appropriate insert tool. Word will insert as many rows or columns as you have selected.

Word 2013 also includes a new method for inserting one or more rows or columns. Just select the number of rows or columns to insert with the mouse, and then move the mouse pointer to the side of the selection where you want to insert the new rows or columns. As shown in Figure 13.17, a divider with a plus button appears. Click the plus to insert the specified number of rows or columns at the divider. In the example in Figure 13.17, because two columns are selected and the divider is to the right of the selection, clicking the plus would insert two new columns to the right of the selection.

FIGURE 13.17

Click the plus button that appears to insert new rows or columns in the specified position.

Sizing Chart	X-Small	Small	Medium	Large	X-Large
Chest	34-35	36-38	39-41	42-45	46-48
Neck	14-14½	15-15½	15½-16	16½-17	17-17½
Sleeve	32	33	34	35	36
Waist	28	29-30	31-33	34-36	38
Inseam	31	31	32	33	33

To insert cells, select the cell(s) adjacent to where you want the new one(s) to appear, and click the dialog box launcher in the bottom-right corner of the Rows & Columns group in the Layout tab. You'll see a dialog box containing the identical options shown in Figure 13.16. Choose your desired action and click OK.

Controlling how tables break

Sometimes you don't particularly care how tables break across pages, but sometimes you do. When you need to keep certain rows together on a page:

1. **Select the rows in question.**
2. **Click Properties in the Table group of the Layout tab (or right-click the selection and choose Table Properties from the shortcut menu).**
3. **Click the Row tab, and under Options uncheck the Allow row to break across pages check box.**
4. **Click OK.**

To force a table to break at a particular point, move the insertion point to anywhere in the row where you want the break to occur, and then press Ctrl+Enter. Note that this doesn't simply force the table to break at that point; it actually breaks the table into two tables. If the Repeat as header row at the top of each page setting on the Row tab of the Table Properties dialog box is enabled for the first row(s) of the original table, it won't be inherited by the "new" table. You'll have to copy the heading row to the new table and reinstate the setting, if needed.

Merging table cells

Sometimes you need to merge columns, rows, or cells. For example, it's common to merge the cells in the top row of a table to create one larger cell to hold a title for the table. Merging cells is easy. Select the cells you want to merge and click Merge Cells in the Merge group of the Layout tab (refer to Figure 13.15).

TIP

You also can use the table eraser in the Layout tab's Draw group. Click the Eraser tool, and then click on the table gridline or border segment to remove. To turn the eraser off, click its Ribbon button again, or press the Esc key.

Word can't really merge rows or columns. Suppose you need to merge the cells from two columns into a single column on each row. What you want to end up with is the same number of rows with one less column. If you select both columns and click Merge Cells, however, Word treats that as a request to merge all the cells in the selection, and you end up with one big cell with the entries jumbled together. This is illustrated in Figure 13.18. The HIGH and LOW columns were merged, resulting in one big cell of useless data. There is no way around this. To get the desired result, you would have to select the HIGH and LOW column entries on each row and merge them individually.

FIGURE 13.18

Word cannot merge into multiple cells.

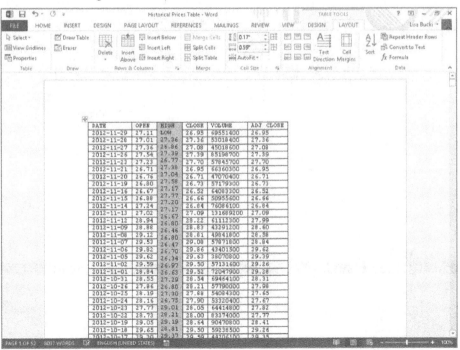

13

> **NOTE**
>
> If you are also an Excel user, you could use Excel to merge columns of data as in the previous example. Excel has functions that enable you to join text from two separate cells into a single entry.

Splitting cells, rows, and columns

At first it seemed that one cell, row, or column was fine, but later you decide that the logic of the table layout calls for two (or more) cells where there once was one If you split a cell that holds text, the text will remain in the left or upper-left cell in the split group. In Figure 13.19, the cell with X-Large in it was split into three cells, as illustrated by the settings in the Split Cells dialog box.

FIGURE 13.19

When you split cells, specify how many rows and columns you want to create.

To perform a split, select the cell(s) to split, click Split cells in the Merge group of the Layout tab, make Number of columns and Number of rows entries as needed in the Split Cells dialog box, and click OK.

Horizontal splits or splits where you start by selecting multiple rows or columns are often harder to control. The trick is to make sure that items are horizontally displayed and separated either by at least two spaces or by a tab (press Ctrl+Tab to insert a tab inside a table). It can still be tedious, but it's a bit more direct than using the dialog box, and you have more control and precision.

Cell size

When you're using a table to lay out a fill-in form, cell measurements sometimes have to be precise, especially when you're trying to align a Word document with preprinted forms. When cell height and width need to be controlled precisely, click the Table Row Height or Table Column Width boxes in the Cell Size group on the Layout tab, shown in Figure 13.20. Note that cell height cannot vary for any cell within any given row.

FIGURE 13.20

Use the Cell Size group on the Layout tab to specify the precise height and width of rows and columns.

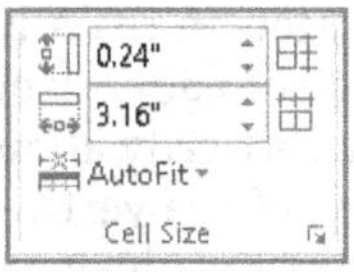

When you need rows to have a uniform height, click the Distribute Rows button to the right of the Table Row Height text box. If rows are of different heights—as sometimes happens when you're converting part of an Excel spreadsheet into a Word table—this command determines the optimal height and equalizes the height of all selected rows or of all rows in the table if no rows are selected.

Similarly, click Distribute Columns (found to the right of the Table Column Width text box) to set selected or all columns to the same width. If different rows have different widths, this command will not equalize the whole table. It works only when all the rows have the same width. If any differ (for example, if row two is 4 inches and all the other rows are 3.5 inches, giving the table a ragged left and/or right edge), it won't equalize them all. To remedy this, drag the right border(s) of shorter or longer rows so that they all align on the left and right.

Alignment

The Alignment group of the Layout tab offers nine cell alignment options, as shown at the left in Figure 13.21. To change how the contents align horizontally or vertically within any cell, click in or select the cells you want to change, and then click the desired tool. As noted elsewhere, many users confuse cell alignment with table alignment. With the whole table selected, this tool will at most set the individual alignment of each cell and won't have any effect on table alignment. Instead, select the whole table and use the Paragraph group alignment tools in the Home tab, or use the Alignment setting in the Table Properties dialog box.

FIGURE 13.21

Word offers nine options for cell alignment, as well as the ability to change text direction and cell margins.

Text direction

To control text direction in selected table cells, click the Text Direction tool in the Alignment group of the Layout tab. This command toggles the text between the normal horizontal layout, to text vertically aligned at the right side of the cell, to text vertically aligned at the left side of the cell. For example, you may prefer to change to one of the vertical alignments when the titles in the top row of the table are wider than the rest of the entries in the column and you're having trouble fitting the table horizontally on the page. Formatting the titles vertically would enable you to make the columns narrower to better fit the table on the page.

Cell margins and cell spacing

Word provides several kinds of controls for cell margins. *Cell margin* is the distance between cell contents and cell walls. Proper margins can keep cells from becoming too crowded and unreadable. Additional spacing can also prevent data from printing over the borders when you're using a table to format data for printing on preprinted forms. To set cell margins and cell spacing, click Cell Margins in the Alignment group of the Layout tab, shown in Figure 13.21. This displays the Table Options dialog box shown in Figure 13.22.

Despite the name of the Default cell margins section of the dialog box, it does not set the *default* cell margins or spacing for tables. It sets the cell margins only for the currently selected table, and the settings you enter apply to all cells in the table.

The Allow spacing between cells setting under Default cell spacing in the Table Options dialog box can be used to create the effect shown in Figure 13.23. This gives the table the appearance of having a distinct box inside each table cell.

FIGURE 13.22

If your table is too crowded, increase the default cell margins.

FIGURE 13.23

Cell spacing can give tables a dramatic appearance.

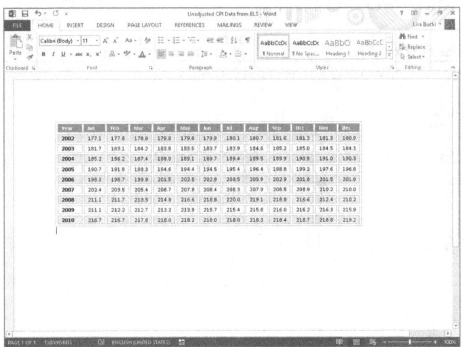

Year	Jan	Feb	Mar	Apr	May	Jun	Jul	Aug	Sep	Oct	Nov	Dec
2002	177.1	177.8	178.8	179.8	179.8	179.9	180.1	180.7	181.0	181.3	181.3	180.9
2003	181.7	183.1	184.2	183.8	183.5	183.7	183.9	184.6	185.2	185.0	184.5	184.3
2004	185.2	186.2	187.4	188.0	189.1	189.7	189.4	189.5	189.9	190.9	191.0	190.3
2005	190.7	191.8	193.3	194.6	194.4	194.5	195.4	196.4	198.8	199.2	197.6	196.8
2006	198.3	198.7	199.8	201.5	202.5	202.9	203.5	203.9	202.9	201.8	201.5	201.8
2007	202.4	203.5	205.4	206.7	207.9	208.4	208.3	207.9	208.5	208.9	210.2	210.0
2008	211.1	211.7	213.5	214.8	216.6	218.8	220.0	219.1	218.8	216.6	212.4	210.2
2009	211.1	212.2	212.7	213.2	213.9	215.7	215.4	215.8	216.0	216.2	216.3	215.9
2010	216.7	216.7	217.6	218.0	218.2	218.0	218.0	218.3	218.4	218.7	218.8	219.2

13

Tables that span multiple pages

When a table spans multiple pages, Word can automatically repeat one or more heading rows to make the table more manageable. When the need arises, select the target table's heading rows (you can have multiple heading rows), and click Repeat Heading Rows in the Data group of the Layout tab. The selected heading rows are then repeated where necessary. The setting can be toggled on or off for each individual table. Because the number of heading rows can vary, this setting cannot be made the default for all tables, nor incorporated into a style definition.

NOTE

If you are preparing a document for the Web and working in Web Layout view, the Repeat Heading rows command has no effect, because web pages are seamless and do not have page breaks in concept.

Sorting table rows

Word provides a flexible and fast way to sort data in tables. To sort a table, select the first column (field) to sort by, and click the Sort button in the Data group of the Layout tab. Word displays the Sort dialog box, shown in Figure 13.24. If the table has headings in the first row at the top of each column, selecting the Header Row option under My list has does two things. First, it provides labels in the Sort by and Then by drop-down lists. Second, it excludes the header row from the sort.

FIGURE 13.24

The Sort command lets you sort by up to three fields.

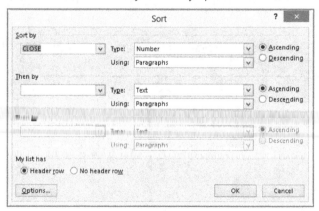

If you did not select a column before opening the Sort dialog box, select the first sort field from the Sort by drop-down list. Open the Type drop-down list and click Text, Number, or Date to match up with the type of data stored in the sort column. Choose Ascending or Descending depending on whether you want to sort from A to Z or lowest to highest or most recent to least recent—or vice versa for any of those. To sort by additional fields, open the two Then by drop-down lists and click a field name to include up to two of them, and set the additional type and sort order settings. Click Options to determine additional settings, including how fields are delimited (for non-table sorts), whether to make the sort case-sensitive, and the sorting language. Click OK to close Sort Options, and then click OK to apply the sort.

Adding table calculations

Word can perform some calculations using the Formula button in the Data group of the Layout tab (refer to Figure 13.19). To use it, first create a cell or row where you want to include formulas, and then select the first cell in which to enter a formula. Note that you only can select multiple cells when the formula will be the same in each one, such as summing all the cells above the selection. Click Formula in the Data group of the Layout tab. Edit the contents of the Formula text box. Or you can click to the right of the equals sign (=) in the Formula text, box and use the Paste function drop-down list to paste in one of the predefined functions and indicate what cells to calculate between the parentheses. If needed, choose a format from the Number format drop-down list; the selection shown in Figure 13.25 formats the number with two decimal places. Click OK to insert the formula in the cell.

13

FIGURE 13.25

These Formula settings calculate an average and set it to display with two decimal places.

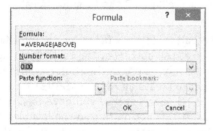

As with Excel, you also can use "cell addresses" to specify which cells to calculate on in a table; the column is column A, and the first row is row 1. Unfortunately, even if you do so, you cannot copy or fill formulas across a row or down a column; you have to insert a new formula in each individual table cell, or copy a formula with Excel-style cell addressing and then edit the field and change the cell addresses. If you use Word for math, double-check all calculations using a calculator or Excel. But if you have Excel and you need complex math in tables, then use Excel. You can then link the results to Word. That being said, here are a few more formula examples to give you ideas of how you might use formulas in your own tables:

- Let's say you work as a freelance personal assistant and want to create an invoice that calculates your billing based on various rates you charge for various tasks. You create a table with four columns and enter **Task, Hours, Rate**, and **Item Total** in the top row. In the second row you enter **Filing, 3.25**, and **10** in the first three cells. You then click in the fourth cell of the second row and display the Formula dialog box (Layout contextual tab, click Formula in the Data group). Edit the Formula text box entry to read **=B2*C2**, because you want to multiply the values in the second and third columns (Hours times Rate) to get the Item Total for the row. Choose a format with the dollar sign and two decimals from the Number format drop-down list, and click OK. The correct total of $32.50 displays for that row. In the next row, you could enter the next Task, Hours, and Rate values, and then use the Formula dialog box to create a formula in the fourth column that calculates **=B3*C3**, incrementing the row number in the formula for each new row. Then, to create an overall total in the final row, you can enter **Total** in the third column, and in the fourth column use the Formula dialog box to enter an **=SUM(ABOVE)** formula, formatted as currency like the formulas above it.

- If you're coaching a little league basketball team, you could create table to calculate quick stats. For example, if you've created a table to track how many points each player scores in each game, you could add a column at the far right and use the Formula dialog box to enter an **=AVERAGE(LEFT)** formula with the 0.00 Number format choice to average the scores. (The formula dialog box will likely suggest the **=SUM(LEFT)** formula; edit to replace SUM with AVERAGE.) In this case, because the formula does not refer to specific cells, you can copy and paste it down the column as needed, and then update the table to make sure all the formulas recalculate. (See the Note below.)

- You could make your little league basketball table more fancy by finding the high player score for each game. Add two rows at the bottom of the table, labeling them **High** and **Low** in the first column, respectively. Then, in the High row, use the Formula dialog box and the MAX function to create an **=MAX(ABOVE)** formula for each column. Calculating the low score is trickier, because you have to skip the High row. In each cell of the low row, use MIN function to find the low player scores by specifying a range of cells within the parentheses. For example, if the player scores are in rows 2-10 and the High scores are in row 11, the first formula in the second column of the Low row (row 12) would be **=MIN(B2:B10)**, the formula in the next column of the row would be **=MIN(C2:C10)**, and so on.

Those are just a few simple examples, and as you might imagine if you've done any work with Excel, you can create more complicated formulas in Word by using parentheses to group multiple functions and calculations. To redisplay the Formula dialog box to edit a calculation, click in the calculation so you see gray shading behind it. And use Layout ➪ Data ➪ Formula to redisplay it.

> **NOTE**
>
> If you change the values that a table is using to perform calculations, then you will need to recalculate the table. The table formulas are inserted as fields, and unlike the formulas in Excel, they do not recalculate automatically. The safest way to ensure that a table's calculations are up to date is to click a table cell, click the table move handle to select the whole table, and then press F9. Chapter 23, "Automating Document Content with Fields," teaches you more about fields, such as how to display field codes so that you can manually edit the field, a trick that may come in handy with table formulas.

Modifying table design

Word 2013 provides a number of powerful tools to help you quickly enhance the look and feel of your tables. One of these tools, Table Styles, features Live Preview. In this section we'll look only at the features contained in the Table Tools ➪ Design contextual tab, shown in Figure 13.26.

FIGURE 13.26

The Design contextual tab provides access to six Table Style Options and a gallery of Table Styles.

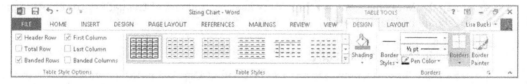

Applying a table style

Word 2013's refreshed and updated preset table styles enable you to change the look of any table with just a few clicks. Table styles provide a wide variety of formatting that you can preview live in your table. You can use styles to ensure a consistent, professional look when you include multiple tables within a single document. You can also modify a table style and save the modified versions for later use.

To apply a table style, click anywhere in the table to format, and then click the Table Tools ➪ Design contextual tab (from here referred to as the Design tab for simplicity. In Table Styles, hover the mouse over various styles and observe the changes to your table. As you move the mouse, tooltips display the name of the selected table style (such as Plain Table 1), as shown in Figure 13.27.

13

FIGURE 13.27

As you move the mouse over various table styles, the currently selected table displays a Live Preview of the formatting.

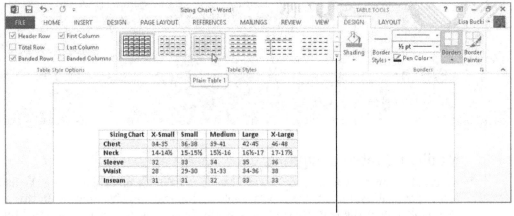

More button

If you see a style you like, click it to apply it to your table. If it's not perfect you can modify it. If you don't see a style you like, click the More button to the right of the table styles. Word displays the full Table Styles gallery, showing Plain Tables, Grid Tables, and (if you scroll down) List Tables categories of table styles, as shown in Figure 13.28. Move the mouse pointer over additional styles to preview their look on your table, and then click the style to apply. Note that you can click Clear near the bottom of the gallery to remove a previously applied table style.

Choosing table style options

The Table Style Options group at the left end of the Design tab provides access to six options, shown in Figure 13.26, that you can apply to your table. For some of these to work, you have to apply a table style that includes shading rather than trying to use them with the plain Table Grid style that is the default for newly inserted tables. After you apply an overall table style, click to check to apply Table Style Options to your tables, or remove checks to turn the corresponding features off:

- **Header Row:** Applies special formatting to the entire top row in your table.

- **First Column:** Applies special formatting to the entire first column.

- **Total Row:** Applies special formatting to the last row, generally a double border above the row as for traditional accounting formatting for numeric totals. The formatting may be omitted for the first cell.

- **Last Column:** Applies special formatting to the last column, except for the top cell.

- **Banded Rows:** Alternates shading in rows to create a horizontal striping effect. This helps the reader focus on specific rows.

- **Banded Columns:** Alternates shading in columns to create vertical stripes, focusing the reader on columnar comparisons.

FIGURE 13.28

The Table Styles gallery enables you to test-drive dozens of built-in table styles.

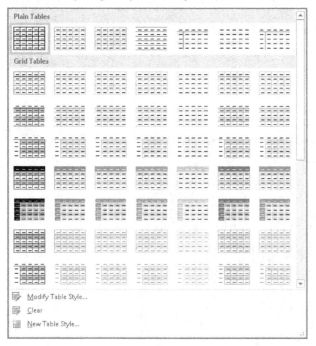

Shading cells

You can apply shading (a background fill color) to individual cells, rows, columns, or to a complete table. You can use shading sometimes to draw attention to one or more elements of a table. For example, if you added a row with calculated averages to the bottom of a table, you might want to call attention to that data with special shading. It's also common to use shading to set off a title row or column.

Select the cells, rows, or columns to shade, and then click Shading in the Table Styles group of the Design tab. Live Preview works with the Shading gallery, as shown in Figure 13.29. Move the mouse pointer over a color to preview it on the selection, and then click when you're ready to apply a color. Figure 13.29 shows light shading applied to the left column of a table, with darker shading being previewed in the top row. Note that when you apply Theme Colors as your shading choices, those colors automatically update whenever you apply a new theme to the document. Use the More Colors command to apply colors that won't change when you change the theme.

FIGURE 13.29

Live Preview works with the Shading choices.

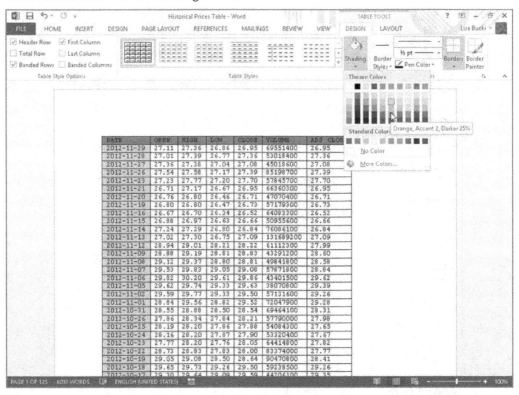

Modifying and saving a table style

To modify the table style applied to the selected table:

1. **Open the Table Styles gallery and click Modify Table Style near the bottom the gallery.** The Modify Style dialog box shown in Figure 13.30 appears.
2. **Type or edit the name in the Name text box if you want to rename the style.** You can use the Modify Style dialog box to apply style formatting, as described in Chapter 7, "Using Styles to Create a Great Looking Document."

FIGURE 13.30

Use the Modify Style dialog box to make changes to a table style.

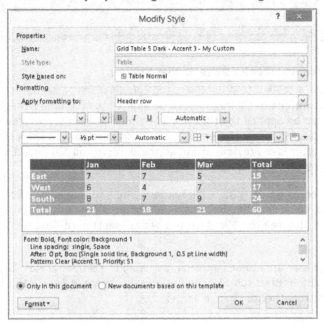

3. **Open the Apply formatting to drop-down list and choose the part of the table for which you want to change formatting.**

4. **Use the formatting choices above the preview to format the selected item.**

5. **Repeat Steps 3 and 4 to change additional parts of the style.**

6. **Check an option to store the style Only in this document or in New documents based on this template.**

7. **Click OK.**

If you want to create a new style rather than modify one of the existing ones—which is a good choice when you want to keep all the original table styles intact—click the New Table Style choice at the bottom of the Table Styles gallery. The Create New Style from Formatting dialog box that appears has the same settings as those in the Modify Style dialog box shown in Figure 13.30. Enter a table Name, and then open the Style based on drop-down list to choose an existing table style to serve as the model or base for your new style. Make formatting adjustments as described in Steps 3 and 4 here, choose where to store the file, and then click OK to finish creating your new style. The new style will appear in a category named Custom at the top of the Table Styles gallery.

> **NOTE**
>
> You can delete a style that you've created from the Table Styles gallery. Right-click the style thumbnail and click Delete Table Style. Click Yes in the message box that appears to confirm the deletion.

Borders and table drawing (border styles, border painter)

Border lines separate a table into cells, rows, and columns. You've seen in other chapters that borders are not unique to tables, and can be applied to characters and paragraphs as well. They also can be applied to other Word document elements, such as text boxes, frames, and graphics. Any of the border tools can be used to control borders in tables. None of the border tools offer Live Preview, although the Borders and Shading dialog box does provide a generic preview.

You have two strategies for working with borders. You can launch the Borders and Shading dialog box. For a detailed description of how to apply borders using the Borders and Shading dialog box, see the "Borders and boxes" section in Chapter 6, "Paragraph Formatting."

The second strategy uses an ad hoc approach, by using the Border Styles, Line Style, Line Weight, Pen Color, and Borders tools in the Design tab, shown in Figure 13.31. Use the border formatting tools together to change borders:

FIGURE 13.31

Use the Borders Styles tool and its friends to make ad hoc changes to table borders.

1. **Select the cells, rows, or columns to which you want to apply borders.**

2. **In the Borders group of the Design contextual tab, choose the settings you want from the Line Style, Line Weight, and Pen Color drop-downs; or click the Border Styles button and click a border style in the gallery.**

3. **Click the Borders button down arrow, and then click to specify where you'd like to apply the borders.** Click Outside Borders to put borders all around the selection, for example.

TIP

Click No Border in the Borders tool menu to remove existing borders from the table selection.

Once you've applied a border style you like to selected cells, you can use Word 2013's new Border Painter tool to copy it to other selections, as shown in Figure 13.32. Click Border Painter, and then drag the painter mouse pointer to apply the specified border to cell, row, and column boundaries. Press Esc to turn the Border Painter off when finished.

TIP

Remember that if you remove all table borders, you may want to turn on table gridlines so that you can see cell boundaries. The View Gridlines setting is in the Table group of the Table Tools Layout tab.

FIGURE 13.32

When the Border Painter is active, drag to copy border settings to other table locations.

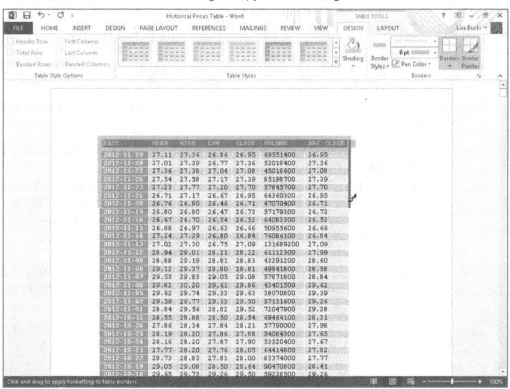

Using the table eraser

The table eraser removes parts of tables. It doesn't merely remove border lines; it deletes the cell boundaries in a table where you specify. You can use the table eraser to turn interior cells into a larger interior cell. Be careful, though. If you try to delete a table's upper-left cell, you might instead delete the whole top row of the table.

To use the table eraser, click in a table and then click Eraser in the Draw group of the Table Tools ⇨ Layout tab. Click on cell boundaries to remove as needed. (Remember to press Ctrl+Z immediately if you inadvertently click the wrong border.) To dismiss the eraser, either click the Eraser tool again to toggle it off, or press Esc. The eraser also deactivates if you click outside a table (in regular text).

Inserting SmartArt

SmartArt provides you with a much wider selection of diagrams to illustrate processes, relationships, organizational hierarchies, and more. SmartArt also features 3-D formatting that's so dimensional it looks like it took hours for a graphic artist to create it.

> **NOTE**
>
> SmartArt, introduced in Word 2007, replaced the Insert Diagram and Insert Organization Chart features of Word 2003 (and earlier).

Here are the basic steps for inserting SmartArt. I'll elaborate on some of the details after the steps:

1. **Click to position the insertion point at the location where you want to insert SmartArt.**

2. **Click the Insert tab on the Ribbon, and click SmartArt in the Illustrations group.** The Choose a SmartArt Graphic dialog box shown in Figure 13.33 appears. It lists eight categories, plus All, which enables you to peruse all the graphic types.

3. **Click a category, and then click one of the graphic thumbnails that appears.** A larger preview and description appear at the right.

4. **When you find a graphic that looks appropriate, either double-click it or click it and then click OK.** Word inserts the shape into your document with the text pane ready to accept information, as shown in Figure 13.34.

FIGURE 13.33

Word features more than 160 SmartArt gallery items divided into eight categories.

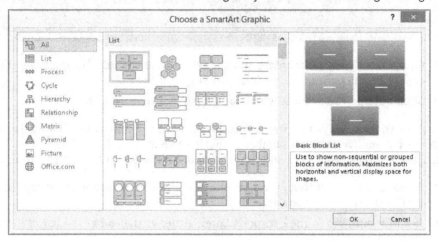

FIGURE 13.34

Enter text to appear in the various shapes in a SmartArt graphic.

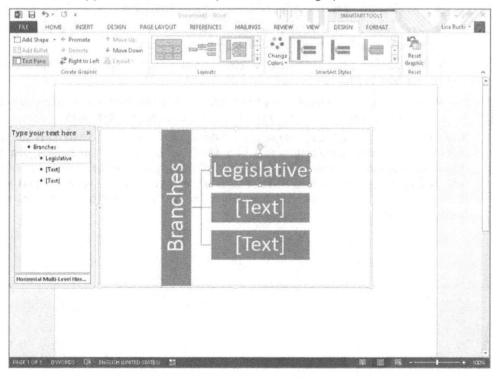

> **TIP**
>
> If the text pane doesn't appear, click Text Pane in the Create Graphic group of the SmartArt Tools Design contextual tab. Click the choice again if you want to hide the text pane after you finish entering text for the graphic.

5. **Click each [Text] placeholder in the text pane at the left.** As you type, the text appears in the corresponding SmartArt shape on the right.

6. **Click outside the graphic when you finish working with it.**

There are a variety of ways to enter and format text in the text pane. The following list, though not exhaustive, offers a number of methods that work. Note that some actions can also be performed via the Create Graphic group in the SmartArt Tools ⇨ Design tab.

- To move to the next item, press the down arrow. Use the other arrow keys to navigate in the text entry box as well.

- To add a new item to the list, press Enter, either at the end of the list of items or above an existing item.

- To demote the current item, if possible, press the Tab key.

- To promote the current item, press Shift+Tab.

- To delete an item, select it and press the Backspace key.

- To change the font for an item, select the text you want to change, mouse over the selection, and use the Mini Toolbar (see Figure 13.35).

- You can also enter text directly, without using the text pane. Click in the SmartArt item and type.

- The text pane can be moved and resized if it's in the way: Drag it to a more convenient location or drag any of the four sides to resize the text area.

Note that basic paragraph and character formatting can be applied to SmartArt shapes. Indents, bullets, and numbering cannot be applied, nor can styles. You can assign a style to the overall diagram; however, effects are limited unless the SmartArt item is In line with text. To change the font used in all the text in a SmartArt object, display the text pane, click in it, press Ctrl+A to select the contents of the text area, and then right-click and set the desired font.

FIGURE 13.35

You also can format text in the text pane or use the Design contextual tab to work with shapes and layouts.

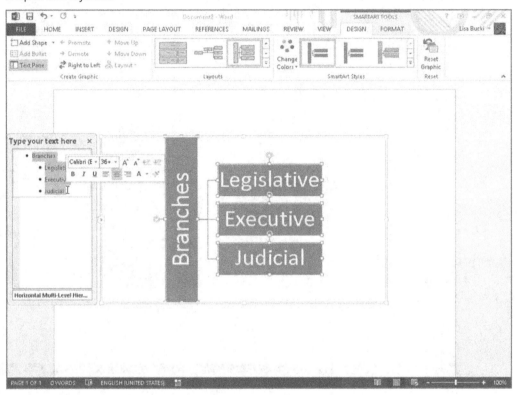

Changing layout, style, and colors

You can change a SmartArt diagram's overall layout, colors, and style at any time using the tools in the Layouts and SmartArt Styles groups of the SmartArt Tools ➪ Design contextual tab. Select the SmartArt graphic by clicking it, and use the Layouts Gallery, shown in Figure 13.36, to choose a different layout. Note that the gallery works with Live Preview. You aren't limited to applying the same class (List, Hierarchy, Process, Cycle,) of layout, either. SmartArt will adapt the different designs using the relationship levels currently applied.

FIGURE 13.36

You can apply any layout to any SmartArt list.

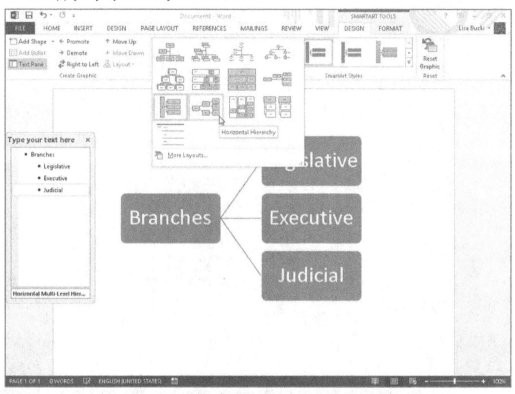

SmartArt Styles enable you to apply a variety of preset formatting to the selected SmartArt diagram. Click the More button to open the gallery and point to any choice—again, Live Preview helps you to make a selection. As shown in the example in Figure 13.37, the styles offer both 2-D and 3-D options, as well as a variety of sophisticated surface treatments.

Open the Change Colors gallery beside the SmartArt styles to preview and select from a variety of color schemes you can apply to the selected SmartArt graphic.

> **NOTE**
>
> When the entire SmartArt graphic is selected, a Layout Options button appears at the right. Click it and then click the setting to use to wrap text around the graphic. Chapter 14, "Adding Pictures and WordArt to Highlight Information," will explain more about wrapping text around various objects in Word.

FIGURE 13.37

The SmartArt Styles gallery gives you choices for updating the look of the selected SmartArt graphic.

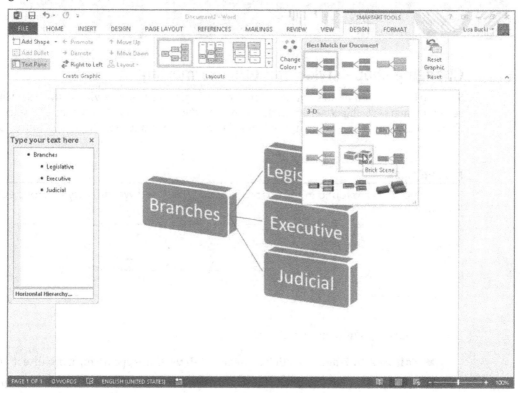

Adding a shape

You have to add and remove shapes in a SmartArt graphic to control the content that appears. You can do so in the text pane as noted earlier. Or you can click the SmartArt diagram to select it, click a shape within the diagram to which the new shape will relate, and then click the Add Shape drop-down list arrow in the Create Graphic group of the Design tab. The choices that appear are Add Shape After, Add Shape Before, Add Shape Above, and Add Shape Below. (Depending on the nature and position of the shape you initially selected, not all of these choices may be active.) Click the desired shape location, and then type the text for the new shape. You also can right-click a shape and use the Add Shape submenu of the shortcut menu to insert a shape.

Changing shape styles and other formatting

SmartArt provides a number of additional tools for formatting individual shapes within a selected SmartArt object. After clicking the SmartArt diagram, click a shape to select it, and then use the applicable tools in the SmartArt Tools ⇨ Format tab, shown in Figure 13.38.

FIGURE 13.38

Formatting tools are found in the Shapes, Shape Styles, and WordArt Styles groups of the Format tab.

Use the Shapes group tools as follows:

- **Edit in 2-D:** When you click a shape, a 2-D version appears for more direct editing.
- **Change Shape:** Change the selected shape into any of dozens of Word's shapes.
- **Larger or Smaller:** Expand or shrink the selected shape.

The Shape Styles group includes these choices for formatting a selected shape:

- **Shape Style Gallery:** Choose from three dozen different patterns of outlines and fill.
- **Shape Fill:** Choose your own custom fill for the selected shape.
- **Shape Outline:** Choose a custom outline for the selected shape.
- **Shape Effects:** Choose from a variety of effects—shadow, reflection, glow, soft edges, bevel, and 3-D—to change individual shapes.

The settings in the WordArt Styles group change the appearance of the text in the selected shape. Chapter 14 describes WordArt formatting settings in more detail.

Chart Basics

Use charts to convey how numeric data compares or trends. Like its companion programs PowerPoint and Excel, Word gives you the ability to create sophisticated charts that make numeric data easier for your reader to interpret. This section introduces you to the essentials for creating and formatting charts in Word.

Inserting a chart in a document

Word offers an extensive set of predefined chart types and styles. To insert a new chart in a document:

1. **Click to position the insertion point at the document location where you want the chart to appear.**

2. **Click Insert and then click Chart in the Illustrations group.** The Insert Chart dialog box shown in Figure 13.39 appears.

FIGURE 13.39

Choose a chart type here.

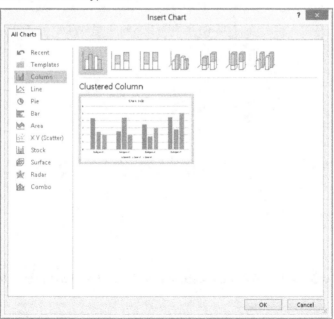

411

3. Click an overall chart type at right.

4. **Click one of the chart subtype thumbnails along the top to view a preview of the chart.**

5. **When you've found the desired chart subtype, make sure it's selected and click OK.** Word inserts the initial chart and opens an Excel-like spreadsheet window with sample data. The sample data suggests how you need to enter your actual data based on the selected chart type.

6. **Type or paste previously copied information into the window.** As in a Word table, press the Tab or arrow keys to move from cell to cell. Simply type over any current entry to replace it, or use Delete and Backspace as needed. Make sure you delete any unneeded example data and that the range selector includes all of the data that you enter. Watch the chart preview as you go to see whether you've done the needed cleanup work.

7. **When the chart has the appearance you want, as in the example in Figure 13.40, click the Close (X) button on the spreadsheet data window to close it.**

FIGURE 13.40

Enter chart data in a separate window.

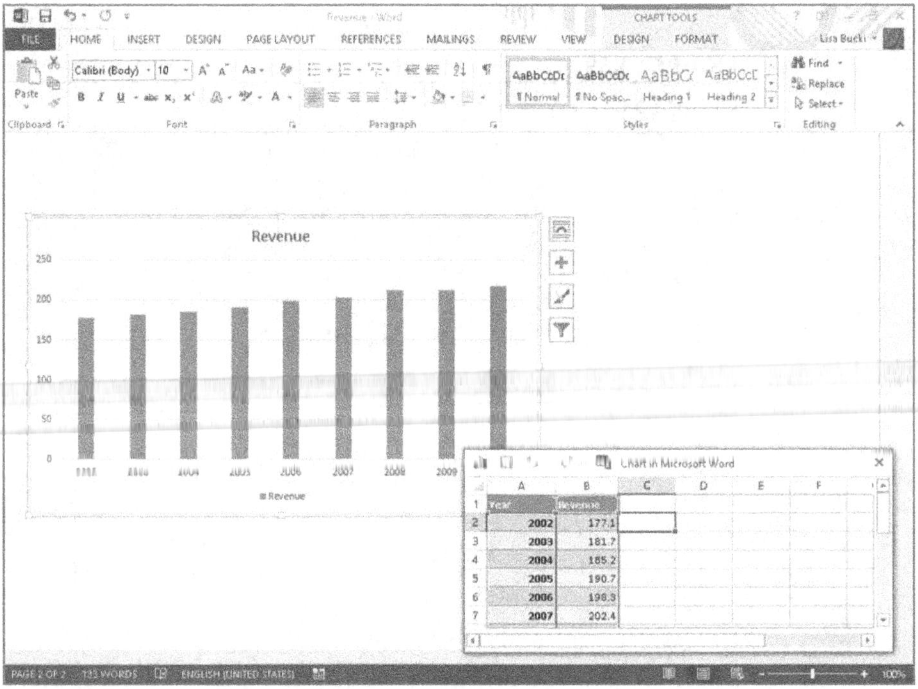

The chart is inserted. Click the chart at any time to reselect it. Notice that when you do, the Design and Format contextual tabs appear under Chart Tools.

Working with the chart design

The Design tab, shown in Figure 13.41, is where you make the major decisions that determine overall design, data, layout, and style. It makes sense to make the major decisions about data presentation first, and then tweak as necessary. Notice also that four buttons appear beside the chart, enabling you to work with its formatting. From top to bottom these are:

FIGURE 13.41

Use the Design contextual tab to change chart appearance.

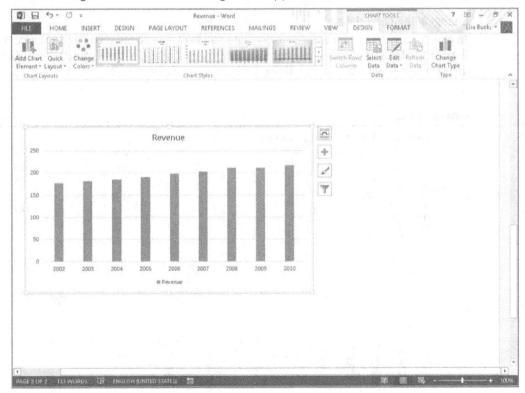

- **Layout Options:** Click to work with text wrapping settings. Chapter 14 explains how object wrapping settings work.
- **Chart Elements:** Use to work with parts of the chart, such as the title or legend.

413

- **Chart Styles:** Work with the chart's overall appearance and colors.
- **Chart Filters:** You can use this tool to temporarily limit the data the chart displays, as described later.

Changing the chart type

If you're not satisfied with the overall type of your chart, you can change it. In the Design tab, click Change Chart Type. The Change Chart Type dialog box appears. It looks identical in most respects (except for the title bar) to the one in Figure 13.39 that you encountered when you inserted the chart, but there is one essential difference. This time, the previews that you see will preview the data you've entered for the chart rather than the sample data. This lets you know whether a given chart type is appropriate for the data you have. Click OK to apply the currently selected chart subtype and finish changing the chart type.

Changing the chart data

To change the chart data after you've created a chart, select the chart and then click Select Data in the Data group of the Design tab. Office highlights the current dataset in Excel, and displays the Select Data Source dialog box, shown in Figure 13.42.

FIGURE 13.42

You can edit the data or change the entire data source.

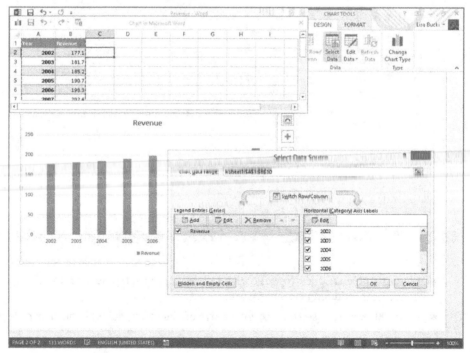

Edit the data in the worksheet window as needed. Or if you want to make larger-scale changes, the Select Data Source dialog box options work as follows:

- **Chart data range:** Specify the range of the worksheet that is used by the chart as data.

- **Switch Row/Column:** Exchange how the data is charted versus the vertical and horizontal axes in the chart; for example, if the rows were previously charted against the horizontal axis, clicking this button rearranges the chart to chart them against the vertical axis. This may not be appropriate for all sets of data. In the example in Figure 13.42, because the chart has only one series, switching would foul up the chart.

- **Add:** Add a new data series (Total Sales versus Revenue?) to the chart.

- **Edit (under Legend Entries):** Make changes to the currently selected data series.

- **Remove:** Exclude the selected data series from the chart.

- **Move Up/Move Down:** Use the buttons to move the selected series in the chart.

- **Edit (under Horizontal):** Edit the horizontal category labels.

- **Hidden and Empty Cells:** Click to see and control hidden and empty cells so you can decide how to handle them (hide them or leave gaps).

- **OK:** Apply the changes to the chart.

> **TIP**
>
> If you simply need to edit the data and not change the data layout, click Edit Data in the Data group rather than Select Data. If you are also an Excel user, you can learn more about working with the Select Data Source dialog box in Excel Help.

Updating the chart layout, style, and colors

Chart layouts, in the Design tab, provide a varying number of different layouts for each chart subtype. To apply a new chart layout, click the Quick Layouts button in the Chart Layout group (or the More button if a gallery already appears), point to a layout to see a Live Preview, and click the desired layout to apply it. For example, Clustered Column, the first chart type in the Insert Chart dialog, has 11 chart layouts, as shown in Figure 13.43.

Click the More button for Chart Styles to open the gallery shown in Figure 13.44. Use the mouse to see a Live Preview of any of the styles, and then click to apply it.

13

FIGURE 13.43

Each chart type has a different number of associated chart layouts, selectable from the Design tab.

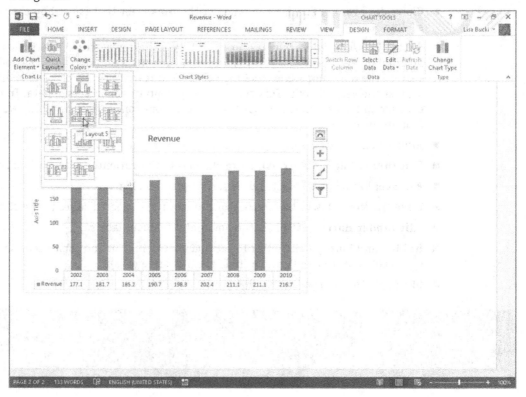

FIGURE 13.44

Change the overall chart style in this gallery.

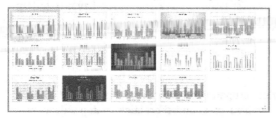

As for SmartArt, you can apply a new color scheme for the chart overall. To do so, click Change Colors in the Chart Styles group of the Design tab, point to a color scheme in the gallery to preview it, and then click the color scheme to apply.

Refining the chart format

The Chart Tools ⇨ Format contextual tab provides tools for selecting and formatting individual components of charts. As shown in Figure 13.45, the Format tab's groups provide myriad controls for fine-tuning your charts.

FIGURE 13.45

The Format tab provides tools for enhancing individual elements in your charts.

Selecting and formatting chart elements

You can click to select elements on a chart such as a series or axis. However, sometimes it's easier and more precise to open the Current Selection drop-down list in the Current Selection group of the Format tab and then click on the element you'd like to select. Then you can click Format Selection to open a dialog box with formatting choices specific to the chart object you selected. Or you can use the tools in the Shape Styles, WordArt Styles, Arrange, and Size groups of the Format tab to make changes to the selected element. Click Reset to Match Style to remove custom formatting from the selected chart element.

Displaying chart elements, including series and axes

Click the Chart Elements button beside the chart to display the flyout shown in Figure 13.46. Use the check boxes to control which labels (chart title, axis titles, legend, and data labels) appear on the chart. When a triangle appears to the right of any option you check, click it to see additional options for formatting the displayed items. To edit label text such as titles, click in the respective text box and make the desired changes. Click outside the text box when you're done.

FIGURE 13.46

You can check which elements you want to appear in the selected chart.

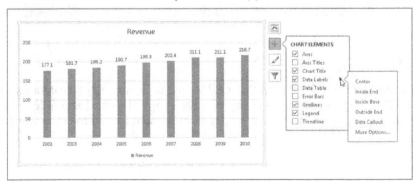

Controlling the background

One common feature of a chart to format is the Chart Area or background. After selecting Chart area in the Current Selection group, click Format Selection to display the Format Chart Area pane at the right. Select a fill type to see options for applying that type of fill. For example, in Figure 13.47 a texture has been applied to the background. Click the pane's Close (X) button to close it when you've finished formatting the background.

FIGURE 13.47

Choosing a relevant fill for a chart background can liven up an otherwise boring chart.

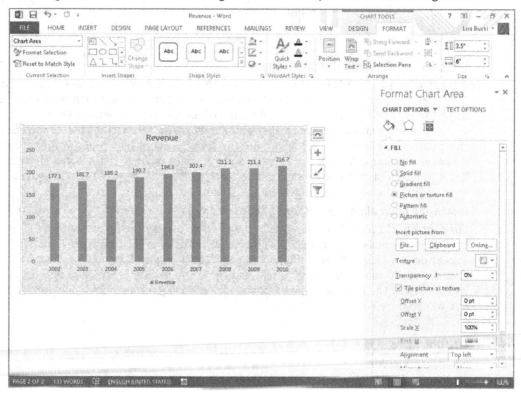

Filtering the chart

Filtering is a new feature in Word 2013 that enables you to temporarily hide data appearing in the chart. This enables you to, for example, make a copy of a chart and hide some of the data in the copy, so you can create a similar chart without having to create and format it from scratch. Click the Chart Filters button beside the selected chart, and then click to clear the check box beside any data you don't want to appear, as shown in Figure 13.48. Then click Apply, and click in the document to close the filtering choices. Use (Select All) to reselect or clear all of the check boxes.

FIGURE 13.48

Clear check boxes to temporarily hide chart data.

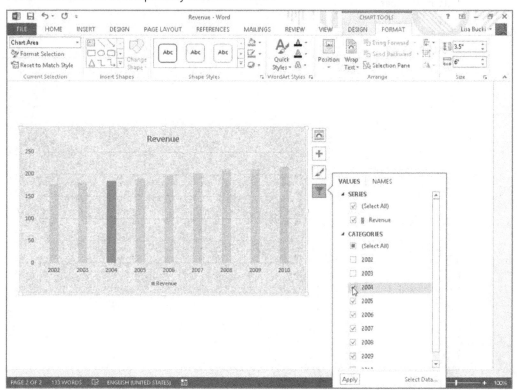

Using the Selection Pane

In Word 2013, you can format graphic objects as invisible, as long as they have a Wrap Text setting other than In Line with Text. To determine whether or not an object is set as invisible, open any .docx document that contains graphics with the right Wrap Text settings. In the Editing group of the Home tab, choose Select ⇨ Selection Pane.

Each object with an applicable Wrap Text setting appears in the Selection pane with an eye icon to its right. Clicking the icon makes the associated object invisible. In Figure 13.49, the top Picture object has been marked as invisible, and the bottom Text Box object remains visible, as indicated by the eye icon still being visible. Use the Show All and Hide All buttons in the pane to show and hide all graphics.

You can use this feature to hide shapes, text boxes, SmartArt, and charts. You cannot unbundle parts of a chart or SmartArt object—it's all or nothing. Click the pane's Close (X) button to close it.

FIGURE 13.49

Use the Selection pane to control visibility for floating (not inline) graphic objects.

Summary

In this chapter, you've learned the essentials you need to know about tables, SmartArt, and charts. You should now be able to do the following:

- Insert a table, SmartArt graphic, or chart into a document
- Copy material from one table into another, even if the dimensions don't match
- Use table styles and other formatting settings to add zest and color to your tables
- Create tables from existing non-tabular data
- Use the Ribbon tools to modify table layout and design
- Add and format the text for a SmartArt diagram
- Change a diagram's layout, style, and colors
- Add shapes where needed
- Choose a chart subtype
- Add and update the text for a chart
- Select and format specific chart items, including the background
- Use new chart tools, such as filtering
- Use the Selection pane

13

Adding Pictures and WordArt to Highlight Information

IN THIS CHAPTER

Inserting pictures from files

Finding pictures online

Controlling how pictures and other graphics wrap

Using live layout and alignment guides

Creating WordArt from existing text

Creating WordArt from scratch

Editing and formatting WordArt

Using Live Preview to change WordArt gallery style and shape

Pictures for their own sake might simply clutter up a document, and make it more time-consuming to send to somebody, and more expensive to print. On the other hand, used carefully, pictures enable you to show the reader what you mean. And in many cases, pictures can be a necessary addition to a document. For example, adding a company logo identifies the source of information, and customers want to see product photos in a catalog. In addition to pictures, you can include special decorative text called WordArt to highlight information in a document.

This chapter shows you where to find pictures if you don't have any, how to insert pictures and WordArt, and how to work with pictures and WordArt once they're in your document. Many of the techniques you learn in this chapter—such as how to move, size, and rotate a picture—apply to other types of graphics such as shapes, too.

Inserting a Pictures from a File

You can insert pictures in Word in several ways, using pictures from a variety of graphics formats. If you have pictures on removable media—such as SD (Secure Digital), CF (Compact Flash), CD, DVD, or USB drive—it's usually best to copy those pictures to your hard drive before you proceed. Although you can insert directly from such sources, or from a network location or over the Internet, you have more options available to you if the files are on your own computer in a location that is always accessible.

You might also have pictures available from a webcam, another camera, or a scanner connected to your computer. To use pictures from these types of devices, save the images to your hard drive first.

Though it's not necessary, you often can save time when pictures, sounds, and other files are where Word and other programs expect them to be. In the case of pictures, the expected location is your Pictures Library (or the My Pictures folder, which the Pictures Library in Windows 7 or 8 integrates by default).

NOTE

This book assumes that you're working with a Word 2010 or Word 2013 .docx file, and not a Word 97–2003 Compatibility Mode file. This matters because in Compatibility Mode, picture file linking is accomplished with the INCLUDEPICTURE field. In a Word 2013 file, linking is accomplished with XML relationships.

Adding the picture

To insert a picture at the current insertion location in a document:

1. **Click Pictures in the Illustrations group of the Insert tab.** The Insert Picture dialog box appears as shown in Figure 14.1, by default showing the contents of your Pictures Library.

2. **If the picture is in an alternate location, navigate to it.**

FIGURE 14.1

When you insert a picture, the Pictures Library contents appear first.

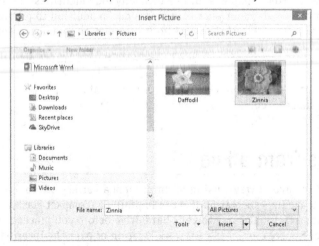

TIP

Notice in Figure 14.1 that SkyDrive appears as a choice under Favorites. This choice appears when you have the SkyDrive for Windows application installed. When you copy a picture to your local `SkyDrive Pictures` folder and then sign in to SkyDrive.com, or upload a picture to your `SkyDrive Pictures` folder, the local and online `Picture` folders sync to have the same contents. In the Insert Pictures dialog box, click SkyDrive and then double-click Pictures to access the local copies of your synced image files.

3. **Once you've found the picture to insert, you can either double-click it to insert it immediately or click it once and choose an insert method from the Insert button drop-down list.** The options for inserting pictures are:

   ■ **Insert:** The picture is embedded in the current document. If the original is ever deleted or moved, it will still exist in your document. If the original is ever updated, however, your document will not reflect the update. The document file will be larger because the original image is stored in the .docx file. If neither file size nor updates are important, this is the best option.

   ■ **Link to File:** A link to the picture is inserted, and the picture is displayed in the document. The document file will be smaller—often dramatically smaller—because the image is external to the Word document. If the original file is moved or deleted, it will no longer be available for viewing in the document, and you will see the error message shown in Figure 14.2 (see the Warning for more information). On the other hand, if the image is modified or updated, the update will be available and displayed in Word. If file size is an issue but the availability of the image file is not, then this is the best option.

FIGURE 14.2

If you rename, move, or delete a linked picture file, Word will not be able to display it.

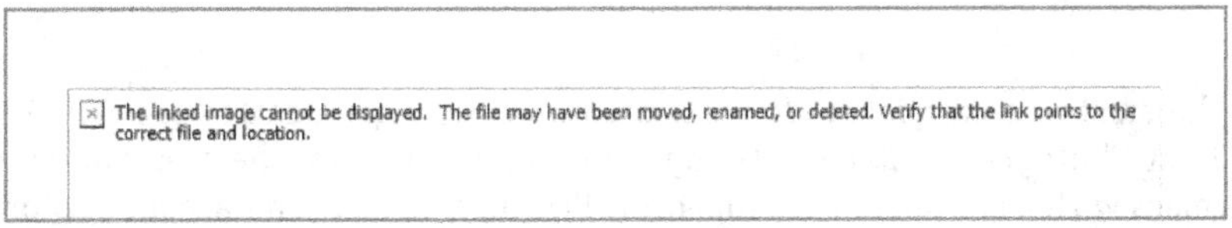

> ☒ The linked image cannot be displayed. The file may have been moved, renamed, or deleted. Verify that the link points to the correct file and location.

   ■ **Insert and Link:** The image is both embedded in the document and linked to the original file. If the original file is updated, the picture in the document will be updated to reflect changes in the original. Because the file is embedded, the document will be larger than it would be if only linked. However, the document will not be larger than it would be if only inserted. If file size is not an issue but updates are, this is the best option.

Supported picture file formats

If the picture you want doesn't appear in Word's Insert Picture dialog box but you know it should be in the current folder, click the All Pictures button in the lower-right corner, and in the list of choices shown in Figure 14.3 click the desired picture (graphic) file format to narrow the list of displayed pictures to ones that match the selected type.

FIGURE 14.3

Word supports a number of popular graphics file formats.

The most popular picture format, used by most digital cameras, is JPEG, which stands for Joint Photographic Experts Group (so if you didn't know before, you do now). Word 2013 comes with a converter that supports JPEG files, which can have a .jpg or .jpeg file name extension. Other Word 2013–supported popular formats include Graphics Interchange Format (.gif), which is heavily used on the Internet due to its support for transparent backgrounds, which makes such images better suited for web page design; Portable Network Graphics (.png); Tagged Image File Format (.tif or .tiff); Windows Metafile (.wmf); Enhanced Metafile (.emf); and Windows Bitmap (.bmp).

If your file format isn't supported natively by Word 2013, your best bet might be to open it in the program originally used to create it, if available, and use Save As to convert it to a graphic file format that Word supports, such as JPEG. This is especially true if you created the image in a relatively esoteric type of design/drafting software or something like that. You could also search the Web for a freeware or low-cost graphics editing program that can convert the desired file format; check the program's capabilities carefully before buying. The freeware program Gimp (www.gimp.org) can open and save to a number of different graphics file formats.

Adding an Online Picture

Prior versions of Word included a locally stored collection of clipart images that you could insert through a Clip Art pane or gallery. Word 2013 does away with that functionality, replacing it with a streamlined Online Pictures tool that enables you find and insert pictures and clipart from Office.com, Bing Image Search, your SkyDrive, or Flickr. (It wouldn't be surprising to see other social media/sharing services added in future updates.)

This section shows you how to search for and select an image from Office.com. The benefit of choosing Office.com over Bing Image Search is that Office.com offers royalty-free images for use in your projects free of charge. (According to 8.1 in the Microsoft Services Agreement, http://windows.microsoft.com/en-US/windows-live/microsoft-services-agreement, you simply can't resell the pictures or any project that relies primarily on them. For example, you might get into trouble if you downloaded an image from Office.com, made 8 × 10 color printouts of it, and then tried to frame them and sell them as art.) Images on Bing Image Search are released under the Creative Commons licensing scheme. This means that the owner of each image or illustration determines the particular licensing. For example, a Creative Commons Attribution-Share-Alike 3.0 License requires that you give credit (attribution) as specified by the creator anywhere you use the image

14

or illustration, and that you share any derivatives or alterations of the work under the same license. When you select a picture or illustration after using Bing Image Search, the information should include a link that you can click to find out about the Creative Commons licensing for the selected item. The Flickr choice enables you to connect with images you've stored in your Flickr account.

Here's how to find and insert an image from Office.com in a document:

1. **Make sure you are signed in and your system is connected to the Internet, and click to position the insertion point where you want to insert the picture.**

2. **Click the Insert tab, and then click Online Pictures in the Illustrations group.** The Insert Pictures window shown in Figure 14.4 appears.

FIGURE 14.4

Use the new Insert Pictures feature to find and download images from Office.com and more.

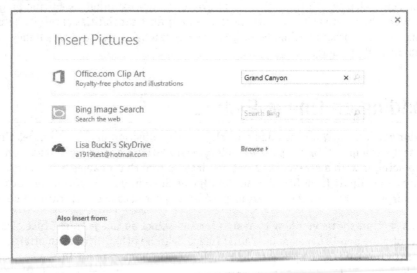

3. **Type a search term in the text box to the right of Office.com Clip Art, and then click the Search (magnifying glass) button at the right.** Insert Pictures finds and displays matching pictures.

4. **Scroll down to preview additional pictures, if needed; click the one you want to insert, as shown in Figure 14.5; and then click Insert.** Word downloads the image or illustration and displays it at the insertion point.

FIGURE 14.5

Select the image or illustration you want to insert, and then click Insert.

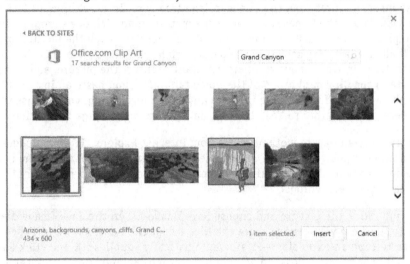

The process for finding a picture with Bing Image Search is similar to the above, except in Step 3 you would type the search term in the text box to the right of Bing Image Search, instead. Then run the search. To insert a picture from your SkyDrive from the Insert Pictures window, make sure you are signed in to Word using your Microsoft account. Open Insert Pictures, and click Browse to the right of your SkyDrive. The window displays the folders in your SkyDrive, including the Pictures folder. Click a folder to display its items, click an image to insert, and then click the Insert button.

> **TIP**
>
> The first time you click the Flickr button at the bottom of the Insert Pictures window, you'll see a prompt to connect to your account. Click Connect, and then enter your account sign-in information when prompted.

Pasting or Snapping a Picture

It may not always be the case that the source image is one stored on your hard disk. You may want to grab an image out of a document you've received from another user and reuse it yourself, or you may have downloaded a PDF file with an image you'd like to reuse. Or you may want to take a picture of what you're doing in another Office program to include in the current document. Let's see how that works.

Pasting a picture

You can also insert pictures from the Clipboard and from your Internet browser (usually, but not always). To use the Clipboard, display the picture in any Windows program that supports graphics, and use that program's controls to select and copy the picture to the Clipboard. If all else fails, try selecting the picture, right-clicking it, and choosing Copy or Copy Picture. Then, in Word, move to where you want to insert the picture, and press Ctrl+V (or click Paste in the Clipboard group of the Home tab). After you paste an image, a Paste Options button appears; if the picture includes any added formatting, you can use the Paste Options to determine whether to keep the original formatting or merge formatting.

Sometimes the copy-and-paste method works from Internet Explorer, Firefox, Google Chrome, and other popular browsers—other times not. When the Clipboard method fails, or when you want a copy of the file itself (not simply the embedded version in a Word document), you can try several things.

In Firefox, right-click the picture and choose Save Image As. In the Save Image dialog box, navigate to where you want to store the file, accept the name shown or type a new one (no need to type an extension—Firefox automatically supplies it), and click Save. In the Windows 7 or Windows 8 desktop version of Internet Explorer, right-click the picture and choose Save picture as. Again, navigate to the desired location, specify a file name, and click Save. In the new Windows 8 Internet Explorer app (launched from the Start screen), start the process by right-clicking the picture and clicking Save to picture library.

> **TIP**
>
> Before reusing pictures from the Internet, however, please make sure that you have a right to do so. Many pictures on the Internet are copyright protected.

There are a number of ways to find pictures on the Internet, from surfing to explicitly searching. Google itself has an Image Search feature. From Google's home page, click Images. In the Image Search page, type the search text (enclose in quotes to search for a whole name), and click Search Images. Another common technique is to include the word "gallery" in the search, although these days you'd probably find a lot of Office 2013 gallery hits! In addition to enabling you to store your own pictures, Flickr enables users to share pictures and make them available for download. It even has a special section of images released under the Creative Commons licensing scheme at http://www.flickr.com/creativecommons/.

Taking a screenshot

Windows itself has long offered the built-in ability to copy a picture of what's onscreen to the Clipboard via the Print Screen or Shift+Prnt scr shortcut keys. Word 2013 (and some of the Office applications) builds on this feature by enabling you to insert a screenshot of other open Office file windows—including Help windows—directly into Word. You might want to take advantage of this feature if you are writing how-to instructions about a task for a colleague, or if you want to show data from an Excel workbook and don't feel that you need to be fussy about copying and pasting specific cells. To snap a screenshot in Word:

1. **After opening the desired application window and switching back to Word, click to position the insertion point where you want to insert the picture.**

2. **Click the Insert tab, and then click Screenshot in the Illustrations group.** The gallery of Available Windows to shoot appears as shown in Figure 14.6.

3. **Click the window to shoot.** A picture of the window appears at the insertion point.

FIGURE 14.6

Insert a picture of another open Office window in the current document.

14

Manipulating Inserted Pictures (and Other Graphics)

After you insert a picture or other graphic into the document, you can use a plethora of tools in Word 2013 to position, style, and otherwise work with the image to integrate it into your document in the most attractive way possible. For example, this section covers the various text wrapping options and their implications.

Controlling picture positioning

Wrapping is the term used to classify the various ways in which pictures (as well as other graphics) appear relative to the text in a Word document. It helps to understand that a

Word document has several different *layers*. Where you normally compose text is called the *text layer*. There are also *drawing layers* that are both in front of and behind the text layer. A graphic inserted in front of the text layer will cover text up, unless the graphic is semi-transparent, in which case it will modify the view of the text. Graphics inserted behind the text layer act as a backdrop, or background, for the text.

Additionally, there is the *header and footer layer*. This is where headers and footers reside. This area is behind the text area. If you place a graphic into a header or footer, the graphic will appear behind the text. Dim graphics placed in the header and footer layer often serve as watermarks. Sometimes the word CONFIDENTIAL will be used in the header and footer layer, branding each page of the document as a caution to readers. See Chapter 17, "Changing Other Page Features," for more information about watermarks.

Setting wrapping and wrapping defaults

The Wrap Text setting determines how graphics interact with each other and with text. Table 14.1 describes the available Wrap Text settings. Knowing how you plan to position a picture should determine the wrapping setting. Wrapping effects and typical uses are shown in Table 14.1. Wrapping comes in two basic flavors: In Line with Text (in the text layer) and floating (in the graphics layer, which includes the other six wrapping formats listed in Table 14.1). *Floating* means that the picture can be dragged anywhere in the document and isn't constrained in the way that pictures in the text layer of the document are.

TABLE 14.1 **Wrap Text Setting**

Wrapping Setting	Effect/Application
In Line with Text	Inserted into text layer. Graphic can be dragged, but only from one paragraph marker to another. Typically used in simple presentations and formal reports.
Square	Creates a square "container" in the text where the graphic is. Text wraps around the graphic, leaving a gap between the text and the graphic. The graphic can be dragged anywhere in the document. Typically used in newsletters and flyers with a fair amount of white space
Tight	Effectively creates a "container" in the text where the graphic is, of the same shape as the overall outline of the graphic, so that text flows around the graphic. Wrapping points can be changed to reshape the "hole" that the text flows around. The graphic can be dragged anywhere in the document. Typically used in denser publications in which paper space is at a premium, and where irregular shapes are acceptable and even desirable.
Behind Text	Inserted into the bottom or back drawing layer of a document. The graphic can be dragged anywhere in the document. Typically used for watermarks and page background pictures. Text flows in front of the graphic. Also used in the assembling of pictures from different vector elements.

Wrapping Setting	Effect/Application
In Front of Text	Inserted into the top drawing layer of a document. The graphic can be dragged anywhere in the document. Text flows behind the graphic. Typically used only on top of other pictures or in the assembling of vector drawings, or when you deliberately need to cover or veil text in some way to create a special effect.
Through	Text flows around the graphic's wrapping points, which can be adjusted. Text is supposed to flow into any open areas of the graphic, but evidence that this actually works is in short supply. For all practical purposes, this appears to have the same effects and behavior as Tight wrapping.
Top and Bottom	Effectively creates a rectangular "container" the same width as the margin. Text flows above and below, but not beside, the graphic. The picture can be dragged anywhere in the document. Typically used when the graphic is the focal point of the text.

To set the wrapping behavior of a graphic, click it and then click the Wrap Text button in the Arrange group of the Picture Tools ➪ Format tab. Choose the desired wrapping from the list menu, as shown in Figure 14.7. The Square wrap setting was previously applied to the selected picture in Figure 14.7.

FIGURE 14.7

Wrapping behavior determines where you can position a picture or graphic in Word.

14

In Word 2013, you also can click the Layout Options button that appears to the right of a selected picture or graphic to access Text Wrapping settings in a flyout, as shown in Figure 14.8. You can click one of the wrap settings under In Line with Text or With Text Wrapping to change the wrapping. Clicking See more opens the Layout dialog box (Figure 14.9); you can use the settings on the Position tab to set a precise Horizontal and Vertical location on the page for the selected graphic, or the Text Wrapping tab to set more general wrapping options. For example, you can use the Distance from text settings to control the white space between the wrapped graphic and surrounding text.

FIGURE 14.8

The Layout Options button also enables you to work with text wrapping.

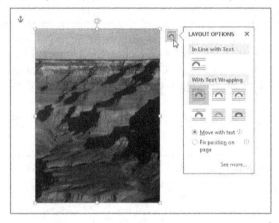

FIGURE 14.9

The Layout dialog box offers settings for precise control over wrapping and graphic positioning.

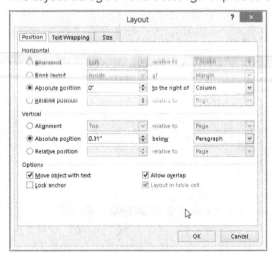

You can also change the default Wrap Text setting. Let's face it, in most cases, having a graphic appear inline wastes space and can interrupt the flow of the text, especially if you weren't precise about positioning when you inserted a graphic. To set the default wrapping style for most graphic objects you insert, paste, or create, choose File ⇨ Options ⇨ Advanced. In the Cut, copy, and paste section, click the Insert/paste pictures as drop-down list arrow, and click the desired default Wrap Text setting. Then click OK.

You should note that when you insert shapes (and hand-drawn text boxes (as described in the next chapter), Word applies the In Front of Text Wrap Text setting by default. If you copy a picture from one part of a document and paste it elsewhere, the copy inherits the wrapping style of the original picture, and won't use your default.

Changing wrap points

When you've applied some of the Wrap Text settings to a picture or an object, you can change the *wrap points*. The wrap points are special handles that enable you to alter the wrapping boundaries for a graphic. Moving the wrap points further away from the graphic puts more space between the graphic and the text. For example, you might move the top corner wrap points for a photo up to add white space above the photo. To edit the wrap points for a graphic:

1. **Click the picture or graphic (you might need to click twice), to select it, and then apply the desired text wrapping setting if needed.**

2. **Choose Wrap Text ⇨ Edit Wrap Points in the Arrange group in the Picture Tools ⇨ Format tab (or from the applicable contextual tab for the selected object).** The object border changes color and the wrap point handles appear.

3. **Drag the wrap point handles to the desired position, as shown in Figure 14.10.** As you can see in the figure, the mouse pointer also changes when the wrap points are active.

4. **Click outside the selected object to deactivate the wrap points.**

14

FIGURE 14.10

Move wrap points to change the way text flows around a picture.

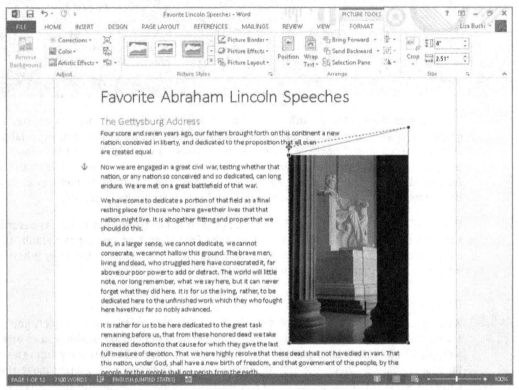

Choosing a position

The Position gallery in the Arrange group of the Picture Tools ⇨ Format tab (or the Drawing Tools ⇨ Format tab) enables you to skip moving a picture or graphic and setting wrapping on your own, and just have Word handle it for you. Select the object to move into position, and then click Position in the Arrange group. The gallery of choices shown in Figure 14.11 appears. Click one of the choices under With Text Wrapping to move the picture to the specified location on the current page.

Moving a graphic

You can move any graphic by dragging it, and some graphics can be dropped anywhere in the document. Graphics with Wrap Text (from the Arrange group in the Format contextual tab) set to In Line with Text, however, can be dropped only at a paragraph mark. All other graphics (in other words, those with wrapping settings that enable them to "float") can be dragged and dropped anywhere. To drag a graphic, click to select it, and then drag it where you want it to go.

FIGURE 14.11

You can tell Word to position a picture or graphic automatically.

> **NOTE**
>
> Word won't let you drag a picture or other graphic into position when Wrap Text is set to In Line with Text, because that wrap setting anchors the graphic to its original inserted location. If you find you can't move a picture to a new location as desired, check the Wrap Text setting and make sure it's set to an option that enables you to move the graphic.

Dragging a graphic with live layout and alignment guides

Word 2013 now provides a more real time preview of how your document will look as you move and resize objects. The *live layout* feature causes text to reflow around a wrapped graphic as you move it around. For example, this can be important if you have automatic hyphenation turned on and want to choose a position for the graphic that causes the least hyphenation. Live layout works hand in hand with the new *alignment guides* feature. One or more alignment guides appear when you drag a graphic and it reaches a position where it lines up with text, such as the top of a paragraph as shown in Figure 14.12, or the left margin, right margin, or center point of the page. If you release the mouse button when an alignment guide appears, chances are the graphic will land in a more pleasing position than you might achieve if purely aligning by eyeball. This method is also faster than using the Layout dialog box to align to the left or right margin.

> **CAUTION**
>
> You can control live layout in Word Options. Choose File ⇨ Options. On the General tab, check or clear Update document content while dragging. The option also appears on the Advanced tab under Display. Click OK to apply the change.

14

FIGURE 14.12

Alignment guides appear as you drag a graphic to enable you to align it precisely with text or other graphics.

Favorite Abraham Lincoln Speeches

The Gettysburg Address

Four score and seven years ago, our fathers brought forth on this continent a new nation: conceived in liberty, and dedicated to the proposition that all men are created equal.

Now we are engaged in a great civil war, testing whether that nation, or any nation so conceived and so dedicated, can long endure. We are met on a great battlefield of that war.

We have come to dedicate a portion of that field as a final resting place for those who here gave their lives that that nation might live. It is altogether fitting and proper that we should do this.

But, in a larger sense, we cannot dedicate, we cannot consecrate, we cannot hallow this ground. The brave men, living and dead, who struggled here have consecrated it, far above our poor power to add or detract. The world will little note, nor long remember, what we say here, but it can never forget what they did here. It is for us the living, rather, to be dedicated here to the unfinished work which they who fought here have thus far so nobly advanced.

— Alignment guide

Nudging

You can also *nudge* a selected floating graphic. Select it, and then use the arrow keys on the keyboard to move it a small distance in any of the four directions. Nudging works well for precise alignments, but alignment guides do not appear when you use this feature, so you will have to go by eye.

To drag in discrete steps using Word's built-in alignment gridlines, hold the Alt key as you drag and drag slowly. You will see the graphic jump in small increments as it snaps to the grid. If you display the gridlines (see Figure 14.13) by checking Gridlines in the Show group of the View tab, however, Alt-dragging works in reverse, making Word ignore the grid. With the grid displayed, arrow key nudging also changes. Now the arrow keys move the picture in grid increments. Press the Ctrl key to nudge in smaller gradations.

The vertical and horizontal gridlines are an eighth of an inch apart, so nudging in any direction with the gridline displayed moves the graphic ⅛ inch at a time. Note that when gridlines are displayed, they will display in all open documents.

FIGURE 14.13

Enable Gridlines in the Show group of the View tab to display the grid for help in planning graphic placement.

Resizing, rotating, and cropping a picture

Resizing changes the physical dimensions of the picture or other graphic as it is displayed in your document. Resizing in Word will not make the associated file (or the image stored in the .docx file) any larger or smaller. If you make it smaller and then later make it larger, you still retain the original file resolution.

Cropping refers to blocking out certain portions of a picture by changing its exterior borders. You can crop out distracting or unnecessary details. Again, cropping in Word does not affect the actual picture itself, only the way it is displayed in Word. The fact that Word doesn't change the actual image is a big plus, because you can undo the cropping if you later change your mind.

CAUTION

Resizing and cropping a picture file in a graphics editing program does change the picture itself. Keep this distinction in mind. Once you've saved a cropped or resized picture in a graphics program, you can't get the original back. If you want to crop graphics outside of Word to keep the file sizes more limited, always make a copy of each picture file and crop the copy.

Resizing and rotating

You can resize a picture by typing the measurements or by dragging. To resize by dragging, click on the picture and then move the mouse pointer so that it's over one of the eight sizing handles. The mouse pointer changes into a double arrow, as shown in Figure 14.14. Drag until the picture is the desired size and then release the mouse button. Note that dragging the corner handles maintains the aspect ratio of the picture, whereas dragging the side handles can be used to stretch or compress the picture.

FIGURE 14.14

Resize a picture or other graphic by dragging any of the eight sizing handles.

Hold down the Ctrl and/or Alt keys while dragging to modify the way resizing occurs:

- To resize symmetrically from the center point of the picture or graphic, causing the picture to increase or decrease by the same amount in all directions, hold down the Ctrl key while dragging.

- To resize in discrete steps, snapping to the alignment gridlines while hidden, press and hold down the Alt key while dragging and drag slowly, so that you can see each size increment as you go; if gridlines are displayed, the Alt key's behavior is reversed, as indicated earlier.

You can combine these options. For example, holding down the Alt and Ctrl keys at the same time while dragging a sizing handle slowly forces Word to resize in discrete steps while resizing from the center.

To specify an exact picture or graphic size, select the entry in the Shape Height and/or Shape Width text boxes in the Size group at the right end of the Picture Tools ⇨ Format tab (or Drawing Tools ⇨ Format tab) of the Ribbon. Type a new value, and press Enter. By default, these settings maintain the aspect ratio automatically, so if you enter a new Height and press Enter, the Width adjusts accordingly. To be able to change the picture proportions via the Size group settings, click the dialog box launcher in the Size group. Remove the check next to Lock aspect ratio as shown in Figure 14.15. (Note that for shape graphics, Lock aspect ratio is turned off by default, so the default setting differs depending on the selected object.)

FIGURE 14.15

To be able to distort a picture's dimensions, clear the Lock aspect ratio check box as shown here.

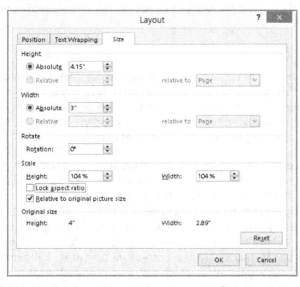

Use the rotate handle with the circular arrow icon above the top center resizing handle (refer to Figure 14.14) to rotate a picture. Select the picture and drag the handle in the direction in which you want to rotate the picture. You also can rotate a selected picture using arrow key shortcuts. Pressing Alt+Left or Right Arrow rotates the picture. If you add Ctrl key and press Ctrl+Alt+left arrow or Ctrl+Alt+Right Arrow, the rotation happens in smaller increments.

If you click the Position tab of the Layout dialog box shown in Figure 14.15, additional options of interest include the following:

- **Move object with text:** Associates a picture or graphic with a particular paragraph so that the paragraph and the picture will always appear on the same page. This setting affects only vertical position on the page. Although Word will allow you to check this option and Lock anchor at the same time, once you click OK the Move object with text option is cleared.

- **Lock anchor:** This setting locks the picture's current position on the page. If you have trouble dragging a picture, verify that it is set to one of the floating wrapping options (anything but In line with text), and that Lock anchor is turned off. Pictures that have been positioned with any of the nine Position gallery presets will also resist dragging.

- **Allow overlap:** Use this setting to allow graphical objects to cover each other up. One use for this is to create a stack of photographs or other objects. This feature is also needed for layered drawings.

- **Layout in table cell:** This setting enables you to use tables for positioning graphics on the page.

Cropping

To crop a picture, click the Crop button in the Size group in the Picture Tools ⇨ Format tab. Cropping handles appear on the selected picture. Move the pointer over any of the eight cropping handles, and when it changes shape to match the handle, drag to remove the part of the picture you want to hide. Click outside the picture to finish applying the crop. Note that pressing the Alt key while dragging slowly crops in discrete steps.

Clicking the down arrow on the bottom of the Crop button reveals other options for customized cropping. You can click Crop to Shape and then click one of the shapes in the gallery that appears to crop the picture to fit within the specified shape, as in the star example in Figure 14.16. Use the Aspect Ratio option to crop the image to standard proportions, such as 1:1 to square the image or 3:5 for a portrait (tall) image. Cropping all the images in a document to the same aspect ratio can lend a more consistent appearance. You can also use the Fill and Fit commands to resize the image within the current picture area. Fill generally snaps the picture back to its original aspect ratio, which may undo the crop depending on how it was applied, and Fit shrinks the picture so previously cropped areas redisplay at a smaller size within the picture area.

FIGURE 14.16

Crop to hide part of a picture or to change its overall shape.

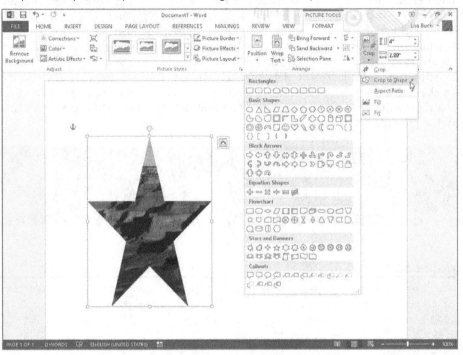

Formatting a picture or shape

You don't have to settle for a picture's original appearance when you insert it into a document. Word offers a variety of tools for making formatting adjustments. Applying uniform styles and effects to the pictures and other graphics in a document creates a unified look. This is the kind of approach that graphic designers use to create the brand identity for a magazine, for example. Here you learn how to find the settings you need to update the appearance of pictures and other graphics in your documents. Word offers dozens of changes that you can apply, so much so that every feature cannot be covered in detail here. Taking the time to explore the settings introduced here can help you make a document's graphics even more interesting.

Applying picture styles

Double-clicking one of the items in the Picture Styles of the Format tab enables you to apply any of a number of preset styles to the selected picture. The styles include various combinations of frames or borders, cropping, glows, shadows, and more. After selecting the picture, click the More button to display all of the gallery's choices. As shown in Figure 14.17, you can move the mouse over each style to see a Live Preview of it on the selected picture (or pictures). Note that the speed of Live Preview may be heavily affected by the size of the graphic file. If the picture is 2 MB, Live Preview is going to be a lot slower than if the file were only 50 KB. When you find the style that you prefer, click it to apply it to the picture.

> **NOTE**
>
> Note that for shapes, the Drawing Tools ⇨ Format tab has a Shape Styles group with a Shape Styles gallery. The choices in that gallery enable you to apply different combinations of fills and borders, based on the applied theme, to the selected shape.

FIGURE 14.17

Use Live Preview to choose a picture style to apply.

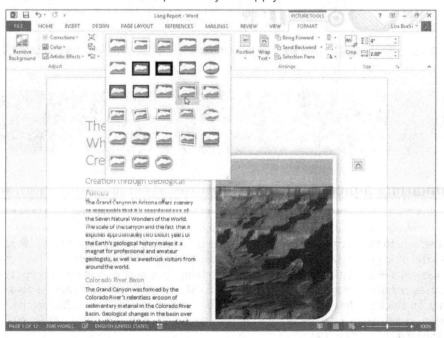

Applying a border or picture effects

You can apply a basic color border to a selected picture using the Picture Border button in the Picture Styles group of the Picture Tools ⇨ Format tab. (For a shape, you would use the Shape Outline tool in the Shape Styles group of the Drawing Tools ⇨ Format tab.) You have the option of using the drop-down that appears to change three settings for the border:

- **Color:** Click one of the Theme Colors or Standard Colors, or click More Outline Colors to choose a custom color. Keep in mind that when you use a theme color, the border color will update if you change the document theme.

- **Weight:** Click this option and then click a border width in the submenu that appears.

- **Dashes:** Click to display a submenu of border styles, and then click the desired style.

Click the No Outline choice in the Picture Border drop-down to remove any previously applied outline.

You can apply and refine additional effects with the Picture Effects tool, also located in the Picture Styles group. You can choose one of the Preset choices that combines effects, or apply any combination of individual effects that you prefer. In Figure 14.18, the picture already has a Reflection choice and a Bevel choice applied, and the Live Preview shows a potential Glow effect.

FIGURE 14.18

Apply any combination of Picture Effects to achieve the look you want.

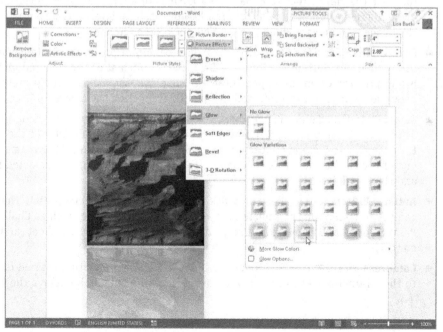

TIP

Use the Picture Layout choice in the Picture Styles group of the Picture Tools ⇨ Format tab to convert a picture to a SmartArt object. See Chapter 13, "Building Tables, Charts, and Smart Art to Show Data and Process," for more about working with SmartArt.

Applying other picture adjustments

Word also features seven tools for adjusting picture attributes, shown in Figure 14.19.

FIGURE 14.19

The Adjust group contains seven tools for additional picture corrections.

Use the tools to accomplish a number of common tasks:

- **Remove Background:** Lets you automatically/selectively remove portions of a picture based on color patterns. For example, this feature can remove everything from a picture except for a single object, such as a flower or a car. After you click this tool, use the Mark Areas to Remove, Mark Areas to Keep, and Remove Mark buttons in the Refine group of the Background Removal tab to determine which portions of the image to remove and keep, and then click Keep Changes.

- **Corrections:** Clicking this button displays a gallery of preset corrections you can use to Sharpen/Soften or adjust the Brightness/Contrast of the selected picture for better printing or onscreen presentation. Move your mouse over the presets to preview their impact on the selected image, and then click the desired preset.

- **Color:** Open this gallery to see Color Saturation and Color Tone correction presets, as well as a variety of Recolor options for changing the overall color of the image. For example, you can apply Grayscale, Sepia, or Washout, or recolor the image using one of the theme colors. Use the mouse to preview a choice on the selected image, and then click it.

- **Artistic Effects:** This gallery provides more than a dozen special presets that you can use to transform the selected picture's overall appearance, such as Chalk Sketch, Paint Strokes, and Film Grain. Use your mouse to Live Preview an effect, and then click it.

- **Compress Picture:** Use this tool to reduce the size of the pictures stored in the file to the minimum needed for a given output. Clicking this tool displays the Compress

Pictures dialog box shown in Figure 14.20. Under Compression Options, clear the Apply only to this picture check box if you want to compress all pictures in the document. Choose a resolution under Target output, and then click OK. If you will need to make high-quality printouts of your document, be cautious when using this feature. Compressing picture size can reduce the image quality, and because the feature discards information during the process, you can't undo it later.

- **Change Picture:** Clicking this tool opens the Insert Pictures window, where you can choose to replace the selected picture with a different one. You can either use Insert from file to select a locally stored replacement image file or search online for a replacement. Picture Styles and Effects applied carry over to the replacement picture, as do changes applied with other tools in the Adjust group. Cropping and resizing, however, do not.

- **Reset Picture:** Removes formatting applied with Picture Styles, Picture Effects, and other Adjust tools (except for Change and Compress). If you open the menu for this option, as noted earlier, you can Choose Reset Picture & Size to restore a cropped picture.

FIGURE 14.20

Compress pictures to reduce the file size of the Word document.

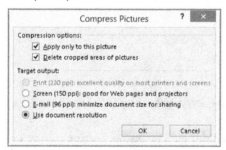

Using the Format Picture pane

If you click the dialog box launcher in the Picture Styles group of the Picture Tools ⇨ Format tab, the Format Picture pane shown in Figure 14.21 appears at the right. You also can display this pane by right-clicking a selected picture and clicking Format Picture. The Format Picture pane in Word 2013 replaces the Format Picture dialog box found in previous Word versions and offers settings for you to fine-tune presets and other format changes made to a selected picture. Click one of the icons at top to choose an overall category of settings, click an arrow to expand particular settings, and then change the detailed settings. For example, Figure 14.21 shows the detailed settings for working with the Reflection preset applied to the selected image. The category icons at the top of the pane include:

FIGURE 14.21

Find more detailed settings in the Format Picture pane.

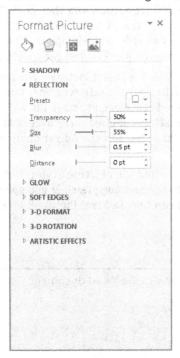

- **Fill & Line:** Use to change the settings for any interior Fill or Line (border) applied to the picture.
- **Effects:** Select to work with detailed Shadow, Reflection, Glow, Soft Edges, 3-D Format, 3-D Rotation, and Artistic Effects settings for the selected image.
- **Layout & Properties:** The Text Box settings here generally are not active for pictures, but you can use the Alt Text choices to add accessibility information.
- **Picture:** Make changes here to Picture Correction, Picture Color, and Crop settings.

> **NOTE**
>
> The Format Shape pane that appears when you click the dialog box launcher for the Shape Styles group of the Drawing Tools ⟡ Format tab offers similar choices for reformatting a selected shape or other graphic such as a text box.

> **NOTE**
>
> For some types of objects, you can display a pane with formatting or other settings by double-clicking, but this technique doesn't work with image files.

Adding Online Video

You can insert a video clip from Bing Video Search, an embed code from another video site or website, or YouTube. For example, if you're writing a report about an Apollo mission, you can find a video clip about it and add it. Video clips of product demonstrations also can supplement a product instruction document that you intend to convert to PDF or HTML web format and post online. You insert all three types of video using the Insert Video window shown in Figure 14.22. If you've already copied a video embed code from another website, click the Paste embed code here text box beside From a Video Embed Code, and then click the Insert button at the right side of the text box. If you select YouTube, it moves up from the bottom of the window to the list of search options, and you can use the search box that appears for it to search for and insert a video.

FIGURE 14.22

Use the new Insert Video feature to find and download video clips using Bing Video Search.

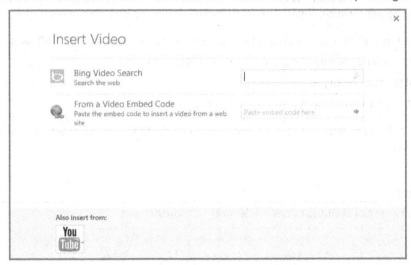

Here's how to find and insert an image from Bing Video Search in a document.

1. **Make sure you are signed in and your system is connected to the Internet, and click to position the insertion point where you want to insert the video.**
2. **Click the Insert tab, and then click Online Video in the Media group.** The Insert Video window shown in Figure 14.22 appears.

3. **Type a search term in the text box to the right of Bing Video Search, and then click the Search (magnifying glass) button at the right.** Insert Video finds and displays matching clips.

4. **Scroll down to preview additional clips, if needed, click the one you want, and then click Insert.** Word downloads the image or illustration and displays it at the insertion point.

If you click the inserted video clip, the Picture Tools ⇨ Format tab appears, and you can use its tools as described earlier to adjust the appearance of the clip. Click the Play button on the clip to play it.

Creating WordArt

If there's something creative you need to do to text, and Word's normal text tools don't even come close to what you need, then WordArt probably has what you're looking for. WordArt enables you to get creative if you need to accomplish unique tasks like these:

- Stretch text diagonally across the page so you can make a CLASSIFIED watermark.
- Make a fancy banner headline for a newsletter or flyer.
- Rotate text to any angle.
- Place text in a circle for making a button.

Figure 14.23 shows several of the text shapes and effects that you can create using Word 2013 WordArt.

FIGURE 14.23

Combine a variety of settings to create decorative WordArt text.

Creating classic WordArt

When you open a Word 97–2003 document in Compatibility Mode, certain features are disabled, such as the ability to insert SmartArt graphics or take a screenshot. You can still insert WordArt in Compatibility Mode using the command described next, but when you display the gallery of WordArt styles, the styles you see are the Classic WordArt styles available in Word 97–2003. The WordArt styles were updated starting with Word 2007. If you attempt to copy a Classic WordArt object to a Word 2013 file or convert a .doc file with Classic WordArt to .docx format, Word 2013 attempts to reformat the WordArt object, and the results may not be appropriate or attractive. So if you want to retain the Classic WordArt styling in a Word 97–2003 document, don't convert it. If you do decide to convert it, however, you will likely need to reapply updated WordArt styles to all WordArt objects.

Creating WordArt from scratch

The WordArt tool makes it surprisingly simple to create decorative text. Here's how to insert a new WordArt object into your document:

1. **Click to position the insertion point where you want to insert the WordArt.**

2. **Click the Insert tab, and then click the Insert WordArt button in the Text group.** Word presents you with the WordArt Style gallery, shown in Figure 14.24.

FIGURE 14.24

Click a style in the WordArt gallery.

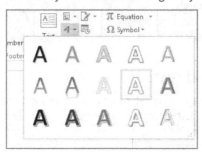

3. **Click a style in the gallery.** Word applies the style to the placeholder phrase Your Text Here in the WordArt object.

4. **Type your text.**

5. **(Optional) Select the text in the object and apply additional formatting as desired.** This step is optional because you also can reselect the WordArt later to change its formatting.

6. **Click Outside the WordArt object to finish it.**

14

The wrap setting applied to a new WordArt object varies depending on whether the document already has text or not. If you insert WordArt in a blank document or one with only other objects, the new WordArt graphic appears in the upper-left corner of the document (although not in the header), formatted with wrapping set to In Front of Text. You can change the wrapping as desired using the Wrap Text choices in the Arrange group of the Drawing Tools ⇨ Format tab, and drag the WordArt text box where you want it.

If you positioned the insertion point in some text or have selected some text before adding the WordArt, it is inserted at the beginning of the current paragraph, also formatted with the In Front of Text wrapping style. You can change the wrapping style to create a decorative effect at the beginning of the paragraph, as shown in Figure 14.25.

FIGURE 14.25

Use WordArt to draw attention to the beginning of the paragraph or create wrapped titles.

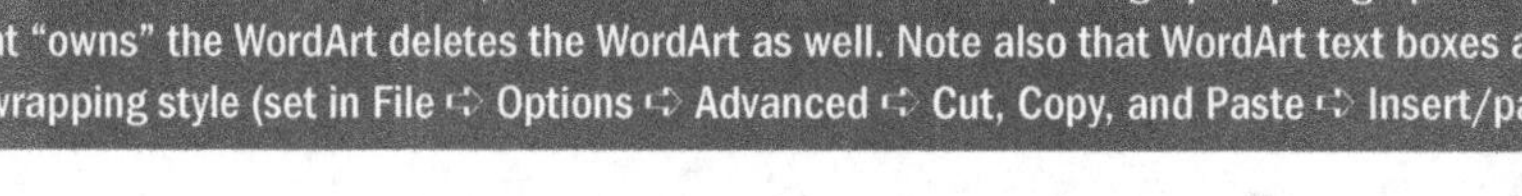

Creation through Geological Forces

The Grand Canyon in Arizona offers scenery so memorable that it is considered one of the Seven Natural Wonders of the World. The scale of the canyon and the fact that it exposes approximately two billion years of the Earth's geological history makes it a magnet for professional and amateur geologists, as well as awestruck visitors from around the world.

> **NOTE**
>
> When you insert WordArt within text, Word anchors it to the current paragraph's paragraph mark. Deleting the paragraph mark that "owns" the WordArt deletes the WordArt as well. Note also that WordArt text boxes are *not* inserted with the default wrapping style (set in File ⇨ Options ⇨ Advanced ⇨ Cut, Copy, and Paste ⇨ Insert/paste pictures as).

Creating WordArt from selected text

If you've already entered all the text for a document or have received a document to format from another person, the text that you want to format as WordArt may already be included in the document. If that's the case, select the text, and then select the WordArt type as described in Steps 2 and 3 in the previous section. The selected text appears in the WordArt object. Unlike in Word 2007 and earlier, the 10-word/200-character limit for WordArt text no longer exists, so it's possible to format entire paragraphs as WordArt. You might want to do this to create a flyer or a pull quote.

Formatting WordArt text

Because WordArt is integrated into Word's main graphics engine, Word displays the Drawing Tools ⇨ Format contextual tab when you select a WordArt object by clicking it and then clicking its border. As shown in Figure 14.26, the tab offers the same text-formatting tools that are available for text boxes and the same shape-formatting tools that are available for all Word shapes. (Chapter 15, "Adding Drop Caps, Text Boxes, Shapes, Symbols, and Equations," covers creating text boxes and shapes.) You will also notice that there is also a lot of overlap of applicable tools when you're working with pictures.

FIGURE 14.26

Word displays the Drawing Tools ➪ Format tab for formatting WordArt.

Use the tools in the WordArt Styles and Text groups to format text. Any of these formatting tools can be applied letter by letter if that is what required. In addition, you can use the normal settings in the Font and Paragraph groups of the Home tab to make changes to the selected WordArt text.

Moving, sizing, and rotating WordArt

WordArt shapes can be formatted like any other picture or shape in Word. The techniques for moving, sizing, rotating and so on described earlier in this chapter work the same for WordArt. WordArt text can be rotated to any angle using the rotate handle above the top center selection handle. You're not limited to the settings offered with the Text Direction tool in the Text group of the Drawing Tools ➪ Format tab. Also, you can reverse WordArt both horizontally and vertically—by dragging top over bottom, side over side, and corner over corner, essentially flipping the object and the text it contains. You can use this method, or you can use the Rotate Objects choice in the Arrange group to rotate and flip the selected WordArt.

Changing WordArt styles

One basic change you may want to make to a selected Word Art object is to change to another WordArt style. To see the gallery, click the Quick Styles button in the WordArt Styles group (if your screen is at a low resolution) or if the gallery appears in the group, click its More button. The available styles are the same as those shown in Figure 14.24, during the discussion about how to create WordArt. Simply click an alternate style to apply it.

The WordArt Styles group also contains the Text Fill, Text Outline, and Text Effects tools. Clicking Text Fill then enables you to click a new color to use as the fill for the WordArt text. Text Outline and Text Effects enable you to change the WordArt text outline and effects, and work just as described earlier for pictures under "Applying a border or picture effects."

Changing 3-D rotation

While there are a number of Effects choices you may want to apply to WordArt, 3-D Rotation is one that can make the WordArt really pop from the page. Click Text Effects ➪ 3-D Rotation to use Live Preview to select a rotation setting as shown in Figure 14.27, and then click it.

Changing the WordArt background

While the tools in the WordArt Styles group of the Drawing Tools ➪ Format tab apply to the text within a WordArt object, the tools in the Shape Styles group enable you to change the fill and outline for the WordArt object's surrounding box, creating a rectangular background for the WordArt graphic. In the example in Figure 14.28, I've added a fill color, as well as used the Soft Edges and Shadow effects to give the object dimension. By combining text formatting and overall shape formatting, you can create interesting effects and special objects such as a newsletter title.

FIGURE 14.27

Rotation controls give you the ability to display WordArt in virtually any position.

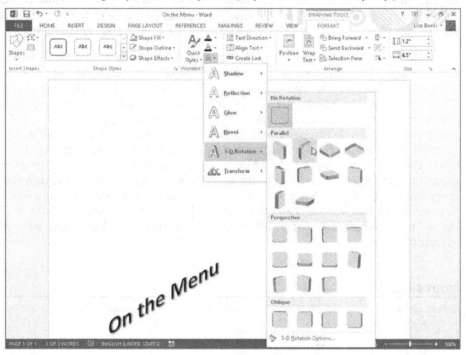

FIGURE 14.28

You also can format the WordArt object's background using the choices in the Shape Styles group.

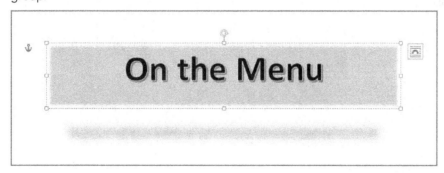

14

Shaping and transforming WordArt

Another important formatting change most users want to know about is how to change the overall shape of a WordArt object. Depending on what you are wanting to accomplish, there are two ways to do this: with the Format Shape pane or with the Transform tools.

If you click the dialog box launcher for either the Shape Styles or WordArt Styles groups in the Drawing Tools ➪ Format tab, the Format Shape pane appears at right as shown in Figure 14.29. You also can right-click a selected WordArt object and click Format Shape to display the pane. The Format Shape pane works just like the Format Picture pane described earlier under "Using the Format Picture pane." One exception appears at the top of the pane, where you see Shape Options and Text Options choices. Click these as needed to flip between formatting the overall WordArt shape and the text in the shape. For example, Figure 14.29 shows the 3-D Rotation Options for the shape text, because Text Options is selected at the top of the pane. The X, Y, and Z Rotation controls let you rotate the text within the object in three dimensions. This allows you to, among other things, rotate text to any angle, as well as to rotate the text vertically and horizontally. (If you selected Shape Options at the top of the pane, rotation changes appear differently.) Click the pane's Close button when you finish choosing settings.

FIGURE 14.29

Select detailed formatting options for the WordArt shape and text in the Format Shape pane.

If using the Format Shape pane doesn't give you the effect you are looking for, you can use the Transform tools. With the WordArt object selected, select Text Effects ⇨ Transform, and point to the different transformations provided. As shown in Figure 14.30, Live Preview shows how the effect would look if applied. When you click a choice, Word applies the new shape and also adds one or more additional controls, which appear as little purple diamonds.

You can use these controls to further shape or warp the text inside. Drag one of the controls, and as you drag a diagram appears showing a preview of the shape. When you like what you see, release the mouse button.

FIGURE 14.30

Use Transform to warp WordArt text.

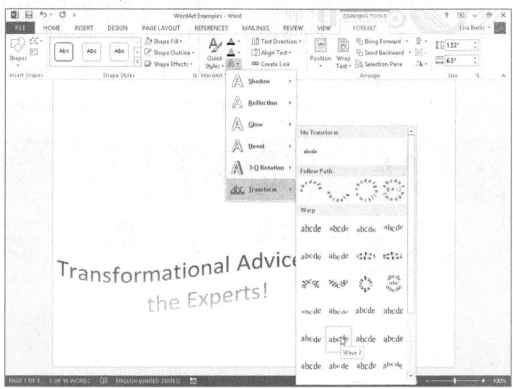

Arranging Pictures and Other Objects

In addition to the Position and Wrap Text tools described earlier in the chapter, the Arrange group of the Picture Tools ⇨ and Drawing Tools ⇨ Format tabs has tools for working with the layering, alignment, grouping, and rotation of various types of Word graphics. These additional tools are:

- **Bring Forward:** When layering objects, moves the selected object one layer forward. Click the arrow to choose the Bring to Front (brings to the top layer) or Bring in Front of Text choices.

- **Send Backward:** When layering objects, moves the selected object one layer backward. Click the arrow to choose the Bring to Back (moves to the bottom layer) or Send Behind Text choices.

- **Align Objects:** Gives you choices for aligning selected objects relative to one another (when Align to Margin is selected). For example, click Align Center to align all objects relative to their center points. You also can choose Distribute Horizontally or Distribute vertically to space the objects equally.

- **Group Objects:** Allows you to group and ungroup selected objects. Grouping object enables you to move them as a unit.

- **Rotate Objects:** Enables you to rotate or flip the selected object by selecting a preset rather than using the rotate handle.

> **TIP**
>
> To select multiple graphic objects before aligning or grouping them, select the first object, and then use Shift+click or Ctrl+click to select more.

In Figure 14.31, I layered a WordArt object over a picture. I applied Bring to Front to the WordArt and Send to Back for the Picture. I selected both objects and used Align Objects ⇨ Align Center and then Align Objects ⇨ Align Top to position them. Finally, I grouped the objects.

FIGURE 14.31

Also use the Arrange choices to arrange objects relative to one another and group them.

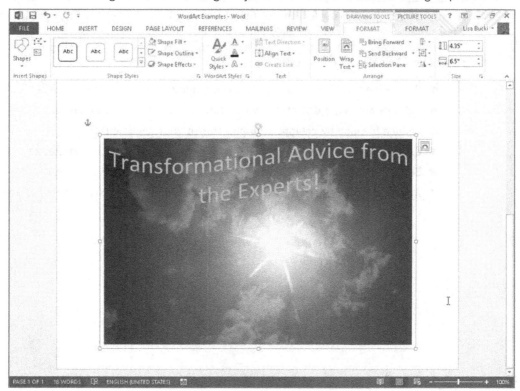

Summary

In this chapter you've learned how to insert pictures into Word documents and how to use Word's tools—new and old—to mold those pictures into art. You've also seen how to find images online and insert them, as well as how to create dynamic text using WordArt. You should now be able to do the following:

- Determine whether Word supports the graphic format of your pictures
- Achieve any wrapping effect when working with text and graphics
- Reduce file size by compressing pictures in your documents
- Use WordArt to create a masthead banner for a newspaper or newsletter
- Bend and curve text in creative ways to help make a point in a flyer
- Apply different colors to WordArt to blend with other artistic aspects of your publication

Adding Drop Caps, Text Boxes, Shapes, Symbols, and Equations

IN THIS CHAPTER

Decorating a document with a drop cap

Understanding text boxes and when to use them

Using a text box preset or drawing your own

Formatting text boxes

Adding and formatting shapes

Adding text to a shape to make it a text box

Inserting symbols and special characters

Inserting built-in gallery equations or creating your own

Editing and numbering equations

This chapter zeroes in on a group features that you can use to add decorative interest or emphasis to text or to incorporate special information in ways not possible through basic typing. The chapter starts by looking at drop caps and text boxes, which you can use to emphasize text. You'll also learn how to insert and format basic shapes. Depending on how you position and format shapes, you can create some interesting effects, including adding text to a shape to make it into your own unique text box.

This chapter also covers symbols, including how to locate the symbol you need and how to insert it into your document. Then it's time to put on your Dexter glasses and look using Word's equation tools to represent often complex concepts in mathematics, statistics, engineering, and other quantitative fields.

Adding a Drop Cap for Drama

When you want to emphasize the beginning of an article or a chapter, try converting the first character or word of the paragraph into a drop cap. This historical technique was developed to call attention to the first part of the document and grew to involve hand-drawn decorations and coloring along with the letter or word itself. At the most basic level, you can create a drop cap by making the letter or word significantly larger than the rest of the paragraph. But you also can use the Drop Cap feature in Word to size and position the selected letter or word as a drop cap in one action. Here's how to add a drop cap in your document:

1. **Select the letter or word to make into a drop cap.** Note that if you intend to position the drop cap beside the text, you should select only a letter, not a word.

2. **(Optional) Apply a different font to the selection to further distinguish it from the rest of the text.**

3. **Click the Insert tab, and click Drop Cap in the Text group.** Note that if your screen is at a higher resolution, the button may appear larger and its name may be visible.

4. **Move the mouse over either the Dropped or In margin choice to see a Live Preview, as shown in Figure 15.1.**

5. **Click to choose the drop-cap style to apply.**

FIGURE 15.1

Add a drop cap at the beginning of an article or chapter.

> **NOTE**
>
> After you insert the drop cap, you can leave it selected and reopen the Drop Cap menu. Click Drop Cap Options. In the Drop Cap dialog box, you can change the Position and Font, and also fine-tune the drop cap by changing the Lines to drop and Distance from text settings. Click OK to apply your changes.

Why Use Text Boxes?

Text boxes are shapes that can contain text. They are containers that themselves can be manipulated as graphics but that can contain text (and some other objects). Text boxes do the following:

- Enable you to place text anywhere on the page, including on top of other text
- Can be bordered or unbordered, filled or unfilled
- Can be chained or linked together so that text flows from one into a second, into a third, and so on
- Can be any shape, although the inside text itself is constrained to a rectangular shape)
- Can be rotated to any angle

When you first insert a text box, it's purely a rectangular container for text. However, you can quickly and easily transform it through a variety of formatting tools, including rotating the text box. There are at least three possible alternatives to text boxes, so it's appropriate to ask why you should use them. Each of the three alternatives offers different capabilities:

- **A single-cell table:** Pro: It can automatically expand as text is added to it. You can selectively border the sides differently, if needed. It can be divided internally into more cells with hidden internal borders for special effects. It can be made into a floating table so that text can wrap around it. Con: It has limited wrapping talents, its wrapping points can't be changed, it cannot be rotated, and it's limited to a rectangular exterior format.
- **A WordArt object:** Pro: Almost infinite possibilities for shaping and contouring text. Fully flexible wrapping capabilities. Con: It is limited to a rectangular exterior shape.
- **A bordered paragraph:** Pro: It is normal text, so it has a full range of regular text properties. It's easy to understand. Con: It has no wrapping capabilities and can appear only in line with other text, since it is regular text. Note that if you insert a bordered paragraph as an object, it will simulate some aspects of a text box. However, manipulation and editing then become correspondingly more tedious. Moreover, it's no longer "normal text" that doesn't require special handling.

Inserting a Text Box

To insert a predefined text box from the Text Box gallery:

1. **Click to position the insertion point to where you want the text box to appear in the document.**
2. **Click the Text Box button in the Text group of the Insert tab.** As shown in Figure 15.2, the gallery of ready-to-use text boxes appears.

15

FIGURE 15.2

You can insert any of more than 30 prebuilt text boxes, or draw your own from scratch.

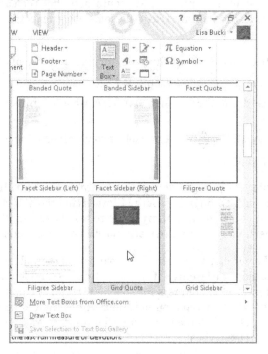

3. **Scroll through the list and, if you see a text box that looks as if it will work for your purposes, click it.** As shown in Figure 15.3, the text box appears approximately at the insertion point.

4. **Type your text to replace the placeholder text.**

The text boxes that come with Word have been preformatted with a variety of attributes that make them suitable for different purposes. You can use them to provide tips in a how-to document or to add a box with a list of topics or scheduled events. A traditional use is to present a quote "pulled" from the text of the document. Often used in magazines, *pull quotes* highlight an interesting portion of the text.

TIP

To make creating your pull quote faster, copy the text you want to quote first. Then create the text box and paste the quoted text in.

FIGURE 15.3

Ready-to-use text boxes are preformatted with borders, wrapping styles, and other formatting attributes that make them easy to use.

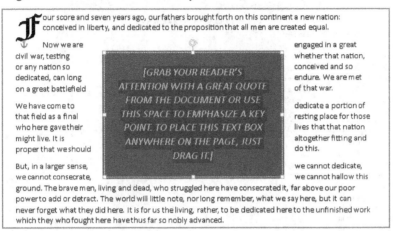

> **NOTE**
>
> The text inside the text box in Figure 15.3 appears in square brackets because it is a content control device. Developers use content controls to create forms and templates that guide you in adding your own text where required. See Chapter 24, "Forms," for more about content controls.

More about prefab text boxes

Word stores all the predesigned text boxes in the Building Blocks gallery. To open it, click the Quick Parts button in the Text group of the Insert tab, and click Building Blocks Organizer. Scroll down until you can see Text Boxes in the Gallery column. As shown in Figure 15.4, you can click a text box Building Block to see a preview at the right. If you create your own text boxes or modify prefab ones that you want to reuse, you can add them to the Text Box gallery, and they will appear both there and in the Building Blocks Organizer. To save a text box as a Building Blocks gallery item, see "Adding a new Building Block or Quick Part" in Chapter 12, "Getting Smart with Text: Building Blocks, Quick Parts, Actions (Tags), and More."

15

FIGURE 15.4

You can insert text boxes from the Building Blocks Organizer if you prefer to see a terser listing.

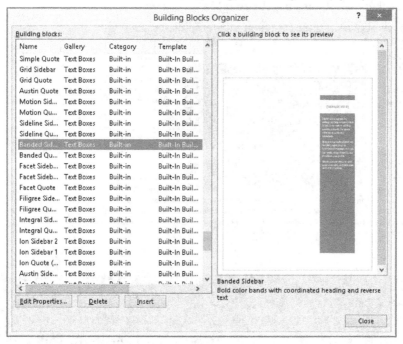

Designing your own text box

You can also insert your own text boxes from scratch. Click Text Box in the text group of the Insert tab on the Ribbon and click Draw Textbox. The mouse pointer turns into a large plus sign. Drag on the document until the text box reaches the size you want, as shown in Figure 15.5. Release the mouse button and you now have your text box. If you click the text box, it will display six sizing handles.

When drawing a text box, you can hold down the following keys to modify the resulting box:

- **Shift:** Forces the box to retain the current aspect ratio.
- **Ctrl:** Forces the box to expand symmetrically in two directions, expanding from the center (up and down or left and right, depending on which way you drag), rather than just in the direction being dragged.
- **Alt:** If gridlines are not displayed, this forces the box to increase in discrete increments that are aligned with the invisible grid. If gridlines are displayed, Alt allows smooth dragging that ignores the grid. With a text box selected, click the Drawing Tools ⇨ Format tab, click Align in the Arrange group, and click View Gridlines to toggle gridlines.

FIGURE 15.5

Drag to create the text box size you want.

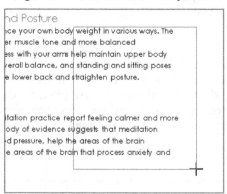

After drawing the new text box, type or paste your text into it. From there, you can format it as needed. One obvious change for a hand-drawn text box is the need to wrap other document text around it. You can change wrapping and other formatting settings for a hand-drawn or preset text box as described next.

Formatting a text box

Click a text box to select it and display its formatting tools, which appear in the Drawing Tools ⇨ Format contextual tab, shown in Figure 15.6. Many of these tools were already covered in Chapter 14, "Adding Pictures and WordArt to Highlight Information," and work just as explained there, so in this chapter, I'll just review the key points you need to recall.

FIGURE 15.6

For all intents and purposes, text boxes can be formatted like other graphics as described in Chapter 14.

To edit or format the text itself—to change font, point size, and other character-formatting attributes—first select the text box and then drag over the text to change. Edit the text or use the tools in the Home tab, the tools in the Mini Toolbar (if text is selected), or keyboard shortcuts, as described in Chapter 5, "Font/Character Formatting." Formatting works

15

for text boxes as it does for ordinary text. Select what you want to format and then apply the formatting. You can apply paragraph and style formatting as well, perhaps even creating dedicated styles for formatting text box text.

Rotating the text box

You can display text box text (as well as table text) in any degree of rotation, as shown in Figure 15.7. Typical applications for rotated text include mirroring text for tent cards, calling attention to a banner headline, and the simulation of index tabs in the right margin. For example, you might include the current chapter number and title in a text box at the right side and rotate the text box so that the text down the side of the page.

FIGURE 15.7

You can rotate a text box to any angle.

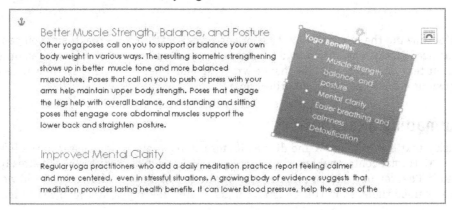

To rotate a text box, drag the rotate handle above the top center selection handle until the text box is in the desired attitude. For very precise or 3-D rotation, right-click the text box border and choose Format Shape. The Format Text Effects pane appears at the right. Leave Shape Options selected at the top of the pane, click the Effects icon (with the pentagon shape), and then click the triangle beside 3-D Rotation to display its options. Use the X, Y, and Z Rotation tools to twist and turn the text box as desired. Or, use the Presets to choose a rotation that fits your needs, or choose one that makes a better starting point before you customize the rotation. Click the pane Close (X) button to close it when you've finished changing Rotation and other settings.

Chaining or linking text boxes

You can use the Create Link button in the Text group of the Drawing Tools ➪ Format tab to chain or link text boxes together. Many users see the name of this tool (Create *Link*) and immediately think about *hyperlinks*. That's not what this feature is about. Instead, the chain tool, as it's more appropriately known, makes text flow from one text box into another. For example, you could use this technique when creating a newsletter. The strategy is to use one or more linked text boxes for each story or article. If you paste the copied story into the first text box and it is too small to display all the pasted contents, you can continue the article in another text box by linking the two.

For example, Figure 15.8 shows two text boxes. Some text was copied and pasted into the left text box, but there is too much text to fit there. With that text box selected, click the Create Link button in the Text group of the Format tab. This turns the mouse pointer into a cup that's tilted sideways with letters spilling out of it. Move the pointer over the text box into which you want that text to "spill," and click to cause text to flow from the first text box to the second.

FIGURE 15.8

With one text box selected, click the Create Link button, and then click the text box into which you want the first text box's text to flow.

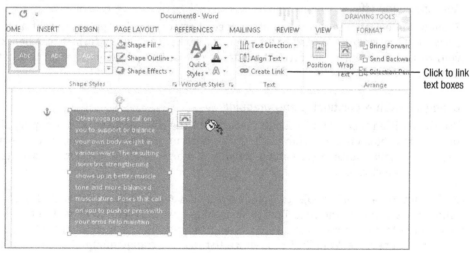

Applying a shape style

The Shape Styles tools, shown in the Shape Styles group of the Format tab shown in Figure 15.6, are used to apply preset combinations of fill, outline borders, shadow effects, and 3-D effects to text boxes. The same styles are available for formatting any WordArt objects, as described in greater detail in Chapter 14. To apply a style, click the More drop-down arrow at the bottom of the Shape Styles gallery, and then move the mouse over the styles. Use Live Preview to determine the style you want, and then click it.

15

You can apply shape styles to multiple objects at the same time. To select multiple text boxes, click the first one you want to select and then Shift+click each additional text box. Once they're all selected you can apply shape styles or other formatting as needed. When you're trying to achieve a particular theme by coordinating the shapes of all included text boxes, this can save you some work.

Changing the fill outline

The Shape Fill and Shape Outline both work with Live Preview, and enable you to change the interior and outline of a shape respectively. As discussed in Chapter 14, rather than use one of the preformatted shape styles, you can apply your own shape fill and outline. You can also start with one of the preformatted styles, and then modify it as you like.

Applying shape effects

Shadow, Reflection, Glow, 3-D and other special effects can be applied to text boxes as shown in Chapter 14. As noted earlier, you can either completely format text boxes on your own or start with a preformatted shape style and then apply different touches as needed.

Changing text box positioning and wrapping

Use the Position tool group to simultaneously set the page position and wrapping of the selected text box. Click Position in the Arrange group of the Format tab, move the mouse over the various choices to see a Live Preview of where it would position the selected text box, and then click OK.

As for pictures and other objects, you generally have to change a text box's default wrapping setting from In Line with Text to something else to be able to move the text box. To change the text wrapping setting for the selected text box (instead of choosing a position), click it and open the Wrap Text drop-down list in the Arrange group of the Format tab, and then choose the desired wrapping setting. Or click the Layout Options button beside the selected box, and then click a choice under In Line with Text or With Text Wrapping, as shown in Figure 15.9. Chapter 14 provides a more detailed explanation of text wrapping.

FIGURE 15.9

Use Layout Options to change text wrapping for the selected text box.

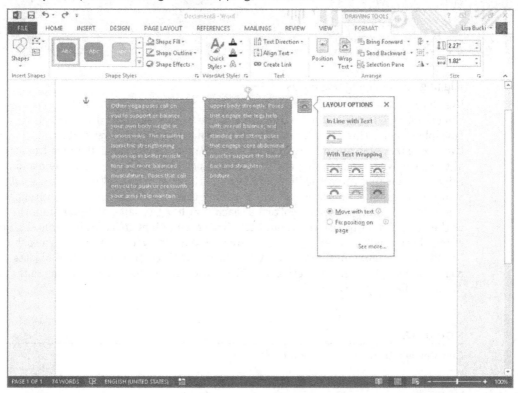

> **TIP**
>
> When you copy or cut and then paste a text box or shape, the Paste Options button appears. You can usually paste the object with its source formatting or paste it as a picture.

Bring Forward and Send Backward

Use the Bring Forward and Send Backward tools in the Arrange group of the Drawing Tools ⇨ Format tab to change the text box's location in the graphics layers of the document. You can, for example, overlap text boxes with other text boxes and/or other graphics to create special effects. As a general technique, click the object you want to have reside at the deepest layer, drag it to where you want it, and then choose Send Backward ⇨ Send to Back. Select the object that will be directly on top of the deepest one, and click Send Backward until it's where you want it. Depending on how many layers you have, you may need to switch among the Bring Forward and Send Backward options.

15

Aligning and grouping text boxes

Use the Arrange group's Align tool options, shown in Figure 15.10, to align multiple selected objects relative to each other and relative to the page or margin. Use Shift+click to select multiple objects. This provides more precision than using your eyes and hands. If you have two text boxes of differing heights and want them to be the same distance from the top of the page, without changing their horizontal positions, select both of them and choose Align ⇨ Align Top. Align Middle would move both objects vertically so that a single horizontal line would cut both in half while leaving their horizontal positions untouched, and Align Bottom would make the bottom of each text box the same distance from the bottom of the page. Similarly, use the Align Left, Center, and Right tools for horizontal alignment of text boxes and/or other objects that are vertically arrayed with respect to each other. Use Distribute Horizontally/Vertically to spread out three or more selected objects on the page. For a single object, the effects of Distribute will be the same as Align Center and Align Middle, respectively.

FIGURE 15.10

Chapter 14 introduced the Align tools.

Use the Group tool to connect two or more text boxes (and/or other objects) so that they act as if they were a single object. This typically is used when you have, for example, pictures that are positioned precisely either inside or relative to a text box and you want their relative locations maintained when the objects are moved or copied elsewhere in the document. To group selected objects, choose Group ⇨ Group in the Arrange group of the Format tab. If you need to move or apply distinct formatting to an object relative to those in its set, click the group and choose Group ⇨ Ungroup. Once you've moved or reformatted the object, choose Group ⇨ Group again to reconnect the group.

The Format Shape pane

When working with text boxes, you can use the Format Shape pane described earlier to make more detailed changes. To display it, right-click a text box's border and choose Format Shape, or click the dialog box launcher in the Drawing Tools ⇨ Format tab's Shape Styles group. As shown in Figure 15.11, choose Shape Options or Text Options at the top to determine whether to format the box itself or the text within. Use the icons that appear below the first selection to determine what category to format such as Fill & Line, and then click a name such as Fill or Line to expand the detailed settings in the pane. Chapter 14 covered more about working with this pane. Explore it to learn about the detailed settings applying to text boxes. Click the pane's Close (X) button when you finish using it.

FIGURE 15.11

Use the Format Shape pane for more direct and precise control over text boxes.

Inserting a Shape

In addition to inserting a rectangular text box into a document, you can insert a pre-defined shape. To add a shape to the current page of the document:

1. **Click the Insert tab, and in the Illustrations group, click Shapes.**
2. **In the Shapes gallery (see Figure 15.12), click a shape in one of the categories: Recently Used Shapes, Lines, Rectangles, Basic Shapes, Block Arrows, Equation Shapes, Flowchart, Stars and Banners, or Callouts.**
3. **Add the shape to the document using one of two methods:**
   - Click to insert the shape at its default size.
   - Drag on the page to specify the size that you want for the shape.

Sizing and moving a shape

When you want to move a shape, you have to first change its wrapping setting to something other than In Line with Text, using either the Wrap Text choice in the Arrange group of the Drawing Tools ➪ Format tab or the Layout Options button that appears by the selected shape, as previously described. You can then drag the shape into the desired position. You also can use Position in the Arrange group to choose a preset location for the selected shape.

FIGURE 15.12

Insert a shape from the Shapes gallery.

Working with smart shape features

In most cases, when you insert a shape and select it by clicking it, one or more yellow handles appear along with the regular selection handles. You can drag these handles to redefine the proportions of individual aspects of the shape within the overall shape boundary. For example, Figure 15.13 shows three copies of the same shape. The left one shows how the shape appeared when originally inserted. It is selected, and the yellow smart handle appears at the left side of the circular center. In the middle copy I dragged the smart handle as far toward the center as possible. In the right copy, I dragged the smart handle as far away from the center as possible.

15

FIGURE 15.13

Use any yellow smart handles that appear to redefine the internal proportions of the shape.

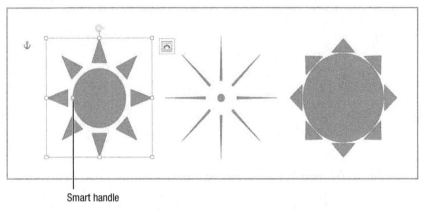

Smart handle

> **NOTE**
>
> Knowing how to use the smart handles is especially important when you are working with the Callouts shapes. Each end of the callout line has a smart handle that you need to use to change the line shape and angle.

Formatting a shape

Formatting a shape works just like formatting a text box or other types of objects as described in Chapter 14. The same Drawing Tools ⇨ Format tab appears when you select a shape, and you can apply settings from the Shape Styles group and the Size group, as well as using the Arrange group tools. Most of the tools pertaining to text won't be active until you add text to the shape as described next.

Adding text to a shape

You can convert any Word shape into a text box. Just right-click it and choose Add Text. Type the text that you need, and click outside it to finish. From there, you can select the shape and use the choices in the WordArt Styles and Text groups of the Drawing Tools Format tab to make changes as desired. For example, in Figure 15.14, I added the Striped Right Arrow shape under Block Arrows in Shapes gallery. I clicked in the shape, typed the text, clicked out of it, and reselected it. I applied the Colored Fill - Dark Red, Accent 1 style from the Shape Styles gallery of the Format tab, and then used the Rotate handle to rotate the shape left to a vertical position, pressing Shift to help snap it into an absolute vertical position. (Note that I rotated the shape itself in this case rather than using the Text Direction tool in the Text group of the Drawing Tools Format tab.)

I then opened the Quick Styles gallery in the WordArt Styles group of Drawing Tools ⇨ Format, and clicked Fill - White, Outline - Accent 2, Hard Shadow - Accent 2 (fourth style in the third row of the gallery). Finally, I changed the Wrap Text setting to Square, dragged the shape into position, and used tools in the Font and Paragraph group of the Home tab to better position the text within the shape. This is just one illustration of the possibilities for creating your own custom text box based on a shape that you could then save via the Building Blocks Organizer.

FIGURE 15.14

A shape converted to a custom text box

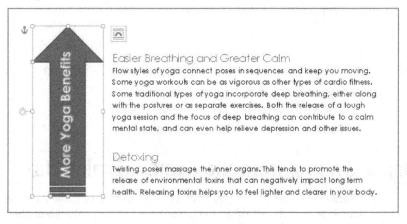

Adding a Basic Symbol

A *symbol* is a character for a font that's not one of the commonly used letter, number, or punctuation characters easily typed in via the keyboard. While technically you can use a character code to type in a symbol, most of us don't have time to memorize dozens of character codes. Symbols include things like trademark and copyright symbols, accented letters from non-English foreign languages, Greek letters, mathematical symbols, foreign currency symbols, arrows and fractions, and other more decorative choices like musical notes, playing card suits, starbursts, and more.

To insert a common symbol, click Symbol in the Symbols group of the Insert tab of the Ribbon. If the symbol you seek is shown in the symbols gallery shown in Figure 15.15, click it to insert it into your document. The first time you access the Symbol gallery, it contains

15

20 commonly used symbols for quick access, as shown in Figure 15.15. Each time you use the tool to insert a symbol, that symbol moves to the first position in the gallery the next time you use the Symbol gallery. Once you've inserted 20 distinct characters using the Symbol tool, the gallery is fully personalized and effectively becomes the "recently used symbols list."

FIGURE 15.15

The Symbol gallery provides quick access to the 20 most recently used symbols.

Inserting a Symbol from the Symbol Dialog Box

If you don't see the symbol you seek in the Symbol gallery, click More Symbols at the bottom of the gallery (see Figure 15.15). More Symbols displays the Symbols tab of the Symbol dialog box, and you can proceed from there:

1. **Click to position the insertion point at the location where you want to insert the symbol in the document.**
2. **On the Symbols tab, make sure that the Font selection is set to the desired font.** For more decorative symbols, choose Webdings, one of the Wingdings choices, or Symbol.
3. **Scroll down until you see the desired symbol, and then click it as shown in Figure 15.16. Or click the desired symbol in the Recently used symbols list.**
4. **Click Insert, and then Close.**

Table 15.1 describes more of the features in the Symbol dialog box.

FIGURE 15.16

Click a symbol for the current font or in the Recently used symbols list.

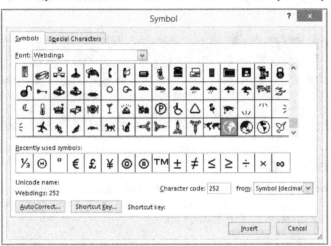

TABLE 15.1 **Symbol Dialog Box Features**

Setting	Description
Font	Drop-down list of all of the fonts installed on your computer. The (normal text) entry shows characters available in the default character font.
Subset	Subset displays only if "from" in the lower-right part of the dialog box is set to Unicode and only if the selected font is a Unicode font.
Character set	The character set is the scrollable list that displays all the characters available for the listed font. If from: is set to Unicode, then Subset is displayed, and the focus changes to reflect the selected subset.
Recently used symbols	The Recently used symbols list contains just that, with the most recent listed first. If your monitor is wide enough, this list can display the 36 most recently used symbols.
Character code	The character code for the selected character using the displayed "from" numbering system.
from	Character system (ASCII and Unicode). ASCII is the traditional 256-character DOS system. Unicode was designed to provide consistent and uniform computer support for all writing systems.
AutoCorrect	Use AutoCorrect to assign mnemonic shortcuts for specific symbols. See Chapter 11, "Cleaning Up with AutoCorrect and AutoFormat," for more about AutoCorrect.
Shortcut Key	Use Shortcut Key to assign keyboard shortcuts for specific symbols. See Chapter 29, "Keyboard Customization."

15

Note that the Symbol dialog box is non-modal, which means that you can move freely between it and the text of your document. This can be handy if you have several characters to enter in different places.

> **TIP**
>
> The Symbol dialog box's non-modality can be handy, but the process of inserting symbols is still rather ergonomically impoverished. It's sometimes easier to insert the characters needed in one place in your document and copy them individually to the Office Clipboard, thereafter using the Clipboard to insert the characters (up to 24) in other locations as needed.

Finding a character's code

Most Word users don't know that you can use the Symbol dialog box not only to insert characters by visual recognition, but also to learn character codes so that you can insert symbols by typing rather than displaying the dialog box.

Let's say you often want to insert a particular symbol from the Webdings font. You can open the Symbol dialog box, change the Font setting to Webdings, and then click the desired character. Make a note of the number or combination displayed in the Character code text box, and then click Cancel to close the dialog box. Then, when you want to insert the symbol into the document by typing, use the Font choice on the Home tab to select the applicable font. Make sure that NumLock is active, and press and hold the Alt key while typing the code you noted earlier.

Finding other marks on the Special Characters tab

The other major feature of the Symbol dialog box is the Special Characters tab. Shown in Figure 15.17, this tab displays 20 characters often needed by Word, their uses, and their respective current shortcut key assignments. Why "current"? The assignments shown aren't necessarily Word's built-in defaults—if you change an assignment, then your assignment will be shown. When you need these characters, using this dialog box is a good way to refresh your memory about how to type them. To use one of the characters here, click it, and then click Insert.

Adding an Equation to Your Document

If you need to insert mathematical equations using many mathematical symbols into a document, use the Equation tool. Click the Insert tab, and then click the Equation drop-down list arrow in the Symbols group. As shown in Figure 15.18, the Equation gallery and additional options appear. (Clicking the Equation button itself or clicking Insert New Equation creates a blank equation; see the "Creating an equation from scratch" section later in this chapter.

FIGURE 15.17

The Special Characters tab shows 20 frequently needed characters, along with their current shortcut assignments, if any.

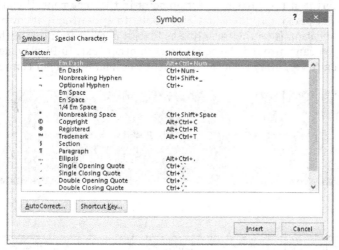

FIGURE 15.18

The Equation gallery features a number of commonly used equations.

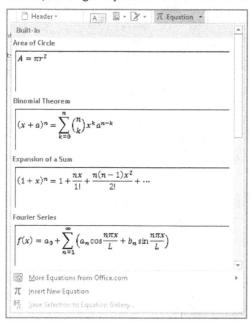

Inserting an equation from the gallery

Use the vertical scroll bar in the gallery to display additional equations. If you see what you want, click it to insert it at the current insertion point in the document. If you insert it into an otherwise empty paragraph, the equation defaults to appearing in its own paragraph, centered; if the equation is on the same line as text, it appears in Inline with Text mode. In Inline mode, you can surround the equation with other text. In Display mode, the equations appear by themselves, away from the document's normal text, as in Figure 15.19.

> **NOTE**
>
> In Display mode, you can center equations individually or you can center them as a group. In the latter case, the longest equation is centered, and the others are left-aligned with it. Use this type of centering when you need to line up coefficients for easier visual comparison. Centering as a group works only when the equations are separated by the newline (Shift+Insert) character instead of by paragraph markers.

FIGURE 15.19

Equations can be shown inline with text or in Display mode; in Display mode, they can be centered individually as shown here.

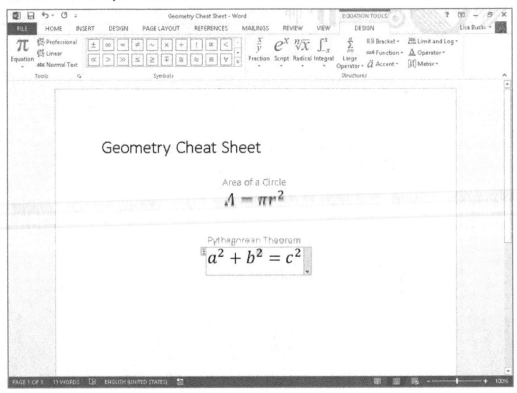

Creating an equation from scratch

To write your own equation, click the main Equation tool on the Insert tab, or simply press Alt+=. Word opens the Equation Tools ⇨ Design tab, shown at the top of Figure 15.19. Use the tools in the Symbols and Structures groups to enter mathematical information within the blank math *content control* that appears, sometimes also called a *math region*. (Chapter 24, "Creating Custom Forms" provides more information about other types of content controls.) Type in anything that doesn't require special symbols or structures. When you finish, click outside the equation control.

> **TIP**
>
> When you're writing and editing equations, it's sometimes hard to detect nuances at the default zoom. Try zooming up to 150% or even 200% to make the details easier to see.

If you want to insert another related equation, press Shift+Enter and continue typing. This ensures your ability to use the Centered as a Group formatting.

Saving equations to the gallery

When you modify the built-in equations or create your own, you can save them to the Equation gallery for future use. If you include an automatic numbering solution such as the one described in the last section of this chapter, you can include the equation plus any formatting. That way, when you add the equation to your document, you won't have to go through any extra numbering steps.

To add an equation to the gallery, select it. Make sure you include any extra elements that play a role in positioning it, such as tabs, paragraph markers, or any other formatting. Click the Insert tab, click the drop-down arrow next to Equation in the Symbols group, and choose Save Selection to Equation Gallery. The selected equation will be appended to the end of the gallery and will be available the next time you're feeling especially mathematical.

> **TIP**
>
> To get started finding more equations online, click the Insert tab, click the drop-down arrow next to Equation in the Symbols group, and choose More Equations from Office.com.

Working with equations

While working with equations is largely intuitive and a matter of getting a feel for the process, some things proceed a bit more easily with a few hints and tips.

15

Take a quick tour of the equation tools, especially the structures. Although many are logical and possibly obvious based on the diagrams and names (assuming you're already familiar with the underlying mathematical concepts and terms), they will seem even more so once you've perused the possibilities. If you need anything highly specialized, verify that it's actually possible with Word's tools. It would be a shame to spend 10 minutes working on an equation only to discover that a lesser-known structure isn't there. It is best to discover that up front.

Linear versus Professional

Word provides two ways to present equations: Professional and Linear, shown in Figure 15.20. Word defaults to Professional (of course), but if you ever need Linear, it's yours with the click of a mouse. Select the equation(s) you want to change, and click the appropriate tool near the left end of the Equation Tools ➪ Design tab.

FIGURE 15.20

Word offers a choice between Professional (top) and Linear (bottom) equation presentation.

$$f(x) = a_0 + \sum_{n=1}^{\infty} \left(a_n \cos\frac{n\pi x}{L} + b_n \sin\frac{n\pi x}{L} \right)$$

$f(x) = a\_0 + \sum\_(n$
$\qquad = 1)^\wedge\infty\blacksquare(a\_n \cos [n\pi x/L]$
$\qquad + b\_n \sin [n\pi x/L] \ )$

Linear mode also enables you to directly modify the structures. Suppose you need a four-by-four matrix, instead of the maximum three-by-three provided. Go ahead and insert a three-by-three, and then switch to Linear view. Replace (&&@&&@&&) with (&&&@&&&@&&&@&&&) Now switch back to Professional mode, and presto! A little experimentation will show you the myriad possibilities.

Math AutoCorrect

Some things can be done in more than one way. For example, if you need *ln x*, there's no need to reach for the mouse. Type **\limit** and press the spacebar. The equation or symbol you want appears.

This happens courtesy of Math AutoCorrect. Choose File ⇨ Options ⇨ Proofing ⇨ AutoCorrect Options, and click the Math AutoCorrect tab. As shown in Figure 15.21, the Replace/With list provides a long list of ways to insert various symbols and structures. (You also can click Recognized Functions to find other functions in the Recognized Math Functions list.) Scroll down the Replace text as you type list to find the shortcuts that Math AutoCorrect will automatically expand to full expressions or mathematical symbols.

FIGURE 15.21

Math AutoCorrect simplifies and speeds work when building equations.

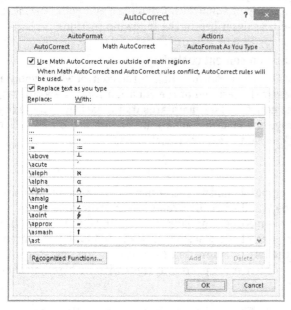

In Chapter 11, you learned how to save your own text AutoCorrect entries. A few math structures already have their own AutoCorrect entries. Some others don't. If you're a statistician, you probably have frequent need for a large sigma with room for the upper, lower, and following elements, or other structures specific to your routine analyses.

To save a custom Math AutoCorrect entry, choose Insert ⇨ Equation to insert a blank math content control to serve as a shell for equation parts you'll need. Use the Equation Tools ⇨ Design tab and typing to build the equation inside the control. Then, inside the math content control, select just the structures or equation parts within the

15

control (not the control itself). Open the Math AutoCorrect dialog box as just described (File ⇨ Options ⇨ Proofing ⇨ AutoCorrect Options ⇨ Math AutoCorrect tab). The With box displays your selection. Type your Replace text, click Add, and click OK. Now delete the structure you created and try out the AutoCorrect entry. Type your Replace name and press the spacebar. Note that this method inserts the equation without the control.

Inserting text before or after an equation

To insert text before or after the equation, press the left or right arrow so that the container disappears, and then type. If you want to retain the equation's initial formatting you have several options. You can apply centered paragraph formatting, which won't necessarily give you identical results if you have a group of equations. Or you can add your normal text inside the equation container itself, as described in the following section.

Inserting normal text inside an equation content control

To add normal text inside the math content control, click in the control where you want the text to begin. In the Tools group near the left end of the Equation Tools ⇨ Design tab, click Normal Text and start typing. The equation now maintains its formatting. Any text you add will be included if you now save the modified equation as a new gallery item. See the "Saving equations to the gallery" section earlier in the chapter.

Working with structures

Word gives you prompts to help you build equation structures. You can start an empty equation, type characters as needed, and then click Tools in the Structures group to display galleries of structures such as the Large Operator gallery shown in Figure 15.22. Click the structure to insert, and then click one of the placeholder boxes and type the contents for it. For example, the equation at the left in Figure 15.22 shows one sum operator with the three placeholders filled in, and another sum operator at right with its blank placeholder boxes.

Look through the structures shown to find the one you're looking for. Note that some might appear quite similar but are actually different, so you'll need to look carefully. For example, can you quickly spot the difference between the summation sign that's selected and the one to its immediate right? The selected one has boxes at the top and bottom to indicate the iteration counter and limit. The one to the right has boxes above and below, but shifted to the right, for superscript and subscript.

Choosing equation options

A number of equation options are not set in concrete. To access the Equation Options dialog box, shown in Figure 15.23, click the dialog box launcher in the Tools group of the Equation Tools ⇨ Design tab. Make the desired choices, and then click OK.

FIGURE 15.22

Make a choice from one of the Structures galleries, such as Large Operator, and then fill in the placeholders in the equation.

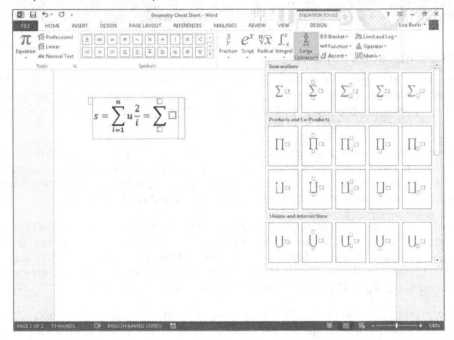

FIGURE 15.23

Use Equation Options to control the way equations are created and inserted.

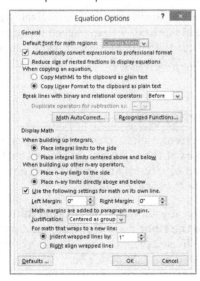

> **TIP**
>
> When you're editing equations, Word provides additional contextual tools that some users overlook. At any location in the equation, right-click to see a shortcut menu with options.

Numbering equations

Many people who work with equations need them numbered. Several approaches can be used in Word, none of them fully satisfactory. Word 2013 does not have a built-in way to number equations. Note that the References ⇨ Captions ⇨ Insert Caption feature does not enable you to add captions for Word 2013 equations.

Although there are several ways to number equations, let's just look at one, which is probably the best way because it's flexible and hard to break. It uses the sequence field code. We'll be looking at fields in detail in Chapter 23, "Automating Document Content with Fields." For now, however, let's look at one field in particular: the SEQ field.

The SEQ field is used for creating sequence numbers. The field code {SEQ name} creates a sequence number in your document. You can substitute anything for name, but consider using eq or equation. Note that this is just a convenient name, and doesn't in any way associate it with equations except in your mind. If you wanted to be willful, for example, you could use {SEQ EQUATION} to number the tables in your document.

In any event, if you include the field code {SEQ EQUATION} inside (or adjacent to) the equation container, it will number your equations. What if you have multiple sets or groups of equations that need to be independently numbered? Well, there's {SEQ EQUATION1} for the first set, {SEQ EQUATION2} for the second, {SEQ SUCCOTASH} for the third, and, well, you get the point.

Consider the example in Figure 15.24. In the blank line after an equation in display mode, I typed **Equation** and pressed the spacebar. On the Insert tab, I then clicked Quick Parts in the Text group, and clicked Field. I selected Seq from the Field names list, typed **eq** after SEQ in the Field codes dialog box, and then clicked OK. That resulted in the numbered field shown above the dialog box in Figure 15.24.

A semiautomatic way to number equations

A common way to number equations in a formal presentation is to center the equations themselves and to right-align parenthetical numbers at the right margin. Armed with this knowledge, let's create a style to use for formatting equations, and an AutoText entry to add the necessary numbering component. To create the style:

1. **Display the horizontal ruler (if it's not already showing) by clicking Ruler in the Show group of the View tab, and observe the right margin setting (and mentally divide it by two for use in Step 3).** In the Home tab, click the Paragraph group dialog box launcher, and then click Tabs to open the Tabs dialog box.

FIGURE 15.24

Use the SEQ field to create numbered equation captions.

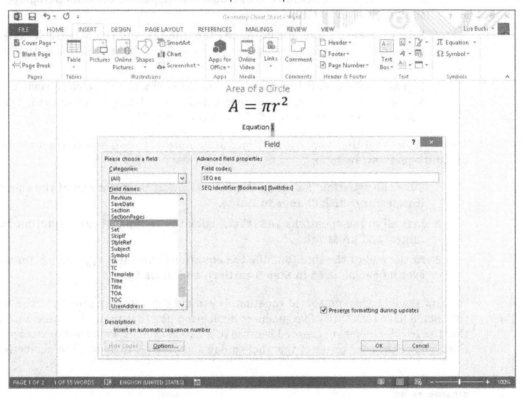

2. **Click Clear All to remove any unneeded tab stops.**

3. **In Tab stop position, type the location of the midway point (often 3.25), click Center, and then click Set.**

4. **In Tab stop position, type the location of the right margin (often 6.5), click Right, and then click Set.** Click OK to close the dialog box.

5. **Assign a style name. Press Ctrl+Shift+S to open the Apply Styles pane.** Type a name for the equation style (Equation Num isn't already taken), and press Enter to apply it to the current paragraph. Close the Apply Styles dialog box.

With the insertion point still in that empty paragraph (now formatted as Equation Num), create the AutoText entry:

1. **Press Ctrl+Tab to insert a tab, and then type ().**

2. **Put the insertion point inside the parentheses, and press Ctrl+F9 to insert field braces.**

15

3. **Inside the field braces, type seq equation and press F9 to update the field. If necessary, press Ctrl+Shift+8 to toggle the display of tabs and paragraph marks so that you can see them.**

4. **Select the entire line, including the tab, the (1), and the paragraph mark at the end of the line.** Choose Insert ⇨ Text ⇨ Quick Parts ⇨ Save Selection to Quick Part Gallery.

5. **Replace the suggested name with something you can remember, such as eqnum.** Set Gallery to AutoText. Set a category and type a description if desired. Leave Options set to Insert Content Only, and then click OK.

You can delete that line now that it's stored as an AutoText item. Now you're ready to number your equations. To do so:

1. **Click the equation, and then click the arrow at the right end of the equation; if necessary, click Change to Inline.**

2. **Left align the equations and labels, click to the right of each equation container, and press Tab.**

3. **At the end of the line (outside the equation container) type eqnum (or whatever name you used in Step 5 earlier), and press F3.**

You now should have a numbered equation. If you did everything according to the steps, you should have something that produces numbering like that shown in Figure 15.25. Note that the selected number is shaded because it is a field code. If you insert or remove equations, you might need to select the whole group and press F9 to update the numbering.

FIGURE 15.25

Use a formatted AutoText entry that contains a sequence numbering field to semiautomatically number equations.

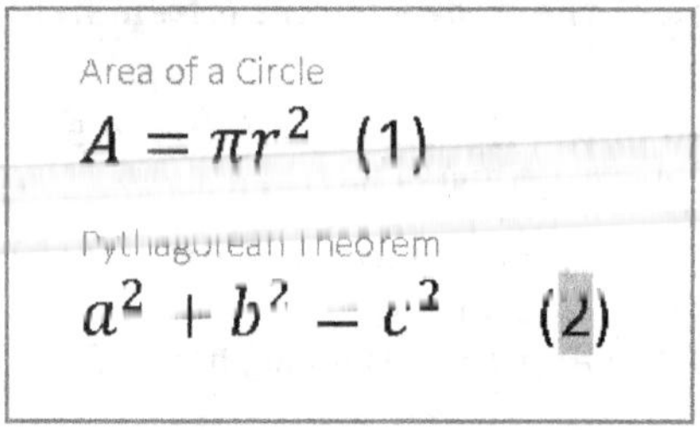

Area of a Circle

$$A = \pi r^2 \quad (1)$$

Pythagorean Theorem

$$a^2 + b^2 = c^2 \quad (2)$$

Summary

In this chapter you've explored creating text boxes and shapes. You learned how to use Word 2013's gallery of text boxes, as well as how to create your own text boxes and shapes. You've seen how to apply existing formats, as well as how to format from scratch. You also learned about symbols and equation editing. You've learned how to insert any of the built-in equations, as well as how to save your own equations to the gallery. You should now be able to do the following:

- Rotate a text box and its text to any angle
- Change the text direction as needed for positioning on different parts of the page
- Use text boxes to design newsletter or other content with text continuing from one text box to another
- Insert and format shapes
- Convert any shape into a text box
- Insert symbols
- Create and edit equations
- Set up a semiautomatic equation numbering solution

15

Part V

Improving Document Setup and Look

Content and form often are depicted as classic combatants in the world of words and publishing. Much of the Bible to this point has focused on content, the basic building blocks of Word documents. Although what you say and how you say it are important, so is how it's presented. Part V focuses on document design, looking at how you put it all together so that what you say actually gets read.

Chapter 16 deals with page setup and issues that require breaking documents into multiple sections, identifying document content with headers and footers, and using columns to help you structure text for special publications such as newsletters and brochures. Chapter 17 explores page background matter, including the use of watermarks and other means of decorating page backgrounds and backdrops. Last but not least in Part V, Chapter 18 shows you everything you need to know about templates, themes, and master documents.

Setting Up the Document with Sections, Headers/Footers, and Columns

IN THIS CHAPTER

Adjusting basic page setup

Working with section breaks and section formatting

Understanding the header/footer layer

Navigating and designing headers and footers

Including page numbers

Creating and changing columns

This chapter examines some concepts that might be a bit challenging if you're new to Word, perhaps even if you're not new to Word. Grasping these concepts, however, enables you to organize and vary the overall setup in your documents as needed.

The chapter starts out by identifying how to use basic Page Setup choices. From there, you learn how to use section breaks to change the page setup as needed for different parts of the document. Next, you learn how to add a header or footer to identify document or section contents and number pages. Finally, the chapter shows you how to use columns to make text more readable in common publications such as newsletters.

Changing Basic Page Setup

The Page Setup group on the Page Layout tab of the Ribbon offers the key settings you might need to change when determining the overall layout of a document. In a basic document without section breaks, most of the Page Setup group choices apply to the entire document. Once you start adding section breaks, as described later in the chapter, you can adjust the Page Setup choices within each individual section as needed.

Using the Page Setup dialog box

Unlike some other features in Word 2013 where traditional dialog boxes have been replaced with panes, Word still offers a Page Setup dialog box that you can use to fine-tune page formatting for the overall document (or current section, if applicable). To open the Page Setup dialog box, click the Page Layout tab, and then click the Page Setup group dialog box launcher. Figure 16.1 shows the Page Setup group choices and the Page Setup dialog box. Work on the various tabs of the dialog box as described throughout this chapter, and then click OK to apply your changes and close the dialog box.

FIGURE 16.1

The Page Setup group of the Page Layout tab enables you to make key document design choices and to open the Page Setup dialog box

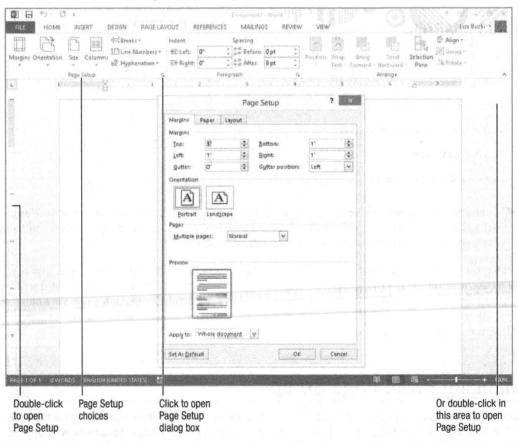

Double-click to open Page Setup

Page Setup choices

Click to open Page Setup dialog box

Or double-click in this area to open Page Setup

> **TIP**
>
> If the Page Layout tab isn't showing, you can also open the Page Setup dialog box by double-clicking the vertical ruler, if it's displayed, or even by double-clicking outside the document area anywhere below the horizontal ruler and above the horizontal scroll bar.

Margins

Click Margins in the Page Setup group of the Page Layout tab to display the gallery of choices shown in Figure 16.2. You can apply one of the available preset margin settings by clicking it. If the document contains multiple sections, the presets will be applied only to the current document section if nothing is selected or only to the selected sections if multiple sections are included in the selection.

FIGURE 16.2

The Margins gallery offers a selection of preset margins.

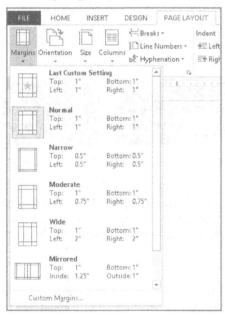

If you want more precise control, choose click Custom Margins, which opens the Page Setup dialog box to the Margins tab, shown back in Figure 16.1. From here you can control all margins as needed and apply the change where you want, which you'll learn more about later in the chapter. You can also adjust the top and bottom margins by dragging the boundary between the shaded and unshaded areas in the vertical ruler at the left side of the document window as shown in Figure 16.3. To increase the top margin, drag the top border down. To increase the bottom margin, draw the bottom border up. In either case, press the Alt key to display the margin setting as you're dragging. You can similarly drag to resize the left and right margins on the horizontal toolbar, but you may need to move the indention controls out of the way.

FIGURE 16.3

Drag the vertical ruler to change top and bottom margins.

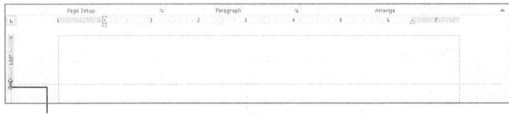

Dragging to resize the top margin

> **TIP**
>
> Often you will choose Margin settings before adding any text to your document. But you can change margins later, and Word will rewrap the text in the document as needed.

Orientation

Orientation refers to whether the page is laid out horizontally (landscape) or vertically (portrait—the default orientation). You might sometimes need to rotate a document to landscape in order to fit wider pictures, charts, tables, or other objects. To change the document orientation, click Orientation in the Page Setup group of the Page Layout tab, and click either Landscape or Portrait as needed.

If you only have only one object or page that has content that is too wide to fit, you can keep the orientation as portrait and rotate the table, chart, or picture instead. For pictures and charts, rotation isn't challenging. With Wrapping (Picture Tools ⇨ Format tab, in the Arrange group) set to anything other than In line with text, simply rotate the picture or chart 90 degrees using the rotation handle, as discussed in Chapter 14, "Adding Pictures and WordArt to Highlight Information." If you rotate only the object, the headers and footers will still display according to the Portrait orientation.

Tables are a bit more challenging, but you have several options. If you're just now creating the table, select the entire table and in the Table Tools ⇨ Layout tab in the Alignment group, click Text Direction to rotate the text so that it can be read if you tilt your head to the right or left. Keep in mind that columns and rows are reversed. It's not necessarily easy to work this way, but it can be done, as shown in Figure 16.4.

FIGURE 16.4

With all text in a table rotated 90 degrees, it's possible to create a sideways table, rather than have to change page orientation within a document.

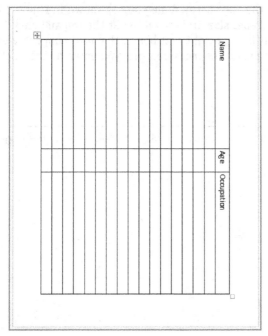

Another option would be to copy a finished table to the Clipboard, choose Paste ⇨ Paste Special in the Clipboard group of the Home tab, and paste the table into the document as a picture. Because it's now a picture, you can choose any floating, wrapping style and then rotate the table as needed so that it fits comfortably, but sideways, in a portrait-oriented Word document page. Headers and footers will display in portrait mode because you haven't changed the paper orientation. The downside is that sometimes the graphics resolution of this technique isn't perfect. You'll have to decide if it's acceptable and legible. Plus, to make changes in the table, you need to maintain a copy of the actual table and remake the conversion as needed.

> **NOTE**
>
> The Page Setup group of the Page Layout tab also contains Hyphenation, which you can turn on document wide. However, most people think of hyphens as a text-related feature, so they are covered in Chapter 11, "Cleaning Up with AutoCorrect and AutoFormat."

Size

The Size choice in the Page Setup group of the Page Layout tab refers to paper size. Click the Size button display a gallery of preset standard sizes, shown in Figure 16.5. Clicking More Paper Sizes displays the Paper tab in the Page Setup dialog box as shown in Figure 16.6. To create your own paper size, open the Paper size drop-down list at the top and click Custom size. Enter the desired sizes in the Width and Height text boxes; the maximum entry for each is 22 inches. Make sure your printer supports the measurements you enter, and then click OK to apply the size change to the document.

FIGURE 16.5

Click a preset paper size, or click More Paper Sizes to display the Paper tab in the Page Setup dialog box.

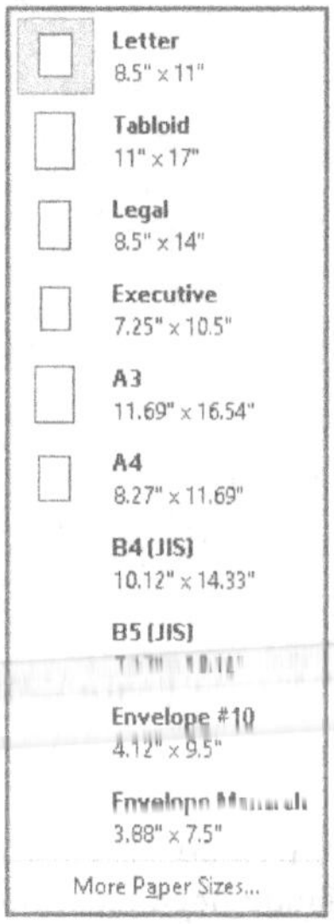

FIGURE 16.6

Choose Custom size and then enter new Width and Height measurements.

Note that you also can change the Paper source settings on the Paper tab of the Page Setup dialog box, as shown in Figure 16.6. For example, if the first page of the document prints on letterhead and the rest prints on plain paper, choose the applicable sources from the First page and Other pages lists.

TIP

In most cases, you will use the Manual Feed Tray to print envelopes. Even when you've inserted an envelope page or section in a document, it's usually easiest to print that page separately from the rest of the document so that you can be careful when feeding the blank envelope into the tray.

Section Formatting

Word uses *section breaks* to separate distinctly formatted parts of a document. Most documents, in fact, start off with and have just a single section. But a more complex document like a product brochure might need different sections if, for example, you want the product description text to appear in two columns on one page and the product specifications to appear in three columns on another page. You have to create new sections when you want to vary the following kinds of formatting within one document:

- **Headers and footers:** Includes changes in page numbering style (except for Different First Page settings)

- **Footnotes:** Can be set to be numbered continuously or set to restart numbering on every new page or section

- **Changes in line numbering style:** Except for suppression on a paragraph-by-paragraph basis

- **Margins:** Indentation can vary within a section, but not margins

- **Orientation:** Landscape versus portrait

- **Paper size:** 8.5×11 (letter), 8.5×14 (legal), 7.25×10.5 (executive), A4 (210.03× 297.03 mm), and so on

- **Paper source:** Upper tray, envelope feed, manual feed, and so on

- **Columns:** Snaking newspaper-style columns, the number of which cannot vary within a document section

> **NOTE**
>
> To work more effectively with sections, make sure that you can see section breaks and other nonprinting formatting characters. Press Ctrl+Shift+8 (Ctrl+*) to toggle them on and off, or click the Show/Hide button in the Paragraph group of the Home tab of the Ribbon. You also may need to show and hide the rulers from time to time with View ⇨ Show ⇨ Ruler. From here on out in this chapter, it's assumed that you have nonprinting characters turned on so you can see section marks and have the rulers on when needed.

Section breaks overview

Word uses four kinds of section breaks. What kind of break you use depends on why you're breaking the text:

- **Next Page:** Causes the new section to begin on the next page

- **Continuous:** Enables the current and next section to coexist on the same page. Not all kinds of formatting can coexist on the same page, so even if you choose Continuous, Word will sometimes force the differently formatted content onto a new page. Section formatting that can be different on different parts of the same page includes the number of columns, left and right margins, and line numbering.

- **Even Page:** Causes the new section to begin on the next even page. If the following page would have been odd, then that page will be blank (unless it has header/footer content, which can include watermarks).

- **Odd Page:** Causes the new section to begin on the next odd page. If the following page would have been even, then that page will be blank, except as noted for the Even Page break.

If you set up a letter in which the first page is to be printed on letterhead but subsequent pages are to be printed on regular stock (using different paper feed methods), the first page should be in a separate document section, because you will probably not want it to display any header or footer information that might overprint the preprinted letterhead contents. If you set up a letter for which the first or last page is an envelope, the envelope must be in a separate section—for multiple reasons, because envelopes typically use a different printer paper source, different orientation (landscape), and different margin settings.

Inserting or deleting a section break

To insert a section break:

1. **Click to position the insertion point at the location where you want the break to appear.**
2. **In the Page Setup group of the Page Layout tab, click Breaks.** As shown in Figure 16.7, Word displays a variety of kinds of breaks, including the four types of section breaks under Section Breaks at the bottom.

FIGURE 16.7

The icons next to the four section break types provide a graphic hint of what the different breaks do.

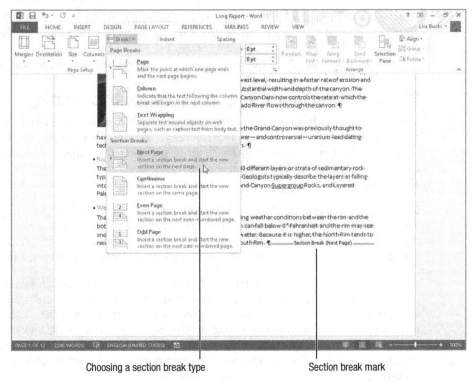

Choosing a section break type   Section break mark

1. **Click the desired section break.** Word adds the section break into the document, and adds one or more new pages as needed depending on the type of break. If nonprinting characters are displayed, you will also see the section break mark in the document.

To delete a section break, press Ctrl+Shift+8 (Ctrl+*). If the section break isn't visible, click the Show/Hide button in the Paragraph group of the Home tab of the Ribbon to toggle the display of nonprinting formatting characters, as shown in Figure 16.7. Click just to the left of the section break to position the insertion point there, press Shift+Right Arrow to select the mark, and then press Delete. If this results in an extra empty paragraph, delete it.

Automatic section breaks

Because some kinds of formatting require a section break in order to vary within a document, Word automatically inserts one or more section breaks when you apply "qualifying" formatting to selected text. Sometimes it gets those breaks right, sometimes not. You'll have to be vigilant if you're going to rely on this feature.

For example, suppose you want an interior set of paragraphs to be formatted in three columns, while the adjacent areas are formatted as a single column. Select the paragraphs you want to differentiate and then set up the columns as described later in this chapter. Word automatically inserts Continuous section breaks before and after the selected text to cordon it off for the distinct formatting.

Sometimes, but not always, Word will insert the wrong kind of section break before and/or after the selected text. It's never quite clear why, but when that happens the best recourse is to press Ctrl+Z to undo the attempt, bracket the target text with the desired type of section breaks, and then apply the formatting to the section you want formatted differently.

Styles, section formatting, and paragraph formatting

Styles can contain font and character- and paragraph-formatting attributes. However, they cannot contain section-formatting attributes. Therefore, for example, you cannot create a style that would enable you to format a given selection with three columns and 1.5-inch left and right margins. Stand by for a few minutes, however, and you'll see how you can indeed effectively create a style for section formatting, although it's not really a style.

Recall that in Chapter 6, "Paragraph Formatting," you learned that the paragraph mark is the repository of paragraph formatting. Similarly, the section break is the repository of section formatting. If you delete a section break, the current section adopts the formatting of the section that follows—that is, the section whose section break is still intact.

Where is the section break in a document that has only one section? In fact, most documents have only a single section, so this is a serious and valid question. There is an implied section break at the end of the document, so if you insert a section break into a single-section document, the formatting for section one resides in that section break, and the formatting for section two effectively resides in the permanent paragraph mark at the end of the document. (If you create a new, blank document with nonprinting characters displayed, you'll see that it contains a paragraph mark you cannot delete.)

Saving section formatting for reuse

If section formatting can't reside in a style, then how can you save it for later use? Suppose you often use a precise set of section formatting attributes—margins and columns, for example—and want to save them for use in other documents. There is a way, but it doesn't involve using what's traditionally called a style. Instead, use a Quick Part or a Building Block. To do this:

1. **Create a new blank document.**

2. **Insert a Continuous or Next Page section break, as needed—to bracket the area to be formatted.** Leave the formatting prior to that first section break as vanilla or typical as possible. This first section break will shield existing text from the new formatting when the Building Block or Quick Part is inserted into an existing document. If it's inserted at the beginning of a document, the first section break can then be deleted.

3. **Press Enter twice or more, and insert another section break of the desired type.** You don't have to insert text between the section breaks because section formatting resides in the section break mark, but you can add text if you want.

4. **Format the area between the section breaks as needed.** (More on section formatting is to come later in the chapter).

5. **Select both section breaks and whatever you've placed between them.**

6. **Choose Insert ⇨ Text ⇨ Quick Parts ⇨ Save Selection to Quick Part Gallery.** The Create New Building Block dialog box appears.

7. **As described in Chapter 12, "Getting Smart with Text: Building Blocks, Quick Parts, Actions (Tags), and More," enter the name and other pertinent information about the new building block.** If you'll need this item frequently, save it to the Quick Parts gallery by choosing Quick Parts from the Gallery drop-down list. Or, if you choose AutoText as the Gallery choice as shown in Figure 16.8, you'll be able to insert it by typing; I've left the space out between 3 and Columns in the Name text box because that will make the AutoText entry more distinct and easier to use.

8. **Click OK to finish creating the building block.**

FIGURE 16.8

Save a Building Block to create reusable section "styles."

505

Now, whenever you want this particular kind of formatting, it's there waiting for you. Choose Insert ⇨ Text ⇨ Quick Parts, and if it's in the Quick Parts gallery, click it to insert it. If it's in AutoText, point to AutoText and click it. Or, if it's elsewhere, choose Building Blocks Organizer to find and insert it. Or, if the first part of the name is unique like the example in Figure 16.8 and you saved it to the AutoText gallery, type it and press F3.

Page layout within a section

You've already seen the Margins and Paper tabs in the Page Setup dialog box. Click within the section where you want to change the settings, and then make choices from the Margins and Paper tabs as described earlier. After you click OK to close the Page Setup dialog box, the changes will apply in the current section only.

The Page Setup dialog box also includes a Layout tab, visible in Figure 16.9, that houses additional settings that are vital for section setup. The choices under Headers and footers enable you to control whether a section uses all the same header/footer information, or whether the footer information is different. See the discussion of headers and footers later in the chapter to learn more about this. The other type settings on this tab will be described shortly.

All three tabs of the Page Setup dialog box include an Apply to drop-down list. If you haven't added any additional section breaks to the document, by default this setting is set to Whole document, although you can open the drop-down list and click This point forward instead. If you've created a section, by default Apply to displays This section, which is why the Page Setup choices apply only to the current section as noted earlier. If you've selected text in one or more sections, the list changes to include Selected sections or Selected text options. The bottom line is that you need to pay attention to the Apply to setting on any of the Page Setup dialog tabs to ensure you've specified the right document location for applying the Page Setup changes.

FIGURE 16.9

The Different odd and even and Different first page under Headers and footers settings enable you to set different headers and footers without using another section break.

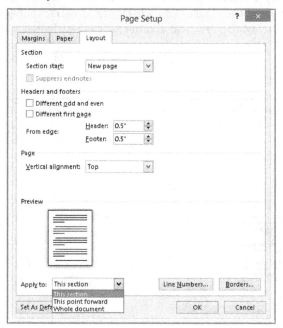

Fixing or changing a section break

The Section start setting shown in Figure 16.9 is a bit cryptic and confusing to many users, but it can be extremely useful. Have you ever ended up with the wrong kind of section break? For example, suppose you want a Continuous section break, but you have a New Page, Odd, or Even section break instead. This can happen either because *you* inserted the wrong kind of break, or because Word inserted the wrong kind of break automatically.

The ordinary impulse is to delete the wrong one and insert the kind you want. Sometimes, however, despite your best efforts, you still end up with the wrong kind of break. This is exactly the situation where you need to use Section start. Click to put the insertion point in the section that is preceded by the wrong kind of break. Open the Page Setup dialog box using any of the techniques described earlier. Click the Layout tab, open the Section start drop-down list, click the kind of section break you want, and click OK.

Vertical page alignment

Another often-unnoticed feature in Word is the Vertical alignment setting under Page near the center of the Layout tab of the Page Setup dialog box. By default, Word sets the vertical alignment to Top, and most users never discover the additional options, which include Center, Bottom, and Justified (which adds line and paragraph spacing to help the text fill the page vertically between the top and bottom margins). For example, the document in Figure 16.10 has been centered vertically to create a more balanced appearance. Because it is a section-formatting attribute, you can set vertical alignment for the whole document or just for selected sections.

FIGURE 16.10

Center a page vertically to balance the white space at the top and bottom of the page.

Vertical alignment can be extremely useful for particular parts of a publication—such as the title page for a format report, booklet, or book—as well as for short letters, brochures, newsletters, and flyers. For title pages, setting the vertical alignment to Centered is almost always more efficient than trying to insert the right number of empty paragraphs above the top line, or trying to set the Spacing Before: to just the right amount in the Paragraph group of the Page Layout tab. For one-page notices, vertical alignment is also often just what the doctor ordered.

For some newsletters and other page-oriented publications, setting the alignment to Justified serves a couple of purposes. Not only does it make the most use of the whole sheet of paper, but it also adjusts line spacing to do it. Hence, the appearance is smoother than it might be otherwise. This setting also lets you optimize the point size if you want to make the font as large as possible without spilling onto another page.

Numbering lines in legal or academic documents

Line numbering, which is different from numbered lists, often is used in legal documents such as affidavits. The numbering allows for ready reference to testimony by page and line number. Line numbering itself, however, is not a paragraph-formatting attribute. It is a section-formatting attribute. Turn line numbering on with the Line Numbers tool in the Page Setup group of the Page Layout tab, or click Line Numbers in the Layout tab of the Page Setup dialog box to open the Line Numbers dialog box, shown in Figure 16.11. Choose the desired settings in the dialog box, and click OK.

FIGURE 16.11

Line numbering is a section-formatting attribute controlled by this dialog box or the Line Numbers choice in the Page Setup group of the Home tab.

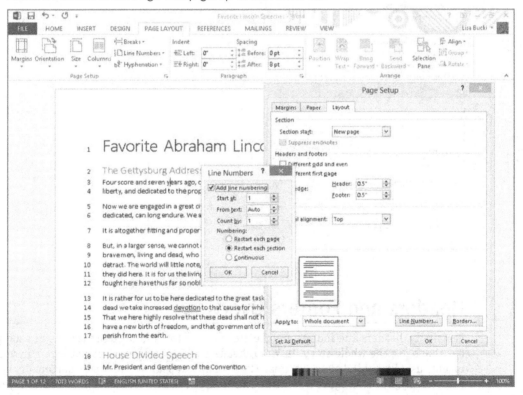

Although line numbering isn't a paragraph attribute, suppressing line numbering *is* a paragraph attribute, as shown in Figure 16.12. (Note that line numbers do not display in Draft or Outline view.) To suppress line numbering in any given paragraph, put the insertion point in that paragraph, display the Paragraph dialog box (click the Paragraph Group dialog box launcher), and enable the Suppress line numbers check box under Formatting exceptions in the Line and Page Breaks tab, as shown in Figure 16.12. Then click OK. Another way to turn off numbering for one or more paragraphs is to select the paragraph(s). Click Page Layout ⇨ Line Numbers, and then click Suppress for Current Paragraph.

FIGURE 16.12

Suppress line numbers on a paragraph-by-paragraph basis.

Headers and Footers Overview

Seemingly, headers and footers are the areas in the top and bottom margins of each page, but that's not the whole story. In Word, headers and footers are distinct layers in your document, usually behind the text area. They usually appear at the top or bottom of the page, respectively, but that's just a convention. Once you're in Word's header or footer layer, you can place text and graphics anywhere on the page. (See "Adding side margin material" later in this chapter for more information.)

This means that in addition to titles, page numbers, dates, and other essential bits of information, headers and footers can contain things such as watermarks, logos, or side margin material.

A second area of misunderstanding concerns how headers and footers are inserted into your Word documents. They aren't inserted—they've been there right from the start. When you "insert" or "create" a header, you're really doing neither. Instead, you're merely adding content to a previously empty or unused area.

The Header and Footer layer

When you're working in Print Layout view, any text in the header and footer layer usually shows up as grayish text at the top, bottom, or side of your document. To access those areas, double-click where you want to edit—even if you don't see any text there. This brings the header and footer areas to the surface, as shown in Figure 16.13.

FIGURE 16.13

Header and Footer tabs clarify what and where headers and footers are. With headers and footers open for editing, the document body text turns gray.

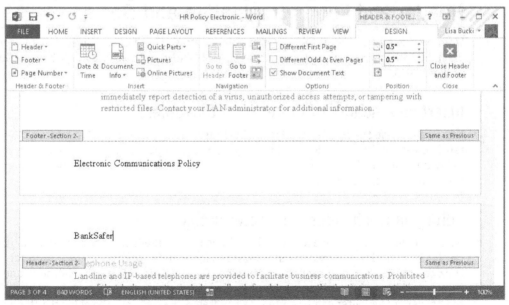

Headers and footers also display in Print Preview. There, however, because the view is supposed to represent what you'll see when the document is printed, the header and footer areas aren't gray and isolated. The same is true in Full Screen Reading view. Note that in Print Preview and Full Screen Reading view, you cannot perform normal editing—neither to normal text nor to text in headers and footers. In Full Screen Reading view, however, you can insert comments. This chapter assumes that you are working in Print Layout view so that all kinds of editing are possible. If you don't see what's shown in the screen shots, then check your view setting.

Coordinating headers and footers and document sections

Figure 16.13 indicates the document section number in the header and footer tabs at the left end of each area. Word documents can be single-section or multi-section. You might use multiple sections for a variety of reasons, particularly in long documents. Some users place each chapter of a document in a separate section, with additional sections being used for front matter (table of contents, table of figures, foreword, etc.) and back matter (index, glossary, etc.).

Section formatting enables you to use different kinds of numbering for different sections. It also allows different header and footer text in different sections. For example, the header or footer might include the name of each chapter, or the word *Index* or *Glossary*.

Header and Footer Navigation and Design

Word provides a number of tools that enable you to control the way headers and footers are displayed and formatted. In this section you'll learn what those are and where to find them in Word 2013.

Inserting a header or footer from the gallery

You also can use the Header and Footer buttons in the Header & Footer group of the Insert tab to create and edit headers and footers. Click either button to display a gallery of predefined headers or footers (Figure 16.14). Scroll down until you see the one you prefer, and then click it to insert it into the document.

Editing in the header and footer areas

When the header or footer area is active, the main set of editing controls appears in the Header & Footer Tools ⇨ Design tab, shown in Figure 16.15. To display the Design tab, double-click the header or footer area in a document. Or, from the Insert tab, choose Header ⇨ Edit Header (or Footer ⇨ Edit Footer). Once the header/footer layer is open for editing, either the header or the footer can be edited, as can items inserted into the side area (for example, page numbers in the side margins) as well as watermarks.

FIGURE 16.14

Choose a predefined header or footer from the gallery.

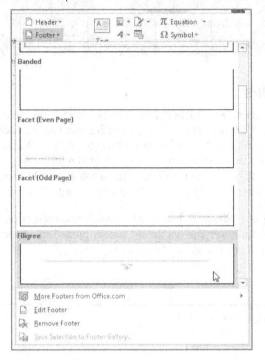

FIGURE 16.15

The Header & Footer Tools ➪ Design tab provides complete control over headers and footers.

Notice the Go to Header and Go to Footer commands in the Navigation group of the tab. You can use those commands to quickly switch back and forth between the header and footer areas, but, as suggested by Figure 16.13, both areas are equally accessible. You do not need to click Go to Header or Go to Footer—you can simply click where you want to edit.

16

Using header and footer styles

If you are creating a header or footer from scratch rather than inserting one from the gallery, Word's headers and footers use built-in paragraph styles named Header and Footer. Each is formatted with a center tab and a right-aligned tab to facilitate placement of text and other items. This enables you to have three distinct components, one each at the left, center, and right within the header or footer, without having to resort to using a table, text box, or other device (although tables and text boxes are perfectly acceptable in headers and footers).

For example, to create a header with a left-adjusted document name, a centered date, and a right-adjusted author's name, you would enter the document name, press Tab, enter the date, press Tab, and finally type the author's name, as shown in Figure 16.16.

FIGURE 16.16

The default header style makes three-part headers easy.

When editing the header/footer layer of a document, you can use the mouse or keyboard keys to navigate as needed. As long as you don't double-click in the text area of the document, the header and footer area remain open for business.

In a long document that contains many sections, however, scrolling can be tedious and imprecise. For greater control and precision you can use the Previous Section and Next Section tools in the Navigation section of the Header & Footer Tools ⇨ Design tab.

Link to Previous

Different document sections can contain different headers and footers. When Link to Previous is selected for any given header or footer, that header or footer is the same as that for the previous section. By default, when you add a new document section, its headers and footers inherit the header and footer settings of the previous section.

To unlink the currently selected header or footer from the header or footer in the previous section (which will allow the current section to maintain a distinct header or footer), click Link to Previous in the Navigation group of the Design tab to toggle it off.

Note that headers and footers in any section have independent Link to Previous settings. While Link to Previous initially is turned on for all new sections that are created, when you turn it off for any given header, the corresponding footer remains linked to the previous footer. This gives you additional control over how document information is presented.

Different First Page

Most formal reports and indeed many other formal documents do not use page numbers on the first page. To keep users from having to make such documents multi-section, Word lets you set an exception for the first page of each document section. To enable this option for any given document section, display a header or footer in that section, and click the Different First Page option in the Options group of the Design tab (refer to Figure 16.15).

Unlike with the Link to Previous option, Different First Page cannot be different for header and footer. You cannot suppress just one. To accomplish that you would need distinct document sections (separated by a section break).

Different Odd & Even Pages

You can, without using section breaks, instruct Word to maintain different headers and footers on odd and even pages. This feature is often used in book/booklet printing, where the header/footer always appears closest to the outside edge of the paper—on the left for left-hand pages, and on the right for right-hand pages. To control whether this feature is enabled, click the Different Odd & Even Pages check box, also in the Options group of the Design tab. Like the Different First Page option, this option applies to both headers and footers in the section, not individually for each header and footer. As Figure 16.17 illustrates, you can set up the headers or footers to mirror one another, such as placing the page numbers to mirror one another on the outside corners of the page.

FIGURE 16.17

Use Different Odd & Even pages to set up mirrored headers or footers for booklet or bound document printing.

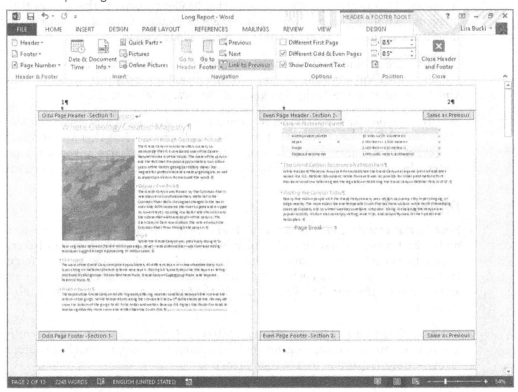

Show Document Text

Sometimes having document text showing is useful and helps provide a frame of reference for headers and footers. At other times, however, it can be distracting and can make it harder to identify header and footer text, particularly if you're actually using gray fonts in the header or footer area. Displayed text also can make it difficult to access graphics that are stored in the header or footer layer.

By default, Show Document Text in the Options group of the Header & Footer Tools ⇨ Design tab is enabled. To hide document text, click to remove the check next to that option.

Setting the distance from the edge of the page

Headers and footers are printed in the margin area. The margin is the area between the edge of the paper and the edge of the text layer in the body of the document. If the header or footer is too "tall" for a given page, Word reduces the height of the text layer on the fly so that the header or footer can be printed. That is, it will be printed if the distance between the top of the header or the bottom of the footer and the respective edge of the paper does not spill into the nonprintable areas of the paper.

Printers have a nonprintable area around the perimeter of the paper (usually 0.25 inches for most printers). This is an area in which it is mechanically impossible for a given printer to print. Windows' printer drivers do a good job of calculating the margin so that the printer does not try to print in the nonprintable region. When the margin is too small, Word will warn you.

Word does not warn you, however, if the header or footer extends too far into the margin. When this happens, all or part of the header or footer is cut off. Everything might look fine in Print Preview, and there is no warning, but part of the footer or header will be cut off in the printout.

You can rein the document in using the Header Position from Top and Footer Position from Bottom settings in the Design tab's Position group. If you find that the header or footer is being cut off, determine how much is being cut off and make that much additional allowance. For example, if 0.25 inches of text is being cut off the footer, then increase Footer Position from Bottom by that amount. You also can use the From edge settings on the Layout tab of the Page Setup dialog box to make these adjustments.

Adding Header and Footer Material

You can put a variety of things into headers and footers, ranging from file names and various other document properties (author, title, date last printed/modified, etc.) to page numbers and even watermarks. Inserting most text and graphics that will actually be printed in the top or bottom margin is straightforward. There are some special cases, however, such as page numbers, side margin matter, and background images and watermarks, that require special attention.

Page numbers

A common use for headers and footers is to display page numbers. To include page numbers in Word 2010, several methods are available—some new as of Word 2007, and some "legacy." This section focuses mostly on the new ways because they provide extraordinary ease, flexibility, and variety not found in pre-Ribbon Word. When the legacy ways are best, however, that's where we'll turn.

Inserting page numbers

Inserting page numbers in Word has never been easier. First, decide where you want the page numbers to appear (top, bottom, or side margin). Then click anywhere on the first page in the document section where you want the number to appear. As noted earlier, documents can contain multiple sections, and each section can have independent headers and footers, which means they also can be numbered independently.

In the Insert tab's Header & Footer group, click Page Number to open its drop-down list, as shown in Figure 16.18, and choose Top of Page, for example. Scroll down the choices as needed, and click the one to insert. Word opens the header and footer layer and displays the inserted page number. Note that you also can use the Page Number button in the Header & Footer group of the Header & Footer Tools Design tab to insert a number when you're already working with the header or footer.

FIGURE 16.18

Word 2013 has extensive galleries with a variety of page number formats from which to choose.

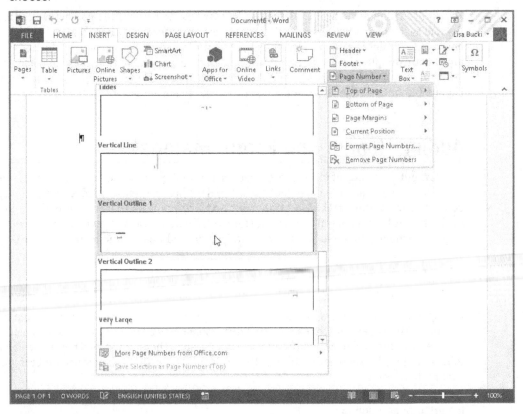

The Page Number menu enables you to select the option that corresponds to where you want the page number to appear:

- Top of Page
- Bottom of Page
- Page Margins (see "Adding side margin material" a little later in this section)
- Current Position (use this option when the insertion point is already exactly where you want the page number to appear)

The bottom of the page is the most common choice for word processing documents, but there are times when the top or side works better for a particular document. Select the desired destination. Word displays a number of preset page number options.

When you find a page number gallery item that suits your fancy, click it to insert the page number into the header or footer (according to which option you chose to get here).

> **NOTE**
>
> To see additional choices for working with a preset listed on any gallery, right click the preset. For example, you can click Edit Properties to work with more detailed settings for the specified page number.

Deleting page numbers

To delete page numbers, move to the document section that contains the numbering you want to remove. In the Header & Footer group of the Insert tab, click Page Numbers ⇨ Remove Page Numbers. You also can remove page numbers via the Header & Footer group of the Header & Footer Tools ⇨ Design tab.

Remove Page Numbers removes all page numbers from headers and footers in the current section—including those in the side margins. It does not remove page numbers from other document sections.

Formatting page numbers

You can choose the page numbering format before or after you insert a page number. On the Insert tab, choose Page Number ⇨ Format Page Numbers (or use the same command in the Header & Footer group of the Header & Footer Tools Design tab), to display the Page Number Format dialog box, shown in Figure 16.19. Options are explained in Table 16.1.

16

FIGURE 16.19

FIGURE 16.19

Word provides flexible page numbering options.

TABLE 16.1 Page Number Options

Option	Purpose
Number format	Specifies numbering scheme: 1, 2, 3; A, B, C; a, b, c; I, II, III; or i, ii, iii. Provides an additional option to bracket Arabic numbers with dashes (to bracket others, edit the header or footer directly.
Include chapter number	Applies a chapter numbering scheme such as I-1, II-5, III-43, where I, II, and III are chapter numbers, and chapters are formatted in a Heading 1 through Heading 9 style, with numbering included in the style definition.
Chapter starts with style	Available only if Include chapter number is enabled. For this option to work, chapter numbers must be formatted in a Heading 1 through Heading 9 style, and numbering must be included in the style.
Use separator	Specifies the separator to use between chapter and page numbers.
Continue from previous section	Indicates whether the current section's numbering is connected with that of the previous section. Use this option when distinct sections are being used for a reason other than to create distinct numbering, such as when switching sections to accommodate changes from portrait to landscape and back again.
Start at	Use this to specify a starting number other than 1.

Additional options that affect page numbers, such as whether headers or footers are displayed on the first page of a document or document section, are discussed earlier in this chapter, in the section "Different First Page."

Adding document information

Word 2013 makes it easier to add key information about the document directly into the header or footer. In previous versions of Word, you had to use field codes to insert such information as the document name, author, or title at the insertion point in the header or footer. Now, it's this easy:

1. **Double-click the header or footer area to open it for editing.**
2. **Click to position the insertion point where you want to insert the document information.**
3. **Click Header & Footer Tools ⇨ Design tab ⇨ Insert ⇨ Document Info.**
4. **Click the desired choice in the menu, shown in Figure 16.20.**

FIGURE 16.20

Inserting document information

Adding side margin material

Textual material inserted in the side margins of a document is inserted in either the header or footer layer. The "trick" is to use something like a non-inline text box to serve as a container for the text. You can use an existing page number preset item that inserts text into the side margin. Or you can insert a text box manually by double-clicking the header or footer area, selecting Insert ⇨ Text ⇨ Text Box ⇨ Draw Text Box, and drawing a text box of the desired shape and size in either the left or right margin. Then insert the page number or other matter there as shown in Figure 16.21. In the document in Figure 16.21, I inserted a circle shape, and then added text to it to make a page number bubble that spills over into the margin.

FIGURE 16.21

Add side margin material by editing the header or footer.

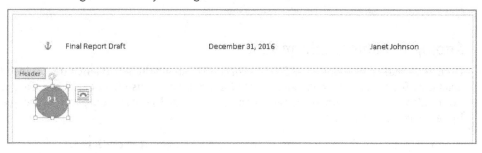

Adding header and footer graphics

Just as you can add a margin text box or graphic on the header and footer layer, you can insert graphics such as a company logo, WordArt, a watermark message such as Not For Distribution, and so on. The graphic will have a "washed out" appearance when you close the header or footer area (as shown in Figure 16.22), but it will print on every specified page for the document or section, depending on the header and footer settings for the section where you inserted it. Use the process just outlined in the previous section for adding a margin text box to add a graphic into the document header or footer.

FIGURE 16.22

Example WordArt added into a header

Considering the Need for Columns

This chapter takes a look at columns and provides you with the information you need to decide whether your document needs columns—and, if so, how many, what kind, and so on. Let's be clear regarding what we're talking about when we say *columns*. Tables have columns, but that's not what we're talking about here. You can also create the appearance of columns by setting up tabs. That's not what this chapter is about either.

In this chapter, *column formatting* refers to dividing the text so that it flows in columns across the page, as shown in Figure 16.23. This kind of formatting sometimes is called *newspaper columns* or *snaking columns,* and is a common format used in journals, newsletters, and magazines, although it's unlikely that those publications use Word's columns feature to accomplish their columnar formatting. Such publications likely use page layout programs because of the precise way in which they feature text, graphics, and advertising.

FIGURE 16.23

Column formatting is sometimes called snaking columns because of the way text zigzags from the bottom of one column to the top of the next.

Why use columns? If you've ever analyzed the way you read or if you've ever taken a speed-reading course, you already know the answer. We use columns because they're easier and faster to read. Contrast reading a wide-format book with reading a newspaper. In a wide-format book each column of text (usually the whole page) is five or more inches wide. In a newspaper, columns typically are only a couple of inches across. We also use columns for a variety of other reasons, such as to utilize space more efficiently or for aesthetic reasons.

Similarly, consider the reason many people prefer to read physical newspapers rather than their online equivalents. While some of it has to do with tactile sensations, a lot of it has to do with chunks of text that are visually more digestible. When text is compacted into a narrow column, it's possible to see an entire sentence in one quick glance. This makes reading a more holistic experience and makes it possible to read with greater comprehension and speed.

The truth is that whether you want columns or not, you already have at least one in every Word document, so the real question is *How many columns do you want?* To answer the question, you should consider the nature of what you're writing, how it will be printed or published, and who will be reading it. Text-dense documents benefit from columns, just as they benefit from graphics. Anything that helps the reader become more engaged with the text is good.

Changing the Number of Columns

Column formatting is a section formatting attribute. Any part of a document that has a different number of columns must be "sectioned off" with section breaks. To insert a section break, choose the desired kind of break by selecting Page Layout ⇨ Page Setup ⇨ Breaks, as described earlier in the chapter.

> **NOTE**
>
> Notice that Column is listed under Page Breaks, not under Section Breaks. Technically, a column break is neither a page break *nor* a section break. To create different numbers of sections in different parts of the same document you must separate them by one of the four breaks listed in the section "Inserting or deleting a section break," earlier in the chapter.

To change the number of columns for the current section (or selected sections or selected text), select Page Layout ⇨ Page Setup ⇨ Columns. The current column formatting (Two, in this case) is highlighted, as shown in Figure 16.24. Remember that if you select a single column of text and format it in multiple columns, Word inserts section breaks as needed.

FIGURE 16.24

Word offers five preset column setups, or choose More Columns to design your own.

If you don't want any of the default, preset column formatting, for additional control click More Columns, which displays the Columns dialog box, shown in Figure 16.25. This dialog box shows the same set of five preset column formats as the Columns drop-down tool, but you can insert as many as two columns per inch of horizontal space between the left and right margins, up to a maximum of 44 columns. For standard paper 8.5 inches wide with one-inch left and right margins, you can have up to 13 columns. To get the maximum of 44 columns you would need paper at least 22 inches wide, assuming no margins and a pretty unusual printer. Note that the Width and spacing controls provide access to only three sets of columns at a time. If there are more than three columns, a vertical scroll bar appears in the Columns dialog box, providing access to additional column settings. When you finish setting up columns, click OK to apply your changes.

FIGURE 16.25

Design your own columns here.

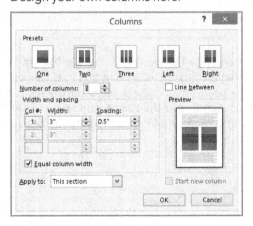

Adding a line between columns

In Figure 16.25, notice the Line between option. Check this option to draw a vertical line between columns. If columns are closely spaced, this can help in maintaining the visual separation of the columns, thereby improving readability. When you're using ragged-right text edges rather than justified text, adding a vertical line can create the appearance of straighter edges and better visual balance.

Formatting columns using the horizontal ruler

You can format column width and spacing using the horizontal ruler. In Figure 16.26, notice that the Left and Right Indent controls can appear in only one column at a time. This doesn't mean that you get those controls only in a single column. It simply means that they are shown only for the active column. To change the width of columns, drag the darker and lighter boundaries between the column spacing and width areas. When you drag to make a column larger, the adjoining space gets smaller, and vice versa. When Equal column width is checked in the Columns dialog box, dragging the boundaries of any column expands or contracts all columns at the same time. The minimum column spacing is 0. Select text in a column to format it individually. For example, in Figure 16.26, I selected the numbered list so I could drag the left indent setting and help its items fill the column better.

Special Column Formatting

If you want part of a document to have three columns and another part to have a single column, those two parts must reside in different sections. (There is a way around the multi-section requirement, by the way, which we'll look at in a moment.) Which one to use? The choice is yours; it should be driven by which works best in each particular situation.

Changing columns using section breaks

Consider the common newsletter format shown back in Figure 16.26. Notice that there is a section break between the top section, which is a single column, and the material that follows, which is in two columns.

One way to create this kind of format is to separate the *masthead* (the big title and other matter that goes with it) from the body using a Continuous section break, as shown in Figure 16.26. Move the insertion point to the beginning of where you want the multi-column formatting to begin, and choose Break ⇨ Continuous in the Page Setup group of the Page Layout tab. Now use the Columns tool or the Columns dialog box to apply the desired column formatting to the new section.

If there's a point at which you want the multi-column formatting to change the number of columns again, insert additional section breaks (choosing Continuous, Next Page, Even, or Odd as needed), and apply the desired column formatting to those additional sections.

Alternatively, let Word insert section breaks automatically. Select the part of the document to which you want a given number of columns applied, and then apply the column formatting. You can do this using the Columns tool or the Columns dialog box, but you will get more consistent and predictable results if you use the dialog box. For some unknown reason Word sometimes inserts Next Page section breaks instead of Continuous section breaks. If this happens, you can always convert the section break to the correct kind using the Section Start setting in the Layout tab of the Page Setup dialog box, covered earlier in the chapter.

16

FIGURE 16.26

Left and Right Indent controls appear above the active column.

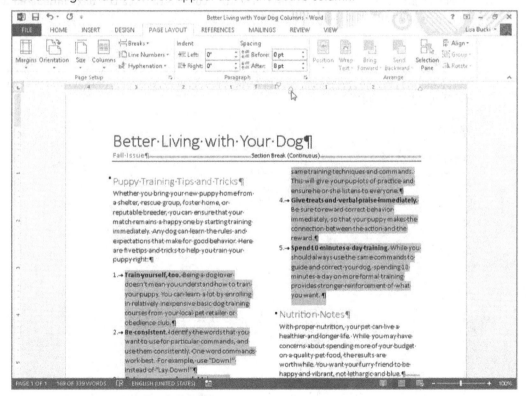

Balancing columns

When you have a multi-column structure, Word treats each column as if it were a page with respect to the flow of text. Ordinarily, text must fill column 1 before it goes into column 2, and must fill column 2 before it flows into column 3, and so on.

A column break is used *within* a column to force text to start at the beginning of the next available column. If you think of columns as mini-pages within a page, then in that sense a column break forces text to the next "page," even though that next page isn't necessarily on a new piece of paper. Problems happen when a column breaks awkwardly. For example, if the column contains a numbered list, you might not want a numbered paragraph to begin at the bottom of one column and continue at the top of the next. The solution is to insert a column break at the beginning of the numbered item. To do so, click to position the insertion point, click the Page Layout tab and click Breaks in the Page Setup group, and then click Column under page breaks, as shown in Figure 16.27. In Figure 16.27, I have already inserted a column break at the end of the first column to force the next numbered item to begin at the top of the second column.

FIGURE 16.27

You can use column breaks to control how columns line up or where text breaks at the bottom of the column.

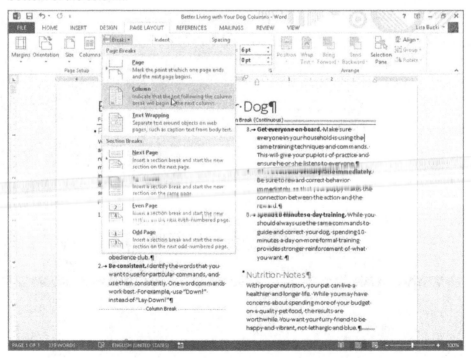

You also can force Word to balance the columns (make them approximately the same height) by inserting a Continuous section break at the end of the last column. When you do that, Word tries to optimize document space to accommodate what comes next, even if nothing comes next. In some cases the columns won't balance perfectly. That's because of other constraints, such as widows and orphans. Nonetheless, symmetrically speaking, it's usually an improvement.

Summary

In this chapter you've learned about the basic page setup choices, what section formatting is, and how the two interact. You also learned what headers and footers are, what they're used for, and how to create them with sections. Finally, you learned about creating columns in a document. You should now be able to do the following:

- Add the right type of section break at the desired location
- Convert a Next Page section break into a Continuous section break, and vice versa
- Vertically align page text in a section of a document
- Change the paper size and paper feed for the section
- Create headers, footers, and page numbers in your documents
- Edit headers and footers
- Set up different headers and footers in different sections of a document
- Add side-margin material and graphics in the header/footer layer
- Create documents with differing numbers of columns
- Change column formatting using the horizontal ruler or Columns dialog box
- Use column breaks

Changing Other Page Features

IN THIS CHAPTER

Putting borders around pages

Adding a color, gradient, texture, pattern, or picture page background

Using watermarks effectively

I f you like the idea of sprucing up the page a little but have never bothered because Word doesn't print page backgrounds by default and doing so can result in paper oversaturated with inkjet ink, you can set those worries aside. Thanks to the Web, PDF, XPS, and ways to share your documents without using paper, adding a background to a document can make sense and can add a needed dimension or personality. If you do want to print decorative page elements, then you can turn on page background printing or consider adding a page border or watermark, instead.

This chapter takes a look at page borders and backgrounds: how to use them, how not to use them, when to use them, and when not to use them. Let's get started.

Adding and Removing Page Borders

A page border is a line, a set of lines, or decorative artwork that appears around the perimeter of the page. You see them a lot on title pages as well as on flyers and brochures. Borders can be formal, discretely colored lines of various weights, or colorful graphics, as in the border for the flyer in Figure 17.1.

FIGURE 17.1

For page borders, you can insert a variety of lines or choose from dozens of built-in art borders.

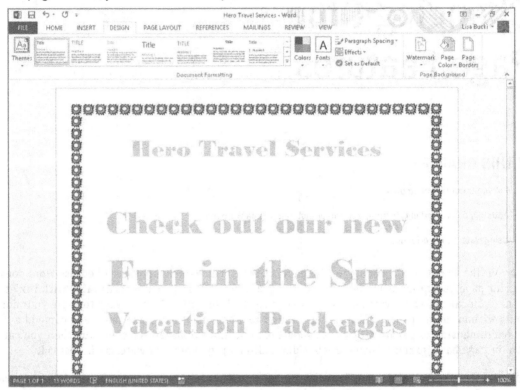

To insert a page border:

1. **Click the Design tab, and then click Page Borders in the Page Background group.** (Refer to Figure 17.1). The Borders and Shading dialog box shown in Figure 17.2 appears. The dialog box offers the same options you saw earlier on the Borders tab in Chapter 6, "Paragraph Formatting," in the "Borders and boxes" section. In addition, however, the Page Border tab includes Art options you can use to create decorative borders, although some of these might not look sophisticated enough for many types of documents.

2. **Click an overall border type under Setting at the left.**

FIGURE 17.2

Choose page border settings in the Page Border tab of the Borders and Shading dialog box.

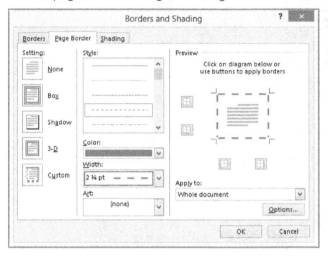

3. **In the center of the dialog box, pick a border Style, Color, and Width; alternately, open the Art drop-down list, scroll to find the style of border art to use, and click it.**

4. **To remove the border from any side, click that side in the border Preview.**

5. **To control which pages in the document have the border, make a choice from the Apply to drop-down list.** For placing a border around a title page, choose This section—First page only. Other options on the list include Whole document, This section, and This section—All except first page.

6. **To control the placement of the page border with respect to the edge of the text or paper, click Options.** The Border and Shading Options dialog box shown in Figure 17.3 appears. Note that when you're setting page borders, paragraph-related options are grayed out.

7. **Make a choice from the Measure from drop-down list to set the distance of the page border either from the Text or from the Edge of page.**

8. **Adjust the Top, Bottom, Left, and Right distance values as desired.**

9. **Click OK twice to close the two open dialog boxes and apply the page border settings.**

FIGURE 17.3

Use Border and Shading Options if your page border crowds the text too much.

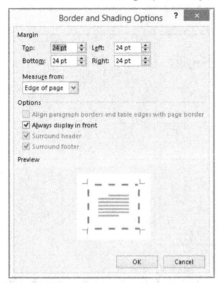

Formatting the Page Background

There are numerous types of page backgrounds, used to add color, personality, or information to a document. They include the following:

- **Background colors and patterns:** Used mostly for decorative purposes, to add color to presentations

- **Background pictures:** Used for decorative purposes or to add some kind of subtle message

- **Decorative watermarks:** Used to "stamp" documents with a particular trademark or symbol

- **Informative watermarks:** Used to add things like CONFIDENTIAL, DRAFT, SAMPLE, or DO NOT COPY to the background of every page of a document to prevent printed versions from being misused or misrepresented

Printed versus onscreen background colors and images

You can include background colors, patterns, images, and messages in both printed and nonprinted documents (those designed to be viewed on a computer screen). For printed documents, take more care with your background selections so that you don't waste ink or create a mess. A practical consideration with many inkjet printers is that ink doesn't dry immediately and paper doesn't necessarily dry flat. A piece of paper saturated with ink is messy and will need to be separated from other paper to dry. It's not unusual for ink to bleed through to the back—an added problem especially when you're doing duplex printing.

You can find special papers designed to withstand such printing, but they are more expensive than regular paper, adding to the cost of printing.

As a result, when designing documents to be printed you should avoid creating documents that will result in saturated paper. Even when you use toner instead of ink, saturation and other bad things can occur, causing smears, buckling, and bulging paper. To avoid saturation, choose a light page background color. If your background is a picture, you can either edit it in advance in a graphics program to reduce its opacity or intensity, or insert it as a custom watermark (see "Using a picture as a watermark" later in the chapter), and use the Washout option to lighten it.

Due to the potential pitfalls of background printing, Word by default does not print background colors and images. To instruct Word to include background colors and images when you print, choose File ⇨ Options ⇨ Display. Under Printing options, click to enable Print background colors and images, as shown in Figure 17.4, and then click OK.

FIGURE 17.4

To enable background colors and images to print, enable the Print background colors and images check box, which is turned off by default. Print drawings created in Word is enabled by default.

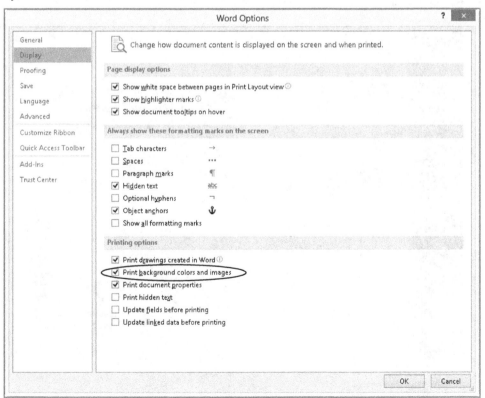

TIP

Notice the option to Print drawings created in Word in Figure 17.4. Ordinarily you might think in terms of shapes and perhaps SmartArt. However, "drawings created in Word" includes WordArt, SmartArt, shapes, and even pictures if they have been modified for printing as a page background or watermark. To fully enable printing of all background colors, images, and watermarks, leave this option enabled, as it is by default. By the same token, to prevent the printing of background colors, images, and watermarks, remove the check marks to disable both of these options.

Note that even when you turn on printing for background colors and images, the capabilities of your printer will determine how much of the background actually prints. Only a printer that supports full bleed or edge-to-edge printing can print all the way to the edges of the paper. Most consumer and small business printers don't support this functionality and instead only print the background as far as the smallest margin allowed by the printer. For example, the printer selected in Figure 17.5 requires a minimum margin of a quarter inch, so the preview accordingly shows a small margin of white space at each edge beyond the printable background area.

FIGURE 17.5

If your printer does not support bleeds, the background prints only within the space allowed by the printer.

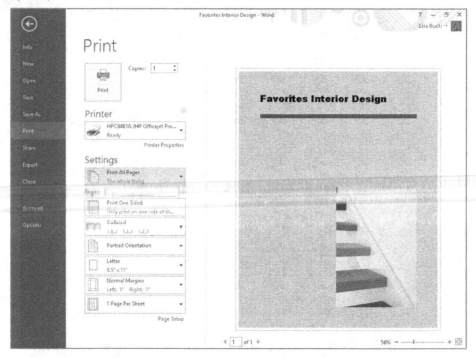

For documents designed to be read on the computer screen, ink and paper aren't a concern. These include documents that "live" on the Internet or on an intranet as various flavors of HTML files, as PDF or XPS files, or even as regular Word documents.

What is a concern with onscreen documents, however, is legibility. Art is important, but so is being able to read what's written. If the color combinations are so bad that they induce eyestrain, or if text gets utterly lost in a background pattern or image, your document won't live up to its potential to communicate via the written word. If you're deliberately trying to obscure the message, on the other hand, a busy background image might work well.

Background versus watermark

It's important to understand the difference between page background and watermarks. Page background is a document-wide setting. You set the page background using the Page Color tool in the Page Background group of the Design tab. You can have only one page background setting in any given document, and the identical page background will appear on every page.

A watermark, on the other hand, applies in the current section only. Though it's common to have only a single watermark in any given document and to have the identical watermark on every page, it is by no means required.

It's important to know that one is a document-wide setting and the other is a section-formatting attribute because it can keep you from beating your head against the wall trying to set a different background for each page using the Page Color tool.

> **NOTE**
>
> If you want a different background for each page, you can make it happen, but not using the Page Color tool. The brute-force way to do it is to create a rectangle, size it to the height and width of the page, position it to fill the page, and fill it with the color, pattern, texture, or picture that you want. Change its Wrap Text setting to Behind Text so that the page text appears in front of the background shape. You can copy the shape and paste it to other pages, changing its fill from page to page as desired. Chapter 15, "Adding Drop Caps, Text Boxes, Shapes, Symbols, and Equations," gives more information about adding and working with shapes.

Applying Page Background Colors, Patterns, Textures, or Pictures

Word 2013 provides a variety of colors, patterns, gradients, and textures for use as document backgrounds. In addition, you can use pictures in any of the graphics formats supported. Formats supported include the graphics filters that come with Office 2013, those installed for earlier versions of Office, and some installed with other Windows programs.

Word applies the backgrounds discussed in this section to the entire document, not to specific document sections. Therefore, whatever background you choose should be coordinated with text and other graphics in all parts of the document.

Colors

To apply a background color to a document, click Page Color in the Page Background group of the Design tab on the Ribbon. Doing so displays the palette shown in Figure 17.6. If you want your background to vary when you change the document theme, click one of the colors under Theme Colors. If you don't want your background to change when you change themes, click one of the choices under Standard Colors or click More Colors.

FIGURE 17.6

To specify a page color that will not change if you change themes, choose from the Standard Colors or click More Colors.

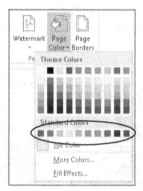

To remove the background color at any time, choose Design ⇨ Page Background ⇨ Page Color ⇨ No Color.

More Colors

If the Standard Colors don't provide the color you're looking for, click More Colors to display the Colors dialog box shown in Figure 17.7. The Standard tab enables you to choose from among 144 colors and shades of gray. The Custom Colors tab enables you to select one of up to 16,777,216 colors (that's the number available when the computer is set up for 24-bit color, which most current systems support). To set a custom color, click on a color that looks close to the one you want in the Colors area. When you get close, you can drag the triangle along the color bar at the right to choose different shades of the selected color. Alternately, you can choose a Color model, and then enter the values that represent a precise color. For example, you could leave RGB selected and enter **170** for Red, **120** for Green, and **170** for Blue to create a dark lavender color. On both the Standard and Custom tabs, the New and Current preview indicator shows both the current background (bottom) and the background you'll get by clicking OK.

FIGURE 17.7

Use either of the tabs in the Colors dialog box to specify a custom page background color that won't change if you change themes.

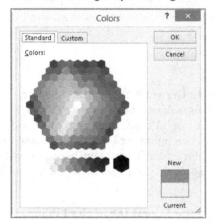 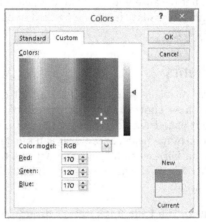

Colors and themes

As alluded to earlier, there are two general approaches to applying color page backgrounds. The first approach is to apply Theme Colors, in which case colors and other elements will change when you apply different themes, as discussed in Chapter 18, "Saving Time with Templates, Themes, and Master Documents." The second approach is to choose a color or other type of background that isn't dependent on the applied theme and therefore will not change when you change themes.

For example, in the default Office theme, Text 2 is a shade of blue-gray with RGB values of 68, 84, and 106. If you like that color for a background and don't want theme changes to affect it later, don't use Design ⇨ Page Background ⇨ Page Color ⇨ Blue-Gray, Text 2 setting to set your background color.

To set the color in a way that is immune to theme changes, first select it using the theme color you want. Then click Design ⇨ Page Background ⇨ Page Color ⇨ More Colors ⇨ Custom. Once on the Custom tab of the Colors dialog box, make a slight change in the color by setting one of the Red, Green, or Blue numbers one notch higher or lower and then returning it to the original value. This convinces Word that you've made a change when you haven't, but, more important, it makes Word think you applied a non-theme color. Then click OK.

The result is that you've set a custom color that happens to be the same as one of the theme colors, but because you used the Custom color dialog box to do it, it is now not connected with any particular theme, and will stay as is when and if you change the overall theme or theme colors.

Gradients

Gradient or *image gradient* is a term that refers to the gradual blending of colors, not unlike those shown in the Custom tab of the Colors dialog box (refer to Figure 17.7). A gradient page background adds dimension versus a solid color, and gives you the opportunity to arrange page contents so you put text on the lighter or brighter areas and graphics on the darker areas. Or, you can vary the text color on the page to ensure the text remains readable versus the gradient color at any given point on the page. To set a gradient page background:

1. **In the Page Background group on the Page Layout tab of the Ribbon, choose Page Color ⇨ Fill Effects.** The Fill Effects dialog box opens.

2. **Click the Gradient tab.** When you first choose this dialog box tab, the initial offering is based on the current page's background setting. If you haven't yet applied any color, you'll see gradients based on black and white (that is, shades of gray).

3. **If the base colors of the displayed gradients aren't to your liking, click a choice in the Colors section, and then make choices from the gradient color options that appear in that section, which will vary depending on which option button you select.** One color blends between white and the Color 1 color you select from the drop-down that appears. Two colors enables you to make selections from the Color 1 and Color 2 drop-downs that appear to create the gradient. Click Preset colors and then make a choice from the Preset colors drop-down list that appears. Figure 17.8 shows one of the presets selected, with the Sample box at the lower right previewing the selected Colors options for the gradient.

4. **In the Shading styles section, choose one of the available options until the sample preview appears as desired.**

5. **Click OK.**

FIGURE 17.8

A gradient page background can be a color, a blend of two colors, or a choice of 24 preset combinations.

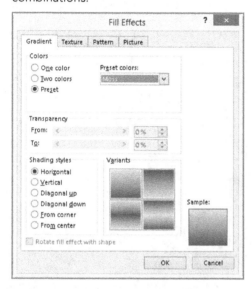

Textures

Texture refers to a variety of subtle pictorial backgrounds—everything from wood to different fabrics to marble. Word offers 24 built-in textures and enables you to insert your own from existing graphics/picture files.

To use a texture as your page background, on the Design tab in the Page Background group, choose Page Color ⇨ Fill Effects, and then click the Texture tab, which displays the Fill Effects dialog box choices shown in Figure 17.9. Click a texture and click OK, or click Other Texture to load a picture file as a texture. When you do this the picture is temporarily added to the list of textures shown. To actually use the picture, you need to select it once it's in the Texture gallery and then click OK.

FIGURE 17.9

You can choose from 24 built-in textures, or click Other Texture to use a file of your own.

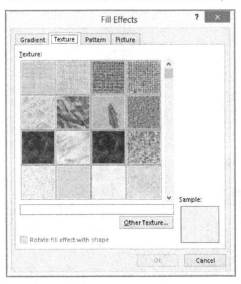

> **NOTE**
>
> When you choose a picture file to use for a texture, depending on the size and resolution, Word may tile the image. This means that if the image isn't large enough to fill the space, multiple copies will be used. With a small graphic you might end up with hundreds of that image as your background. For tiling to work, the edges need to be designed so that they blend seamlessly (unless you want your background to look tiled). Otherwise the image has to be large enough that tiling isn't necessary.

Patterns

Word provides 48 preset patterns you can use for the background. To use a pattern for your page background, click the Design tab, and in the Page Background group choose Page Color ⇨ Fill Effects, and then click the Pattern tab (see Figure 17.10). Click the desired pattern, choose Foreground and Background colors, if desired, and then click OK.

> **CAUTION**
>
> Text placed on top of a bold pattern can be nearly impossible to read. If you really want to use a pattern as the page background, choose light, subtle colors and dark, bold text formatting to ensure that the text will be readable.

FIGURE 17.10

By combining different colors with Word's 48 built-in patterns, you can create literally millions of different backgrounds.

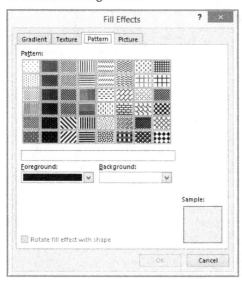

Pictures

You also can use a picture for the document or section background. The result and the considerations involved are identical to those for setting a background texture or pattern. To use a picture as your document background, click the Design tab, and in the Page Background group choose Page Color ⇨ Fill Effects, and then click the Picture tab in the Fill Effects dialog box. Click Select Picture. The Insert Picture window that appears gives you the option of clicking Browse to find and open a picture locally or to add an online picture as described in Chapter 14, "Adding Pictures and WordArt to Highlight Information," in the section, "Adding an Online Picture." If you click Browse beside From a file, navigate to the desired picture and select it, click Insert, and then back in the Fill Effects dialog box, click OK. Otherwise, search Office.com Clip Art or Bing Image Search, or select an image from your SkyDrive as covered in Chapter 14, and then click OK. Figure 17.11 shows an Office.com Clip Art image, selected and ready to become the page background.

FIGURE 17.11

You can use downloaded or local pictures as the page background via the Picture tab of the Fill Effects dialog box.

Adding a Watermark

A *watermark* is a special faded text graphic (similar to WordArt) that appears underneath the document text, usually on every page of a document. It might contain a picture or text, such as the huge word CONFIDENTIAL.

Choosing a preset watermark

To insert a preset text watermark, click the Design tab, and in the Page Background group, click Watermark. Word 2013 provides a dozen or more ready-made watermarks. Scroll down the Watermarks gallery and see if there's one that suits your needs. Click it to insert it. It now appears as the backdrop for your document's page. If you want a text watermark other than what you see in the Watermarks gallery, skip down to Other Text Watermarks.

As shown in Figure 17.12, the watermark actually is a WordArt object inserted on the header and footer layer of the document. (Note the presence of the WordArt Tools ➪ Format and Header & Footer ➪ Design contextual tabs.) To learn how to adjust a watermark WordArt object as you need, see Chapter 14.

FIGURE 17.12

Word 2013 creates ready-made text watermarks as WordArt on the header and footer layer.

Other text watermarks

If the Watermarks gallery doesn't have a preset text watermark that suits your needs, you can choose Watermark from the Page Background group of the Design tab, and then click Custom Watermark. The Printed Watermark dialog box shown in Figure 17.13 appears. Use the Text drop-down list to select alternate text. Or, select the entry in the Text text box and type your own custom text to replace it.

Choose the desired Font, Color, Size, and Layout, and decide whether you want the watermark to be Semitransparent or solid (the unwritten alternative). For Size, you're generally best off leaving it set to Auto, as that will choose the largest possible font that works for the chosen text and the current paper/margin sizes.

FIGURE 17.13

Create your custom watermark by entering new Text and changing other settings as you want.

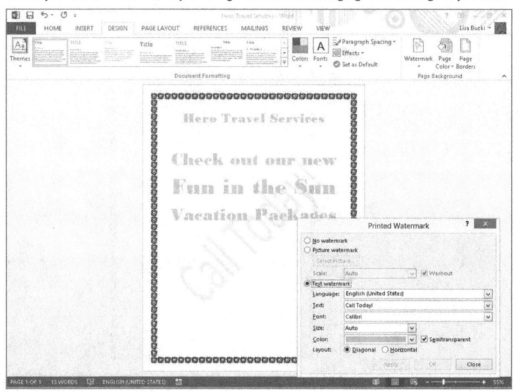

Although the Printed Watermark dialog box doesn't provide Live Preview, it does let you click Apply without closing the dialog box so you can get an idea of what the watermark will look like. Figure 17.13 also shows an example of this. When you click Apply, the Cancel button turns into a Close button. Hence, once you've clicked Apply, the change has been made in your document. If necessary, make changes until you're satisfied and click Apply again. Click OK or Close when you're done. Pressing Ctrl+Z (Undo) once the Printed Watermark dialog box has been dismissed will undo only the most recent change. If you clicked Apply more than once while experimenting, it will take multiple presses of Ctrl+Z to get you back to where you were before you displayed the Printed Watermark dialog box.

Using a picture as a watermark

To use a picture for your watermark, click to select the Picture watermark option button in the Printed Watermark dialog box in Figure 17.13. Click the Select Picture button that becomes active. Then as before, use the Insert Picture window that appears (Figure 17.14) to select a picture. Click Browse beside the From a file choice to open the Insert Pictures dialog box, or click Browse beside your SkyDrive to display a window with the folders on your SkyDrive; use either to find and select a pictured file either in your local folders or in your SkyDrive folders, and then click Insert. Or, enter search word or phrase beside Office.com Clip Art or Bing and click the Search button to search for an image. Click the picture you want to use in the search results, and then click Insert. Back in the Printed Watermark dialog box, set the desired scale and click the Washout check box to lighten the picture, unless your picture is already suitably light for a background. As before, you can click Apply to see if the picture appears as you want, changing pictures or options until you're satisfied. Clicking Apply changes the Cancel button into a Close button. When you're ready, choose OK or Close.

FIGURE 17.14

The Insert Pictures choices also appear when you want to select a picture to use as a custom watermark.

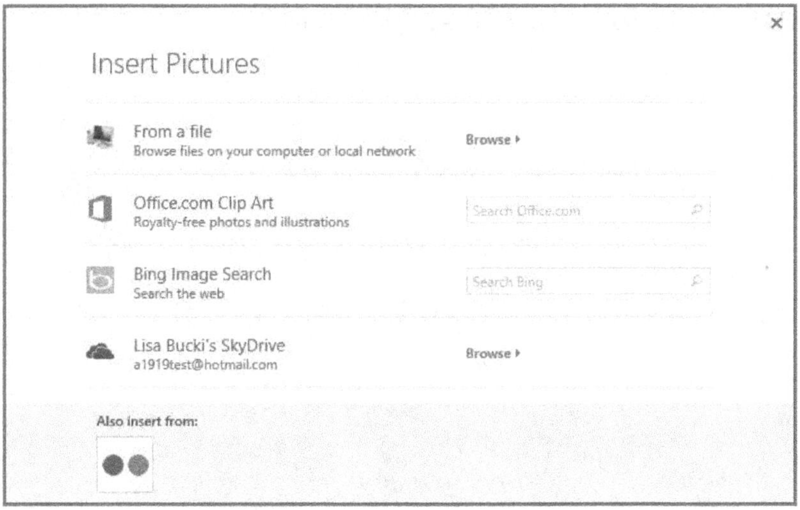

Removing Watermarks and Page Backgrounds

The commands you used for adding page backgrounds and watermarks are the same choices that you can use to remove those items. When you want to remove a watermark, in the Page Background group of the Design tab, click Watermark ⇨ Remove Watermark.

If you try to remove a watermark and it doesn't go away, it's not a watermark. It's probably a page background instead. To remove a page background—even if it's a picture, gradient, or pattern—in the Page Background Group of the Design tab, choose Page Color ⇨ No Color.

Summary

In this chapter you've learned how to add page borders and backgrounds to your documents. You've also seen that you need to be careful to maintain a balance between art and legibility. You should now be able to do the following:

- Add a simple or artistic page border
- Create colored backgrounds and control whether or not Word prints them
- Distinguish between page backgrounds and watermarks
- Match a page background color exactly by using RGB or HSL settings
- Add an informative watermark to the document
- Quickly remove a watermark or a page background

Saving Time with Templates, Themes, and Master Documents

IN THIS CHAPTER

Templates and themes are the foundation when it comes to creating, formatting, and maintaining Word documents. They supply the professional styling and formatting you need so that you don't have to start from scratch for every document, as well as providing example content (when it comes to templates). Using the styles provided in a template enables you to format and reformat a document much more quickly than you otherwise could, and then update it globally just by changing the theme or a component of the theme. Similarly, the master document feature enables you to repurpose content that you and your collaborators have already created. When you combine multiple documents in a master document, you can organize the information as desired and provide uniform formatting to create a cohesive final product.

This chapter looks at templates, themes, and master documents. It shows you how to create and manage your own templates, change key theme components, and create and work with a master document. Read on to learn how you can exploit each of these tools to the max.

Creating Your Own Templates

Word users need a clear understanding of the relationship between templates and themes. You can think about templates and themes as different layers of formatting. When you create or open a document, you start with the formatting that's assigned via styles in the underlying *template*. (As you'll recall, the default document template in Word is Normal.dotm.) You can then layer on top of those formats the colors and other elements provided by the *theme*. The default theme for new blank documents is Office, but you can change it as needed. Applying a new theme or Style Set doesn't change the underlying template. It merely changes certain aspects of the formatting, enabling you to quickly change the overall look of a document, as described in more detail later in the chapter.

Not only can templates include styles and basic formatting, but they also can include *legacy fields* and *content controls* that prompt you (or another user) to enter information, as in the example in Figure 18.1. After you add the fields and/or controls and protect the document, the user can only enter information where specified, and will in some instances see an error message if they enter the wrong type of data, such as entering text in a date field. Chapter 24, "Forms," explains how to set up and protect a fill-in document like this. In addition, templates can include macros (see Chapter 32, "Macros: Recording, Editing, and Using Them") and other Word fields (see Chapter 22, "Data Documents and Mail Merge," or Chapter 23, "Automating Document Content with Fields"). The more formatting, content, and automation you build into a template in advance, the more work you'll save later—but that doesn't mean that you can't save even a very simple document that you use frequently as a template.

The primary way to create your own template is via the Save As command:

1. **Make the desired modifications to the document or template you want to save as a template.** You can either open and alter an existing document or create a new one from scratch.

2. **Choose File ⇨ Save As ⇨ Computer ⇨ Browse, and from Save as type, choose one of the Word Template options (Word Template, Word Macro-Enabled Template, or Word 97-2003 Template).** The new template will be 100 percent identical to the current file, and will contain any text, formatting, macros (assuming the correct type is selected), and styles that the original contains—limited, of course, by compatibility issues if you're saving from a Word 2013 type to a Word 97-2003 type (for example, a Word 97-2003 template cannot retain Word 2013 Building Blocks Gallery items; they are converted to AutoText items).

3. **Edit the name in the File name text box as desired, but leave the current folder selected.** As shown at the top of Figure 18.2, when you start saving templates, Word creates a Custom Office Templates folder within your My Documents folder in your personal folders in Windows 7 or 8. (The My Documents folder contents appear in the Documents library.) Leaving this folder selected ensures that you will be able to access it from the PERSONAL choices in the Word Start screen or the Backstage choices that appear when you choose File ⇨ New.

4. **Click Save.**

FIGURE 18.1

In addition to custom styles, formatting, and example text, you can add legacy fields and content controls before saving as a template.

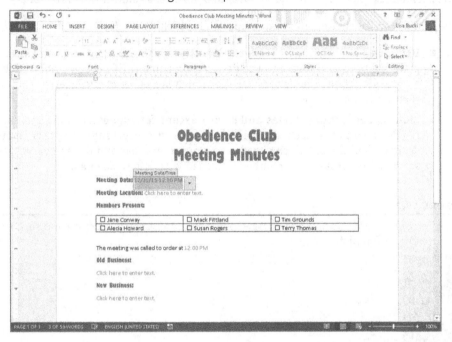

FIGURE 18.2

Choose Word Template from Save as type and enter a file name, but leave the default folder selected.

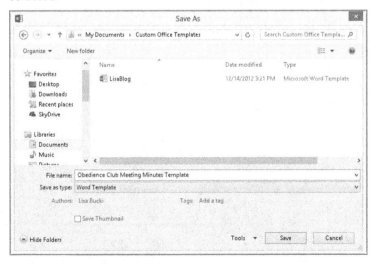

To ensure that you properly saved the template and it's now available for use, choose File ⇨ New, and click Personal under Suggested searches. The templates in your Custom Office Templates folder appear and are available for use, as shown in Figure 18.3.

Other valid ways to create new Word template files include the following:

- **Using any folder window from the Windows desktop:** Right-click an existing template file to copy it, move to the destination window (if needed), right-click, and click Paste. Then rename the new file, which is a clone of the original that you can then modify as desired.

- **Cloning everything (styles and so on) except for suggested text:** Open an existing document or template, press Ctrl+A to select everything, and press Delete. If desired, double-click in the header and/or footer areas and delete everything there as well. Then resave and rename as needed with File ⇨ Save As.

FIGURE 18.3

Click Personal after choosing File ⇨ New to find the templates you create and save to Custom Office Templates.

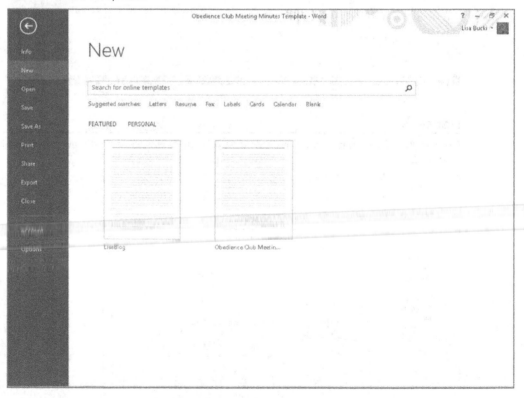

- **Cloning everything except for text and nonstyle formatting:** Press Ctrl+N to create a new blank document, and then choose File ➪ Options ➪ Add-Ins. Open the Manage drop-down list, click Templates, and then click Go. In the Templates and Add-Ins dialog box, click Attach on the Templates tab. In the Attach Template dialog box, select a template in the current folder, or navigate to your Custom Office Templates folder. Select the desired template and click Open. Click to check and enable the Automatically update document styles check box as shown in Figure 18.4, and then click OK. Then resave and rename as needed with File ➪ Save As. Top-level formatting, such as page and section formatting, is not copied to the new document, but any styles, macros, and Building Block items (limited by version compatibility considerations) will be available in the new template.

18

FIGURE 18.4

Click Automatically update document styles to add the styles from the template into the current document, including any blank document you want to resave as a new template.

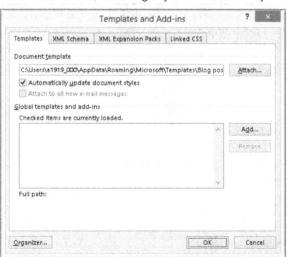

For each of these methods, in order for the templates to be available from the New screen, you need to save them to your Custom Office Templates folder within My Documents. Templates saved elsewhere can still be used, but you need to navigate to them in order to use them.

Using the Organizer

Use the Organizer to move styles and macro projects between open files. You can also use it to delete and rename macro projects (except for built-in styles, of course).

To open the Organizer, use one of two methods:

- Choose File ⇨ Options ⇨ Add-Ins. Open the Manage drop-down list, click Templates, and then click Go. In the Templates and Add-Ins dialog box, click Attach on the Templates tab

- Or, if the Developer tab is displayed on the Ribbon, click Document Template in the Templates group.

The Organizer dialog box appears in Figure 18.5. On the Styles tab, use the two Styles available in drop-down lists to choose the source and target document(s) and/or template(s). (On the Macro Projects Items tab, the lists are named Macro Project items available in.) If either the target or source isn't available on the drop-down list, click either of the Close File buttons to close either currently open file. The button immediately changes to Open File. Use the Open dialog box to navigate to the desired file, and then click Open. Of course, when you finish making any of the following changes, click Close to close the dialog box.

FIGURE 18.5

Use the Organizer to copy styles and macros between documents and templates, or to rename and delete specific styles and macros.

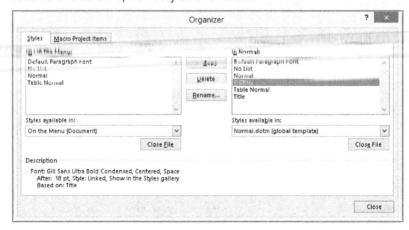

Copying styles and macros

To copy styles or macro project items, use standard Windows list-selection techniques to select the items you want to copy in the source (In) list—the moment you select an item, the opposite pane's preposition changes from In to To, as shown in the left list in Figure 18.5. Click Copy to copy the selected item(s) to the To file. You aren't limited to one direction—either pane can become the "To" pane depending on which pane contains the selection.

Deleting styles and macros

One common reason for deleting a style is when you intend to save a new style in the current file or a template you're updating and mistakenly save it to Normal.dotm. As a result, you may want to clean it out of the default template. To delete items, select the items you want to delete and then click Delete. Click Yes to confirm the deletion. You can delete only one item at a time. You cannot delete built-in styles such as Heading 1 and Normal.

> **CAUTION**
>
> If you delete a user-created style, all text formatted with that style will be reformatted as Normal. If you want to assign a new style to that text, do it *before* deleting the old style. Better still, if the new style doesn't yet exist, simply rename the unwanted style using the new name. As noted in the next section, however, you cannot rename built-in styles.

Renaming styles and macros

To rename an item, select it and click Rename. In the Rename dialog box, type a new name and click OK. Note that built-in styles cannot be renamed—all you can do is add alternative, or *alias*, names. For example, if you type **1h** into the Rename dialog box when trying to rename Heading 1, it will be renamed to Heading 1,1h. This feature is not without utility, mind you, since it then lets you press Ctrl+Shift+S, type **1h**, and press Enter to apply Heading 1 to the current paragraph. You can add multiple aliases to any style.

Removing style aliases

To remove a style name's alias, select the style and click Rename. In the Rename dialog box, delete the portion of the name that you want to remove. Continuing with the preceding example, if you no longer want to be able to refer to Heading 1 as 1h, delete **,1h** and leave the Heading 1 portion. If a style has multiple aliases, remove just the ones you no longer want, keeping in mind that the built-in name, if there is one, will survive regardless of what you try to do.

18

Modifying Templates

You can modify or customize any template on your computer; you first have to open the template file itself, rather than just creating a document based on the template. To do so:

1. **Choose File ⇨ Open ⇨ Computer ⇨ Browse, and from the drop-down list to the right of File name, choose All Word Templates.**

2. **Navigate to the folder holding the template to edit, such as the Custom Office Templates folder in the Documents Library.** Other templates may reside in the `C:\Users\`*user name*`\AppData\Roaming\Microsoft\Templates` folder, or its custom Word Templates subfolder.

3. **Click the desired template to select it.**

4. **Click Open.**

Once you have the template open, make the desired changes, and then save and close the edited file. If you don't want to open the template file and make the changes directly, there are a few ways to make changes indirectly:

- **Via styles:** Modify styles in the Modify Style dialog box as shown in Chapter 7, "Using Styles to Create a Great Looking Document," taking care to enable the New documents based on this template check box before clicking OK to apply your changes. When and if prompted, click Yes to saving changes in the underlying template file.

- **Organizer:** As described earlier, after opening the template file, open the Organizer. Make sure the template is one of the selected files, and then use the choices on the Styles and Macro Project Items tabs to copy, delete, and rename styles and macros as needed. When you're done, click Close.

- **Building Blocks Organizer:** Use the Building Blocks Organizer to move Building Blocks Gallery items between templates, as shown in Chapter 12, "Getting Smart with Text: Building Blocks, Quick Parts, Actions (Tags), and More."

Working More Effectively with Themes

Like many other Word features, Themes work with Live Preview. Unless a document explicitly uses theme-based formatting, such as styles relying on colors and fonts specified by the theme, changing themes will appear to have no effect. Themes are housed at the left end of Word 2013's Design tab, shown in Figure 18.6. The rest of the tab's Document Formatting group contains other theme-related features that you'll learn more about in the following sections.

FIGURE 18.6

Theme settings color-coordinate document contents and change other overall features.

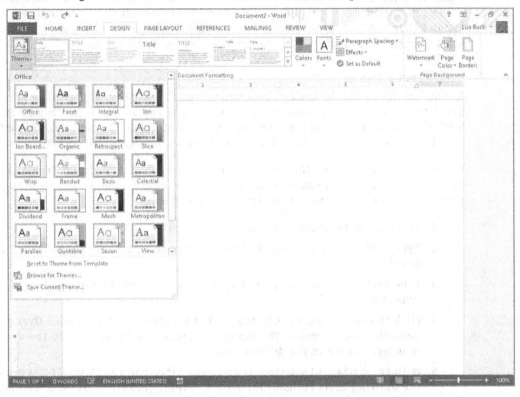

What are themes?

Themes are coordinated sets of colors, fonts, table formats, and other graphic elements used to change the overall look of a document while leaving its content unchanged. Word comes with 21 built-in themes, some of which are shown in Figure 18.6. Although the applied theme's impact hinges on using certain Word 2013 formatting features such as styles and theme colors, themes are not part of style formatting. There is no way to associate or assign a theme with a particular style. Themes are applied to the entire document, wholly apart from styles, and affect many different aspects of document formatting.

Understanding themes

As noted in the earlier discussion about themes versus templates, the template provides the base level of formatting through styles, page setup, and so on. The theme applies the next level of formatting on top of the template. The theme includes theme colors, theme fonts, and theme effects, each of which you'll learn more about later in this section.

The best way to understand themes and what they bring to the document design table is to use them on documents designed with themes specifically in mind. Follow these steps as a practice example to see how a theme impacts a document:

1. **Press Ctrl+N to create a new blank document.**
2. **Type** Heading 1, **and apply the Heading 1 style from the Style gallery of the Home tab.**
3. **Type** Heading 2, **and apply the Heading 2 style from the Style gallery of the Home tab.**
4. **Click the Insert tab, click Shapes in the Illustrations group, click Oval under Recently Used Shapes at the top of the gallery, and then click in the document to insert a circle in the default size.**
5. **With the circle still selected, click Shape Effects in the Shape Styles group of the Drawing Tools Format tab, point to Preset, and click Preset 5 (second row, first column).**
6. **Click a blank area of the document.**
7. **Click the Themes button in the Document Formatting group of the Design tab (refer to Figure 18.6), and note the names of the themes—Facet, Integral, Ion, Ion Boardroom, Organic, and so on.**
8. **Click Integral.** Note the changes in the example document. The text formatted with heading styles changes color and font, and the circle color change as well. Figure 18.7 shows the example document with the new theme applied.
9. **Close the document without saving changes, or if you want to save it for future practice feel free to do so.**

FIGURE 18.7

The Integral theme applies new heading fonts and more in the quickie practice document.

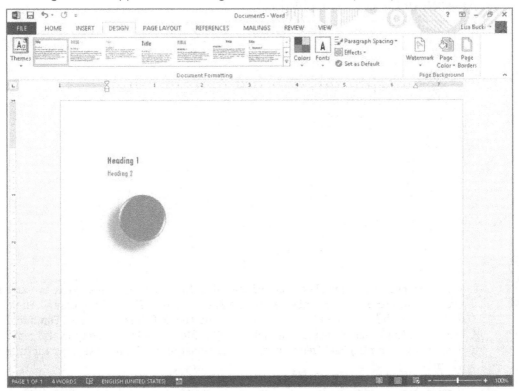

Differences between themes and templates

Word templates are stored in .dotx and .dotm files, and contain styles, macros, QAT settings, and keyboard customization settings. Templates are essentially documents, so they can contain text, graphics, and formatting as well.

Themes, on the other hand, transcend the boundaries of traditional Word structures. They instead owe their existence to .thmx files stored in the C:\Program Files (x86)\ Microsoft Office\Document Themes 15 folder (32-bit version) or C:\Program Files\Microsoft Office\Document Themes 15 folder (64-bit version). Like Word's .docx files, .thmx files are actually compressed .zip files that contain a number of subfolders and files. The structure of the Slice.thmx file is shown in Figure 18.8. Note that this theme file's name was changed to include a .zip extension so that its contents could be viewed by Windows Explorer (Windows 7) or File Explorer (Windows 8). For Word to recognize the file as a theme file, the .zip part of the name would need to be deleted.

FIGURE 18.8

Word gets its theme information from .thmx files, which are compressed .zip files that contain the XML structure and supporting files.

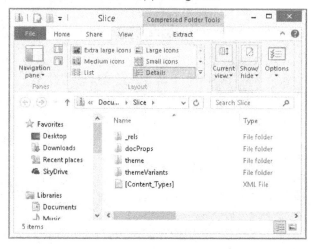

Another piece to this puzzle are additional files (for example, Green Yellow.xml and Grunge Texture.eftx) contained in the Theme Colors, Theme Effects, and Theme Fonts subfolders in the Document Themes 15 folder. The Theme Colors and Theme Fonts folders hold .xml files; the Theme Effects folder holds .eftx files. (The latter file type also represents a compressed .zip file.) Feel free to perform additional research on these file structures at your leisure.

Themes work by adding additional information to the current document, with much the same kinds of results as Style Sets, as discussed in Chapter 7. While the method for themes is different, using XML structures, the result is that the colors, fonts, and effects are added to the current document's formatting.

Theme elements or components

Themes consist of three elements:

- Theme colors
- Theme fonts
- Theme effects

By modifying theme elements, you can apply a new overall look for the document. By creating a new combination of any of these three elements, you effectively create new a new theme that you can save. Here's more about each of these three settings for an applied theme.

Theme colors

While each of the named themes that come with Word has a preassigned set of theme colors, there's no reason you have to stick with that set of colors. If you want the Organic theme but prefer the Slipstream theme colors set rather than the default colors, you can change the theme colors.

To change color sets, in the Design tab, click the Colors button in the Document Formatting group to display the gallery shown in Figure 18.9. Drag the mouse over the various color sets to see a Live Preview, and then click a color set when you see the colors you want.

FIGURE 18.9

After applying a theme, you can apply a different set of theme colors.

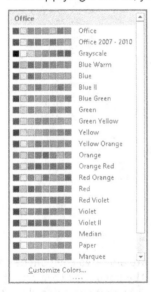

TIP

When you create a style or other template feature with a color other than Automatic, make sure the color you apply is one of the Theme Colors, not one of the Standard Colors in the color gallery. The Theme Colors will change as desired when you change themes, but the Standard Colors won't change.

If you click Customize Colors at the bottom of the gallery shown in Figure 18.9, the Create New Theme Colors dialog box shown in Figure 18.10 appears, where you can customize the colors and create your own theme colors. Click the various color buttons to display the color gallery, and click alternate colors as desired. Enter the theme colors set name in the

Name text box, and then click OK. The file will be saved in .xml format in C:\Users*user name*\AppData\Roaming\Microsoft\Templates\Document Themes\Theme Colors. (This folder is created the first time you save a theme.)

FIGURE 18.10

Create a custom set of theme colors here.

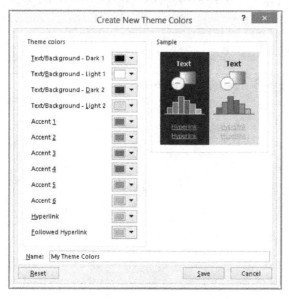

Theme fonts

Theme fonts are a bit simpler to understand because there are only two components: the heading font and body text font. Click the Fonts button in the Document Formatting group of the Design tab to change theme fonts. Notice in Figure 18.11 that the Arial Black-Arial theme fonts are selected. For each theme, the larger font shown is the one that will be applied to Heading styles (Heading 1, Heading 2, etc.), and the smaller one is the one that will be applied to body text.

> **TIP**
>
> The theme fonts for the currently applied theme appear in the Theme Fonts group at the top of Font drop-down list in the Font group of the Home tab.

FIGURE 18.11

For each theme, the Theme Fonts gallery shows the fonts used for headings and body text.

As for theme colors, you can create new theme font sets. Click Theme Fonts in the Document Formatting group of the Design tab, and then click Customize Fonts below the gallery choices, as shown in Figure 18.11. In the Create New Theme Fonts dialog box, shown in Figure 18.12, choose the Heading font and Body font, enter an informative name, and click Save. The theme font will be saved in .xml format in C:\Users*user name*\AppData\Roaming\Microsoft\Templates\Document Themes\Theme Fonts.

FIGURE 18.12

When you create new theme fonts, it's useful if the name you choose either describes the purpose for the fonts or includes the font names.

18

Theme effects

Theme effects are a bit harder to grasp than other theme elements, mostly because they're used a good deal less often by the average user. In the Design tab, click the Effects button in the Document Formatting group to display the gallery of options shown in Figure 18.13. If you study the different theme effects, you will see sometimes subtle and sometimes not-so-subtle differences among the elements shown. For example, the Office set looks soft-edged and perhaps a little blurred with shadows at the edges. Grunge has mottled fills applied. (It's unlikely you can see this in the picture in the book, so look onscreen.)

FIGURE 18.13

Apply theme effects to SmartArt, WordArt, Charts, and Shapes.

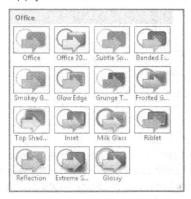

The easiest way to see theme effects in action is to create an example shape or graphic and use Live Preview to see the various effects.

You have seen how to save custom theme colors and theme fonts. The Word 2013 interface does not provide a built-in, direct way for you to save custom theme effects. You can indirectly save them, however, by saving the whole theme, as shown shortly.

Style Sets and paragraph spacing

The Document Formatting group of the Design tab includes a couple of additional settings along with all the theme settings. Chapter 7 discussed Style Sets, which enable you to change the style fonts used throughout the document. Although they are not technically a component of the applied theme, the fonts in the available Style Sets do change when you apply a different theme to the document. Change Style Sets using the Style Sets gallery in the Document Formatting group of the Design tab.

That group also includes a Paragraph Spacing gallery, shown in Figure 18.14. Choose one of the presets from the gallery to apply the combination of line and paragraph spacing that looks appropriate in the current document. For example, you may want to use the Relaxed preset to space out the paragraphs and lines in a flyer document to fill the page better.

FIGURE 18.14

Change overall document paragraph spacing with the Paragraph Spacing choices on the Design tab.

Saving custom themes

Using the Colors, Fonts, and Effect controls in the Document Formatting group of the Design tab, it's possible to create sets of theme elements that you want to preserve for future use. As indicated, you can save custom colors and fonts. In addition, you can save entire themes. To save a custom theme, in the Document Formatting Group of the Design tab, choose Themes ⇨ Save Current Theme. In the Save Current Theme dialog box, shown in Figure 18.15, type a descriptive name and click Save.

Alternatively and additionally, you can include other elements, such as text, styles, pre-built headers and footers, and other document elements, and save the entire setup as a template. When you do that, any custom themes employed automatically become part of the saved template. See the "Creating Your Own Templates" section earlier in this chapter for additional information on saving document templates.

FIGURE 18.15

Overall themes, theme colors, theme fonts, and theme effects are saved in the same folder set by default.

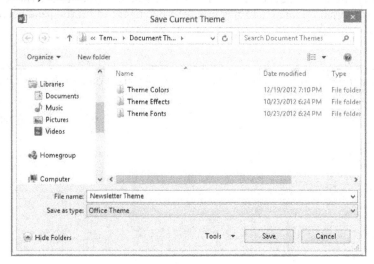

Setting the default theme

In previous Word versions, changing the default theme was a hassle. In Word 2013, open a new blank document, display the Design tab, choose a theme from the Themes gallery in the Document Formatting group, and then click Set as Default in the same group. To change the default theme for a particular template file, open the template file, change the theme, and then save and close the template.

Building on an Existing Foundation with Master Documents

A *master document* lets you create a single container file that provides access to, and control over, a number of smaller documents called *subdocuments*. Using a master document potentially solves a number of problems, including managing a complex assortment of cross-references when different sources are housed in a variety of documents. Other problems potentially solved include creating inclusive tables of contents, indexes, and tables of figures, as well as coordinating headers, footers, page numbers, footnotes, and endnotes.

Another potential advantage in all this is the possibility that different users can edit different subdocuments of the master document. Someone in one office might be working on

Chapter 1, someone else working on Chapter 2, and so on, all at the same time. Then, in theory, the edits to multiple subdocuments would appear the next time you opened the master document.

> **CAUTION**
>
> The master document feature has had a reputation for a propensity for document corruption as well as crashes. In part this may be attributed to trying to link between too many documents and storage locations. To minimize issues, it's a good practice to store all the subdocument files in a single location along with the master document. Also keep a current backup of that location to facilitate recovering files, if needed.

Because the master document itself is a smaller document that serves as a control center for all of the subdocuments, the expectation was that it would use less system memory and result in overall documents that were easier to handle. As it turned out, however, master documents often required at least as much memory as the most conspicuous alternative—which is to put all of the document components into a single document. Depending on the size of the individual components, as well as what they contain (such as numerous tables, equations, and graphics), using a master document can be about as easy as trying to steer an aircraft carrier through the aisles of your neighborhood grocery store.

But that wasn't the worst of it. The worst of it was that the master document feature tended to corrupt the component documents. All of the coordination advantages in the world aren't worth anything if there is a fairly strong likelihood that the document components are going to become so hopelessly corrupted that they can't be opened.

Here are a few tips to reduce the risks and enhance your chances for success when using master documents:

- Use the same template for all documents that will be components for the master document.

- For individual document control, if you have access to a SharePoint server, put the component documents themselves onto a SharePoint server (for example), and let *it* handle the check-ins and check-outs.

- Master documents' potential strength is in coordinating things such as tables of contents, indexes, page numbering, and cross-references. Page numbering, tables of contents, and indexes are easy to redo if the master document feature fails. Cross-references are not. Although it's more work, create cross-references from the individual component documents, and don't rely on the master document itself. It may be more work, but it's less work than having to redo everything if the master document feature fails.

- Use Word's Heading 1 through 9 styles for formatting your headings, keeping in mind that they will need to be coordinated at the top level. If the master document is organized into chapters, with each chapter residing in a single document, reserve Heading 1 for chapter titles, rather than for major headings within chapters.

18

Creating a Master Document

You have essentially two approaches to creating a master document:

- **Organize from existing files:** Create a master document from a container file, and then insert and coordinate existing files with heading styles/outlining applied. Remember to back up those files before turning them into subdocuments.

- **Convert an existing formatted document:** When a document that you've formatted with heading styles (and thus outlining) has become unwieldy, convert it into a master document, converting major sections into subdocuments.

Before we launch into how to do this, it's helpful to be familiar with the available tools. Let's take a look.

The Master Document group

In theory, the Master Document view is the Outline view on steroids. In the View tab, or in the Views section of the status bar, click the Outline choice. To display the Master Document tools, click Show Document in the Master Document group of the Outlining tab, as shown in Figure 18.16.

FIGURE 10.16

Click Show Document to display all of the Master Document tools. Most tools are grayed out until a master document has been created.

568

Tools in the Master Document group of the Outlining tab include:

- **Show Document:** Toggles the display of all master document tools except for Show Document and Collapse Subdocuments.

- **Collapse Subdocuments:** Toggles between showing the path and name of the subdocument and showing the subdocument content itself.

- **Create:** Transforms selected outline items into subdocuments. Each major outline division becomes a separate file.

- **Insert:** Inserts an independent file into the master document as a subdocument. Use this approach to assemble existing files into a master document.

- **Unlink:** Deletes the link to the subdocument and copies the subdocument contents into the master document. If you do this for all subdocuments, the resulting document is no longer a master document.

- **Merge:** Combines multiple subdocuments into a single subdocument. The newly combined subdocument inherits the name of the first subdocument in the selection.

- **Split:** Splits the selected subdocument into new subdocuments at the next lower level of organization. For example, if the subdocument has one Heading 1 but multiple Heading 2 styles, there will be one subdocument for each Heading 2 in the selection.

- **Lock Document:** Toggles the write state of subdocuments in the selection on and off.

Creating a master document from existing documents

It's pretty typical for people from different departments in an organization to be fielding different parts of an RFQ (Request for Quotation), RFP (Request for Proposal), annual report, or other types of documents, such as applications for company-wide certifications such as ISO. These are exactly the types of situations that the master document feature was intended to assist with. Each department's portion of the overall task can be assigned to a single person charged with preparing the text. Then, the overall point person for the project can gather the documents provided by the other team members, insert them into the master document, and tweak the finished product.

To create a master document from existing files, follow this process:

1. **Press Ctrl+N to create a new blank document to serve as the master document, or create the master document from an existing template file.** It isn't essential, but it will greatly simplify document formatting if the master document itself and each of the component files are all based on the same document template and have a relatively similar outline structure applied.

2. **Type a title and any other setup text you might need or insert a cover page, and then position the insertion point where the first subdocument should be inserted.**

3. **Click the View tab of the Ribbon, and click Outline.**

18

4. **In the Master Document group, click Show Document.** The Master Document group expands to show the rest of the Master Document tools.

5. **Click Insert in the Master Document group.** The Insert Subdocument dialog box appears.

6. **Navigate to the file to insert, click it, and click Open.**

7. **Repeat Steps 5 and 6 to insert additional subdocument files.**

8. **Save and name the master document file.**

> **NOTE**
>
> If an inserted subdocument's template is different from that of the master document, Word notifies you in a message box, and you can click OK to continue.

If the subdocument and master document contain user-created styles of the same name, you will be prompted about how to handle the styles, as shown in Figure 18.17. Even if the styles are identically defined, Word offers you an opportunity to rename the incoming styles to something else. Rename the incoming style if the styles really *are* different and used for different things.

FIGURE 18.17

Word offers to rename any user-created styles that exist in both the subdocument and master document.

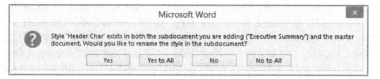

The options are as follows:

- **Yes:** Word automatically renames the incoming style, and then prompts about the next one. Word appends a 1 to the end of the style name (GX1, in this case). In later subdocument insertions, Word increments as needed (that is, GX2, GX3, and so on).

- **Yes to All:** Word automatically renames all incoming styles.

- **No:** Word skips the noted style and prompts about the next one. Word applies the master document's version of the style to the associated text.

- **No to All:** Word skips all of them, and uses the master document's version of all user-created styles for the associated incoming text.

Once you've added all of the files you want to insert, when you save, the master document assumes command and control of the subdocuments, and saves them whenever changes are made to the master document.

Converting an existing file into a master document

You can also create a master document from a single existing file organized with outlining. When you do this, Word enables you to use the Heading 1–9 styles as a basis for identifying how to separate the content of a single document into a series of subdocuments, as follows. Because Word will make major changes to your document, it is a good idea to make a backup copy. Then follow these steps to break it into subdocuments:

1. **Open the outlined file you want to break into subdocuments.**

2. **Switch to Outline view and, in the Master Document group of the Outlining tab, click Show Document.**

3. **Use Show Level in the Outline Tools group to select the heading level that will help you to subdivide the document.** Displaying one level below the level that you will use as the dividing line ensures you will include the right level of detail.

4. **Drag to select headings you want to include in a subdocument, and click the Create button in the Master Document group of the Outlining tab.** As shown in Figure 18.18, a box appears around the new subdocument.

FIGURE 18.18

The box identifies the new subdocument.

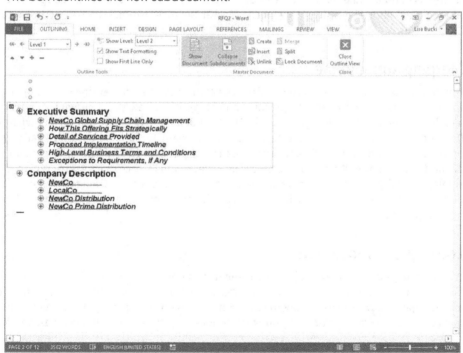

5. **Repeat Step 4 to identify additional subdocuments.**

6. **Click Save on the QAT.** When you save the master document, each of the subdocuments will be assigned a name based on the beginning text of each subdocument. If you don't like the names, you can rename them.

Working with Master Documents

Working with master documents can have some unexpected speed bumps. For those without infinite patience, this section's mission is to lift the veil as much as possible, so you can use master documents effectively without inadvertently introducing issues.

Converting subdocuments into master document text

When working with master documents, text can reside either inside the master document itself or within the subdocuments. If you start seeing "Too many files are open" errors because you've included too many subdocument files in the master document, or if you realize that some subdocument content would logically work better as master document text instead, you can convert a subdocument into master document text.

To convert subdocuments into master document text, click or select the subdocument to convert, and click the Unlink tool in the Master Document group of the Outlining tab in Outline view.

Merging subdocuments

You can merge subdocuments to simplify the structure of a master document, or if you want to combine subdocuments so that you can assign a new subdocument to a team member for revision. To merge, while in Master Document view (Outlining tab with Show Document selected), select the subdocuments you want to merge, ensuring that you include each subdocument in its entirety, and click the Merge tool in the Master Document group of the Outlining tab. When you do this, the several subdocument icons are replaced by a single one. All of the merged subdocuments are combined into a single file that keeps the name of the first subdocument in the group selected. Save the master document file to finish the process.

Locking subdocuments

When managing a complex project, you sometimes don't want parts of a master document changed. You can lock all or part of a master document against write access. When locked, a lock appears next to the subdocument icon, as shown in Figure 18.19. To lock subdocuments, select the subdocuments you want to lock and click Lock Document in the Master

Document group of the Outlining tab. Note that Lock Document is a toggle; if you click different locked and unlocked subdocuments, the Lock Document tool looks flat for unlocked subdocuments, and pushed-in for locked subdocuments. To unlock a locked subdocument, select it and click Lock Document again.

FIGURE 18.19

Locked subdocuments can be opened, but changes can't be saved.

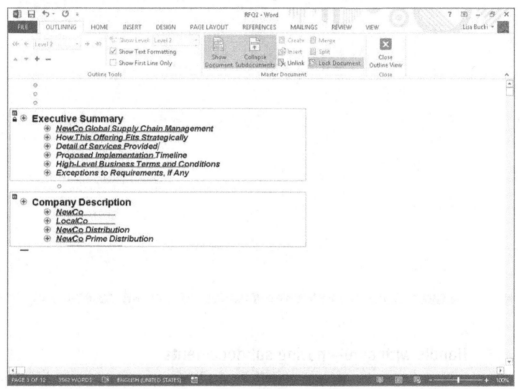

Expand/collapse subdocuments

When you reopen a master document, it doesn't initially show the contents of the subdocuments in expanded form. Instead, it shows the links to the inserted subdocuments, as shown in Figure 18.20. Click the View tab, click Outline in the views group, and then click Expand Subdocuments in the Master Document group to redisplay the outline. You can later use the Collapse Subdocuments button in the Master Document group to collapse one or more subdocuments back to a link.

FIGURE 18.20

When you open a master document, all subdocuments appear as links because the master document is collapsed.

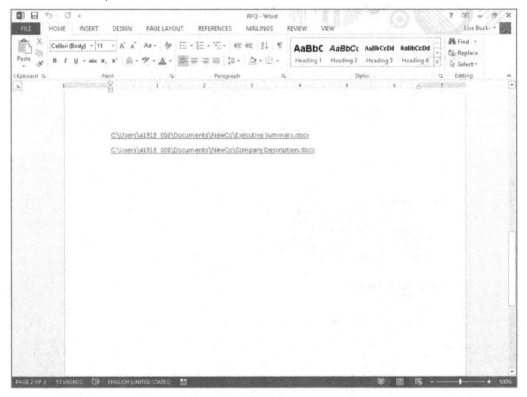

Handle with care—moving subdocuments

In Chapter 3, you learned how wonderfully easy it is to organize documents in Outline view. In addition, you need to know that Word encases each subdocument within section breaks, a feature covered in Chapter 16, "Setting Up the Document with Sections, Headers/Footers, and Columns." When you move a subdocument, it is imperative that the opening and closing section breaks be moved as well. If one of them is left behind, the moved section will suddenly become part of another subdocument, so select with care, and drag and drop with even greater care.

It is almost impossible to properly move a subdocument unless section breaks are visible (toggle on and off with Ctrl+* [Ctrl+Shift+8]). Make sure you turn section breaks on before trying to select and move a subdocument.

Summary

In this chapter you've seen what templates are, how to use existing templates from a variety of sources, and how to create and modify templates. You've also learned about Word 2013's theme feature, how to apply themes and theme elements, and how to save custom themes. Finally, you saw how to create a master document to combine content from various authors and standardize formatting for a cohesive result. You should now be able to do the following:

- Understand the relationship between themes and templates
- Create a new document template
- Copy styles and macros from one template to another
- Change document themes at will, and understand why a theme might not have any effect on a document
- Change theme component settings, and save a custom theme
- Create a master document from existing multiple documents
- Break a single large file into subdocuments
- Lock and merge subdocuments when the need arises

18

Part VI

Enhancing Documents with Reference Features

Tradition and common sense suggest that in a long document, you should help your eventual reader by including navigation aids, summary information, and references to sources. Part VI shows you how to add all the expected and underexploited tools that make working with a long document faster and easier.

Chapter 19 begins with tools useful for both referencing and navigation: bookmarks, hyperlinks, and cross-references. You'll see how to use the first two to move between locations and documents, and more, and the latter to help the reader find and go to relevant information within the document. Next, Chapter 20 shows you how to add summary and organizational information in a document, including a table of contents; captions, and a document index. For the academics among you, Chapter 21 tells you everything you need to know about footnotes and endnotes, as well as how and when to use Word's citations and bibliography tools, and how to set up for and create a table of authorities.

Enhancing Navigation with Bookmarks, Hyperlinks, and Cross-References

IN THIS CHAPTER

Working with bookmarks

Creating bookmarks

Using Word-created bookmarks

Displaying and hiding bookmarks

Fixing broken bookmarks

Adding an automatic hyperlink

Creating hyperlinks to jump within and between documents

Creating a hyperlink that starts an email message

Creating cross-references to headings, numbered items, bookmarks, footnotes, endnotes, and more

This chapter dials you in to the great tools for navigating in and referencing other locations within a long document. You'll learn how to use a bookmark to create a location you can jump to from any location. You'll learn how to add hyperlinks that enable you to jump to another document location or another document, or even spawn a new email message. Finally, the chapter explains how cross-references build on bookmarks, by enabling you to denote relevant information found elsewhere in the document.

Working with Bookmarks

A *bookmark* is a way of naming a point or a selection in a Word document so that it you can easily locate it or refer to in some way. Bookmarks can be used for something as simple as a place marker. You could create bookmarks for:

- Key headings in a document to make them easier to go to

- Specific objects such as all the tables of data in a scientific document that users may want to find quickly

- Locations you may need to reference in a macro (Chapter 32, "Macros: Recording, Editing, and Using Them," covers macros)

Bookmarks make great go-to locations when you want to create a dynamic document. You can manually insert bookmarks as needed to create reference points or to be able to refer to or replicate text elsewhere in a document. Bookmarks are also essential when you want to use cross-references (covered later in the chapter) to refer to parts of a document else-where—referring to a figure number in the text, for example. When you create a cross-refer-ence, Word automatically inserts a bookmark as well. Word also creates automatic bookmarks when you use other features, such as pasting Object Linking and Embedding (OLE) objects. Some of these automatic bookmarks can be made visible, and some are always hidden.

Displaying bookmarks

One way to make sure that you don't accidentally delete a bookmark that is crucial to some other feature working properly is to know where the bookmark is when possible. By default, Word does not display any indication of bookmarks. To display bookmarks, choose File ➪ Options ➪ Advanced, and in the Show document content section, click to place a check next to Show bookmarks, as shown in Figure 19.1.

When Show bookmarks is checked, square brackets ([ ]) display around the bookmarked text, as in the example in Figure 19.1. If you insert a bookmark without making a selection, such as when you want to mark a point for navigation purposes, the bookmarked point appears as an I-beam, as shown in Figure 19.2. (The left and right bracket characters merge together so that the vertical components coincide, with the resulting representation look-ing like a large I.) Word-created hidden bookmarks don't display in the document, but you can specify that they should show up in the Bookmark dialog box, as you'll see shortly.

Information, as they say, is power. It cannot be overemphasized how important it is for you to *know* what's in your document. If your document contains bookmarks—whether you put them there or not—it's helpful and useful to know that they're there, if for no other reason than to keep from deleting them or changing them when other features depend on their being there and not changing. In this spirit, the chapter assumes you have enabled the dis-play of bookmarks to work with them.

FIGURE 19.1

Check next to Show bookmarks to display bookmarks in your document.

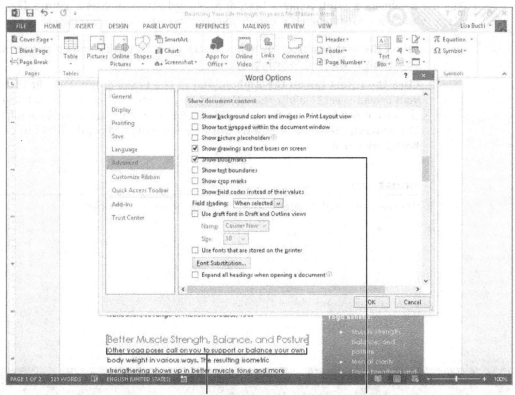

Square brackets around bookmarked text   Check to display bookmarks

FIGURE 19.2

Bookmarks display as gray square brackets or an I-beam, but they do not print.

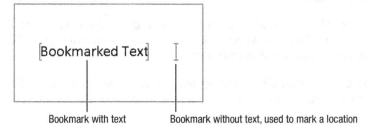

Bookmark with text   Bookmark without text, used to mark a location

Marking bookmarks

You can bookmark a point, selected text, or a selected object such as a picture. Use these steps to add bookmarks where needed in your document:

1. **Select the text or object, or to bookmark a point, click to position the insertion point in the desired location.**

2. **Click the Insert tab on the Ribbon, and in the Links group, click Bookmark.** If your screen is set to a low resolution, you may need to click the Links button and then click Bookmark, as shown in Figure 19.3. Alternatively, press Ctrl+Shift+F5. The Bookmark dialog box appears, with any existing bookmarks listed under Bookmark name.

FIGURE 19.3

Choose Bookmark or press Ctrl+Shift+F5 to insert a bookmark.

3. **Type a name for the new bookmark in the Bookmark name text box as shown in Figure 19.4, and click Add or press Enter.** See the "What's in a name?" section next to learn more about naming bookmarks.

Bookmarked text can be formatted like any other text, either before or after creating the bookmark. So don't think twice about bookmarks as you design your document.

FIGURE 19.4

Use the Bookmark dialog box to Add, Delete, and Go To bookmarks.

What's in a name?

Unless you're creating a temporary placeholder and there's no chance for confusion, it's worth giving some thought to the names you specify for bookmarks so you can remember them. It's true that the Bookmark dialog box shows you the existing bookmarks, but if you have a lot of them, you might need to visit the various locations to be sure what's what.

Word also has rules for naming bookmarks. Bookmark names:

- Cannot include spaces.
- Can include any combination of letters (including accented letters), numbers, and the underscore (_) character.
- Are not case-specific. Many users mix uppercase and lowercase to make bookmarks easier to read, and because they don't like typing or looking at the _ character.

- Must be unique. If you add a bookmark named ThisPlace and create another one by the same name elsewhere in the same document, Word deletes the original one. You do not need to explicitly delete a bookmark to use the same name elsewhere. You can, of course, reuse the same bookmark names in different documents, because bookmark names are specific to the current document.

> **TIP**
>
> A clue that you've included an illegal character such as a space in a bookmark name is that the Add button will be disabled (grayed out). Eliminate the character to make Add active.

Overlap and redundancy

You can have any number of bookmarks in a document. Bookmarks can overlap each other as well as be contained within other bookmarks. For example, suppose the word *overlap* was bookmarked as Example1 in the preceding sentence. You could also bookmark *overlap each other* as Example2. In addition, you could bookmark *each other as well* as Example3. The Example1 bookmark is fully contained within the Example2 bookmark, and the Example1 and Example3 bookmarks overlap. This example demonstrates what can be done but doesn't fully demonstrate the utility. Being able to overlap and contain bookmarks within other bookmarks gives you the flexibility to create references within other references, as well as to refer to different material in a variety of ways.

You can use bookmarks with the cross-reference feature to repeat a selection in a document. Though you could simply copy the text, this has a disadvantage. If the source material is updated, the pasted copy would not reflect the updates. You can also give the identical material multiple bookmark names. You'll see a practical strategic example of why you might want to do this in "Finding Word-created bookmarks," later in this chapter.

Copying and pasting bookmarked text

If you paste or insert text from a Word document, any bookmarks included in it come along for the ride, with two exceptions. First, if you paste as unformatted text, any bookmarks the text contains aren't pasted. Second, if you are pasting from a different document and the current document has bookmarks by the same name, the current ones are preserved, and the pasted bookmarks are eliminated.

> **CAUTION**
>
> When pasting text containing bookmarks into text containing bookmarks by the same name, Word does not warn you or advise you. Also, if you've created a cross reference to a bookmark and copy the cross reference to another document without copying the bookmarked text, as well, the cross reference link no longer works.

Table 19.1 summarizes what happens when you add text to and delete text from items containing or marked with bookmarks, by typing, copying, cutting, deleting, or pasting. This summary assumes that you are not pasting as unformatted text.

TABLE 19.1 **Working with Bookmarks**

Action	Result
Type, paste, or otherwise insert text or graphics anywhere within a bookmarked area.	The added material is included in the bookmark, and all references to that bookmark will reflect the addition when they are updated.
Delete or copy material containing part of a bookmark (beginning or end, but not both).	Partial bookmarks are not copied. If deleting/cutting material that includes part of a bookmark, the original bookmarked area is shrunk to reflect the removal of material.
Copy material containing entire bookmarks to another part of the same document.	The bookmarks are not copied because there is no mechanism for giving them new names.
Copy material containing entire bookmarks to another document.	The bookmarks are copied unless the document contains bookmarks with the same names.
Move material that contains entire bookmarks.	The bookmarks are moved to the destination (by cutting/pasting).
Delete all material between the beginning and ending bookmark brackets.	The bookmark is deleted.
Type or insert material immediately before an opening bookmark bracket or immediately after a closing bookmark bracket.	The material is not included in the bookmark area.

> **NOTE**
>
> There is no way to add text or other material before a bookmark that's at the beginning of the document. To effectively place new unbookmarked material before the bookmark, you need to redefine the bookmark.

19

Navigating bookmarks

There are two main ways to navigate to a bookmark:

- You've already seen that the Bookmark dialog box has its own Go To button. Select a bookmark in the Bookmark name list, click Go To to select the contents of that bookmark in the document, and then click Close.

- Another vehicle is the Go To tab in the Find and Replace dialog box. Press Ctrl+G or F5 to open the Find and Replace dialog with the Go To tab selected. Click Bookmark in the Go to what list at the left. Open the Enter bookmark name drop-down list, click a bookmark name (Figure 19.5), and then click Go To. Click Close to close the dialog box.

FIGURE 19.5

The Go To tab in the Find and Replace dialog box also enables you to go to a bookmark.

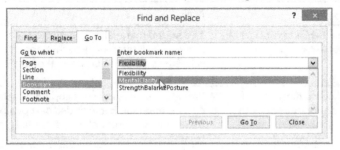

Finding Word-created bookmarks

As indicated earlier, Word sometimes inserts bookmarks automatically. Some of these are hidden, and some are not. When creating a TOC, for example, Word automatically inserts a hidden bookmark for each heading so it can use that item for creating a reference. As shown in Figure 19.6, most Word-created bookmarks have an underscore at the beginning of the name. You cannot display a hidden bookmark in the document. Often, the only hint of its presence is when you click the Hidden bookmarks check box in the Bookmark dialog box. Use the Hidden bookmarks check box to toggle hidden bookmarks on and off in the Bookmark dialog box.

FIGURE 19.6

The bookmarks beginning with the underscore were automatically inserted by Word's TOC feature.

Recall that earlier in this chapter you read that you can assign different bookmarks to identical passages. If you discover hidden bookmarks in your document, you can make them visible by inserting redundant bookmarks. For example, in the Bookmark dialog box, select a bookmark beginning with an underscore and click Go To. That selects the bookmarked passage. With the Bookmark dialog box still open, type a new name in the Bookmark name text box, perhaps adding **visible** before the underscore. Then click Add. The hidden bookmark is still hidden, but you now know where it is in the text because *your* bookmark is visible.

Broken bookmarks

When you or Word use bookmarks in your documents, you may encounter bookmark errors. You need to be vigilant about two types of bookmark errors.

Error! Bookmark not defined

The first and most common error is the dreaded "Error! Bookmark not defined." or "Error! Reference source not found." Any time a bookmark is deleted, any reference to that bookmark will, when updated (by pressing F9 with that field selected), yield one of those pleasant little messages. When that happens, you have several options. You can repair or reinstate the missing bookmark. If that's not possible, you can reinstate the earlier displayed result and either lock the field against updating or convert it into regular text.

Regardless of which choice you make, when you see the "Error! Bookmark not defined" message, immediately press Ctrl+Z. This undoes the update and restores the original text. Right-click the errant field, and choose Edit Field. Examine the field in the Field dialog box to see if you can determine where the problem lies. If you realize what happened, often you can go to the relevant document and passage, and repair the damage by reinstating the bookmark.

If the document referenced by the field is gone, you can lock the field against further updates, and return the underlying document to the necessary location later. To lock the field, select it and press Ctrl+F11 (Lock Fields). You can later unlock the field by selecting it and pressing Ctrl+Shift+F11 (Unlock Fields).

If the referenced document or passage is gone with no hope of return, you can convert the current field result into hard text. With the field selected, press Ctrl+Shift+F9 (Unlink Fields). See Chapter 23, "Automating Document Content with Fields," to learn more about fields.

Unwanted or unexpected results

The second type of error occurs less often but is also harder to spot. This kind of error occurs when the bookmark still exists but the text and other material it contains has changed. This can happen for a variety of reasons, the most common being bad memory. Suppose, for example, that years ago you bookmarked different paragraphs in a report or contract so you could use them as boilerplate text in other documents.

19

Now, you rediscover the source documents with the boilerplate text, which had bookmark display turned off (so you don't even know they're there), and decide that the document will work quite nicely for something else, with just a few edits. You make your additions and deletions, expanding the text contained in some bookmarks, reducing the text in others, and perhaps even deleting a few along the way. After all, without bookmarks displaying, they might as well not even be there.

Later, you notice that some of the dependent documents have changed unexpectedly. After pressing F9, that home sale contract suddenly has a maternity clause in it! Oops!

When this kind of error happens, the source material usually is too far gone to fix. Again, Ctrl+Z is your friend. Press Ctrl+Z to undo the F9 update, select the reference field, and press Ctrl+Shift+F9 to convert the passage into actual text. Let's just hope you noticed the error before sending the revised document to anyone.

Hyperlinks

Anyone who surfs the Internet is familiar with hyperlinks. Hyperlinks often appear as underlined text that is a different color from the surrounding text. When you hover the mouse over a hyperlink, the status bar in the current program or a tooltip displays the location of the content associated with the link. If you click a link, your computer attempts to display the information contained at the indicated address using the program that's associated with it.

In Word, there's only one thing that's technically called a *hyperlink*—references created using the Hyperlink tool in the Links group of the Insert tab. In a broader sense, however, any link in a document is a hyperlink if clicking it results in the display of information from another document or location. This section looks at hyperlinks inserted using the Hyperlink tool in the Links group on the Insert tab, as well as hyperlinks that are inserted automatically or through the use of other features.

Automatic hyperlinks

To create a basic hyperlink to a web page, you don't need to use the Hyperlink tool. First, make sure that AutoCorrect As You Type (covered in detail in Chapter 11, "Cleaning Up with AutoCorrect and AutoFormat") is set up to convert URLs that you type into hyperlinks.

Choose File ⇨ Options ⇨ Proofing ⇨ AutoCorrect Options. Click the AutoFormat As You Type tab, and under Replace as you type, make sure Internet and network paths with hyperlinks is checked. Click OK twice.

With that option enabled, if you type a web address or URL such as www.wiley.com, and press any kind of separator (space, comma, period, and so on), Word automatically converts what you type into a fully functional hyperlink. Word adds the http:// protocol to the beginning of the link address, although that part will not be displayed. Similarly, if you type an email address, such as donaldduck@disney.com or santa@northpole.com, they are converted into fully functional clickable (or Ctrl+clickable) *mailto* links. Correctly specified network paths are also converted into hyperlinks (for example, \\\\ tomjones\\c\\reports\\jan2113report.docx). Figure 19.7 shows a URL that was typed on a line below a table and converted into a hyperlink by Word.

FIGURE 19.7

Word can automatically convert a URL you type into a working hyperlink.

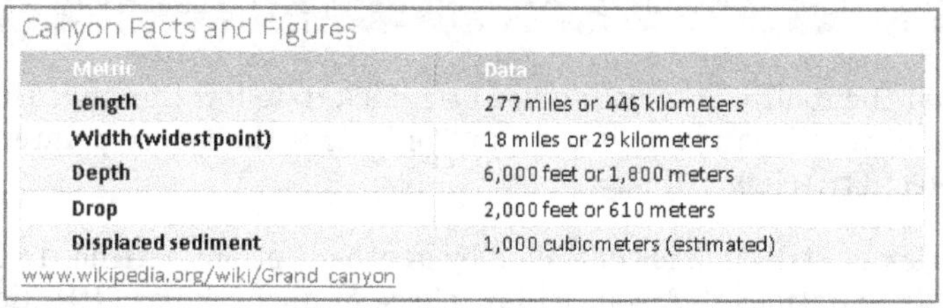

Canyon Facts and Figures

Metric	Data
Length	277 miles or 446 kilometers
Width (widest point)	18 miles or 29 kilometers
Depth	6,000 feet or 1,800 meters
Drop	2,000 feet or 610 meters
Displaced sediment	1,000 cubic meters (estimated)

www.wikipedia.org/wiki/Grand_canyon

NOTE

HTTP, which stands for Hypertext Transfer Protocol, is the set of computer instructions for transferring information over the World Wide Web, which makes up a large portion of the Internet. *mailto* is the proper beginning of a fully formed email hyperlink. Clicking an email hyperlink opens a new message in your system's default email program, using the hyperlinked email address as the destination address.

19

Using and displaying hyperlinks

Sometimes you explicitly insert hyperlinks. Other times, Word creates hyperlinks for you. A number of Word features by default automatically produce clickable hyperlinks. When you create a table of contents, by default, the resulting entries are hyperlinks to the headings associated with them. When you move the mouse over a table of contents entry, a tooltip tells you how to go to the associated content, as shown in Figure 19.8. Other hyperlinks display in a similar fashion, but whether a tooltip displays at all, and whether you click versus Ctrl+click to follow a link are options you can change.

FIGURE 19.8

A tooltip indicates that something is a hyperlink, the location of the content, and how to get there (Ctrl+click, in this case).

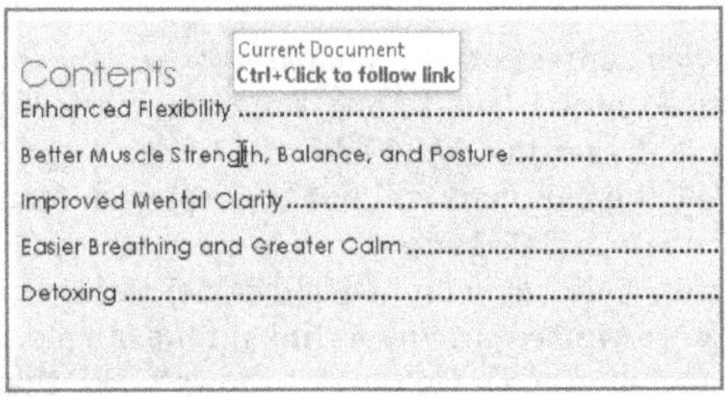

NOTE

Tooltips are displayed by default. If you don't see a tooltip when you hover the mouse over a link, either it does not contain tooltip text or tooltips are turned off. To enable tooltips, choose File ➪ Options ➪ Display ➪ Show document tooltips on hover under Page display options, and then click OK.

Note in Figure 19.8 that the tooltip tells you to use Ctrl+click to follow the link. This is the default method for using or following a hyperlink in Word. Move the mouse pointer over the hyperlink, and select Ctrl+click.

Whether you simply click or Ctrl+click is controlled by another Options setting. To change this setting, choose File ➪ Options ➪ Advanced tab, check or uncheck Use Ctrl+Click to follow hyperlink under Editing options as desired. Then click OK. When you're editing a document, it can be distracting and counterproductive if you inadvertently activate a link when you're actually trying to select it rather than follow it. If you're reading a document, on the other hand, it can be annoying to have to reach for the keyboard to follow a link. Pick a setting that works for you, and change Word's behavior if it doesn't fit how you work.

Inserting hyperlinks

As indicated, some Word features automatically insert hyperlinks by default. These include inserting a table of contents, cross references, certain objects, and footnotes and endnotes. Some of these, along with hyperlinks inserted directly, yield a tooltip telling you to click or Ctrl+click to follow them, such as table of contents and cross-references, whereas others such as footnotes and endnotes don't. This section shows you how to create your own hyperlinks. Using the methods covered here, rather than just typing, enables you to set up more aspects of how the hyperlink looks and behaves.

You saw the Hyperlink tool back in Figure 19.3. Click Insert, click Links in the Links group if needed, and then click Hyperlink. The Insert Hyperlink dialog box shown in Figure 19.9 appears. The contents of the Insert Hyperlink dialog box vary depending on what is selected along the left-hand side under Link to. Use the choices for the various link types as described next, and then click OK to insert the hyperlink.

FIGURE 19.9

Use Insert Hyperlink to create a variety of hyperlinks.

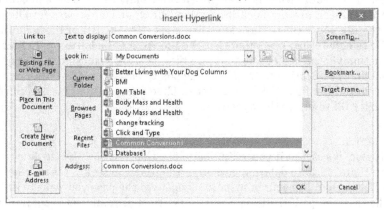

Link to Existing File or Web Page

In the Insert Hyperlink dialog box, set the Link to option to Existing File or Web Page to link to any file on your computer, your network, or the Internet. Any given URL ultimately corresponds to a file. Available options shown in Figure 19.9 are described in Table 19.2.

TABLE 19.2   Insert Hyperlink Dialog Box Options and Controls

Option	Use
Current Folder	Use in conjunction with Look in, Up One Folder, and Browse to File to select the file of interest.
Browsed Pages	Use to select a URL from a list of recently browsed web pages.
Recent Files	Use to select a recently opened Office or HTML file.
Text to display	With a file selected, the name of the file is displayed in the Text to display field. You can replace that text with something more informative if you like.
ScreenTip	Use the ScreenTip control to tell the reader what the link will do. This is especially useful if the link does something unexpected, such as open a different application (especially something other than a browser).
Bookmark	If the selected file is a Word document or an HTML document, click Bookmark to target the hyperlink more narrowly, as shown in Figure 19.7. In "Select a place in this document," click the bookmark you want to link to, and then click OK.
Target Frame	Complex web pages can contain multiple frames for controlling how content is displayed. When using frames, use this setting to specify the frame in which you want the linked content to appear.

19

Linking to a local file

To link to a local file on your own computer (which can be any file—you are not limited to linking just to Word files), use the Look in, Up One Folder, and/or Browse for File tools to navigate to the file you want to link, and then click it in the list of files. Figure 19.9 shows a local file selected. Most users find that the Browse for File button to the far right of the Look in list provides a better way to locate files, because you can use Files of Type or provide a partial file specification in the File Name box to help you narrow the list of files you see. When you find the file, click it to select it. Choose any options, as described in Table 19.2, and click OK to insert the hyperlink.

Linking to a web page

To link to a web page, it's easiest if you're linking to one that's recent. Use the Browsed Pages control shown in Figure 19.10 to determine whether the page you seek is there. If not, click the Browse the Web button. Use your browser to navigate to the page you want to link. When you return to the Insert Hyperlink dialog box, the URL from your browser is automatically copied into the Address field. Choose any options, and then click OK to insert the link.

FIGURE 19.10

Click Browsed Pages and use the list to select a recently visited website to link to.

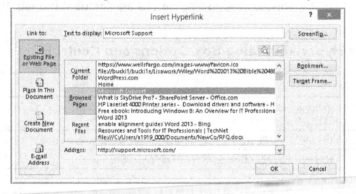

> **TIP**
>
> With your browser open to the link you want to insert, if you click in your browser and click in the Insert Hyperlink dialog box, the URL is automatically copied to the Address field in the Insert Hyperlink dialog box. Alternatively, even if the Insert Hyperlink dialog box isn't open, you can click the icon at the beginning of the address in your browser window and drag that address into the Word window to insert a hyperlink.

Link to Place in This Document

When using a hyperlink to another place in the same document, you're not limited to using bookmarks as the destination. In the Link to section of the Insert Hyperlink dialog box, click Place in This Document. As suggested by Figure 19.11, you can link to any bookmark or heading in the document. For the latter, all text formatted using the styles Heading 1 through Heading 9 is presented under Select a place in this document. Note that non-Heading text with Level formatting applied is not included.

FIGURE 19.11

You can hyperlink to a heading or bookmark in the current document.

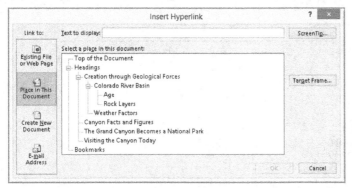

If the bookmark or heading name doesn't meet your needs as the display text, modify or replace the Text to display text box entry as needed. Click ScreenTip, if appropriate for the document, choose any other options you need, and click OK.

> **NOTE**
>
> Every hyperlink is inserted as a field code. You can click in the hyperlink and press Shift+F9 to toggle between the field code and hyperlink display.

Link to Create New Document

Sometimes the document to which you want to link does not yet exist. You can use the Create New Document option in the Link to section of the Insert Hyperlink dialog box to create a placeholder document, with contents provided later, or you can create the document now, as shown in Figure 19.12. Use the Change button if necessary to navigate to a different folder in which you want to store the new file.

The usual reason for using this feature is to create a placeholder, in effect, for a file that has content you will provide later. You are not limited to linking to an existing Word file. However, if you choose the Edit the new document now option as shown in Figure 19.12, Word's ability to transfer control to a capable program might be limited. For other Office documents such as PowerPoint and Excel, there shouldn't be a problem, as long as the

19

program is installed. If you choose Edit the new document now, when you click OK, Word creates a hyperlink to the file, and then starts the appropriate application. Do what's needed to create the file and then save it. Word will properly link to it when you Ctrl+click (or click, depending on your settings) on it later.

FIGURE 19.12

Use Create New Document to create either a new document or a placeholder for one that will be created later.

If the file you specify is something else, however, such as a .mid or .mp3 file, it could be problematic transferring control to a program to create the file. Though Word usually knows how to display such files, it might not know how to create them, in which case you might see the error shown in Figure 19.13. Click Yes to create an empty file, and then manually open the program you need to create or otherwise download or obtain the needed file.

FIGURE 19.13

If the method for creating a given file type is unknown to Word, you can create an empty file now and create its contents later

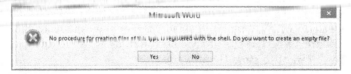

Link to E-Mail Address

The final kind of hyperlink you can insert using the Link to section of the Insert Hyperlink dialog box is a *mailto* (email) link. This sort of link often is inserted into web pages and other documents as a head start for an email that is being suggested in the document, as shown in Figure 19.14.

FIGURE 19.14

Setting up a hyperlink that creates an email message

When you insert an email address in the E-mail address text box, Word includes the mailto: specification used for Internet email addresses. This is standard HTML syntax for including an email link in a web page or other document. Such links work in Word, too.

If you Ctrl+click an email hyperlink in a Word document, Windows opens the default email program and creates a new message with the information you specified in the Insert Hyperlink dialog box when creating the link. For example, if you have Outlook installed and click an email hyperlink link, a new Outlook message opens, as shown in Figure 19.15.

FIGURE 19.15

When you follow an email hyperlink, your default email program starts a new message with the To and Subject lines filled in.

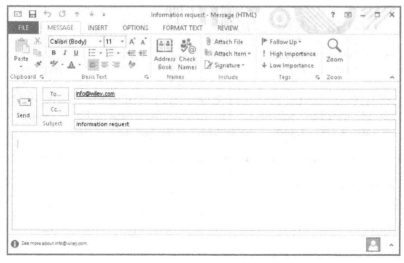

19

Changing a hyperlink

If the insertion point already contains a hyperlink, clicking the Hyperlink button from the Insert tab displays the Edit Hyperlink dialog box. It is similar to the Insert Hyperlink dialog box, but it also contains a Remove Link button. You can use this button to restore a hyperlink to normal text. You also can find Remove Hyperlink, along with additional hyperlink commands, by right-clicking a hyperlink. The shortcut menu options for working with hyperlinks appear in Figure 19.16.

FIGURE 19.16

Right-clicking a hyperlink produces a variety of hyperlink-related commands.

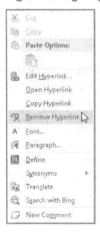

Inserting Cross-References

Just as a hyperlink can serve as a type of cross-reference, Word's cross-references can also serve as a type of hyperlink. A cross-reference displays the specified information at a second location in the document. For example, If you've added a numbered caption to a table or inserted picture, inserting the cross-reference would redisplay the number. Or, if you bookmarked a heading in the document, adding a cross reference to the bookmark displays the heading text at the cross reference location.

Word's cross-reference feature enables you to create cross-references to each of the following:

- Numbered items
- Headings
- Bookmarks
- Footnotes

- Endnotes
- Equations
- Figures
- Tables

The overall method for creating a cross-reference to one of these items is similar for all of them, although the options offered diverge once you make a selection. Here's the general process:

1. **Create and setup the item to be cross-referenced, such as creating the book-mark or adding a caption to a table.** (Chapter 20, "Identifying the Contents and Terms in Your Document: TOC, Captions, and Indexing," covers captions.)

2. **Click to position the insertion point at the location where you want to insert the cross-reference.**

3. **Click the Insert tab, click Links in the Links group if needed, and click Cross-Reference.** (Refer to Figure 19.3.) The Cross-reference dialog box shown in Figure 19.17 appears.

FIGURE 19.17

The Cross-reference dialog box appears here with Table selected as the reference type.

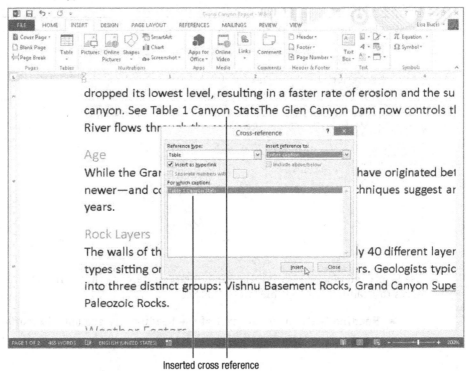

Inserted cross reference

4. Make a selection from the Reference type drop-down list, choose settings, and click Insert.

5. **Click Close.**

6. **Add punctuation and spaces after the inserted reference as needed.**

To use a hyperlinked cross-reference, Ctrl+click it to jump to the hyperlinked location.

> **NOTE**
>
> When you leave Insert as hyperlink selected when inserting a cross-reference, it is not underlined and formatted with the Hyperlink style. That's because it isn't a hyperlink field, and you cannot apply the hyperlink style to something that's not a hyperlink. If field code shading is displayed, the "link" will display as shaded. Other than that, no formatting is applied.

Headings

To insert a cross-reference to a heading, choose Heading from the Reference type list in the Cross-reference dialog box. As shown in Figure 19.18, the dialog box displays all headings (everything formatted with Heading 1 through Heading 9 styles) under For which heading.

FIGURE 19.18

Cross-reference settings for Headings

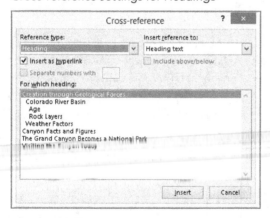

Use Insert reference to control the kind of cross-reference that is inserted. For cross-references to headings, the options are as follows:

- **Heading text:** The actual text of the heading (for example, Executive Summary).
- **Page number:** The page number on which the cross-referenced item begins.

- **Heading number:** If paragraph numbering is used, this displays the heading number relative to the cross-reference's location in the numbering structure. For example, if the cross-reference to 2.(b)(ii) is inserted within 2.(b)(i), the number used is (ii).

- **Heading number (no context):** A cross-reference to 2.(b)(ii) will always be inserted as (ii) from anywhere in the document.

- **Heading number (full context):** This option always displays the complete number; for example, 2.(b)(ii) regardless of where the cross-reference is inserted.

- **Above/below:** The word *above* or *below* is inserted to show the location of the cross-reference relative to the insertion point. For example: See the Executive Summary, *above*.

Numbered items

You can insert cross-references to any item that has Word's numbering applied to it. Note that this does not include sequence numbers or the different AutoNum numbering fields. It includes only items that use Word's numbering, whether applied directly or using a style.

To insert a cross-reference to a numbered item, choose Numbered Item from the Reference Type list in the Cross-reference dialog box. When you open the Insert reference to list, the options, shown in Figure 19.19, are very similar to those that appear for headings.

FIGURE 19.19

Numbered item reference options are similar to heading reference options.

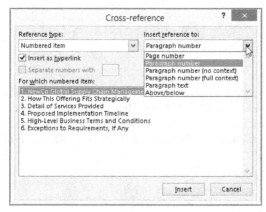

Note that if the Separate numbers with option (shown in Figure 19.19) is available and checked, adjacent number levels will use the separation character specified. For example, if the character is /, then 1)a)iv) would display as 1)/a)/iv). It is sometimes useful to use a space as the separator to clarify which level is which.

Bookmarks

If you were looking for a reason to use a cross-reference rather than a hyperlink, you might find that cross-referencing bookmarks has a slight edge. Notice in Figure 19.20 that the list under For which bookmark includes several with names that begin with an underscore (_). This is a telltale sign that these are hidden bookmarks inserted by Word. Recall that when inserting a hyperlink to a bookmark, the listing did not include hidden bookmarks. (Note that hidden bookmarks appear in the Cross-reference dialog box only if Hidden Bookmarks are checked in the Bookmark dialog box.)

FIGURE 19.20

Separate numbers with can help the reader tell when one number ends and the next begins.

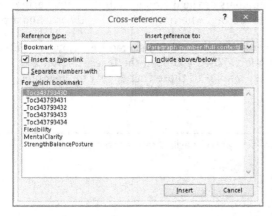

Notice also that Separate numbers with is available for the Paragraph number (full context) Insert reference to choice. As noted, it is available only for that reference, and only for bookmarks and numbered item reference types. The Insert reference to options are similar to those already shown. See the discussion under "Headings" for the explanation of what each type does.

Footnotes and endnotes

When you choose Footnotes or Endnotes from the Reference type drop-down list in the Cross-reference dialog box, the Insert reference to choices change accordingly. If you choose Footnote number, the reference is just to the number. If you choose Footnote number (formatted), the reference number will appear just as it does when the footnote is inserted into the text. This enables you to reuse the same footnote in multiple places in your document. This can be handy when the same footnote can fill multiple shoes. Or you can choose Page Number or Above/Below.

Equations, figures, and tables

Cross-references for equations, figures, and tables are identical. Note the Insert reference to options shown back in Figure 19.17. Use the Captions feature described in the next chapter to add numbered captions to Figures (pictures) and tables, and then insert cross-references to them using the Cross-reference dialog box.

> **NOTE**
>
> If you already read Chapter 15, "Adding Drop Caps, Text Boxes, Shapes, Symbols, and Equations," you know that there is no wonderful built-in equation numbering solution for Word's equations. Automatic captioning does not work for it either, so if you want to refer to a numbering system you cobbled together, you can take advantage of the cross-reference feature only if you use SEQ Equation to number your equation creations. See Chapter 23 for more on using fields.

Summary

In this chapter, you've seen bookmarks in all their radiant splendor. You should have an idea of how to insert them and where they came from when you didn't insert them, and know a few of the reasons why they're useful and occasionally essential. In this chapter you've gotten the inside scoop on hyperlinks and cross-references, including how they're created and how to use them. You should now be able to do the following:

- Turn on the display of bookmarks so you know where they are
- Insert, delete, and redefine bookmarks
- Use bookmarks to replicate text elsewhere in a document
- Use damage control to deal with the most common broken bookmarks
- Use bookmarks to navigate through a document
- Assign redundant bookmarks to hidden bookmarks so that you know where they're lurking
- Create hyperlinks to just about anything in Word
- Cross-reference anything in Word, including to hyperlinks (hint: you can cross-reference or hyperlink anything that's bookmarked)
- Hyperlink to anything you can browse to

19

Identifying the Contents and Terms in Your Document: TOCs, Captions, and Indexing

IN THIS CHAPTER

Creating tables of contents based on styles and outline levels

Creating a table of contents manually

Working with TOC styles

Inserting captions manually and automatically

Customizing caption labels

Adding a table of captioned items

Marking index entries and subentries

Compiling an index

Long documents such as proposals, detailed project quotations, annual reports, technical whitepapers, product user manuals, and so on require formal features to help the reader navigate the document and find and understand information. This chapter looks at some features that you will likely need to include in formal documents like this: a table of contents; captions for infographics such as tables, charts, and other illustrations; a table of captioned items; and an index of key terms and the pages that discuss them. Adding any of these items to a formal long document can be a sign of professionalism.

Automating Table of Contents Creation

A table of contents is a heading-oriented list of what's in a document, and on what page each heading (or other table of contents entry) occurs. If you use Word's built-in heading styles, you can insert a table of contents quickly and might never have to worry about some of the finer points of working with tables of contents. If, on the other hand, you need additional flexibility, you can use other styles as the basis for your table of contents, as well as entries you mark directly, to create a table of contents.

Tables of contents and heading styles

By far, the easiest way to create a table of contents is to use Word's built-in Heading 1 through 9 styles to organize the headings in a document and then to generate the table of contents based on those headings. As discussed in Chapter 3, "Working Smarter, Not Harder, in Word," and Chapter 7, "Using Styles to Create a Great-Looking Document," using heading styles and the Outline view (which automatically applies heading styles) are among the most practical time-saving methods you can use when creating long documents in Word. Not only does it give you instant access to Word's powerful tools for organizing and formatting a document, it gives you the inside track on creating tables of contents as well. To create a table of contents using heading styles:

1. **Position the insertion point where you want the table of contents to appear.** In a formal report or proposal, you will typically insert the table of contents at the top of the page immediately after the cover page.

2. **If the formatting standard you are using requires a page break after the table, use Page Layout ⇨ Page Setup ⇨ Breaks ⇨ Page Break or Next Page (under Section Breaks), and then press the Up Arrow to move the insertion point back up to the blank page.** If you insert the table without the page break and then insert the page break afterward, you would then need to update the table as described later under "Updating or Deleting a Table of Contents."

3. **In the Table of Contents group on the References tab, click Table of Contents.** As shown in Figure 20.1, the gallery offers three built-in options:

   - **Automatic Table 1:** Inserts a title (Contents) followed by a table of contents field

   - **Automatic Table 2:** Inserts a title (Table of Contents), a table of contents field, and a page break

   - **Manual Table:** Inserts a title (Table of Contents) and a dummy table of contents, ready for you to edit and replace with your own text and page numbers

4. **Click the desired choice.** Word inserts the table of contents in a Table of Contents content control. (Chapter 24, "Creating Custom Forms," covers more about inserting and working with other types of content controls.)

5. **If you inserted the third type of table from the gallery, click each heading control and type the desired content; to add more headings at a desired location, select and copy the line for another heading at the same outline level, position the insertion point, and paste.** Figure 20.2 shows an automatic table of contents inserted in the document. When you move the mouse pointer over it, gray field highlighting appears as shown in Figure 20.2. Clicking the table displays its content control.

FIGURE 20.1

The Table of Contents gallery offers three built-in options.

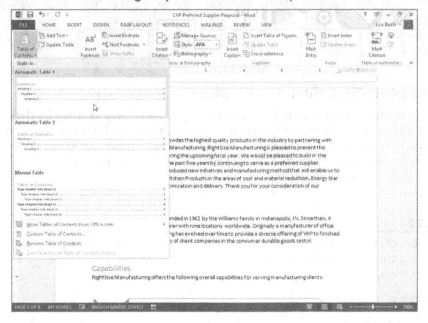

FIGURE 20.2

Word created this table of contents based on the heading styles applied throughout the document.

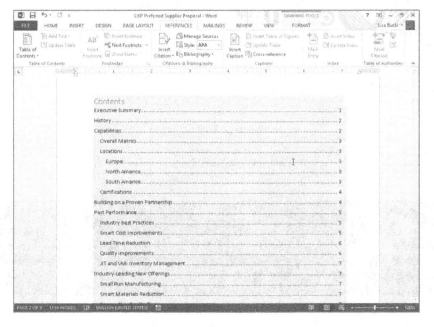

605

Table of contents defaults and options

If none of the tables of contents in the gallery in Figure 20.1 meets your needs, click Custom Table of Contents at the bottom of the gallery, which displays the Table of Contents dialog box, shown in Figure 20.3. The dialog box shows approximate Print and Web previews, without the actual table of contents material. Instead, it shows what styles will be used based on the settings shown in the dialog box.

FIGURE 20.3

Word's table of contents feature defaults to showing three heading levels and using hyperlinks for easy onscreen navigation.

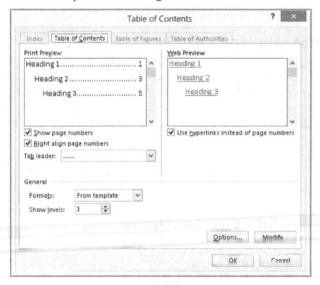

Word's table of contents defaults include the following:

- Show page numbers enabled
- Right-align page numbers enabled
- Separate table of contents heading text from numbers using dot leaders (...)
- Use TOC style formatting from the current template
- Show levels 3 (uses Heading 1 through Heading 3, plus anything else assigned to those levels)
- Use hyperlinks instead of page numbers in Web Layout view (see the preceding note)

If you click the Options button in the Table of Contents dialog box, the Table of Contents Options dialog box shown in Figure 20.4 appears. You can use it to:

- Build table of contents from styles and outline levels
- Determine whether to use Table entry fields
- Reset all of the Table of Contents settings to the defaults by clicking the Reset button shown at the lower left in Figure 20.4

FIGURE 20.4

You can use the built-in outline level assignments or assign levels to other styles.

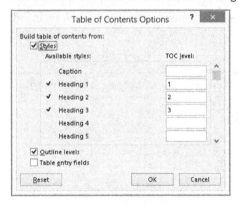

By default, with both Styles and Outline levels checked as shown in Figure 20.4, the TOC level list at the right has a number from 1 through 3. The styles Heading 1 through Heading 3 are assigned TOC levels 1–3, respectively. You can annotate the TOC level list either to change the default assignments or to assign levels to additional styles. Suppose, for example, that you have used the built-in Title and Caption styles in the document, and that you also want them included in the table of contents, as levels 1 and 4, respectively. Scroll down the TOC level list and enter a **1** next to the Title style, and then scroll back up and enter a **4** next to

20

the Caption style. When you do that and click OK, the Show levels setting in the Table of Contents dialog box shown in Figure 20.3 is automatically reset to 4.

Setting levels using the controls shown in Figure 20.4 does not affect the formatting of the paragraphs. It affects only how the TOC field treats the corresponding styles in compiling the table of contents.

If you don't want to use styles (Heading 1 through 9 or otherwise) for the table of contents, reopen the Table of Contents Options dialog box (Figure 20.4) and remove the check next to Styles. If you do want to use styles but not Headings 1 through 9, remove the default numbers from the TOC level list, and place 1, 2, 3, and so on next to the styles you want to use for the corresponding levels in the table of contents.

If your document doesn't use heading styles or other identifiable styles that you want to use for establishing TOC heading levels, you will have to use another method to build the TOC. See "Manually Creating a Table of Contents," later in this chapter.

Understanding the Add Text tool

In the References tab Table of Contents group, notice the Add Text item, shown in Figure 20.5. It functions as a References tab alternative for assigning Outline levels. It has its limitations, but if you understand how to use it, it may come in handy from time to time. Note that this tool does not automatically create table of contents entries. However, if you reformat text using this tool and have built your table automatically using table styles as described earlier, you can then update the table of contents so that the newly reformatted text will be included.

FIGURE 20.5

Add Text does not create fields for manual table of contents entries; it merely formats text.

NOTE

The number of levels shown in the Add Text tool reflects the Show levels setting in the Table of Contents tab in the Table of Contents dialog box shown in Figure 20.3. The default setting is 3. Increase the setting to 9 to include all nine heading styles in the TOC and to enable the Add Text tool to apply all nine levels of heading styles.

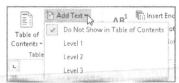

The Add Text tool's behavior depends on whether the selected paragraph(s) are formatted with a Heading 1 through 9 style, as well as whether the TOC level has already been manipulated directly.

Applying a command from Add Text has the following effects:

- If you choose Add Text ➪ Do Not Show in Table of Contents, the style of the selected paragraph is changed to Normal.
- If you choose Add Text ➪ Level 1 through Level 9 and the selected paragraph is formatted with the corresponding Heading 1 through 9 style, the command has no effect.
- If you choose Add Text ➪ Level 1 through Level 9 and the selected paragraph is formatted with a Heading 1 through 9 style with a different level, the command applies the corresponding numbered Heading style. For example, if you apply Level 2 to a paragraph formatted as Heading 4, the paragraph will be reformatted as Heading 2.
- If the selected paragraph is not formatted with a Heading 1 through 9 style, using Add Text ➪ Level 1 through 9 reformats that paragraph with the corresponding numbered Heading style.

NOTE

If you have the Styles pane open while using Add Text, you may see that the numbered heading style corresponding to the level you apply may not be selected immediately. In some cases you have to click off the text you just formatted with Add Text, and then click back in it to verify that the appropriate numbered heading style is applied.

Using outline levels for the table of contents

In addition to using the Heading 1 through 9 styles, the Table of Contents feature automatically uses styles that have outline levels assigned to them. Such styles show up with levels already assigned to them in the Table of Contents Options dialog box shown in Figure 20.4. If you want to use these, you don't have to do anything further, because Word uses them by default.

If you don't want to use non-Heading 1 through 9 styles that have outline levels assigned to them, remove the check next to Outline levels, shown in Figure 20.4. For additional information on assigning outline levels to non-heading styles, see "Creating custom levels for non-heading styles" in Chapter 3.

Changing TOC formats

The Table of Contents dialog box that appears when you click the Table of Contents button and then click Custom Table of Contents as discussed earlier includes a Formats drop-down list in the General section. Click the Formats drop-down list arrow to display additional

20

formatting options, shown in Figure 20.6. After you click one of the Formats choices, the Print Preview and Web Preview previews change to show the new formatting. For example, in Figure 20.6 the Modern choice centers the TOC entries and includes a border below Heading 1 entries. Click OK to close the Table of Contents dialog box and apply the formatting. If you had already inserted and selected a table of contents before choosing a format, a message box appears to ask you to confirm whether to replace the selected table of contents. Click Yes to do so.

FIGURE 20.6

You can use TOC styles from the applied document template or choose from among presets.

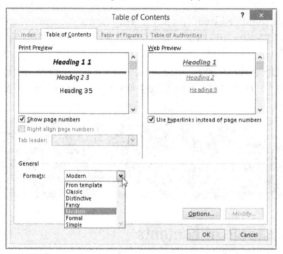

The hyperlink field used by Word to create an automatic table as described earlier, and the TOC field, which you can use to create a table of contents manually, both use styles named TOC 1 through TOC 9 to format the table of contents. By default, they use the settings for TOC 1 through TOC 9 that are stored in the current document template. If you choose one of the Formats alternatives in the Table of Contents dialog box, the TOC styles are redefined according to your selection.

CAUTION

Applying a different Format setting redefines the TOC styles in that document. If you later delete the TOC entries, your TOC styles remain redefined. If, for example, your table of contents styles previously used Times New Roman as the basic font, and Modern uses Calibri as the font, the latter Calibri font will be kept for the TOC 1-9 styles, even if the table of contents field is deleted. Thereafter, the From template and Modern formats will yield the same result. If you save that document, the table of contents styles in it are permanently changed. The only way to get back the former styles would be to reattach the underlying template and choose the Automatically update document styles option.

Working with TOC Styles

As noted in the previous section, Word uses nine built-in styles to format the table of contents: TOC 1 through TOC 9. If you don't like the way the table of contents looks, the best way to "fix" it is not by formatting the table itself. The best way is to change the TOC 1–TOC 9 styles. If you tried to modify TOC formatting manually, it would be possible to introduce inconsistences. For example, you might end up with one TOC 1 line formatted with a 0.4 indent and 12-point Comic Sans and have the rest of the TOC 1 lines formatted with an 0.8 indent and 10-point Cambria. This would tend to confuse your reader as to what text is at what level in the document. When you modify a TOC style instead of formatting table of content text directly, you ensure that all items using that style change to use the same formatting.

> **CAUTION**
>
> One of the mistakes users sometimes make with tables of contents is trying to manually reformat them because they don't like the appearance. This is a mistake because your manual efforts will be wiped out when the table of contents is updated to reflect the latest changes in document content as will be described shortly.

To modify the TOC 1–TOC 9 styles, you can use the methods described in Chapter 7. Alternatively, you can use the Modify button in the bottom-right corner of the Table of Contents dialog box (refer to Figure 20.3) to change style formatting as follows:

1. **In the References tab Table of Contents group, choose Table of Contents ➪ Custom Table of Contents to open the Table of Contents dialog box.**

2. **Click Modify.** If the Modify button is disabled, choose the From template. The Style dialog box appears with just the TOC styles, as shown in Figure 20.7. By default, TOC 1–TOC 9 are formatted using the default paragraph font. The only difference in their formatting is the left indentation setting.

3. **Select different styles, and review their settings.** Notice that the Preview and Description change very little, except that the +Body preview scoots to the right as the level increases.

4. **To change the style definition for a TOC style, select the style and click Modify.** The familiar Modify Style dialog box appears, as shown in Figure 20.8.

5. **To make changes to the table of contents style, choose Format and proceed as described in Chapter 7.**

6. **When you finish making changes, click OK three times to close all open dialog boxes and apply your changes.**

> **TIP**
>
> If you find the perfect blend of formatting for your tables of contents, when modifying each style you change, click to enable New documents based on this template in the Modify Style dialog box. This will make your changes available to future generations of tables of contents when using that template (which might or might not be `Normal.dotm`).

20

FIGURE 20.7

By default, TOC 1–TOC 9 are formatted identically except for the amount of the left indent.

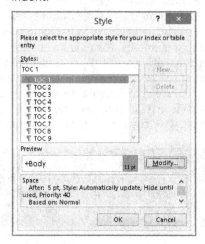

FIGURE 20.8

All of the TOC styles default to Automatically update.

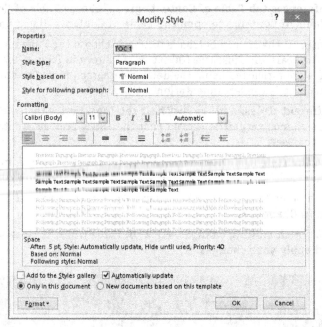

Manually Creating a Table of Contents

Manually creating a table of contents requires two steps. First you have to mark the heading or other items you want to include in the table of contents. Then, use the Table of Contents dialog box to instruct Word to use those marked items, rather than or in addition to styles, and insert the TOC.

Marking entries for the table of contents

The most efficient way to mark entries is to mark them all at once when your document is just about finished. However, if you prefer, you can mark them as you go along. It's your choice.

Assuming that what you want in the table of contents is exactly what you have in the text, the easiest way to mark entries is to select the entry and then display the Mark Table of Contents Entry dialog box, shown in Figure 20.9. The built-in keystroke for this is Alt+Shift+O. (If you prefer a button to the keyboard shortcut, add the Mark Entry command from Commands Not in the Ribbon to the QAT or Ribbon. Chapter 30, "Customizing the Quick Access Toolbar and Ribbon" explains how to add command buttons.) If necessary, make any changes in the Entry field and set the Level to the desired TOC level in the finished TOC. Click Mark, and Word inserts a TC field to the right of the selection to identify it as a marked table of contents entry. In the example in Figure 20.9, the numbered list items are marked as level 2 TOC entries, because ordinarily, numbers in a list would not be included in the TOC. Also note that only the first sentence for each list item is marked; including these items in the TOC by style (List Paragraph) would result in all of the list text being included in the TOC, which is not the desired outcome.

If you have a lot of entries to mark, you will quickly discover why using Heading 1 through 9 styles is so much more efficient than manually marking entries. The Mark Table of Contents Entry dialog box is nonmodal, so it doesn't go away when you click Mark. If all of your entries are ready to be marked, a good strategy is to select what you want to use for an entry, click Mark, select the next entry in the document, click on the dialog box to reactivate it, click Mark, and so on until you're done. If you have hundreds of these to do, you might consider writing a macro, and you most certainly will give styles serious consideration the next time you confront a document like this one.

> **NOTE**
>
> TC fields are formatted as hidden text. If Hidden text is displayed via Word options, TC fields are displayed as field codes all the time, and you can't turn them off using the Show/Hide button in the Paragraph group of the Home tab. You have to choose File ➪ Options ➪ Display, and then uncheck Hidden text under Always show these formatting marks on the screen. Make sure they don't print by unchecking Print hidden on the Display tab under Printing Options. Click OK to apply the changes. If TC fields are hidden from view, you run a substantial risk of accidentally deleting them, so think twice before hiding them.

20

FIGURE 20.9

By default, the table of contents field uses Table identifier C as shown in the Mark Table of Contents Entry dialog box; change the Level setting as needed.

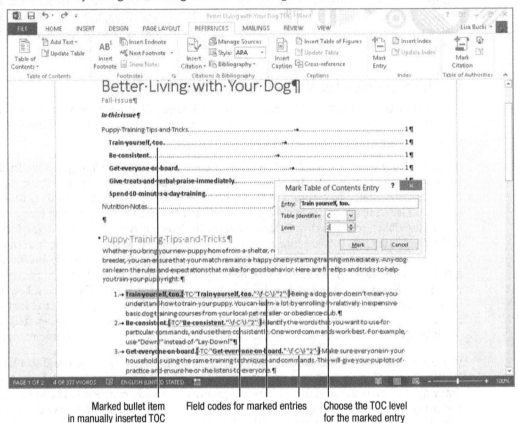

Marked bullet item   Field codes for marked entries   Choose the TOC level
in manually inserted TOC   for the marked entry

Inserting a table of contents using marked entries

After you have marked the desired entries for the TOC, follow these steps to insert the table in the document.

1. **Click to position the insertion point in the location where you'd like to insert the table of contents.** As when inserting a TOC automatically, insert page or section breaks if desired to set off the TOC from other document text.

2. **In the Table of Contents group on the References tab, choose Table of Contents ⇨ Custom Table of Contents.** The Table of Contents dialog box opens with the Table of Contents tab selected.

3. **Click Options to open the Table of Contents Options dialog box.** Refer to Figure 20.4.

4. **If your marked entries are supplementing styles and outline levels, click to add a check next to Table entry fields; if you're using entries instead of styles and/or outline levels, clear the Styles and/or Outline levels check boxes as needed.**

5. **Click OK twice to insert the table of contents.**

6. **If needed, add a title above the inserted table of contents.**

Updating or Deleting a Table of Contents

Generally, you need to perform two types of maintenance on a table of contents. One is to update the table of contents when the contents of the document have changed. The need for updating occurs when the headings have changed or when anything moves to a different page (because material has been added to or removed from the document).

To update the table of contents to reflect changes in the document, click anywhere in the table of contents (in the content control for an automatic table or the field code for a custom table) and press the F9 key or click the Update Table button in the Table of Contents group of the References tab. If you inserted the table manually, right-click anywhere in the table of contents and choose Update Field. Word displays the Update Table of Contents dialog box shown in Figure 20.10. If none of the headings have changed but only the page numbers, and/or you've manually reformatted a table of contents, you can save a little time and preserve that manual formatting by choosing Update page numbers only. If more substantial changes were made—such as headings added or removed, or additional items marked for inclusion—choose Update entire table. With this option, if you have made manual formatting changes other than through the TOC 1 through TOC 9 styles, those changes will be lost. Click OK to finish the update.

FIGURE 20.10

The Update page numbers only option preserves any touch-up editing you might have done.

The other type of maintenance occurs if you want to change the way you present the table of contents. Perhaps you were including only levels 1 through 3, and now want to include level 4 as well. Perhaps you've changed your mind about hyperlinks or some other aspect. To edit the table of contents settings, select the entire table of contents, then choose Table of Contents ⇨ Custom Table of Contents. Make any changes you need to make in

20

the Table of Contents and Table of Contents Options dialog boxes as described earlier, and then then click OK as needed to close the dialog boxes. Word may now prompt as shown in Figure 20.11. If you're sure that you want to replace the table with your changes, click OK.

FIGURE 20.11

Click OK to confirm that you want to replace the table and use new settings.

To delete a table of contents, click in it and choose Table of Contents ⇨ Remove Table of Contents in the Table of Contents group of the References tab. Or for an automatic table contained in a content control, click in the table. On the control tab or toolbar, click the Table of Contents button, and then click Remove Table of Contents, as shown in Figure 20.12. Word doesn't prompt you to confirm the table deletion, but you can press Ctrl+Z automatically when you need to undo a deletion.

FIGURE 20.12

An automatic table content control also enables you to access the commands for working with a table, such as the Remove Table of Contents command.

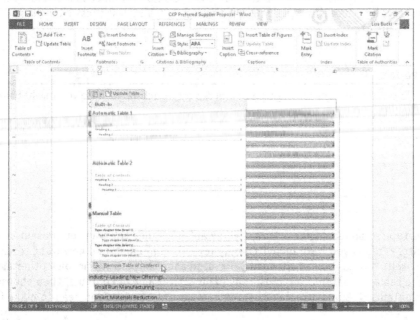

Converting a Table of Contents into Text

Sometimes it's desirable to convert the table of contents into actual text, rather than a field code. In some cases, you will want to have the table of contents in a separate document. You can always reinsert the field code if needed later, using the techniques shown in this chapter. To convert a table of contents into actual text, select the entire table of contents and press Ctrl+Shift+F9 or Ctrl+6.

> **TIP**
>
> Have you ever wanted just a document's outline in a separate file? When you display a document in Outline view, the whole document is really there. You can select what you see and then paste it elsewhere to get just the outline. To get a separate copy of the outline, insert a table of contents using the outline levels you need to see, and then use Ctrl+Shift+F9 to convert it to actual text. Instant outline! You might want to create an outline in this way and then import it into PowerPoint to make a presentation that covers the content in the Word document.

> **TIP**
>
> Once you get a table of contents format just the way you like, you can save it for later use. Select the table of contents and in the Table of Contents group on the References tab, choose Table of Contents ✧ Save Selection to Table of Contents Gallery. In the Create New Building Block dialog box, type a name for the table of contents, leave Gallery set to Table of Contents (so it will show up in the list when you first click Table of Contents in the References tab), and set Save In to the desired location (usually the template on which the document is based or the Building Blocks template). You might want to consider setting Options to Insert content in its own page, because tables of contents usually are on a separate page. Click OK to add the table to the gallery.

The TOC Field Code

When you insert an automatic or manual table, Word creates the table of contents using a TOC field code. If you've never looked at the table of contents field code, you might be surprised that such a simple little code could be so powerful. By default, the table of contents field code that Word uses to create an automatic table is as follows:

```
{ TOC \o "1-3" \h \z \u }
```

In fact, it could be as simple as `{ TOC }` and still produce a serviceable table of contents. To fully understand what each of the switches means, click the Insert tab, and in the Text Group, choose Quick Parts ➪ Field. In the Field dialog box, under Field names, scroll down and click TOC, but don't click the Table of Contents button or you'll be taken to the Table of Contents dialog box—and you've already made that particular pilgrimage in this chapter. Click Field Codes instead. This displays the TOC field with no switches in the Field Codes box. Click the Options button to see a list of the possible switches, shown in Figure 20.13.

20

FIGURE 20.13

The TOC field code has 16 different switches you can use.

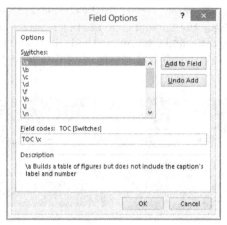

Look at the three switches shown earlier in the default TOC field code:

- \h: Creates a hyperlink for each TOC entry and page number within the table of contents
- \u: Uses the paragraph outline levels to compile the TOC
- \z: When shown in Web Layout view, displays the TOC without page numbers

Click each of the switches to see additional options. You never know when they might prove useful. In this case, for example, you see that hyperlinking and hiding page numbers, combined into the single Use hyperlinks instead of page numbers option shown in Figure 20.3, are two distinct options. If you want one but not the other, you can have it by editing the field code switches

In the document, display the table of contents and press Alt+F9 to toggle field code display. Remove the unwanted switch and press Alt+F9 to toggle field code display off. Right-click the field and choose Update Field (or simply press F9), choose the desired option in Figure 20.10, and click OK

Captions and Tables of Captioned Items

Captions are snippets of text that number and identify pictures, equations, tables, charts, and other items in your document. Word can automatically insert captions for you, automatically numbering such items as they are inserted. By being systematic in how you insert captions in your documents, creating a table of figures, equations, or tables (for example) is a snap, as is numbering them. If you insert or remove a numbered item, Word can automatically renumber all of the items that follow. When you need numbered items in a formal long document, Word's automation can save you loads of time.

Captions settings reside in the Captions group on the Ribbon's References tab, shown in Figure 20.14. Other tools in this group include Insert Table of Figures, Update Table, and Cross-reference. Note that "Table of Figures" is a generic label. In your mind, substitute "whatever things I want a table of" for the word *Figures*. In other words, it can be a table of equations or a table of tables. Figures include any type of graphic you want to add a caption to: inserted pictures, charts, SmartArt graphics, and so on.

FIGURE 20.14

Control captions with the settings in the Captions group.

Strictly speaking, the Cross-reference tool in the Captions group is not just about captions. Though you can use it to refer to captioned items, you can use it to refer to just about anything else as well. With respect to captions, use it to insert references like "See Figure 3." Why would you use a special feature for this rather than just type that text? Sometimes figures are moved, added, or removed. What referred to Figure 3 this morning might refer to Figure 17 this afternoon. By using Word's captioning and cross-referencing features, when figures, references to them, and text are shuffled around in a document, their respective numbers remain correct. Word automatically updates, increments, and decrements the captioned and cross-referenced items as needed.

Inserting a caption

To insert a caption, follow these steps:

1. **Select the object or table for which you want to add a caption.** For a table, this means selecting the table move handle. For an equation, click the equation, and then click the button at the right side of the control twice.

2. **Choose Insert Caption in the Captions group in the References tab of the Ribbon.** As shown in Figure 20.15, the Caption dialog box appears.

   No matter what kind of object is selected, Word will always propose the most recently chosen Label, defaulting to Figure if this is the first caption you're creating.

3. **If you want a different type of label, select it from the Label drop-down list.**

NOTE

You'll learn more details about working with the New Label, Numbering, and Delete Label options in the upcoming sections.

20

FIGURE 20.15

The Caption dialog box helps you create consistent captions.

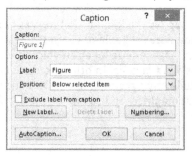

4. **Open the Position drop-down list and choose Below selected item or Above selected item as desired.**

5. **Edit the text in the Caption text box as needed.** Standard practice is to add a period and space following the caption label and number, along with some text describing the captioned item.

6. **Click OK to insert the caption.** Word formats it using the Caption style in the current document template.

> **NOTE**
>
> A caption usually consists of more than just the label and number. As demonstrated in the book you're reading, captions also exist to tell the reader what they're looking at or why it matters in the context of the document. Caption length is limited. You can include 253 characters in addition to the caption label and number.

Labels

If you want to use a *label* for your captions other than the default Figure setting, open the Label drop-down list under Options in the Caption dialog box. By default, Word offers three label options: Equation, Figure, and Table. You are not limited to those three. To add labels of your own, click New Label. In the New Label dialog box shown in Figure 20.16, type a name for the label you want to create and click OK twice. Label naming is generously liberal. There are no restrictions on what you can type.

Labels you create are remembered by Word across multiple sessions. The next time you open Word and click Insert Caption, Word offers the last label you used, as well as any you've created in the Label drop-down list. For example, if you've used Widget, Picture, and Diagram, Word will offer those in addition to the default three. If you believed the preceding paragraph's assertion that there are no restrictions on label names and typed something embarrassing, select that label and click Delete Label. Then either proceed with captioning the selected item or click Cancel to close the dialog box.

FIGURE 20.16

You can create whatever custom label you need: Photo, Picture, Chart, Graph, Snapshot—you name it.

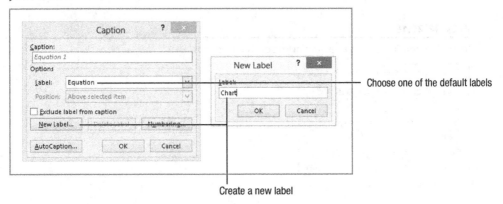

Choose one of the default labels

Create a new label

Adding numbering

By default, Word numbers captions using 1, 2, 3, and so on. If that scheme doesn't meet your needs, click Numbering in the Caption dialog box to display the Caption Numbering dialog box shown in Figure 20.17. Use the Format drop-down list to see if one of the five numbering options offers what you want. If you need options for more custom numbering, jump ahead to "How numbering is done" to find some fresh alternatives.

FIGURE 20.17

Word offers five numbering styles.

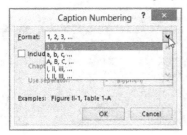

If you use the Multilevel List button in the Paragraph group of the Home tab to apply numbering along with the numbered heading styles, you also can include chapter numbers along with the regular caption number. As shown in Figure 20.18, click Include chapter number in the Caption Numbering dialog box to enable this feature. Choose the appropriate numbered Heading style from the Chapter starts with style drop-down list. The Separator

20

choice enables you to determine what character appears between the chapter and caption number, choose from among the following: hyphen, period, colon, em dash, or en dash.

FIGURE 20.18

You also can include a chapter number in a caption.

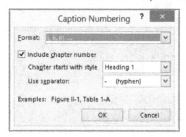

How numbering is done

Word creates and maintains caption numbers using a SEQ field, SEQ identifier, where the selected label is used as the *identifier*, for example, SEQ figure, SEQ equation, or SEQ table, and so on. If you choose the Include chapter number option, the chapter number is inserted by using a STYLEREF field. For example, with field codes showing (Alt+F9), a typical caption might appear as follows:

```
Figure { STYLEREF 1 \s }- { SEQ Figure \* roman \s 1 }
```

Chapter 23, "Automating Document Content with Fields," provides more detailed coverage of fields and how to work with switches to get the desired formatting displayed with the field results.

> **NOTE**
>
> If you move captioned items around in a document, you'll need to update the captions. Select the text holding the captioned items and press F9 to perform the updates. (Because captions use fields, you press F9 to update them as for any other field.) You can select an individual caption and use F9 to update it, or press Ctrl+A first and press F9 to update the entire document. However, if the document includes a table of contents, table of captioned items, index, bibliography, or other features based on fields, they will update as well.

Eliminating the numbers

You probably noticed that *None* is not one of the numbering options. Excluding numbers from your captions is easy, however. To insert an unnumbered caption, position the insertion point where you want it to appear and apply the Caption style. Type the caption label you want to use. In other words, if you don't want numbered captions, you don't need the caption feature. The whole idea of using the caption feature is to coordinate and automate the process of numbering the dang things. If you don't want numbered captions, then this feature has nothing to offer you.

Removing the label

If you have only one type of figure (or whatever) in your document and want to exclude the label, you can. In the New Label dialog box shown in Figure 20.16, click to place a check next to Exclude label from caption. Why would you want to do this? That's a private matter between you and your document.

The Caption style

As noted earlier, Word provides a caption-oriented style named Caption. It is a paragraph style, and it is applied to the entire paragraph. There is no way to change the style that Word applies to captions inserted using the caption feature. You can, however, modify the Caption style. With a caption selected, press Ctrl+Shift+S and choose Modify. Modify the style as described in Chapter 7.

Note that by default the Caption style is color-coordinated with the current theme. By default, the Caption style uses the Text 2 theme color to the Caption style. Keep this in mind if your caption text suddenly changes color when you apply a new theme. For more about themes, see Chapter 18, "Saving Time with Templates, Themes, and Master Documents."

Turning on AutoCaptioning

You can also instruct Word to automatically insert captions when you insert particular kinds of graphics and other objects. If you have a lot of installed applications with object types that Word recognizes, it can be a little daunting, however, trying to figure out what's what.

As of this writing, the list of things for which AutoCaptioning works is short: Microsoft Equation 3 (the Word 2003 version), Word tables, and Microsoft Graph Chart, and perhaps a few others. It does not work for SmartArt, pictures, WordArt, charts, or a vast majority of other object types.

AutoCaption must be enabled for the specific objects for which you want to use it. To enable it, on the References tab, choose Insert Caption in the Captions group, and then click AutoCaption in the Caption dialog box to display the AutoCaption dialog box, shown in Figure 20.19. In the Add caption when inserting list, click to check each kind of item you want to AutoCaption. Make choices as before from the Use label and Position drop-down lists, or click New Label to add a new label to the list of labels you use. Click OK. Word will now use those settings to add captions for all objects of the specified type.

20

FIGURE 20.19

AutoCaption must be enabled for each type of object you want captioned.

> **NOTE**
>
> If you insert a table by pasting one from the Clipboard, AutoCaption will insert a caption only if the Clipboard contains just a table. If the Clipboard contains additional text or other objects, AutoCaption is suppressed. Inserting a table from the Quick Parts Gallery or the Building Blocks Gallery also does not insert an AutoCaption. If you want either of those to contain a caption, you should save a caption with the table when you save it as a Building Block or a Quick Part. In addition, AutoCaption doesn't work for every kind of object. If the object type you seek isn't listed, you'll have to continue manually inserting captions for that type.

Adding tables of captioned items

Word can insert a table of captioned items that appear in the document. Word bases the table on caption labels. Hence, if you have used the Figure label for different kinds of things, they will all be included in the table. If you have used a variety of labels—Figure, Table, and so on—you will have to create a table for each different label type. That's why it's important to think about how you want to label your captions when inserting them, based on whether you want all captioned items listed in a single table or want separate tables to distinguish different types of items.

To insert a table of captioned items:

1. **Click to position the insertion point in the location where you want to insert the table.**

2. **In the Captions group of the References tab, choose Insert Table of Figures. The Table of Figures dialog box appears with the Table of Figures tab selected, as shown in Figure 20.20.**

FIGURE 20.20

Insert Table of Figures means "figures" in a generic sense and can be used to insert a table of any type of captioned item.

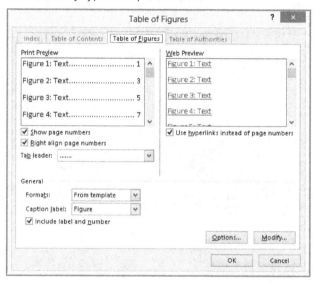

3. **Open the Caption label drop-down list and choose the caption label (that is, Table or another choice rather than Figure) for which you want to compile the table.**

4. **Specify other options on the tab as needed.** These options work the same as those for a table of contents described earlier in the chapter, and include:

   ■ Show page numbers

   ■ Right-align page numbers

   ■ Tab leader (separate table of contents heading text from numbers using...leaders)

   ■ Formats (use From template to use TOC style formatting from the current template)

   ■ Use hyperlinks instead of page numbers in Web Layout view

   ■ Caption label

   ■ Include label and number (clear this check mark to suppress the display of these items in the final table)

5. **Click OK to insert the table.** As shown in the example in Figure 20.21, if you click the table, the field highlighting appears. A table of captioned items is inserted as a series of hyperlinked fields, with an overall TOC field controlling the table.

20

FIGURE 20.21

This inserted table of figures resembles a table of contents and is similarly compiled using fields.

Options for creating the table

For additional options, shown in Figure 20.22, click the Options button in the Table of Figures dialog box. By default, Word builds the table based on occurrences of the selected label formatted with the Caption style. If you haven't used the Caption style but used styles named Normal or Table of Figures instead, click the drop-down arrow to the right of the Style box and click the alternate style used.

FIGURE 20.22

You can base a table of figures on different styles or on table entry fields.

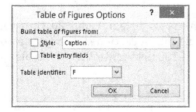

In addition to or instead of basing a table of figures on the presence of a given label for-matted with a given style, you can build a table of figures based on the presence of table entry fields. Recall that earlier in this chapter you learned that Word defaults to a table identifier of C for the table of contents. For the table of figures, it defaults to a table identi-fier of F. As you learned earlier in the section "Marking entries for the table of contents," you can select an item to mark, and press Alt+Shift+O to open the Mark Table of Contents Entry dialog box. For a table of captioned items, change the Table identifier drop-down list choice to F and click Mark. After marking all the entries, insert the table of figures, open the Table of Figures Options dialog box, check Table entry fields, and click OK before click-ing OK in the Table of Figures dialog box.

Updating the table of figures

When you insert captions using AutoCaption or the Insert Caption command, Word automati-cally updates all of the relevant numbering fields for other captions in that series. If you move tables, figures, and so on around, or delete them manually, however—using copy, cut, and paste—the numbers are not automatically updated. Assuming you don't have unrelated field-based numbering systems that you *don't* want updated, you can update the captioned items by pressing Ctrl+A to select all of the text in the document and pressing F9. You can also update caption numbering fields individually, which you may want to do to avoid mistakenly updat-ing other field-based elements in the document, such as a table of contents, either by selecting each and pressing F9 or by right-clicking the selection and choosing Update Fields.

Indexing a Document

For paper books, especially reference books, the index is the key to whether readers will find the book useful as a reference. Word enables you to create indexes (or indices, if you prefer) in a variety of formats and styles. For online documents, indexes are less impor-tant because readers are able to search for what they're looking for. Even there, however, an index can help steer readers to more substantive discussions as opposed to incidental mentions of a given topic or keyword.

Unlike with tables of contents and figures, the indexing process can't be fully automated, although there are some things you can do as you're writing to make things easier. We look at some of those in this section, along with how you set up a document for indexing and how you insert an index.

As a feature set, indexing lives in the Index section of the References tab, as shown in Figure 20.23. Tools provided there are as follows:

- **Mark Entry:** Use to mark locations in the text you want indexed as well as to specify how each location is treated.
- **Insert Index:** Use to insert and format an index.
- **Update Index:** Updates the index. This command is available only when the insertion point is located somewhere within an index.

FIGURE 20.23

In the References tab, use the Index group to mark items for including in the index as well as to insert and update indexes.

Indexing is a two-step process:

1. **Create the index entries—words and phrases in the text you want indexed, as well as categories and subentries—by marking text for indexing.**

2. **Compile and format the index.**

Marking Index Entries

You mark index entries by inserting an index entry field (XE). You can do this in three ways:

- Use the Mark Entry tool in the Index group of the References tab.
- Use the Mark All tool from the Index dialog box.
- Insert an XE field directly either manually or by using Insert Field.

This section describes how to use the Index tools in the References tab. See the "Index field codes" section later in this chapter, and Chapter 23, for more information on fields.

Creating index entries using Mark Entry

Index entries are items you want in the index. For example, if you were to go about indexing a mention of the word *table*, you might simply include that word in the index. Or, if tables were mentioned frequently in the book, and in a variety of contexts, you would probably want to have a main index entry for tables, along with *subentries* about each of the different kinds of tables (table of contents, table of figures, and so on). Examples of an entry and subentries are shown in Figure 20.24. Note that the subentries are indented below the main entries.

To create an index entry and/or subentry:

1. **Select the text you want indexed, or click at the beginning of the section you want indexed.** This ultimately will insert a tag into the text that will move with that location if text is added or removed before the entry location. This enables the index to refer to the correct page even if the document is heavily edited, as long as the index entry itself is not deleted. Note that selected text will always go into the Main entry box. There is no built-in way to make selected text go into the subentry field.

2. **Click Mark Entry in the Index group of the References tab, press Alt+Shift+X, or click Mark Entry from the Insert Index dialog box.** This displays the Mark Index Entry dialog box, shown in Figure 20.25. If text is selected, it will automatically be displayed in the Main entry field. This dialog box is nonmodal and can be kept onscreen as you navigate, so you can mark multiple items without having to dismiss and resummon the dialog box.

FIGURE 20.24

Use subentries to provide detail when a topic is covered extensively.

3 **If the Main entry text box is blank or does not contain the entry you want, type the desired index entry.** Word will use the capitalization and formatting you supply. Use character formatting shortcut keys to format the text boxes (Main entry, Subentry, and Cross-reference) as you want them to appear in the index. For example, select text in the dialog box text fields and press Ctrl+I, Ctrl+B, Ctrl+U, Ctrl+Shift+D, and so on.

4. **If desired, enter a subentry.** If the text you want to enter in the Subentry text box is in the Main entry text box, follow these steps:

    a. **To change the marked text to a Subentry, select and cut it (Ctrl+X) from the Main entry text box.**

b. **Type the appropriate main entry.**

c. **Click in the Subentry text box and press Ctrl+V to paste the subentry.**

FIGURE 20.25

Use the Mark Index Entry dialog box to create index main entries and subentries.

This will become a category within the Main entry, as shown in Figure 20.24. See the section "Working with subentries and styles" later in this chapter for more information on subentries.

5. **If desired, select Bold or Italic for the Page number format.** In some publications, key entries are formatted differently (for example, where a concept is defined or introduced) so they can be found more readily.

6. **To refer to another entry, choose Cross-reference and supply the text needed.**

7. **To specify a page range rather than a single page, bookmark the range of pages prior to inserting the index, choose Bookmark in the Mark Index Entry dialog box, and use the drop down arrow to indicate which bookmark to use.**

8. **Click Mark to insert an index entry field either at the insertion point or next to the text that was selected.** If you want to mark every instance of text matching the Main entry (whether it is selected or not), click Mark All.

When you click Mark or Mark All, the Mark Index Entry dialog box remains onscreen. An XE field is inserted as hidden text into the document. If hidden text is showing, XE fields always display as field codes. They never collapse into field results. This enables them to be conspicuous, as shown in Figure 20.26, and less subject to accidental deletion. When proofing or reading a finished document, they can be distracting, however. Toggle hidden text on/off using File ➪ Options ➪ Display as described earlier in the chapter for manually marked TOC entries if you find glaring XE fields distracting.

FIGURE 20.26

Index entry (XE) fields are inserted as hidden text.

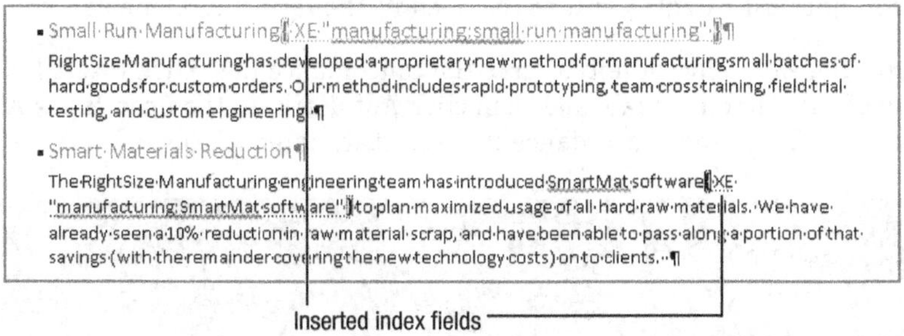

- Small·Run·Manufacturing{·XE·"manufacturing:small·run·manufacturing"·}¶
  RightSize·Manufacturing·has·developed·a·proprietary·new·method·for·manufacturing·small·batches·of·
  hard·goods·for·custom·orders.·Our·method·includes·rapid·prototyping,·team·cross·training,·field·trial·
  testing,·and·custom·engineering.·¶
- Smart·Materials·Reduction·¶
  The·RightSize·Manufacturing·engineering·team·has·introduced·SmartMat·software{·XE·
  "manufacturing:SmartMat·software"·}·to·plan·maximized·usage·of·all·hard·raw·materials.··We·have·
  already·seen·a·10%·reduction·in·raw·material·scrap,·and·have·been·able·to·pass·along·a·portion·of·that·
  savings·(with·the·remainder·covering·the·new·technology·costs)·on·to·clients.···¶

Inserted index fields

TIP

Because the Mark Index Entry dialog box is nonmodal, you can move readily between it and the text area. If you select text in the document, when you click back in the Mark Index Entry dialog box, the selected text is automatically copied to the Main entry field.

Automatically marking index entries using AutoMark

If you have a long document with numerous entries, marking them manually can prove tedious. A simple solution is to create a list of words (called a *concordance file*) you want indexed, and use the AutoMark feature to insert the XE entries for you.

To do this, you first create the concordance file using Word. A concordance file should contain only a two-column table. The first column contains the text you want indexed, using the exact capitalization, punctuation, and formatting you want to appear in the index. The second column contains the XE field you want used. When you run the AutoMark command, Word finds each occurrence of every word or phrase in the list and inserts the XE field from the second column. The concordance file is saved in Word format and should resemble the example shown in Figure 20.27.

FIGURE 20.27

Use a concordance table to automatically insert index entry (XE) fields into your document.

prohibit	{xe "prohibit"}
concurrent	{xe "concurrent"}
compensation	{xe "compensation"}
disabled	{xe "disabled"}
retirees	{xe "retirees"}

20

Notice that Figure 20.27 does not show any subentries. That's because subentries do not work when applied using a concordance file. If you attempt to use subentries, separated by colons, only the rightmost category will be included in the resulting XE fields.

To run AutoMark (the Word procedure that uses the concordance file), click Insert Index from the Index group of the References tab, and then click AutoMark. In the Open Index AutoMark File dialog box, navigate to the concordance file, select it, and click Open.

> **NOTE**
>
> If you get the No index entries were marked message, it usually means that no instances of the words in the first column of the concordance file match anything in the document. It can also mean that the concordance file is defective in some way, often meaning that it contains something other than the expected table with XE fields.

Compiling and Inserting an Index

Compiling an index means collecting all of the XE entries and putting them into the form of an index. Once the XE entries have been inserted using the methods described earlier in this chapter, use these steps to insert the index:

1. **Move the insertion point to where you want the index inserted, perhaps setting it off with a page break or section break (Page Layout ⇨ Page Setup ⇨ Breaks).**

2. **In the Index group of the References tab, click Insert Index, which displays the dialog box shown in Figure 20.28.**

3. **Change settings as desired:**

   - **Print Preview:** This shows an approximate preview of the finished index using the current settings.

   - **Right align page numbers:** Moves page numbers to the far right. With indexes, this sometimes makes it difficult to associate entries and page numbers, even with leaders. Unless you're using narrow columns of text, right-aligned is usually not a good choice.

   - **Tab leader:** When right-aligning page numbers, specify a leader to help the reader connect the dots between the index entry and the page number.

   - **Formats:** Choose the From template option to use Index 1 through Index 9 styles defined in the current template, or choose one of the preset options available through the Formats drop-down control.

- **Type:** Indented or Run-in. Subentry levels can be indented or presented in the same line as the main entry (assuming there's room). The former usually results in a neater and more organized appearance. The latter generally results in a more compact index that's sometimes easier for readers to follow, because all of the entry/subentry category information is presented in one place, eliminating the need to visually backtrack to figure out where a given entry originated.

- **Columns:** Word can organize the index into snaking columns. Narrower columns, as long as entries are fairly terse, often are easier to follow, and use paper more wisely. The default is two columns, and you can specify up to four columns.

- **Language:** If you have indexes in multiple languages, be sure to associate the correct language with each for proper proofing.

- **Modify:** Use this option to modify built-in Index 1 through 9 styles when Formats is set to From template. See "Working with subentries and styles" a little later in this chapter.

4. **Click OK to compile and insert the index.** Word responds by inserting an INDEX field in the document, using switches corresponding to the options selected in the Index dialog box.

FIGURE 20.28

Use the Index dialog box to launch Mark Entry or AutoMark, to modify index styles, or to format and insert an index.

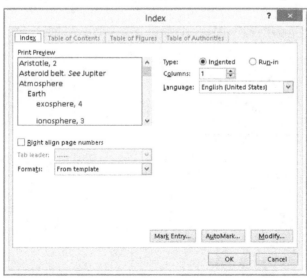

20

Index field codes

Unlike index entry fields, the INDEX field itself does display a field result. With field codes displayed, a typical run-in index field might appear as follows:

```
{ INDEX \r \h " " \c "2" \z "1033" }
```

To see what the switches mean, choose Insert ➪ Text ➪ Quick Parts ➪ Field. Select Index in the Field Names list, click Field Codes in the bottom-left corner, and then click Options to open the Field Options dialog box shown in Figure 20.29. Alternatively, if the index has already been inserted, right-click it and choose Edit Field ➪ Options. The switches used here are as follows:

- \r: Keeps index subentries on the same line as the main entry
- \h " ": Separates groups in the index with a blank line formatted with the Index Heading style
- \c "2": Specifies the number of columns (2) to use for the index
- \z "1033": Specifies the language ID (1033 means U.S. English)

FIGURE 20.29

Field options for the Index field

Working with subentries and styles

You are not limited to just one subentry level. You can have up to nine levels in an index, which means up to eight subentries below the main entry. To designate additional subentry levels, mark the text that will be the index entry, and then edit the field code to indicate the entries by level, separating each level with a colon. In the following example, **manufacturing** is at the main entry index level, **new product line pilot** is at the first subentry level, and **green** is at the next subentry level (third level overall in the index):

```
{ XE "manufacturing:new product line pilot:green" }
```

You can format different subentry levels differently. Word uses built-in styles named Index 1 through Index 9. By default, the only formatting differentiation is indent levels. If you want to change the associated formatting, in the References tab choose Insert Index and then click the Modify button in the Index dialog box, which displays the Style dialog box. Click on Index 2 through Index 9; notice that, by default, only the Left Indent setting changes. To change the indentation or differentiate in other ways, click Modify to change the selected style. For information on modifying styles, see Chapter 7.

Updating an index

If you revise a document, adding and deleting pages and marking additional index entries, you'll need to update the index contents. To do so, click in the Index and press F9, or click Update Index in the Index group of the References tab.

Creating Multiple Indexes

Word lets you create up to 26 separate indexes for a document. However, no automatic support for this is provided in the Index group on the References tab. To create separate indexes, you must include the \f*index* switch in each of the XE fields you insert, where *index* identifies the index in which the item would be included. These 26 indexes can be designated as *a* through *z*, *alpha* through *zulu*, or *artichokes* through *zucchini*, the point being that they must start with the letters a through z, and that the names themselves aren't important.

When you insert the index, you also include a \f*index* switch in its field code. The { index \fa } generates an index for index entries such as { XE \fa "finches" }, { index \fb } for index entries such as { XE \fb "larks" }, and so on.

20

Summary

In this chapter you've seen how to add important reference features to a long document, including tables of contents, tables of captioned items (such as figures), and indexes. You've learned how to mark TOC and index entries manually, as well as how to insert captions manually, and you should have a good understanding of how a TOC, table of figures or other captioned items, or index is compiled. You should now be able to accomplish the following in finishing your document:

- Insert an automatic table of contents based on heading styles in your document
- Mark table of contents entries for manually creating a table of contents
- Selectively use non-heading styles in a table of contents
- Save a custom table of contents to the Table of Contents Gallery for reuse
- Perform custom edits to the TOC field to change features to which the Table of Contents dialog box doesn't provide access
- Create new labels for captioning a variety of objects
- Change the caption numbering style
- Insert a table of figures, tables, and so on using caption labels
- Mark captioned items manually and insert a table using table entry fields
- Use the Mark Entry dialog box to mark index entries
- Insert and update an index

Documenting Your Sources

IN THIS CHAPTER

I n addition to including tools to help a reader navigate a long, formal document as you learned in Chapter 20, "Identifying the Contents and Terms in Your Document: TOC, Captions, and Indexing," it's necessary to document the sources you've used to develop the document content. In academic reports, scientific publications, legal documents, and more, crediting your sources is a matter of ethics and professionalism. You enhance your own credibility and avoid any appearance of plagiarism by giving credit where credit is due.

This chapter covers the automated features for crediting sources in Word. It shows you how to insert footnotes and endnotes, the two most basic ways of crediting sources. From there, the chapter moves on to cover how to create and insert citations within text, and how to compile cited sources into a bibliography, a feature often required for scholarly books or publications. Finally, the chapter shows how to insert a table of authorities, used to cite legal rulings, statutes, and other information within a legal document.

Footnotes and Endnotes Basics

Footnotes and *endnotes* contain material that, if presented in the text, tends to disrupt the reader's train of thought. In some types of documents—academic, professional, and legal, for example—footnotes or endnotes are mandatory. In these types of documents, the footnotes or endnotes typically identify the source for quoted or paraphrased information. In less formal documents, footnotes and endnotes can be used to cite sources or to share the author's thoughts or other side commentary.

Footnotes appear at the bottom of the same page where the reference is made. In certain citation-heavy documents, such as legal and scientific documents and papers, it is not uncommon for footnotes to begin on one page and extend onto one or more additional pages. Though a bit awkward for readers, it is often less awkward than having to search for an endnote at the end of the document to find an explanation for what was said in the text.

Endnotes are compiled at the end of the document. In a book, endnotes often occur at the end of each chapter. In magazines and journal articles, they usually occur at the end of the article.

Word enables you to use footnotes, endnotes, or both. You can also determine how they are presented, up to a point. Word even enables you to specify the footnote and endnote separators, continuation separators, and the continuation notice itself. Because many publishers and publications are rather specific about how to present footnotes and endnotes, Word's flexibility usually helps you conform to those varying specifications.

The Footnotes group of the References tab on the Ribbon, shown in Figure 21.1, holds the tools for working with footnotes and endnotes. Figure 21.1 shows the entire References tab, as you'll be working with more of its tools throughout the rest of this chapter.

FIGURE 21.1

Use the Footnotes group to insert footnotes and endnotes and to launch the Footnote and Endnote dialog box.

Footnote and endnote options

Open the Footnote and Endnote dialog box by clicking the dialog launcher button in the lower-right corner of the Footnotes group shown in Figure 21.1. You can also display the Footnote and Endnote dialog box by right-clicking a previously added footnote or endnote area in the document and choosing Note options. The options in the Footnote and Endnote dialog box, shown in Figure 21.2, are explained in Table 21.1. After making the desired changes, click Apply, or click Insert to insert a new footnote or endnote using the specified settings.

FIGURE 21.2

Change footnote and endnote options using the Footnote and Endnote dialog box.

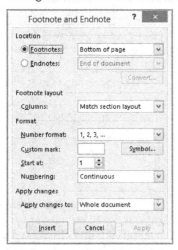

TABLE 21.1 Footnote and Endnote Options

Option	Choices
Footnotes under Location	Bottom of page or Below text. Bottom of page puts the footnotes inside the bottom margin area, above any footer. Below text puts them above the margin area at the end of the text on the page where they occur, making it easier for the reader to find the footnotes on short pages.
Endnotes under Location	End of document or End of section. Notes begin at the end of the document or the section in which they occur, immediately after the text, above the margin area.
Columns under Footnote layout	If the section holding the insertion point is formatted in more than one column, this setting becomes active. The Match section layout option formats the notes in the same number of columns as the section. Or choose 1 column, 2 column, 3 column, or 4 column to specify the number of columns for the notes.
Number format under Format	Endnote and Footnote number formats are independent of one another. Both offer identical numbering formats (1, 2, 3/a, b, c/A, B, C/i, ii, ii/I, II, III, and legal footnote symbols). When specifying the legal symbols, they will double, triple, and so on, if the list of available marks is exhausted.
Custom mark under Format	Choose a custom mark to use for the footnote or endnote symbol. You can specify only one. If you choose the ever-popular *, you will get *, **, ***, and so on, for the first, second, third, and so on, notes.

Continues

TABLE 21.1 *(continued)*

Option	Choices
Start at under Format	Specify the number where you want footnote or endnote numbering to start. This is usually used in conjunction with the Apply changes to this section setting.
Numbering under Format	Can be continuous throughout the document, restarted each section, or restarted each page.
Apply changes to under Apply changes	Options are Selected sections, This section, and Whole document.

Inserting a footnote

To insert a footnote, put the insertion point immediately after the character where you want the footnote reference mark to appear (usually a superscripted number or symbol that appears in the text immediately to the right of the material being cited), and press Alt+Ctrl+F, or click Insert Footnote in the Footnote group of the References tab on the Ribbon. If you're composing in Print Layout view, the insertion point jumps to the footnotes area, as shown in Figure 21.3. If you're composing in Draft view, the Footnotes pane, shown in Figure 21.4, opens.

Type the footnote, including any desired formatting and punctuation. Then click back in the text to continue typing.

FIGURE 21.3

In Print Layout view, footnotes are composed in the footnote area, either under the text or at the bottom of the page.

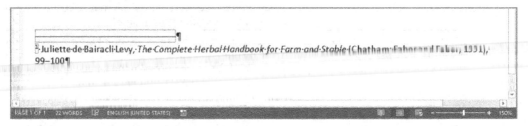

FIGURE 21.4

In Draft view, footnotes are composed in the Footnotes pane.

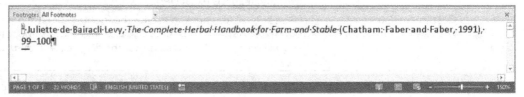

TIP

To get back to where you were in the text when entering footnotes or endnotes, you usually can press one of the GoBack keyboard shortcuts, Shift+F5 or Alt+Ctrl+Z. Most speed typists prefer this to having to reach for the mouse—you can either double-click the footnote number or click in the text where you want to continue writing. If you're composing in Draft view, you can close the Footnotes pane by pressing Alt+Shift+C or clicking the X in the upper-right corner of the Footnotes pane.

Inserting an endnote

To insert an endnote, with the insertion point where you want the reference mark to appear, press Alt+Ctrl+D or click Insert Endnote in the Footnotes group of the References tab on the Ribbon. As with inserting footnotes, where the insertion point jumps to depends on whether you are in Draft or Print Layout view. Type the endnote text, and then return to the document text using one of the same methods previously described for footnotes.

Displaying and editing footnotes and endnotes

You have several ways to display and access footnotes and endnotes, depending on your settings. In both Print Layout view, as shown in Figure 21.5, and Draft view, you can hover the mouse pointer over a footnote or endnote reference mark in the text to display the text of the note in a tooltip. Note that the hover method does not work if you have customized Word not to display tooltips. In File ⇨ Options ⇨ Display tab, under Page display options, verify that Show document tooltips on hover is checked, and click OK.

FIGURE 21.5

Hover the mouse over a footnote/endnote reference mark to display a tooltip containing the note contents.

To edit a footnote or endnote, use either of the following methods:

- In the References tab Footnotes group, click Show Notes. In Print Layout view, this provides access just to the notes on the current page. In Draft view, this provides access to all notes, using the notes pane.

- In the text, double-click on the reference mark for the note you want to edit. This opens the note or the notes pane, depending on the current view.

When the footnote or endnote you want to edit is displayed, edit it using ordinary editing techniques.

For navigating footnotes, in the Footnotes group of the References tab, you can use the drop-down arrow by the Next Footnote tool to select Next Footnote, Previous Footnote, Next Endnote, or Preview Endnote. When the insertion point is in the text, this moves you to the indicated reference mark in the text area. When the insertion point is in the notes area or notes pane, this moves you to the next or previous footnote or endnote.

Deleting footnotes and endnotes

Deleting footnotes and endnotes is easy, but potentially confusing. Among many users, the first impulse is to delete the most visible aspect of the footnote/endnote—the footnote/endnote itself. However, that deletes only the text of the note, stranding the footnote or endnote reference mark in the text.

To delete a footnote or endnote, select the note reference mark in the text area of the document and press Delete or Backspace. This removes the reference mark as well as the footnote or endnote.

Converting footnotes and endnotes

If you change your mind and decide that a given endnote/footnote should really be a foot-note/endnote, respectively, you can make the change easily. Double-click the reference mark for the footnote or endnote to display it in the footnote/endnote area in Print Layout view or the notes pane in Draft view, right-click anywhere in the footnote or endnote you want to convert, and choose Convert to Footnote or Convert to Endnote, as shown in Figure 21.6, whichever is appropriate.

> **NOTE**
>
> If you click Go to Footnote (or Go to Endnote) in the shortcut menu, the insertion point moves to the location in the text where the reference mark occurs.

> **TIP**
>
> If you want to convert all footnotes or endnotes, the quickest way is to switch to Draft view. Then, either click Show Notes in the Footnotes group of the References tab or double-click any reference mark in the text. This displays the Endnotes or Footnotes (notes) pane. Use the drop-down arrow at the top of the pane to select All Footnotes or All Endnotes. Press Ctrl+A to select the entire contents of the pane, right-click, and choose the Convert To option.

FIGURE 21.6

You can easily convert between footnotes and endnotes.

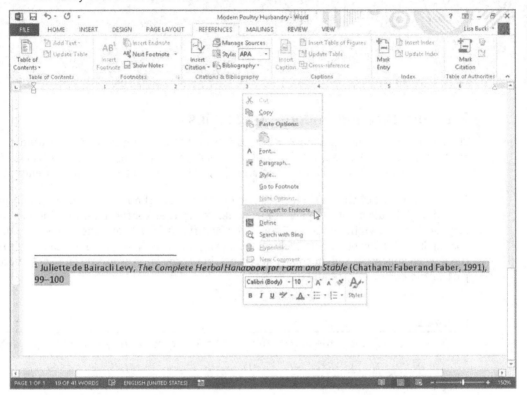

Working with Footnote and Endnote Styling

As for many of the reference elements you learned about in Chapter 20, a set of default styles apply to footnote and endnote formatting. Although you can format footnotes and endnotes directly, it is much more effective—not to mention easier and more consistent—to change the styles involved. Of course, if you want an italic or bold word, direct formatting is fine. For underlining or italicizing references, however, you'd be better off using character styles, just in case somebody suddenly tells you that you need to reformat them all according to the East Podunk Manual of Style.

> **CAUTION**
>
> Note that the footnote and endnote styles do not help with the character formatting and punctuation required by the citation style (for example, MLA or Chicago) that you're using when making formal citations via footnotes or endnotes. If the style calls for italicizing a book title, you will need to apply the formatting manually. When the style calls for including quotation marks, a colon, or other punctuation at a particular location, you will need to type that information into the footnote.

Footnote Text and Endnote Text styles

The Footnote Text and Endnote Text styles control the basic appearance for footnotes. These are both linked styles that can be used to format paragraphs or smaller selections of text. Typically, however, you would use them for formatting the entire footnote or endnote.

To modify either of these, the easiest way is to display the note for editing, and press Ctrl+Shift+S to display the Apply Styles pane. Verify that Footnote Text or Endnote Text is displayed, as shown in Figure 21.7, and click Modify. Use the techniques shown in Chapter 7, "Using Styles to Create a Great-Looking Document," to modify the style, taking care to enable the New documents based on this template setting if you want the style change to become part of the document's template.

FIGURE 21.7

The Apply Styles pane (Ctrl+Shift+S) provides handy access when you want to quickly modify a style.

Reference mark styles

The footnote and endnote numbers themselves are controlled by the Footnote Reference and Endnote Reference styles. Unlike the Footnote/Endnote Text styles, the reference styles are character styles. These two styles are used to format the reference marks in the body of the document as well as at the beginning of the actual footnotes and endnotes themselves. To modify the style for either of these, select a reference mark—in the text area or in the notes area—and press Ctrl+Shift+S as indicated previously, click Modify, and so on.

Separators and Continuation

When you use footnotes and endnotes, Word uses a combination of separators and continuation notices to identify the footnote and endnote sections for the reader. If the built-in separators and continuation notices don't meet your needs, you can specify different ones.

To change, set, or reset separators and continuation marks, you must be in Draft view. On the References tab in the Footnotes group, click Show Notes. If the document contains both endnotes and footnotes, a Show Notes dialog box prompts you to specify which area you want to view. Click View footnote area or View endnote area, according to which one you want, and then click OK.

Using the drop-down arrow shown in Figure 21.8, pick the item you want to change. It will appear in the pane. Reformat what's shown or delete it and insert your own. Note that with any separator or continuation item selected, a Reset button appears to the right of the drop-down arrow. If you want to revert to Word's default for the displayed item, click Reset. When you're finished making changes, click the X to close the notes pane.

FIGURE 21.8

The notes pane can display a variety of notes-related items.

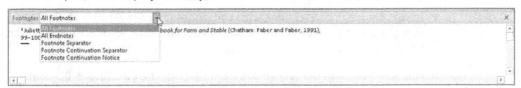

Making a Bibliography

In Word 2013 it is easy to add cited sources into a document so they'll always be available. Once you've added a source, you can insert a citation to that source anywhere in the current document. Then, when you finish adding citations, you can tell Word to insert the bibliography with all the sources used in the current document.

To develop this feature, folks from Microsoft spent countless hours interviewing undergraduate students, graduate students, professors, and researchers in a variety of disciplines to see how they work and what their needs are. The result is a set of citation and bibliography tools that can save many academic and professional writers a lot of time.

> **NOTE**
>
> To be honest, Word's bibliographic capabilities, while being just the ticket for high school students, most college students, and a number of professionals with modest needs, won't please everyone. Among the significant gaps is the lack of an Abstract field for storing document abstracts. If you have hundreds or even thousands of sources, it's unlikely that you will remember what each and every article and book are about. If you are working on your Ph.D. dissertation or are otherwise engaged in heavy-duty research, you may want to reach beyond Word's capability to something such as RefWorks or EndNote, products used by many graduate students and researchers.

Identifying the Sources for Your Bibliography

To be able to use citations in your Word documents, you need the bibliographic information (title, author, and so on) for each source you want to cite. Word's citation and bibliography feature enables you to use several methods to enter that information into your document:

- Insert a source from scratch using the Create Source dialog box. This inserts the source into your Master List as well as in your Current List. The Current List is just for the current document, and the Master List is all the sources you've ever created.

- Copy an existing source from the Master List to the Current List.

- Import sources you exchange with colleagues (or even set up a shared source list that you and colleagues can all access and contribute to) or sources you find in online libraries.

The citation and bibliography features are available in the Citations & Bibliography group in the References tab of the Ribbon, shown back in Figure 21.1. You use the tools in this group to add sources, insert citations in the current document, initiate library searches, manage sources using the Manage Sources dialog box, choose the style for the references in the current document, and insert a bibliography into the current document.

Style first

Before you begin to insert citations, it is helpful to first choose the appropriate bibliographic style as required. In this case, style does not refer to the text formatting, but instead to a standard or convention dictating what details are included in the citation and how they are presented when the citation is inserted and included in a bibliography. Before selecting a style, be sure you understand what citation style is required by your school or publisher. The MLA style (Modern Language Association) is widely used for research reports and publications. Also for research papers, APA style (American Psychological Association) is often required for documenting reports in the fields of psychology and sociology. Writers in the fields of literature, history, and the arts generally use Chicago style (*Chicago Manual of*

Style) citations. In addition to these three widely used styles, Word offers several other styles, some of which pertain to other specific disciplines or areas of study.

If you later need to repurpose an article or paper, you can change styles when needed. Because citations and bibliographies are inserted using field codes, when you change styles, all citations and bibliographical entries are reformatted to match the selected style.

To set the style, click the drop-down arrow next to Style in the Citations & Bibliography group on the References tab. As shown in Figure 21.9, Word has several common styles from which to choose. Click to choose the style needed for the current document. If you've already inserted citations, they will automatically be reformatted to match the selected style.

FIGURE 21.9

Choose the citation style required for your publication.

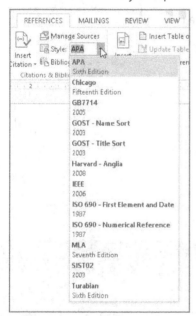

Inserting sources from scratch

You have two ways to insert a source from scratch. You can use Insert Citation ⇨ Add New Source, or you can use the New button from the Manage Sources dialog box. The former adds the source and inserts a standard citation into the document at the insertion point. The latter adds the source but does not immediately cite it.

Adding a new source

To add a new source and cite it at the same time:

1. **Click in the document to position the insertion point where you need to insert the citation.** As with footnotes and endnotes, this typically means clicking just to the right of the material being cited.

2. **Click the References tab, and in the Citations & Bibliography group, choose Insert Citation ⇨ Add New Source.** This displays the Create Source dialog box, shown in Figure 21.10.

FIGURE 21.10

Use the Create Source dialog box to add a new source.

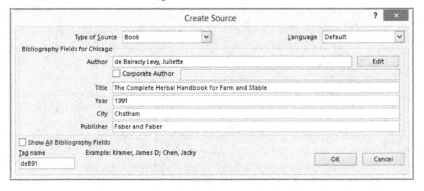

3. **Open the Type of Source drop-down list and choose the source publication type, if needed.** This choice determines the fields available. The list also enables you to select a digital source such as a web page. Note that if you are required to prepare a more detailed bibliography or want to store more details about a source

---

TIP

Key fields to keep in mind are Author, Title, Tag name, and Year. In the Source Manager, which you'll see shortly, you can sort sources by those fields, which makes them useful organizational resources. This might not matter when you have a dozen sources. When you have hundreds, however, it will matter.

---

for your own purposes, you could click the Show All Bibliography Fields check box near the lower-left corner of the dialog box to see all available bibliography fields.

4. **In the Bibliography Fields for section, make an entry in each text box.** After you click in each field, check the Example at the bottom to see how to enter it properly for the given style. For example, as shown in Figure 21.10, author names should be entered as last name, a comma, and then first name and multiple author names separated by semicolons in the Chicago style. You also can click the Edit button beside the Author text box and use the Edit Name dialog box that appears to add authors. After entering the information for each name, click Add. Use the Up, Down, and Delete buttons to work with the selected name in the Names list, and click OK to finish adding Names.

5. **Click OK.** Word finishes creating the source and inserts the citation, including parentheses, using the selected bibliographic style (APA, Chicago, MLA, and so on). Figure 21.11 shows an example citation. Keep in mind that the citation format differs from the source information and does not include all the source information; the more detailed source information is used when you compile a bibliography.

FIGURE 21.11

The citation appears in parentheses to the left of the insertion point.

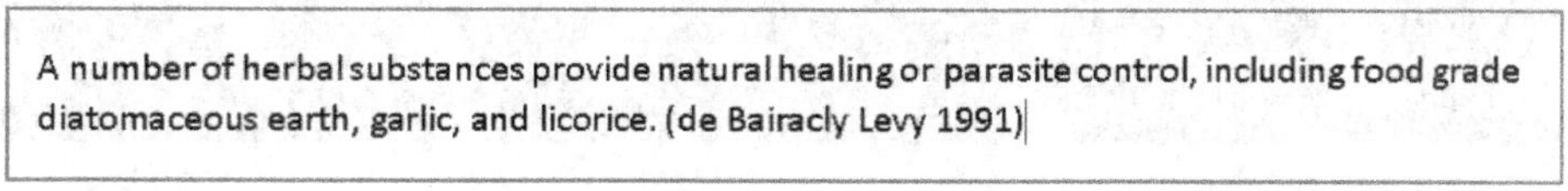

> A number of herbal substances provide natural healing or parasite control, including food grade diatomaceous earth, garlic, and licorice. (de Bairacly Levy 1991)|

NOTE

With Show All Bibliography Fields enabled, red asterisks appear next to some field names, indicating that they are *recommended* for the selected style. Though the fields available for entry do not vary according to which style is selected, the position of the asterisks does change. Therefore, although it's not essential that you pick the style before creating a source, doing so ensures you will fill in the correct recommended fields. Remember also that if you use the same source with a different style, different data elements might be emphasized. Therefore, as time permits, it pays to add as much information as possible when creating a source.

Less visibly, as shown in Figure 21.12, the source is added to the Insert Citation gallery, and will be available the next time you choose Insert Citation from the References tab. At the same time, the source is added to both the Current List and the Master List in the Source Manager, which you'll learn about shortly.

FIGURE 21.12

As you add sources in the current document, they are listed in the Insert Citation gallery.

Adding new sources using the Source Manager

You can also add sources using the Source Manager, which creates the source without inserting a citation in the document. In the Citations & Bibliography group of the References tab, click Manage Sources to display the Source Manager dialog box shown in Figure 21.13. From there you can:

- **Add a new source:** Click New to open the Create Source dialog box (refer to Figure 21.10), and add the source as described earlier. Once you click OK to add the new source, it appears in the Source Manager (Current and Master Lists) as well as in the Insert Citation gallery.

- **Copy a source from the Master List to the Current List (current document's sources):** In the Master List at the left, select the source(s) you want to copy. You can use Shift+click or Ctrl+click to select multiple sources, if desired. Notice that the Copy button arrow now points to the Current List at the right. Click Copy to add the selected items to the Current list.

Note in Figure 21.13 that the Current List shows a check mark to the left of any source for which you've inserted a citation in the current document. Click Close to close the Source Manager dialog box when you finish using it.

FIGURE 21.13

Use the Source Manager to create new sources as well as copy sources between the Master and Current Lists, among other things.

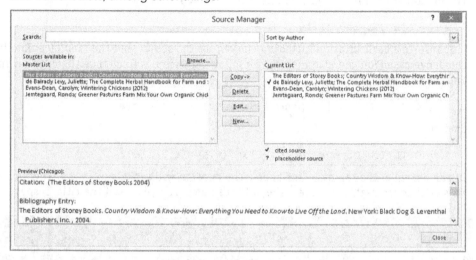

Inserting existing citations

In addition to creating citations from scratch, as shown in the preceding section, you can use existing citations. As noted previously and shown in Figure 21.12, once you have created a source—either directly using Insert Citation ⇨ Add New Source, or by clicking the New button in the Source Manager—that source is added to the Insert Citation gallery. To insert a citation of a source:

1. **Click to position the insertion point at the location where you want to insert the citation.**
2. **Click the References tab, and click Insert Citation in the Citations & Bibliography group.**
3. **Click the source to insert in the gallery.**

TIP

By convention, you should include a citation for any source material you have quoted, paraphrased, or summarized.

NOTE

Word's Citations & Bibliography tools can create only parenthetical citations. The tools are not geared to creating footnotes or endnotes. If you need a footnote or endnote, insert the parenthetical citation, cut it to the Clipboard, insert a footnote/endnote, paste the Clipboard contents into place, and delete the parentheses.

To create citations, Word inserts a citation field code. The Insert Field dialog box provides no explanation of the switches for this type of field. However, here's a little help with that. The default syntax for the citation field is as follows:

{ *CITATION tag* \l 1033 }

This inserts a basic citation including the tag for the source and the language; English, in the above case. You can also include the following switches to change the citation appearance as needed:

{ *CITATION tag* [\s *pages* \n \y \t] \l *language* }

Example:

{ CITATION Cooper \s "p. 233" \n \y \t \l 1033 }

In the example, the tag name is Cooper. The citation will include p. 233. The \n, \y, and \t switches are used to suppress the author's name, the year, and the title, respectively.

> **NOTE**
>
> The CITATION field inserted by the Insert Citation command is locked programmatically so that you cannot edit it by hand in the document. However, if you right-click it and click Edit Field, you can add field switches in the Field codes text box and then click OK to update the field.

Inserting a placeholder citation

When writing, if you stop to insert a citation it often interrupts your train of thought. It's often more creatively efficient to insert a temporary placeholder and then come back to it later. To insert a placeholder citation at the insertion pint, choose Insert Citation ⇨ Add New Placeholder. In the box provided, shown in Figure 21.14, type a name for the placeholder and click OK. Placeholder names have some silly rules—the same rules used for bookmark names. Names can include letters (including accented letters), numbers, and the underscore character. That's it. No dashes, no spaces. Names are case sensitive (for example, Cooper, COOPER, and cooper are different placeholder names), so be careful with that Shift key.

FIGURE 21.14

Remind yourself to find a citation later, and then continue writing.

When you create a placeholder, Word doesn't add it to the Master List (although you can add placeholders using the Source Manager), but it does get added to the Citation gallery.

Edit Source and converting a placeholder to a source

21

If information about a source changes, or if you simply get new information, as happens when you are converting placeholders into ready-to-use sources, it is easy to edit the source. When you need to update the information about a source (or to convert the placeholder into an actual source), you have several ways to proceed:

- Right-click any occurrence of the citation in the document and choose Edit Source.
- Click the citation or placeholder to display its container, click the drop-down arrow at the right end of the container, and choose Edit Source.
- Open the Source Manager, select the source or placeholder, and choose Edit. (A placeholder appears in the Current List choices and incudes a question mark to the left of its name.)

However you proceed, you'll see the Edit Source dialog box, which is virtually identical to the Create Source dialog box shown in Figure 21.10. Add the source information as described earlier in "Adding a new source," and click OK. When you do this, all citations in the current document are updated with the new information.

If the identical source (identified by Tag name) is included in both the Master List and the Current List, you will be prompted about which lists should be updated, as shown in Figure 21.15. Say No if you want to update only the list associated with the method you used to access the Edit Source process. If you accessed Edit Source by using a citation in the document and now click No, only the Current List version of the source will be updated. If, on the other hand, you selected the source in the Master List from the Source Manager and clicked Edit, clicking No will update only the Master List version of the source.

FIGURE 21.15

Click Yes to update both the Master List and the Current List. Click No to update just the Master List.

When and why might the entry in the two lists differ? The two versions of the source might be different, for example, if the Master List includes a whole book, whereas the Current List item includes only one chapter.

Editing Citations

You might have noticed that when you insert a citation, you aren't provided with any options. A minimal citation is inserted based on the selected bibliography style. Suppose, for example, that you're using the same citation in different parts of a paper and want to focus the reader's attention only on certain pages of a particular book or article. You could handle this by creating different sources, but that approach tends to make the list of sources rather unwieldy and confusing later. A better way is to edit the citation to add the additional information.

To edit a citation, right-click the citation or click the citation container's drop-down arrow and choose Edit Citation. In the Edit Citation dialog box, shown in Figure 21.16, type the page number, or click to check citation details you might want suppressed. Note that when adding page numbers, Word does not supply the p. or pp. in the resulting citation. You'll need to type any desired abbreviation yourself in the Pages text box of the Edit Citation dialog box, as in the example in Figure 21.16.

FIGURE 21.16

Edit the citation to provide page numbers or to suppress Author, Year, or Title.

NOTE

When you edit a citation in this way, you're probably wondering what happens later when/if you edit the source. Because of the way that the edits are added—using field switches, the main citation itself can be updated independently of the edit. Hence, if you later edit the source, the citation will be updated, but any additional information provided or suppressed through editing is preserved.

Deleting sources

Ordinarily, you probably won't need to delete sources from your Master List. However, if you acquire source lists from other people, you sometimes will discover that you have different versions of the same source, with one being slightly more complete than the other or each having details that the other lacks. There is no built-in way to consolidate such "duplicates" into a single item that uses information from all available sources. Given that the quality of the information might vary as well as the quantity of information, it's not even clear that you would *want* Word making such decisions about which source to believe.

Therefore, you would need to sort through the information manually by inspecting the different sources, copying missing details to the pick of the litter, and then deleting the inferior versions. When you're ready to delete a source, choose Manage Sources, select the source(s) you want to delete from either the Master List or Current List, and then click Delete.

You might want to delete from the Current List if you discover you have duplicates with different tag names. You might also want to delete from the Current List if you decide not to use a given source. Keep in mind, however, that Word is capable of distinguishing between sources consulted and sources cited (see "Inserting a bibliography"), so don't delete sources you consulted but didn't cite. The fact that you consulted a source might ultimately prove useful, even if you don't include it in the list of sources cited that you include with the finished document.

Acquiring external sources

Word stores the sources you create in a single .xml file: C:\Users*user name*\AppData\ Roaming\Microsoft\Bibliography\Sources.xml. As suggested earlier, you're not limited to sources that you develop and enter. You can exchange source lists with colleagues, download sources from libraries that adopt Word 2013's bibliographic standard, as well as establish source lists on local/organizational servers. For example, a colleague could create a copy of his or her own Sources.xml file, rename the copy, and provide it to you to use with your own documents.

To load a new list of sources you've acquired:

1. **Open the document for which you want to use the sources.**
2. **Click Manage Sources in the Citations & Bibliography group of the References tab.** The Source Manager dialog box opens.
3. **Click Browse.**
4. **Use the Open Source List dialog box to navigate to the alternate source file, click it, and click Open.**
5. **Verify that the new sources appear in the Master List.**
6. **Delete any unneeded entries from the Current List and add entries from the Master List there as needed.**
7. **Click OK.**

When you want to revert back to your original sources if they don't load automatically, repeat the above process and select your Sources.xml file.

Ordinarily, Word users might expect that additional source files copied to the C.\Users\ *user name*\AppData\Roaming\Microsoft\Bibliography folder would automatically be loaded by Word. Not so in this case. Word automatically loads only the Sources.xml file, so if you copied a file to the same folder expecting it to be opened automatically by Word, that won't work. The process for getting external sources to be permanently available in Word is unintuitive and a bit tricky. It requires two overall operations: loading the .xml file of new sources into Word, and then using a blank document to copy them to the Master List along with your own sources, as follows:

1. **Open the file with the new sources as described earlier, and then close the Source Manager dialog box.**

2. **Open a new blank Word document.**

3. **Click Manage Sources in the Citations & Bibliography group of the References tab.**

4. **Use the Source Manager to copy the "guest" sources from the Master List into the Current List as described earlier in the section "Adding new sources using the Source Manager."** They should now be listed in both places.

5. **Click Close to close the Source Manager.**

6. **Save and close the Word document that now has the "guest" sources associated with it.**

7. **Close Word.**

8. **Open Word and reopen the Word document into which you copied the sources.**

9. **Click Manage Sources in the Citations & Bibliography group of the References tab.** Verify that your default sources now reappear in the Master List and that the imported sources are in the Current List.

10. **In the Current List, select the sources and click Copy.**

11. **Click Close to close the Source Manager.**

12. **Save and close the file, and close Word again.** The next time you reopen Word, the Source Manager should include the copied external sources in the Master List.

> **CAUTION**
>
> If you don't want the imported sources to be merged with your default sources, don't perform these steps. Instead just use the Source Manager dialog box to load the alternate source file on an as-needed basis.

Compiling the Citations into a Bibliography

Just as you saw when you learned how to insert a table of contents in Chapter 20, Word enables you to use automated choices to insert a bibliography. This section explains how to choose what type of list to insert, as well as how to maintain, delete, and work with the inserted list.

Inserting a bibliography

To insert a bibliography, first select the location for the bibliography. In most documents, you need to insert the bibliography on its own page at the end of the document. Use the Breaks button in the Page Setup group of the Page Layout tab to insert either a Page break or Next Page section break, and then position the insertion point on the new page. Click the Bibliography drop-down arrow in the Citations & Bibliography group of the References tab. Word offers the Bibliography gallery alternatives shown in Figure 21.17.

- **Bibliography, References, or Works Cited:** Inserts a list of all sources associated with the document, whether cited or not, and includes Bibliography, References, or Works Cited as the title. The list is contained within a content control.

- **Insert Bibliography:** Inserts a list of all sources associated with the document, whether cited or not, and does not include a title or content container.

FIGURE 21.17

Word by default offers three Built-In bibliography alternatives in the gallery.

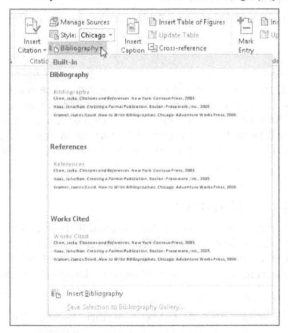

NOTE

If you need your bibliography to include only sources directly cited in the document, then you will have to use the Source Manager to delete the unneeded sources from the Current List at right. At present, Word doesn't provide an automated way to distinguish between sources that have been cited or not in the compiled bibliography, regardless of whatever title you choose when inserting it. If you need to have both *Works Consulted* and *Works Cited* lists in your document, the easiest way is to leave all the consulted sources in the Current List in the Source Manager. Use the Bibliography gallery to insert two Works Cited lists. In the first, change the title to Works Consulted. In the second, delete the individual entries for sources that weren't cited. Then, Restrict Editing as described in Chapter 26, "Managing Document Security, Comments, and Tracked Changes," to prevent any updates to the edited Works Cited list.

Updating a bibliography

Ordinarily, there should never be a need to edit or update a bibliography inserted using Word's Citations & Bibliography commands. When you add sources and/or cite them, any bibliographies are updated automatically. The only time you might *need* to update a bibliography would be if you need to fix an accidental edit.

To update any type of bibliography list:

1. **Click in the list to display its content control.**
2. **On the tab at top, click Update Citations and Bibliography, shown in the example in Figure 21.18.**

Deleting a bibliography

To delete a bibliography, click in it; then click the three dots at the left of the content control tab and press the Delete or Backspace key. If only part of the bibliography field is selected, the text will be deleted. However, the next time any citation or source change occurs in the document, the edit will be undone. If you want to perform manual edits to a bibliography and have the edits survive updates, you will need to convert the bibliography into static text.

Converting a bibliography into static text

Bibliographies, like citations themselves and some other features you learned about in Chapter 20, are inserted using field codes. To convert a bibliography into static text, click in it to display its content control, click the three dots at the left end of the tab to select the entire list, click the Bibliographies button, and choose Convert bibliography to static text, as shown in Figure 21.19.

Note that once you convert the bibliography into static text, the static text version of the bibliography is still within the content control container. If you want to remove a bibliography from the whole citation process, after unlinking it copy the contents of the field to the Clipboard, making sure that no part of the container is selected. Then, paste it somewhere outside of the container and delete the container.

FIGURE 21.18

The tab at the top of the bibliography control enables you to update its contents.

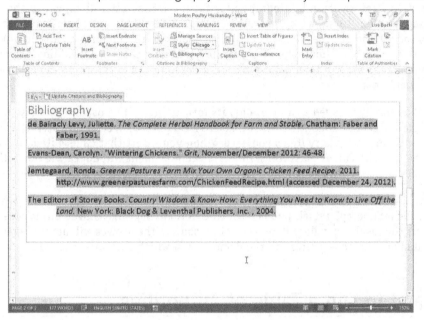

FIGURE 21.19

To copy a bibliography elsewhere, convert it to static text. (Filter Languages appears only if you have multiple languages installed on your computer.)

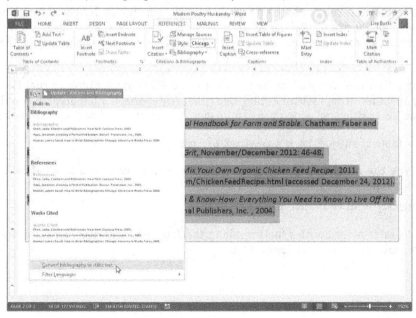

21

Save Selection to Bibliography Gallery

You can save a reformatted bibliography for future use, and it will appear in the Bibliography gallery along with the built-in items. To do this, select the bibliography and any formatting or other text (including page breaks, section breaks, and so on), and from the Citations & Bibliography group of the References tab, choose Bibliography ⇨ Save Selection to Bibliography Gallery. The bibliography you're adding to the gallery can be a field or static text.

If the bibliography is saved as a field, only its formatting will be used, not any source content. If you determine that you need a title, a section break, special formatting, and so on, you can include it in gallery items you save. When you insert that gallery item, it will then determine how the Current List items in any given document will appear. It won't display the sources that were in the bibliography used to create the gallery item.

You can, however, convert a gallery to static text before saving it to the gallery. When you do that, the bibliography itself (along with title, formatting, text, and so on) is saved. When you insert the resulting gallery item, the actual sources themselves will appear, even if they aren't cited or otherwise sourced in the document in which they are inserted.

Understanding a Table of Authorities

Unless you work in the legal field, you probably will never need to care about tables of authorities. However, if you're an attorney, a paralegal, or a legal assistant, you will likely work with tables of authorities on a frequent basis.

A table of authorities is a list of references in legal documents, such as briefs, certifications, court orders, and decisions. References include court cases, decisions, statutes, ordinances, articles, books, rules, and regulations, along with additional details necessary to enable the reader to see the connections being asserted.

A table of authorities works a bit like the Citations & Bibliography tools in that there are citations and a resulting table of authorities (like a categorized bibliography) that lists the references (authorities) on which your arguments, assertions, and billing statements rely.

Creating a table of authorities is a two-step process:

1. **Type the citation into the document and then mark it as a table of authorities citation.**
2. **Insert/build the table of authorities.**

Word 2010's table of authorities tools reside in the Table of Authorities group in the References tab, shown back in Figure 21.1.

Creating Citations for a Table of Authorities

The first step, as noted in the preceding section, is to mark the citations. Citation entries come in two flavors:

- **Long:** Long citations are the full legal reference that actually appears in the table of authorities itself. These include the name of the authority (case name or statute name, for example) and the full legal reference for it. You use a long citation the first time an authority is cited. An example of a long citation is *Boutilier v. Immigration & Naturalization Service, 387 U.S. 118 (1967)*.

- **Short:** Short citations are informative but shorter versions of long citations. These are used subsequent to the first time an authority is cited, and are not used in the table of authorities itself. These are very similar to the kinds of citations shown earlier in this chapter. An acceptable short version for the long citation of the case just cited would be *Boutilier v. INS (1967)*.

Marking citations

To begin, enter the citation in the document, and then follow these steps:

1. **Select the citation you want to mark (this isn't essential, but usually saves time).**
2. **Click the Mark Citation button in the Table of Authorities group in the Reference tab, or press Alt+Shift+I.** As shown in Figure 21.20, the selected text is copied to both the Selected text and the Short citation text fields in the Mark Citation dialog box.

FIGURE 21.20

Word copies the selected citation text to two text boxes in the Mark Citation dialog box.

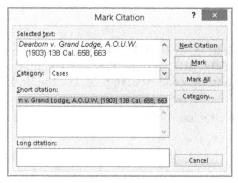

3. **The full selected citation was also copied to the Short citation field; edit it so that it matches all occurrences of the short citation in other parts of the document.** Note that character formatting keystrokes do not work in the Short citation field.

4. **Open the Category drop-down list and click the appropriate one for the authority being cited.** If there is no category that fits, click the Category button. As shown in Figure 21.21, click one of the number placeholders (8 through 16) and type a new category name in the Replace with text box. Click Replace to replace the number with the category you type. You can replace additional ones as well while the dialog box is open. When you're ready, click OK. Back in the Mark Citation dialog box, ensure that the correct category is selected.

FIGURE 21.21

Word has several built-in authorities categories. You can add several additional categories.

5. **Click Mark to mark the current citation, or Mark All to mark all citations matching the text in the Short citation field.** After clicking Mark or Mark All, the contents of Selected text moves down into the Long citation field, and the Mark Citation dialog box remains open.

6. **Click Close to finish marking the citation.**

Removing citations

The table of authorities interface does not provide a neat way to remove or edit citations. You might need to remove a citation if it contains an error, or if you no longer refer to it in the text. Notice in the Mark Citation dialog box that there is no Edit, Delete, or Remove button. If you need to remove citations, you simply delete the field code at the location where you marked the citation in the text. To completely remove all citations of a given authority/source, if there are multiple citations, you have to remove all occurrences of that field code.

Citation fields

When you mark a citation, it is inserted as a noncollapsible field code with hidden text formatting applied. To see the citation fields, which all begin with TA, you might need to toggle the display of hidden text as described under "Marking entries for the table of contents" in Chapter 20. A typical TA field appears as follows:

```
{ TA \l "Carey v. Brown, 447 U.S. 455, 467 (1980)" \s "Carey v. Brown
(1980)"
 \c 1 }
```

TIP

Use Find and Replace to remove unwanted citations. You might want to take a quick look at the full table of authorities to ensure that you don't have multiple cases with similar names. If you do, specify as much of the field as needed in the Find what field to ensure a correct hit. Press Ctrl+H to display the Find and Replace dialog box with the Replace tab active. In Find What, type **^d ta** followed by as much of the beginning of the citation as you need in order to find it (you might want to copy TA and what follows from inside an existing TA field, and then paste it into the Find what box after the ^d). Notice that you need a space between ^d and ta. For the case citation shown in the "Citation fields" section, for example, you might use ^d ta \l "Carey v. Brown." The ^d tells Replace to search for a field code. The space and what follows are what's contained within the field braces.

Clear any text or formatting that might be in or associated with the Replace with field. Try Replace a few times to ensure that it's finding the citations you want to remove, and then click Replace All if you're sure you're matching the right citations.

Inserting the Table of Authorities

To insert a table of authorities, first click to position the insertion point at the location where you need to insert the table, inserting a page or section break first, if needed. Click the Insert Table of Authorities button in the Table of Authorities group on the References tab. As shown in Figure 21.22, the Table of Authorities dialog box appears. Make your selections and then click OK to insert the table of authorities.

FIGURE 21.22

Use the Table of Authorities dialog box to insert a table of authorities for any or all categories.

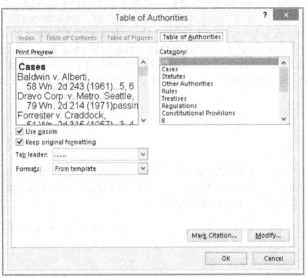

Category

Word can insert tables for any one or all categories. You can't pick and choose multiple categories to insert using the Category list of the Table of Authorities dialog box (except by repeatedly using Insert Table of Authorities). If you click All, Word inserts only those categories that actually occur in the document. Word inserts a separate TOA field with a heading for each category. For example, Figure 21.23 shows the TOA entries with the Cases category assigned.

FIGURE 21.23

This table of authorities shows the Cases category entries.

```
Cases
Asso Contractors, Inc. v. McNamara & Peepe Lumber Co. (1976) 63 Cal.App.3d 202,
    295 ........................................................................................................................ 2
Butler Bros. v. McColgan (1941) 17 Cal.2d 664, 673, affd. (1942) 315 U.S. 501 ............... 3
Dearborn v. Grand Lodge, A.O.U.W. (1903) 138 Cal. 658, 663 .................................... 2
Edison California Stores v. McColgan (1947) 30 Cal.2d 472, 480 ................................. 3
Rain Bird Sprinkler Mfg. Corp. v. Franchise Tax Bd. (1991) 229 Cal.App.3d 784, 787 ...... 3
```

Use passim

Passim is commonly used in a table of authorities to indicate that a case is cited multiple times throughout the document. Specifically, if the Use passim option shown in Figure 21.22 is enabled, Word replaces the page number with *passim* in the table of authorities.

Formatting

When you select a citation and use Mark Citation, Word uses any character formatting that is applied to the selection when it copies that text to the Selected text field. You can make any modification you need in the Selected text field as noted earlier. Once you click Mark or Mark All, from then on, Word ignores the formatting of the original item in the document, and "original formatting" thereafter refers to the formatting that appears in the Long citation field.

Use the Keep original formatting option in the Table of Authorities dialog box to apply the formatting specified in the Long citation field when Word creates the table of authorities. If this option is turned off, Word uses only the formatting specified in the Formats drop-down list.

Tab leaders are used to connect listed legal sources with the page numbers. Use the Tab leader drop-down list in the Table of Authorities dialog box to choose one of the available styles.

For overall formatting of the table of authorities, Word offers a choice between the current template table of authorities styles (TOA Heading and Table of Authorities) and one of the four preset formats shown in Figure 21.24.

If none of the preset formats suits your needs, leave From template selected in the Formats drop-down list, and then choose Modify, which displays the dialog box shown in Figure 21.25. Word uses the TOA Heading style for each category (for example, Cases, Statutes, Regulations, and so on), and uses the Table of Authorities style for the individual authorities cited. Click the style you want to change, and then click Modify to use the Modify Style dialog box to change the selected style. See Chapter 7 for more information on modifying styles.

FIGURE 21.24

Choosing a different Format choice applies the specified template's TOA Heading style to each category heading and the Table of Authorities style to the individual cases/sources.

FIGURE 21.25

Choose a different style for the table of authorities, if desired; click Modify to change the formatting of the selected style.

Updating a table of authorities

To update the table of authorities, right-click the section you want to update and choose Update Field. Alternatively, if the References tab is showing, click the Update Table button in the Table of Authorities group. To update the entire table of authorities, select all of the components. Now you can press F9, click the Update Table of Authorities tool in the Reference tab, or right-click the selection and choose Update Field.

Removing page numbers

In many legal documents, the accepted standards do not use page numbers. This is especially true in short briefs for which the use of page numbers isn't particularly useful. Unfortunately, Word's table of authorities feature makes no provision for suppressing page numbers entirely. The \n switch, which so neatly suppresses page numbers in a table of contents field, has no effect in a table of authorities.

If you need to suppress page numbers in a table of authorities, wait until the document is finished. Edit the TOA entries to delete the page numbers and any dot leader displays. Then protect the document against edits and updates as described in Chapter 26.

Summary

In this chapter, you've learned about the automated tools Word provides for inserting and managing footnotes and endnotes, marking citations and making a bibliography, and marking legal citations in a legal document for inclusion in a table of authorities. You should now be able to perform the following tasks to document sources in long documents:

- Insert and edit footnotes and endnotes
- Change the appearance of footnotes and endnotes by modifying their respective styles
- Control and set footnote and endnote numbering and location on the page
- Convert footnotes to endnotes and vice versa
- Use the Style tool to apply a variety of bibliography styles (APA, Chicago, and so on) to an article or paper
- Insert properly formatted parenthetical citations to sources used in a research paper
- Import sources from other source lists
- Insert a bibliography that contains all sources
- Mark legal citations
- Format long citations to control how they appear in a table of authorities
- Create short citations so that they match all occurrences in a document
- Insert and format a complete table of authorities
- Remove page numbers from a table of authorities as needed

Part VII

Making Documents Work for You

Hand-addressing your holiday cards lends a personal touch that many recipients will appreciate. But in most cases, hand-addressing a mass mailing to friends or clients takes more time than you have to spend. Word offers features that you can use to create documents that take care of some tedious tasks for you.

Chapter 22 launches this part by showing you to create a mail-merge document that combines a data source and data document. Chapter 23 explains how to add fields to a document to supply content automatically or prompt the user for content. Finally, Chapter 24 shows you how to use Word's form capabilities to collect data.

CHAPTER

22

Data Documents and Mail Merge

IN THIS CHAPTER

Reviewing data sources you can use with Word

Formatting source data

Attaching a data source to a data document

Editing data

Assembling a data document

Merging to a printer

Using the Mail Merge Wizard

This chapter shows you how to create specialized types of documents—such as envelopes, labels, form letters, mass email, catalogs, and directories—by combining a main document with a list called a data source. Merging can save a lot of time once you are familiar with the process, but it does require careful setup for both the data source and the main document. This chapter covers how to bring your data and document together without errors so you can save time and let Word do some of the heavy lifting for you.

Previewing the Mail Merge Process

Let's say you need to send a letter about a new product to 20 clients, and you already have the client names and addresses typed into Excel. Rather than manually retyping each name and address into a separate copy of the letter, you can write the letter, specify where the name and address information from the list should go, and perform the *mail merge* to create 20 versions of the letter—each personally addressed for a specific recipient. Even better, you can quickly create a matching set of addressed envelopes or labels to use for the mailing.

You also can use mail merge to create updateable versions of other long documents. For example, let's say you maintain a directory of contact information for your department at work. You have access to the main employee database from the HR department, but you only need to list the employees for your department. During the merge process, you can select which items to use based on certain criteria, so Word easily pulls out just the list of colleagues from your department for the merge into the main directory document you've set up.

Setting up a mail merge *main document* and *data source* and merging them together involves a number of steps, some of which must be done before others can happen:

1. **Set the document type for the main document: letter, email, envelope, labels, and directory.**

2. **Associate a data source with the document: new, Outlook contact, or some other source.** The data source file holds the *records* of information, such as one recipient's name and address, that will be inserted into the main document at specified locations.

3. **Design your main document by combining ordinary document features with Word *merge field codes*.** Each merge field corresponds to a *field* in the data source document, such as Fname, Lname. In this way, Word customizes each copy of the main document with information from a single record of the data source.

4. **Preview the finished document by testing to see how it looks with different data records.**

5. **Finish the process by merging the data document with the data source, creating a printed result, a saved document, or an email document.**

Data Considerations

It might seem odd to discuss the data source first, but the data source is often the most important consideration for a merge and typically receives the least attention. Once you've identified and correctly set up your data source, the rest of the merge process is made much easier.

Some data considerations, such as usability (does the data set contain what you need?) and accuracy pretty much go without saying. Other considerations are equally important, such as whether the data source will be available when you need it, the ease of updating the data source, and access to the data source both for other data users as well as data creators.

Sometimes, your computer isn't the only device that needs to access data. For some documents, you will need access to data in other places (for example, on a notebook or laptop, for a presentation while traveling, on a different desktop computer at home, or elsewhere).

You can take several approaches to solving the need to either access data from another location or take the data with you. For the former, especially if the data source is large, unwieldy, or nonportable for other reasons, some kind of server solution will provide the answer. This might take the form of a data file residing on a SharePoint or other server, or you might place it in your SkyDrive so you can download it and reattach it as needed from any location. To see what's involved with using your SkyDrive, see Chapter 27, "Collaborating in the Cloud with SkyDrive." If you work in an enterprise, your company might have other kinds of server facilities that can serve as data sources for Word.

For portability, the answer often will be to extract a portion of a full data set—either a limited number of data records or a sample containing just the data fields you need. Every database has some unit or focus, such as individuals (for example, contact records) or products. Each person or product in a given database is called a *data record*.

Each piece of information about a person or product is called a *data field*. For example, a person's name, telephone number, address, email address, and date of birth each would be data fields. For a product, data fields typically include name, SKU, shipping weight, price, color, description, and cost.

Unless a data set was constructed explicitly for a single purpose, most data sets will contain more records than you need, as well as more data fields than you need for a specific data-driven Word document. Often, it's possible to extract just what you need and take it with you. You have a variety of ways of doing that, as you see in this chapter.

TIP

To extract a portion of a larger database for use at a remote or inaccessible location, create a directory document using the mail merge feature, specifying only the records and fields you need. When you complete the merge, the resulting directory (or data document) will become the input data you need for associating with another data document.

Reviewing Data File Formats

Word enables you to use data from a variety of formats. You can create a data source directly from Word as part of the mail merge process or use an existing source. If you use an existing data source document, your options include the following:

- Outlook contacts
- Office Database Connections (*.odc)
- Access 2010 and later Databases (*.accdb, *.accde)
- Access 2007 Databases (*.mdb, *.mde)
- Microsoft Office Address Lists (*.mdb)
- Microsoft Office List Shortcuts (*.ols)
- Microsoft Data links (*.udl)
- ODBC File DSNs (*.dsn)

22

- Excel Files (*.xlsx, *.xlsm, *.xlsb, *.xls)
- Web Pages (*.htm, *.html, *.asp, *.mht, *.mhtml)
- Rich Text Format (*.rtf)
- Word Documents (*.docx, *.doc, *.docm, *.dot)
- Text Files (*.txt, *.prn, *.csv, *.tab, *.asc)
- Database Queries (*.dqy, *.rqy)
- OpenDocument Text Files (*.odt)

> **NOTE**
>
> Several older file formats are not directly supported in Word 2013, including Microsoft Works Databases (*.wdb), Outlook Personal Address Books (*.pab), Lotus 1-2-3 files (*.wk?, *.wj?), Paradox files (*.db), and dBASE files (*.dbf). Note that if you still have the old software, you can often export from those formats to a delimited *.txt or *.csv file that you can then use for the merge.

Using most of the data source formats works in a similar fashion, so there's no need to go through each and every type in detail. However, we will go through the most common formats. Keep in mind that although the chapter examples repeatedly use names and addresses, you're by no means limited to those. Your list could be a list of products, an inventory, planetary information for a school project, and more. The idea is to use Word to present and format data in some fashion; it doesn't matter to Word what the data pertains to.

To begin, in the Mailings tab, and in the Start Mail Merge group click the Select Recipients tool, exposing the options shown in Figure 22.1.

FIGURE 22.1

When selecting a data file, you can create it from Word, use a variety of other formats, or select data from Outlook Contacts.

> **NOTE**
>
> This section explains how to set up the various types of data source files. You'll learn how to attach the data source during the merge process later in the chapter.

Typing a new list

To create a new list (a somewhat generic euphemism for "data document") in Word for a mail-merge document:

1. **Click the Mailings tab, and in the Start Mail Merge group, choose Select Recipients ⇨ Type New List.** The New Address List dialog box shown in Figure 22.2 appears.

FIGURE 22.2

Build your merge data source in this dialog box.

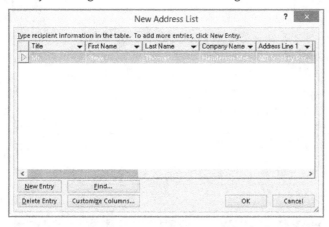

2. **Type your data into the fields shown, tabbing or clicking to get to the next entry field.**
3. **To accept the current entry and enter a new record, click New Entry.**
4. **To remove an entry, click it and then click Delete Entry.**
5. **When you're finished entering data, click OK.** The Save Address List dialog box prompts you to save the file as a Microsoft Office Address Lists file, as shown in Figure 22.3. Note that this is the only Save as type option.
6. **Type a name in the File name text box and click Save.**

FIGURE 22.3

Word saves new data source lists in the Microsoft Office Address Lists format.

While you're working in the New Address List dialog box, if you've entered a lot of data and need to find a particular entry, click Find to display the Find Entry dialog box shown in Figure 22.4. Type the search text into the Find field. To search in a particular field, click the This field option button and select the desired field from the accompanying drop-down list. Click Find Next to find the next entry that matches the Find text in the field(s) specified. Click Cancel to dismiss the dialog box.

FIGURE 22.4

Once your data set is a bit larger, you might need some help finding a record.

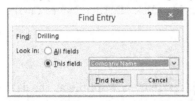

If you want to create a list that consists of data other than a name and address list, click the Customize Columns button near the bottom of the New Address List dialog box. As shown in Figure 22.5, you can use the tools in the Customize Address List dialog box that appears to change the fields in your list. To add a field, select the field above where you want to add the new field, and click Add. Type the field name in the Add Field dialog box that appears, and click OK. To delete a field, select the field and click Delete; click Yes in the dialog box that prompts you to confirm the deletion. To rename a field, select it, click Rename, type a new name in the To text box of the Rename Field dialog box, and click OK. (To add a field at the beginning, select the first field and click Add, as before. The added field will be second on the list, not first. Select the added field and then click Move Up.)

FIGURE 22.5

Use Customize Address List to specify your own fields for a merge data source.

To rearrange the fields, click a field you want to move, and then click Move Up or Move Down, as needed. When you're done customizing the list fields, click OK. Then you can make entries in the list as described earlier.

Word and text files

You can also use a Word document as your data source. Using a Word file as the data source usually works best when the data is stored in a table, but that's by no means essential. You can use a plain Word document in which the fields are separated by tabs, commas, slashes, or another delimiter. Plain text (*.txt) or comma-separated value (*.csv) files also should be delimited. Regardless of how the data file is formatted, Word assumes that the data file contains a header row or a header line containing the field names. The header itself should be formatted the same way the data is formatted—separated by tabs, commas, in a table row, and so on.

Figure 22.6 shows a merge data source properly entered as a table in Word. Notice that the first row of the table is the header row with the field names. Each column holds a single field (such as Restaurant), and each row holds a single record (all the fields for one restaurant).

Headerless data files

After you attach a data source file, you can check it by clicking Edit Recipient List in the Start Mail Merge group of the Mailings tab. (You'll learn more about editing a data source later in the chapter.)

Word assumes that the first row of data contains the column headers. If your data source file doesn't include column headers in the first data record, you'll run into problems, as shown in the Mail Merge Recipients dialog box in Figure 22.7. And if a field in the top record is empty, Word displays AutoMergeField as the field title.

If the recipient list doesn't look as expected, click OK to close the Mail Merge Recipients dialog box. Open your data source document, and add the missing header row. Then return to the main document and reattach the file.

FIGURE 22.6

A merge data source document created as a Word table

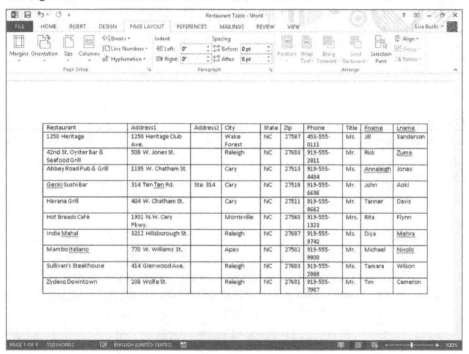

22

FIGURE 22.7

Beware of data files that don't contain a header row!

Understanding delimited files

Figure 22.8 shows a comma-separated value (*.csv) file opened in Word. The first row has the field names separated by commas, and each subsequent row contains one record, with the record's field entries separated by commas. Note that if a field is empty, two commas appear to keep the fields properly synchronized. When you attach a delimited file, you may be prompted to convert the file and confirm the encoding to use. In most cases, you can simply click OK to continue.

FIGURE 22.8

A delimited data source file can use commas, tabs, or another type of separating character.

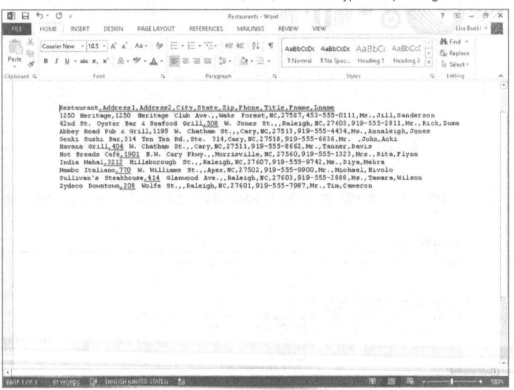

If your data file is not properly delimited or Word is unclear on the delimiter used, the Header Record Delimiters dialog box shown in Figure 22.9 appears when you attempt to attach the data source file. If not, select the proper delimiters from the Field delimiter and Record delimiter drop-down lists, and click OK.

FIGURE 22.9

If the data file doesn't contain a table, Word asks you to confirm the nature of the field and record delimiters (separators).

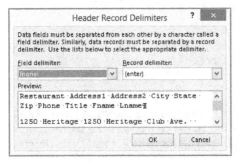

CAUTION

It's been my experience that when the Header Record Delimiters dialog box appears, chances are the file wasn't delimited properly. If you see that dialog box, click the Edit Recipient List button in the Start Mail Merge group of the Mailings tab to check the fields.

NOTE

Only use the comma delimiter when the field contents themselves don't contain commas. For example, if your data includes commas in company names (as in Widgets, LLC or Widgets, Inc.) use another type of delimiter. If you need to include a field that may be blank in some instances, such as a suite/apartment number, consecutive commas indicate the blank field in the delimited file, as in "2424 Main St.,," versus "2424 Main St., Apt. 3,".

Outlook

You can use contacts that you've entered in Outlook to perform a merge. To use data from Outlook, click Select Recipients in the Start Mail Merge group and select Choose from Outlook Contacts. The first time you do so, the Choose Profile dialog box may appear. Select a Profile Name and click OK. In Select Contacts, shown in Figure 22.10, if multiple contact folders are displayed, click the one you want to use and click OK.

FIGURE 22.10

When you select an Outlook contact folder, Word imports it.

After you click OK, the Mail Merge Recipients list appears, as shown in Figure 22.11. Notice in the lower-left corner that the Data Source list shows Contacts as the source for the records. See the later section "Selecting recipients" to learn how to select and limit which contacts you use from the list.

FIGURE 22.11

Imported Outlook contacts display correctly.

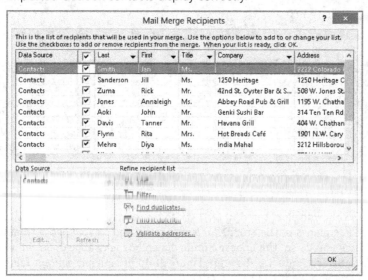

Excel

As in a Word table used for a data source, each column should hold one field and each row a single record; if you would like to include field names in row 1 as the header row, you can, but this is optional with Excel. If the workbook file has multiple tabs, the Select Table dialog box shown in Figure 22.12 appears. Click to select the table containing the data you want, and check or uncheck First row of data contains column headers as applicable.

FIGURE 22.12

Before attaching an Excel data source to a Word document, select the table you want to use.

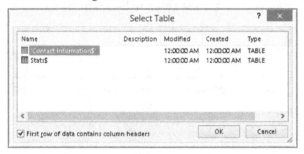

Access

As for Outlook contacts, when select an Access file or another type of database as the data source, generally Word will have no trouble interpreting the data, as it's by definition set up correctly. Similar to when you attach an Excel data source, when you attach an Access data source, you will need to select the table or query that holds the records to merge. In the Select Table dialog box, click a table or query, and then click OK.

HTML files

When working with HTML files as data sources, note that they cannot reside on the Internet. You must first save the file to your local hard drive (or at least somewhere on your LAN or in your workgroup).

In addition, using HTML files as data sources almost never work unless the data has been carefully formatted. For best results, the data should be in a table and should contain a header row, and there should be no information above the table. If there is, the Header Record Delimiters dialog box shown in Figure 22.9 will appear, cuing you that the data won't import correctly.

Another problem occurs if Word can't recognize a consistent data pattern in the file or when the data source is inconsistently formatted, such as when some rows (records) contain different numbers of columns (data fields). When that is the case and you try to attach the file, an error message like the one shown in Figure 22.13 appears. Unfortunately, when this happens, the only recourse might be to edit the file to fix the problem, which ultimately means that the original data source is probably not going to be a reliable source of additional data or updates.

FIGURE 22.13

Word displays this message when different data records contain different numbers of data fields.

Choosing the Data Document Type

After you're sure you've properly set up your data source file, you can move on to work with the main data document. Either open the document to use or start a new blank file. To choose the type of data document, in the Mailings tab click Start Mail Merge in the Start Mail Merge group, as shown in Figure 22.14. Some of the options are obvious; others are not. There are basically two kinds of data documents you can design. For one kind, each data record in the data source will result in a personalized copy of the data document, such as a form letter, a mass email, a product specification sheet, or an invoice. For the other kind, a single document is produced in which multiple records can appear on any given page. This approach is needed for creating directories, catalogs, and sheets of labels.

Contrast, for example, using an envelope (with a different address on each envelope) with using a sheet of labels (with a different address on each label). If you have only one address and want to print only one envelope or label, you don't need a data document. All you need are the procedures described in Chapter 12, "Getting Smart with Text: Building Blocks, Quick Parts, Actions (Tags), and More." When you plan to crank out stacks of envelopes, each with a different address, or sheets of labels for which no two contain the same information, you need the approach described in this chapter.

FIGURE 22.14

Letters, email messages, and envelopes use one record per output document, whereas labels and directories use multiple records for each output document.

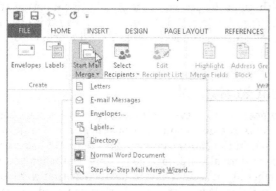

As shown in Figure 22.14, Word offers five flavors of the two basic types of data documents:

- **Letters:** Use this option for composing and designing mass mailings for which only the recipient information varies from page to page. Use this approach too when you're preparing sheets containing product or other item specifications with one piece of paper per product or item. You might use this approach, for example, not only when sending out a form letter or invoices, but also when producing a job manual wherein each page describes a different job title, and job information is stored in a database.

- **E-mail Messages:** This is identical in concept to the form letter, except that it is geared to paperless online distribution. Contrast this with using multiple email addresses in the To, Cc, or Bcc field. Using E-mail merge, each recipient can receive a personalized email. Using multiple addresses, each recipient receives the identical email.

- **Envelopes:** This is also identical in concept to the form letter, except that the resulting document will be envelopes. As a result, when you choose this option, Word begins by displaying the Envelope Options dialog box.

- **Labels:** Use this option to print to one or more sheets of labels. This combines Word's capability to print to any of hundreds of different label formats, as shown in Chapter 12, with the capability to associate a database with a document, printing many addresses (data records) on the same page, rather than the same address on each label.

- **Directory:** This is similar in concept to labels, in that you print from multiple data records on a single page. Use the directory approach when printing a catalog or any other document that requires printing multiple records per page.

To specify the kind of document, choose Start Mail Merge in the Mailings tab, and click the kind of document you want to create.

If you want step-by-step guidance through the process, note an additional option at the bottom of the Start Mail Merge list—Step-by-Step Mail Merge Wizard. Use this option if you're unfamiliar with the mail merge process. The Mail Merge Wizard process is described later in this chapter.

Restoring a Word document to Normal

Sometimes, by accident, temporary need, or whatever, a Word document becomes associated with a data file, and you want to restore the document to normal non–mail-merge status. To restore a Word document to normal, in the Mailings tab, choose Start Mail Merge in the Start Mail Merge group, and then click Normal Word Document. Note that when you restore a document to normal status, a number of tools on the Mailings toolbar that were formerly available become grayed out as unavailable. If you later decide that you need to again make the document into a data document, you will need to reestablish the data connection.

> **TIP**
>
> If there's a chance that you'll later need to restore a data connection, and if document storage space isn't a concern, rather than break the data connection for a document, save a copy of the document, giving it a name that lets you know that it has a data connection. Though establishing a data connection isn't all that difficult or time-consuming, you can usually save some time and guesswork by not having to reinvent that particular wheel.

Attaching a Data Source

To associate a Word file as the data file:

1. **Click the Mailings tab of the Ribbon, and choose Select Recipients in the Start Mail Merge group.**

2. **As shown earlier in Figure 22.1, click Type a New List, Use an Existing List, or Choose from Outlook Contacts.** If you choose the first or third option, you can proceed as described for those data sources earlier in the chapter.

3. **In the Select Data Source dialog box (Figure 22.15), change the All Data Sources list to a particular file type if desired.**

4. **Navigate to the location of the file, select it, and click Open.**

5. **Respond to any additional prompts as needed, such as selecting a delimiter or table as described earlier, and click OK.**

FIGURE 22.15

Selecting a data source for a merge

Note that once you've attached a data source to the document, Edit Recipient List and a number of other tools on the Mailings tab are no longer grayed out. If you plan to use the entire database, you can skip the following section.

Selecting recipients

If you don't plan to use the entire database, you can use the Mail Merge Recipients dialog box, shown in Figure 22.16, to select just the recipients you want to use. To open the dialog box, click Edit Recipient List in the Start Mail Merge group of the Mailings tab. Use the check boxes shown to include or exclude records. To quickly deselect all records, clear or select the check box at the top of the list, just to the right of Data Source.

Editing a data source

Depending on your data source, you sometimes can edit the contents of the file by clicking the file in the Data Source box of the Mail Merge Recipients dialog box and then clicking Edit. Make the changes you need in the Edit Data Source dialog box, and click OK. Then click Refresh to ensure the data is updated for the merge. When your data source is Outlook contacts, note that Edit is not an option. To change your Outlook data, you must use Outlook. Once you've made your change in Outlook, you can then refresh the records you see in the Mail Merge Recipients list by highlighting the data source and clicking Refresh.

FIGURE 22.16

Select just the target recipients using the Mail Merge Recipients dialog box.

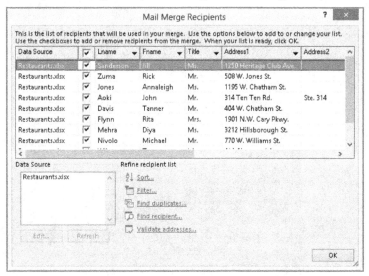

Sorting records

When editing non-Outlook data, you can sort using Word controls. Click the arrow next to a field to drop down a list of sort options, shown in Figure 22.17. For example, if you want to filter out records for which the contents are blank, click the drop-down list arrow for that field and choose Blanks. To select only records for which the email address is *not* blank, click Nonblanks. To restore the list to show all records, choose the All option.

To sort by multiple fields at the same time, in the Mail Merge Recipients dialog box, choose Sort under Refine recipient list. This displays the Filter and Sort dialog box, shown in Figure 22.18. Use this dialog box to sort by multiple criteria. For example, if letters are being hand-delivered within a company, it might be useful to sort by floor and then by room number, assuming those are separate fields. (Often, sorting just by room number accomplishes both at the same time.)

> **NOTE**
>
> If you want to take advantage of bulk mailing rates, then your pieces need to be sorted by ZIP code. Also, the USPS prefers that mailing names and addresses be entered in all capital letters. The USPS.com website includes a lot of guidance about how to prepare you mailings, including this article: http://pe.usps.com/businessmail101/addressing/deliveryaddress.htm.

FIGURE 22.17

Quickly select records for which the current field is blank or nonblank by choosing Blanks or Nonblanks.

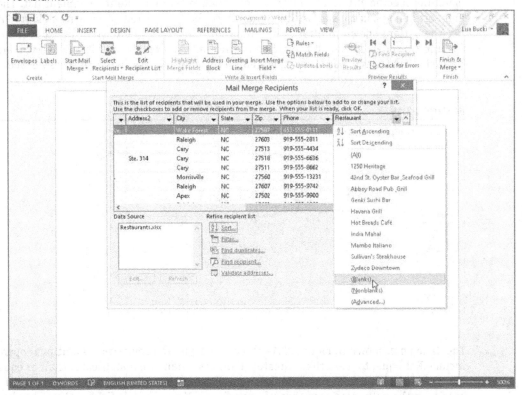

FIGURE 22.18

You can sort by up to three fields.

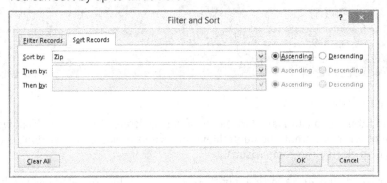

Filtering records

Word also enables you to filter records to either include or exclude records with data fields matching specific criteria. To filter records, click Filter under Refine recipient list. The Filter and Sort dialog box appears with its Filter Records tab selected, as shown in Figure 22.19. Use the options shown to filter by specific values. As shown here, you can use it to include specific Zip codes. Although the dialog box initially shows just six filter fields, you are not limited to that many. Just keep applying filters, and new rows will appear as needed.

FIGURE 22.19

You can specify multiple filter criteria.

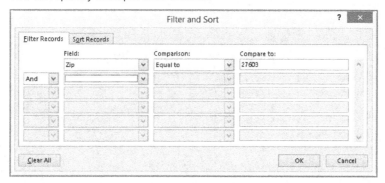

The dialog box shown in Figure 22.19 shows the Equal to comparison. Additional operators include Not equal to, Less than, Greater than, Less than or equal, Greater than or equal, Is blank, Is not blank, Contains, and Does not contain. The latter entries help you filter by text entries in the field. Also note that you can filter a list using the field's column heading, as shown in Figure 22.17. Click the column heading drop-down list entry, and then click the column contents to filter for. To remove the filter, reopen the drop-down and click (All).

> **TIP**
>
> When filtering by ZIP code, if your database contains nine-digit ZIP codes, use the Contains filter rather than the Equal to filter. Using Equal to, you would need to specify all nine digits in the filter, and specifying as many as 9,000 different filters doesn't seem like a productive use of your time.

Understanding And and Or

When setting up filters, you can make two kinds of comparisons: *And* and *Or*. If all we had were one or the other, there would be no problem, but we have both, and we don't have parentheses to help clarify the comparisons.

It helps to understand that *And* and *Or* apply to each pair of rules. You also need to understand that the *And* rule is harder to satisfy in that it requires that two conditions be met.

Depending on what comes before or follows, each and/or effectively divides the list of filters into sets of filters that are being evaluated. However, by being careful with filters, you can avoid combinations that are impossibly difficult to understand.

Suppose the filters contained the comparisons shown in Table 22.1. The first *And* applies to the Alexandria and VA filters. The second *And* applies to the Hampton and VA filters. This set of filters requires that records must be in Alexandria, VA, *Or* in Hampton, VA.

TABLE 22.1 Understanding Or and And Operators

Operator	Field	Comparison	Compare to
	City	Equal to	Alexandria
And	State	Equal to	VA
Or	City	Equal to	Hampton
And	State	Equal to	VA

Finally, understand that it's perfectly possible to set up filters that make no logical sense. Hence, Table 22.1 could have been set up with all of the Operators set to *And*. There would be no matching records, of course. It's up to you to examine the collection of resulting data records to make sure that your logic is being applied as you think it should be.

Duplicates

Databases often contain duplicate records. When mailing or emailing, especially, you want to avoid sending the same person duplicate messages. When sending invoices to large companies, this can cause problems, especially if they are received and processed by different people, resulting in double payment, and further paperwork downstream.

To find duplicates, click the Find duplicates link in the lower section of the Mail Merge Recipients dialog box. Word displays the Find Duplicates dialog box, shown in Figure 22.20. Remove the checks beside a valid duplicate to exclude it from the data merge. Look carefully, however, because Word's criteria for what constitutes a duplicate might be different from your own.

Validating addresses

The Validate addresses choice in the Mail Merge Recipients dialog box works with third-party software, such as that provided with stamps.com and other electronic postage services. If you don't have such software installed, you'll see an error message if you click the link. These services vary, but basically they check against a huge database of valid street addresses to determine whether the selected address and ZIP code combination really exists. This can save considerably on costs, because it can prevent you from mailing to addresses that don't exist or are missing information such as suite number.

FIGURE 22.20

Uncheck duplicate records to exclude them from the merge.

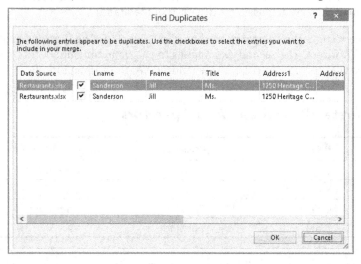

Assembling a Merge Document

Regardless of which merge document type you choose (letter, email, envelopes, labels, or directory), the process for building it is similar. There are some additional considerations for multi-record-per-page documents, however, so we will look at those separately after discussing the common elements.

When designing a letter or email you plan to send to multiple recipients using the merge feature, it's often a good idea to draft the document as you want it to appear, using placeholders in square brackets for information pertaining to the intended recipient, as shown in the following example:

Dear [name]:

We are writing to inform you that the warranty for:

[product]

which you purchased on:

[purchasedate]

will expire on [expirationdate].

If you would like to extend your warranty, you must take advantage of our extended warranty coverage plans before [expirationdate]. Costs for extending the warranty are:

1 Year: [oneyearwarranty]

2 Years: [twoyearwarranty]

3 Years: [threeyearwarranty]

Please use the enclosed card and envelope to extend your warranty before it's too late!

Yours truly,

[salesagent]

When you're done, edit your document and substitute merge fields for the placeholders.

Adding merge fields

After setting the data document type (using Start Mail Merge), associating a database with it (using Select Recipients), narrowing the list of recipients or records just to those records you plan to use, and drafting the data document, the next step is to insert merge fields into your document where you want the corresponding data fields to appear.

> **NOTE**
>
> *Merge fields* are special Word fields that correspond to the data fields in the attached data source file. For example, if you have a data field called Company, then you would insert the company name into your data document by using a MergeField field code with the name Company in it: `{ MERGEFIELD Company }`. In your data document, that field displays either as «Company» or as the name of the company associated with the current record in the data set. Use the Mailings tab's Preview Results in the Preview results group button to toggle between the merge field name and actual data.

To insert a merge field, position the insertion point where you want the field to appear (or select the placeholder if you're replacing a placeholder with a merge field). From the Mailings tab, choose Insert Merge Field, as shown in Figure 22.21. Click the field you want to insert. Using a combination of text and merge fields that you insert, complete the assembly and wording of your document. Note that in addition to individual merge fields that you can insert using the Insert Merge Field tool, you can use special sets of merge fields to save time: Address Block and Greeting Line.

> **TIP**
>
> When you insert individual merge fields, be sure to include the proper punctuation, such as spaces between fields or a comma after a greeting line. Also, you can format a field code just as you can any other text, and the merged information will appear with that formatting. For example, you could bold a merge field code to make sure the merged information appears in bold for emphasis.

FIGURE 22.21

Merge fields are data tokens that you use where you want actual data fields to appear in the data document.

Address Block

You can insert an Address Block field, which can contain a number of elements that you can select from the Insert Address Block dialog box. To determine the contents of the Address Block, position the insertion point where you want to insert the field and click Address Block in the Write & Insert Fields group of the Mailings tab. The Insert Address Block dialog box shown in Figure 22.22 appears.

Notice that it contains three sections for selecting, previewing, and correcting your address block information (if there are problems). Make your selections as indicated, and then click OK.

- **Specify address elements:** Use this section to tell Word how to define the address block. You can include the recipient's name (click one of the listed formats to select it), the company name, the postal address, as well as the country or region. If desired, you can suppress the country or region, always include it, or include it only if it's different from the country selected. You can also tell Word to format the address according to the destination country or region.

- **Preview:** Use the First, Previous, Next, and Last buttons to preview different addresses as they will appear with the selected options. It's a good idea to preview a good sampling in case some parts of the address are treated differently from how you expect, or if there are problems with missing data that will leave "holes" in the address block. (Click Preview Results if you see merge field names instead of data.)

- **Correct Problems:** If the preview isn't what you expect, click Match Fields. Use the drop-down lists in the Match Fields dialog box to change the different data elements with which each of the fields listed is associated, as shown in Figure 22.23. If you plan to reuse the address block data either for the same database or for other databases that contain the same field names, click to enable the Remember this matching... check box. Then click OK.

FIGURE 22.22

Use the Address Block tool in the Write & Insert Fields group of the Mailings tab to launch the Insert Address Block dialog box.

22

FIGURE 22.23

Use the Match Fields dialog box to associate each of 11 items with data fields from your database for the Address Block.

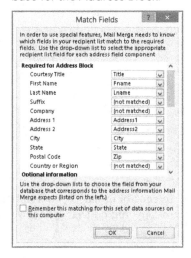

After you finish choosing Address Block settings, click OK to insert the field in the document.

Match Fields

If you preview your recipients and the merged data still looks off, click Match Fields in the Write & Insert Fields group of the mailing tab to display the Match Fields dialog box shown in Figure 22.23. Change the specified fields from your data source as needed to match up with the field names that Word uses for merge elements, and click OK.

Greeting Line

The Greeting Line merge field, like the Address Block field, is a collection of different data elements and plain text designed to save you entry time when composing data documents. Click Greeting Line in the Write & Insert Fields group of the Mailings tab. This displays the Insert Greeting Line dialog box shown in Figure 22.24. Use the Greeting line format choices to set up the greeting line, and choose a greeting line for invalid recipient names. Use the Preview buttons to test your selected greeting line options against your actual data. If something doesn't look quite right, click Match Fields, use the previously shown controls to associate the Greeting Line components with the correct merge data fields, and click OK. Back in the Insert Greeting Line dialog box, click OK to insert the Greeting Line field code at the insertion point.

FIGURE 22.24

Set and preview greeting line components.

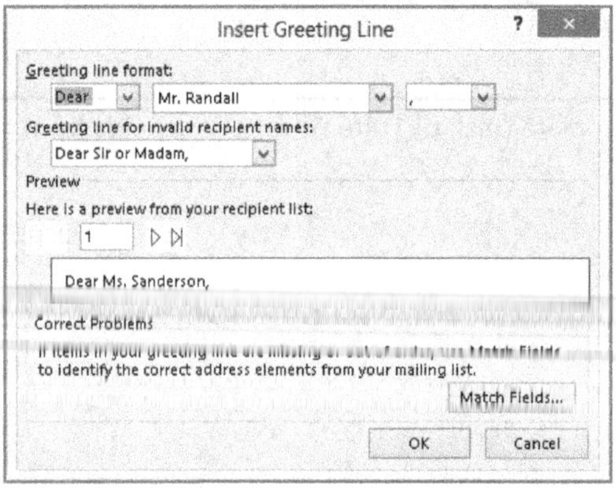

Rules

In assembling a data document, you sometimes need to control or modify how data and records are processed. Word provides nine commands to help you do that, as shown in

Figure 22.25. The entries shown in the Rules drop-down box show how those rule keywords are displayed in the data document.

FIGURE 22.25

Use the Rules drop-down list of Word fields to control how data is merged with the data document.

These rules, which are tied to specific Word field codes, are explained in Table 22.2. (Chapter 23, "Automating Document Content with Fields," explains more about field codes.) Note that many of these are supported by dialog boxes that guide you through proper syntax, making them easy to use and understand.

TABLE 22.2 **Merge Rules**

Field	Usage/Purpose
ASK	This field prompts you to provide information and assigns a bookmark to the answer you provide; the information is stored internally. A reference to the bookmark can then be used in the mail-merge document to reproduce the information you type. A default response to the prompt can also be included in the field. The ASK field displays as an empty bookmark in the mail-merge document. You might use this field in conjunction with an IF field to prompt for missing information during a merge.
FILLIN	This field prompts you to enter text, and then uses your response in place of the field in the mail-merge document. This is similar to the ASK field, except that the information can be used only in one place.
IF	This is used in mail-merge documents to control the flow and to create a conditional statement that controls whether specific mail-merge fields are printed or included in the merged document.

Continues

TABLE 22.2 *(continued)*

Field	Usage/Purpose
MERGESEQ	This field provides a counter of mail-merge documents that actually result from a merge. If you merge the entire database and do not change the base sorting, and if no records are skipped, then MERGESEQ and MERGEREC will be identical.
MERGEREC	When doing a mail merge, the MERGEREC field serves as a counter of records in the data file and doesn't count the number of documents actually printed. This field is incremented by the presence of NEXT and NEXTIF fields. If you skip records using SKIPIF, MERGEREC is incremented nonetheless.
NEXT	The NEXT field is used to include more than one record in a given document. Ordinarily, when doing a mail merge, one document is printed for each record. With the NEXT field, however, you can include multiple records in a single document. This can be useful when you need to refer to several addresses from a data file. When doing a label merge, the NEXT field is provided automatically, and appears as «Next Record».
NEXTIF	The NEXTIF statement works like the NEXT field except that it advances to the nevxt record only if an expression being evaluated is true. A typical use is to skip a given record if a particular key field is blank. For example, in an email merge, if you haven't otherwise excluded records with blank email addresses, you can use NEXTIF to do it.
SET	The SET field is used to change the text referred to by a bookmark. SET often is used in conjunction with IF to conditionally change how particular text is defined based on external factors, such as the current date, or internal factors, such as the value(s) of particular fields.
SKIPIF	The SKIPIF field is used to cancel processing of the current database record during a mail merge. For example, you might use it to screen out a particular ZIP code.

Update Labels

When the data document type is Labels, the process for properly populating the fields into the document differs a bit. After selecting Labels from the Start Mail Merge drop-down list, the Label Options dialog box appears so you can select a label type and other options, as described in Chapter 12. After you do so and click OK, use these steps to set up the label merge document:

1. **Click View gridlines in the Table group of the Table Tools ⇨ Layout tab.** It's easier to work with the label layout when you can see the label boundaries.

2. **Return to the Mailings tab, and use Select Recipients in the Start Mail Merge group to select the data source as described earlier in the chapter.**

3. **Insert field codes for the address in the upper-left table cell.**

4. **Format the field codes in the upper-left cell as desired.** For example, you may want to remove the extra spacing between lines and make the font size a bit larger.

5. **Click Update Labels in the Write & Insert Fields group of the Mailings tab.** Word copies all text, merge fields, and formatting from the first cell into each of the other cells, after the Next Record control, as shown in Figure 22.26. The result is that each sheet of labels will contain data from the same number of label cells. A sheet containing nine labels will use data from nine database records.

FIGURE 22.26

When you insert a merge field into the first label cell, Word automatically puts the Next Record control into each of the other cells.

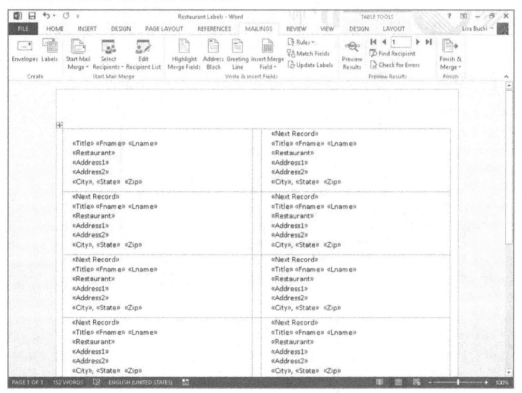

Preview Results

At any time as you go along, if you want to see what actual data will look like in your document, click the Preview Results button in the Preview Results group of the Mailings tab to toggle between the merge field codes in double angle brackets and actual data. Figure 22.27 shows field codes, while Figure 22.28 shows the preview data. Use the First, Previous, Next, Last, and Go To Record tools in the Preview Results group to move between the data records, and click Preview Results again to return to viewing field codes.

In Figure 22.28, you can see that the restaurant's address appears in the body of the document, where you clearly want the restaurant's name to appear. This can happen due to an error in either the field or the data record. You can check both and correct whichever is necessary. This shows how valuable Preview Results can be. To more easily catch errors, you can also use Highlight Merge Fields and Check for Errors, which will be discussed in the next few sections.

FIGURE 22.27

Data merge fields appear in double angle brackets.

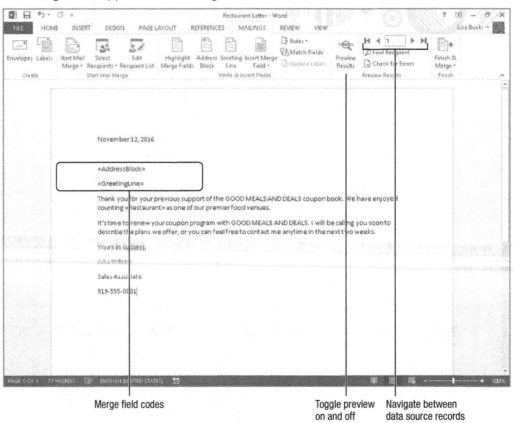

Merge field codes   Toggle preview   Navigate between
                           on and off   data source records

FIGURE 22.28

Use the Preview Results tools to ensure that the merge will produce the results you want.

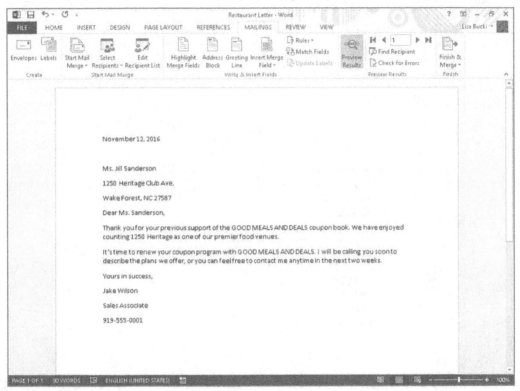

Find Recipient

To search for a specific data record or for records whose data you want to preview (with the Preview button active), click the Find Recipient tool in the Preview Results group. This displays the Find Entry dialog box shown in Figure 22.29. Type the search text in the Find field, choose All fields or click This field and select a specific field, and then click Find Next. Note that the search is not case sensitive. If there are matches, Word highlights the first matching document, and the Find Entry dialog box stays onscreen. Click Find Next to move to successive matches in the merged information, and then click Cancel when finished.

FIGURE 22.29

Use Find Entry to search for a matching record in the merged data.

Return to this tool later, after your data document has been constructed, to preview specific data records. It's better to iron out problems before committing your merge to paper or email.

Highlight Merge Fields

Use the Highlight Merge Fields tool in the Write & Insert Fields group of the Mailings tab to highlight all of the merge fields when previewing data, as shown in Figure 22.30. This can be useful if you're working on a complex document and need to recheck the logic and placement of merge fields. If, for example, you expect a given merge field result to appear in two places in the document, this tool enables you to find those locations more easily so you can verify that the correct text appears. If you're using conditional rules, such as Skip Record If, Next Record If, and If, this also helps you focus on the results so you can verify that the rules are working as expected.

FIGURE 22.30

When previewing, you can turn on highlighting to see which data is merged.

Check for Errors

To avoid wasting paper and other resources, when you think you're done, click Check for Errors in the Preview Results group of the Mailings tab to display the options shown in Figure 22.31.

FIGURE 22.31

Rather than waste paper or send out errant emails, use the error checking tool to avoid logical errors or other unwanted surprises.

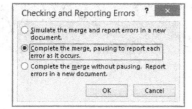

The options in the Checking and Reporting Errors dialog box work as follows:

- **Simulate the merge and report errors in a new document:** Use this option to examine any and all errors in a new document.

- **Complete the merge, pausing to report each error as it occurs:** Use this option once you've determined that there are errors, so you can observe the error in action.

- **Complete the merge without pausing. Report errors in a new document:** Use this option to go ahead and complete the merge without stopping at each error, sending the error report to a new document.

Finishing the merge

Once the data document is ready and has been thoroughly debugged and certified as error free, it's time to go through the final motions. The Finish & Merge drop-down list in the Finish group of the Mailings tab provides three options, shown in Figure 22.32, *regardless of the type of data document chosen.*

> **CAUTION**
>
> Be careful about clicking Send E-Mail Messages. You don't want to accidentally send sensitive information like a list of preferred clients to the wrong recipients. You also don't want to email information that would be otherwise confusing or embarrassing, such as a set of labels.

FIGURE 22.32

It's usually a good idea not to send a merge directly to a printer until the results have been thoroughly examined.

> **NOTE**
>
> Don't forget to save and name your original merge document in addition to any documents based on it.

Editing individual documents

From the Finish & Merge drop-down list in the Finish group of the Mailings tab, choose the Edit Individual Documents option if you want to save your merged results for future use. For example, suppose you have a set of labels that seldom changes and which you need to print out every week. Rather than go through the mail-merge exercise each week, save the merge labels in a separate Word document, and then print them each time you need them. That way, you don't need to go through the whole mail-merge routine unless the underlying database has changed.

You might also choose this option if you don't trust other ways of proofing the results. Instead of printing from the Mailings tab, send the results to a new document where you can examine each of them, and then print when you're ready.

When you choose this option, Word displays the Merge to New Document dialog box shown in Figure 22.33. If you want Word to create a limited number of output documents, choose either Current record or indicate a From/To range. Click OK to create a new Word document with the merged data.

FIGURE 22.33

Select the desired records to merge and click OK.

Printing documents

From the Finish & Merge drop-down list in the Finish group of the Mailings tab, choose the Print Documents option when you're certain that the merge will give you the results you want. When you click Print Documents, Word displays a dialog box with similar options to those shown earlier in Figure 22.33, this time sporting a Merge to Printer title bar. Specify which records to merge and click OK to launch the Print dialog box. Make any additional choices and decisions, including which printer to use, cross your fingers, and click OK.

> **TIP**
>
> If you don't trust all of the previews and error checks at this stage, you've probably been burned by mail merge in the past. If you still want to be sure before wasting a tree, use the Name drop-down list in the Print dialog box to see whether you have an option that produces electronic images of printed pages, rather than actual printed pages. Using Office 2013 and Windows 8, you should at the very least see Microsoft XPS Document Writer, which is Microsoft's answer to PDF files. Then you can review what actually amounts to your best possible print preview.

Sending email messages

From the Finish & Merge drop-down list in the Finish group of the Mailings tab, choose the Send E-Mail Messages option if you're working on an email merge. When you click Send E-mail Messages, Word displays the Merge to E-mail dialog box, shown in Figure 22.34.

FIGURE 22.34

A Subject line for the merged email messages here

In addition to the Send Records options (All, Current Record, and From/To), Word provides three additional options for which you should make selections before clicking OK to merge and send the messages:

- **To:** Select the data source field that holds recipient email addresses.

- **Subject line:** This is very important. Studies show that 73.4 percent of all non-spam email merges sent omit the subject line. Don't become a statistic! Replace that blank subject line. (This statistic was made up by the author. Nonetheless, don't send subjectless emails!)

- **Mail format:** Many email recipients wisely have their email options set up to read all email as plain text (this gives them a shot at preventing any automatic naughtiness from being executed when email is opened). Options provided are Attachment, Plain Text, and HTML, the latter being the default. Though Attachment seems like a good compromise for formatted email, this option provides no way for you to include any message text for the body of the email. When and if you use that option, make sure the subject line isn't blank.

Mail Merge Pane/Wizard

If you'd rather not use the individual tools in the Mailings tab of the Ribbon and prefer a little more assistance when performing a mail merge, Word provides the Mail Merge Wizard. Start a new blank document (or open a document you want to use as the basis for a data document). Click the Mailings tab, click the Start Mail Merge button in the Start Mail Merge group, and choose Step-by-Step Mail Merge Wizard. This opens the Mail Merge pane, shown in Figure 22.35. Just follow along its steps from there.

FIGURE 22.35

Choosing the Wizard opens the Mail Merge task pane.

Step 1: Select Document Type

In Step 1, shown in Figure 22.35, choose the type of data document you want to create under Select document type. Click the Next: Starting document link at the bottom of the pane to move to the next wizard step.

Step 2: Starting Document

The Mail Merge task pane next presents three options under Select starting document. Note that when you choose any of these options, Word explains the option in the lower part of the task pane. The options are as follows:

- **Use the current document:** Start from the current document and use the Mail Merge wizard to add recipient information (merge fields).
- **Start from a template:** Start from a template, which you can customize as needed by adding merge fields and/or other contents. If you choose this option, click Select Template to be shown a list of all of the available templates (at least the ones that Word knows about). Note that despite the option's wording, it does *not* present you with a list of "ready-to-use mail merge" templates.
- **Start from existing document:** Open an existing mail merge or other document and change it to fit the current need by changing the contents or recipients. Recent mail merge documents, if any, will be listed. If the one you want isn't listed, click Open to navigate to the one you want, select it, and then click Open.

After making your selection, choose Next: Select recipients at the bottom of the task pane.

Step 3: Select Recipients

In Step 3, select from Use an existing list, Select from Outlook contacts, and Type a new list. These options, shown in Figure 22.36, correspond to the identical options described in detail earlier in the chapter. If you leave Use an existing list selected, click Browse to find the data source file, and choose a table or worksheet if prompted. In the Mail Merge Recipients dialog box that opens, use it to work with the records as described earlier. Click Next: Write your letter at the bottom of the pane to move on.

Step 4: Write Your Letter

In Step 4, you are greeted with four options:

- **Address block:** This enables you to insert an Address Block field as described earlier. See the discussion under "Address Block" for additional details.
- **Greeting line:** The Greeting line option enables you to insert a Greeting Line merge field. See the "Greeting Line" section for more information.
- **Electronic postage:** As indicated previously, the functioning of this option requires the installation of third-party software that enables you to apply postage to items you send.
- **More items:** This option displays the Insert Merge Field dialog box shown in Figure 22.37. Leave Database Fields selected to see the fields in your data source. Before displaying Insert Merge Field, move the insertion point to the document location where you want a merge field to appear, click More items, select the field,

and click Insert. Dismiss the dialog box and repeat this series of actions for each merge field. In practice, however, if you know which fields you want to insert, select (with Shift+click or Ctrl+click) and insert them all at once, and then cut and paste them where you want them to go.

FIGURE 22.36

Select the desired recipients option and then click Next: Write your letter.

FIGURE 22.37

The associated fields in your data source are listed when you choose Database Fields.

Step 5: Preview Your Letters

In Step 5, shown in Figure 22.38, use the controls shown to move from record to record in your database. Note that the « and » tools correspond to the Previous and Next button in the Mailings tab. When you finish previewing the merge, click Next: Complete the merge.

FIGURE 22.38

Use the final wizard steps to preview the data document and complete the merge.

Step 6: Complete the Merge

The contents of the final Mail Merge pane vary depending on the document type. When the document type is a letter, the options are to send the merged results to the printer or to send them to "individual letters." Actually, that's not at all what the option does. Instead, it sends all of the merged letter results to a single new document, in which the individual letters are separated by section breaks.

Summary

In this chapter, you've learned about data considerations when preparing a data source document in Word or another application. You then learned how to use each of the mail merge tools in the Mailings tab to begin a mail merge document, attach a data source with records to a merge document, insert merge fields, and complete a data merge. You've also seen that this feature isn't just for mail merge, but has many other uses as well. You should now be able to do the following:

- Create a new data source file and prepare data from various sources
- Create a new data source list within Word
- Use Outlook contacts as a source for mail merge data
- Select a Word, HTML, Access, Excel, and other data file for the merge data source
- Select just the records you want for the merge
- Insert composite merge fields, such as the Address Block and Greeting Line, as well as control how those fields are constituted
- Integrate the merge fields with your other document content
- Update labels
- Finish by merging to a document or printer
- Use the Mail Merge Wizard

22

Automating Document Content with Fields

IN THIS CHAPTER

- Understanding field codes
- Inserting fields with the Field dialog box
- Customizing fields
- Using field syntax and switches
- Reviewing available fields by category

This book has touched on fields several times, but only in relation to their role in other Word features. You've seen fields used to insert dates and page numbers, to number equations, and a few other things. So far, however, the book hasn't delved into fields and how to use them to automate document content.

A number of tasks that required fields in Word 2003 and earlier can now be performed more efficiently and elegantly with content controls (contained in the Controls section of the Developer tab; see Chapter 24, "Creating Custom Forms"). If you work with complex documents in compatibility mode, you are much more likely to encounter fields than when working in the .docx format.

Moreover, a number of linking tasks that require the use of fields in a compatibility-mode document can be performed in ways that are more robust (harder to break) in the XML-based Word .docx format, so when you insert links you're less likely to see field codes than before. Instead, much is done behind the scenes with XML technology.

Yet some Word 2013 features—dates, page numbers, mail merge, tables of contents, indexes, and some others—still do rely on fields. This book covers a number of the field-dependent features elsewhere. This chapter's mission is not to redundantly cover those other features. Rather, it is to provide a strong background and foundation that helps you thoroughly understand the relationship between fields and specific features, and how you can insert fields manually to make a document easier to use and update. Equipped with this information, you'll be in a solid position to take advantage of the power of fields when needed, to choose between legacy and newer approaches when the option presents itself, and to deal with the occasional challenges that inevitably creep in.

And Field Codes Are ... ?

Field codes are special sets of instructions in Word documents. They sometimes tell Word to display the current date, the number of pages in a document or a document section, an index, a table of contents, the contents of all or of part of a linked document, or the file name and folder where the current document is stored. Field instructions (called *switches*) also tell Word how to display the specified information.

Word enables you to update most fields. When the source information for a field changes, you can update the field so it displays the latest information. This enables you to turn documents into more dynamic information containers, rather than static documents that always contain the same information. To update a field, click it and press F9. Other update methods are available as well, as you will see later in this chapter.

You can format fields just like regular text. You can apply font, paragraph, and other formatting to field results so that they blend in with your document. Sometimes you don't even know information is in a field code until you look more carefully. As you will see, however, for the person working on the document, knowing that something is a field is critically important.

Many fields can be unlinked easily and turned into permanent content that doesn't change. This enables you to create a snapshot, rather than dynamic content. This means that you can use the convenience of a field to insert today's date, but then lock that date in so that when you look at a letter years from now it will have the original date, rather than some date in 2018. That way you'll know when the letter was written, but if you repurpose a copy of that letter, you can unlock the date field so it can be updated.

Mastering Field Basics

As suggested earlier, sometimes fields are inserted automatically as part of some other process, such that you aren't even specifically aware that fields are involved. For example, in the Insert tab's Text group, click the Insert Date and Time field button, as shown in Figure 23.1.

FIGURE 23.1

Some features such as Insert Date and Time insert a field.

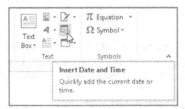

In response, the Date and Time dialog box springs to life. If you choose a format and click OK, you'll get just the date and/or time in the format selected, and not a field. If you enable the Update automatically option indicated in Figure 23.2 before clicking OK, Word instead inserts a DATE field.

FIGURE 23.2

Update automatically instructs Word to insert a Date field code instead of just the date and time.

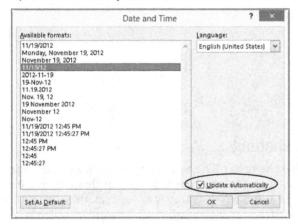

Updating fields

The word *update* has been used several times because it's impossible to talk about fields other-wise. Updating a field simply means forcing Word to reevaluate that field in light of any changes that might have occurred either to it directly or to source materials on which it is based.

To update a field, select it and do one of the following:

- Press F9.
- Right-click it and choose Update Field.
- If the field is in a special container that has an Update button, click the field to display the Update button, and then click that button (see Figure 23.3). Containers are discussed further in the next section, "Controlling field display shading."

Update a field when it has been created or edited manually or when the source or circumstances have changed. Circumstances can include a wide variety of things that affect context. You will learn more about them throughout this chapter.

FIGURE 23.3

Date fields are enclosed in special containers to alert you to their special status. Notice the Update button.

Controlling field display shading

When you insert a date field using the Insert Date and Time button, it initially looks like a simple date (depending on your settings—more about that later in this section). However, if you select the date or use the mouse to hover over it, you see something very different, as shown in Figure 23.3. The gray container shown is a special means by which Word displays some fields and a number of other features so that you realize you're not dealing with ordinary text. Not all fields display this way; in fact, most do not. Because date fields have been a frequent source of confusion and problems in the past, however, Microsoft has chosen to display them this way in recent versions of Word.

Most other fields, such as tables of contents and indexes, don't display in containers. How or whether those fields display in a special way is up to you.

To change the way fields are displayed, choose File ➪ Options ➪ Advanced. Scroll down to Show document content, and note the setting for Field shading, shown in Figure 23.4.

In addition to using special containers for some fields, Word can shade fields so that you're aware of their presence in your document. The options are as follows:

- **Never:** This is not a good choice for everyday work; see the accompanying Warning.
- **Always:** This is a great choice if you're prone to accidentally editing field results by mistake. Use this option if the presence of shading isn't too distracting.
- **When selected:** The default; this is a good compromise choice for most users. This means that when a field is contained in your document, you won't necessarily know it until you click on the field and try to edit it.

FIGURE 23.4

To avoid accidentally deleting or mishandling fields, it's a good idea not to set Field shading to Never.

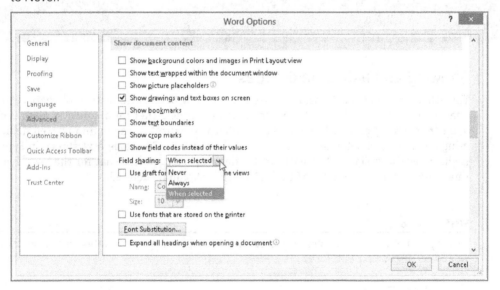

The When selected option provides a nice balance of information and aesthetics, as shown in Figure 23.5. With Field shading set to display When selected, Word shades only the field holding the insertion point. If Always had been selected, all four fields would have been shaded.

FIGURE 23.5

The default setting shades only the field you click in

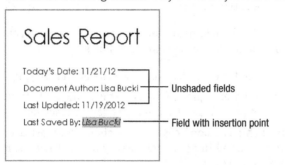

Sales Report

Today's Date: 11/21/12 ——┐
Document Author: Lisa Buckl ——┤—— **Unshaded fields**
Last Updated: 11/19/2012 ——┘

Last Saved By: *Lisa Buckl* —————— **Field with insertion point**

> **CAUTION**
>
> With Field shading set to Never, it's possible to edit the interior of a field's displayed results without realizing it. This frequently happens with dates and tables of contents. The next time you update fields (which can even happen automatically when you print a document), however, your careful edits get zapped! If you have a tendency to do this, consider changing to the Always setting for field shading.

Showing and hiding field codes

The other major option shown in Figure 23.4 is Show field codes instead of their values. Enable this option to display the underlying field code either for diagnostic reasons or so you can manually edit it. If you don't see what you expect to see in an inserted field, toggling a field code display on can help solve the mystery. The same text shown in Figure 23.5 is shown again in Figure 23.6 with field codes displayed. Notice that for the Last Updated line, there is an extra field, LASTSAVEDBY, that should be deleted.

FIGURE 23.6

Displaying field codes enables you to see what's happening behind the scenes and figure out what's causing unexpected results.

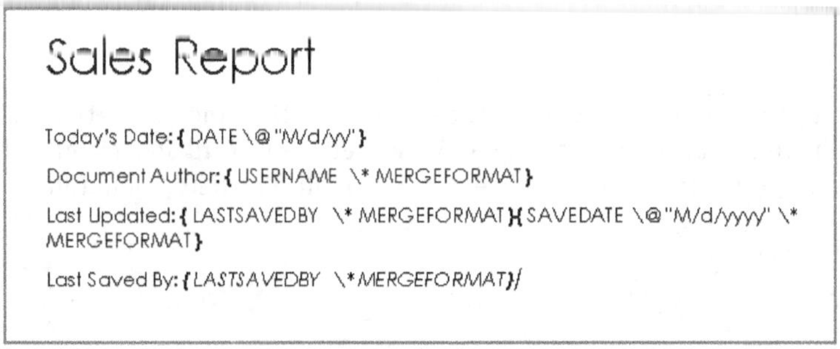

Sales Report

Today's Date: { DATE \@ "M/d/yy" }

Document Author: { USERNAME * MERGEFORMAT }

Last Updated: { LASTSAVEDBY * MERGEFORMAT }{ SAVEDATE \@ "M/d/yyyy" * MERGEFORMAT }

Last Saved By: { LASTSAVEDBY * MERGEFORMAT }

The Show field codes instead of their values option shown in Figure 23.4 displays all field codes, not just the one in question. To see just the one in question, right-click it and choose Toggle Field Codes, as shown in Figure 23.7. If you select text holding multiple fields before right-clicking, this command will toggle all fields in the selection. Toggling one or several field codes can be helpful when you're trying to understand what's happening with a particular set of related fields. If you are familiar with the syntax of the field, you can also edit the field directly, rather than editing it with the Field dialog box or using other indirect methods (such as Insert ⇨ Text ⇨ Date and Time or Page Number).

FIGURE 23.7

Right-click a field (or a selection that contains multiple fields) and choose Toggle Field Codes to show the underlying field codes for fields in the selection.

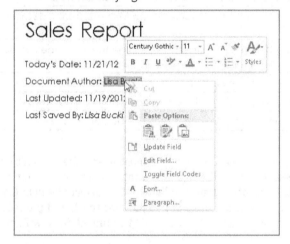

23

Field keyboard shortcuts

When you need to display all the fields as codes, rather than having to drill into the File ⇨ Options ⇨ Advanced settings, it's much simpler and quicker to press Alt+F9. Other field-related shortcut keys incorporating F9 or F11, as listed in Table 23.1, perform such actions as updating fields.

TABLE 23.1 Field Keyboard Shortcuts

Shortcut	Action
F9	Update fields—updates all fields contained in the current selection.
Ctrl+F9	Insert field characters—inserts new field code braces for manually inserting fields.
Shift+F9	Toggle field display—toggles field code display for fields contained in the current selection.
Alt+F9	View field codes—toggles field code display for all fields in the entire document.
Ctrl+Shift+F9	Unlink fields—converts all qualifying fields in the selection into hard text; once this action is done, the field can't be updated anymore.
Alt+Shift+F9	Do field click—alternative to double-clicking MacroButton and GoToButton fields.
F11	Next field—selects the next field in the document. Field codes do not need to be displayed for this command or the next.
Shift+F11	Previous field—selects the previous field in the document.
Ctrl+F11	Lock fields—prevents fields in the selection from being updated.
Ctrl+Shift+F11	Unlock fields—unlocks fields so that they can be updated.

In Table 23.1, notice the last two commands. Unknown by most users, these aren't used nearly enough, but they are exceedingly useful when you want to control whether a date field, a link to bookmarked text, or some other field can be updated. Select the field (in fact, if it's the very next field in the document you can press F11 to go right to it), and press Ctrl+F11. Press F9 to try to update it. It doesn't work! Press Ctrl+Shift+F11 to unlock it. Now F9 works.

TIP

If you want a good test field for trying out such behavior, insert a Time field, using an option that includes displaying seconds. That way you'll never have to wait more than a second before the field is out of date.

Recall from the beginning of this chapter that some field operations have been replaced by XML relational linking—such as when you insert a link to a picture. In Word 97–2003 compatibility mode, you still get an INCLUDEPICTURE field, but not in a Word 2013 .docx file. What's interesting is that the F9 key works to update the non-field picture links, but Ctrl+F11 does *not* work to lock them. Worse, once you've updated such a link by pressing F9, Ctrl+Z won't undo the update.

Other shortcut menu tools

In addition to the Toggle Field Codes option shown in Figure 23.7, there are other contextual commands. Note that these appear only when a field is selected:

- **Update Field:** See "Updating Fields" earlier in this chapter.
- **Edit Field:** This command opens the Field dialog box for the selected field, as shown in Figure 23.8. This enables you to use the interface to make changes in the field, rather than edit the field directly. Use this option if you're uncomfortable with direct field editing and/or you're unfamiliar with the needed syntax. Note that Edit Field does not work with all fields in the same way. For example, it doesn't work with the Table of Contents (TOC) field unless the entire table of contents is perfectly selected. If you get a generic Field dialog box rather than the specific one you're looking for, verify that the selection doesn't include something other than a field code, or return to the original command that created the field (such as Insert ⇨ Table of Contents).

FIGURE 23.8

The Field dialog box's Field properties section enables you to pick the options, and it builds the field code behind the scenes.

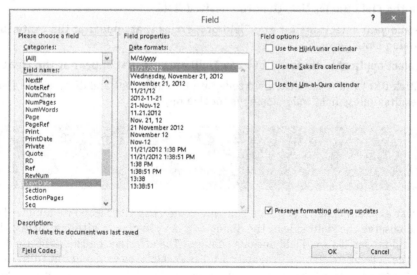

Using the Field Dialog Box to Insert a Field

In the Field dialog box, you choose the options you want and Word automatically builds the necessary field code for you. Here's how to use the dialog box to create a field:

1. **Click Insert, click Explore Quick Parts in the Text group, and then click Field to display the dialog box shown in Figure 23.8.**

2. **Under Please choose a field, open the Categories drop-down list, and click a field category.** If you choose All, all the different possible fields (at least the ones to which the interface provides access) are shown under Field names. The dialog box also provides several categories that can help steer you in a particular direction.

3. **In the Field names list, click the desired field.**

4. **Make your selections for any Field properties that appear at the center of the dialog box.**

5. **Select applicable choices from any Field options that appear at the right.**

6. **Click OK.** Word inserts the field code into the document and displays the field results (unless field code display is toggled on).

If you're just exploring the Field dialog box, you could click the second item under Field Names and observe the right side of the dialog box. As you choose different fields, the array of Field properties and Field options changes. The offerings on the right are determined by the type of field and its capabilities. For example, some are designed to work with bookmarks, and a list is offered accordingly. Others work with dates, and corresponding date formats are shown from which you can choose.

Caveats for Mergeformat

Note that many fields have an option to Preserve formatting during updates, seen in the lower right in Figure 23.8. When you select this option Word adds a * MERGEFORMAT switch to the field code. For example, a DATE field code with this option might look like this:

```
{ DATE \@ "MMMM d, yyyy" \* MERGEFORMAT }
```

The * MERGEFORMAT switch tells Word to preserve any formatting you might have applied so that in a subsequent update your formatting will be preserved. That is the theory, and it works quite well for some fields, including dates. For example, if you make that date bold, it will stay bold in subsequent updates.

However, it doesn't necessarily work for REF fields to bookmarks for which the contents change, or for a number of other fields. Consider what happens if the bookmarked passage is:

[Now is the time for all good men to come to the aid of their country.]

You can use a REF field to reproduce that text elsewhere in the document. If the bookmark's name is "countrymen," the field code { REF countrymen * MERGEFORMAT } could reproduce the original text elsewhere in the document. Suppose you add italics to the word *good* in the reproduced text, but it's not italicized in the original. With the * MERGEFORMAT switch in place, updating the field will leave "good" alone. Without the switch, "good" reverts to its original form.

Now consider what will happen if you completely rewrite the original text so that it no longer contains the word *good* at all, but still uses the same bookmark. In this case, Word arbitrarily formats the seventh word in italics when you update the REF field! Keep this odd behavior in mind before you rely heavily on the Preserve formatting option. It's best when formatting field results to use only formatting that applies to the entire field result, rather than to individual words.

Field Codes and Hide Codes

Looking back at Figure 23.8, with Categories set to (All) and Field Names set to SaveDate, notice the Field Codes button in the lower-left corner. If you click it, the button face now says Hide Codes. The right part of the dialog box now says Advanced field properties, and includes a Field codes text box with the field information in it, as shown in Figure 23.9.

23

FIGURE 23.9

With the Field codes box displayed, the Field dialog box provides a place for you to enter the field code, and displays the syntax model below the fill-in box.

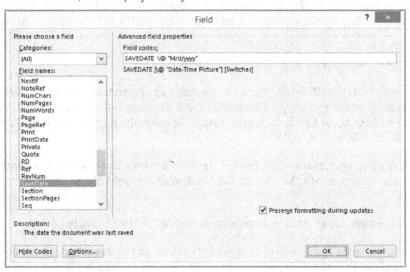

The *syntax model* shown below the Field code text box provides information how to manually edit the field. For some fields, the Options button next to Hide Codes is grayed out as unavailable. That doesn't mean that no options are possible for this field code; you can just click Hide codes to redisplay the previous options for the field in the dialog box. When the Options button is active, clicking it opens the Field Options dialog box shown in Figure 23.10.

FIGURE 23.10

Field Options enables you to customize a field without memorizing complicated syntax.

Click a listed option on either the General Switches or Field Specific Switches tab, review the Description that appears near the bottom of the dialog box to determine whether you've selected the appropriate option, and then click Add to Field. Repeat as needed, and then click OK to return to the field dialog box. Click OK again if you are finished editing the field.

The next section explains more about field switches, regardless of whether you want to enter them in the Field dialog box or display a field code in the document and edit it manually.

Using Switches to Customize a Field

Some fields are very simple. Their only syntax is the keywords by which they're identified. The field { BIBLIOGRAPHY } for example, uses no parameters whatsoever. Other fields can be rather complex, requiring both parameters and switches to achieve the desired effect. Furthermore, for some reason known only to Microsoft, some fields require quotes around literal arguments, whereas others do not.

Although syntax can vary substantially for various field types, a number of general rules apply. The general form for the field statement is as follows:

```
{ keyword [instructions] [switches] }
```

> **NOTE**
>
> Technically, Word distinguishes slightly between what appears in the middle brackets and shorter field-specific switches. But because the Field Options dialog box calls them all switches, this chapter follows suit.

Note that anything inside brackets [] is optional. Anything not in brackets is required.

The keyword can be any the field types (including field types created by third parties for Word add-ins; those fields can be used only if the corresponding add-in has been installed). The field character pair, which you can insert by pressing Ctrl+F9, can also be used to enclose just a bookmark reference, such as {duedate}. In such cases, the REF keyword is implied, and is almost equivalent to {REF duedate}. I say *almost* equivalent, because the two fields behave differently sometimes. For example, if you apply formatting to a REF field code's displayed results, Word adds a * MERGEFORMAT switch to the field. If you apply formatting to a plain bookmark field that doesn't use REF, Word will not add the switch. If you right-click a REF bookmark field and choose Edit Field, you'll get the full services of the REF field, replete with a list of bookmarks and switches. If you right-click a plain bookmark field, you'll get no services at all.

Anytime the first word in a field statement isn't one of the recognized keywords, Word tries to interpret the field as a bookmark. When manually inserting a field code, if you mistype or if the bookmark name isn't otherwise defined, when you try updating the resulting field Word informs you that something is wrong by yelling "Error! Bookmark not defined." If you see this error message, it means that you've mistyped a keyword or a bookmark or that a bookmark has been deleted.

The actual ordering of arguments and switches matters sometimes, but not always. As a general rule, switches that affect the entire field precede any arguments. A switch that affects a particular parameter usually appears immediately after the parameter it affects.

You can use three types of general switches. These can be used with a number of different fields and they affect how the results of fields are displayed:

- Text format
- Numeric format
- Date format

Text format switches

Text format switches use the following syntax:

```
\* format
```

They are used to affect how certain text will appear. The format options can be any of the keywords that follow.

> **NOTE**
>
> Each switch only works with certain fields. For example, adding the * firstcap switch to the AUTHOR field does not change the capping of the username information used by that field.

- *** alphabetic:** This switch converts the numerical result of an expression into lowercase letters, producing an alphabetical numbering result. For uppercase letters, capitalize the first letter of the * alphabetic switch: Alphabetic. The numerals 1 through 26 produce a through z, 27 through 52 produce aa through zz, and so on. For example, {= * alphabetic 2} displays as a single lowercase b. If you add 26 to it (28), it displays as two b's, etc. The maximum number you can display this way is 780, which displays as 30 z's. Use this if you're planning a nap.

- *** Arabic:** This switch is the default and results in normal Arabic numerals. For example, {=2^16 * Arabic} displays as 65536.

- *** caps:** Any text in the resulting expression is displayed in initial caps. For example, with the SET bookmark field {SET greeting "dear senator"}, the corresponding bookmark reference {greeting * caps} would result in Dear Senator.

- *** cardtext:** This switch displays a numeric expression in cardinal form. For example, {=666666 * cardtext} displays as six hundred sixty-six thousand six hundred sixty-six. This can be handy if you use Word to write legal documents in which numerical amounts and dates sometimes are spelled out.

- *** CHARFORMAT: and * MERGEFORMAT:** The * CHARFORMAT switch affects the character format of text that's displayed. If neither * CHARFORMAT nor * MERGEFORMAT is specified, the text is displayed exactly as it appears in its original form. If * CHARFORMAT is specified, the displayed result has the same character formatting as the first character in the field keyword or bookmark name. This lets you permanently set the formatting of the displayed result. If * MERGEFORMAT is specified, the displayed result takes on the character format of the current result the next time the field is updated. When no format switch is used, note that a reformatted field always reverts to the original format when updated. If you change the text contained in the bookmark when * MERGEFORMAT is specified, any new formatting done to the displayed field result will be applied to the field when it is updated. Without * MERGEFORMAT, the displayed formatting of the field will revert to that of the text it references. Use the following guidelines when you have to decide which switch to use:

  - Use no switch at all when you want to preserve original formatting. You might want to do this for such things as business logos whose original appearance must not vary by context.

  - Use * CHARFORMAT when you want to ensure that the display result matches what you're typing right now, such as boilerplate text, an address, or the signature line in a letter. The first letter of the bookmark will be in your current font and point size (unless you explicitly change it), pretty well guaranteeing that the displayed text will blend in.

  - Use * MERGEFORMAT when you plan to reformat the displayed text and want the formatting retained. You might use this approach for special text—such as a book title or product name—for which the font might vary markedly depending on where you're using it.

- *** dollartext:** The dollartext format is a variation of cardtext, producing the kind of result you might want when writing the amount in long form on checks. For example, { = 4577.89 * dollartext} would result in four thousand five hundred seventy-seven and 89/100.

- *** firstcap:** The firstcap format capitalizes the first word only in the displayed result. For example, {QUOTE * firstcap "now is the season of our discontent"} would result in Now is the season of our discontent. Note that with the * firstcap switch you would still get the identical result even if the text inside the field were all capitals or alternating capitals and lowercase.

- *** hex:** The hex format switch displays a number in hexadecimal form. For example, { = 16384 * hex } displays as 4000. The largest number that can be displayed this way in Word 2013 is 65,535 (FFFF).

23

- *** lower:** The lower format setting displays text in all lowercase. For example, {QUOTE * lower "WHAT DO YOU MEAN 'STOP YELLING!'"} results in what do you mean 'stop yelling!'

- *** ordinal:** The * ordinal switch adds st, nd, rd, and th endings to numbers. For example, { =5283 * ordinal} produces 5283rd.

- *** ordtext:** Ordtext adds ordinal endings to the text versions of numbers. For example, {= 999999 * ordtext} yields nine hundred ninety-nine thousand nine hundred ninety-ninth. That, by the way, is as high as Word will go. The number 1,000,000 results in an error.

- *** ROMAN:** The * ROMAN switch dresses your text up in a toga. Just kidding. It yields a Roman numeral. The expression Microsoft Office { =2010 * ROMAN } results in Microsoft Office MMX. Incidentally, the highest you can go is 32,767, which results in MMMMMMMMMMMMMMMMMMMMMMMMMMMMMMMMDCCLXVII. Higher numbers are met with an error message. The lowest you can go is 1 because, as every math student learns, the Romans had no zero. If you try to display 0, you'll get only a simple space. Try a negative number, and you'll get an error message.

- *** upper:** The * upper switch causes the field's text to display in all caps. For example, {QUOTE * upper "tHiS iS mIxEd Up"} rather disingenuously proclaims THIS IS MIXED UP.

Numeric format switches

Numeric format switches, sometimes called numeric picture switches, have the following syntax:

```
\# format
```

These are quite versatile, enabling you to format numbers in a wide variety of ways.

(number placeholder)

The # parameter is sometimes a source of confusion. That's because in addition to being used as the overall numeric format switch (\#), it can also be used as a specification or argument within the switch — for example, {=6765.44 \# $#,.##}. Note that the \# in this field is the numeric switch. The additional # parameters specify how the number should appear. In this case, the noted field would produce $6,765.44. The $ means that the result will be preceded by $. The next # is a placeholder for any significant digits to the left of the decimal point. The comma means that commas will be used every three places to the left. The remaining .## reserves two significant digits to the right of the decimal point. The number 6765.444444 would therefore be displayed as $6,765.44.

0 (zero placeholder)

The numeral 0 is used as a placeholder to guarantee the same order of precision in numbers. This is useful when you have multiple formula fields that ordinarily might yield different precisions. For example, it's generally unacceptable to list the same statistic for different individuals using different precisions, such as in the following table:

Courtney	4.216
Ryan	3.7
Colleen	4.4
Matt	4.7231

Suppose these numbers were all exact, and the result of calculations performed by Word. By using the same numeric switch in all the calculation fields (for example, {=59/14 \#0.000}), you ensure that all the results are shown to thousandths, with a leading 0 for any that are less than 1 (for example, 0.412 instead of .412).

x

When x is used at the left edge of any other arguments, Word truncates additional digits that don't fit in the reserved space. For example, {=42753 \# x#.00} results in 53.00 because x# reserves only two places to the left of the decimal point. When used to the right of the decimal point, x serves the same purpose as #.

. (decimal point)

The decimal point is used in conjunction with # and 0 placeholders to specify the precision of the displayed result.

, (commas for three-digit groups)

The comma is used to insert commas to separate three-digit groups (thousands) to the left of the decimal point. If you want only commas and numbers, the comma and any other number placeholder (except for x) will work. You don't need {=55000 \# ###,###} to get 55,000. A simple {=45000 \# #,} works just as well.

+ (forcing the plus sign to display)

Include the plus sign to force the positive or negative display of the number. No sign is displayed for 0. Consider the following example:

The temperature in Frostbite Falls, Minnesota, was {=sum(weathertable[A1]) \# +#}.

If the A1 cell in a table bookmarked as weathertable says –57, it will display as –57. If it's 37 in the table, then the field result will display +37, and the residents will be putting on their shorts and T-shirts.

; (semicolon)

The semicolon is used to specify different formats for positive, negative, and 0. If a single semicolon is used, the picture format to the left controls the display of positive and zero values, and the picture format to the right of the semicolon controls the display of negative numbers. If two semicolons are used, the first argument specifies positive format, the second specifies negative format, and the third specifies zero format.

For example, consider the switch \# *+###*;^+###^;=0.#=. The numbers 65, –7, and 0 would display respectively as *+65*, ^–7^, and =0.0=. Why would you do that? Because you can!

' (single quote)

Single quotes are used to insert literal text into the number display when the text contains characters otherwise reserved for use as part of the format switch. When you do this, the entire numeric format must be enclosed in double quotes.

Enclosing reserved characters in single quotes prevents the single-quoted text from being interpreted as a numeric switch argument. For example,

```
{ =8.9 \# "Please add #.0% sales tax"}
```

displays as

Please add 8.9% sales ta

Recall that x is a switch argument. For this to work properly, the x in *tax* must be enclosed in single quotes:

```
{ =8.9 \# "Please add #.0% sales ta'x'" }
```

You can, of course, enclose the entire literal text in single quotes. Minimum quoting is used here to demonstrate why it's necessary. Alternatively, move to a state that doesn't have a sales tax.

Date format (date-time picture switches)

Date-time picture switches have the following syntax:

```
\@ format
```

They enable you to format dates in a variety of ways, as detailed in Table 23.2.

23

TIP

You can specify a desired default format using the Date and Time dialog box. Choose Insert ⇨ Text ⇨ Date and Time. Highlight the format you want to use for the default and click Default. Choose Yes to confirm. Back in the Date and Time dialog box, click OK to insert a date, or Cancel if you're simply changing the default. The default was changed when you confirmed changing the default; canceling doesn't cancel the change.

TABLE 23.2   Time and Date Picture Switch Format Elements

Characters	Effect
AM/PM or am/pm	AM and PM or am and pm, respectively
A/P or a/p	A and P or a and p, respectively
D	Date, with no leading zero
Dd	Date, with leading zero
Ddd	Abbreviated name of the day of the week (SUN, MON, etc.)
Dddd	Full name of the day of the week (Sunday, Monday, you know the rest)
H	Hour, 12-hour format with no leading zero
Hh	Hour, 12-hour format with leading zero
H	Hour, 24-hour format with no leading zero
HH	Hour, 24-hour format with leading zero
M	Numeric month, no leading zero
MM	Numeric month, leading zero
MMM	First three letters of month (Jan, Feb, etc.)
MMMM	Full name of month (March, April, etc.)
M	Minutes, no leading zero
Mm	Minutes, leading zero
S	Seconds, no leading zero
Ss	Seconds, leading zero
y or yy	Year, two-digit format (07, 08, etc.)
Yyyy	Year, four-digit format (2013, 2014)

Date formats use key letters to represent parts of dates and times, as shown in Table 23.2. These key letters affect only the component that is displayed, not the capitalization. You must add the appropriate * switch to achieve different forms of capitalization. The field {date \@ "MMM"} produces Aug (an uppercase M produces months, while a lowercase m produces minutes). You would need to add * upper to get AUG. See the following section for other exciting ideas.

Switch combinations

Some of the switches can be combined. For example, * CHARFORMAT or * MERGEFORMAT can be combined with any other format. The field {quote * CHARFORMAT * ordtext "9"} produces *ninth* (in italics because the *q* in *quote* is in italics). However, none of the numeric arguments can be combined with case arguments, except for alphabetic.

Categories

The Field dialog box separates the fields into several categories. In this section we will look at each category, the fields they contain, and what those fields are used for.

Date and Time

Word provides six different date and time fields. Of the six, note that only the Date field itself, which provides the current date, uses the special document control container.

- **CreateDate:** The date the document was created
- **Date:** The current date
- **EditTime:** Cumulative time that the document has been open
- **PrintDate:** The last date that the document was printed
- **SaveDate:** The last date the document was saved
- **Time:** The current time

All of these except for EditTime can be used as either Time or Date fields depending on the picture switches applied. Note also that for each of the Time and Date fields, when you display the dialog box, as shown in Figure 23.11, the top format is shown (such as 11/21/2012), even if the selected field name is Time.

If you select the field and then just click OK, accepting the default date format, that may not be the format displayed by the field. In the case of Date, you will get the default date format (which you can change as shown earlier). In the case of Time, you will get just the time. For CreateDate, PrintDate, and SaveDate, however, you will get a combination of the default date and the time. Therefore, if you want one of those three—and you generally want the time as well—you don't need to build a formatting switch. It's already been done for you, the dialog box's display notwithstanding.

FIGURE 23.11

The Field dialog box enables you to set up any of the date and time fields (except for EditTime) using any combination of date and time elements.

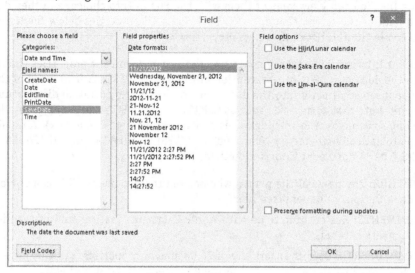

Document Automation

The document automation fields are used mostly in building automated forms. The fields can be used to perform logical operations and to allow the user to run a macro, send special instructions to the printer, or go to a bookmark. Six fields are provided:

- **Compare:** Used in mail merge operations to test the values of data fields.
- **DocVariable:** Used to display the contents of a document variable that was created by a macro.
- **GoToButton:** Used to transfer the insertion point to a bookmark location. This field has been superseded by the Hyperlink field.
- **If:** Often used in mail merge documents to control the flow and to create conditional statements that control whether specific mail merge fields are printed.
- **MacroButton:** Used to run a macro.
- **Print:** Used to send special codes to your printer.

23

Document Information

Document information fields are taken from the Document Properties stored behind the scenes for a file. You can view some of them with the File ⇨ Info choice, and they display at the right side of the screen that appears. Click Show All properties below the list of Properties to see the full list of available properties.

The Document Information category contains a variety of document properties that you can insert into the document. With the exception of the DOCPROPERTIES field, each of the field codes can be inserted directly into the document to display the corresponding datum about the document. Note that some fields such as COMMENTS, SUBJECT, and TITLE generally must be entered by someone (using the document panel or Properties dialog box). A number of these are automatically created by Word, such as FILESIZE, NUMCHARS, NUMPAGES, and NUMWORDS. The 14 document information fields are as follows:

- **AUTHOR:** The name of the person who created the document. This comes from the File ⇨ Options ⇨ General settings.
- **COMMENTS:** Has nothing to do with Word's Comments feature, and instead is any comments entered.
- **DOCPROPERTY:** Used to insert any of 26 document properties into the current document, not just the list included in the document information fields.
- **FILENAME:** The name of the current file, optionally including the path.
- **FILESIZE:** The stored size of the file, available in several different formats.
- **INFO:** Used to insert any of 17 summary information items.
- **KEYWORDS:** Any document keywords that happen to have been inscribed in Document Properties.
- **LASTSAVEDBY:** The name of the user who last saved changes to the document.
- **NUMCHARS:** The number of characters in the document, excluding white space.
- **NUMPAGES:** The total number of physical pages in the document
- **NUMWORDS:** The number of words in the document.
- **SUBJECT:** The subject document information field, if populated.
- **TEMPLATE:** The name of the currently attached document template.
- **TITLE.** The title of the document, if one has been assigned. This is not the same as the filename.

Equations and Formulas

This group is used to perform calculations, manipulate characters, construct equations, and display symbols. Though the formula (=) field will still attract a few diehard users in Word

2013, for the most part the functionality offered by this group is for backward compatibility. Four fields are provided:

- **= (Formula):** Used to perform calculations and format numbers.
- **Advance:** Used to position characters for special effects and for simulating characters not available through the user's installed fonts.
- **Eq.:** Used to create equation-like effects. This is provided for backward compatibility. Use Insert ⇨ Symbols ⇨ Equation instead.
- **Symbol:** Used to insert symbols. Use this approach instead of Insert ⇨ Symbols ⇨ Symbol if you need to retain information about the exact nature of the symbol being inserted.

Index and Tables

The index and tables fields are used to build and maintain tables of contents, indexes, and tables of authorities. The seven fields in this category are as follows:

- **Index:** Creates an index based on XE fields
- **RD:** Creates an index, table of contents, table of figures, or table of authorities using marked entries or heading styles in multiple documents
- **TA:** Used to mark a table of authorities entry
- **TC:** Used to manually mark a table of contents entry
- **TOA:** Creates a table of authorities based on TA fields
- **TOC:** Creates a table of contents using outline levels (heading styles) or TC entries
- **XE:** Used to mark index entries

Links and References

These fields are used to link content into Word documents from external files as well as from other parts of the current Word document. Fields are provided in those cases both for backward compatibility and to allow for different methods if other options are preferred. The 11 fields in this category are as follows:

- **AutoText:** Inserts the contents of a Building Blocks gallery item into the current document. You might use this rather than insert an entry using the Building Blocks gallery or Quick Parts gallery if the contents/value of the underlying entry changes. For example, the item might contain an address, a telephone number, or boilerplate text that is subject to being updated. If you include a reference to the AutoText instead of the AutoText itself, the document can be more dynamic and updateable.

23

- **AutoTextList:** Creates a shortcut menu based on AutoText entries in a template that's currently available. The entry list can be based on the styles applied to the AutoText entries. For example, if you have a style named Color Choices, any entry formatted with that style will appear in the list. When the user right-clicks the AutoTextList item, the list of Color Choices appears. If you click one of the items, the AutoTextList field is replaced by the AutoText item chosen.

- **Hyperlink:** Inserts a hyperlink to a URL, file, or other location available on a disk, a network location, the Internet, or an intranet.

- **INCLUDEPICTURE:** Used to link to a supported graphics file. Word 2013 defaults to an XML link instead of using INCLUDEPICTURE, although the field is still supported. An advantage of the INCLUDEPICTURE field is that it can be locked with Ctrl+F11 to prevent accidental updates and unlinking. When working in compatibility mode, Word defaults to INCLUDEPICTURE links because the XML method is not supported in earlier versions of Word.

- **INCLUDETEXT:** Similar to INCLUDEPICTURE, but used to link to a nongraphic file. Word 2013 still uses the INCLUDETEXT field when you insert a link to a file, however.

- **LINK:** This field links information you copy and paste from another application to the original source file using OLE (object linking and embedding). You typically would use Paste ➪ Paste Special, choose the desired object type, and enable the Paste link option.

- **NOTEREF:** Used to insert a footnote or endnote reference mark that's been bookmarked so you can make multiple references to the same note, or to cross-reference footnotes or endnotes.

- **PAGEREF:** Inserts the page number of a bookmarked location; used for cross-references.

- **QUOTE:** Used to insert literal text. This field often is used with the IF field to conditionally insert different text based on a comparison with data from a database of some kind.

- **REF:** Used to insert bookmarked text. For example, you might bookmark the table number in a table caption and use that reference in the text. If other tables are inserted or deleted and the numbering changes, the REF field that refers to the bookmarked table number can be updated.

- **STYLEREF:** Used to insert the text of the nearest occurrence (searching up or down) of a style relative to the location of the STYLEREF field, or some datum related to that style occurrence. Often used in making dictionary-type headings wherein the first and last words defined on the page appear at the top of each page.

Mail Merge

The fields included in the Mail Merge group are used in constructing mail merge documents of the type shown when you choose Start Mail Merge in the Mailing dialog box. See Chapter 22, "Data Documents and Mail Merge," for the full scoop.

Some of the fields in the Mail Merge category are also shown under Document Automation. The 14 Mail Merge fields are as follows:

■ **ADDRESSBLOCK:** This field inserts a mail merge address block. Using the ADDRESSBLOCK field is an alternative to specifying the address elements individually. You generally insert this field by clicking Address Block in the Mailings Ribbon tab. See Chapter 22 for additional information.

■ **ASK:** This field prompts you to provide information. It assigns a bookmark to the answer you provide, and the information is stored internally. A reference to the bookmark can then be used in the mail merge document to reproduce the information you type. A default response to the prompt can also be included in the field. The ASK field displays only as an empty bookmark in the mail merge document, so don't be surprised if you don't see a result.

■ **COMPARE:** See the field of the same name under "Document Automation."

■ **DATABASE:** This field inserts data into your document in the form of a Word table. When you create the field, you are prompted for a database from which records can be filtered and selected. The result can appear either as a normal Word table or as a field masquerading as a table. One use for this field is to extract data into a file that can then be used for mail merges. You might want to do this when the larger dataset is tied to a server and will be inaccessible to the ultimate mail merge users. You might also do this simply to present data in a table in a Word document. If you keep the database result in the form of a field, it can be updated when and if the underlying data change.

■ **FILL-IN:** This field prompts you to enter text and then uses your response in place of the field in the mail merge document. This is similar to the ASK field, except that the information can be used only in one place.

■ **GreetingLine:** This field inserts a greeting line into your mail merge document. It usually is inserted by means of the Greeting Line button in the Mailings tab. See Chapter 22 for additional information.

■ **IF:** See the field of the same name under "Document Automation."

■ **MERGEFIELD:** This is used as a token placeholder for a mail merge field inserted from a database. For example, rather than Dear John, you might see Dear <<FirstName>> in your document. Or you might instead see <<GreetingLine>>. See Chapter 22 for additional information.

23

- **MERGEREC:** When you're doing a mail merge, the MERGEREC field serves as a counter of records in the data file and doesn't count the number of documents actually printed. This field is incremented by the presence of NEXT and NEXTIF fields. If you skip records using SKIPIF, MERGEREC is incremented nonetheless.

- **MERGESEQ:** This field provides a counter of mail merge documents that actually result from a merge. If you merge the entire database and do not change the base sorting, and if no records are skipped, MERGESEQ and MERGEREC will be identical.

- **NEXT:** The NEXT field is used to include more than one record in a given document. Ordinarily, when you're doing a mail merge, one document is printed for each record. With the NEXT field, however, you can include multiple records in a single document. This can be useful when you need to refer to several addresses from a data file.

- **NEXTIF:** The NEXTIF statement works like the NEXT field except that it advances to the next record only if an expression being evaluated is true.

- **SET:** The SET field is used to change the text referred to by a bookmark. For example, an occurrence of the text July 4, 2014, might be bookmarked as dayoff in one part of the document, and dayoff might be referred to in other parts of the document with a REF field. If you want to change the date referred to by the bookmark, you can either change the original underlying text at the site of the original bookmarked instance of July 4, 2014, or you can use a SET field to change it.

- **SKIPIF:** The SKIPIF field is used to cancel processing of the current database record during a mail merge. For example, you might use it to screen out a particular ZIP code.

Numbering

Numbering fields are used to insert certain kinds of numbering into your documents. The 10 field codes in the Numbering category are as follows:

- **AUTONUM:** The AUTONUM field inserts an automatic paragraph number field. The resulting numbers are displayed as 1., 2., 3., and so forth. AUTONUM is incremented in each paragraph. If you include multiple AUTONUM fields within the same paragraph, they will all display the same number. General formatting switches are ignored by this field, and updating is automatic—you don't need to press F9. The AUTONUM field is designed for numbering paragraphs or sections of a document. Some users find it less flaky than Word's Numbering tool and automatic list numbering, especially in legacy documents from Word 2003 and earlier.

- **AUTONUMLGL:** AUTONUMLGL inserts an automatic paragraph number field code whose results are displayed in legal style as 1., 1.1., 1.1.1., etc. AUTONUMLGL is tied to Heading level styles (Heading 1 is 1., Heading 2 is 1.1., and so on). All general format switches are ignored by this field and updating is automatic each time a paragraph is inserted or deleted. AUTONUMLGL displays the same as AUTONUM when used in non-Heading-style paragraphs.

- **AUTONUMOUT:** AUTONUMOUT inserts an automatic paragraph number field code whose results are displayed with traditional outline numbering (I., A., 1., a., and so on). Like AUTONUMLGL, AUTONUMOUT works with Heading level styles, and updating is fully automatic.

- **BARCODE:** This field inserts a BARCODE into the current document. If you see a Bookmark not defined error code instead of a bar code, toggle field codes and remove the \b switch. According to Word this feature has been removed. It has and it hasn't. Other parts of the Word interface no longer provide access to it, but it remains as a field code for two reasons: a) for compatibility with legacy documents and b) to annoy the post office. Use it at your own risk.

- **LISTNUM:** This field inserts a set of numbers anywhere in a paragraph. Unlike the AUTONUM fields, LISTNUM is incremented each time you use it. Also unlike the AUTONUM fields, LISTNUM supports several switches that enable you to control how numbering is performed, the starting number, and the list level: 1), a), i), (1), (a), (i), and so on (feel free to experiment to see what each level produces). A common instance in which you'd use LISTNUM is when you're numbering things within a paragraph and don't want to worry about having to renumber them when you insert or remove items. For example, "I needed to 1) make a list of things to do, 2) do the things on the list, and 3) add additional things to the list." In this case, a LISTNUM field would be used to create 1), 2), and 3). Like AUTONUM, LISTNUM is updated instantly and automatically anytime another LISTNUM field is inserted or deleted. If you make a to-do list, however, LISTNUM won't do the things on the list for you.

- **PAGE:** Use this field to insert the current page number. It's used most often in creating page numbers in headers and footers.

- **REVNUM:** The REVNUM field comes from the Advanced Properties Statistics tab. The revision number is incremented each and every time the document is saved. For the average paranoid but savvy Word user, this makes REVNUM essentially worthless. For example, REVNUM indicates that this particular chapter has now been saved 212 times. Note that REVNUM is unrelated to the Versions feature from Word 2003 (which Word 2013 does not support).

- **SECTION:** The SECTION field inserts the section number of the current section. This can be useful in setting up some kinds of compound numbering that numbers pages by section, but in which numbering is not being applied to a Heading style that varies by section.

- **SECTIONPAGES:** The SECTIONPAGES field inserts the number of pages in the current section. When you're numbering by section and want to include the length of each section, a common page numbering setup would be Page {section}-{page} of {sectionpages}.

23

- **SEQ:** The SEQ field is used to insert a sequence number into a document. SEQ is used to number chapters, tables, figures, illustrations, lists, or anything else not already covered by a built-in numbering system. Though it's more complex than Word's built-in numbering system for numbered lists, many users found that in past versions of Word, the SEQ field was a lot more predictable and dependable than the numbered lists feature, and that its use resulted in fewer problems. You can create any number of independent numbering sequences in a document, and switches provide full control over numbering features.

User Information

User information corresponds to the User Name and Initials fields in File ⇨ Options ⇨ General, as well as to the Mailing Address field found in File ⇨ Options ⇨ Advanced ⇨ General. The three user information fields are as follows:

- **USERADDRESS:** Your mailing address, if you chose to enter it
- **USERINITALS:** Your initials, if you entered your name in the Personalize settings
- **USERNAME:** Your name, if you entered it in the Personalize settings

Summary

In this chapter you've learned about field codes: what they are, how to insert them, and why you might want to. You've learned about numerous fields available in Word and how to use them. You should now be able to do the following:

- Insert a date field
- Use various methods to toggle field code display, Ctrl+Shift+F9 to convert a field result into actual text, and other shortcut keys for working with fields
- Insert a field using the Field dialog box, including specifying options and switches for the field
- Edit a field manually or in the Field dialog box
- Decide when to use the * CHARFORMAT or * MERGEFORMAT formatting switches
- Lock a date field to keep it from being unintentionally updated
- Use field codes to set up a variety of different kinds of page numbering
- Understand the difference between a FILLIN and an ASK field, and when to use each
- Use the LISTNUM field to a) set up this kind of numbering within a paragraph and b) avoid having to renumber this kind of within-paragraph numbering when you add or remove an item

Creating Custom Forms

IN THIS CHAPTER

Understanding Legacy form fields versus modern content controls

Working in Design mode

Creating forms using legacy tools

Creating templates using content control tools

Importing Word forms into InfoPath

I t seems that just about every time you turn around, someone has a form you need to fill out. There are job applications, credit applications, school forms, medical forms, subscription forms, tax forms... the list goes on and on. All these forms aren't just on paper, either. Many of the same forms—and plenty more, to boot—are now online.

Word's form-building capabilities have evolved over time. Word currently provides multiple methods for creating forms. Each approach has its own strengths, as you'll see in this chapter. Let's dive in.

Forms Basics

Word 2013 has three different sets of tools that can be used to create electronic forms:

- Content control tools
- Legacy form fields from Word 2003 and earlier
- ActiveX form controls

Ostensibly, legacy form fields and ActiveX form controls are included with Word 2013 only to provide limited support for legacy documents. However, because while Word 2013's Help focuses on the new content control features when you ask it how to create forms, Word's other options give you reasons you may want to use legacy form fields from Word 2003 and earlier (and not the ActiveX tools).

Two Word options—designed to save forms data and print only forms data—work only with forms having legacy controls. Choose File ➪ Options ➪ Advanced ➪ When printing this document. Notice the option that says Print only the data from a form. A little further down, under Preserve fidelity when sharing this document, notice the option that says Save form data as delimited text file. Both of those options work only with legacy Word 2003 form fields, so if you choose to use the new content controls, you'll have to use other means to gather the data collected from the form files. Later sections in this chapter will show you how to work with both types of form controls. I suggest that you read through both sections before starting any important form project, as you'll want to have a clear understanding of which of the form tools will better suit your needs.

One way to think about a form is as a kind of reverse mail merge. Whereas the objective in a mail merge is to display data in a particular way, often combining data and document elements, the objective in using forms typically is to obtain data. Hence, document elements are combined with empty slots for the form recipient to use to type in the data manually. *Document elements* are instructions telling the form user what kind of information is being sought. Such forms often are used for job applications, placing online orders, filling out surveys, and a host of other purposes.

> **NOTE**
>
> In Word 2013, forms have another purpose: to create document templates in which the objective is not specifically to obtain data. Rather, the purpose is to provide a method for constructing content-oriented templates. Extracting data from these new documents requires considerably more effort, as well as the talents of a programmer who knows his or her way around VBA (Visual Basic for Applications, which is the macro/scripting language that Word uses for its macros) and XML. While Word provides the ability to view XML structure via the XML Mapping Pane button in the Mapping group of the Developer tab on the Ribbon, most of the useful XML editing capabilities were removed from Word due to litigation. For that reason, XML is not covered in this book.

Creating and using forms: general steps

In Word, you create a data collection form using the following general steps:

1. **Combine text instructions and content controls (or legacy form fields) in a Word document.**

2. **Protect the document, enabling entry only in content control or legacy form field areas.** Do not protect the document or template for fill-in forms when the goal is to create a template that is not data oriented.

3. **Save the form as a Word template.**

To use a form, you use the form template to create a new document. That document (or the original template.) can then be sent out to be filled in, posted online, emailed, and so on. Make sure to provide users with any applicable saving and naming instructions, as well as instructions for how to return their completed forms to you or another person or online location.

You can also create a form or template that isn't data-oriented per se. Rather, it contains strategically placed content controls to help users to create a document more quickly and to use precise formulations of text and formatting (in some instances) to promote consistency and accuracy.

Form tools and controls

Word's form tools and controls are located in the Developer tab of the Ribbon. To display the Developer tab, choose File ➪ Options ➪ Customize Ribbon. In the Main Tabs list at the right, click the Developer check box to check it, as shown in Figure 24.1, and click OK.

FIGURE 24.1

The Developer tab does not appear by default; turn it on in Word Options.

The primary tools used for creating and working with forms are in the Controls group of the Developer tab, shown in Figure 24.2. In addition to the nine content control tools, the Legacy Tools control provides access to the legacy forms tools from Word 2003 (and earlier), as well as ActiveX tools. Note that using ActiveX tools requires additional programming knowledge that is beyond the scope of the *Microsoft Word 2013 Bible*. For information about programming and forms, visit www.mousetrax.com, or search for help on the Internet. To access legacy forms tools and ActiveX controls, click the Legacy Tools drop-down arrow. Both Legacy Forms tools and ActiveX tools are also shown in Figure 24.2.

FIGURE 24.2

Content controls and access to legacy form and ActiveX tools is provided in the Controls group on the Developer tab.

Content control tools

Word 2013 provides nine content control tools in the Controls group. If the control icons aren't self-explanatory enough, move the mouse pointer over the control to see a ScreenTip telling what it does. The controls are:

- **Rich Text:** Provides an area in which the user can type formatted text.

- **Plain Text:** Provides a plain-text area that cannot contain formatting.

- **Picture:** Provides a control in which the user can insert or paste a picture.

- **Building Block Gallery:** Provides a drop-down menu of Building Blocks. This enables you to include larger selections of boilerplate and other preset text than otherwise can be selected using the other controls. This can be handy for more complex forms.

- **Check Box:** Provides a check box that can be toggled checked/unchecked by clicking.

- **Combo Box:** Provides a combination of preset options and user entry.

- **Drop-Down List:** Provides a list of preset options only.

- **Date Picker:** Provides a drop-down menu that enables you to pick the date using a calendar.

- **Repeating Section:** Enables you to organize the form by creating a section or area to hold other controls.

Unlike Word's legacy form fields, the content controls are not specifically designed to facilitate data collection. Rather, they are present in Word to facilitate constructing document templates. You can protect a content control–based document or template, permitting entry of data only in content controls. Therefore, you can send such a document to users so they can fill in the blanks, so to speak. However, extracting data from them is not supported by Word 2013 directly and requires a fair amount of programming effort.

If you don't need to extract data directly from such documents, or use them to print data only onto preprinted forms, and if you find these tools more accessible than the legacy tools, then feel free to use them.

If you do need a systematic way to extract data from your forms, however, use the legacy tools described in the following section.

Legacy form tools

Click the Legacy Tools button in the Controls group of the Developer tab to access Word's legacy form field tools:

- **Text Form Field:** Insert a text form field; use can be controlled to prevent non-numeric or non-date entry in a text form field.
- **Check Box Form Field:** Create a clickable check box.
- **Drop-Down Form Field:** This tool enables users to choose from a list of preset options.
- **Insert Frame:** Insert an old-style Word frame as a container for manipulating form fields.
- **Form Field Shading:** Toggle shading of form fields, which enables you to quickly identify where form fields are located in a document.
- **Reset Form Fields:** Restore all form fields in a forms document to their default entry settings.

The legacy tools are used to create forms from which you will need to extract or print just data. One use for such tools is to create a specific pattern of data you can use to print onto preprinted forms (such as tax forms, order forms, and so on). Another use is so you can save just the data to a delimited text file, with each text file containing one record. You would then need to collect the text files into a single data file, wherein each file would be the basis for a single record in the data file. The details of how to print and save data only are provided later in this chapter.

ActiveX controls

The third set of controls is the ActiveX controls (refer to Figure 24.2). Like content controls, ActiveX controls are of limited utility to most Word users from a data standpoint. They require a skilled programmer to use properly and are therefore beyond the scope of this book.

Like the legacy tools and content control tools, the ActiveX controls can also be used to record a document user's responses to questions. Like the content control tools, however,

24

the ActiveX controls do not have the ability to save or print just data. If your document contains such controls, any responses recorded in them will not be retained when printing or saving just data. That talent belongs exclusively to the legacy tools.

Forms protection

Protecting forms documents has been mentioned several times in this chapter without any explanation. Like so many concepts in Word 2013, it's difficult to talk about any one concept without mentioning others. When you protect a document for forms in Word, that means the user cannot edit any of the static text. The only places where the user can type or otherwise interact with the document's contents are in the form controls themselves.

Consider the simple document shown in Figure 24.3. The shaded second column contains a series of form fields. When the document is protected after you create all the form information, you can type only in the form fields. If displayed, the Restrict Editing pane informs you that you are only allowed to fill in the form. The prompt or label text (Name, DOB, City, and so on) is off-limits.

FIGURE 24.3

When you protect a document for forms, you can type only in the form fields.

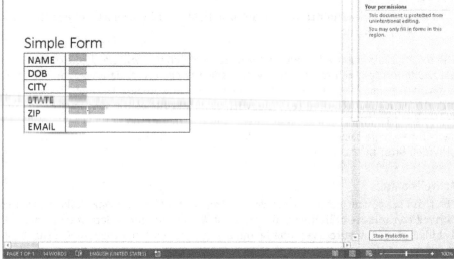

To protect a document for forms editing, in the Controls group of the Developer tab, first make sure that the Design Mode button is not selected or turned off (you cannot protect a form if Design mode is active). Then, click Restrict Editing in the Protect group, which displays the Restrict Editing pane, shown in Figure 24.4. In section 2, Editing restrictions, click the Allow only this type of editing in the document check box to check it, open the drop-down list, and click Filling in forms. When you're ready to begin enforcement, click Yes, Start Enforcing Protection.

FIGURE 24.4

Choose the Filling in forms editing restriction when creating your forms.

Word displays the Start Enforcing Protection dialog box, shown in Figure 24.5. You can include a password if you like—the choice is yours. Type it in the two text boxes prompting for it, and click OK. Note that the User authentication option appears only if you're using Word 2013 in an enterprise environment, such as with Office 365. An authenticated user is one who is logged on to the computer or network to which the computer is attached—and only on certain kinds of networks. Don't be concerned if this option is grayed out or missing completely.

24

FIGURE 24.5

A password isn't mandatory, but it's often not a bad idea to avoid confusing and/or tempting users.

> **CAUTION**
>
> Most users don't know how to enable or disable forms protection. If they do turn off protection via the Review tab, then at worst they will mess up the document and won't give you any useful information. If you set a password and forget it, you will have completely lost the capability to modify the document or template, probably with no hope of recovery. If it's a complex document, you're going to have to redo all that work. Make sure you record your form passwords and store them in such a way that you will always be able to retrieve them.

Determining when to protect a document

If the document you are creating is not being used for data collection of some kind, but rather uses content control to drive the creation of a document, you do not need to protect the document for fill-in forms. In fact, if you do, the template will not be terribly useful.

Removing form protection

To remove protection for fill-in forms, if the Restrict Editing pane isn't displayed, in the Developer tab, choose Restrict Editing in the Protect group. At the bottom of the Restrict Editing pane, click Stop Protection. If a password has been set, type the password and click OK or press Enter. If you forgot the password, unfortunately, you will not be able to remove the protection.

Creating a Fill-In Form Using Legacy Tools

Now that you know the basics about forms, it's time to create one. In addition to using the legacy tools to create basic forms, you must use the legacy form tools in the following two situations:

- When you want to be able to print only the field data that the user inputs, because you already have preprinted paper forms. (Turn on the Print only the data from a form options in Word's Advanced options for this to work.)

- When you want to be able to save the field data that the user inputs as a comma-delimited text file so that you can easily compile the user responses. (Turn on the Save form data as delimited text file in Word's advanced options.) When you set the form file up to do this as described in the warning below, when the user enters their responses in the form five and then saves it, only the responses are saved in a single delimited line in the the Plain Text (.txt) file format. You can then use the Insert ⇨ Text ⇨ Object arrow ⇨ Text from File command to insert the response file from each user into a new line to create a single delimited document. Save that file in the Plain Text format, and then you can import its data into Excel or Access for analysis.

One of the most common uses for online Word forms is subscriptions and order forms. In this section you learn how to create a simple order form template using Word's legacy form tools. The basic steps are as follows:

1. **Draft or sketch what you want the form to look like.** This will speed the process of designing your form.

2. **Create a document that contains instructional text and form fields in which the user can provide answers to questions and save the file as a Word document.**

CAUTION

If you need to enable the legacy options under File ⇨ Options ⇨ Advanced, Save form data as delimited text file and Print only the data from a form, you will need to leave the form saved as a Word document (not a Word template). Then create a VBA macro that turns on these options when the user opens the original Word file, because these options can only be set in the current file, and a template spawns a new file which then disables the options. Save the macro in the form Word file. You can then right-click the first form Text control in the Word file, and click Properties. In the Text Form Field Properties dialog box that appears, open the Entry list under Run macro on, and click the name of your macro. Click OK and proceed with creating the form, but do not save it as a template.

---

3. **Turn on protection for fill-in forms.**

4. **Save the document as a template, if you are able to do so based on the previous warning.**

5. **Create a new document based on the template.**

6. **Make the new document available to customers so they can fill it out with the needed information.**

In addition, legacy form fields provide the following advantages and features that content controls do not:

- The ability to control the type of data entry (for example, to reject non-date data from a date field and non-numeric data from a numeric field)

- The ability to automatically perform calculations

- The ability to specify numeric formatting

Creating the form document

In a new Word document, type any prompts or labels (instructional text) you need. Often, setting up a form is easiest when you create a table, including your labels in one column and the fill-in or other legacy fields in a second column, as shown in Figure 24.6. To create the form shown here, I inserted a 2×13 table. I merged the top cell to add the company information and split the lower-right cells to hold the numeric calculations (see Chapter 13, "Building Tables, Charts, and Smart Art to Show Data and Process," for more information on working with tables).

FIGURE 24.6

Tables help in the organization and positioning of form fields and other information.

Generic Paint Supplies, LLC	
121 Side Street	
Indianapolis, IN 46219	

DATE:	1/1/2016
SHIP TO:	All orders ship UPS. UPS will not ship to a P.O. Box.
NAME	Customer Name
STREET ADDRESS	Shipping Address
APT.	
CITY	City
STATE	Select State from List
ZIP	5 Digit ZIP Code

ITEMS ORDERED	**QUANTITY**	**PRICE**
BRUSH SET	0	$0.00
PAINT SAMPLER	0 2 OUNCES EACH, 5 COLORS	$0.00
TOTAL		$0.00

Turning on nonprinting formatting characters and form field shading

To facilitate working with form fields, it helps to display nonprinting formatting characters and form field shading. It sometimes helps to turn on the display of bookmarks as well, although bookmarks are turned off here so that you can read the field contents better.

NOTE

Legacy form fields use bookmarks as their names. You can customize the bookmark names to enable the fields to be used by other fields for calculations and logic tests. This topic is discussed more a little later in this chapter.

To toggle the display of nonprinting formatting characters, press Ctrl+Shift+8 (Ctrl+*) or click Show/Hide in the Paragraph group of the Home tab. To turn on the display of form field shading if it is not already on, in the Controls group of the Developer tab choose Legacy Tools ⇨ Form Field Shading (the second item from the right under Legacy Forms).

To turn on the display of bookmarks, choose File ⇨ Options ⇨ Advanced. Under Show document content, ensure that Show Bookmarks has a check next to it, and click OK.

Inserting a text form field with date format

Word's legacy text form fields actually provide a lot more than just a place to type text. To create the date field shown in Figure 24.6, in the Developer tab's Controls group choose Legacy Tools ⇨ Text Form Field. If field shading and nonprinting formatting marks are displayed as instructed earlier, the text form field includes five little circles that are special spaces. If you press Ctrl+Shift+8 (Ctrl+*), the circles disappear. If you do that and turn off form field shading, the entire field becomes invisible (for now). This can make working with such form fields rather difficult.

Double-click the text form field to open the Text Form Field Options dialog box. This is where you make the field more specific and choose display settings and behavior. Open the Type drop-down list and choose Date, as shown in Figure 24.7.

FIGURE 24.7

You can set a text form field to any of six types of data.

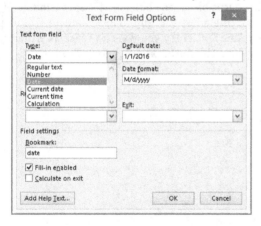

When you set the type to Date, notice that the default and format settings titles change to Default date and Default format. For the date style shown in Figure 24.6, set Date format to m/d/yyyy. If the user types **7-31-16**, Word automatically converts it to July 31, 2016. You can also type an entry such as **1/1/2016** in the Default date text box to help prompt the user to enter the date in the default format. Click OK to finish setting up the field. If the user types something other than a date and presses Tab or Enter, Word prompts for a valid entry, as shown in Figure 24.8.

24

FIGURE 24.8

When the text form field type is set to Date, Word will not accept any other type of entry in the form field.

If you want to be able to use the date elsewhere, use the Bookmark text box under Field settings in the Text Form Field Options dialog box to assign a bookmark to it. You might want to change the bookmark to something more memorable that offers a better reference point, such as OrderDate. You can then use { REF OrderDate } to insert that date elsewhere in the file. Ensure that Fill-in enabled is checked if you want the user to be able to type a date.

If a field requires special instructions, click Add Help Text. In the Form Field Help Text dialog box, shown in Figure 24.9, you can specify two kinds of help: Status Bar and Help Key (F1). When the form field is selected (by clicking on it or tabbing to it), the status bar Help message (up to 138 characters) is displayed on the status bar at the bottom of Word's window. If you press F1 while the form field is selected, your Help Key text (up to 255 characters) is displayed in a message box. If you have an existing AutoText entry you want to reuse as either your Status Bar or your Help Key text, select it from the AutoText entry drop-down list.

FIGURE 24.9

Word enables you to provide two flavors of Help for form fillers.

Click OK to close the Form Field Help Text dialog box, and then click OK again to finish setting up the field and close the Text Form Field Options dialog box.

Inserting a regular text form field

When you insert a text form field, Word defaults to using the Regular text type. Position the insertion point where you want the field to appear. Then in the Developer tab's Controls group, choose Legacy Tools ⇨ Text Form Field. Double-click the form field (gray rectangle) to open the Text Form Field Options dialog box (refer to Figure 24.7). Type should already be set to the default Type. Under Default text, you can reinforce an instruction such as NAME by including some default text, such as **Please type your name here.** If the name field ultimately will be used by a process that has a length limit, use the Maximum length control to set a limit. Note that because this is a simple example, there is only one field for name. Ordinarily, however, you might invest a few more minutes and include separate fields for first name, last name, middle initial, title, and suffix. For title and suffix, you might use drop-down fields (which you'll see shortly) instead of text fields, both to facilitate entry and to restrict the entry to the range of options you want to accommodate.

> **TIP**
>
> Anytime you create a form field that has reuse potential, save it as a Building Block Gallery item. You might consider creating a new Category (for example, Form Fields) expressly for this purpose and to make them easier to find when you are designing forms.

If the ultimate data handler can benefit from specific text formats (for example, uppercase, lowercase, first capital, or title case), choose a specific Text format. Otherwise, as long as it doesn't exceed the maximum length you set, the text form field will accept anything you type. Ensure that Fill-in enabled is checked, add Help text, if needed, and then click OK to accept the changes.

Inserting a drop-down list

To insert a drop-down list, in Legacy Tools in the Controls group of the Developer tab, click the Drop-Down Form Field tool (refer to Figure 24.2). With form field shading turned on, this inserts a gray rectangle, as for the other field types so far.

Double-click the Drop-down form field to display the Drop-Down Form Field Options dialog box. As shown in Figure 24.10, type each item you want to add into the Drop-down item text box, and then click Add. The item then appears in the Items in drop-down list. Continue adding items until you're done, or until you reach 25, which is the limit. As shown in the Figure 24.10, the first item you add can serve as a prompt to tell the user what to do.

24

FIGURE 24.10

You have to build the list of items for a drop-down list field as shown here.

Inserting numeric and calculation fields

Some form fields are designed to work together. In the example form shown in Figure 24.6, the Price form-field uses the contents of the Quantity field to perform a calculation. The user doesn't type a value into the Price field; the form calculates that field automatically.

To insert a number field like the Brush Set Quantity field shown in Figure 24.6, position the insertion point and click Legacy Tools in the Controls group of the Developer tab, and then click Text Form Field as before. Double-click the gray form-field box to open the Text Form Field Options dialog box. Set the Type field to Number, and enter 0 in the Default number text box. Maximum length determines how many characters the user can enter in the field, so choose a length that's reasonable (for example, if your inventory is 50, it wouldn't make sense to allow more than two digits as shown in Figure 24.11). Open the Number format drop-down list and click 0. In the Bookmark text box under Field settings, drag over the Text# bookmark name and type a descriptive name that you'll remember for use in calculations. Let's call this one *brush*, but this makes sense only for the example shown here. Ensure that Fill-in enabled is checked. Figure 24.11 shows the finished settings for this field. Click OK to apply them and finish setting it up.

FIGURE 24.11

Example settings for a Number type text form field

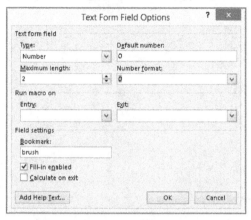

Now, insert a calculated field like the first Price field in the example in Figure 24.6. As before, position the insertion point and use the legacy Text Form Field from the Controls group of the Developer tab to insert the field. Double-click the form field to open the Text Form Field Options dialog box. Set Type to Calculation. In Expression, you want to calculate the price to display based on the number of items in the first row (Brush Set) shown under Quantity. If the quantity field is bookmarked as *brush*, and the price of a brush set is $9.99, then you would enter the expression as **=brush*9.99** in the Expression text box, as shown in Figure 24.12.

For a calculated field, leaving Maximum length set to the default Unlimited setting makes sense because the control needs to be able to display as many characters as needed for the calculated result and formatting. Make a choice from the Number Format drop-down list. Change the bookmark name to something you can remember because the result of this calculation is going to be used in another one later. In this example the bookmark name is brushtot. Notice that Fill-in enabled is grayed out. That's because this is a calculation field, and you want it to be automatic. Check the Calculate on exit check box; otherwise the field will not perform the calculation. If needed, you can add some help text. Whether you should do that depends on the complexity of the information being presented. Click OK to finish setting up the form field.

FIGURE 24.12

When Type is set to Calculation, enter the calculation Expression.

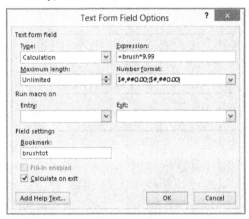

Once the prices for other items have been determined, a third calculation field would also be needed to compute the total. This one would be the simple sum of the other two prices (in this example, **=brushtot+painttot**).

After setting up all your form fields, remember to enable form protection as described earlier. Then, the form user can press Tab to move between and fill in fields. The user may have to press Tab a few extra times after filling in the form data to ensure that all calculated fields recalculate as needed.

Run Macro On

Up until now, we've ignored the Run Macro On drop-down lists in the Form Field Options dialog boxes. If the current document or template contains macros, you can select them using the Entry and Exit drop-down lists. You can use macros to perform setup/housekeeping tasks when a given form field is selected, as well as when the insertion point leaves that field.

For example, suppose somewhere else in the form is a form field for selecting a country. When entering a drop-down field, if the country selected is Canada, it doesn't make sense to have a list of US states. Rather than have a longer list that combines both US states and Canadian provinces, an entry macro could redefine the options for this field.

Suppose also that your business has offices in a number of states and therefore must charge sales tax in those states. Similarly, for international sales, shipping would be different. You might use an exit macro to take care of those details once a state, province, or other destination has been selected.

And as noted earlier, you may need to use macros to set Word Options for saving and printing the form. For an introduction to writing macros, see Chapter 32, "Macros: Recording, Editing, and Using Them."

Using Content Controls

Content controls, unlike Word's legacy tools, are of limited utility for data collection by most Word users. That's because in order to use them, you need the services of a programmer who understands how to extract data from the resulting Word XML file.

If you have InfoPath, another scenario is to design data collection forms using Word, and then import those into InfoPath. They can then be published to a SharePoint, InfoPath, or other server, where they can be downloaded, filled out, and returned.

Word's content controls are useful, however, in developing document templates. This section looks at several of the controls and how they might be used to put together a document template.

Design mode

For full access to content controls, you need to be in Design mode. In the Controls group of the Developer tab, click Design Mode to enable it.

Design mode provides full access to content controls. For example, if a content control is protected against deletion, you can delete it only in Design mode. Placeholder text can also be changed only in Design mode. Additionally, when Design mode is turned on, the content control itself gains horizontal scroll controls (beginning and end of text), as shown in Figure 24.13. To change the placeholder text, select the existing text and edit it or type over it.

FIGURE 24.13

Design mode is needed to edit placeholder text.

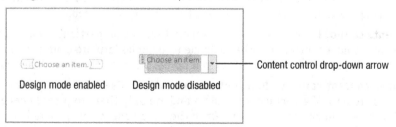

Content control drop-down arrow

Design mode enabled Design mode disabled

Once you're finished designing your form and are ready to save it, turn Design mode off. This enables forms to function properly. Note that you will not be able to protect a document for fill-in forms unless Design mode has been turned off (assuming you want to; if the document you are designing isn't a fill-in form for data collection, you don't need to protect it in this way).

Content control tools

Word 2013 has nine content control tools, described earlier in this chapter. Each of these has an associated Properties dialog box that enables you to control most aspects of the content control. The Properties dialog box for the Rich Text control is shown in Figure 24.14.

FIGURE 24.14

Content Control Properties for different controls have a number of common settings.

Though each Properties dialog box has some differences, they also share a number of common features and settings:

- **Content control cannot be deleted:** Enable this setting when you are planning to use the resulting document for data collection and programmatic data extraction. Extracting the data depends on the data fields being identified.

- **Contents cannot be edited:** Use this setting to lock in a particular value. If you are assembling a contract or other document using boilerplate contained in content controls, there are some aspects that you do not want an end user changing.

- **Remove content control when contents are edited:** Use this option if the content controls are part of a document template and are only there to provide general guidance as to document structure. Once the document is done, there is no harm in removing the content controls. (This option is not present for the new Check Box content control.)

Now you will explore each specific content control.

Rich Text content control

Use the Rich Text content control to reserve a place for the user to enter formatted text. The term *rich text* is sometimes confusing. Here, the term stands not in contrast to HTML (which it usually does) but simply to indicate that formatting is allowed. You are not limited to character formatting. A Rich Text content control can contain paragraph formatting, styles, headings (as in the example in Figure 24.14), columns, equations, and so on. It can also contain paragraph breaks, page breaks, and even section breaks. If you want to get thoroughly obsessive about it, a single Rich Text content control could contain a whole multipage, multisection document, with pictures, tables, and charts.

To change a Rich Text content control's default settings, right-click anywhere in the content control and then click Properties (or click the content control and click Properties in the Controls group of the Developer tab), which displays the dialog box shown in Figure 24.14. A Title entry isn't essential unless you plan to export the document to InfoPath or otherwise plan programmatic access to the data fields. If you're just putting together a document template and the controls are there more for guidance than for control, a title isn't essential. Title adds a little ID label at the top of the content control container that identifies the control when it's selected.

Tag is used for identifying XML data. Again, if you're using content control to provide guidance in a document template, a tag isn't useful. If you're using content control to collect or present data that will be repurposed or otherwise used in an XML process, then you should supply a useful tag. It's not unusual for tags and titles to be the same.

The Use a style to format text typed into the empty control option is used to limit some of the variation just discussed. When this setting is enabled, you cannot have variations in style, and only the style chosen will be used. Click OK after entering your settings to finish formatting the controls.

Plain Text content control

Use the Plain Text content control to contain text in which you do not want formatting variation. Any formatting applied affects all text in the control. The Properties dialog box for the Plain Text content control is almost identical to that for the Rich Text control, with one additional option: Allow carriage returns (multiple paragraphs)

This option is disabled by default. With this option enabled, you still can't really insert carriage returns per se. Instead, Word now allows you to insert new line (Shift+Enter) breaks, as well as page breaks and column breaks (but not section breaks). Oddly enough, with or without this setting, Word allows Plain Text content control content to be formatted into columns.

24

Picture content control

Use the Picture content control to provide a place for the user to insert a picture. In setting up a data collection form, this control might be used for inserting a picture of the respondent (or whatever other item is appropriate). The Picture content control is inserted in line with text, and the wrapping cannot be changed. If you try to drag the picture control to a new location, the control will be copied to the new location instead.

The picture control's Properties dialog box, shown in Figure 24.15, offers fewer options than any of the others. Use the Locking check boxes, if desired, to prevent the picture control from being deleted or to prevent the picture itself from being replaced or edited, and then click OK.

FIGURE 24.15

The picture Content Control Properties dialog box offers limited options.

Drop-Down List content control

Use a drop-down list to restrict user responses only to those that are provided in the drop-down list. One of the most common applications for this is a list of state abbreviations, as shown in the earlier example for a legacy drop-down list field. Hence, for users, Virginia could select

VA rather than type it. Drop-down lists can make using and processing data faster and easier, as you don't have to allow for a lot of strange variations and possible ambiguity.

Setting up a drop-down list is a little different from the content controls discussed so far. Until now, the controls discussed are pretty much ready-to-use straight off the rack, so to speak. A drop-down list, however, requires additional setup. In the Developer tab, click the Drop-Down List content control, shown in Figure 24.2. Right-click the control and then click Properties, which displays the dialog box shown in Figure 24.16.

FIGURE 24.16

Use the Drop-down content control to limit the user's range of options.

To add drop-down options, click Add. In the Add Choice dialog box, shown in Figure 24.17, in the Display Name field type the name that will be displayed as the drop-down option. Notice that as you type the name, Word adds the name as the value. You're not stuck with that value, however. Press the Tab key to move to the Value field, type the desired value, and click OK. Click again to apply the field options and finish setting up the field.

FIGURE 24.17

Adding choices for a drop-down list control

761

Despite the fact that the default placeholder text and the default first item both are Choose an item, setting the default first item to something different does not change the place-holder text. To change the placeholder text to match any instructional text you might have included as the first drop-down item, with Design mode turned on, drag over the content control's placeholder text, type new text, and click on another part of the control.

Combo Box content control

A combo box is a combination of a text box and a drop-down list. The idea is to provide the most common options in the drop-down list but allow for the possibility that one size doesn't fit all. When you do this, of course, you open yourself up to the problem indicated earlier, in which you might end up with a lot of different responses to handle.

To create a combo box content control, click the Combo Box tool shown in Figure 24.2. Then right-click it in the document, and click Properties, which displays the Combo Box Content Control Properties dialog box. Follow the same procedure shown for the Drop-down content control to add drop-down options, or choices. Click OK to finish the control set up.

You might also notice that the properties for the Combo Box and the Drop-down control are identical. The only difference is in behavior, in that you can overwrite the choice shown in the Combo Box to provide your own.

Date Picker content control

Use the Date Picker to insert a calendar control, like the one shown in Figure 24.18, for choosing the date. Use the arrows shown to go to the next/previous month. Click a date to enter it into the date control. Note that there is no easy way, for example, to jump to the year 2016. You basically have to repeat clicking the Next Month control until the desired year appears.

To insert the Date Picker content control in Design mode, click the Date Picker button in the controls group of the Developer tab, and then right-click it and click the Properties button to display the Date Picker's Content Control Properties dialog box, shown in Figure 24.19. Note that the selections that appear under Locale are determined by which languages you have installed. Calendar type will include only Western unless you've installed support for certain Asian calendars. For the final option, check with your IT department to determine whether you need to use a particular format.

FIGURE 24.18

The Date Picker inserts a GUI control for entering dates.

FIGURE 24.19

You can set the date format, locale, calendar, and format for storing the date in XML.

Building Block Gallery content control

The Building Block Gallery content control enables the form user to access to the Building Block gallery. One way to leverage this feature is to create a specific category designed to work with the form or template you are designing, using items created in a specific gallery. Then, using the Properties dialog box, limit the content control to using that specific gallery and category. You would need to set up the categories and content separately.

Click the Building Block Gallery tool in the Controls group of the Developer tab to insert the content control in Design mode. Right-click the control and then click Properties to display the Properties dialog box for the Building Block Gallery content control, shown in Figure 24.20. Type a title, if useful; choose any options you need; make the appropriate Gallery and Category selections; and then click OK. Now, the chosen gallery items will be available for drop-down insertion into your document.

FIGURE 24.20

Use the Building Block Gallery content control tool to enable form users to insert boilerplate text.

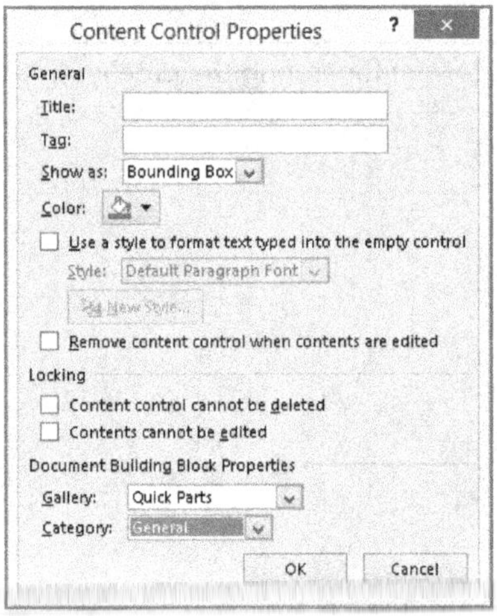

> **TIP**
>
> Note that all the content control properties dialog boxes now include a Color choice. You can click it and then click a color to color-code your content controls or help them stand out from other form content.

Check Box content control

Use the Check Box content control to insert a clickable check box into your document. Unlike the legacy check box, you do not need to protect the document for the check box to function. By default, "checked" displays an X in the box. In the Content Control Properties dialog box, use either Change button to choose different characters for Checked and Unchecked.

Repeating Section content control

Use the new Repeating Section content control to insert a control that can hold content that you want to repeat, as well as other controls. When you want the user to be able to give multiple responses to a form question or prompt, as shown in the example in Figure 24.21, you would insert a Repeating Section content control. To add another answer, the form user would simply click the plus (+) button at lower right. (Notice how the text above this control explains how to use it.) The Properties for this control for the most part resembles those you've seen for other controls, but you need to make sure that Allow users to add and remove sections is checked under Repeating Section Properties to ensure that the user can add rows with the plus (+) button. While in Design mode, edit the prompt text within the control, and add any other controls or contents within the Repeating Section control. For example, you could insert a table and then insert additional controls within the table.

FIGURE 24.21

A Repeating Section content control enables the user to click the plus (+) button and enter more data.

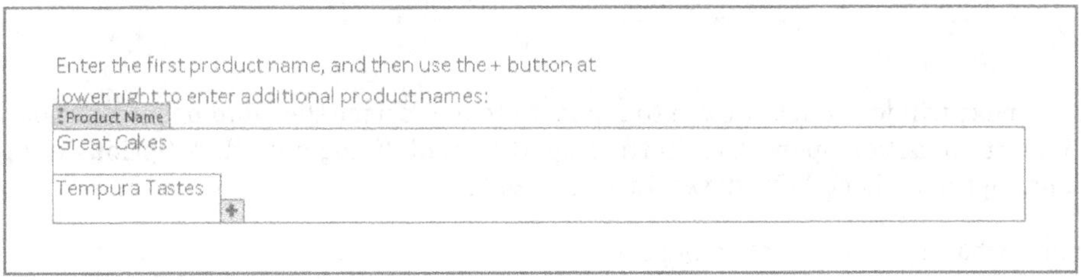

Importing a Word Form into InfoPath

There are a number of deficiencies in Word's ability to create and handle forms. The most glaring deficiency is the nearly complete inability to perform data validation without resorting to macros/VBA. If you have InfoPath 2013, however, you can easily avoid many of those problems by designing your basic form in Word 2013 (assuming you're most comfortable using Word), importing the form into InfoPath, and adding data validation and other missing features using InfoPath's capabilities.

InfoPath 2013 can import forms created in Word, provided that any of the following file formats are used: .doc, .dot, .xml, .rtf, .docx, .dotx, .docm, or .dotm. Design your form in Word, and save it to one of those formats.

Start InfoPath Designer 2013. From the New screen in Backstage view (choose File ⇨ New to return there if needed), choose Convert Existing Form under Advanced Form Templates. Then click the Design Form button at the right. This starts the Import Wizard. Click InfoPath importer for Word documents as the import method as shown in Figure 24.22 and click Next.

FIGURE 24.22

Use InfoPath's Import Wizard to import a form created by Word or Excel.

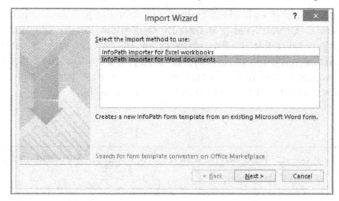

In the next window, click Browse to navigate to and select the Word document you want to import, and click Open. Back in the Import Wizard dialog box, click Options to open the Import Options dialog box, shown in Figure 24.23.

Choose what/how you want to import:

- **Layout only:** Choose this option if you want to insert the form fields from within InfoPath and abandon any that were inserted using Word. This option requires familiarity with InfoPath, or a willingness to learn. If you're familiar with InfoPath and plan to convert a normal Word document into a form, your best bet is to skip using Word's form tools, import the document, and choose Layout only (there won't be any form fields to import anyway).

- **Layout and form fields (default conversion):** In most cases, this option results in the least work and reinventing of the wheel.

- **Layout and form fields (custom conversion):** Choose this option if you need to deviate from the defaults. When you click this option, the checked settings you see at first reflect the defaults.

FIGURE 24.23

When you click the Custom Conversion option, the checked options are the ones InfoPath uses by default.

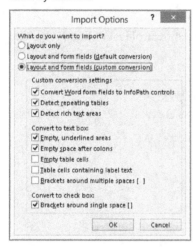

When you've selected any options you need, click OK to continue, and then click Finish back in the wizard. Note that it's not unusual to see a message that says there are potential issues, and to use the Design Checker to review them. More often than not, there are simple formatting issues that InfoPath was able to resolve. You might also see a message saying that tracked changes were discarded. It's not unusual to see this message even when the document didn't contain any tracked changes. It's simply InfoPath's way of asserting its independence.

NOTE

Once your form is done, whether it is in Word format or InfoPath format, you can publish it to a SharePoint server, as you would any other document, to make it available to the users in your organization.

24

Summary

In this chapter, you've learned that Word has access to three sets of form tools. You've learned how to use Word's legacy form fields to create an order form, and you should be able to translate those techniques into creating a variety of different forms. You've also learned about Word's content controls feature, and how you can use content controls to create a document that basically tells the user what to type. And you've been exposed to Word's ActiveX controls, which are of limited use but can be explored further. You should now be able to do the following:

- Decide what set of form tools to use, based on your level of knowledge and your support resources
- Create a form for collecting information
- Use content controls to create a document template
- Protect and unprotect a document for forms entry

Part VIII

Publishing, Collaboration, and the Cloud

The modern workplace requires an unprecedented level of collaboration, and software such as the Microsoft Office suite increasingly includes tools and options to facilitate team document development and sharing. This part of the *Microsoft Word 2013 Bible* shows you how to integrate your Word work with the work of others and other programs.

Chapter 25 explores file formats that enable users to view documents outside Word and how to publish your work online. Chapter 26 shows you how to protect your documents so you can control what happens to them and see who did what, as well as exploring the various ways to compare and combine collaborative documents, even when Word's tracking features weren't being used. Chapter 27 shows you how to share documents and other resources among different computers and users, using SkyDrive in particular. Finally, Chapter 28 shows you how to use Word hand-in-hand with other Office 2013 applications, such as Outlook, Excel, and PowerPoint.

Sharing and Publishing Documents

IN THIS CHAPTER

I n this chapter we look at Word's ability to save files in either of two competing printer-ready formats: PDF and XPS. Each is a more or less open file format that aspires to be the industry standard for distributing documents in such a way that they appear identical to the reader regardless of platform—PC, Macintosh, Unix, Linux, and so on. Word 2013 adds the ability to edit PDF files.

The chapter also looks at other ways of digitally sharing information, including emailing a Word file to others and presenting a document online. Finally, this chapter looks at publishing for the Web in the form of HTML (Hyperttext Markup Language) and blogging (short for web logging, a web log being a journal published to the Web).

Working with PDF Files in Word

PDF stands for *portable document format*. It is an open-standard file format owned and developed by Adobe Systems. PDF is designed so that any given document looks identical regardless of the operating system and other software used to display or print it.

A Word document you send to someone else will look different depending on a variety of circumstances, including the following:

- Whether the reader has Word or is using different software to view the document.
- Whether the reader is running Word on Windows or on a Mac makes a difference, as well as whether the document is being viewed in an older version of Word via a converter.
- Whether the reader has the template on which the document was based.
- The capabilities of the printer and printer driver on the reader's system.
- Whether the reader's system has the fonts needed to display the file.

The PDF format is designed to make those conditions irrelevant. Each PDF file contains everything that's needed to completely display/render the file so that it looks reasonably identical for each person who views it, regardless of operating system or computer hardware. A PDF also enables you to encrypt and password-protect a document so that it can be read only by those with the password, preventing it from being copied, printed, or otherwise modified (even with Adobe Acrobat Pro, the premier PDF-authoring program).

Furthermore, when the resulting files are printed, regardless of what kind of computer or operating system is being used, the printed results should be more or less identical. Whether the documents are viewed onscreen or printed, all readers have essentially the same reading experience. Yes, there are always going to be variations caused by hardware capabilities, but to the greatest extent possible, those variations are minimal.

Viewing PDF files in Word

Previously, to view PDF files you needed a PDF reader, such as Adobe Reader (http://get .adobe.com/reader) or another PDF reader of your preference. Windows 8 now also includes the built-in Reader app, accessible from the Start screen, although its tools for viewing and working with document content are much more limited than those found in Adobe Reader.

Now you can open PDF documents directly in Word to view and work with them. The new feature called *PDF Reflow* enables Word to open PDF files directly so that you can read, edit, and reformat the contents in Word. Open a PDF in Word using these steps:

1. **Choose ⇨ File ⇨ Open ⇨ Computer ⇨ Browse.** The Open dialog box appears.
2. **Click All Files to the right of the File name text box, and then click PDF Files.**
3. **Navigate to the folder holding the file.** As shown in Figure 25.1, only PDF files appear due to the choice you made in the prior step. (You can use the Change your view button located at left just below the Search text box in the Open dialog box to change to the Details view, which includes the Type column, as shown in Figure 25.1.)

4. **Click the file, and then click Open.** Word displays the message shown in Figure 25.2, informing you it will convert the file so that you can edit it in Word.

5. **Click OK to continue and open the file.** The file appears in Word.

FIGURE 25.1

Choose the PDF Files file type to make it easier to locate PDF files in the Open dialog box.

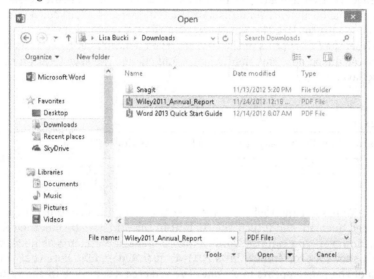

FIGURE 25.2

Word informs you it will be performing a conversion to make the PDF file editable.

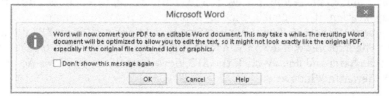

Editing PDF files

If the PDF file is one that you've created yourself in Word or another program, it opens immediately for editing.

Word treats PDFs that you've downloaded from the Web, received as an email attachment, or opened from a potentially unsafe network location a little differently. In such instances, the converted PDF file initially opens in Protected View in Word, as indicated by the Protected View Message Bar that appears (see Figure 25.3). Click the Enable Editing button to continue working with the document. Word displays another message about converting the file. Click OK. It's a good idea to click the Save button on the QAT right away, because even though the file name from the PDF appears in the title bar, the file hasn't yet been saved in Word format. In the Save As dialog box, edit the file name and change the save location as needed, and then click Save.

FIGURE 25.3

The converted PDF file initially appears in Protected View.

| PROTECTED VIEW Be careful—files from the Internet can contain viruses. Unless you need to edit, it's safer to stay in Protected View. | Enable Editing | × |

You can use Word's editing tools to make changes to the file's contents. Depending on the methods used to create and format the content in the original PDF file, the conversion results may vary. However, you can use Word's tools to make adjustments as needed. For example, Figure 25.4 shows a page from Wiley's 2011 Annual Report PDF. Note that some of the text at the top of the page appears in a table. I've selected a sentence in the right column and applied bold for emphasis. I've also displayed the rulers and am dragging the Left Indent tool on the Horizontal ruler to fix the indention issue in the right column.

Understanding and Viewing XPS Files

XPS stands for *XML paper specification*. It is Microsoft's response to PDF—intended to provide a computer-independent method for distributing files so that they look the same to anyone who opens them for viewing or for printing. XPS is a potential competitor of PDF, but perhaps only in the long term.

Windows 7 and 8 enable you to view XPS files directly, but each uses a different viewer or reader application. If you double-click an XPS file in a Windows Explorer window in Windows 7, the file opens in the XPS Viewer application. If you double-click an XPS file (or OpenXPS file) in a File Explorer window in Windows 8, it opens in the Reader app. You also can use the Search charm and double-click the XPS Viewer tile under Windows Accessories to use the XPS Viewer in Windows 8.

FIGURE 25.4

You may need to make some corrections to the formatting of the imported PDF file, but you generally will be able to use Word's tools to edit and format it as needed.

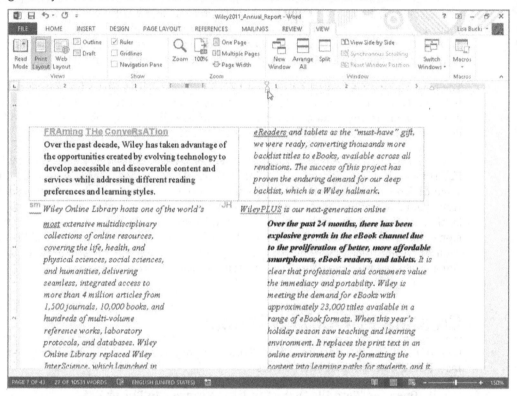

NOTE

In both Windows 7 and Windows 8, you can open the Print capability from any application (including Word) and select Microsoft XPS Document Writer as the printer. Then when you click Print, the Save Print Output As dialog box appears and asks you for a file name and save location. After you specify those, click Save. In Windows 7, this saves the file as an XPS document with the `.xps` file name extension. In Windows 8, the file is saved as an OpenXPS document with the `.oxps` file name extension. OpenXPS is the next-generation, more open variation of XPS, and you can view OpenXPS in the Reader app or XPS Viewer in Windows 8.

Deciding Which Format to Use for Output

If you are distributing documents for a more controlled environment in which document permissions are being set (where Windows Rights Management Services is in use, a subject that's beyond the scope of this book) or the environment for some reason has standardized on XPS, then XPS might be the way to go. If you need to create documents for the widest possible audience, at this time at least, the decision is a no-brainer: PDF.

The best way to determine whether Word 2013's PDF capability works for your documents is to try it. Does the resulting PDF look the way you expect it to look? Is it legible? Are the colors correct? Is anything missing or distorted? Are all of the graphics—including borders—present and accounted for? Is the file size acceptable?

Of course, if you have Adobe Acrobat or other PDF-writing software, you can try saving a PDF from both it and Word using similar quality settings and compare the results. Although small differences may be present in the sample pages, generally speaking a PDF generated from Word 2013 will be adequate for onscreen viewing and everyday printing. It might well be that for a document with tables, SmartArt, WordArt, and a variety of other document elements, Acrobat or another converter that offers more options such as PrimoPDF might even be outperformed by Word. (Of course, given that Acrobat is the standard for professional high-end printing, Word won't match its capabilities in that arena.)

Creating PDF or XPS Output

Creating a PDF or XPS document from Word is as easy as saving a file, but likely not quite as fast. Here's how to handle the process:

1. **Open the Word file that you'd like to convert to PDF or XPS.**
2. **Choose File ⇨ Export ⇨ Create PDF/XPS Document ⇨ Create a PDF/XPS.** The Publish as PDF or XPS dialog box shown in Figure 25.5 appears.
3. **Open the Save as type drop-down list, and click PDF or XPS Document as needed.** When saving as XPS, the main Publish as PDF or XPS dialog box offers the same options for PDF format.
4. **Change the File name if the one suggested isn't acceptable.**
5. **If you want to preview the resulting PDF file, make sure Open file after publishing is checked.** (If this option is grayed out, then your default PDF or XPS viewer either does not exist or is not installed correctly.)
6. **(Optional) Choose Optimize for and Options settings.** (These are described further in the upcoming sections.)
7. **Click Publish.** After conversion, the file opens in the default PDF viewer.

FIGURE 25.5

Creating a PDF/XPS is not an ergonomic exercise.

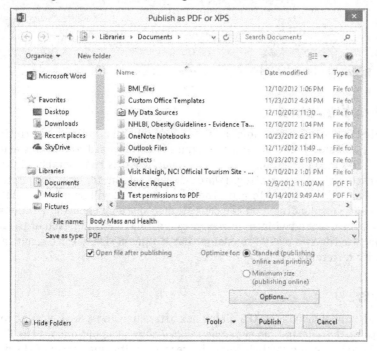

If you try to save a password-protected Word file as a PDF, the warning shown in Figure 25.6 appears and tells you the password protection will be removed. You can click No and then Cancel to back out of the PDF save process. Remove the password protection in Word. Return to the Publish as PDF or XPS dialog box, and then use Options as described shortly to add a password when creating the PDF.

FIGURE 25.6

Saving as a PDF removes any password assigned to the source Word document.

> **CAUTION**
>
> Although you can save from Word to PDF and then open your new PDF again in Word as a converted Word document, be careful about editing and saving back to PDF from there. Though Word's conversion capabilities work pretty well, if you have a source Word document with complex formatting and copious graphics and tables, it's best to edit in the original Word document (not the one reimported from PDF) to ensure your formatting remains as intended.

Choosing the optimization

In Figure 25.5, note the Optimize for choices: Standard (publishing online and printing) and Minimum size (publishing online). Graphics typically do not need resolutions above the current screen's DPI (usually 96) for display onscreen, whereas considerably higher resolutions are needed for quality printing. (Word's default setting for graphics resolution is 220 PPI or DPI.) If you don't intend to print the document or it will be made available online for viewing and downloading, you can save storage space by choosing Minimum size (publishing online). It's never a bad idea, however, to create a PDF using each of the settings and then compare the two results to ensure that Minimum size doesn't result in an unacceptable quality difference.

Setting options

Click Options in the Publish as PDF or XPS dialog box after choosing a Save as type to view additional settings for the selected file type. Figure 25.7 shows the options for the PDF file type. Use the Page range and Publish what choices to specify what parts of the document to print. Under Include non-printing information, you can choose whether to include Document properties and Document structure tags for accessibility. Word also can automatically generate bookmarks in the PDF if you check Create bookmarks using, and then choose whether the bookmarks should come from Headings (assuming you've formatted with heading styles) or Word bookmarks (that you already created in the document).

Under PDF options, you generally will find that checking ISO 19005-1-compliant (PDF/A) produces files that are significantly larger (often as much as 80 percent larger) than those produced by the default Bitmap text when fonts may not be embedded option. At the same time, the fidelity is greater as well. Note that choosing the ISO option grays out the Document properties option under Include non-printing information, as well as the Bitmap text... and Encrypt the document... options.

When you need to password-protect the PDF file, check Encrypt the document with a password. After choosing options as needed, click OK to return to the Publish as PDF or XPS dialog box. If you checked Encrypt the document with a password, the Encrypt PDF Document dialog box shown in Figure 25.8 appears. Type the desired password in the Password and Reenter password text boxes, and click OK.

FIGURE 25.7

Options for publishing a PDF file

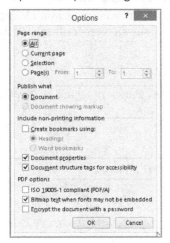

FIGURE 25.8

You can apply a password while saving to PDF.

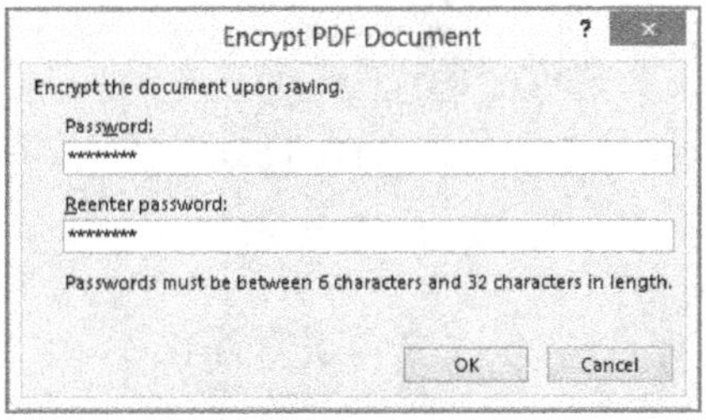

TIP

If you use PDF format often, you can save steps by adding the Publish as PDF or XPS command to your Quick Access Toolbar. Right-click the QAT and choose Customize Quick Access Toolbar. Set Choose commands from to All Commands. Scroll down to Publish as PDF or XPS and click Add, then OK.

If you've chosen the XPS Document format in the Publish as PDF or XPS dialog box, when you click Options, most of the choices in the Options dialog box are the same. You can specify a Page range or make a choice under Publish what, as well as determine what to check under Include non-printing information. The bottom section holds the only difference. There, under XPS Document options, you can check Preserve restricted permissions in XPS if available. Select any options you need, and click OK to return to the Publish as PDF or XPS dialog box.

Emailing a Document

Word enables you to send the current file directly to an Outlook message as a file attachment. This makes it easy to shoot a document over to a colleague for feedback. To email a document as a file attachment:

1. **Open the Word file that you'd like to send.**
2. **Choose File ⇨ Share ⇨ Email.** The Share choices shown in Figure 25.9 appear in Backstage view.

FIGURE 25.9

Word provides choices for how to format the attached file.

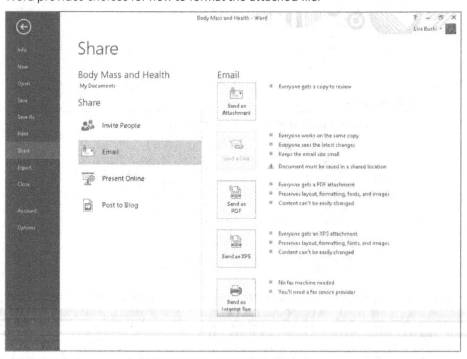

3. **Click Send as Attachment under Email at right.** Only use Send as PDF or Send as XPS if you want to both convert and send the file. However, for normal collaboration, sending the file in its native Word document format works best. Word opens an Outlook message window with the file already inserted as an attachment, as shown in Figure 25.10.

FIGURE 25.10

The initial email message with a Word file attached

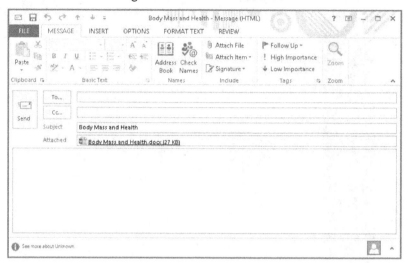

4. **Enter the recipient email addresses in the To field, edit the Subject field as needed, and type a message in the body text area.**

5. **Click Send.** The message goes to the Outlook Outbox folder and will be routed to the recipients the next time messages are sent and received, either automatically or manually.

> **NOTE**
>
> The steps for emailing documents assume you have an email account configured in Outlook. If you don't, you will see a message prompting you to set one up after you click Send.

Presenting a Document to an Online Audience

Microsoft offers a free online platform called the Office Presentation Service that you can use to present documents from some Office applications online. You can show a Word document to your audience page by page over the Web while simultaneously holding a conference call, which is a great way to encourage greater buy in and audience interaction. Here's how to present a Word document online:

1. **Open the Word file that you'd like to present.**

2. **Choose File ⇨ Share ⇨ Present Online.** The Present Online choices shown in Figure 25.11 appear in Backstage view.

FIGURE 25.11

Share a presentation online through the Microsoft Presentation Service.

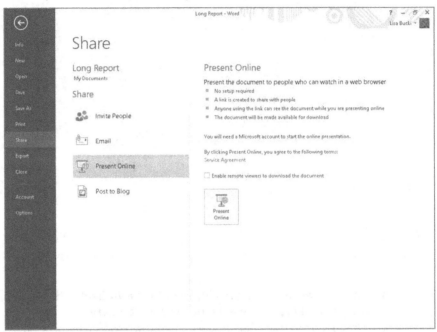

3. **(Optional) Click Enable remote viewers to download the document to check it.** Enabling this option enables the colleagues who you invite to view the presentation to choose to download a copy of the file for later viewing in Word.

4. **Click Present Online.** The Present Online window shown in Figure 25.12 appears. After it prepares the online presentation, it displays the link that you can use to invite colleagues to your online presentation. You can use Copy Link to copy the link so you can paste it into an IM message (such as in Microsoft Lync), or click Send in Email to open an Outlook message window with the link in the message body. Address and send the message.

5. **After you've invited recipients and given time for them to be ready to join the online presentation, click Start Presentation.** The Present Online tab appears on the Ribbon, as shown in Figure 25.13.

6. **Use Page Down and Page Up on your keyboard or the vertical scroll bar on the right side of the screen to move through the document.**

7. **If you need to make changes or comments, click Edit in the Present Online group, make the desired changes, and then click Resume in the Online Presentation Paused Message Bar.**

8. **When you finish, click End Online Presentation in the Present Online group of the Present Online tab.**

9. **In the message box, click End Online Presentation to confirm.**

FIGURE 25.12

The online presentation is ready to go at this point.

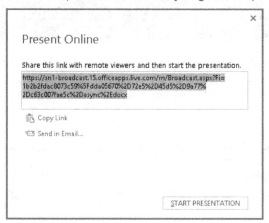

FIGURE 25.13

Use the Present Online tools and other Word tools to work with the presentation.

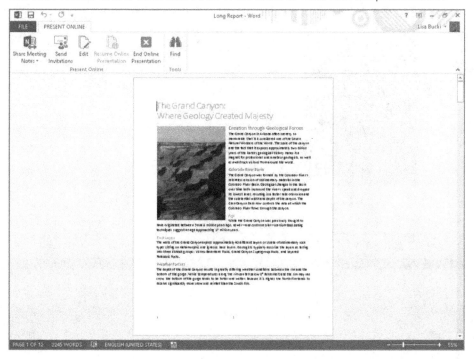

NOTE

The idea is that you and colleagues viewing the show will be conversing by conference call or Lync as you're viewing the document online.

If you've received an invitation to view a document presented online, simply click it to launch your system's web browser and go to the shared file. You can click the tab to open the Comments pane, where you can review questions, as in the example in Figure 25.14.

FIGURE 25.14

Viewing the document and a comment online.

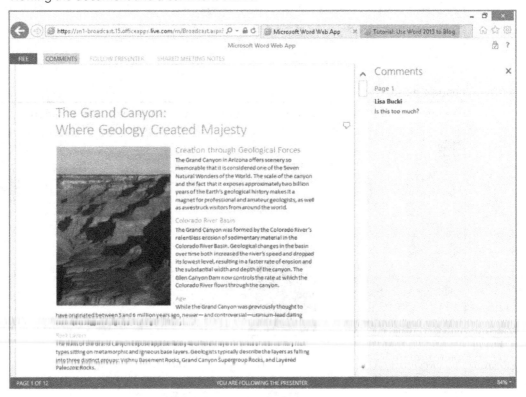

HTML Overview

HTML (Hypertext Markup Language) is the primary language of the Web. Most basic web pages are saved as HTML files, with the `.html` or `.htm` file name extension. Why *markup?* Imagine that you have some text that someone has edited or *marked up* to indicate which words are bold, which are italicized, which are larger, and so on. The markup aspect of HTML involves the insertion of tags that tell a web browser how to display the text.

Suppose, for example, that a browser, such as Internet Explorer, Chrome, or Firefox, encounters the following:

```
<b>This</b> is a <i>test</i>.
```

The bits between the angle brackets are called *tags*. `<b>` is a tag that means bold. `<i>` means italics. The `<b>` tag means "begin bold"; `</b>` means "end bold." The tags tell the browser where certain kinds of formatting begin and end. For example, a browser would display the preceding example line as follows:

This is a *test*.

Tags also are used to perform other chores, such as displaying pictures or hyperlinks, the beginning and ending of paragraphs, numbering, bullets, centering, and a variety of other attributes. The word *hyperlink* is where the *hyper* part of HTML's name comes from. Clicking a hyperlink causes a browser or other HTML-content displayer to jump to that link. Hyperlinks have revolutionized the way people use computers over the past two decades. (If you want to learn how to code HTML, sources abound, including many free resources on the Web. A simple search will lead you in directions and to places that this book isn't going.)

To save a Word file as HTML:

1. **Design the file as desired and preview it in Web Layout view.**
2. **Choose File ➪ Save As ➪ Computer ➪ Browse.**
3. **Choose a save location, set Save as type to Web Page, and edit the File name as needed.**
4. **Click Change Title, enter a page title in the Page title text box, and click OK.**
5. **Click Save.**

You can then upload the resulting *filename*`.htm` file and its matching *filename_files* folder to your site folder on your web host using a service such as FTP or your host's online uploading tools.

Understanding differences in Word's HTML

Using Word to save a document for the Web (thus creating an HTML file) is tempting, especially if it's the only means you have for doing so. Just save any file in HTML format. Nothing could be easier.

However, that's where the advantages begin and end. Why? Let's begin with a simple example. Consider the Hello, World, a common phrase used in programming and design examples (we'll instead use Hello, Word). The raw truth is that if you put that phrase into a plain text editor and name the file `hello.htm`, any web browser can display it. You don't need anything other than those 12 characters (including punctuation and spaces). Yes, there are additional elements that browsers want to see, but there's a difference between wanting and needing.

If you use SharePoint Designer and feed it those 12 characters, it's not quite so frugal, but it's not so bad. Here's what you get:

```
<title>Untitled 2</title>
</head>
<body>
<p>Hello, Word.</p>
</body>
</html>
```

SharePoint Designer is designed to produce HTML, so we would expect it to be good at what it's designed to do.

Now, say you press Ctrl+N in Word to start a new Document window and try the same thing. Type **Hello, Word.**, and then choose File ⇨ Save As ⇨ Computer ⇨ Browse, set Save as type to Web Page, accept the proposed name (Hello), and click Save. To see what this file really looks like, you could then open it in a text editor such as Notepad.

Remember that simple phrase "Hello, Word."? Converted into HTML by Word, it now has hundreds of lines, tags, and properties, as shown in Figure 25.15. But that's not the end of the story. At the same time, Word also created a folder named `Hello_files`, which contains three additional files—the infrastructure for a much more complex HTML file than the one we created.

786

FIGURE 25.15

Word converts a 12-character text message into a highly complex HTML file.

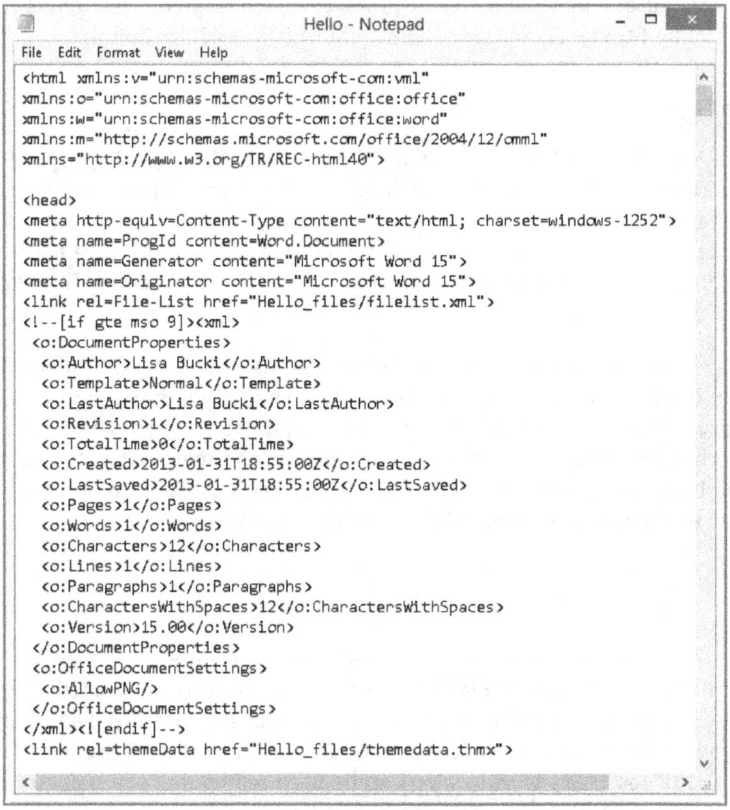

```
Hello - Notepad                                    - □ ×
File  Edit  Format  View  Help
<html xmlns:v="urn:schemas-microsoft-com:vml"
xmlns:o="urn:schemas-microsoft-com:office:office"
xmlns:w="urn:schemas-microsoft-com:office:word"
xmlns:m="http://schemas.microsoft.com/office/2004/12/omml"
xmlns="http://www.w3.org/TR/REC-html40">

<head>
<meta http-equiv=Content-Type content="text/html; charset=windows-1252">
<meta name=ProgId content=Word.Document>
<meta name=Generator content="Microsoft Word 15">
<meta name=Originator content="Microsoft Word 15">
<link rel=File-List href="Hello_files/filelist.xml">
<!--[if gte mso 9]><xml>
 <o:DocumentProperties>
  <o:Author>Lisa Bucki</o:Author>
  <o:Template>Normal</o:Template>
  <o:LastAuthor>Lisa Bucki</o:LastAuthor>
  <o:Revision>1</o:Revision>
  <o:TotalTime>0</o:TotalTime>
  <o:Created>2013-01-31T18:55:00Z</o:Created>
  <o:LastSaved>2013-01-31T18:55:00Z</o:LastSaved>
  <o:Pages>1</o:Pages>
  <o:Words>1</o:Words>
  <o:Characters>12</o:Characters>
  <o:Lines>1</o:Lines>
  <o:Paragraphs>1</o:Paragraphs>
  <o:CharactersWithSpaces>12</o:CharactersWithSpaces>
  <o:Version>15.00</o:Version>
 </o:DocumentProperties>
 <o:OfficeDocumentSettings>
  <o:AllowPNG/>
 </o:OfficeDocumentSettings>
</xml><![endif]-->
<link rel=themeData href="Hello_files/themedata.thmx">
```

In fairness to Word, we didn't use the optimal approach to saving HTML. Selecting the Web Page, Filtered Save as type results in a much more compact file.

Although Microsoft has put a lot of effort into including HTML in Office and Word, the truth is that there are other programs that are much better at HTML—from an authoring standpoint, from a publishing standpoint, and from a maintenance standpoint. Moreover, Word has rightfully earned a reputation in the HTML world for producing HTML documents that don't necessarily play well with modern web tools such as CSS, scripting, and various menuing tools. So, depending on your needs and capabilities, you can go with something other than Word—something such as SharePoint Designer, Microsoft Expression Web, Dreamweaver, or something else.

HTML is an endlessly deep subject about which a great many books have been written. Doing any sort of justice to it is well beyond the scope of the *Microsoft Word 2013 Bible*. If you want to explore all of the capabilities of HTML in depth, a great resource is *HTML, XHTML, and CSS Bible*, by Steven M. Schafer (Wiley, ISBN: 978-0-470-52396-4).

What Is MHTML?

The Single File Web Page Save as type is based on MIME HTML. MIME (Multipurpose Internet Mail Extensions) is the standard format in which email is sent over the Internet. Its specification includes the capability to encode graphics and other binary attachments into plain text so they can be transmitted over older computers that support only plain text (the original 128 characters known as ASCII, or American Standard Code for Information Interchange).

If you choose to save a Word document for the Web using the Single File Web Page format, it assigns the .mht file name extension. The idea here is that if you have pictures, sound files, or other binary content, it's often better to encapsulate them within the body of the HTML file itself so that when you email the file to someone, the recipient will have all the ingredients needed to properly display it. MHTML is an emerging standard. That means that not every browser will display the same MHTML file identically.

Blogging

The Post to Blog feature enables you to publish directly from Word to supported blogs, which include SharePoint Blog, WordPress, Blogger, Telligent Community, and TypePad. Simply put, blogging enables you to share your own articles and ideas online without maintaining a separate website. Each post you make to your blog can be followed by and often commented on by your readers. The different blog sites offer different levels of functionality, so you may want to visit each of them before deciding which one to sign on with. Create your account with the desired blog provider before moving on to the next steps for registering your blog account with Word.

Registering with a blog platform

The first time you choose File ➪ Share ➪ Post to Blog, and then click the Post to Blog button in Word 2013, it prompts you to register for a blog account, as shown in Figure 25.16. Click Register Now. The New Blog Account dialog box shown in Figure 25.17 appears. If you already have a blog provider, select it from the Blog drop-down list, click Next, and follow the prompts to enter your sign-in information. (The procedure will vary depending on your provider.) Figure 25.18 shows example information entered for a WordPress account.

FIGURE 25.16

Click Register now to sign up for or specify a blog account.

FIGURE 25.17

Select your blog provider and click Next, or click I don't have a blog yet.

FIGURE 25.18

Enter blog sign-in information, and then click OK.

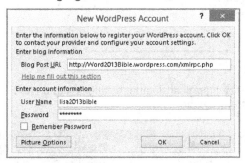

Click OK to finish registering, and then click Yes in the warning about account information. If you succeed, you'll see a message box saying that account registration was successful. Click OK to start blogging!

Composing and publishing your blog entry

For each blog post, you should start by creating a new document for it in Word. You can do this in one of two ways:

- Choose File ➪ Share ➪ Post to Blog ➪ Post to Blog.
- Choose File ➪ New. Scroll down the templates, and click Blog post. Click Create in the description window that appears (Figure 25.19).

FIGURE 25.19

Use File a New a Blog post a Create to begin a new blog post.

No matter which method you use, the empty blog post document appears and the Blog Post tab appears on the Ribbon, as shown in Figure 25.20.

NOTE

When you choose File ➪ New ➪ Blog post ➪ Create, Word opens a new document window based on the Blog.dotx template. See Chapter 18, "Saving Time with Templates, Themes, and Master Documents," for more information about templates.

FIGURE 25.20

When you start a blog document, Word displays the Blog Post tools.

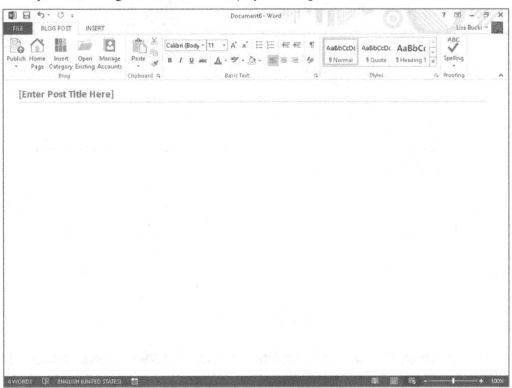

Create your post, replacing the post title placeholder text and adding body text as desired. When you're done, save a copy of the post as a Word document, if desired. Note that the Publish button in the Ribbon is a split button. Click the top half to publish immediately. Use the bottom half to choose between Publish and Publish as Draft. Enter you username and password in the Connect to dialog box that appears; click OK, then Yes in the message that appears. When you publish you'll see a notification bar above your blog entry indicating that posting was successful, as shown in Figure 25.21.

FIGURE 25.21

Word lets you know that a blog entry was successfully published. Log on to your blog account to verify that it actually worked.

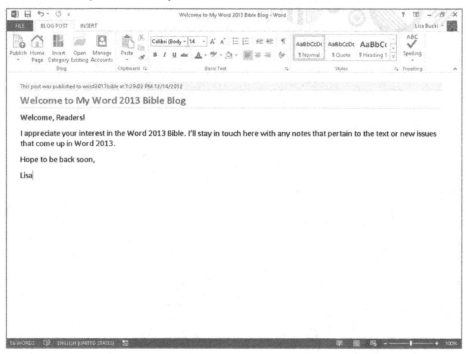

If a blog post fails, you'll see an error message box. That usually just means a temporary communication issue. Try to post again in a few minutes, and it will usually work fine.

> **CAUTION**
>
> Do you have a business and a personal blog? If so, be careful not to accidentally post to the wrong one. It's extremely easy to do, and if your blog is syndicated through RSS, there's absolutely no way to guarantee that an "Oops!" entry won't be read by someone you don't want reading it. If there's any risk of this happening, set the *least harm* blog as your default. Better still, create a throwaway blog somewhere—one that nobody else can read—and set that one as your default. That way, if you inadvertently forget to choose a destination, there's no harm done.

Taking advantage of other blog tools

Other useful blog-related items in the Blog Post tab include Home Page and Insert Category—both in the Blog group. The Home Page tool opens your browser to the main web page for the currently selected blog account.

Use the Insert Category tool if your blog supports categories for organizing your posts. When you click Insert Category, you'll be prompted to sign in to your blog account, and then a Category drop-down appears under the post title placeholder. Select a category from the category drop-down list or type a new one into the text box.

NOTE

To register additional accounts, or to manage existing ones, click Manage Accounts in the Blog group of the Blog Post tab. In the Blog Accounts dialog box, use the New button to add a new account. Select an account in the list, and click Change to edit it, Set As Default to make it the default account, or Remove to delete it.

Using Open Existing to correct and revise

The best way to find errors in a blog is to publish the blog online and then read it. A post you moments ago pronounced "good-to-go" may contain errors upon a second read.

To edit an existing post, click Open Existing in the Blog group of the Blog Post tab. (Start a new blank blog entry first if you need to display the Blog Post tools.) Sign in to your blog account when prompted. In the Open Existing Post dialog box (Figure 25.22), scroll to the desired post if needed, select it, and click OK. Sign in again if prompted. At the top of the post, an information bar displays the publication time and date as shown in Figure 25.21. Make any changes you see fit, click Publish, and sign in. Word will now display the **re**-publication time and date in the information bar at the top of the post, above the title.

FIGURE 25.22

Select an existing post to edit and republish.

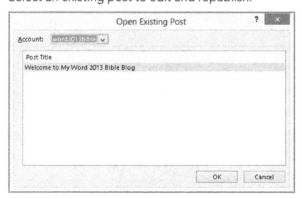

There is a limited number of existing posts that Word can fetch in this manner. You might be able to increase this number using your blog settings (from the Web interface—not from Word). If the existing post does not show up in the Open Existing Post dialog box, however, you will need to edit the post using your Web interface to make changes. Or if you require Word's capabilities, you can sometimes trick the post into appearing in the Open Existing Post dialog box by changing the posting date using the Web interface.

Summary

In this chapter you've explored the difference between PDF files and XPS files. You also learned about sharing a document via email or an online presentation, and how to publish your work as an HTML file or blog post. You should now be able to handle these tasks:

- Decide whether to use PDF or XPS format
- Decide whether to use higher-quality or lower-file-size PDF or XPS files
- View PDF and XPS files
- Create PDF and XPS files, optimizing and setting options as needed
- Email a Word document to colleagues
- Present a document online
- Convert a Word document to an HTML file
- Register any of a number of popular blog hosts for blogging directly from Word
- Blog from Word 2013
- Use Open Existing to correct and revise existing blog posts

Managing Document Security, Comments, and Tracked Changes

IN THIS CHAPTER

Document protection

Using digital signatures and signature lines

Protecting a document with a password

Inserting comments

Tracking changes

Reviewing comments and changes

Comparing two documents using "legal blackline"

Combining documents that contain tracked changes

Word offers a variety of kinds of protection (although nothing is 100 percent secure). Some of the protection tools work hand in hand with other tools that facilitate collaboration and reviewing. For example, you can limit formatting or allow users only to enter tracked changes or comments.

This chapter looks at the types of document protection and review tools available to Word users and describes how to use them.

Protection Types

Word 2013's privacy settings aren't centrally located. To save you the trouble of searching to find what you can control, here's the definitive list of the different types of protection (and pseudo-protection) Word 2013 offers and where to find them:

- **Permission:** Restrict a document so it can be opened and/or changed only by specific individuals. Select File ⇨ Info ⇨ Protect Document ⇨ Restrict Access. For this to work, your system must be set up for Information Rights Management so it can connect to a Digital Rights Management server, a topic that's beyond the scope of this book.

- **Digital signature:** Sign a document with a digital signature to provide assurance that you are the source of the document. Select File ⇨ Info ⇨ Protect Document ⇨ Add a Digital Signature.

- **Inspect Document:** Inspect the document to see if it contains private or sensitive information or data. Select File ⇨ Info ⇨ Check for Issues ⇨ Inspect Document.

- **Mark as Final:** Mark a document as final to let recipients know that the document is considered the final revision. This setting makes the document read-only and makes it unavailable for additional typing, editing, proofing, or tracking changes. Note that this setting is advisory only—you can click the big Edit Anyway button— this removes the Mark as Final setting. Recipients with earlier versions of Word who have installed the Office 2010 Compatibility Pack won't even see the file as read-only. Hence, this kind of gentle protection would have to be combined with something more substantial to be meaningful. Select File ⇨ Info ⇨ Protect Document ⇨ Mark As Final.

- **Style formatting restrictions:** Limit formatting to a selection of styles as well as block Theme, Scheme, or Quick Style Set switching. Protection here is by password, and is therefore less secure and robust than when using permissions. Select File ⇨ Info ⇨ Protect Document ⇨ Restrict Editing ⇨ Limit formatting to a selection of styles.

- **Editing restrictions—Read only:** This offers password protection, which is not very secure, along with exceptions of specific areas of the document. Exceptions can be made wholesale, or you can limit them to individuals with specific Microsoft account–associated email addresses. Select File ⇨ Info ⇨ Protect Document ⇨ Restrict Editing ⇨ Allow only this type of editing in the document ⇨ No changes (read only).

- **Editing restrictions—Tracked changes:** This type of protection allows only tracked changes to be made. Select File ⇨ Info ⇨ Protect Document ⇨ Restrict Editing ⇨ Allow only this type of editing in the document ⇨ Tracked changes.

- **Editing restrictions—Fill-in forms:** This type of protection allows filling in of form fields and content controls. Select File ⇨ Info ⇨ Protect Document ⇨ Restrict Editing ⇨ Allow only this type of editing in the document ⇨ Filling in forms.

- **Editing restrictions—Comments:** This type of protection allows only comments. Exceptions can be made for selected areas of the document, for everyone, or for specific individuals (using Microsoft account ID–associated email addresses). Select File ⇨ Info ⇨ Protect Document ⇨ Restrict Editing ⇨ Allow only this type of editing in the document ⇨ Comments.

- **Password to open/modify:** This type of protection lets you specify a password to open and/or modify the document. This protection is not the same as the Editing restrictions' No Changes setting. You must choose one or the other. Select File ⇨ Save As ⇨ Computer ⇨ Browse ⇨ Tools ⇨ General Options.

NOTE

Some of these controls are also available using the Protect group on the Developer tab.

The rest of this section looks at these settings, showing how you enable protection and assessing the degree of protection provided.

Information Rights Management

A relatively new and strong way to protect your documents uses an Information Rights Management server to authenticate users who create or receive documents or email that have restricted permissions. If your organization uses a Rights Management Services (RMS) server, your system administrator must enable Windows and Office 2013 to work with RMS. You then choose File ⇨ Info ⇨ Protect Document ⇨ Restrict Access, and click Connect to Digital Rights Management Services and get templates to get started. From there you can use the File ⇨ Info ⇨ Protect Document ⇨ Restrict Access commands to restrict access to the document to specified user accounts, or remove previously applied restrictions.

Using digital signatures

A *digital signature* is an electronic certificate that provides a way for recipients to verify that a document or email actually came from the sender. Digital signatures do not provide 100% guaranteed authentication that a document is from a non-malicious sender, but generally speaking, a document signed by someone you know and trust is likely to be more trustworthy than an unsigned document from an unknown or suspicious source.

NOTE

Carefully check any document with a digital signature. If you receive something important and the validity of the signature is an issue, pick up the telephone and call the sender to verify the document's contents. Never share private information such as account numbers or passwords on the basis of a digital signature alone.

Before you can digitally sign a document, you must have a digital signature installed on your system. To get a signature, choose File ⇨ Info ⇨ Protect Document ⇨ Add a Digital Signature. If this is the first time you've used this feature, Word displays the dialog box shown in Figure 26.1. Click Yes to obtain a certificate. Your system's web browser launches and displays Microsoft's Available Digital IDs page, listing partner organizations though which you can obtain a digital ID and download and install a certificate on your system.

FIGURE 26.1

If you don't already have a digital signing certificate, click Yes to learn about for-fee and for-free services.

NOTE

You also can use the Office SelfCert utility to create your own digital certificate. SelfCert certificates are for personal use only on the computer on which they were created. To learn more about working with digital certificates on your system, see the TechNet topic "Manage Certificates" at http://technet.microsoft.com/en-us/library/cc771377.aspx. To learn how to create a SelfCert signature, see "Installing and running SelfCert" in Chapter 32, "Macros: Recording, Editing, and Using Them."

How to digitally sign a Word document

After you've obtained a digital signature, follow these steps to digitally sign a Word document:

1. **Choose File ⇨ Info ⇨ Protect Document ⇨ Add a Digital Signature.** If the document has not been saved, you are prompted to save the file as a Word document. Click Yes, enter a File name, and click Save. Word then displays the Sign dialog box, shown in Figure 26.2.

2. **Open the Commitment Type drop-down list and click the desired commitment type.**

3. **Type a Purpose for signing this document entry if desired.**

4. **To enter more information about yourself as the signer, click Details, add entries in the text boxes in the Additional Signing Information dialog box as desired, and then click OK.**

5. **If the Signing As identity/certificate isn't the one you want to use, click Change, click an alternate certificate in the Windows Security dialog box, and click OK.**

6. **Click Sign.** The Signature Confirmation message appears, as shown in Figure 26.3.

7. **Click OK to finish applying the signature.** This also marks the document as final, a feature you'll read about soon. As shown in Figure 26.4, the Backstage view indicates that the document has been signed and marked as final.

FIGURE 26.2

Specify signature details here.

FIGURE 26.3

Don't sign a document until you're finished making changes to it.

FIGURE 26.4

Backstage view now identifies the file as a signed document.

Removing a signature

Once you've signed a document, the document is locked against further changes until the signature is removed. Unlike document permissions, a digital signature can be removed from a Word document by anyone with the appropriate version of Word. Once a signature has been removed, however, only be signed again by the owner of the original signing certificate. Hence, if I send you a signed file and you remove my signature, you can edit the file I sent you and make any changes you want to. However, you will not be able to restore my signature.

> **CAUTION**
>
> There are ways to make a forged signature look valid, and not everyone is sufficiently skeptical. Make sure you know and trust the sender before you open a signed document.

When you open a signed document, the messages shown in Figure 26.5 appear at the top of the document. You can click Edit Anyway if you want to make changes to the document.

FIGURE 26.5

Messages tell you when a document you open has been marked as final and signed.

To view and work with signatures in the document, click the View Signatures button in the Message Bar, or choose File ⇨ Info ⇨ View Signatures. The Signatures pane opens at the right side of the document window. To remove a signature, move your mouse pointer over it, click the drop-down list arrow that appears, and click Remove Signature as shown in Figure 26.6. (Note that you also can view details about the signature.) At the prompt that asks whether you want to remove the signature permanently, click Yes.

Don't let the words "permanently" and "cannot be undone" in the Remove Signature message box throw you. This simply means that you can't remove someone's signature, change that $1,000 fee to $100,000, and then reaffix their signature. Once you remove someone's signature, only they can put it back.

FIGURE 26.6

View and work with digital signatures in the Signatures pane.

Adding a signature line

Word 2013 now includes the ability to specify a signature line to prompt for a recipient's signature. You can include a signature line on a contract, a proposal, a change order verification, or any other type of document that requires a signature to indicate agreement or approval. To add a signature line in a document:

1. **Click to position the insertion point in the location where you want the signature to appear.**

2. **Click the Insert tab, and in the Text group, click the Add a Signature Line button.** (If you click the button's down arrow, instead, click the Microsoft Office Signature Line command.) The Signature Setup dialog box shown in Figure 26.7 appears.

3. **Enter the desired information.** You can enter only a Suggested signer, or you can add other information as needed depending on what you want to include in the signature.

4. **Click OK.** Word inserts the signature line in the document.

FIGURE 26.7

Set up the signature information here.

As shown in Figure 26.8, the signature line is a special object in the document. To use it to sign the document, double-click it. The Sign dialog box appears. If you previously scanned your actual signature and saved it as a graphic file, you can click Select Image and use the Browse choice, in the Insert Picture window that appears, to select and insert the signature file. Otherwise, just click in the text box, type your signature, and click Sign.

FIGURE 26.8

Double-click the signature line to open the Sign dialog box so you can add your signature.

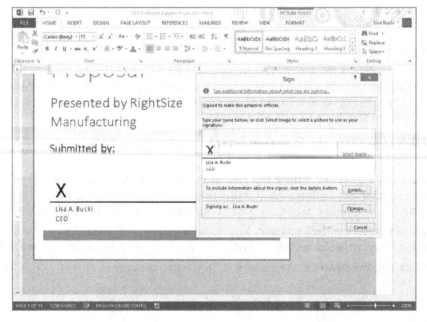

TIP

To change the information included with a signature, right-click it and then click Signature Setup to reopen the Signature Setup dialog box.

Document Inspector (removing private/personal information)

You can use the Document Inspector to see what private or personal information resides in a file and remove it. The Document Inspector checks for the kinds of information and content shown in Figure 26.9. To display the Document Inspector, choose File ➪ Info ➪ Check for Issues ➪ Inspect Document ➪ Inspect Document. By default, all eight areas are checked. Remove checks if you don't want those kinds of information removed. For example, if the purpose for sending a document to someone is to convey the XML data it contains, then remove the check next to Custom XML Data. On the other hand, if the document might contain "colorful" comments about someone's draft, you probably do want to inspect it for those. When the right checks are checked and the wrong checks are unchecked, click Inspect.

FIGURE 26.9

Use the Document Inspector to remove private/proprietary information before passing a document along to someone else.

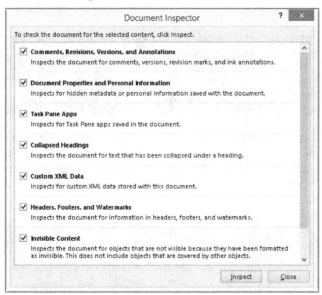

The Document Inspector inspects the current document for each of the types of material or data indicated. If it finds any, the Document Inspector dialog box is redisplayed, with Remove All buttons next to each type of content that was found, as shown in Figure 26.10.

FIGURE 26.10

A red exclamation mark means that the Document Inspector found potentially sensitive content, and the check mark indicates that the specified type of content was not found.

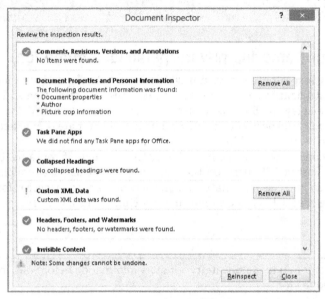

> **CAUTION**
>
> Make a backup copy of the document before using Remove All. Once you remove the content using the Document Inspector, you can't get it back using Undo. Particularly for comments and data, if they are content you need to preserve, make a backup copy of the document.

The Document Inspector does not provide further details about exactly what it found. You have two options: click Remove All to remove the found items, or click Close and review the types of items found by Document Inspector. You can remove the content yourself manually or you can return to the Document Inspector and use Remove All once you're satisfied that you want something removed.

> **NOTE**
>
> Unlike the Selection pane, which you can use to make objects visible or hidden in a document as described in Chapter 13, "Building Tables, Charts, and Smart Art to Show Data and Process," when you click Remove All in the Document Inspector, it actually does remove the hidden objects from the document—it doesn't just toggle their visibility. So, exercise caution if you really do need those objects; it's a good idea to create a for-distribution copy of the document.

Formatting and editing restrictions

The Restrict Formatting and Editing settings can provide a measure of protection for your document. You can limit the type of formatting that users can apply, limit the types of changes most users can make, and apply exceptions for trusted users. Specify these settings in the Restrict Editing pane, which you can display in one of two ways:

- Choose File ⇨ Info ⇨ Protect Document ⇨ Restrict Editing.
- Click the Review tab, and click Restrict Editing in the Protect group.

Limit formatting to a selection of styles

To limit formatting to certain styles, in the Restrict Editing pane shown in Figure 26.11, click to place a check next to Limit formatting to a selection of styles. To choose which styles, click Settings. The Formatting Restrictions dialog box now appears, also shown in Figure 26.11.

FIGURE 26.11

With Limit formatting to a selection of styles checked, click Settings to choose those limits.

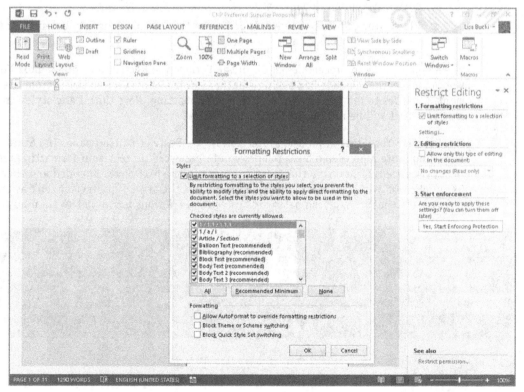

The Formatting Restrictions dialog box provides the following options:

- **Checked styles are currently allowed:** Place a check next to each style you want to allow. Remove checks for styles you want to disallow. Note that the styles listed might be limited based on settings in the Manage Styles dialog box, discussed in Chapter 7, "Using Styles to Create a Great Looking Document," so consult that earlier discussion if you need to display additional styles here. Note that Normal is not included in the list. As much as you might like to, you can't deny access to the Normal style.

- **Recommended Minimum:** If the list is too inclusive, click Recommended Minimum, and then add or remove checks as needed.

- **None:** If the style list is way too inclusive, then choose None, and place a check next to just those you want to allow.

- **All:** If the style list is way too restrictive, then click All and remove the check next to those you want to disallow.

- **Allow AutoFormat to override formatting restrictions:** If AutoFormat's rules and practices are sufficiently rigorous for your purposes, click to allow this option.

- **Block Theme or Scheme switching:** Choose this option to limit formatting to the currently applied theme or scheme.

- **Block Quick Style Set switching:** Choose this option to use style definitions from the current document and template only.

When you're ready to proceed, click OK in the Formatting Restrictions dialog box. Next, Word displays the message box asking whether to remove disallowed styles from the document. Click Yes to remove disallowed styles or formatting. Note that if any styles are removed, text will be reformatted using the Normal style.

Finally, click Yes, Start Enforcing Protection in the Restrict Editing pane. The Start Enforcing Protection dialog box prompts you to password-protect your formatting restrictions, if desired. Either type the password twice in the text boxes provided and then click OK, or click OK without entering passwords. Even if the level of protection isn't as strong as rights management, applying passwords to your restrictions is still better than nothing.

> **NOTE**
>
> Why would you want to impose formatting restrictions? Some publishing processes depend upon only certain styles being used. There are macros or other programs that process files so that they can be fed into other parts of the publishing process. If other styles are used, the process breaks down and requires manual intervention. Hence, it's better if only the allowed styles are used. In other cases, enterprise-wide formatting standards are strictly imposed to ensure that all documents have a consistent and professional look. Enforcing style restrictions is one way to do that.

With formatting restrictions applied, a number of formatting tools, commands, and key-strokes on the Home tab are grayed out as unavailable.

No changes (Read only)

You can protect all or part of a document against changes. You can make different excep-tions for different users. Suppose, for example, that you have a document that has been written by a group of people. You want each individual to be able to edit his or her own section, but not that of others. At the same time, you don't want to have to manage differ-ent documents.

The solution is to create a document with a specific area for each individual. You make the entire document read-only, but you make an exception for each individual's section so that the individual responsible can make changes as needed.

To set a document as read-only, open the Restrict Editing pane. In the Editing restrictions section, click the check box to Allow only this type of editing in the document, and use the accompanying drop-down list to set it to No changes (Read only).

To make an exception, select the part of the document to which you want to allow changes by someone (or everyone). This selection can be any part of the document—a single letter, word, sentence, line, paragraph, and so on. If you want the exception to apply to everyone, click the check box next to Everyone. Or, if other groups are listed, you can place a check next to any of them.

To make an exception for individuals, if they are listed, click to place a check by their names. If the individuals aren't listed (or if no individuals are listed at all), click More Users. In Add Users, type the user IDs or email addresses for the individuals you want to exempt from the read-only proscription, and click OK. Word attempts to verify the names/addresses you added. If they are verified, they are added to the list of individuals.

Back in the Restrict Formatting and Editing pane, you need to place a check by the name(s) and email address(es) you added. As shown in Figure 26.12, Word highlights and bookmarks the text that you've indicated the checked user can edit. Add exceptions for other users as desired, and then click Yes, Start Enforcing Protection. Add and confirm a password if desired, as shown in Figure 26.13, noting that the document is not encrypted and is sus-ceptible to hacking by malicious users. If you enable User authentication, Word will use Information Rights Management to control the permissions. Click OK to finish applying the permissions.

FIGURE 26.12

The user a1919test@hotmail.com has been granted an exception to edit the Executive Summary information.

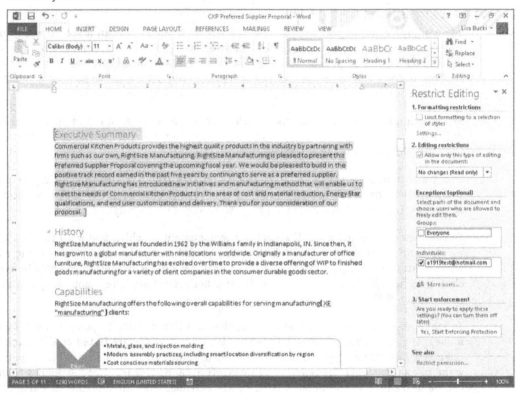

FIGURE 26.13

Applying a password to the protections

Comments

Choosing this protection option from the Editing restrictions drop-down list in the Restrict Editing pane results in protection identical to the No changes (Read only) option, except that all users can insert comments wherever they want to. Refer to the preceding discussion to see how to apply this protection, substituting Editing restrictions at the appropriate point.

Tracked changes

Another option is to allow editing but only tracked changes. That way, you can see who changed what, and when. This is an important feature in controlling the editing/revision process. To protect a document for tracked changes, open the Restrict Editing pane, click to enable Editing restrictions, and choose Tracked changes.

To turn protection on, click Yes, Start Enforcing Protection. The Start Enforcing Protection dialog box appears, where you can set and confirm a password. Note that User authentication is not available for this kind of protection. When you click OK, protection is enabled, and the document switches into Track Changes mode. To turn protection off—which is necessary for accepting/rejecting tracked changes—click Stop Protection at the bottom of the Restrict Editing pane.

Filling in forms

Forms protection is discussed in Chapter 24, "Creating Custom Forms." In particular, see the section "Forms protection."

Applying a password to open/modify a Word document

A final kind of password protection is well hidden in Word 2013. This legacy feature offers the same weak protection already noted in that passwords aren't impossibly difficult to hack and crack. The bottom line: Rely on this kind of password protection at your own risk. It offers minimal, if any, protection. Worse, it offers the illusion of protection, and thinking a document is well protected when it's not is perhaps worse than no protection at all, because you are unlikely to be as careful with the document as you would be if you knew it were completely unprotected.

You can set two different passwords: one that enables a user to open the document, and another that enables the user to make changes. To enable this kind of password protection, choose File ⇨ Save As ⇨ Computer ⇨ Browse. In the lower-right corner of the Save As dialog box, choose Tools ⇨ General Options, to display the General Options dialog box shown in Figure 26.14. Type a password in Password to open, and/or in Password to modify. Both are optional.

FIGURE 26.14

Applying open and modify passwords to a Word document.

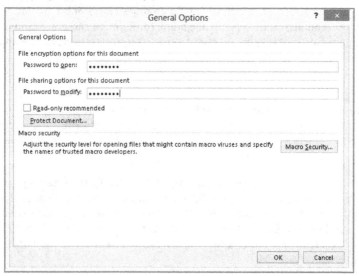

The Read-only recommended option applies only if there is no password for modifying the document. If this option is enabled, the user is provided a read-only recommendation when the file is opened and an easy way to select read-only.

When you click OK, you are prompted to confirm any passwords and are returned to the Save As dialog box. Click Save to save the document with the password settings.

> **NOTE**
>
> The Protect Document button is irrelevant to this dialog box and serves mostly to let the user know that there are other and better protection options. If you click this button and the Restrict Editing pane is not already showing, it is displayed behind the Save As dialog box, and the General Options dialog box goes away. If the Restrict Editing pane is not already showing, clicking the Protect Document button simply causes the General Options dialog box to close.

When you try to open a password-protected file, Word prompts you to enter the relevant passwords. If you know the password to open but not the password to modify, you can click Read Only to open the document in "read only" mode. Why the quotes? Because it's only the file itself that is read only. The document window can be edited willy-nilly, unlike when using other kinds of protection discussed earlier. If you save the file under a new name, the new file will inherit the password settings, but if you copy the file to the Clipboard and save under a new name, the protection is history.

> **TIP**
>
> You also can use File ⇨ Info ⇨ Protect Document ⇨ Encrypt with Password to apply a password to the document.

Comments and Tracked Changes

Comments and tracked changes are two ways Word provides for reviewing others' Word documents. Comments themselves are easy to explain: they are notes, questions, suggestions, and other details that a reader offers to the author of the Word document. Although a commenter might suggest a particular edit within a comment, the Comments feature does not integrate any edits or changes into the text. It's not unusual to copy the text of a suggestion from inside a comment and paste it into the text, but comments themselves aren't part of the flow.

Tracked changes, however, are part of the flow. Tracked changes are insertions and deletions made to a Word document. You can see what was inserted or deleted, by whom, and when. That way, if you have multiple reviewers making changes in a document, you can see who made which changes, which helps in deciding how to integrate inconsistent edits.

Viewing comments and tracked changes

Because comments are not part of the main text, Word has a lot of flexibility in how it can display them. This section looks at your display options, as well as how to add and work with comments as needed. Use the choices in the Tracking and Comments groups of the Review tab to work with comments.

Word includes two views for working with comments and tracked changes: Simple Markup (the new default view) and All Markup. Choose the overall view using the Display for Review drop-down menu in the Tracking group of the Review tab.

In the default Simple Markup view, shown in Figure 26.15, a comment balloon in the right margin shows you that there's a comment. A red line appears in the left margin beside any line(s) with tracked changes. To see the comment text and author, click the comment balloon. Click the balloon again to hide the comment information.

FIGURE 26.15

Simple Markup view initially hides comment text and tracked changes.

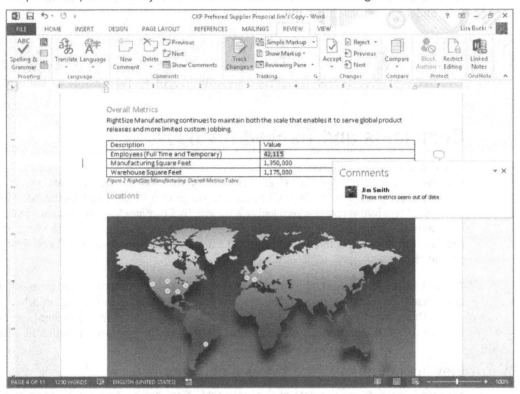

In All Markup view, shown in Figure 26.16, a comment area appears at the right side of the screen, and comment text appears there with a dashed line and highlight showing you the selected text that the comment refers to. These are also considered comment "balloons," although they don't look as much like balloons as they do in Simple Markup view. Tracked changes are marked up using a highlight color, strikethrough for deleted information, and underlining for inserted information. If you move your mouse pointer over a tracked change, a tooltip appears to show you who made the change and when.

If you also want tracked changes to display as balloons in the right margin, in the Review tab's Tracking group, choose Show Markup ➪ Balloons ➪ Show Revisions in Balloons. To set comments to display inline (which isn't really correct, because comments themselves do not display inline), choose Show Markup ➪ Balloons ➪ Show All Revisions Inline. When you make this choice, no comment balloon of any type appears. Instead, the commented text is high-lighted and the reviewer's initials appear in brackets beside the comment. You can right-click the initials and click Edit Comment to see the comment in the Revisions pane at left. For the sake of consistency, this chapter assumes you are not working in the Revisions pane.

FIGURE 26.16

Hover the mouse over a tracked change to find out who made the change.

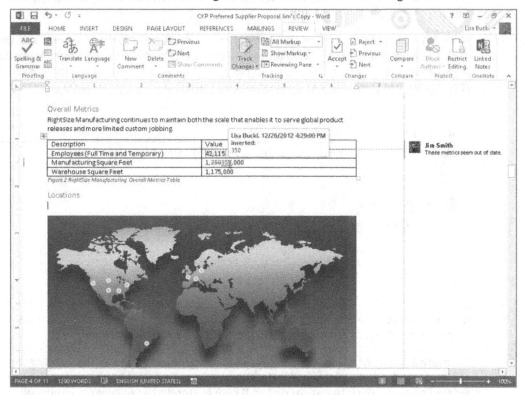

Inserting, editing, replying to, and deleting comments

To insert a new comment, first select the text that you want to comment about. In some cases, you can even click on a graphic object and insert a comment about it, but that doesn't work in all instances. Click the Review tab, and then click New Comment in the Comments group. In Simple Markup view, type your comment inside the yellow Comments box that opens, and then click the Close (X) button on the box. In All Markup view, a balloon appears in the right comment area. Type the comment, and then click in the text to return to normal editing.

To edit a comment, click its balloon in either Simple Markup or All Markup, and make changes in the comment box, and then click the Close (X) button or click in the text to finish.

Word 2013 includes the new ability to reply to a comment. Click the comment, and then click the Reply button (page with an arrow) at the right side of the box (see Figure 26.17). Type the comment text in the reply comment that appears, as shown in Figure 26.17, and then click Close (X) or click in the text to continue.

FIGURE 26.17

Click the page with the arrow in the Comments box to reply to a comment.

If you've taken the action recommended in a comment and want to leave it it place but indicate that it is no longer active, you can right-click the comment in the comment balloon or box, and click Mark Comment Done. This grays out the comment text.

To delete a comment, click the comment in either view, and then in the Comments group of the Review tab, click Delete. In All Markup view, you can right-click the comment and click Delete Comment. Click the arrow on the Delete button in the Comments group and then click Delete All Comments in Document if you're ready to remove all changes.

Tracking changes by various editors

Unlike comments, tracked changes can be displayed inline. You also have a variety of options regarding which aspects of tracked changes to display.

Track Changes Options

To see the main set of tracking options, click the dialog box launcher in the Tracking group of the Review tab. In the initial Track Changes Options dialog box that appears (see the left side of Figure 26.18) you can change some overall options such as what to show or hide. If you click Advanced Options, more detailed choices appear in the Advanced Track Changes Options dialog box shown at the right in Figure 26.18. Make the desired changes, and then click OK to close each dialog box. Options in the Advanced Track Changes Options dialog box include:

- **Markup:** These options control the formatting and colors to use when displaying insertions, deletions, and comments, as well as how to display lines indicating where changes have been made. The default formatting is to use underlining for insertions and strikethrough for deletions. If Color is set to By author, Word automatically chooses different colors for different authors. Note, however, that whereas your comments might display as green on your computer, they might display as magenta on somebody else's. Therefore, if you're describing a change in a phone conversation, don't assume the other party is seeing exactly what you're seeing.

- **Track moves:** These options control the formatting and colors to use when displaying text that was moved from one location to another in the document. If you don't want to track moves, remove the check next to Track Moves.

FIGURE 26.18

Use Track Changes Options to change how/if changes are tracked and displayed.

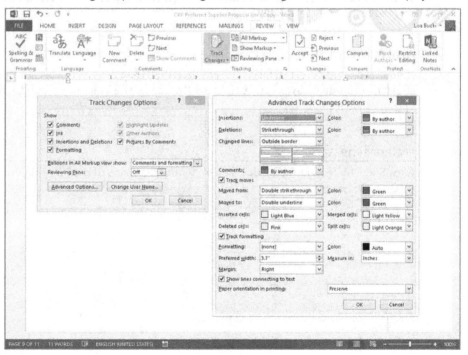

- **Track formatting:** These options control how formatting changes are represented. If you don't want to track formatting changes, remove the check next to Track formatting. Note that this doesn't affect the *display* of tracked formatting. It controls whether formatting is tracked at all. When you turn this off, existing tracked formatting changes remain in the document, but subsequent formatting changes are not tracked at all. To hide tracked formatting changes, choose Show Markup in the Tracking group of the Review tab and remove the check next to Formatting.

Turning on Track Changes

To enable tracked changes, click the Track Changes button in the Tracking group of the Review tab. Notice that the upper and lower portions of that button are separate. Use the upper portion to toggle tracked changes, and use the lower portion to choose Track Changes or Lock Tracking. Lock Tracking enables you to add a password to prevent other users from turning off change tracking.

Alternatively, if Track Changes is displayed in the status bar, you can click it to toggle tracking on and off. If Track Changes is not displayed, right-click the status bar and click to place a check next to Track Changes. Then click outside the menu to close it. Once it's on the status bar, click Track Changes to turn tracking on or off. Track Changes can also be toggled using Ctrl+Shift+E.

Show Markup

If your comments don't display, it's possible that they are turned off. In the Review tab, click the drop-down arrow next to Show Markup in the Tracking group to display the options shown in Figure 26.19.

FIGURE 26.19

Click Show Markup in the Review tab to control the kinds of markup that Word displays.

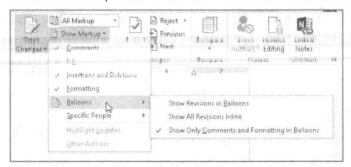

Show Markup options affect only the display of markup. They do not affect whether changes are tracked. Display options are as follows:

- **Comments:** Choose to display or not display comments.

- **Ink:** When using a tablet, touch-enabled, or other system that supports pen annotations, use this option to choose whether to display the original ink markup (in addition to the text conversion thereof).

- **Insertions and Deletions:** Use this setting to control the display of textual edits (insertions and deletions). Some users prefer to deal separately with textual and formatting edits. With this option enabled and Formatting display turned off, you can selectively focus.

- **Formatting:** Use this setting to hide or show formatting changes.

- **Balloons:** Use this setting to control the use of balloons for revisions and comments as described earlier.

- **Specific People:** Use this setting to selectively show or hide specific reviewers' edits and comments.

- **Highlight Updates:** When you are co-authoring a document on a SharePoint server or Office365, this option highlights updates by the other author(s).

- **Other Authors:** When you are co-authoring, this option lists other authors currently working on the same document.

> **TIP**
>
> You can click one of the vertical bars (lines) in the left margin of Simple Markup view to display or hide tracked changes and comments.

Display for Review

Use the Display for Review menu in the Tracking group of the Review tab to determine exactly what displays when a document contains tracked changes. As noted earlier, you use this drop-down to change between All Markup and Simple Markup views, which were discussed in the "Viewing comments and tracked changes" section earlier. Its other two options are:

- **No Markup:** All markup is hidden, and you see the document as it would appear if all changes were accepted. This view is useful when a document has been heavily edited. You can read a "clean" copy of the new version without the change tracking markup slowing you down.

- **Original:** All markup is hidden, and you see the document as it appeared before any markup occurred. This is how the document would appear if all changes were rejected.

> **TIP**
>
> It's often hard to gauge the effects of changes. It can be helpful to switch between Final and Original so you can properly assess the full impact of changes, especially when comparing paragraphs that have undergone substantial editing.

Accepting and Rejecting Changes

Use the Changes group of the Review tab, shown in Figure 26.20, to review changes to determine whether you want to accept or reject them. Use Next or Previous to navigate to the nearest comment or change. Use Accept and Reject to integrate or remove changes. You can also right-click a change and choose Accept or Reject.

FIGURE 26.20

Accept All Changes Shown is available only when some changes are hidden.

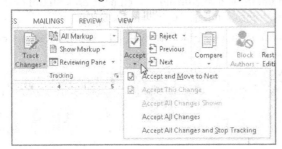

Here is a brief overview of what happens when you choose Accept or Reject:

- When you accept an insertion, it is converted from a tracked change into regular text.
- When you reject an insertion, it is deleted.
- When you accept a deletion, it is removed entirely from the document.
- When you reject a deletion, the original text is restored.
- When you accept formatting changes, they are applied to the final version of the text.
- When you reject formatting changes, the formatting is removed.

Note that the Accept and Reject buttons in the Changes group of the Review tab both have upper and lower sections. The lower section of the Accept button features the options shown in Figure 26.20. Reject has similar options. Note that the third option, Accept All

Changes Shown, is available only if one or more kinds of changes are hidden in the Show Markup tool.

> **NOTE**
>
> You cannot accept or reject a comment per se. Accepting a comment leaves it alone. Rejecting a comment deletes it.

Combining Collaborative Documents

Word can compare and combine different versions of the same document. If the document was revised without tracking turned on, you learn how to compare the two different versions. If a document was revised by multiple people, whether or not Track Changes was turned on, you learn how to combine all of the different edits into a single (hopefully manageable) document.

Comparing Documents

Word enables you to compare two documents, usually different versions of the same document, using what Microsoft calls *legal blackline*. Basically, you feed Word two documents, designating one as the original document and the other as the revised document. Microsoft then creates a third document (the default setting) with markup indicating the changes. Perhaps not surprisingly, this new document contains tracked changes, and you can use Word's Review tab tools to manage the document, to decide what to keep and what to zap.

In a nutshell, suppose that you have two versions of the same document, and the second was accidentally edited without Track Changes turned on. The Compare feature enables you to correct that "oversight" by creating a new document that shows what the original document would look like if the revisions had been made with Track Changes turned on.

> **NOTE**
>
> If you have only two documents you want to compare, and neither displays tracked changes, use the Compare feature. If you have two or more documents that contain tracked changes, and you need to keep track of who changed what and when, use the Combine feature, described later in this chapter.

To initiate the comparison, in the Review tab, click Compare in the Compare group.

Word displays the Compare dialog box. Click the More button to display the full Compare Documents dialog box shown in Figure 26.21. When you first click the More button, you see the default settings for Compare. By default, all of the Comparison settings are enabled: Show changes at is set to Word level, and Show changes in is set to New document. Use the

Original and Revised document drop-down arrows to choose the documents you want to compare. If the documents you seek aren't in the alphabetical list of recent files shown, choose Browse, either in the list or by clicking the Browse button to the right of the drop-down list.

FIGURE 26.21

By default, the result of the comparison is placed into a new document.

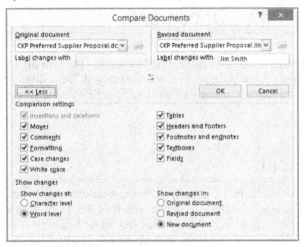

Under the Revised document choice, Label changes with is set to the current default user-name (from Word's Popular Options). You can change that to whatever you like—it doesn't even have to be a user's name.

Under Comparison settings, choose the elements you want included in the comparison. Under Show changes at, you can choose to compare character by character or word by word. Choose Character level if you want to see the exact edits that were performed. For example, if the original document has "word" and the revised document has "world," in which the "l" was inserted, then the Word level setting would simply show you that "word" was replaced by "world," whereas Character level would show the fact that an "l" was inserted.

> **NOTE**
>
> The Insertions and deletions item is always grayed out and always checked. This is by design. When you use Compare or Combine, insertions and deletions will always be compared. Microsoft left this in because it might not be obvious. Hence, it displays as always checked, and it cannot be changed.

As noted, by default, Compare puts the changes into a new document. However, if it suits your purposes better, you can route the changes into the document designated as either the Original document or the Revised document under Show changes in at lower right. Note that if you've now changed your mind about which is which, you can click the Swap Documents tool.

When you're ready to make the comparison, click OK. If either of the two documents being compared contains tracked changes, for purposes of the comparison, Word displays a message telling you that it assumes that the changes are accepted. Click Yes to continue the comparison.

Word arranges the Compared Document (the Show changes in document), the Original, and the Revised into a document window, along with the Revisions pane, as shown in Figure 26.22. If you chose the Save to a new document option, notice that the tentative file name is Compare Result #.

FIGURE 26.22

Word shows you exactly what editing has taken place.

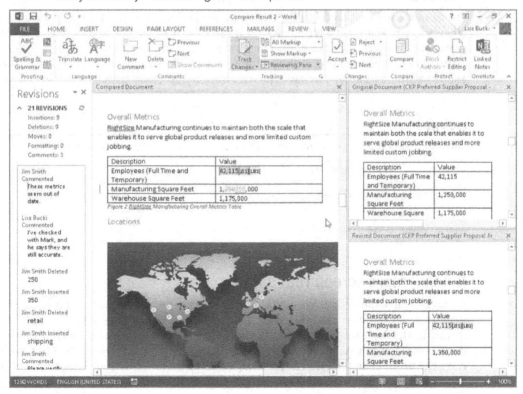

In this view, notice that the three document windows scroll at the same time. The idea is to show the original, revised, and resulting edits at the same time. Depending on screen size as well as how large the Word window is, this can be difficult. However, Word makes a valiant effort.

Use the Review tab tools, as described earlier in this chapter, to set the view as needed, and to move to the Next or Previous changes, accepting or rejecting changes as you see fit. When you're done, if you want to save the compared result, choose File ⇨ Save As (or Save, but read this section's Warning first), and save as usual.

> **CAUTION**
>
> Before you click Save, keep in mind that if you chose Original or Revised as the document in which to show changes, saving now will replace the corresponding document with the compared version. Once done, there's no going back. If you think you'll have a need for all three versions of the document, choose Save As, and give the compare results version a new name.

Protection

You cannot compare two documents if either of them is protected for tracked changes. When you try, Word will advise you that it can't "merge" the documents due to document protection. In fact, any kind of document protection will produce the objection shown in Figure 26.23. If you see this message, unprotect the documents you are trying to compare and try again, assuming you have the necessary permissions to unprotect the documents.

FIGURE 26.23

You can't compare two documents if either of them has protection enabled.

Gaining more screen real estate

If you find that the default view offered by the Compare feature doesn't give you enough room to maneuver, you can selectively display (or not) the Original and Revised documents. In the Compare group in the Review tab, click Compare, and then click Show Source Documents. You can click Hide Source Documents to close those windows. You can also close the Original and Revised documents by clicking the Xs. If you change your mind, click Compare ⇨ Show Source Documents and click Show Both to redisplay the source documents.

Combining Documents That Contain Tracked Changes

When you have multiple documents containing tracked changes and you need to keep track of who changed what (and when), use the Combine command to merge the tracked changes two at a time until all of the different reviewers' changes have been incorporated into one document. As with the Compare command, documents are combined two at a time. If any document in the paired combinations is protected, you cannot continue. Before you invest a lot of time doing comparisons, make sure that you can use the documents you're planning to compare.

Combining multiple documents containing changes

When combining or merging changes from multiple documents, it doesn't matter if the changes have been tracked. At the end of the process, changes attributable to any given reviewer will be tracked due to the way the documents are combined.

> **NOTE**
>
> The only loss for untracked changes is that you won't know exactly when the changes were made. For example, if a reviewer was making changes at 4:00 a.m., you won't know that. Depending on the reviewer, that could matter a lot, affecting how seriously you consider such sleep-deprived comments.

Suppose, for example, that document A is the original document written by Lisa Bucki, and that document B has changes that were made by Jim Smith—some of them tracked and some of them not. When you combine document A and document B, everything that is different in document B will be attributed to Jim Smith, whether tracked or not.

When you combine documents, you have the same options you have when you compare them, in terms of where the combined changes go. It works best if you always combine changes into the same document, preferably the original to which the other changes were applied. Suppose that you start with document A and give it to four reviewers. Each of them takes a whack at it at the same time, so you end up with four different revisions to document A. Let's call those revisions Bob, Jim, Ted, and Lisa. There is no temporal sequence, and it doesn't matter when each is compared with the original, A.

One way to proceed is as follows (keeping in mind that the order for combining with Bob, Jim, Ted, and Lisa doesn't matter):

- Compare A with Bob's version, putting the results in A. Save A.
- Compare A with Jim's version, putting the results in A. Save A.
- Compare A with Ted's version, putting the results in A. Save A.
- Compare A with Lisa's version, putting the results in A.

At the end of the process, A will contain tracked changes from each of the four reviewers. It won't necessarily be easy to sort out, but all of the changes *will* be in a single document.

> **NOTE**
>
> An alternative way to proceed is to insert an additional step before saving A. You could, depending on the nature of the edits, resolve each set of edits one at a time. First, examine Bob's changes and accept or reject each. Then, use the resolved version of A for the next comparison, and continue in this fashion. This might seem less cluttered and confusing, but there is a logical problem. By the time you get around to Lisa, her changes might be moot if the text she revised was deleted by Jim. Ultimately, you'll need to decide which method works best, although most users find it least confusing when they can see all of the suggestions at once. At the end of the day, however, most Word users conclude that simultaneous editing by four reviewers is a nightmare that should be avoided. Sequential edits are a lot easier to manage.

Running the Combine Documents command

To kick off the process, in the Review tab's Compare group, click the Compare button arrow, and then click Combine. The Combine Documents dialog box that appears is essentially identical to the Compare Documents dialog box in Figure 16.21. Set Original document to the earliest version you have, and set Revised document to a revised version of the original. Choose the desired options and set Show changes in to New document or Original document (but make a backup copy of the original before you combine the documents). Click OK to combine that set.

> **NOTE**
>
> Before you begin, be aware that Word cannot retain multiple formatting revisions. Therefore, after each Combine operation, if you are including formatting in the Comparison settings you enable, you should set Show Markup (in the Review tab) to just Formatting, and use Next/Previous/Accept/Reject to resolve all of the formatting changes before proceeding to the next Combine.

After the Combined Document appears, resolve any formatting changes and then repeat the process for the next revision. Continue until each of the revised versions has been combined. Finally, you'll have a version that contains all of the changes, as well as the reviewers' names. If the originals contain tracked changes, you'll also have the times the changes were made. For untracked changes in the revised versions, the revision time will be the time that the combine operation occurred for that revision and hence won't be meaningful.

Summary

In this chapter, you've learned about the many different kinds of document protection and security available in Word. You should now have a good idea about which forms of protection and security are useful, and which ones give only partial security. You've also learned about tracking changes and commenting on Word documents, as well as how to compare and combine documents. You should now be able to do the following:

- Protect a document so that only a specific kind of editing can be performed
- Use Word's legacy password protection, while understanding its limitations
- Add comments and enable Track Changes in a document
- Navigate and work with comments and tracked changes
- Set options that let you display a variety of elements when tracking changes in a document
- Compare two documents that contain no tracked changes, automatically marking up one so you can review the changes
- Combine an original document with independently revised versions to create a version that contains tracking

26

Collaborating in the Cloud with SkyDrive

IN THIS CHAPTER

Learning the difference between SkyDrive and SkyDrive Pro

Saving to your SkyDrive and sharing files

Working with SkyDrive Pro

Using SkyDrive Pro with Office 365

Word 2013 includes features that integrate it into the cloud more than ever before, and this chapter serves as your roadmap for navigating them. The Microsoft account that you use to sign into Windows 8 and to Word includes free SkyDrive storage. You store files in your SkyDrive and share them from there directly, using the Save or Save As command on the File tab. If needed, you also can install client software to integrate SkyDrive with your Windows desktop file storage. Most versions of Office 2013 also include the SkyDrive Pro application. SkyDrive Pro works with a separate cloud-based service called Office 365 as well as SharePoint. It enables you to sync files from your online library to a local folder. Finally, the chapter concludes by showing a few more things you can accomplish in your Office 365 account in the cloud.

Understanding SkyDrive Pro and SkyDrive for Windows

SkyDrive is cloud-based service that offers you online storage and an online workspace. You automatically receive a SkyDrive account when you create a Microsoft account to sign into Windows 8 or Office 2013. Your free SkyDrive account includes 7 GB of free online storage space, accessed through your Microsoft account sign-on information. You can upgrade your SkyDrive account for a fee to include even more storage. But once your account is established you can share files and folders and use SkyDrive as your personal gateway for sharing files and folders.

Most versions of Office 2013 include an application called *SkyDrive Pro*. SkyDrive Pro does not work with the SkyDrive account associated with your Microsoft account, but instead works with your library on your organization's *Office 365* site (as well as SharePoint and SharePoint online sites, but this book focuses on Office 365). Office 365 is a more team-oriented type of cloud-based sharing and requires a subscription. This is discussed further in the "Accessing Your SkyDrive Pro Library on Office 365" section later in this chapter.

You need to understand that SkyDrive syncing and SkyDrive Pro syncing are two distinct things. SkyDrive syncing uses the SkyDrive for Windows application. It sets up a copy of the cloud-based SkyDrive folders associated with your Microsoft account on your computer's hard disk, and keeps files synced between those local folders and your online SkyDrive. SkyDrive Pro syncing, in contrast, uses the SkyDrive Pro 2013 application included with some versions of Office, and syncs the online library associated with your Office 365 account with a location you specify on your computer's hard disk. You'll learn about each type of syncing later in the chapter.

Saving to the Cloud with SkyDrive

You can save to your SkyDrive storage directly from Word. As long as you are signed into Word using the account that has the same sign-in settings as the SkyDrive account (Microsoft account) you want to save to, the process should work seamlessly. If you have separate SkyDrive accounts for personal and work purposes, or if you using a system where a colleague or family member is signed in, you could inadvertently upload sensitive files to the wrong account. In such instances you'll need to be a little more careful about saving your files.

The rest of this section covers the two SkyDrive operations you can perform within Word: saving to your SkyDrive, and saving and sharing a file.

Saving

Saving to your SkyDrive is as easy as saving to your system's hard disk. SkyDrive has three top-level folders by default: Documents, Pictures, and Public. By default, the Documents and Pictures folders are not shared, but the Public folder is. So it's a good policy to save any file that you want to share with other users to the Public folder. Once you get comfortable working with your SkyDrive online, you'll learn how to create other folders and share them. Follow these steps to save a file to your SkyDrive:

1. **Open the file that you want to save to your SkyDrive, or save and name the current file.** While you can save a new file to the SkyDrive, chances are you will want both a local copy on your computer and a cloud copy, so saving is a manual way to make sure you have the local copy.

2. **Choose File ⇨ Save As.** The Save As choices appear in Backstage view.

3. **In the middle pane, under Save As, click your SkyDrive if needed.** As shown in Figure 27.1, the right pane lists any Recent Folders you've used. You can click one to save to it and skip to Step 6, or go on to Step 4.

4. **Click Browse.** You may see a message that Word is contacting the (SkyDrive) server for information. After the connection is made, the Save As dialog box appears as shown in Figure 27.2. Note in the address bar that the current folder name is a series of letters and numbers. That's because Word has prepared a virtual copy of the file to upload.

FIGURE 27.1

Choose your SkyDrive after clicking Save As.

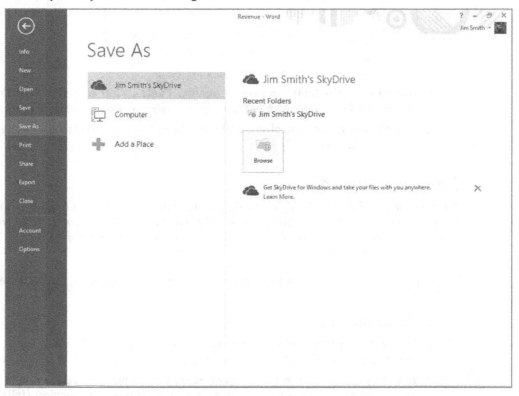

FIGURE 27.2

Specify a save location as you would for any file, and then click Save.

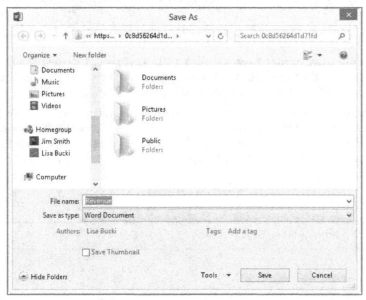

5. **Double-click the folder to save to, such as Public.** After contacting the SkyDrive server, the Save As dialog box displays the contents of that folder, if any.

6. **Edit the file name as desired, and click Save.** Word uploads the file to the specified folder on your SkyDrive.

Saving and sharing

When you *share* a file stored on your SkyDrive with other users, the process sends an email message with a link they can follow to see and download the file from your SkyDrive via a web browser. The process works differently depending on whether you've saved the file to your SkyDrive during the current Word work session.

If you've just saved the file to your SkyDrive using the preceding steps, follow these steps to share:

1. **Choose File ➪ Share.**

2. **In the middle pane, under Share, click Invite People.** As shown in Figure 27.3, the right pane enables you to enter recipient email addresses and a message.

3. **In the Type names or e-mail addresses text box, enter or specify one or more email addresses, separating addresses with a comma or semicolon (followed by an optional space).** As you type, a list of suggestions may appear.

FIGURE 27.3

Sharing a file via SkyDrive

4. **(Optional) To enable the user to view but not edit the file, click Can edit to open the drop-down list, and then click Can view to change the setting.**

5. **If enabled, type a personal message in the space provided.**

6. **To require the recipients to sign in with a Microsoft account to view the files, click the Require user to sign in before accessing document check box to check it.**

7. **Click Share.** SkyDrive sends the sharing email message. After that, each recipient's name appears under Shared with on the Share page.

If you haven't just saved a file to your SkyDrive and choose File ⇨ Share ⇨ Invite People, you'll see the Save To Cloud button shown in Figure 27.4. Click it, and then follow the prompts that appear (which resemble the previously described processes to save and then share the file).

FIGURE 27.4

If you try to share a file before saving to your SkyDrive, the Save To Cloud button appears.

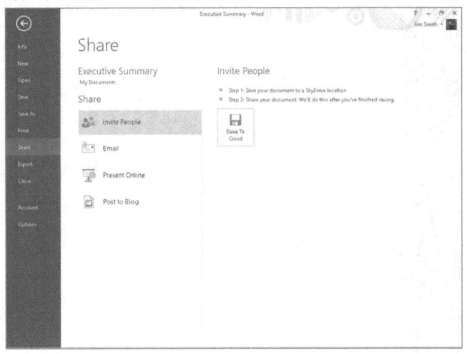

SkyDrive for Windows Application versus SkyDrive in Office

Using SkyDrive as described in the previous section has a limitation. The files you upload to SkyDrive exist independently of the copies on your hard disk. If you or another user with whom you've shared the file (with Can edit enabled) makes changes to a file via Word Web App on your online SkyDrive, you may need to sync the files manually. As shown in Figure 27.5, the Save button on the QAT changes to include a refresh indicator. (If you want to be able to compare the changes that were made online to the local copy of the file, make a copy of the local file and rename the copy. Then, when you refresh the shared file with the changes from the SkyDrive version, you can use the Compare Documents feature to compare the two files. See the section called "Comparing Documents" in Chapter 26, "Managing Document Security, Comments, and Tracked Changes.")

Microsoft has created another way to take your SkyDrive file syncing to a more secure and flexible level: the SkyDrive for Windows client application. And even limiting it to SkyDrive "for Windows" is not strictly accurate. You also can download a SkyDrive app for computers running the Mac OS X Lion operating system and mobile SkyDrive apps for Windows Phone, iOS, and Android. The various client apps will keep your files synced between your SkyDrive and any computer or mobile phone device where the app is installed. This means you have access to the latest version of your files from any device at any time.

FIGURE 27.5

Save a shared document from the QAT to update it with all user changes.

Some versions of Windows 8 are now shipping with SkyDrive for Windows already installed. If you are running Office 2013 on Windows 7 or for some reason don't have it in Windows 8, you can install it. You can verify whether you have SkyDrive for Windows by opening a folder window from the desktop. As shown in Figure 27.6, expand the Favorites in the Navigation pane at the left and see if SkyDrive is listed. If it is, the SkyDrive client is installed and you can see the local copies of your SkyDrive folders and files.

FIGURE 27.6

When SkyDrive for Windows is installed, it appears under Favorites in File Explorer (Windows 8) or Windows Explorer (Windows 7).

To download the SkyDrive desktop client (or to learn about and find the versions for the other platforms noted here), go to http://windows.microsoft.com/en-US/skydrive/download and click the Download button. You can then double-click the downloaded file to install it. The rest of this section assumes you have the client installed and are read to work with it.

> **TIP**
>
> In Windows 8, you also can access and work with files on your SkyDrive using the SkyDrive Windows 8 app on the Start screen. Display the Start screen and click the SkyDrive tile to start that app and connect with your SkyDrive.

Saving and viewing your files

Even with the SkyDrive client installed, the process for saving a Word file to your SkyDrive is the same as described earlier. The only difference is that when you click Browse, the Save As dialog box displays your local SkyDrive folders (see Figure 27.7), versus the virtual location shown earlier (see Figure 27.2). When you save to one of the online SkyDrive folders, Word again contacts the SkyDrive server and saves the file there, but it also saves a copy to the corresponding local SkyDrive subfolder.

FIGURE 27.7

Your local SkyDrive client folders are part of your user personal folders.

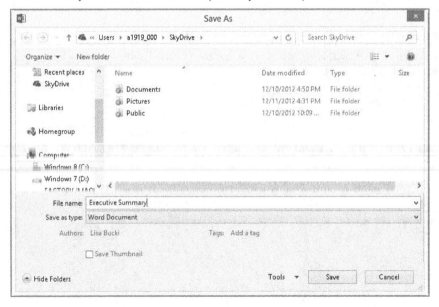

To view the files in a local SkyDrive folder, click SkyDrive under Favorites, and then double-click folders as needed to navigate to the desired location in the window. The files appear as in any folder window. Once you've navigated to a file, you can share it via the local SkyDrive folder. Right-click the file to share, point to SkyDrive, and click Share, as shown in Figure 27.8. After you do so, your SkyDrive opens in your web browser. Even though your SkyDrive and the file will appear, click Sign in to continue the sharing process. At that point, the screen shown in Figure 27.9 appears, so you can address and send an email message sharing the file. Enter the desired recipient email addresses and a message and click Share.

FIGURE 27.8

You also can share a file from your local SkyDrive client folder.

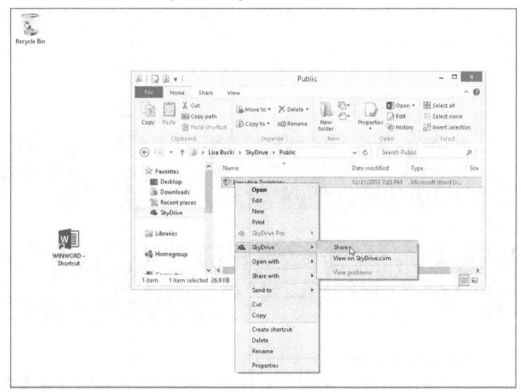

FIGURE 27.9

Finishing the share online on your SkyDrive

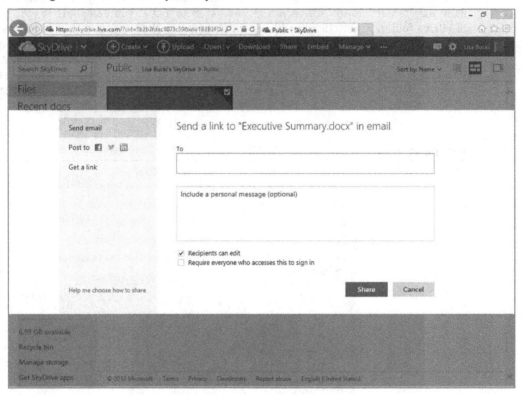

> **NOTE**
>
> Be careful about saving any linked files such as mail-merge data source files to your local and cloud SkyDrive folders and then deleting the files from the original location. When you change storage locations in that way, it breaks the links between files and can create the need for you to find and reestablish file relationships.

Syncing your files

You also can copy files and paste them into the local SkyDrive client folders via Windows by copying and pasting. The local SkyDrive folders should automatically sync with the SkyDrive folders in a matter of minutes. In Figure 27.10, the bottom file, Long Report, was copied within Windows. As shown by the check mark on its file icon, it has been automatically synced to the online SkyDrive. Assuming you are logged into Windows with the Microsoft account that corresponds to your SkyDrive, the syncing should occur automatically.

FIGURE 27.10

The Long Report file was copied to the local SkyDrive subfolder in Windows; the check on the file icon shows that it has synced automatically with the online SkyDrive.

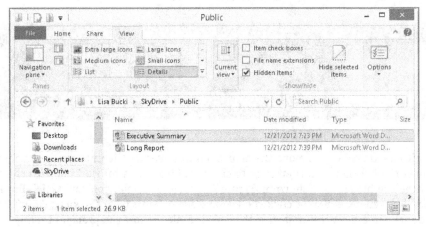

Viewing and working with SkyDrive files online

SkyDrive initially offered convenience because you could access your files via any web browser and Internet connection. That holds true—the integration with Word 2013 and its companion Office applications just adds another level of convenience. You can access your SkyDrive folders via the Web at any time.

There is one detail to be aware of at this point. Microsoft is in the process of rebranding a number of its online services. Previously its hotmail.com domain provided email and file support. Then Microsoft moved on to the Windows Live branding, so you could sign on for services at home.live.com, and it added skydrive.live.com from there. The new branding is Outlook.com. Right now, there is legacy support for all of these. So if you go to hotmail.com, home.live.com, skydrive.live.com, or Outlook.com and sign in, you should be taken to the main email screen for Outlook.com.

NOTE

Even if you used a non-Microsoft (that is, not live.com, hotmail.com, or outlook.com) email address when creating your Microsoft account, you will still have a SkyDrive account and be able to log into it using the email address for your Microsoft account.

After you sign in to your account, whatever its branding, click the down arrow icon to the right of Outlook at the upper right to display the choices shown in Figure 27.11, and then click SkyDrive. The Files section at the center displays the folders in your SkyDrive. Double-click the tile for a folder to display its files.

FIGURE 27.11

At the main Outlook.com screen, click the arrow beside Outlook, and then click SkyDrive.

To work with a particular file, move the mouse pointer over its tile until you see a check box in the upper-right corner, and then click to check it. Commands for working with the file appear above the file tiles, as shown in Figure 27.12. For example, you could click Download to download the checked file, or click the Manage down arrow (also shown in Figure 27.12) to see additional choices for working with the selected file. Follow the prompts that appear to perform the desired action on the file.

FIGURE 27.12

Managing a file in your SkyDrive

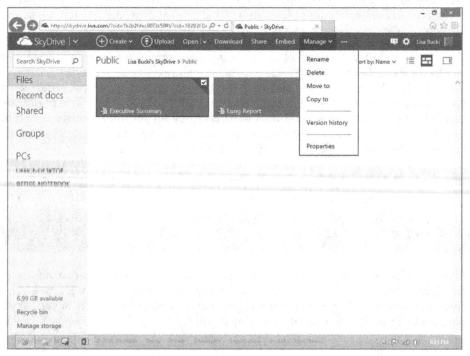

Touching up a document in the Word Web App

Your SkyDrive account also includes access to the Office Web Apps. These cloud-based versions of the Office applications aren't fully featured, but they do allow you or your collaborators to make some of the most important types of edits—changes to the text—online without even needing to have Word installed. Here's how:

1. **Double-click the tile for a file when viewing it in SkyDrive via your web browser.**
2. **In the Microsoft Word Web App window that appears, click Edit Document, and then click Edit in Word Web App (see Figure 27.13).**
3. **Use the controls that appear (see Figure 27.14) to change the document as needed.**

27

FIGURE 27.13

Choose to edit a document stored in your SkyDrive using Word Web App.

FIGURE 27.14

The Word Web App Ribbon choices are a subset of the full Word 2013 choices.

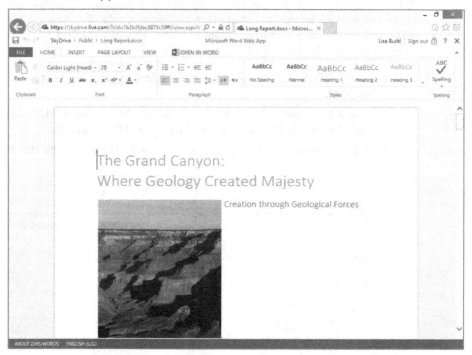

4. **Choose File ➪ Save to save your changes.** The file changes are saved in your SkyDrive. If you have SkyDrive for Windows installed, the next sync will also place the edited version of the file in your local SkyDrive folder.

5. **Click SkyDrive above the Home tab to return to SkyDrive.**

TIP

Click Open In Word to the right of the main Word Web App tabs to download and open a SkyDrive file in Word for editing.

> **NOTE**
> Office 365, described next, also enables you to edit documents with Office Web Apps.

Accessing Your SkyDrive Pro Library on Office 365

Office 365 is a completely separate animal from SkyDrive. Office 365 is a licensed service that provides a platform for team members in an organization to access email, share files, and more. The Office 365 file sharing capability is based on the SharePoint platform, an enterprise collaboration platform.

Office 2013 can interface directly with an Office 365 SharePoint-based team storage site, assuming the user is signed in to Office using the same sign-on information as for his or her Office 365 account. In addition, most Office versions include a SkyDrive Pro client by default. This client is specifically created to sync files between a file library on Office 365 and a local folder on your computer.

> **NOTE**
> The SkyDrive Pro also works with SharePoint Online and proprietary organization SharePoint sites, but describing all the variations of using SkyDrive Pro with these various resources is beyond the scope of this book.

This final section of the chapter gives you an introduction to SkyDrive Pro and how it works with your Office 365 sign-on. To have an Office 365 sign-on, the administrator of an Office 365 account must add you as a user and provide your account sign-in information. If your Office 365 administrator has not added a private domain for the Office 365 setup, the sign-in email addressed to you might be a variation of the onmicrosoft.com domain, as in mycompany.onmicrosoft.com.

Saving

Saving a file to your Office 365 account so that you can sync it via SkyDrive Pro in the future works much like saving to your SkyDrive:

1. **Open the file that you want to save to your Office 365 Library, or save and name the current file.**
2. **Choose File ⇨ Save As.** The Save As choices appear in Backstage view.

3. **In the middle pane, under Save As, click your Office 365 location (identified with a SharePoint icon).** As shown in Figure 27.15, the right pane lists any Recent Folders you've used. You can click one to save to it and then skip to Step 6, or go on to Step 4.

FIGURE 27.15

Saving to an Office 365 location

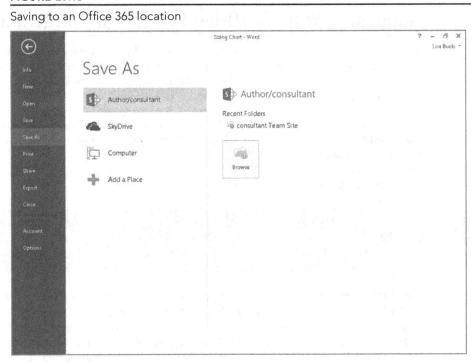

4. **Click Browse.** You may see a message that Word is contacting the server for information. After the connection is made, the Save As dialog box shows various libraries on the Office 365 team site, as shown in Figure 27.16.

5. **Double-click the location to save to, such as Documents.** After contacting the SkyDrive server, the Save As dialog box displays the contents of that library, if any.

6. **Click Save.** Word uploads the file to the specified Office 365 Library.

CAUTION

All these individual accounts can become confusing. To be able to save directly to an Office 365 location from Word, you must be signed into Word with your Office 365 sign-in information, which may be different than the Office account you sign in with every day. Click your username at the upper right, and click Switch account. In the window that appears, click Organizational account and follow the prompts that appear to sign in with your Office 365 account information provided by the system administrator.

FIGURE 27.16

Save locations on an Office 365 team site

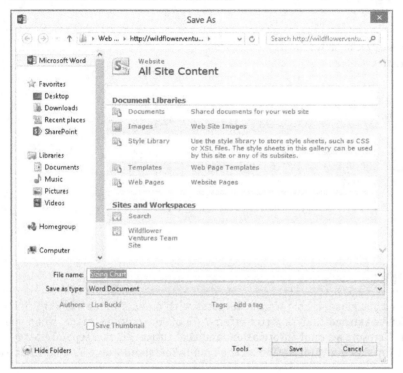

Changing the sync folder, syncing files, and viewing local files

As you and other users view and edit your files via Office 365, you can use SkyDrive Pro 2013 to sync the files to a local folder and view the files. You can even change the local folder that you want to sync to. Here's the overview of how to accomplish all of that:

1. **While signed in to Windows using the same account information as your Office 365 account, start the SkyDrive Pro 2013 application.** In Windows 7, start it from the Start menu. In Windows 8, used the Search charm to start it under Microsoft Office 2013.

2. **If needed, click the Change sync folder link and specify another folder.**

3. **Enter the URL for the Office 365 team site to sync with.** If you don't know the URL, you can get it from your Office 365 system administrator.

4. **Click Sync.**

5. **As SkyDrive Pro is syncing files, it tells you, as shown in Figure 27.17.**

6. **To view the local copies of the synced files in a folder window, click Show my files.**

FIGURE 27.17

FIGURE 27.17

Use SkyDrive Pro to sync with Office 365 cloud storage.

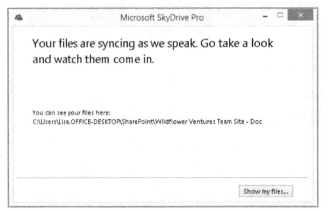

Summary

In this chapter you've seen how Word integrates with cloud storage via SkyDrive and Office 365. You've learned that SkyDrive offers 7 GB of free online storage, when you sign in with your Microsoft account information, and that Office 365 is a separate team-based environment for sharing information in the cloud. You should now be able to do the following:

- Save a document to your SkyDrive from Word
- Use Word to share a document from your SkyDrive
- Use the SkyDrive for Windows client to manage and sync files between your system and the cloud from your desktop
- Understand the difference between Office 365 and SkyDrive
- Use SkyDrive Pro to sync files from your Office 365 library to a local folder

Integration with Other Office Applications

IN THIS CHAPTER

Sending data between Excel and Word

Copying tables between Excel and Word

Exchanging outlines between Word and PowerPoint

Using the Outlook Address Book in Word

I n some ways, using the Office suite is like using a single multipurpose program. Features from the different programs mesh together almost seamlessly. For example, when you create a chart in a Word 2013 document, the data also lives in Excel 2013, almost as if Excel were an extension of Word.

In this chapter, you explore the ways in which Excel, PowerPoint, Word, and Outlook communicate with each other. Some things are perfectly intuitive, and others aren't. The casual PowerPoint user might never stumble on how to send outlines back and forth with Word. Do you ever wonder about the array of picture options available to you when copying images between Word and other programs? Which format should you use, and what are the consequences of using this one or that? How can pasting a 40 KB picture into a Word file add 900 KB to its size? In this chapter, the focus is on the less intuitive, to get you over some hurdles and stumbling blocks, and to make sense of some of those little mysteries that can make using Word seem like a struggle.

Excel

Although sharing work between Word and Excel often works well, differences in how the two programs operate can produce confusing results. This can be addressed by becoming aware of those differences, and working in a way that accommodates them and smoothes the way. This section looks at Word and Excel and ways to share text, data, tables, and graphics.

Using Excel content in Word

Word offers a variety of ways to share and exchange content with Excel:

- **Clipboard:** Copying content to the Clipboard, and then using Paste or Paste Special to insert the contents into Word or Excel. Commandment: When in doubt, use Paste Special.
- **Chart:** Using Office 2013's Chart feature to create a chart inside Word using Excel's facilities.
- **Object:** Using Insert ⇨ Text ⇨ Object ⇨ Create New tab or Create from File tab to embed all or part of an Excel worksheet into a Word document.

A common method that also works is drag-and-drop. You can select data or other content in Excel and drag it into Word. Make sure you press and hold the Ctrl key while dragging. If you do not see the plus with the mouse pointer as shown in Figure 28.1, the selection will be cut from Excel rather than copied. By default, the Excel data becomes an embedded object in the Word document, and you can double-click it there to display Excel tools for making changes. If you want the data to become a table in Word instead, use the Clipboard as described next.

FIGURE 28.1

Press Ctrl when dragging from Excel to Word to copy the range.

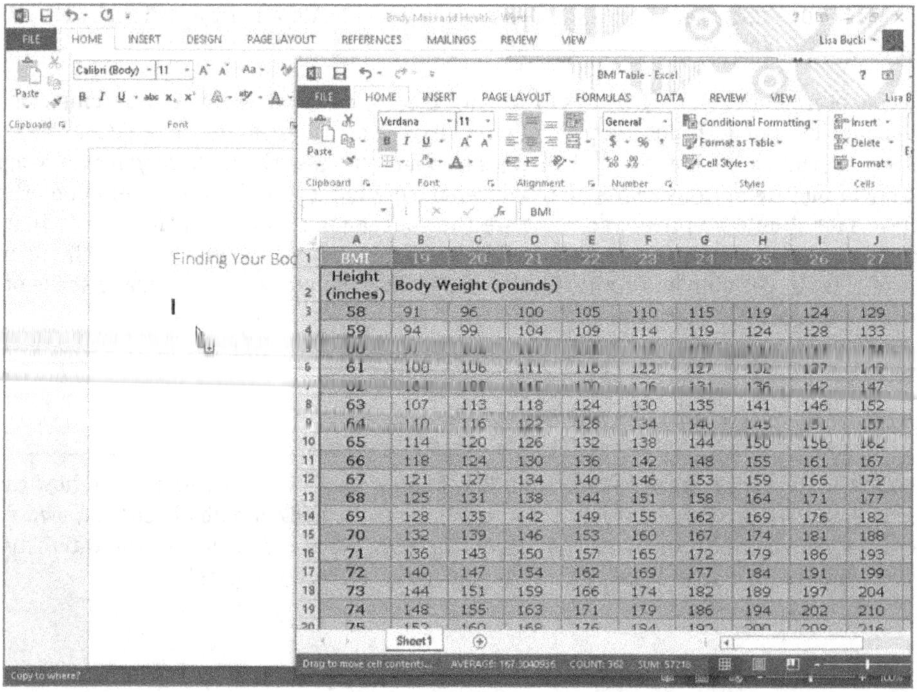

Read on to learn more about using the Clipboard, Chart, and Insert ⇨ Object features.

Clipboard

Excel's Clipboard works slightly differently from the Clipboard in most other Office programs. When you select cells in an Excel worksheet, they are highlighted. At this point, they are merely highlighted and cannot be moved or otherwise acted upon. You need to copy (or cut) the selection to the Clipboard, by pressing Ctrl+C or Ctrl+X, or right-clicking and choosing Copy or Paste. As in Word, you also can use the tools in the Clipboard group of Excel's Home tab to cut, copy, and paste a selection. After you cut or copy a selection of cells in Excel, an animated border appears around the selection, as shown in Figure 28.2.

FIGURE 28.2

The animated marquee around a selection in Excel shows you that you have cut or copied it.

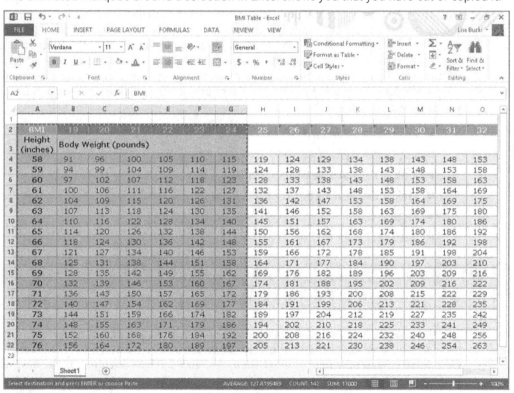

28

If you press Esc in Excel or double-click elsewhere (or perform any of a dozen or more other actions in Excel), the animated border disappears and you cannot paste the selection. Even if the data has actually been copied to the Clipboard, you still can't use the Paste button unless the animated border still appears in Excel. Dismissing the animated border also disables Paste Special, which is a helpful tool to use to determine how to paste Excel data.

> **TIP**
>
> There is one exception to this behavior. You can open the Clipboard pane in either Word or Excel by clicking the dialog box launcher in the Clipboard group of the Home tab. This will ensure that the Office Clipboard will collect the copied or cut data and keep it even if you press Esc or take another action that removes the animated border. (However, the Paste Special options still won't be available.) You can set the Office Clipboard to collect copied and cut selections in this way even if it is not open. To do so, click the Options button at the bottom of the Clipboard pane, and make sure that Collect Without Showing Office Clipboard is checked.

With the selection active in Excel, click where you want the data to appear in Word. If you simply click the Paste button in the Clipboard group of the Home tab, the cut or copied Excel selection pastes into Word as a Word table. As shown in Figure 28.3, the Paste Options button appears. You can click it to reveal options for how to paste the data. Move the mouse pointer over a paste option to see a description of what it does and a Live Preview of it on the pasted data. From left to right, the Paste Options for pasting Excel data and the key you can press to apply each are:

- Keep Source Formatting (K)
- Use Destination Styles (S)
- Link & Keep Source Formatting (F)
- Link & Use Destination Styles (L)
- Picture (U)
- Keep Text Only (T)

> **TIP**
>
> The Paste Options also are available when you click the Paste Special arrow, under Paste Options.

You also can use the Paste Special dialog box to paste and control how Word formats the data and whether the data stays linked to the source data in Excel. This method provides a few different format choices than the Paste Options button, but the downside is that you don't see a Live Preview of the pasted data. To use Paste Special, click the Paste button's down arrow (the bottom half of the button), and choose Paste Special (or press Ctrl+Alt+V). The Paste Special dialog box, shown in Figure 28.4, appears. Notice that the default is HTML format.

FIGURE 28.3

With a straight paste, the Excel data appears as a table, but you can use Paste Options to control how the pasted data appears.

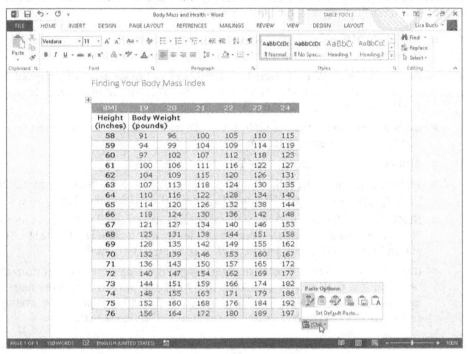

FIGURE 28.4

When using Paste Special to paste a selection of cells from Excel into Word, you'll have several options regarding how to paste.

28

At the end of the day, both HTML and RTF retain both formatting and table structure, but there are differences. They might seem subtle, or they might seem substantial, depending on your needs. There also are differences among other options that might seemingly appear similar. Different Paste Special options are as follows:

- **Microsoft Office Excel Worksheet Object:** Inserts the selection as a complete mini-worksheet, complete with Excel editing if you double-click the object.
- **Formatted Text (RTF):** Inserts formatted text as a table, retaining the cell, column, and row formatting in effect in the Excel file. This option often misinterprets cell shading and other colors.
- **Unformatted Text:** Inserts plain text with no attributes. Tabs are used to separate text that originated in different cells.
- **Bitmap:** Inserts a .bmp picture file.
- **Picture (Enhanced Metafile):** Inserts an .emf picture file that is essentially identical in appearance to the Windows Metafile but is slightly smaller in size.
- **HTML Format:** Retains text formatting, but doesn't retain all of the table formatting. This usually results in a table that is smaller in width than the RTF table. This option inserts cell shading and colors more accurately than RTF.
- **Unformatted Unicode Text:** Usually, this yields the same result as unformatted text. Unicode goes well beyond ASCII and ANSI and provides for many more characters and languages. If you find that linguistic information is being lost when pasting as unformatted text, then switch to unformatted Unicode text.

Click the Paste link option button to the left of the list of formats if you want copied Excel data to be linked to its source. This means that any changes you make to the Excel data will appear in Word when you reopen the Word file. Click OK to finish the paste.

> **NOTE**
>
> Generally speaking, you can right-click linked data and click Update Link to refresh the data. Or in the shortcut menu, you can click the command for the linked object (such as Linked Worksheet Object for linked Excel data), and then click Links. The Links dialog that appears gives you options for working with the linked data, including a Break Link command for removing the link.

Chart

If you simply paste a chart from Excel to Word, the chart is pasted as an unlinked, embedded chart. Once the chart is in Word, when you click it, the Chart Tools contextual tabs—Design and Format—appear. If you need to change the data, choose the Chart Tools Design tab, and then click Select Data or Edit Data in the Data group of the tab, as shown in Figure 28.5.

FIGURE 28.5

Clicking Edit Data in the Chart Tools Design tab selects and opens the data in Excel.

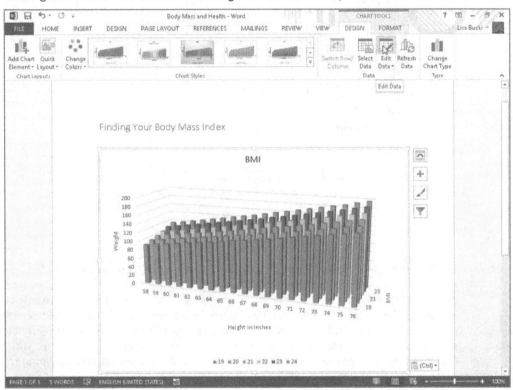

When you make changes to the data, the chart in Word is updated automatically to reflect the data changes. If there's a chance that you'll need to undo changes, leave the Excel window open. As long as it remains open, Ctrl+Z will work if you want to undo a change. If you close the Excel window with the data, changes to the chart and data are saved automatically, and Ctrl+Z will no longer undo changes you might have made.

When you copy graphics such as charts from Excel to Word with Paste Special, the rules change a bit. Right-click the chart or graphic and choose Copy. This time, you don't get the dashed selection because you're not copying cells—so it's a bit simpler, and once something has been copied to the Clipboard, the Paste Special options remain available. Switch to Word, click the Paste Special arrow or press Ctrl+Alt+V, and you'll see the options shown in Figure 28.6.

FIGURE 28.6

When you're copying graphics such as charts from Excel to Word, most of the formats presented are picture formats.

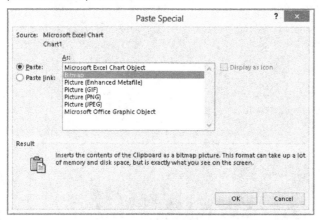

The first option, Microsoft Excel Chart Object, inserts the chart as an embedded object, which I'll discuss more in the next section. To find out about any of the other formats—various picture formats—click the format to see a description of it under Result at the bottom of the dialog box. For example, Figure 28.6 shows the Bitmap format selected and its description. The different picture formats each result in a different appearance for the pasted object in the Word document, so you might want to experiment to see which format gives you the best appearance in your document considering how it's going to be presented—online versus on paper.

> **NOTE**
>
> Even though you can use Paste Special to change a picture format when pasting into Word, for best results you should still use a dedicated graphics program for working with various file formats and other graphics modifications.

Object

A third way to use Excel data in a Word document is as an object. In Word, choose Insert ⇨ Text ⇨ Object. The Object dialog box appears. To use an existing Excel worksheet, click the Create from File tab. To create a new Excel object, stay on the Create New tab. Each tab is described next.

Create from File

On the Create from File tab, click the Browse button to navigate to the target file. As described in Chapter 12, "Getting Smart with Text: Building Blocks, Quick Parts, Actions (Tags), and More," choose Link to file and/or Display as icon, according to your needs, and click OK.

NOTE

Typically, you would use Display as Icon when the purpose is to provide access to the contents of the Excel file rather than to display it. For example, suppose you have a number of tax tables that you want to provide to the reader. Some readers need one table, others need another, and so on. A document will be much less cluttered if users can click a link to open the data set of interest in Excel, rather than make all readers have to look through all of the data files to find the one they want.

Create New

In the Create New tab of the Object dialog box, select the desired type of Excel object, as shown in Figure 28.7. Choose Display as icon, if desired (click Change Icon, if appropriate), and then click OK. Use Excel's tools to create the desired object, as shown in Figure 28.8, and then click outside the object (or close Excel, depending on the object type).

FIGURE 28.7

The Change Icon button appears only if Display as icon is checked.

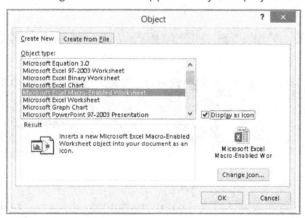

FIGURE 28.8

Creating an Excel worksheet object in Word

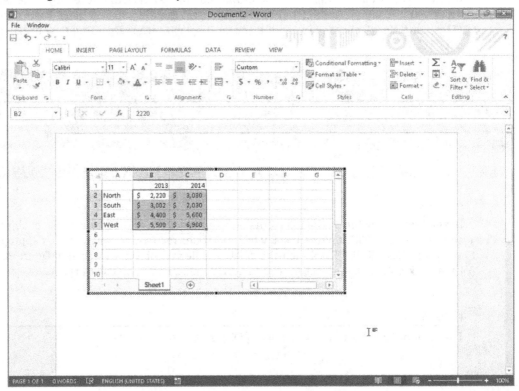

TIP

Notice that saving is controlled within the Word process. If you would like to have an independent version of the Excel object that is accessible from Excel without using Word, copy the contents of the "objectized" Excel worksheet to the Clipboard, open the full Excel application, paste your work into it, and save it.

From worksheet to table

As noted earlier, directly pasting formatted Excel data into Word creates a new table automatically. Sometimes, however, you need to insert data into a table that already exists. Typically, two problems can occur. First, sometimes the pasted cells don't go exactly where you want them to go. Second, no matter what you do, the formatting in the table never ends up exactly as you want.

To handle the first problem, the dimensions (rows and columns) of the source must be identical to the destination and the destination cells must be selected. For example, if you are pasting a selection of cells that contains 5 rows and 4 columns, then the destination must also be 5×4, and you must select the destination cells. If you try to paste in the top-left cell (which seems logical, right?), Word will paste the entire selection into that cell, so you end up with a table within a table.

> **TIP**
>
> If you are inserting new cells into an existing table (as opposed to replacing existing material), insert blank rows so you have empty cells that you can select and into which you can paste the incoming cells.

There is no perfect way to handle the second problem. Even if you choose the setting File ⇨ Options ⇨ Advanced ⇨ Pasting from other programs to Match Destination Formatting or Keep Text Only, *something* in the formatting will be messed up—usually the spacing.

Your best bet, assuming you're using a style, is to choose Keep Text Only from either Paste Options or the Paste Special button, and then reapply the style to the pasted cells. Alternatively, if there are table cells that contain the correct formatting, use the Format Painter to reformat the pasted cells as desired.

> **NOTE**
>
> The Paste Options differ slightly when pasting into an existing table. Nest Table (N) enables you to paste all the cells from the copied data into a single cell; or if you selected multiple cells before pasting, each of the selected cells receives a full copy of the pasted data. Insert as New Rows(s) creates new rows to hold the data for you and pastes beginning at the first column, which can lead to a ragged right side if the pasted selection has more or fewer columns than the destination table. Overwrite Cells (O) replaces any existing content in the selected destination but may alter the formatting. Keep Text Only (T), mentioned earlier, pastes without any text formatting but doesn't impact cell formatting.

28

Using Word content in Excel

Going from Word into Excel isn't quite as tricky as going from Excel into Word, although the setup of the Word content matters more in terms of how it pastes into the destination cells in Excel.

Clipboard

If you simply copy content from Word and paste it into Excel—using the Paste button or Ctrl+V—the setup of the original data controls how it is distributed in the destination cells in Excel. When you paste text that includes one or no paragraph marks, Excel inserts all of the text into the selected cell. If the selection contains multiple paragraphs, it is inserted into consecutive cells in the target column. For example, if the Clipboard contains three paragraphs and you paste into cell A1 (Row 1 Column 1), the three paragraphs are inserted into cells A1 (Row 1 Column 1), A2 (Row 2 Column 1), and A3 (Row 3 Column 1), respectively.

When pasting all or part of a table or text delimited with tabs into Excel, the cells are inserted into separate cells matching the original selection in Word. (Point to the table and then click the table move handle that appears to select the entire table or drag over cells to select them before clicking Copy or pressing Ctrl+C.) You only need to select the cell in the upper-left corner of the destination range. For example, to copy a 5×4 table from Word to Excel, select the table and copy or cut it to the Clipboard. In Excel, right-click in the upper-left cell of the 5×4 area where you want the table to appear and choose Paste or press Ctrl+V. By default, any formatting or shading from the original table appears when you paste to Excel.

Paste Options (also available via the Paste Special arrow) are a bit more limited, as shown in Figure 28.9. In this case, the two options are Keep Source Formatting (K) or Match Destination Formatting (M).

FIGURE 28.9

You also can choose Paste Options when pasting from Word to Excel.

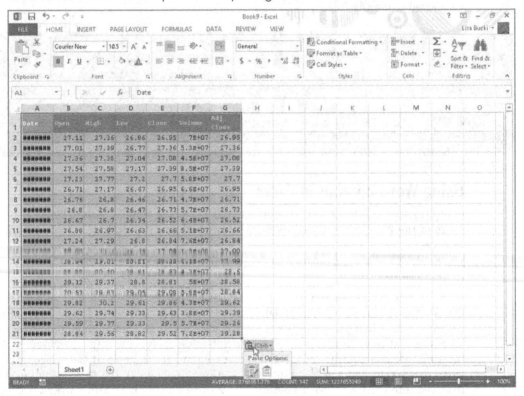

Notice in Figure 28.9 that you may need to make adjustments to column widths and number formatting. Columns A and F in the pasted data in the figure need to be widened. In the case of column A, the column is too narrow to display the date information, so pound signs appear instead. In the case of column F, the numeric values appear in scientific notation because the column is too narrow. Double-clicking the right border of the column heading (beside the column letter) AutoFits the column to the appropriate width. Also, the dollar values shown would have their decimal points vertically aligned with Accounting or Currency number formatting applied. Use the tools in the Number group of Excel's Home tab to work with the number formats for pasted data.

Caution

Note that even if you press Ctrl+A (Select All) to select the entire document and then copy, certain elements will not be copied. That's because Ctrl+A excludes content such as headers, footers, and footnotes. If you want to see the entire file, insert it as an object as described later.

When you paste a picture from Word into Excel, it is inserted into Excel's drawing layer rather than into cells. Note that Excel does not have text wrapping options for graphics, because cell text can't wrap around them.

Drag-and-drop

Unlike when copying via drag-and-drop from Excel to Word, when you do so from Word to Excel, you also need to press and hold Ctrl while dragging. Otherwise the text will be moved from Word. When dragging and dropping a table, drag from within the table; attempting to drag via the table move handle doesn't work. And if you drag and drop a table without using Ctrl, an empty table remains in Word after you move the contents to Excel.

Note

If you try dragging and dropping to Word and it doesn't work, make sure dragging and dropping is enabled in Word Options (File ⇨ Options ⇨ Advanced ⇨ Editing Options ⇨ Allow text to be dragged and dropped).

Object

You can insert a new or existing Word document into an Excel file as an object. In the destination file in Excel, click the cell where you want it to reside. Click the Insert tab, click the Text button to display the Text group if needed, and click Object. Click the Create from File tab and, as described earlier, use the Browse button to select the file to insert. Select Link to file and Display as icon, as needed, and then click OK. The inserted document looks like a picture object on the worksheet, but if you double-click it, you can edit its contents.

28

PowerPoint

In some ways, Word and PowerPoint were meant to work together. That's because PowerPoint uses heading levels that are similar to Word's Heading styles. When creating a PowerPoint presentation, for example, it's a simple matter to convert a Word outline into a PowerPoint presentation (or at least the basis for one), or to use a PowerPoint presentation as an outline for a Word document.

Converting a Word outline to a PowerPoint presentation

Converting a Word document outline into a PowerPoint presentation is simple—as long as you've used Word's Heading styles for your outline or created it in Outline view, which automatically applies the heading styles. Unfortunately, PowerPoint is not able to extract just the outline from a Word document with body text under the headings, so you would have to strip out the body text manually yourself if the document has already been written. Also keep in mind that you need to have saved and named the file. PowerPoint opens the outline from a saved file rather than using a copy type of process.

> **TIP**
>
> A quick way to strip body text from a Word document that was formatted using Heading styles is to copy the entire document to new blank file. Click a paragraph using the main style for body text. In the Editing group of the Home tab, click Select, and then click Select All Text with Similar Formatting. Press the Delete key to remove the text. Repeat the process to select and delete text formatted with other styles representing content not needed in the presentation. Save the file under a new name, and then create the PowerPoint presentation from it.

To convert a Word outline into a PowerPoint presentation, in PowerPoint start a new PowerPoint presentation (Ctrl+N). In the Slides group of the Home tab in PowerPoint, click the New Slide button arrow, and click Slides from Outline, as shown in Figure 28.10. In the Insert Outline dialog box, find the document containing your outline, select it, and click Insert.

> **NOTE**
>
> Once you've inserted an outline into a PowerPoint presentation, you'll often discover that stray or extra paragraph marks insinuate themselves prominently in the PowerPoint presentation, creating unsightly gaps. You can fix them in PowerPoint, or, if it's easier, press Ctrl+Z to undo the insert, clean up the outline in Word, and then try again. Or change to PowerPoint's Outline view by clicking the View tab and then clicking Outline View in the Presentation Views group. Note that Tab and Shift+Tab demote and promote outline levels in PowerPoint's Outline view as they do in Word's Outline view.

FIGURE 28.10

You can use a Word outline to create a PowerPoint presentation.

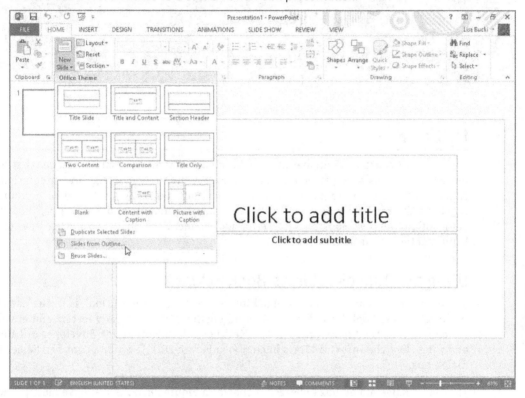

Converting a PowerPoint presentation to a Word document

You can also go in the other direction, using a PowerPoint presentation as a starting outline for a Word document. In PowerPoint, choose File ➪ Save As. After selecting the save location from Backstage or clicking Browse and entering a name if needed in the File name text box, open the Save as type drop-down list and click Outline/RTF—near the bottom of the nonalphabetized list—and then click Save.

In Word, choose File ➪ Open ➪ Computer ➪ Browse, navigate to the .rtf file you just created, and open it. Then switch to Outline view. The top level for each slide was assigned Heading 1, the next level Heading 2, and so on.

Outlook

Outlook 2013 contains a number of tools for creating and formatting messages that greatly resemble the tools for creating and editing documents in Word 2013. This integration of functionality in both programs should make it comfortable for you to use both programs together. You've already seen in Chapter 22, "Data Documents and Mail Merge," how to use your Outlook Address Book contents for a mail merge. Read on to learn other ways that Word and Outlook interact.

Using the Outlook Address Book in Word

One of the more conspicuous relationships between Word and Outlook is in the use of the Outlook Address Book for addresses in Word documents—especially letters and envelopes. For example, in the Create group of the Mailings tab in Word, click Envelopes or Labels, and then click the Insert Address button (see Figure 28.11), which opens the Select Name dialog box.

The Select Name dialog box appears, as shown in Figure 28.12. If you have multiple address books set up, click the Address Book drop-down arrow and choose the one you want. Note that the Search option enables you to search the Name only or More columns. When you use Name only, the dialog box displays only names that start with what you type.

Alternatively, click More columns, type what you're looking for, and click Go. This search feature searches for occurrences of the search text anywhere in any contact field. If that still gives you too many hits, click Advanced Find. Use the Find dialog box to search for names containing text you type. When you find the person or business whose address you want, select it and click OK.

Once the address you need is selected in the Select Names dialog box, click OK, finish selecting settings in the Envelopes and Labels dialog box, and then click OK again.

FIGURE 28.11

You can access the Outlook Address Book using the Insert Address button.

FIGURE 28.12

Insert addresses for Word envelopes or labels via the Address Book.

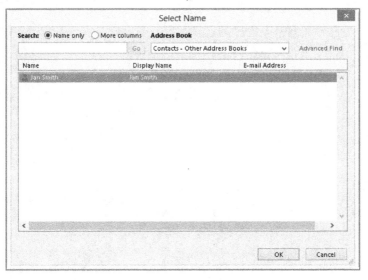

28

Summary

In this chapter, you've learned several ways to exchange data between Word and Excel. You've also seen how to convert Word outlines into PowerPoint presentations, and how to create a Word outline using a PowerPoint presentation. Additionally, you've looked at several ways that Outlook and Word stay in contact with, well, Contacts. You should now be able to do the following:

- Insert Excel content in a Word document and vice versa using a variety of different methods
- Use the Clipboard and drag-and-drop to copy or move content between Word and Excel
- Exchange outlines between Word and PowerPoint
- Use the Address Book tool to insert a contact's address in Word envelopes or labels

Part IX

Power and Customization

The success of any piece of software is the degree to which it does what you want it to do. If a program works the way you want it to, you'll keep using it. If not, chances are good that you'll find another program that meets your needs. Fortunately, Word provides dozens and dozens of ways you can customize it to help it perform tasks as they need to be performed. Part IX shows you how to change the aspects of Word you don't like, to sculpt Word into a word processing environment that fits the way you work.

Chapter 29 shows you how to take full advantage of Word's greatest and most flexible asset, the keyboard. Chapter 30 focuses on the Quick Access Toolbar and the Ribbon, so you can put the commands that you need front and center. One of Word's most powerful yet confusing features is its dizzying array of options and settings, which you tackle head-on in Chapter 31. Chapter 32 gives you a running start with Word's most powerful feature—macros, which are based on Microsoft's Visual Basic for Applications.

IN THIS PART

Keyboard Customization

To a Word power user, one of the most amazing pieces of Word trivia is that most users don't take advantage of the option to customize Word's keyboard. A power user knows that there's no need to drill down through multiple layers of choices from the Ribbon to choose a command or option that could easily be assigned to a simple keystroke.

Using the mouse may be more intuitive for many people, but it can actually slow a fast typist down. As your fingers fly along, it takes less time to add in a shortcut key combination than it is to move your hand off the keyboard, move the mouse around, and then return to the keyboard. If you possess good keyboard skills, creating your own keyboard shortcuts makes sense and can help you stay efficient. This chapter shows you how to take greater command of Word through the keyboard.

Understanding Customization Boundaries

The first thing you need to know when you consider customizing your keyboard is that Word effectively does not reserve any keys for particular commands. Unlike a lot of programs, in which you have no choice or little choice about what keystrokes you can assign to which commands, in Word your options are wide open. If you would rather that Ctrl+H be used to highlight selected text (yellow marker style) than be used for Replace, you can make that change. If Ctrl+T really doesn't work for you, mnemonically speaking, for hanging indent (or, better still if you had no clue that that's what Ctrl+T does), feel free to reassign Ctrl+T to the thesaurus, or to something else.

You have a variety of ways of remapping the keyboard. This chapter starts by showing you the shortcut methods for customizing the keyboard, and then moves on to the more complicated ways of doing so.

Viewing and Assigning Keyboard Shortcuts with the Cloverleaf Method

You can use a keyboard shortcut combination to quickly find out what almost any keystroke does, and to assign and remove keyboard shortcuts. Here's how:

1. **Press Ctrl+Alt+Plus Sign (on the number pad).** This runs the Customize Keyboard Shortcut command which is one of the Commands Not in the Ribbon found in the Word Options dialog box when you customize the Ribbon or Quick Access Toolbar. The mouse pointer turns into the cloverleaf shown in Figure 29.1.

FIGURE 29.1

Press Ctrl+Alt+Plus Sign to display the cloverleaf mouse pointer, and then click a tool to work with its keyboard shortcuts.

2. **Click any tool that has a command or macro assigned to it.** The Customize Keyboard dialog box appears, shown in Figure 29.2.

FIGURE 29.2

Use the Customize Keyboard dialog box to add and remove keyboard shortcuts.

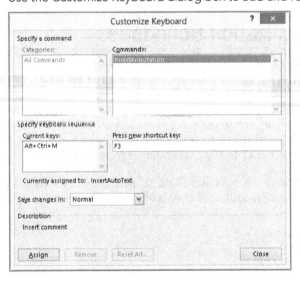

3. **Type the new keyboard shortcut to assign to the command you clicked.** In Figure 29.2, I pressed F3 (the Insert AutoText keystroke), so it appears in the Press new shortcut key text box.

4. **Click the Assign button.** This moves the new keyboard shortcut into the Current keys list.

> **NOTE**
>
> Before clicking Assign, ensure that the Save changes in setting is set to the correct template. If you're customizing a particular template, use it. Or use `Normal.dotm` if you want the assignment available all the time.

5. **Click Close to dismiss the dialog box.**

There are numerous instances where changing a keyboard shortcut can come in handy. Suppose, for example, that you have just clicked the Navigation Pane check box on the View tab for the thousandth time, and really would rather have a shortcut key assigned to it. Press Ctrl+Alt+Plus Sign, and then click Navigation Pane in the Show group of the View tab of the Ribbon. The Customize Keyboard dialog box appears. Under Current keys, nothing is currently assigned. Decide what you want to assign (if you never use Normal view, for example, you might consider Ctrl+Alt+N), press that key combination, click Assign, and click Close.

Note that the Customize Keyboard dialog box also includes a Remove button. You can display the dialog box, click a shortcut to remove in the Current keys list, and then click Remove to undo a keyboard shortcut assignment.

> **NOTE**
>
> If you are working on a notebook computer that doesn't have a numeric keyboard with the plus sign, you can access the Customize Keyboard Shortcut command by adding it to the Ribbon or Quick Access toolbar. See Chapter 30, "Customizing the Quick Access Toolbar and Ribbon," for more about that type of customization.

Choosing the Storage Location for Keyboard Shortcuts

You can specify whether to store any keyboard shortcut assignments within the current documents or the default template. The default Save changes in setting as shown in Figure 29.2 is Normal (`Normal.dotm`), but you can open that drop-down list and choose to save a keyboard assignment in any of three locations:

- **The current document.** Click the document name in the drop-down list. If you save a key assignment in the current document, that key assignment will be available only when editing that document.

29

- **The template on which the current document is based (if different from Normal.dotm).** Shortcut key assignments saved in the current template are available only when editing documents based on that template. Assignments in that template take precedence over assignments in `Normal.dotm`, but not over assignments in the current document (if they are different).
  - **Normal (Normal.dotm).** This makes the keyboard shortcut assignment available in not only all current documents, but any new documents that you create.

As a general strategy, therefore, any key assignments you want to be available throughout Word, you should save in `Normal.dotm`. If an assignment is relevant only while editing a particular document or template, then save to the current document or template. For example, if you have a newsletter template that requires aligning numerous graphics and headings, you may want to assign a keyboard shortcut to the Gridlines check box in the Show group of the View tab and save the keyboard assignment in the template. Then you will be able to use the keyboard shortcut as needed to show and hide gridlines while creating each new edition of the newsletter.

Multi-Stroke Key Assignment

Ordinarily, most users think about keystrokes in terms of Ctrl+S, Alt+B, Shift+F5, and so on. Word does enable you to create these kinds of shortcuts, but you can also create another kind, such as Ctrl+S,1 or Ctrl+T,Z. For these assignments, you would press the initial keystroke, such as Ctrl+S, and then (after releasing the Ctrl and S keys) you would type an additional character, such as a 1.

Why would you want to do this? You might want to do this because it greatly expands the number of shortcut keys you can create for any given Ctrl, Alt, Shift + key combination. It also lets you do so in a logical and methodical way. For example, by default, Headings 1 through 3 are assigned to Ctrl+Alt+1 through 3. For some of us, that's not exactly an easy combination to press with one hand. Moreover, what about Heading 4 through 9? Many people use those styles as well.

What if, instead of those three difficult-to-press assignments, you could instead press Ctrl+Shift+X followed by 1 through 9? (By default, Ctrl+Shift+X toggles XML tags, so if you're not an XMLer, this might work for you.) That then gives you the much easier Ctrl+Shift+X to press, and easy-to-remember 1 through 9 for the respective heading styles.

Or suppose you frequently work with mail merge. Very few of the Mailings Ribbon tools have built-in key assignments. You might consider assigning Ctrl+M,S to Select Recipients, Ctrl+M,E to Edit Recipients List, and so on.

To create a multi-stroke assignment, open the Customize Keyboard dialog box for the desired command or tool, press the first combination, release the keys, and then tap the next key. The assignments will appear as Ctrl+M,S or Ctrl+M,E; the latter is shown in Figure 29.3. Click Assign and Close, and you're off and running.

FIGURE 29.3

Create a more robust or easier-to-reach shortcut using multiple keystrokes.

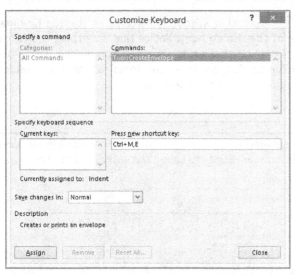

> **NOTE**
>
> Although Word supports multi-stroke keyboard shortcuts, it generally does not allow you to assign a single key to a shortcut, because that would undermine the keystroke's normal usage. For example, suppose Word were to let you assign the "e" key to a command. That might cause problems. You likely need the "e" key for typing things like "Help!" So, you can't reassign the "e" key as a shortcut. Moreover, the Tab key is used as a navigation key within the dialog box itself, so if you press Tab while in the Press new shortcut key box, the focus is shifted to the Save changes in box. Therefore, that tab key is taboo, at least in the Customize Keyboard dialog box. Other keys, such as Enter, F1, Shift+Enter, and Esc, are also off-limits in the Customize Keyboard dialog box, so if you need to assign the off-limits keys, you'll need to do so using VBA (Visual Basic for Applications, the language used for recording and writing Word macros). See Chapter 32, "Macros: Recording, Editing, and Using," for more details about VBA.

29

Customizing Keystrokes through Word Options

The cloverleaf method only enables you to set keyboard shortcuts for commands that appear on the Ribbon. Some commands aren't available in any of the ribbon tabs, and other commands are available only indirectly (for example, from inside a dialog box). When the quick cloverleaf method isn't available or otherwise doesn't work, you can use the Word Options dialog box to make the desired shortcut assignments. From it, you can assign almost any key to just about any command:

1. **Choose File ⇨ Options ⇨ Customize Ribbon ⇨ Customize (beside Keyboard shortcutsat the bottom of the dialog box).** Notice that this time, the Categories and Commands lists display more choices, as shown in Figure 29.4. That's because previously, as shown in Figure 29.2, you used the cloverleaf pointer to select a single command prior to displaying the dialog box.

FIGURE 29.4

When you open the Customize Keyboard dialog box from Word Options, you can use the Categories and Commands lists to select the command for which you want to add a shortcut.

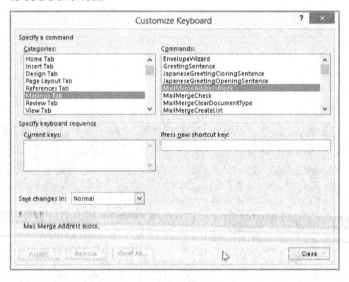

2. **Click the category that holds the command for which you want to add a short-cut key.** The commands in that category appear in the Commands list at the right. Note that I've selected the Mailings tab category in Figure 29.4.

3. **Click the desired command in the Commands list.** Figure 29.4 shows the MailMergeAddressBlock command selected.

4. **Click in the Press new shortcut key text box, and press the desired keyboard shortcut.**

5. **Click Assign, and then Close.**

That's the overview of how it works. Now let's examine the Categories and Commands lists of the Customize Keyboard dialog box a bit more closely.

Categories

The Categories list starts by organizing commands into a number of categories corresponding to the tabs on the Ribbon: File Tab, Home Tab, Insert Tab, Design Tab, Page Layout Tab, References Tab, Mailings Tab, Review Tab, View Tab, Developer Tab, and so on. If you're looking for a command that resides on the Home tab, try setting Categories to Home Tab. If you're looking for a References command, set Categories to References Tab.

As you scroll down the list of categories, the choices move from the main ribbon tabs and go to the specialized tabs, such as Add-Ins. Just in case you're wondering, Add-Ins corresponds to the commands you'll find in File ⇨ Options ⇨ Add-Ins. You'll next find a category entry for each of Word's contextual tabs, such as SmartArt Tools | Design Tab, Chart Tools | Design Tab, and Ink Tools | Pens Tab.

A little further down, you come to a very useful category: Commands Not in the Ribbon. This category is home to a number of legacy Word commands. If there's a tool from Word 2003 or earlier that you liked using and want to continue using in Word 2013, take a look in this category to see if you can find it.

Further down still, you'll come to All Commands, which has almost all of Word's commands in it, but not quite. Though it might seem easier to look in smaller categories, it's sometimes frustrating, because there's no guarantee that the command you seek is in the category that seems most logical to you. Your logic might not be the same as the Microsoft programmer who designed the categories. For that reason, sometimes your best shot is to aim for the All Commands list. If it's not there, then it's not anywhere.

At the bottom, the Categories list includes Macros, Fonts, Building Blocks, Styles, and Common Symbols. You can assign keyboard shortcuts to make these tools and settings more accessible.

Commands

With so many nice categories, you might think it would be simple to find the command you're looking for. The difficulty in determining what a particular command is called might explain in part why so few Word users take full advantage of the option to customize the keyboard.

To help you in this quest, notice the Description section of the Customize Keyboard dialog box (refer to Figure 29.4). As you scroll through the commands, a description of the command is listed there. That might help you when trying to locate the command you're looking for.

29

Here are a couple of tips that can help you zero in on a command more quickly:

- Run the ListCommands command to generate a list of all Word commands, and then search through that list to find the name of the command. See the next section for more on this method.

- Record a macro to do what you want, and then look at the macro's VBA listing to see what the commands are called. See Chapter 32 to learn how to create macros and view their contents.

List Commands

Word has a built-in command that few Word users know about: List Commands. This command creates a new Word document that contains a full list of Word's commands. Because it's a Word document, it is completely searchable and provides a handy way to find out what a particular command is called. Here's how to create a commands list document.

1. **Choose File ⇨ Options ⇨ Customize Ribbon, click to check Developer in the Main Tabs list, and then click OK.** This displays the Developer tab of the Ribbon.

2. **On the Developer tab in the Code group, click Macros.** The Macros dialog box appears.

3. **Click in the Macro name text box, and type** ListCommands. As shown in Figure 29.5, the Run and Step Into buttons become active. That means that the command or macro name you've typed actually exists in Word.

FIGURE 29.5

When you type the name of a command or macro that exists, the Run button becomes available.

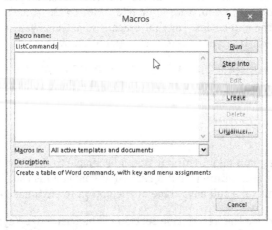

4. **Click Run.** This causes the List Commands dialog box to appear, as shown in Figure 29.6.

FIGURE 29.6

Choose All Word commands to create a list of all Word commands and key assignments. Choose Current keyboard settings to see just a list of commands that already have key assignments (built-in and user-customized).

5. **To list all commands, click All Word commands, and then click OK.** Word responds by creating a new Word document (see Figure 29.7) with a three-column table: Command Name, Modifiers, and Key. Modifiers are the shifting keys you press, and Key is the main active key you press. For example, Alt+Ctrl+ and M, which you see for Annotation (unless you've changed it), means that you would press Alt+Ctrl+M to insert an annotation. (Press Ctrl+Z if you just did that and inserted an unwanted annotation into the current document.)

FIGURE 29.7

The resulting document lists Command Name, Modifiers, and Key in a table.

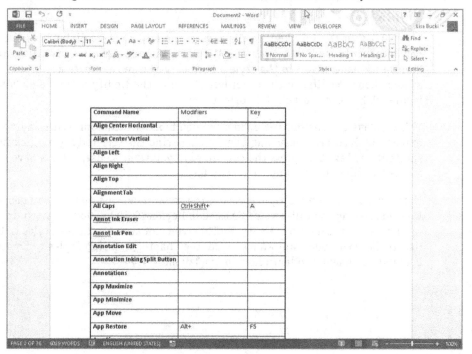

Command Name	Modifiers	Key
Align Center Horizontal		
Align Center Vertical		
Align Left		
Align Right		
Align Top		
Alignment Tab		
All Caps	Ctrl+Shift+	A
Annot Ink Eraser		
Annot Ink Pen		
Annotation Edit		
Annotation Inking Split Button		
Annotations		
App Maximize		
App Minimize		
App Move		
App Restore	Alt+	F5

The listing contains all built-in commands as well as macros and all current key assignments. If you've changed an assignment, your assignment will be listed. When there are multiple assignments, there will be separate rows in the table for each assignment.

What you're interested in here, however, is command names, rather than assignments. Suppose, for example, that you remember a command in an earlier version of Word—one you haven't been able to discover in the latest version's interface. Search the list for words or word fragments that are related to the command you seek. There's a good chance that you'll find the command.

When you find a command name, open the Customize Keyboard dialog box, set Categories to All Commands, and look for the command name in the list of commands. As you search, keep in mind that Word commands don't contain spaces. Once you find the command you seek, you can assign it to a keystroke.

Other Methods for Assigning Keyboard Shortcuts

The Customize Keyboard dialog box isn't the only way to assign keystrokes to Word commands and tools. Word provides additional assignment methods that are available from other dialog boxes.

Styles

You can assign shortcut keys to styles from the Modify Style dialog box. Click the dialog box launcher for the Styles group in the Home tab or press Alt+Ctrl+Shift+S to display the Styles task pane. Scroll to the style for which you want to create a shortcut, right-click it, and choose Modify. In the lower-left corner of the Modify Style dialog box, shown in Figure 29.8, choose Format ⇨ Shortcut key.

This displays the Customize Keyboard dialog box, with Categories displaying only the grayed-out Styles category, and Commands listing the selected style. Click in the Press new shortcut key text box, press the combination you want to use, set the Save changes in box as needed, click Assign, and then click Close.

If you want to assign multiple styles at the same time, this method can get old quickly. Instead, display the full-service Customize Keyboard dialog box as shown in the previous section, and set Categories to Styles. Then you can access multiple styles in the Commands list. If the styles you want aren't listed, see Chapter 7, "Using Styles to Create a Great Looking Document," to learn how to display more styles.

FIGURE 29.8

Use the Format menu to start assigning a shortcut key to the selected style.

Symbols

A number of symbols already have default shortcut keys assigned to them. For a list, choose Insert ➪ Symbols ➪ Symbol ➪ More Symbols ➪ Special Characters. To assign a symbol that doesn't have a built-in shortcut, choose Insert ➪ Symbols ➪ Symbol ➪ More Symbols ➪ Symbols. Using the techniques described in Chapter 15, "Adding Drop Caps, Text Boxes, Shapes, Symbols, and Equations," find the symbol you want to assign and then click the Shortcut Key button at the bottom of the Symbol dialog box (see Figure 29.9).

The Customize Keyboard dialog box appears, with Categories set to Common Symbols, and Commands listing the symbol you selected. Click in the Press new shortcut key text box, press the desired shortcut keystrokes, click Assign, and then click Close.

For access to multiple symbols, you can go through the full-service Customize Keyboard dialog box, setting Categories to Common Symbols. However, this will not give you complete access to all of the symbols you get when you go through the Symbol dialog box. Hence, if you're looking for something in particular and require the associated encoding, you'll need to go the Symbols route.

29

FIGURE 29.9

Apply a shortcut key combination to the selected symbol in the Symbol dialog box.

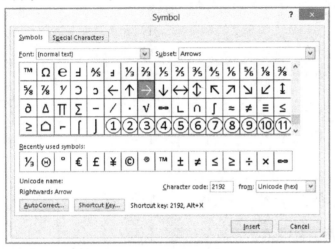

Record Macro

When you record a new macro, you can assign a keystroke to the resulting macro. In the Code group of the Developer tab (File ➪ Options ➪ Customize Ribbon, click to check Developer in the Main Tabs list, and then click OK), click Record Macro. Or, if the Developer tab hasn't been displayed, you can click the Record Macro button in the status bar. (To enable macro recording and playback from the status bar, right-click the status bar, click to check Macro Recording, and then press Esc.) Or, you can click the View tab, click Macros in the Macro group, and then click Record Macro.

When the Record Macro dialog box appears, as shown in Figure 29.10, type a name that will help you identify the macro later, add a description in the Description box, set Store macro in as appropriate, and then click Keyboard. This displays the Customize Keyboard dialog box, with the macro name listed. As before, click the Press new shortcut key text box if needed, press the combination, click Assign, and click Close.

If you forgot to assign a keyboard shortcut to a macro when you recorded it, you can open the Customize Keyboard dialog box through Word Options, as described earlier. Select Macros in the Categories list, click the desired macro in the Macros list at right (see Figure 29.11), and then add the shortcut key as previously described.

FIGURE 29.10

The best time to assign a shortcut assignment to a macro is when the macro is created.

FIGURE 29.11

Go through Word Options to assign a shortcut to a macro at a later time.

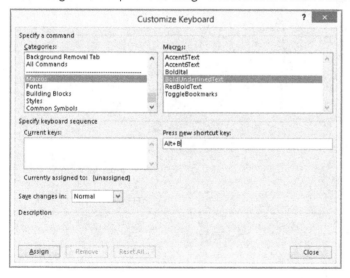

29

Summary

In this chapter you've seen a number of ways to assign keyboard shortcuts to a variety of tools, commands, styles, symbols, and other Word features. You should now be able to do the following:

- Use the cloverleaf method to quickly determine whether a given Ribbon tool already has a shortcut key assigned or to make a new assignment
- Assign keyboard shortcuts to fonts
- Make multi-key assignments to conserve Ctrl/Alt/Shift keys as well as to create logical systems of shortcuts
- Locate long-lost commands and assign keyboard shortcuts so you can start using them again
- Assign a shortcut to a macro that you are creating

CHAPTER

30

Customizing the Quick Access Toolbar and Ribbon

IN THIS CHAPTER

Customizing the QAT

Adding Ribbon groups to the QAT

Rearranging the QAT

Resetting the QAT to the factory defaults

Finding Ribbon customization settings

Adding and removing tabs and groups with the desired commands

Exporting and importing Ribbon customizations

The Quick Access Toolbar, or QAT, and Ribbon in Word 2013 present the most essential commands in Word front and center. Research has shown that the Pareto principle (80-20 Rule) often applies when it comes to software: 80 percent of users only use 20 percent of the features. If you are part of the 20 percent of users who need to explore the commands beyond what you see on the QAT and Ribbon, you can customize each of them to put the commands that are your personal essentials at your fingertips.

In this chapter, you learn how ridiculously easy it is to customize the QAT and Ribbon—how to remove commands that you don't use and how to replace them with tools that better match your needs. You also learn how to share Ribbon customizations by exporting what you create or by importing other customizations.

The QAT?

The *Quick Access Toolbar* (QAT) is the collection of tools that appears above the Ribbon (by default) in the upper-left corner of the Word screen, shown in Figure 30.1. The default tools are Save, Undo, and Repeat. (The far-left button controls the application window; clicking it displays choices for working with the window size or closing Word.) Like the Ribbon, the QAT is somewhat context-sensitive. The Undo command is only available once you've performed an action that can be undone. The same applies for Repeat. If you do an action such as typing a word and pressing Spacebar, you can click Repeat to repeat that action for a period of time. If you click Undo, the Repeat button changes to the Redo button, and the ScreenTip for the Repeat button becomes "Repeat Bold."

FIGURE 30.1

The default QAT appears above the Ribbon and contains just three tools.

> **TIP**
>
> The arrow on the button for the third QAT button in repeat mode is circular. When it is in Redo mode, it's a mirror image of the shape of the arrow on the Undo button.

There is no practical upper limit to the number of tools the QAT can contain. However, when it holds too many to display all at once, a More controls button appears at the right end of the QAT as shown in Figure 30.2. Clicking it displays the additional tools in a bar to the right and below. The Customize the Quick Access Toolbar button appears at the right end of the bar with the additional QAT tools.

FIGURE 30.2

When the QAT is full, clicking the More controls button displays additional tools.

As for many other customizable features in Word, you can choose where you want to store changes you make to the QAT. Many users place all of their everyday tools onto the QAT and store them in Normal.dotm. This makes the custom set of tools available all the time.

As an alternative, you can store special tools used only some of the time in templates and documents in which you need them. For example, you might use some tools only when creating forms. There's simply no reason for them to clutter up your QAT the rest of the time. In that case, store those tools only in forms templates.

Other tools might be useful only when writing long documents that have a bibliography, footnotes, and citations. Why not store those tools only in the templates you typically use for creating such documents?

Of course, if the only template you ever use is Normal.dotm, the issue of where to store tools is moot. If you heed the advice of this book, however, you will make use of a variety of templates. As you discover task-specific tools you need, consider having those tools at the ready only when they're needed.

Changing the Buttons on the Quick Access Toolbar

As suggested at the beginning of this chapter, customizing the Quick Access Toolbar could hardly be any easier. You can add any tool on the Ribbon directly from their location. Otherwise, you may have to open the Word Options dialog box, and then the only difficulty may be determining the proper name for the command you need to add.

Adding commands to the QAT

To help you hit the ground running, Word makes it easy to place up to 11 popular commands on the QAT without having to visit the Quick Access Toolbar customization choices in the Word Options dialog box, which you'll see shortly. At the right end of the QAT, as shown in Figure 30.3, click the Customize Quick Access Toolbar button. By default, three popular commands are already checked. Click to check (enable) or uncheck (disable) any or all of the commands shown.

30

FIGURE 30.3

Check or uncheck any of the 11 commands listed on the Customize Quick Access Toolbar menu.

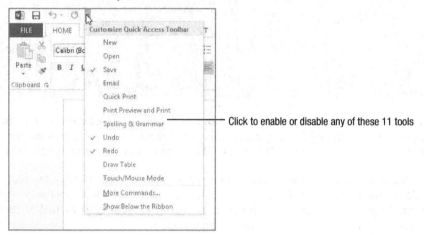

Click to enable or disable any of these 11 tools

To add a command/tool to the QAT directly from the Ribbon, right-click the command/tool and choose Add to Quick Access Toolbar, as shown in Figure 30.4.

FIGURE 30.4

Right-click almost any Ribbon tool and choose Add to Quick Access Toolbar to add a tool to the QAT.

Adding groups

You can also add entire sections or command groups to the QAT. This might be useful, for example, when creating a special QAT in a particular document template. To add a group to the QAT, right-click the title for that group and choose Add to Quick Access Toolbar.

When you add a group to the QAT, the individual tools aren't added. Rather, a tool representing the group as a whole is added. When you click that tool, the group is then revealed, much the same way that the More controls button reveals tools that do not fit on the QAT.

When you add the Styles group (from the Home tab) to the QAT, it appears as shown in Figure 30.5. Clicking its button opens the whole Styles group, just as it appears in the Home tab. When you think about it, you could probably add the Ribbon groups you use most frequently to the QAT and never display the Ribbon at all. (Press Ctrl+F1 to toggle the Ribbon off and on, or double-click any Ribbon tab.)

FIGURE 30.5

You can add entire groups to the QAT.

Removing commands

Removing commands or other items from the Ribbon is even easier than adding them, because you don't have to go looking for them. Right-click the offending item and click Remove from Quick Access Toolbar.

The Customize Quick Access Toolbar Dialog Box

So far, the chapter has focused on the easy methods customizing the Quick Access Toolbar. When you know exactly what command to add and where it is in the Ribbon, it's very simple to add it. When it's not directly accessible on the Ribbon (for example, available only from inside a dialog box or other control) or not obviously available at all (as in the case for certain legacy commands), finding the correct command name takes a bit more effort. The chore isn't made any easier by the fact that command names used for the Quick Access Toolbar are not always the same as command names used in the Customize Keyboard dialog box. Hence, the cloverleaf method for discovering a command's name doesn't always help when it comes to the Quick Access Toolbar.

Displaying the main QAT customization dialog box

To display the main dialog box for customizing the QAT, right-click the QAT and choose Customize Quick Access Toolbar. Note that you can also get here by choosing File ➪ Options ➪ Quick Access Toolbar, but that takes more steps. Open the Choose commands from drop-down list to see the categories holding the commands, as shown in Figure 30.6, similar to the

30

Customize Keyboard categories you saw in Chapter 29, "Keyboard Customization." Of course, after you finish making the various QAT adjustments described next, click OK to close the dialog box and apply your changes.

FIGURE 30.6

To customize the Quick Access Toolbar, you can choose from among a number of categories.

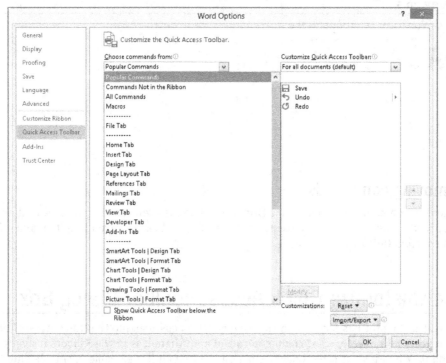

Setting the storage location for the QAT

The customizations for the QAT can be stored in the current document or in Normal.dotm. As shown in Figure 30.6, the default storage location selected in the drop-down list under Customize Quick Access Toolbar at the upper right is called For all documents (default). This means Normal.dotm.

If you want to store the QAT changes in another document, such as a template you're creating, open that document before displaying the Word Options dialog box Quick Access Toolbar settings. Then open the drop-down list under Customize Quick Access Toolbar and click For *Document Name*. The changes that you make will then be saved in the specified document; if the document is a template, the custom tools will appear in any document based on that template.

Finding and adding commands

After you choose a category from the Choose commands from list, the list in the left half of the Word Options dialog box adjusts to display only the commands in the specified category. For commands ending in an ellipsis (...), you can hover the mouse over a command to see the full name and the Ribbon location of the command. The steps for reaching the command, usually indicated with ⇨ in this book, are indicated using the | character, as shown in Figure 30.7.

FIGURE 30.7

If you hover the mouse pointer over a command, a tooltip tells you where the command "lives" and its full name.

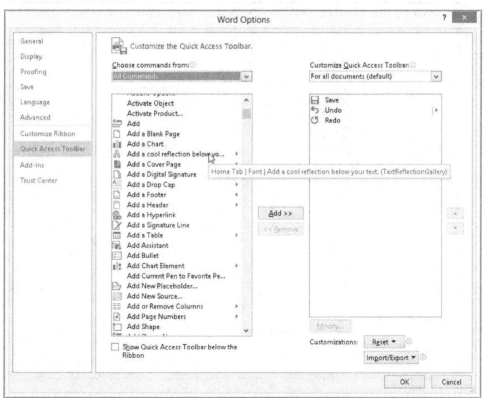

To add a command to the Quick Access Toolbar, select it in the left list in the dialog box and click the Add button between the lists. Then, as noted earlier, use the up and down buttons to move the tool to where you want it.

Adding a separator

You can add one or more separators to group commands. For example, you might want to separate formatting commands from other commands. To add one, scroll to the top of the left list of commands, click <Separator> at the top of the list, and click Add.

Rearranging the QAT buttons

Work with the right list of the dialog box to change the order of the tools on the QAT. Click to select the command you want to move. Click either the Move Up (up arrow) or Move Down (down arrow) buttons to the right of the list as many times as needed to move the item into the desired position. As shown in Figure 30.8, you also can move inserted separators using the same method.

FIGURE 30.8

Use Move Up and Move Down buttons to rearrange the QAT to suit your needs.

Removing tools from the QAT

To remove a tool from the QAT via the Word Options dialog box, click the tool in the right half of the dialog box and click the Remove button between the lists. Note that it's usually easier to remove a button directly from the QAT by right-clicking and choosing Remove from Quick Access Toolbar as described earlier. You might use the Customize Quick Access Toolbar method when you're doing a number of changes at the same time.

Resetting the QAT to the default

If you decide for any reason that you want to remove all customizations made to the QAT, it's easy. With the QAT customization dialog box showing, first set the location of the QAT you want to reset by using the drop-down list under Customize Quick Access Toolbar at the upper right in the dialog box and then click either For all documents (default) to reset the QAT stored in `Normal.dotm`, or For *Document Name* to select another open document or template. Then click the Reset button below the right list and click Reset Only Quick Access Toolbar. Word prompts as shown in Figure 30.9; click Yes to confirm.

FIGURE 30.9

Word prompts to confirm before resetting customizations.

> **NOTE**
>
> After clicking Yes, you're still not done. If you click Cancel (or press Esc) rather than OK, the reset action will not be done. This gives you a fallback option if you change your mind.

Making Changes to the Ribbon

If you're willing to invest a few minutes, you can turn Word 2013's Ribbon into a collection of tools that better suit your needs. If you're truly evil, you can even make your colleagues think they're going crazy. But, since this is a Bible, I'll leave the evil entirely up to your own devices.

Customizing the Ribbon

The easiest way to start is by right-clicking the QAT, any blank area in the Ribbon, or any Ribbon tab, and clicking Customize the Ribbon, as shown in Figure 30.10. This opens Word

30

Options to the Customize Ribbon tab, shown in Figure 30.11. As for changes to the QAT, be sure to click OK when you finish making the various customizations to close the Word Options dialog box and apply your changes.

FIGURE 30.10

Right-click the QAT or a Ribbon tab for quick access to Ribbon customization settings.

FIGURE 30.11

The Customize Ribbon tab is also where you go to customize the keyboard.

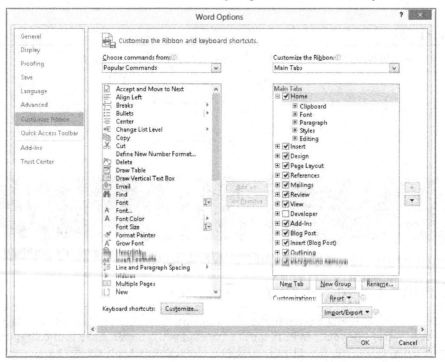

Adding a custom group

You can't add or remove tools within an existing tab group. If an existing group contains tools you never use and the tools that you do want don't appear, build your own custom group and make room for it on the tab by hiding the unwanted built-in group.

Suppose that you never use the Online Video tool in the Media group of the Insert tab. Instead, you'd rather have the 5-Point Star tool in that slot. To do this, you would add a new group—which you might rename Star. Then, add the 5-Point Star tool to the group. Finally, hide the unneeded built-in group.

To add a group in the Customize Ribbon tab of the Word Options dialog box:

1. **Choose Main Tabs from the Customize the Ribbon drop-down list at right.**

2. **In the right Main Tabs group, click the plus (+) beside the tab you want to customize to expand its groups.**

3. **Right-click the group you want to replace and click Add new group; or click the group and click the New Group button below the right list.** If you don't need to replace a group, select the group to the right of which you want to insert the new group. The new group appears with a placeholder name, New Group (Custom).

4. **With the new group still selected, either right-click the new group and choose Rename, or click the Rename button.** The Rename dialog box appears as shown in Figure 30.12.

5. **Type the group name into the Display name text box, and click OK.** For example, Figure 30.12 shows **Star** entered as the new group name. Note that clicking an icon in this dialog box does not have any impact.

6. **Add commands to the group as described later in the "Finding and adding Ribbon commands" section.**

7. **Finally, right-click the built-in group you want to remove, if any, and click Remove; or you can click the group and click the Remove button between the lists.**

8. **Click OK to see your customized group.** The example in Figure 30.13 shows a new Star group near the center of the Insert tab.

30

FIGURE 30.12

Replace the placeholder name for the custom group.

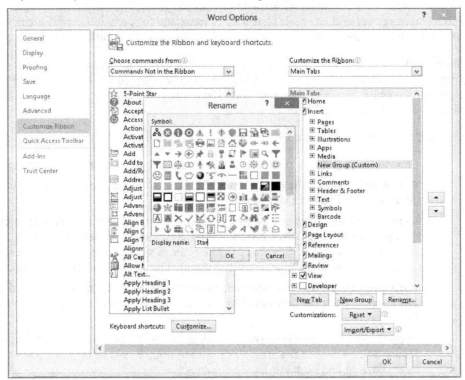

FIGURE 30.13

A customized Insert tab with a group named Star.

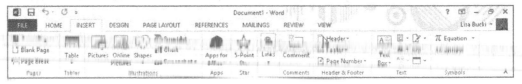

Adding a custom tab

You could rebuild Word's interface completely, if needed, with the exception of the File tab, which cannot be user modified. You can replace all of the built-in tabs and groups with your own. As a practical matter, this might be useful for a specialized project and/or to reduce the amount of learning time needed by a certain set of users in your organization.

To add a custom tab:

1. **Right-click a Ribbon tab and click Customize the Ribbon.** The Customize Ribbon tab in the Word Options dialog box appears.

2. **Choose Main Tabs from the Customize the Ribbon drop-down list at right.**

3. **In the right Main Tabs group, click a tab to specify the location where Word will insert the new tab.** The new tab will appear immediately below the selected tab in the list, and will appear to the right of it on the Ribbon.

4. **Click the New Tab button below the list; or right-click the selected tab and choose Add New Tab.** It has the placeholder name New Tab (Custom) and contains a group with the placeholder name New Group (Custom). See Figure 30.14. You cannot add commands to a tab outside of a group, so Word automatically includes the first new group for you on the new tab.

FIGURE 30.14

When you create a new tab, it automatically includes a new group.

5. **If you don't like the location, use the Move Up (up arrow) and Move Down (down arrow) buttons to the right of the right list to move the tab where you want it.** Or drag it to the desired location.

6. For both the tab and group, click the placeholder name, type a new name in the Display name text box of the Rename dialog box that appears, and then click OK.

7. Add commands to the group as described next in the "Finding and adding Ribbon commands" section.

8. Click OK to see your new customized tab.

Finding and adding Ribbon commands

As shown earlier in the chapter during the discussion about customizing the QAT, use the left Choose commands from list of the Customize Ribbon tab in the Word Options dialog box to select the commands and macros you want to add to the Ribbon. Use the Choose commands from drop-down list to specify a category. If you don't know exactly where the command you seek resides, choose All Commands. On the other hand, if you have an idea of where the command resides, selecting the appropriate category or tab can save some time.

When looking for commands, click in the command list and press the first letter of the command name you're looking for to scroll down to that part of the alphabet. Unfortunately, the command list is not searchable, and it sometimes takes a bit of hunting to find any given command.

If you're looking for a command that normally resides in a specific tab, set Choose commands from to All Tabs. This organizes the list of commands by tab, showing only commands that are already somewhere in the Ribbon. Suppose, for example, that you're looking for the Bring Forward tools. After selecting All Tabs, click the plus (+) beside the desired tab, and then expand the desired group to see its commands.

Once you've found the desired command at left, use these steps to add it to the desired existing or custom group at the right:

1. Click the command or tool to add to the Ribbon in the left list once you've navigated to it.

2. Choose Main Tabs from the Customize the Ribbon drop-down list at the right.

3. In the right Main Tabs group, click the plus (+) beside the tab that holds the group where you want to add commands.

4. Within the tab you selected, expand the destination group if it has a plus sign beside it, and then click the group name to select it.

5. Click the Add button tvo add the command or tool selected in Step 1 to the selected group in the right Main Tabs list.

6. **Continue the general process to add more commands from thve left list to the selected location as needed.** Figure 30.15 illustrates several commands added to a custom Lists group in a custom Lisa's Favorites tab. You also can use the Move Up

(up arrow) and Move Down (down arrow) buttons to rearrange the commands in the group you're working with in the right Main Tabs list.

7. **Click OK when you've finished adding commands to groups.**

FIGURE 30.15

Select commands from the left list to add to the selected group in the right Main Tabs list.

30

Turning tabs on or off

Rather than completely removing a tab and then having to figure out how to reinstate it, you can use the check boxes that appear with the tab names after you select Main Tabs from the right Customize the Ribbon drop-down list in the Customize Ribbon tab of Word Options. If you want to hide the tab, clear its check box and then click OK. To redisplay the tab, check its check box and then click OK. The ability to display and hide tabs enables you to create a library of custom tabs, essentially, and to turn them on or off as needed.

The Developer tab frequently gets turned on and back off by more experienced Word users. By default, Word has the Developer tab turned off, because it contains commands for creating and editing macros and other custom controls. Many Word users never need it, but a few more experienced Word users may need it from time to time. If you haven't yet turned it on, right-click a Ribbon tab and choose Customize the Ribbon. Make sure that Main Tabs is selected from the right Customize the Ribbon drop-down list, and note that Developer appears between View and Add-Ins in the list. Click the check box beside Developer to place a check in it, and then click OK. Suddenly, the Developer tab appears in the Ribbon!

Removing tabs and groups

You cannot remove built-in tabs, but you can hide them by unchecking them as just described. User-created custom tabs, however, can be hidden or removed.

Often, it's more likely that you don't use specific tools or groups, rather than entire Ribbon tabs. As noted earlier, even built-in groups can be removed when not needed, as well as easily reinstated

To remove a group or custom tab, expand the tab if needed to display the group. Right-click the group or custom tab and then, as shown in Figure 30.16, click Remove. Then click OK to close the Word Options dialog box.

FIGURE 30.16

Right-click a group and click Remove to deep-six it from a Ribbon tab.

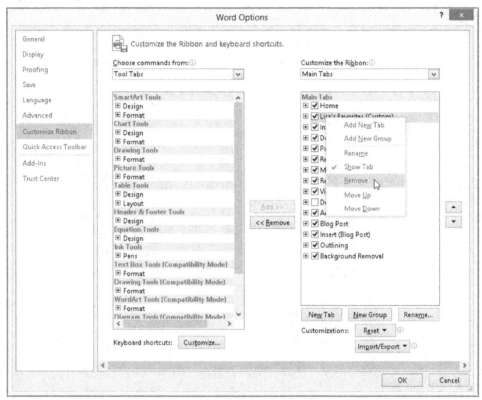

Resetting tabs and removing all customizations

If you decide that you want to remove all customizations from a Ribbon tab, you do not need to remove them one at a time, or drag any removed items back to the tab. In the right panel in the Customize Ribbon dialog box, right-click the tab you want to restore and choose Reset Tab, as shown in Figure 30.17.

You can reset the selected tab using the Reset button drop-down list below the right Customize the Ribbon list. Click the button, and then click Reset only selected Ribbon tab to undo all customizations to the tab selected in the right list.

Not only can you reset a tab, you can, in fact, remove all Ribbon customizations as well. Click the Reset button near the bottom of the Customize Ribbon dialog box and choose Reset All Customizations. The message box shown in Figure 30.18 appears. Note that this option also deletes all QAT customizations, so be sure you want that to happen as well before clicking Yes.

30

FIGURE 30.17

Restoring a tab to its default contents is just a right-click away.

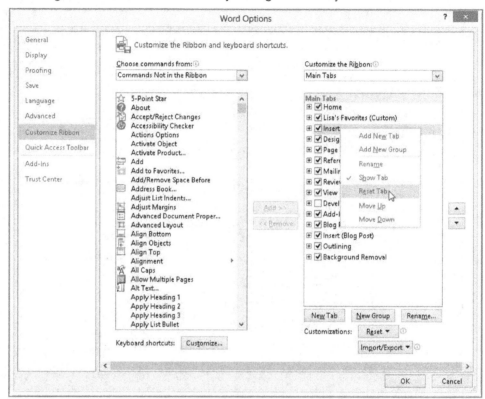

FIGURE 30.18

Reset All Customizations applies to the Ribbon and to the Quick Access Toolbar.

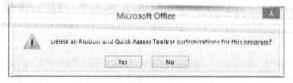

Note that as with other Ribbon customizations, the changes do not take effect until you click OK to close the Word Options dialog box. If you click Cancel instead, the reset won't happen.

Importing and Exporting Ribbon Customizations

You can export and import customizations. Doing so allows you not only to share your custom interface changes, but to quickly load either your own stored custom interface or one provided by someone else. To export your Ribbon customizations, right-click a Ribbon tab and click Customize the Ribbon. Below the right Customize the Ribbon group, click the Import/Export button, and then click Export all customizations. Word saves the file in Exported Office UI file (.exportedUI) format, saving to your My Documents folder within your Documents library.

To open a saved customization file, choose Import/Export, and then click Import customization file. The .exportedUI format is the only one supported so you should see your previously exported file of that format in the Document Library location that appears in the File Open dialog box. Click the customization file that you want to use, and then click Open.

Summary

In this chapter you've learned the easy ins and outs of modifying the Quick Access Toolbar and customizing the Ribbon. You've learned how to add and remove QAT commands, how to save QAT changes only to the current document, and how to reset your changes. For the Ribbon, you've learned how to copy built-in groups to different tabs, create your own groups and tabs, and rearrange custom tabs to suit your needs. Among many other things, you should now be able to do the following:

- Rearrange QAT commands
- Place the QAT above or below the Ribbon
- Work largely without the Ribbon by careful selection of QAT commands
- Find commands in the QAT Customization dialog box
- Turn built-in Ribbon tabs and groups on and off
- Create custom Ribbon tabs to house commands you need
- Effectively move anything around after creating your own tabs and groups

30

Word Options and Settings

IN THIS CHAPTER

Personalizing Word

Changing display options and Save options

Understanding advanced options

Managing add-ins

Using Trust Center settings

I f you don't like something about the way Word works, there's a good chance that you can change it. The problem usually isn't whether you can change something. Rather, the issue is finding out where to change it.

In this chapter, you learn about all of the different options you can change in Word. In a few cases, you are referred to more detailed discussions in other parts of the book. For the most part, however, you'll find everything you need to know about changing Word's options in this chapter.

Opening Word Options

Word 2013 consolidates most of its customization settings in the Word Options dialog box that you first saw in Chapter 1, "Taking Your First Steps with Word," and have revisited from time to time throughout the book. To open the Word Options dialog box, choose File ⇨ Options. Some feature-oriented options can still be found in other locations—such as those for labels, various formatting defaults (for example, the default font), styles, and captions. Most settings and options, however, can be found under the Word Options umbrella, shown in Figure 31.1.

Word Options is divided into 10 tabs, or sections:

- General
- Display
- Proofing
- Save
- Language

- Advanced
- Customize Ribbon
- Quick Access Toolbar
- Add-Ins
- Trust Center

FIGURE 31.1

The Word Options dialog box enables you to control how Word goes about most of its business.

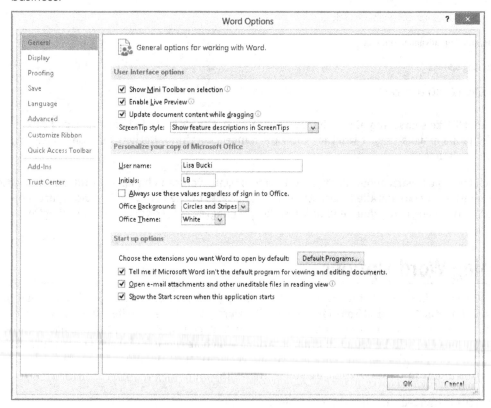

Although these tab names indicate what you'll find and where to find it, they are by no means perfect. For example, General contains a number of display-related settings. Display contains a number of printing options. Moreover, Advanced contains settings of just about every variety.

If you're looking for a particular setting, start on the General tab. If one of the other tabs besides Advanced looks promising, check that tab next. If you don't find the desired setting, take a look in the Advanced tab options, divided into a number of subsections.

In addition, to save wear and tear on your patience, rather than repeatedly say "Choose File ➪ Options" for the rest of this chapter, I'm going to assume that you know how to open the Word Options dialog box and that the relevant tab is onscreen as it's being described. That said, click File ➪ Options ➪ General to get started. And make sure you click OK to apply your setting's changes every time.

Another route to Word Options

While File ➪ Options opens the main Word Options dialog box, the Options button from other dialog boxes sometimes takes you there as well. For example, if you click the dialog box launcher in the Page Setup group of the Page Layout tab to open the Page Setup dialog box, clicking Print Options on the Paper tab transports you to the Display tab in the Word Options dialog box. The bottom subsection of the Display tab is called Printing Options.

Those aren't all of the printing options, of course. You can find many more in Word Options' Advanced tab, under Print and When Printing This Document. Some of these options affect only the current document, not Word as a whole.

Option ScreenTips

As you scroll through different sections of the Word Options dialog box, notice that several icons feature a lowercase "i" in a circle. Hover the mouse over these, as shown in Figure 31.2, to see a ScreenTip describing the feature to the left of the "i."

FIGURE 31.2

Hover the mouse pointer over information icons to see a ScreenTip description of the option.

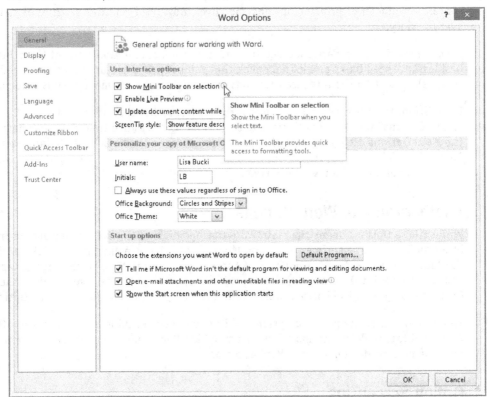

General

The description for the General tab, shown at the top of Figure 31.2, indicates that it offers General options for working with Word. Note that while it says "with Word," some of these, indicated in the following list, affect all of Office 2013, not just Word. The General options and how they behave when enabled (checked) are:

- **Show Mini Toolbar on selection:** The Mini Toolbar appears beside selected text and contains a number of common formatting tools. See the discussion in Chapter 1, and especially Figure 1.15.

- **Enable Live Preview:** Live Preview shows the effects of specific formatting options in the current document. See Chapter 1 for an introduction to Live Preview.

- **Update document content while dragging:** This option gives an animated view of how moved, resized, or rotated objects will look when you finish.

- **ScreenTip style:** This provides three different options regarding how to display ScreenTips: Show feature descriptions in ScreenTips (the default, which shows the most detail in the ScreenTips); Don't show feature descriptions in ScreenTips (which shows only the command name); and Don't show ScreenTips (which suppresses them entirely). This setting affects all of Office 2013.

- **User name and Initials:** Enter the User name and Initials you want Word to use when it identifies who's making comments and editing changes, as well as for certain document properties, such as author. This setting affects all Office 2013 applications that use username and initials.

- **Always use these values regardless of my sign in to Office:** This tells Word to always use the specified User name and Initials values, even when you sign into Office with Microsoft account information that might be different.

- **Office Background and Office Theme:** The choices on these drop-down lists enable you to customize how Office programs look onscreen. Choose one of several backgrounds to appear above the tabs and either the White, Light Gray, or Dark Gray theme.

- **Choose the extensions you want Word to open by default:** Clicking the Default Programs button beside this choice opens the Windows Control panel to its Set Program Associations choices for Word; you may need to click a flashing icon for Control Panel to bring the window to the front. (See Figure 31.3 for the Windows 8 version.) To stop Word from opening files with one of the checked extension types, clear the check box for that extension. For example, you might clear the .rtf extension check box if you prefer to open that type of file in WordPad. Click Save to save your changes and return to the Word Options dialog box.

- **Tell me if Microsoft Word isn't the default program for viewing and editing documents:** You might install another program and it makes itself the default editor for documents. When this option is checked and that happens, on startup Word displays a message asking if you want to reinstate it as the default document editor.

- **Open e-mail attachments and other uneditable files in reading view:** By default, when you click a Word document attachment in an email message, Word opens that attachment in Reading view. If you dislike this default, clear this check box to turn it off.

- **Show the Start screen when this application starts:** If you'd prefer the traditional Word startup that takes you directly to a document, rather than stopping at the Start screen to select a template, clear this check box.

FIGURE 31.3

Files with the checked type of extension automatically open in Word.

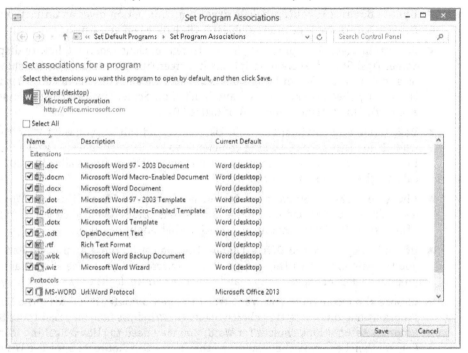

Display (and Printing)

The Display settings, shown in Figure 31.4, affect how certain aspects and attributes are displayed and printed. The most popular among these include the display of nonprinting formatting marks. If the settings you seek aren't here, check in the Advanced tab, where a number of additional display and printing settings are listed under Show document content, Display, Print, and When printing this document.

FIGURE 31.4

A number of Display tab settings affect printing, too.

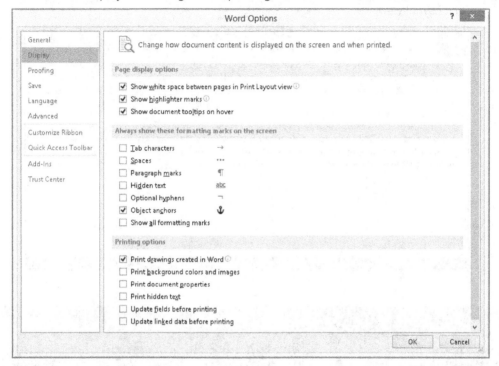

Page display options

Common Page display options are as follows:

- **Show white space between pages in Print Layout view:** This setting is enabled by default, and provides an accurate page preview. Turn this feature off if you'd rather see more text at one time—for example, when proofreading text for continuity and flow—as shown in Figure 31.5.

- **Show highlighter marks:** If the text contains any highlighting, when this setting is enabled highlighting is displayed onscreen as well as printed.

- **Show document tooltips on hover:** This controls the display of a wide variety of tooltips, including tracked changes, footnotes, and endnotes. This does not affect the display of ScreenTips.

FIGURE 31.5

With Show white space between pages in Print Layout view disabled, you see more text in Print Layout view.

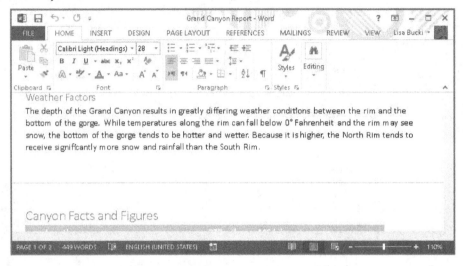

Nonprinting formatting marks

Nonprinting formatting marks often help you uncover formatting problems or oddities in documents. The formatting marks also include additional characters not mentioned in the list, such as page breaks, column breaks, and section breaks. Some are controlled by specific settings in the Always show these formatting marks on the screen subsection shown in Figure 31.4, while others are controlled by the Show all formatting marks check box also found in that subsection, regardless of the individual settings. The Show all formatting marks check can be toggled by pressing Ctrl+Shift+8 or by clicking the Show/Hide button in the Paragraph group of the Home tab on the Ribbon, which you learned about in an Chapter 4, "Zapping Word's Top Annoyances."

Marks included, shown in Figure 31.4, are as follows:

- **Tab characters:** This includes tab characters inserted by the user as well as tabs inserted by the Bullets, Numbering, and AutoFormat tools.

- **Spaces (regular and nonbreaking):** In addition to spaces, this check box controls page breaks.

- **Paragraph marks:** This setting also controls the display of the newline character and cell markers inside tables.

- **Hidden text:** In addition to hidden text formatting (Ctrl+Shift+H), this check box toggles the display of index, table of contents, and table of authorities entries, which are formatted as hidden text.

- **Optional hyphens:** Also called *discretionary hyphens*, these are manually inserted hyphens used along with Word's hyphenation feature.

- **Object anchors:** These indicate the paragraph to which graphics are attached (or anchored).

When you check any of the above options, the indicated characters appear all the time, and Show/Hide will not toggle them on and off. Note that column breaks and section breaks are toggled by Show all formatting marks, but are not associated with any of the individual settings. Hence, there is no way to display column and section breaks all the time, independent of Show/Hide.

Printing options

Word provides a number of options that enable you to control what is printed. Additional options are located in the Advanced tab, under Print and When printing this document. Options in the Display tab are as follows:

- **Print drawings created in Word:** This controls whether Word prints a variety of graphical objects. When this option is turned off, Word will not print any graphic that is in the drawing layer. Only graphics with a Wrap Text setting of In Line with Text can be printed, and not all of those. With wrapping set to In Line with Text, pictures inserted from files, some clipart, and WordArt can be printed even if this Word Option is turned off. With this setting turned off, even if set to In Line with Text, Word will not print SmartArt, shapes, text boxes, or charts. This setting also affects whether images used as watermarks are printed.

- **Print background colors and images:** This determines whether Word prints web-style background colors and images. This does not affect watermarks.

- **Print document properties:** When enabled, this causes an additional page to be printed at the end of the document (and not integrated into the page number structure). The additional page contains a number of document properties: file name, directory, template, title, subject, author, keywords, comments, creation date, change number, last saved on, last saved by, total editing time, last printed on, number of pages, number of words, and number of characters.

- **Print hidden text:** This setting determines whether hidden text (index, table of contents, table of authorities entries, and text formatted as hidden by you) is printed.

- **Update fields before printing:** If enabled, all fields are updated when the document is printed, except for fields that are locked (using either the LockFields keystroke command, Ctrl+F11, or a locking switch).

- **Update linked data before printing:** If enabled, non-field-based links are updated when the file is printed. This includes data linked using XML methods.

Proofing

Proofing options control what kinds of things Word considers to be errors, and what it does about those errors. The Proofing tab has five sections:

- **AutoCorrect Options:** See Chapter 3, "Working Smarter, Not Harder, in Word," and Chapter 11, "Cleaning Up with AutoCorrect and AutoFormat," for a complete discussion of AutoCorrect options.

- **When correcting spelling in Microsoft Office programs:** This subsection holds options that affect all Office 2013 programs that use the proofing tools. See Chapter 10, "Reviewing a Document with Language Tools," for a discussion of these options.

- **When correcting spelling and grammar in Word:** This subsection offers additional spelling and grammar options available in Word that can be set in addition to what might be set in other Office 2013 programs. For example, SharePoint Designer has a "Check spelling as you type" option that is independent of Word's. See Chapter 10 for more on these options.

- **Exceptions for:** Leave the current document selected or choose All New Documents from the drop-down list. Then use the check boxes described next to indicate which exceptions apply to the current document or new documents you create.

- **Hide spelling errors in this document only and Hide grammar errors in this document only:** Check the appropriate option to hide spelling or grammar error onscreen markup as desired. Making an exception can be especially useful when you are using a lot of technical terms in a document, for example.

Save

The Save tab, shown in Figure 31.6, houses a number of settings relating to how Word saves your documents. The Advanced tab has additional save settings.

FIGURE 31.6

Use Save options to keep your documents better organized and safer.

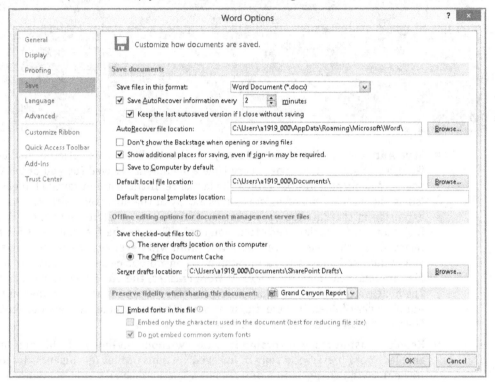

Save documents (backup options)

The Save documents section shown near the top of Figure 31.6 provides five important settings:

- **Save files in this format:** Use this setting to set Word's default save format. Ordinarily, to take full advantage of Word 2013's features, you'll want to save in .docx format. However, if you work in an office with mixed installations of different versions of Word and/or other word processors, it can be helpful to default to saving files in a different format. Or sometimes you need to save in a specific format when working on a particular project. In any case, you have more than a dozen default formats from which to choose.

- **Save AutoRecover information every *x* minutes:** When this option is enabled, Word starts an internal timer every time a document is saved (by you or by Word itself). When *x* minutes pass since the last save, if there are unsaved changes (since the most recent save) Word saves a copy of the document with an .asd extension in the AutoRecovery location, and includes a reference to the original file's name and location. Each time you explicitly save the file, the .asd file is removed and the time is reset. Note that Word will never automatically save the actual file itself—just the .asd version. When Word is closed normally, all .asd files are removed from this folder. If Word crashes, the .asd files aren't removed. The next time Word starts, Word checks whether there are any .asd files in the AutoRecovery folder. If there are, it presents them to you as file versions on the File ➪ Info tab, as described in Chapter 3.

- **Keep the last autosaved version if I close without saving:** With this option enabled, Word preserves a copy of unsaved versions of files (documents closed without saving changes) in a drafts folder. These are available as versions in File ➪ Info, under Versions. These files are saved in C:\Users*user name*\AppData\Local\Microsoft\Office\UnsavedFiles. You cannot change this location. Windows 7 and 8's own file versioning feature does provide additional resources for recovering older saved versions of files. Consult the Help system in your version of Windows to learn how to turn on and use this valuable protection.

- **AutoRecover file location:** Word defaults to a location in your personal folders for your Windows user account (this location can vary depending on what version of Windows you are using). Under some circumstances, you might want to specify a backup drive or a network drive for this location. Either way, it should be a location that is available when Word restarts.

- **Don't show the Backstage when opening or saving files:** Turns off the Backstage so you can go directly to the Open or Save As dialog boxes.

- **Show additional places for saving, even if sign-in may be required:** Controls whether the File ➪ Save As page in Backstage includes your SkyDrive or Office 365 cloud storage locations that you can choose when saving.

- **Save to Computer by default:** Makes the computer (instead of the cloud) the default location when you choose File ⇨ Save As.

- **Default file location:** This is the location where Word saves files and looks for files. You might want to change the location from the default for better organization and control over your files, and to use subfolders.

- **Default personal templates location:** If you want to save templates you create to a default location other than the one that Word uses, enter the folder path here.

Offline editing options for document management server files

These options control what Word does when you check out files from a document management server, such as SharePoint. These settings can affect performance. Under most circumstances, the best performance will be obtained if Word makes a local copy of the file on your own computer. Under some circumstances, however, security requirements might be such that specific documents need to reside on the server. Note that if you choose to save the checked out file to a web server, you will still need to check that document back in for others to see your changes and/or to access it themselves for editing. The Server drafts location can be on your own computer, some other location on your LAN or WAN, or an Internet location.

Preserve fidelity when sharing this document

The last set of options default to affecting only the current document, but you can set it to another open document or All New Documents using the drop-down list. Then set the specific options to apply to the current or new file:

- **Embed fonts in the file:** Enable this check box if you're using unusual fonts, and/or the fonts are essential to proper display and interpretation of the document. This option can be crucial when the document is being printed by a commercial printing service. When you choose to embed, you have the following additional options:

  - **Embed only the characters used in the document (best for reducing file size):** Any given font set potentially can contain hundreds of characters. If the others need fonts only for displaying and printing a file, enable this option to keep file size low. If others will need fonts to edit the file, don't use this option.

  - **Do not embed common system fonts:** This is another space-saving option. It prevents common Windows fonts, such as Arial and Times New Roman, from being embedded, thereby saving on file size.

> **NOTE**
>
> Not all fonts are licensed to permit embedding. Fonts that come with Office 2013 do permit embedding. If you paid a third party for fonts, check your license agreement. If your document contains such fonts, and if the document recipient (for example, a commercial printing service) doesn't have the correct fonts, you will need to provide the necessary fonts in some other way (for example, using removable media).
>
> Some fonts are licensed only for preview. If you embed preview-only fonts, others will be able to view and print the file but will not be able to make changes.

Language

Word-controlled language settings have expanded in Word 2013. Language settings work along with proofing tools and other features in Word, so you may need to change them from time to time if you work in a multilingual environment. Note that you typically have to restart Word for language changes to take effect.

Choose Editing Languages

Use the choices here to determine what languages work with the spelling and grammar checking tools in Word. Chapter 10 gave you the detailed steps for installing an additional language.

As shown in Figure 31.7, in addition to installing a language, you may need to enable the Keyboard Layout for it so you can more easily type in that language. Click Not enabled beside the language. This opens the Language settings in Control Panel so that you can install the needed display and keyboard layout language in Windows. Consult the Help system in your version of Windows to learn how to install additional languages. You may also be prompted to download and install a language pack, depending on the language and dialect you select. When you finish, save your changes in Control Panel and close Control Panel.

> **NOTE**
>
> You can insert accented characters using the default US keyboard. For example, press Ctrl+' followed by e to produce é.

Once you've added additional editing languages, a keyboard icon should appear in the Windows taskbar. Click it to choose the desired language.

Choose Display and Help Languages

This section lets you independently choose the language for the interface (button labels, menu, and so on) and Help. The default is for the interface to match Windows' language, and for Help to match the display language. If you need additional languages, click the "How do I get more Display and Help languages from Office.com?" link.

FIGURE 31.7

Add editing languages to work with Word's proofing tools.

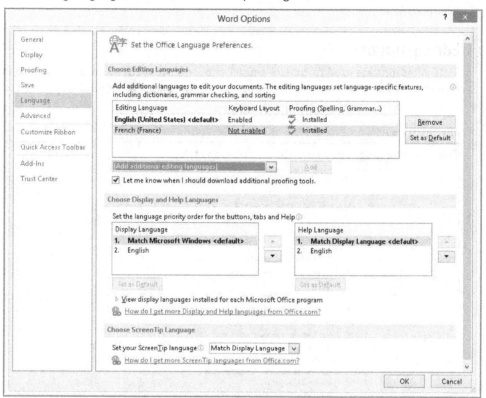

Choose ScreenTip Language

By default, the Set your ScreenTip language drop-down choice matches the current display language. Unlike display and Help languages, this is not tied to complete language interfaces. If you installed Spanish and/or French proofing tools when you installed Office 2013, then ScreenTips for those languages will be available and you can select either choice from the drop-down list. If you need ScreenTips for a different language, then click the "How do I get more ScreenTip languages from Office.com?" link to find out how.

Advanced

The Advanced tab contains more than 140 option settings (if we include the Layout Options at the bottom of the tab). Though many of these are options you will never need, let alone care about what they are, each and every one of these settings is important to *somebody*. You'll have to scroll down the tab to find all the subsection options available on the Advanced tab.

Editing options

Editing options are used to control a number of what to many Word users are essential features but which to others are annoyances. They are shown in Figure 31.8.

FIGURE 31.8

Change editing options to match your working style.

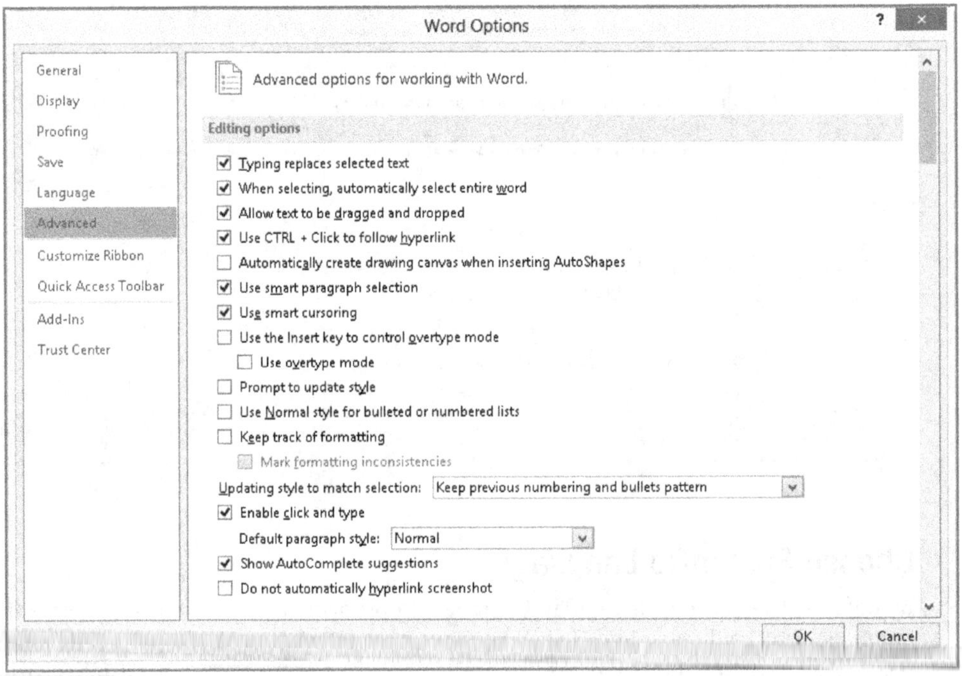

The Advanced Editing options are as follows:

- **Typing replaces selected text:** This is Windows' default. Word supports a different option that Windows doesn't support. If this setting is turned on and text is selected, when you type another character the selection is replaced by the first character you type (or by the contents of the Clipboard if you are pasting over a selection). If this option is turned off, text you type or paste is inserted to the left of the selection, and the selection highlight is removed.

31

- **When selecting, automatically select entire word:** For selection purposes, this affects only the mouse. When enabled, when you select from the interior of a word and drag to expand the selection to include additional material, the original selection start point is moved to encompass the entire word. This setting also affects formatting. When the setting is enabled and nothing is selected, if you apply character formatting anywhere in a word the formatting is applied to the entire word (no matter how the formatting is applied, that is, pressing Ctrl+B, clicking a formatting tool, or using the Font dialog box).

- **Allow text to be dragged and dropped:** When this setting is turned off, when you click to try to drag selected text the selection highlighting is removed instead.

- **Use Ctrl+click to follow hyperlink:** When this setting is turned off, clicking follows a hyperlink, which can make selecting text rather difficult.

- **Automatically create drawing canvas when inserting AutoShapes:** This controls whether Word inserts the drawing canvas when you add shapes and other graphics to a document. Most users prefer to leave this setting turned off, but you may want to turn it back on when creating more complex graphics.

- **Use smart paragraph selection:** When enabled, if you select a paragraph, the paragraph mark is automatically included.

- **Use smart cursoring:** This controls what happens when you scroll using the scroll bars. When this setting is enabled and you scroll so that the insertion point is no longer showing, Word automatically moves the insertion point to the top of the page that is displayed. When turned off, the next character is inserted at the insertion point, which might be miles from where you are looking. Though this is annoying to some, to others it's actually useful. You can scroll to look for something in your document, and then press the Left and Right arrows to return to the insertion point to resume typing.

- **Use the Insert key to control overtype mode:** This is the Windows default. In Word, however, it's not. This setting evolved due to people accidentally pressing the Insert key and toggling Overtype on, which replaces old text—character for character—as new text is typed.

- **Use overtype mode:** Use this setting to toggle Overtype on/off. If the status bar displays Overtype status (right-click the status bar and choose Overtype), you can also toggle this by clicking Overtype or Insert in the status bar.

- **Prompt to update style:** This controls whether Word reapplies the current style or prompts to update the style, when the current style and the formatting of the selection are different. See Chapter 7, "Using Styles to Create a Great Looking Document," for a more complete discussion.

- **Use Normal style for bulleted or numbered lists:** When this setting is enabled and you click the Numbering or Bullets tools, Word uses Normal to format the list. When the setting is disabled, Word instead uses List Paragraph style.

- **Keep track of formatting:** When enabled, variant formatting information is added to the Plus section in the Style Inspector. See Chapter 7 for more about the Style Inspector.

- **Mark formatting inconsistencies:** When this setting is enabled, Word analyzes your formatting and underlines text it considers to be inconsistent using a blue zigzag. This analysis is not instantaneous and sometimes can take several minutes before it appears.

- **Updating style to match selection:** Lets you choose between Keep previous numbering and bullets pattern or Add numbering or bullets to all paragraphs with this style. If you have a series of paragraphs—some numbered/bulleted and some not—but all using the same style, Keep previous... will allow the formatting pattern to remain if the style definition is updated. If Add numbering or bullets... is enabled, then if you update the style definition, the previously unnumbered and unbulleted paragraphs will acquire bullets or numbers. If you typically apply bullets and numbering by using the tools in the Home tab's Paragraph section (rather than by explicitly applying dedicated styles), then changing to Add numbering... will likely have a major impact on your formatting and will cause unintended numbering/bullets in your document. If you typically use dedicated bullet or numbering styles, then the Add numbering... feature will help you maintain the strict use of styles.

- **Enable click and type:** When this setting is enabled, you can double-click anywhere and start typing. Word will add the necessary tabs and paragraph marks to allow you to start typing where you double-click.

- **Default paragraph style:** Use this setting to specify the default style that is applied when you use Click and Type.

- **Show AutoComplete suggestions:** This setting controls whether Word provides an AutoComplete suggestion when it recognizes a date or an AutoText entry.

- **Do not automatically hyperlink screenshot:** When you take a screenshot, this setting prevents it from being automatically hyperlinked.

Cut, copy, and paste

Cut, copy, and paste settings, shown in Figure 31.9, are used primarily to control what happens when pasting.

The first four options control the following pasting behaviors:

- Pasting within the same document
- Pasting between documents
- Pasting between documents when style definitions conflict
- Pasting from other programs

FIGURE 31.9

Cut, copy, and paste settings can save you work if they stop Word from automatically doing something you always have to fix.

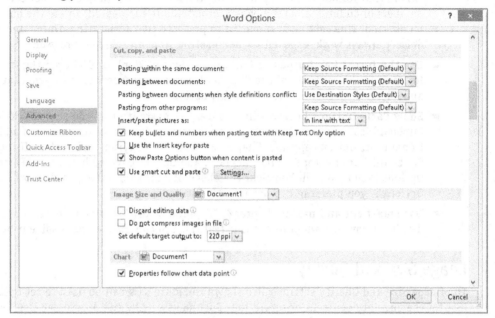

Word offers the same three options for each of those four, and a fourth when style definitions conflict:

- **Keep Source Formatting:** Use this option when pasting things such as book and article titles.
- **Merge Formatting:** The style name(s) in the original text are kept, but the destination style definitions are used. Use this option when repurposing text, such that the original formatting is moot.
- **Keep Text Only:** This is the equivalent of choosing Paste Special ⇨ Unformatted Text. It removes all formatting and graphics.
- **Use Destination Styles:** This option is provided only when pasting between documents and style definitions are in conflict.

Additional cut, copy, and paste options are as follows:

- **Insert/paste pictures as:** Use this to set the default wrapping style for pictures and many other (but not all) graphic objects.

- **Keep bullets and numbers when pasting text with Keep Text Only option:** Ordinarily, when pasting formatted text that contains bullets and formatting (where that formatting is applied using HTML or RTF techniques, rather than actual numbers of bullet characters), when formatting is suppressed, so are the bullets and numbering. This setting is supposed to preserve that formatting. Unfortunately, it doesn't always work, especially when pasting from an Internet browser.

- **Use the Insert key for paste:** Antique versions of Word for DOS used the Insert key for pasting the contents of the Clipboard. Some users were loath to give that up, and Microsoft accommodated with this option.

- **Show Paste Options button when content is pasted:** After you paste, a little Clipboard icon appears. If you hover the mouse pointer over it, a menu of additional paste options appears. Chapter 8, "Cutting, Copying, and Pasting Using the Clipboard," or Chapter 9, "Find, Replace, and Go To," covered how to use Paste Options in more detail. You clear the check box for this setting to turn off Paste Options if you prefer not to use it.

- **Use smart cut and paste:** Chapter 4, "Zapping Word's Top Annoyances," covered the details of how and when to use this feature. You can enable and disable it here.

Image Size and Quality

The Image Size and Quality settings also shown in Figure 31.9 can be used to set options just for the current document or for All New Documents, using the drop-down list beside the subsection name. From there, choose how these options apply.

- **Discard editing data:** Choose this option to tell Word not to save editing information when you crop/resize/recolor or otherwise edit images. Choosing this option reduces file size, but it also means that you can't later revert or undo edits without going back to the original image file.

- **Do not compress images in file:** Choose this option to keep full resolution data from images. This option increases file size, but it maximizes the available resolution. This can improve image quality especially when printing.

- **Set default target output to:** Choose this option when you need to precisely control the resolution of images. Choices are 220, 150, and 96 ppi. If your files are going to be viewed onscreen only, there's no need for resolution above 96 ppi. On the other hand, if the documents are going to be printed, 220 ppi will provide higher quality with less graininess.

Chart

This section can be set to apply to an open document or All New Documents using the subsection title drop-down list. From there, click to enable or disable Properties follow chart data point as needed. When enabled, this setting ensures that data labels will be repositioned properly if you edit chart data.

Show document content

Shown in Figure 31.10, the Show document content subsection options affect how a variety of Word features are represented onscreen. Some of the following options are for information purposes only, such as text boundaries and crop marks, whereas others can affect performance when memory and other resources are tight.

FIGURE 31.10

When pictures disappear and odd things show up in your documents, Show document content settings often explain why.

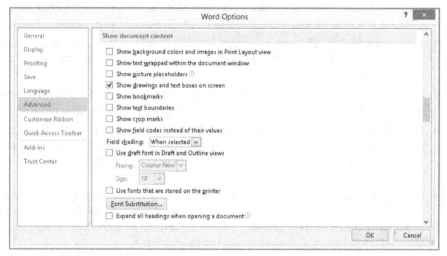

- **Show background colors and images in Print Layout view:** Choose this option to display background colors and images in the document. This affects the display of Page Color settings in the Page Layout tab of the Ribbon but does not affect the Watermark settings. This setting is independent of the similar Print setting in the Display tab.

- **Show text wrapped within the document window:** Choose this option to wrap text to the document window so that horizontal scrolling isn't needed. This setting works only in Draft view.

- **Show picture placeholders:** Choose this option to display empty boxes instead of pictures in your document. This option does not affect the printing of pictures—just whether they are displayed in Word. Using this option makes displaying documents containing pictures faster, and requires less memory. This option does not affect the display of Word shapes, drawings, and text boxes. If multiple documents are open, this setting affects only the currently displayed document and documents opened thereafter.

- **Show drawings and text boxes on screen:** This option controls whether Word displays objects created using Word drawing tools when in Print Layout or Web Layout view. This option does not affect the printing of drawings and text boxes.

- **Show bookmarks:** This option displays bookmarks by placing brackets around bookmarked text. The brackets display as [bookmark] when text is bookmarked or as an I-beam when a single point is bookmarked. This option is for screen display purposes only and does not affect how the document is printed.

- **Show text boundaries:** This option displays hash lines around text margins, columns, and paragraphs. This feature is useful for document layout purposes. The hash lines are not printed and disappear when the document is displayed in Print Preview.

- **Show crop marks:** This option causes Word to display crop marks at the corners of your document. They are used for layout purposes, like text boundaries, and are not printed.

- **Show field codes instead of their values:** Use this option to display field codes instead of field results. You can toggle this setting on/off by pressing Alt+F9.

- **Field shading:** Use this option to control when and if fields are displayed as shaded. Choose Always or When Selected to shade your fields. Using some kind of shading is a good idea because it makes fields easy to see and can help prevent accidental editing and deletion.

- **Use draft font in Draft and Outline views:** Use this option if you don't want to see font variations onscreen. This can be handy if the chosen fonts and point size make the document hard to read or are distracting. Because the display is less complicated, this option also uses fewer system resources.

- **Name and Size:** Choose the font and size used to display Draft view when you've enabled the above check box. Even if you don't want Draft view right now, you can enable Draft view, choose your draft font/size, and then remove the check next to Use draft font. Word will remember your settings.

- **Font Substitution:** Use this button to open the Font Substitution dialog box, shown in Figure 31.11. If no fonts in the current document are missing, a message box informs you of that fact. This option is also a useful way to discover whether the current document contains formatting using fonts not present on your computer. Choose Convert Permanently if there is no reason to maintain the different font and little chance of obtaining it.

- **Expand all headings when opening a document:** If you had collapsed headings when previously working with a document in Outline view or another view, checking this option ensures that Word will expand the headings and display their text the next time you open the document.

FIGURE 31.11

Use Font Substitution to tell Word how to display text formatted using fonts not available on your system.

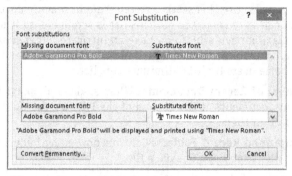

Display

Whereas the Show document content settings mostly affect the interior parts of a document, the Display settings, shown in Figure 31.12, affect the working environment.

FIGURE 31.12

If the Display tab doesn't contain the setting you seek, try the Advanced tab's Display section.

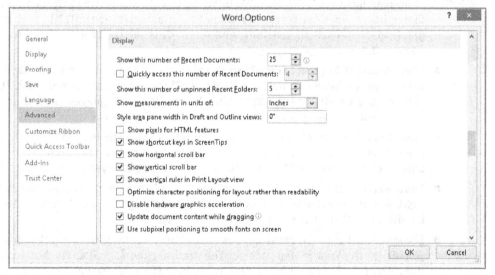

Word's Advanced Display options are as follows:

- **Show this number of Recent Documents:** When you choose File ⇨ Open, Word displays a list of recent documents. Use this setting to tell Word how many documents to remember. The number can vary from 0 to 50. This list is scrollable, so it might make sense to enter the max, particularly if you have an intricate folder structure that's tedious to navigate, and you work with lots of files. On the other hand, as a security/privacy matter, some users limit or eliminate this list.

- **Quickly access this number of Recent Documents:** When enabled, displays the specified number of recent documents at the bottom of the File tab, so you don't even have to click Open to find them.

- **Show this number of unpinned Recent Folders.** Controls how many folders appear in the Recent Folders list when you open or save a file.

- **Show measurements in units of:** Use this setting to choose the measurement units that are used for the rulers dialog boxes. This does not affect font point size selection. Measurement options are inches, centimeters, millimeters, points, and picas.

- **Style area pane width in Draft and Outline views:** Setting a non-zero value causes Word to display a pane at the left side of the Word document, showing the names of the applied styles. Once visible, the pane's width can be varied by dragging its right boundary. Drag all the way to the left to close it. Once closed, it can't be reopened by dragging and must be reopened using this setting.

- **Show pixels for HTML features:** Use this option to set pixels as the default unit of measurement for HTML features in dialog boxes. This setting affects a variety of dialog boxes, even for features you might not associate with HTML, such as paragraph spacing, table dimensions, and so on. This setting is not related to the document view.

- **Show shortcut keys in ScreenTips:** Use this option to display shortcut keys in ScreenTips. Compare this option with ScreenTip Scheme in the General tab. It provides an additional display option when ScreenTips are displayed but has no effect when ScreenTip Theme is set to Don't Show ScreenTips.

- **Show horizontal scroll bar:** Use this option to display the horizontal scroll bar at the bottom of the document window. In Print Layout view, the scroll bar displays only when the document is wider than what can be displayed at the current zoom.

- **Show vertical scroll bar:** Use this option to display the vertical scroll bar at the right side of the document window. When this setting is enabled, the vertical scroll bar displays all the time, regardless of the zoom.

- **Show vertical ruler in Print Layout view:** This option controls whether the Ruler setting (in the View Ribbon) toggles the vertical ruler as well as the horizontal ruler. You can also toggle the rulers by clicking the ruler icon at the top of the vertical scroll bar. You can display just the horizontal or vertical ruler by moving the mouse pointer over the top or left edge of the document window, respectively.

- **Optimize character positioning for layout rather than readability:** Use this option for exact character positioning when creating high-end brochures and other publications for which correct kerning is needed. For best onscreen reading, turn this option off, because it can result in the crowding of narrower letters such as the lowercase "i."

- **Disable hardware graphics accelerations:** For some video adapters, hardware acceleration prevents Word from displaying some graphics or other features correctly. If you notice display problems, try using this option to suppress hardware graphics acceleration to see if it eliminates the problem. If it does, see if you can update your video driver, and then retry with acceleration to see if the update eliminates the problem.

- **Update document content while dragging:** This feature essentially gives Word the ability to give you an animated Live Preview as you move, rotate, or resize objects.

- **Use subpixel positioning to smooth fonts on screen:** Depending on the capabilities of your graphics adapter, enabling this option can result in smoother-looking onscreen fonts.

Print

Print options, shown in Figure 31.13, are used to set a number of printing defaults, in addition to the settings in the Word Options ⇨ Display tab.

FIGURE 31.13

Print settings control a variety of printing defaults; use When printing this document settings to control only the active document.

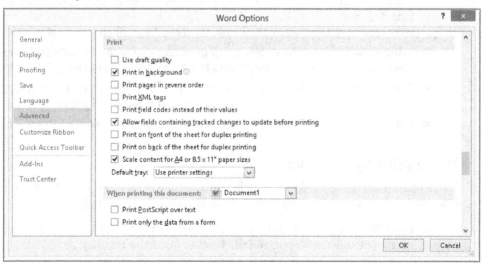

Advanced Print options include the following:

- **Use draft quality:** This option instructs Word to print the document using the printer's draft mode (assuming it has one). This can save ink/toner and time, when all you need is a paper copy to review the text. Some printers do not support draft printing.

- **Print in background:** This option allows printing at the same time you continue working. Don't confuse this "background" with the Print background colors and pictures option discussed earlier. If you have a slow computer, this option can make working even slower. Usually, however, this setting is moot because the document is quickly handed off to Windows.

- **Print pages in reverse order:** Use this option if your printer stacks the document face up, first sheet on the bottom. Select this option also if you need to have sheets reversed for some reason.

- **Print XML tags:** Use this option to print XML tags for XML elements applied to an XML document. For this to work, a schema must be attached to the document.

- **Print field codes instead of their values:** This option causes Word to print field codes instead of field results. This can be useful when you are checking the logic and links in a document, rather than the content.

- **Allow fields containing tracked changes to update before printing:** This option ensures that the "latest" version of a link/field is used when printing. Turn this option off to ensure that what you're looking at is what will print. If you're unsure about what will print, Print Preview (in the right panel when you choose File ➪ Print) or saving in XPS or PDF format are good ways to be sure about printed results before committing to paper.

- **Print on front of the sheet for duplex printing:** Use this setting to simulate duplex printing by printing to the front of each sheet when printing on a printer that does not have duplex capability. Pages are printed in reverse order so that when you turn them over, the backs are ready to print in the correct order.

- **Print on back of the sheet for duplex printing:** This is the flip side of the immediately preceding option. Select this option to finish the simulated duplex printing operation.

- **Scale content for A4 or 8.5 × 11 paper sizes:** Use this option to automatically adjust the size of the output for European or U.S. standard paper sizes.

- **Default tray:** Use this option to tell Word which printer tray or slot to use by default.

When printing this document

These options can be applied to a specific open document or to All New Documents. Use the drop-down arrow to set the target as desired. The options are as follows:

- **Print PostScript over text:** When a Word document has PRINT fields that contain PostScript codes, this option tells Word to print the text first, and to then overlay the results of the PostScript command on top of the already printed text. PRINT fields aren't used very often, and show up mostly in documents converted from Word for the Mac.

■ **Print only the data from a form:** Use this option to print only the data in a form, without printing the protected text. This option works only with legacy Word fields, and not with Word 2007/2010/2013 content controls.

Save

Word's Advanced Save options, shown in Figure 31.14, set four options in addition to those found in the Save tab. These can affect certain features and performance, as well as interact with other Word features, so you should consider the consequences before using them.

FIGURE 31.14

Advanced Save options change the defaults for all Word documents.

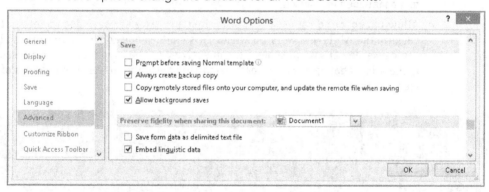

The Save options in the Advanced tab are as follows:

■ **Prompt before saving Normal template:** With this option enabled, when you close Word, if Normal.dotm has changed, you are prompted to save changes to Normal .dotm. You will also see this prompt when you choose Save All, if Normal.dotm contains unsaved changes (see the note about Save All following the description of the Save options). As a security measure, this is an option you should enable. Not only does it let you say No if you were experimenting with settings and don't really want to save the changes, but it also alerts you if something else has unexpectedly changed Normal.dotm.

■ **Always create backup copy:** This option causes Word to create a backup copy of every document you change—including templates. Each time you save changes to a document, Word replaces any existing backup copy by copying the most recent, previously saved version of the file to a file named Backup of *current name*.wbk. This file is saved to the same folder as the original. A problem is that this feature creates a backup copy every time you save, so if you follow best practices and save frequently, the backup copy won't be the version of the file as it was when you first opened it. It will always be what the file looked like just a few minutes earlier. If corruption occurs, you likely won't find out until long after the current document and the backup copy are both corrupted.

- **Copy remotely stored files onto your computer and update the remote file when saving:** This option tells Word to temporarily store a local copy (that is, on your own hard drive) of files that are retrieved from/stored on a network or removable drive. When you save the local copy, changes are saved to the remote file as well. If the original file isn't available, you are prompted to save to a different location to avoid losing the changes. When the file is closed, the temporary version is removed. This option improves performance. The difference between this option and the Offline editing options for document management server files detailed in the Save tab discussion is that the Advanced Save option affects files that aren't on a document management server.

- **Allow background saves:** This option instructs Word to save documents in the background while you work on them. This enables you to continue working but can cause slower saving times. If connectivity to the save location is an issue, or if there is a chance of power loss, using this option increases the chances of document corruption and data loss.

> **NOTE**
>
> In Word 2003 and earlier, you can display the Save All command in the File menu by holding the Shift key when you click File. (The Save All command saves all open documents, so it's a great timesaver.) This does not work in Word 2013. Instead, if you're a fan of Save All, you can add it to the Quick Access Toolbar or the Ribbon. You'll find it in Commands, not in the Ribbon. See Chapter 30, "Customizing the Quick Access Toolbar and Ribbon," for more information about customizing the QAT and the Ribbon.

Preserve fidelity when sharing this document

The Preserve fidelity options, shown in Figure 31.14, can be applied to any open document or to All New Documents. Use the drop-down arrow to change the target as needed.

The options here are as follows:

- **Save form data as delimited text file:** Use this option to save only the data when saving a forms-protected document that contains legacy form fields. Note that this feature affects only legacy form fields and does not work on content controls.

- **Embed linguistic data:** Use this option to save linguistic data, such as speech and handwritten text, in the file.

General

The General options in the Advanced tab, shown in Figure 31.15, defy categorization. At least, they don't fit the taxonomy otherwise offered. They do, however, provide access to a great tool that expands what you can do with Word, "Confirm file format conversion on open." For more on this setting, see the bulleted descriptions.

FIGURE 31.15

The General settings in the Advanced tab provide access to some useful features.

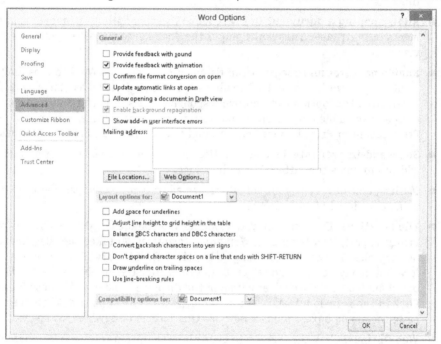

General options in the Advanced tab are as follows:

- **Provide feedback with sound:** Use this option to play different sound effects when performing a number of actions, such as when deleting, pasting, and so on. In order for this setting to work, you need the Microsoft Office Sounds add-in. A dialog box will inform you of that fact, and offer to initiate a site visit so you can download it. Click Yes to do it or No to change your mind. If you say Yes, download and run the file (`sounds.exe`) to install the add-in, following the directions and prompts in the wizard.

- **Provide feedback with animation:** Use this option to animate your pointer in Word and other Office programs that support animation. (It's not clear that this feature actually does anything. I've never seen it make any difference whatsoever.)

- **Confirm file format conversion on open:** Use this option to be able to select the converter to use when opening a file that's not a native Word file. This can be handy when you want to deal with XML, HTML, or even RTF files directly, rather than with Word's interpretation of them. If this option is unchecked, Word automatically determines which converter to use. If you have this feature unchecked but get the Convert File dialog box anyway, either the file isn't in a format recognized by Word or it is corrupted.

- **Update automatic links at open:** Use this option to update all linked content when a file is opened. This affects field-based links, OLE links, and XML-based links.

- **Allow opening a document in Draft view:** Use this option to enable opening documents in Draft view. This works only if the document was last saved while in Draft view.

- **Enable background repagination:** Using this option tells Word to repaginate documents as you work. If you don't really care about pagination as you're working, deselecting this option can improve responsiveness and performance in Word. This option is available only in Draft and Outline views; otherwise, it is grayed out. In Print Layout or Print Preview, background pagination is automatic, not optional.

- **Show add-in user interface errors:** Use this option to display error messages from add-in programs that affect Word's interface.

- **Mailing address:** Type your default return address for envelopes and letters when using associated Word features.

- **File Locations:** Use this button to examine and change the default folders for documents, clipart, User templates, Workgroup templates, AutoRecover files, Tools, and Startup files. To examine or change a location, click Modify. To change to a new location, navigate to it and select it, and then click OK. To obtain the location without changing it, right-click any item in the displayed folder and choose Properties. Click in the Location item, select it, and copy it to the Clipboard. Then press Esc to close the dialog boxes. You can now use that location elsewhere, as needed.

- **Web Options:** Click this button to open the Web Options dialog box, where you can set a variety of options to control how Word creates web pages.

Compatibility and Layout options

Use the Layout and Compatibility settings to control a variety of more obscure Word formatting behaviors. Most are self-explanatory:

- Add space for underlines
- Adjust line height to grid height in the table
- Balance SBCS characters and DBCS characters

- Convert backslash characters into yen signs
- Don't expand characters spaces on a line that ends with SHIFT-RETURN
- Draw underlines on trailing spaces
- Use line-breaking rules

Compatibility options only appear when you open a document from an older version of Word and you see [Compatibility Mode] in the title bar. There are dozens of options, and most are clearly marked for the prior file format they work with, such as Use Word 97 line-breaking rules for Asian text.

Customize Ribbon

The Customize Ribbon tab provides access to customization options for the Ribbon and keyboard. See Chapter 30 for the details.

Quick Access Toolbar

Use this tab to customize the Quick Access Toolbar. See Chapter 30 for details.

Add-Ins

Use the Add-Ins tab to view and control various Word add-ins. For most users, most or all of the add-ins listed won't really seem like add-ins to you. That's because they come with Office 2013. Most of us consider something an add-in if we explicitly and separately install it. None of the add-ins shown in Figure 31.16 were explicitly added by the user.

Add-ins are grouped into the following four sections:

- **Active Application Add-ins:** Add-ins currently in use that affect all of Word.
- **Inactive Application Add-ins:** Word-wide add-ins that are available but currently not being used.
- **Document Related Add-ins:** Available document-specific add-ins in use in the current/active document.
- **Disabled Application Add-ins:** Add-ins disabled by you or by Word. If an add-in causes Word to crash or hang, it can automatically be disabled by Word.

FIGURE 31.16

Add-Ins are grouped into four sets.

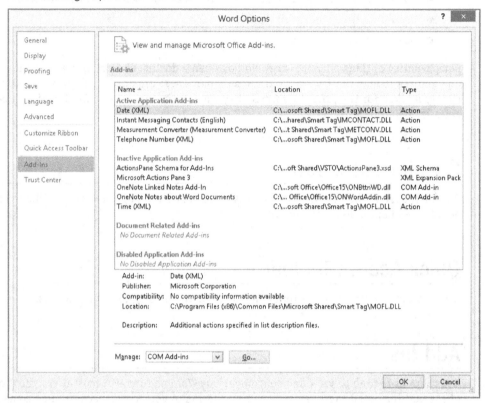

Use the Manage drop-down list to load, unload, disable, and enable add-ins. Select which type of add-in to load from the Manage Tasks list, which includes: COM Add-ins, Actions, Word Add-ins, Templates, XML Schemas, XML Expansion Packs, and Disabled Items. After making your choice, click Go, make selections from the dialog box that appears (which will vary depending on the type of add-in selected), and then click OK twice to finish loading the add-in. Applicable add-ins have been discussed in earlier chapters.

> **NOTE**
>
> *Component Object Model* (COM) is Microsoft's platform for adding software components to Windows. It encompasses OLE, OLE Automation, ActiveX, COM+, and DCOM (distributed component object model).

Under ordinary circumstances, you should not have to be concerned with the Add-ins tab. However, if Word crashes due to an add-in, once any problems have been addressed (such as by updating the add-in), you can return to Add-ins to re-enable the disabled item. Under Manage, choose Disabled Items, and then click Go. In the Disabled Items dialog box, click the disabled item, and then click Enable ⇨ Close.

Trust Center

Trust Center (Figure 31.17) contains information as well as a variety of settings relating to document privacy and security. Under most circumstances, you will not need to change these settings. However, it can be useful to know what's under the hood, so to speak, so that you understand that these settings can be tweaked if necessary.

FIGURE 31.17

Access security and privacy settings from the initial Trust Center tab.

> **NOTE**
>
> The Trust Center options affect all of Office 2013, not just Word.

If you work in an enterprise environment, note that what you see in the Trust Center Settings might be different from what's shown here. Even if it is not different, there might be organizational policies that dictate what you can and cannot change. Consult your IT department if you are unsure. Note that changing settings can affect how Word works, as well as whether or not some features work at all.

In the Trust Center tab, note that most of what you see are links to additional information about privacy and security. Examine these if you like—all of the blue links will open your default browser.

To access Trust Center settings, click the Trust Center Settings button. This displays the Trust Center dialog box, as shown in Figure 31.18. By default, the Trust Center dialog box displays Macro Settings, which is the most common set of trust settings that sometimes require user intervention. As for Word Options, be sure you click OK when finished to save your new Trust Center settings. The rest of this chapter reviews the settings found on each of its tabs.

FIGURE 31.18

Trust Center settings are organized into 11 tabs; the Macro Settings tab displays initially by default.

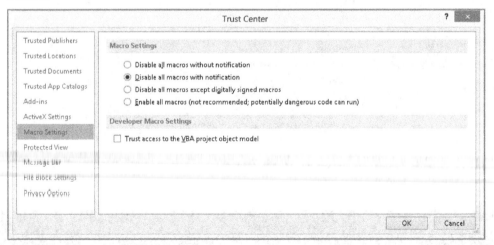

Trusted Publishers

Trusted publishers are developers who have created macros, add-ins, application extensions, or other custom facilities that you can use. When you install such items, their publishers may be added to the Trusted Publishers list as part of the installation process. For most users, however, most of the time your Trusted Publishers list will be empty or have only one entry in it. If you install third-party add-ins from Office.com, they might be listed.

> **CAUTION**
>
> A *digital signature* is an encrypted allegedly secure stamp of authentication on a macro or document. By convention, only specific organizations can issue digital signatures. The digital signature is supposed to confirm that the macro or document originated from the signer and has not been altered. What's to stop someone with a valid digital signature from digitally signing malicious code? I don't know. Bottom line: Before you accept any digital signature, use some independent means to verify that the macros/add-ins you are effectively authorizing are really safe.

Trusted Locations

Trusted Locations provide another way of handling the security of macros you know to be safe. The Trust Center is paranoid by design. The Trust Center's default behavior is to trust only digitally signed macros. If there are macros that you trust, but which the Trust Center doesn't, rather than lowering your security setting and thereby putting your files at risk, it's better to put the template that contains those macros into a trusted location.

> **CAUTION**
>
> Many users don't know about Trusted Locations and often wonder why a macro works, even though security settings are set relatively high. The reason is because the macros are in a template that is stored in a trusted location. Therefore, think twice before you put an add-in into a trusted location. The foot you shoot may be your own.

Think of Trusted Locations as a secure area. Once inside that area, armed guards no longer check ID or shine a flashlight at security certificates. Instead, they assume that those macros wouldn't be inside the compound unless somebody high up (you) had vouched for them. Put another way, it's *your* foot. If you trust yourself not to shoot yourself there, who is the Trust Center to argue?

The Trusted Locations tab, shown in Figure 31.19, enables you to add, remove, and modify locations. That way, if you don't want to co-mingle templates from different sources, you don't have to. By default, Word creates three trusted locations: User templates (templates that are on your computer because you put them there), Application templates (templates that are there because Office's setup program put them there), and StartUp templates (templates and other add-ins that are there because you or someone you trust—an add-in you installed, for example—put them there). In an enterprise, your IT folks might also have created one or more trusted locations using Windows' policy settings. If so, Policy Locations won't be vacant as it is in Figure 31.19.

FIGURE 31.19

Trusted Locations essentially override other macro security settings, so make sure macros are safe before putting a template into a trusted location.

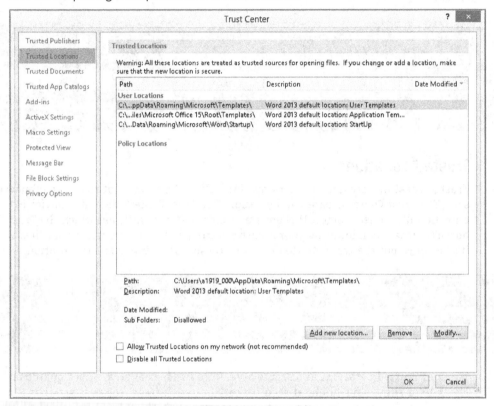

To add a new location, click Add new location. In the Microsoft Office Trusted Location dialog box, shown in Figure 31.20, use the Browse button as needed to locate and select the folder to add. Note that you can add only locations in this way, and not specific files. Click OK when you find the location you want to add. In the Microsoft Office Trusted Location dialog box, note the option Subfolders of this location are also trusted. Click this option only if you really trust any and all subfolders, and then click OK.

FIGURE 31.20

Make sure a folder's subfolders contain only safe add-ins and templates before checking the Subfolders of this location are also trusted option.

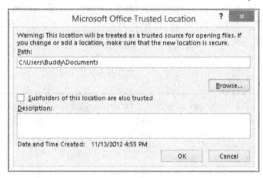

To remove a trusted location, under Path, click the location you want to zap and click Remove.

To modify a location, click the location you want to modify and click Modify. You can use Modify not only to change a location, but also to turn on/off the option to include subfolders as trusted locations.

> **TIP**
>
> To save time and effort, rather than remove a location and add a new one, it's sometimes faster to use the Modify button. This is especially true when the new location is in a branch of the same tree as the one you're replacing.

There are two additional options at the bottom of the Trusted Locations section in the Trust Center:

- **Allow Trusted Locations on my network (not recommended):** Sometimes, locations on your network will be listed under Policy Locations. Other times, such as when explicitly adding a workgroup location (File ⇨ Options ⇨ Advanced ⇨ File locations), you might want to add that location as a trusted location as well. Microsoft doesn't recommend adding network locations to the Trusted Location list, but sometimes it's necessary. As noted earlier, it's *your* foot.

- **Disable all Trusted Locations:** Use this option if you don't trust the files in Trusted Locations, if you suspect that a rogue macro is running amok and you are trying to find it, or if you want to explicitly identify the source of macros that are being run on your computer. With this option enabled, only files signed by Trusted Publishers will be trusted.

Trusted Documents

This tab, shown in Figure 31.21, enables you to preemptively just say No to all trusted documents (Disable Trusted Documents) as well as documents on a network (Allow documents on a network to be trusted). Click the Clear button and then Yes in the message box that appears to reset documents previously marked as trusted documents.

FIGURE 31.21

The Trusted Documents feature allows you to trust specific documents on a one-by-one basis. It also lets you disallow the Trusted Documents entirely.

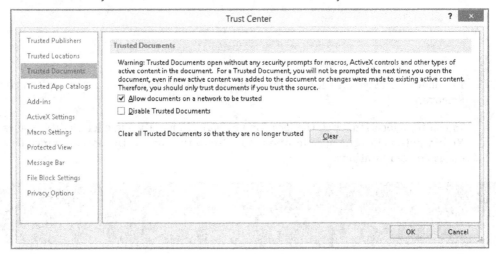

When trusted documents have been disabled or cleared, you will see the Security Warning shown in Figure 31.22 when you reopen a document with macros. Click Enable Content only if you need the active content and only if you trust whoever created it. If the document is on a network, you then may also see a prompt about whether to make it a trusted document.

FIGURE 31.22

Do not click Enable Content unless you are positive that the document is 100 percent safe.

Trusted App Catalogs

New to Office 2013 is the ability to download Office apps that extend functionality within Word and some of the other Office applications. On this tab, you can prohibit apps from running by checking the Don't allow any apps to start or Don't allow apps from the Office Store to start options. If you know a source that has a catalog of apps and trust that source, you can enter the full URL for the catalog (it must be from a secure site using the HTTPS protocol, which also must be typed with the URL), and then click Add catalog.

Add-Ins

Use the Add-ins tab to set the additional security settings shown in Figure 31.23.

FIGURE 31.23

The Add-ins settings often are used in troubleshooting.

Three options are available:

- **Require Application Add-ins to be signed by Trusted Publisher:** Choose this option to tell Word not to use add-ins unless they have been digitally signed. If an unsigned add-in is encountered, Word's message bar displays a notification that the add-in has been disabled (unless the following option is checked).

- **Disable notification for unsigned add-ins (code will remain disabled):** This check box is disabled unless the preceding option is also checked. Add-ins that aren't signed are disabled, but the user isn't notified.

- **Disable all Application Add-ins (may impair functionality):** Click this check box if you don't trust any add-ins. All add-ins are disabled, the other add-in check boxes in this dialog box are grayed out, and you will not be notified when specific add-ins are denied access. This setting does not take effect until all Office 2013 programs have been closed. The settings then take effect when Office 2013 programs are restarted.

ActiveX Settings

Use the ActiveX settings, shown in Figure 31.24, to enable or disable ActiveX controls. Note that these settings do not apply to ActiveX controls contained in files that are in Trusted Locations.

FIGURE 31.24

Use ActiveX settings to limit/enable the availability of ActiveX controls.

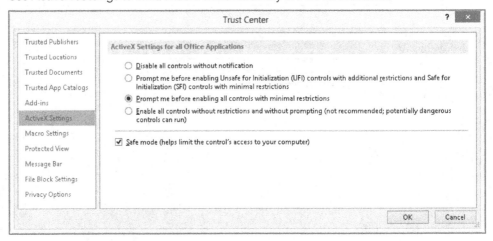

- **Disable all controls without notification:** Choose this option to prevent all ActiveX controls from running. Select this option if either you don't trust the ActiveX controls or you don't want them running for some other reason. When you choose this option, all ActiveX controls in all Office documents are disabled. They are replaced by a red X or a picture of the control. The application message bar will not advise you that ActiveX controls are disabled.

- **Prompt me before enabling Unsafe for Initialization (UFI) controls with additional restrictions and Safe for Initialization (SFI) controls with minimal restrictions:** The effects of this option depend on whether documents that contain ActiveX controls also contain VBA projects. If they contain one or more VBA projects, then all ActiveX controls are disabled, but a message bar appears that lets you selectively enable them. If there is no VBA project, SFI controls are not blocked, and there is no prompt. UFI (unsafe for initialization) controls are disabled, but a message bar prompt will let you enable them.

- **Prompt me before enabling all controls with minimal restrictions:** This is the default option. Effects vary (as in the preceding option) depending on whether the ActiveX's container document also contains one or more VBA projects. If VBA is present, ActiveX controls are disabled with notification and the options to enable them. When you click Enable, all ActiveX controls (both SFI and UFI) are enabled. If there is no VBA project, all ActiveX controls are enabled, period.

- **Enable all controls without restrictions and without prompting (not recommended, potentially dangerous controls can run):** Click this option if you don't value your foot. This enables all ActiveX controls, period. Seriously, use this option only if you work in a 100 percent controlled environment in which there is no possibility of rogue controls being present (for example, if you are not connected to a network or the Internet and never copy files from removable media).

- **Safe mode (helps limit the control's access to your computer):** Use this check box to enable only SFI ActiveX controls that have been marked by the developer as "safe." Note that this "safe mode" has nothing to do with starting Word in safe mode. They are different concepts.

Macro Settings

The options contained in the Macro Settings dialog box, shown in Figure 31.25, control how Word and other Office 2013 applications (the ones that support macros) handle macros.

FIGURE 31.25

Office 2013 must be closed and restarted for these and a number of other Trust Center settings to take effect.

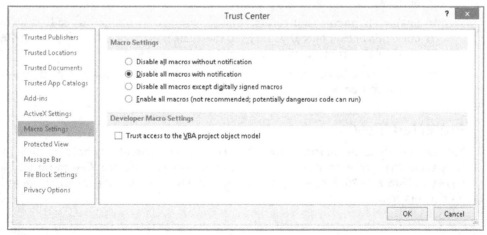

> **CAUTION**
>
> One of the most frustrating things about macro settings is something that the dialog boxes don't tell you: Settings that affect whether macros run do not take effect until you close any macro-aware Office 2013 applications that might be open and then restart the programs of interest.
>
> You might meticulously change all of the settings that affect macros—disabling trusted locations, disabling trusting the VBA project object model, disabling macros, and even removing trusted publishers—yet macros continue to run just fine (or not run at all, if you're trying to enable them). You might even try closing and reopening just Word. Still no dice. What they forget to tell you is that these settings don't take effect until Office 2013 has been closed.

We've already looked at a number of Trust Center settings that affect whether macros run. Macro Settings (refer to Figure 31.26) provide two additional settings. The first is a choice of four levels of macro security. The second is an independent check box that tells Office whether or not to trust access to the VBA project object model:

- **Disable all macros without notification:** Choose this option to prevent all macros from running. They won't run, and you won't hear about them, except that the word *all* doesn't really mean *all*. Macros in a trusted location run regardless of this setting, because documents and templates in trusted locations are not checked by the Trust Center security system. If you change this setting but macros in non-trusted locations still run, close all Office 2013 programs and try again.

- **Disable all macros with notification:** This is identical to the preceding setting, except that Word tells you that macros are being suppressed. You can choose whether or not to run them.

- **Disable all macros except digitally signed macros:** This setting is the same as the first option, except for macros that are digitally signed by publishers in the Trusted Publishers list. If the publisher is not in the trusted list, you are notified, and you can add the publisher to the list. Unsigned macros are disabled without notification.

- **Enable all macros (not recommended, potentially dangerous code can run):** Click this option only if you like to live dangerously, or your computer is 100 percent isolated from possible sources of malicious macros.

- **Trust access to the VBA project object model:** Choose this setting if you develop your own macros.

Protected View

This feature offers an additional line of defense against potentially harmful files, particularly those that arrive as attachments. If you've noticed Protected View warnings like that shown in Figure 31.26, Protected View settings are where you come for relief—or at least for an explanation.

FIGURE 31.26

By default, Word warns you when opening documents that might contain harmful active content.

The appearance of this kind of warning is controlled by the Protected View settings, shown in Figure 31.27.

FIGURE 31.27

Protected View settings control whether you are warned when opening "foreign" attachments.

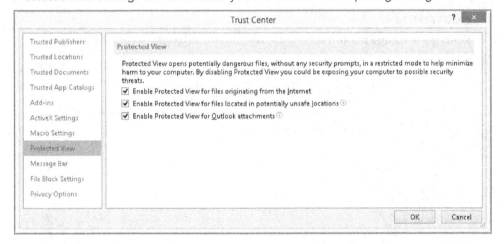

Options are:

- **Enable Protected View for files originating from the Internet:** This option notes the original source for files, including those contained in ZIP and other archives, and gives the Protected View warning if the file was downloaded from the Internet (for example, using a web browser).

- **Enable Protected View for files located in potentially unsafe locations:** Among other things, this setting enables Protected View for files residing in your Temporary Internet folder. Note that this is different from disabling active content, which is controlled by (among other things) Trusted Locations. For Trusted Locations, active content is blocked. For Protected View, any editing at all is blocked.

- **Enable Protected View for Outlook attachments:** This setting warns you that a file originated as an Outlook attachment. This can also serve as a reminder to save it in a known user location rather than in your Temporary Internet files location.

Message Bar

The message bar, shown in Figure 31.26, informs you if macros have been stopped from running for any reason. This is an Office 2013–wide setting. In Trust Center (Figure 31.28), choose Show the Message Bar in all applications when active content has been blocked to display the bar shown in Figure 31.26. It displays at the top of the Word window. If you never want to receive notification, choose Never show information about blocked content.

FIGURE 31.28

Keep the message bar turned on unless you want to ignore security warnings.

The option to Enable Trust Center Logging is used to keep track of all blocked content. The log is a text file kept in the TCDlog folder, which usually is at C:\Users\user name\ AppData\Local\Microsoft\Office\TCDlog.

File Block Settings

File Block Settings allow you to control how Word treats files of specific types, shown in Figure 31.29. The bottom options control how Word interprets the check marks:

- **Do not open selected file types:** Word will not open the files at all. Instead, you will receive an error notice telling you that the file type is blocked by File Block Settings and telling you how to unblock it.

■ **Open selected file types in Protected View:** This setting allows you to open and view checked file types, but does not have an Enable Editing button in the Protected View message bar. There is a "Click for more details link" that leads to the Info tab in Backstage, and a link there to File Block Settings.

■ **Open selected file type in Protected View and allow editing:** This setting allows you to open the files and provides an Enable Editing button.

FIGURE 31.29

Use File Block Settings to control how or if Word opens and saves specific file types.

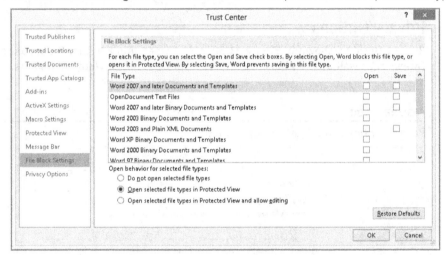

Use the Open check boxes to choose which files to prevent or interfere with opening and editing. For each of the File Block Settings options, if Save is checked, you will not be allowed to save in that format.

Suppose, for example, that your office is trying to explicitly avoid using .doc format anymore, except when absolutely necessary. If you check the Save boxes for all of the pre–Word 2007 formats, Word will effectively remind you that you're not supposed to save in those formats if you should happen to try.

By the way, in Figure 31.29, "Word 2007 and later Binary..." refers to .doc and .dot files that were saved by Word 2007 or Word 2010. While neither has their own "binary" format, internally, Word 2010 differentiates among different .doc/.dot files and can tell Word 2003–saved files from those saved by Word 2007 or Word 2010.

> **NOTE**
>
> What are binary formats? In the list of file types, *binary* means `.doc` or `.dot` format. A bit of a misnomer, binary is used to refer to files that do not contain just plain ASCII text. Notice that the top Word 2007 and later...item does not contain the word "binary," whereas all of the other Word document formats do. So, implicitly, `.docx`, `.docm`, and other x-formats must be plain ASCII. Right? To see why this is silly nomenclature, try opening a `.docx` file using Notepad, which is a plain-text editor. Do `.docx` files look like plain text to you? Not to me, either. That's because they're really ZIP files, which is not a plain-text format. They contain a combination of `.xml` files (which are plain-text files that contain XML tags) and graphics files (which, by their definition would have to be binary). So much for nomenclature. I'll save the lecture on why *binary* is itself a misnomer for a different book.

Privacy Options

Privacy Options, shown in Figure 31.30, affect when and whether Word connects to the Internet, as well as the kinds of data that can be saved in Word documents.

FIGURE 31.30

Privacy Options aren't just about privacy.

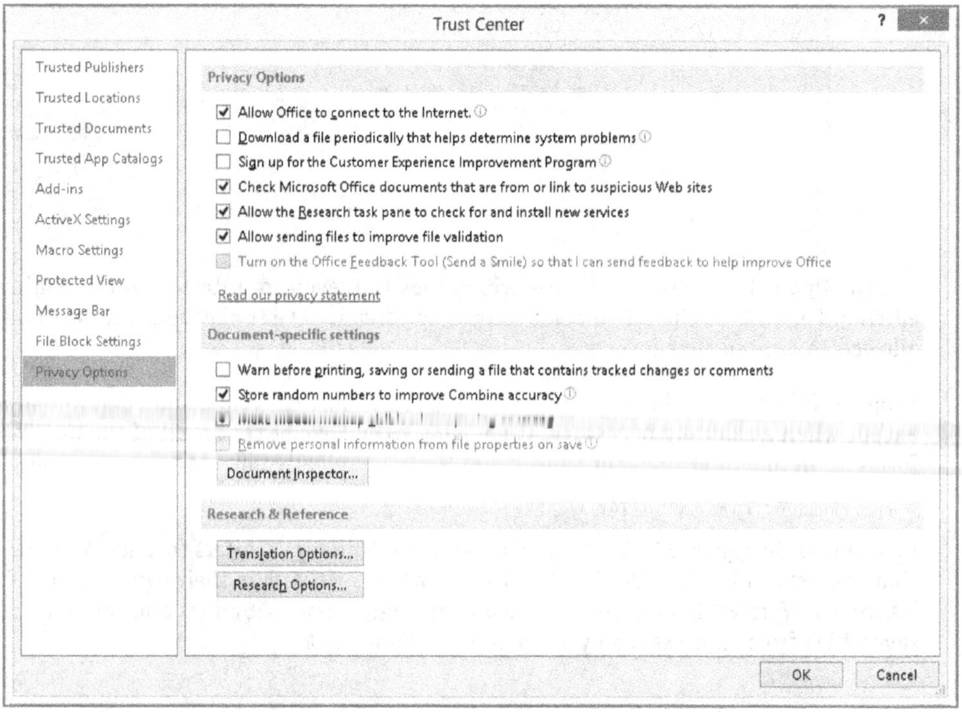

Editor and Macros dialog box, shown in Figure 32.1. To access macro recording without the Developer tab showing, enable the Macro Recording tool on Word's status bar. To do so:

1. **Right-click the status bar.**
2. **Click Macro Recording to check it, as shown in Figure 32.2.** This displays the macro recording (Record Macro) button on the status bar, also shown in Figure 32.2.

FIGURE 32.2

Enable macro recording via the status bar.

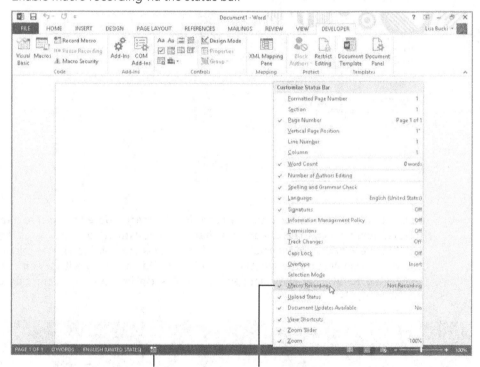

Click to start recording a macro   Check to enable the status bar control for macro recording

Recording a macro

To begin recording a macro, select some text or an object that you want to perform the recorded steps on. You can make selections with the keyboard while macro recording, but those selections are recorded as part of the macro, which may not be what you want. Say you want your macro to apply to a selection, no matter what its size—word, sentence, or paragraph. If you start your macro without making a selection and press Ctrl+Shift+Right

Arrow to select one word, the macro will always select just one word and apply the rest of the recorded steps to it.

After making a selection, if needed, click the Record Macro button, either in the Code group of the Developer tab or on the status bar. This displays the Record Macro dialog box, shown in Figure 32.3.

FIGURE 32.3

Replace the default macro name with one that will help you identify it later.

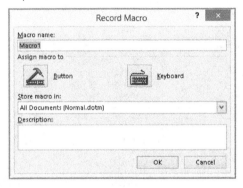

In the Macro name text box, type a name for the macro. Note that macro names can contain letters, numbers, and the underscore character but cannot contain spaces. By default, Word numbers new macros sequentially, but those names are not descriptive enough to enable you to tell one macro from another. Replace the Macro# entry with a name that indicates something about what the macro will do. In Description, type a succinct description of the macro's intended purpose.

NOTE

If you give a macro the name of a built-in Word command, your macro will replace the built-in command while the template or document in which the macro is stored is active. To restore a command to its default, simply delete the macro. To see a list of built-in command names, click the Macros button on the Developer tab, and choose Word Commands from the Macros in drop-down list.

Use the drop-down arrow next to Store macro in to set the storage location. Macros can be stored in templates or documents. The default location makes the macro available in all documents and stores the macro in Normal.dotm. If you choose to store the macro in the currently open template file (.dotx) or document (.docx) file, ultimately the file will need to be saved as a .dotm or .docm (macro-enabled) file. This topic is discussed later in this chapter.

In the Record Macro dialog box, so you can easily access and test your macro, assign it to run from either a Quick Access Toolbar button or a shortcut key. Ultimately, it could be assigned to both, but you can only do one or the other from the Record Macro dialog box. Hence, you have three options:

- To run the macro from the Quick Access Toolbar, click Button under Assign macro to. Word displays the dialog box for customizing the QAT. Open the Customize Quick Access Toolbar at the upper right, and click the desired storage location for the customization (for all documents or the current file). In the list, click the only macro listed, and then click Add to move it to the right list. Click OK. You can easily remove the button later, if desired (by right-clicking it on the QAT and choosing Remove from Quick Access Toolbar); see Chapter 30, "Customizing the Quick Access Toolbar and Ribbon," for more on customizing the QAT.

- To assign the macro to run from a keyboard shortcut, click Keyboard under Assign macro to in the Record Macro dialog box. In the Customize Keyboard dialog box, press the shortcut key(s) you want to use. Open the Save changes in drop-down list and click the appropriate location. Click Assign, and then click Close.

- If you choose not to assign the macro to the QAT or a keyboard shortcut, you can click OK.

After you make an assignment or click OK, Word displays the Recording Macro pointer. In addition, on the status bar, the Record Macro tool changes to a white square. Figure 32.4 shows the recording pointer and Stop Recording button.

When recording is in progress, your mouse options are restricted. You can select commands from the QAT and Ribbon using the mouse, but you cannot use the mouse to select text or perform other editing. For selection and other editing, you need to rely on a combination of the keyboard, Ribbon, and QAT.

NOTE

Experts in VBA recommend creating a template file in which to store a macro before recording the macro. You can then save the macro directly to the template file.

FIGURE 32.4

Word has two ways to indicate that macro recording is in progress.

Let's record an example macro to toggle the display of bookmarks, both because there is no built-in command to do it and because doing it using the Word Options dialog box requires a number of steps:

1. **Open or create a document and add at least one bookmark so you'll be able to see the effect of the macro.**

2. **Start macro recording by clicking Record Macro on either the Developer tab or the status bar.** The Record Macro dialog box opens.

3. **For this example, type** ToggleBookmarks **in the Macro name text box.**

4. **Leave All Documents (Normal.dotm) selected for Store macro in.**

5. **Click OK.** The macro recording begins.

6. **Choose File ⇨ Options ⇨ Advanced.**

7. **Scroll down to Show document content and click to reverse the setting of Show bookmarks, regardless of its current setting.**

8. **Click OK.**

9. **On the status bar, click the white square (Stop Recording button), seen in Figure 32.4.** The macro recorder stops.

At this point, you have a macro that sets the current state of bookmark display to the selection you made in Step 7—either enabling or disabling bookmark display. To make the macro useful, you need to edit it to turn it into a toggle instead. Ideally, when you record a macro, it will work without further intervention. Sometimes, however (as in the current example), you need to edit it to make it do what you want.

> **CAUTION**
>
> There are certain actions that the macro recorder cannot capture, such as applying a theme color to text. In these instances, as in the example macro you just created, you have to learn a little about VBA to write your macro.

Editing a macro

To edit a macro, click the Macros button in the Code group of the Developer tab. This displays the Macros dialog box, shown in Figure 32.5. Select the macro to edit (select the ToggleBookmarks macro you just recorded if you're following along with the example) and click Edit. If you didn't store the macro in the default location (Normal.dotm), you might need to set Macros in to the correct location for your macro to appear in the list.

CAUTION

Make sure you click Edit to edit a macro. If you click Create rather than Edit, you will be prompted to replace the existing macro.

FIGURE 32.5

Select a macro in the Macro name list and click Edit.

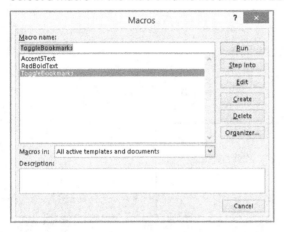

When you click Edit, Word opens the Visual Basic Editor, as shown in Figure 32.6. The section on the left is called the Project Explorer. Because the macro was saved in Normal.dotm, it shows up in the NewMacros module. Ultimately, there could be many macros stored in that module. If the macro is to become a permanent addition to your tools, you probably want to create a module that contains common tools you create (for example, Toggles) and copy the ToggleBookmarks macro into it, rather than leave it in NewMacros to get lost as your library of macros grows. You look at how to create a new module and move a macro into it later in this chapter.

The right side of the window shows the contents of the NewMacros module. The example in the screenshot contains three macros. The blinking insertion point appears in the ToggleBookmarks steps, because the example macro has been selected for editing. You can use the drop-down arrow next to the current macro at the upper right (ToggleBookmarks in this case) to display a list of macros in the current module and click another macro name to scroll the window to that macro.

FIGURE 32.6

When you edit or create a macro, Word opens the Microsoft Visual Basic Editor.

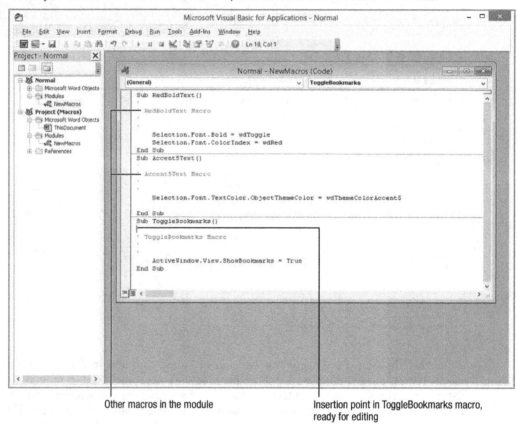

Other macros in the module

Insertion point in ToggleBookmarks macro, ready for editing

To turn the example macro you recorded earlier into a toggle, you're going to have to make a slight change to its contents. Consider the following statement shown in the ToggleBookmarks macro in Figure 32.6:

```
ActiveWindow.View.ShowBookmarks = True
```

This statement instructs Word to set `ActiveWindow.View.ShowBookmarks` to `True`. `ActiveWindow.View.ShowBookmarks` is the state of the `ShowBookmarks` setting. If you set it to `True`, bookmarks will be displayed. If you set it to `False`, they won't be displayed. What you *want* to do is set it to the opposite of its current state.

As it turns out, this is ridiculously easy, and it might even seem that way if you enjoy and understand mathematics. The opposite of:

```
ActiveWindow.View.ShowBookmarks
```

is:

```
Not ActiveWindow.View.ShowBookmarks
```

Therefore, you can turn this macro into a toggle by replacing `True` with the latter statement:

```
ActiveWindow.View.ShowBookmarks = Not ActiveWindow.View.ShowBookmarks
```

Make that change in the Visual Basic Editor window.

> **TIP**
>
> It's notoriously easy to mistype Visual Basic commands. Whenever possible, take advantage of existing code and make generous use of the Clipboard to copy and paste as needed. Here, copy `ActiveWindow.View .ShowBookmarks` to the Clipboard, and paste it over `True` on the right side of the `=`. Type `Not` in front of it, as shown in the preceding example.

32

Testing a macro

You can test a macro without closing the Visual Basic Editor. If you assigned the macro to a QAT tool or to a keyboard shortcut, switch over to the Word editing window and display something you know to be bookmarked. If the current document doesn't contain any bookmarks, then type some text, select it, press Ctrl+Shift+F5, type a bookmark name, and click Add.

Now run your macros such as the example toggle macro by clicking the corresponding QAT tool or pressing the assigned shortcut key. If it works, you should see the bookmark brackets toggling on and off.

If you didn't assign a keystroke or QAT tool, you can still test the macro, but it's a bit clumsier. Position the Visual Basic Editor window and the Word window so you can see both. Make sure that your macro (ToggleBookmarks in this example) is still selected from the drop-down list in the upper-right corner of the code window. In the Visual Basic Editor toolbar, click the Run button shown in Figure 32.7.

FIGURE 32.7

When you run a macro using the Run Sub/UserForm button, its steps happen in the corresponding open Word document window.

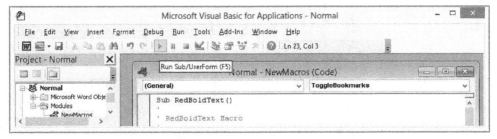

Managing Macros

To maximize the utility of macros, there are some things you can do. As mentioned earlier, one thing you can do is create a special module for containing your macros—something other than NewMacros, which can quickly become cluttered. Another thing you can do is sign your macros so you can choose higher levels of security and still be able to run your own macros.

Copying macros to a new module

You can create new modules in `Normal.dotm` or you can create a new template for storing your macros and put that macro into your startup folder (see "Global Add-Ins" later in this chapter). Using `Normal.dotm` is easier because it requires less work.

To create a new module in `Normal.dotm`, in the Project Explorer right-click Modules under Normal and choose Insert ⇨ Module, as shown in Figure 32.8. If the Project Explorer is not showing, choose View ⇨ Project Explorer (Ctrl+R). To rename the module, from the default Module# name click the module and choose View ⇨ Properties (F4). Next to (Name), select Module# (for example, Module1) and replace it with a new name, such as **Toggles** or **MyTools** (the name can contain numbers, letters, and the underscore character). Click the X to close the Properties window.

FIGURE 32.8

Right-click Modules in the Project Explorer to insert a new module.

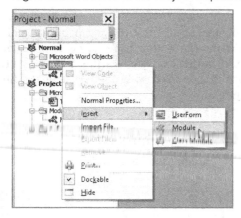

Double-click the NewMacros module in the Project Explorer to display the contents of that module. Drag over the macro contents to select it. If you created the example macro, for example, you could drag from Sub ToggleBookmarks() through End Sub. Right-click and choose Cut (Ctrl+X). Double-click the new module in the Project Explorer to switch back to it. If you've previously added macros to the module, go to the end of an existing End Sub and press Enter. Right-click and choose Paste (Ctrl+V) to insert the macro at that location. If you have additional macros to transfer, repeat the procedure.

To go ahead and save your work now, choose File ⇨ Save Normal (or Save filename, where *filename* is the name of the file in which the currently displayed module resides) or click the Save button on the Visual Basic Editor toolbar. If the Prompt before saving Normal.dotm option is enabled in File ⇨ Options ⇨ Advanced, you might still be prompted to save changes later if key assignments or QAT assignments have been made.

NOTE

If you've been using NewMacros as your macro repository for a while, it might sometimes seem simpler to rename NewMacros rather than create a new module and move macros over after they've been created, debugged, and tested. However, if macros are assigned to the QAT or keyboard shortcuts, those assignments will no longer work. Ultimately, it's the same amount of work, but it will seem like less work if you move macros to their permanent home on an as-you-go basis.

Digitally signing your macros

Signing your macros enables others to verify that they come from a trusted source, if you're in situation where you create templates with macros for colleagues or clients.

Installing and running SelfCert

First, make sure that you can create a certificate for yourself. Open Control Panel and under Programs, choose Uninstall a program ⇨ Microsoft Office 2013 ⇨ Change ⇨ Add or Remove Features ⇨ Continue. Click the + (plus) button beside Office Shared Features. (Note that the name of your Office 2013 installation may vary.) If Digital Certificate for VBA Projects is not set to Run from My Computer, click the Digital Certificate for VBA button, click Run from My Computer in the drop-down, click Continue, and follow the setup instructions. Close the Control Panel window when you're done.

In Windows 7, choose Start ⇨ All Programs ⇨ Microsoft Office ⇨ Microsoft Office 2013 Tools ⇨ Digital Certificate for VBA Projects. In Windows 8, open a File Explorer window, and navigate to C:\Program Files (x86)\Office\Office15 (for 32-bit versions of Office), or C:\Program Files\Office\Office15 (for 64-bit versions of Office). Locate the SELFCERT.EXE command in the folder and double-click it.

In Create Digital Certificate, shown in Figure 32.9, type a name to use on the certificate—usually your own name. Click OK, and you should see a notice indicating success. Click OK to close that message dialog box.

FIGURE 32.9

You can create a certificate for signing your own macro projects.

Signing your macros

If it's not already open, open the Visual Basic Editor (Alt+F11). Expand the template or document that contains the macro project(s) you want to sign, click in the project you want to sign, and choose Tools ⇨ Digital Signature to open the Digital Signature dialog box shown in Figure 32.10. Click Choose. In the Windows Security dialog box that appears, select your signing certificate, and then click OK. Click OK again back in the Digital Signature dialog box.

FIGURE 32.10

Choosing a signing certificate

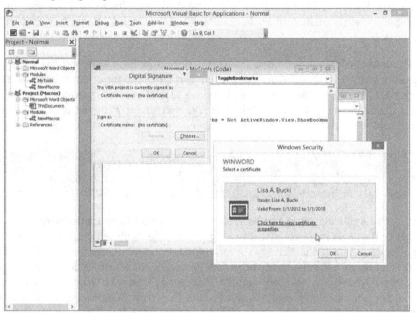

Understanding More about Macro Security

Macro security is one of those areas that has the power to thoroughly confuse and frustrate Word users. One of the primary reasons is that a number of settings are Office-wide and take effect when any macro-capable Office 2013 program is started. When you change settings, the changes often do not take effect until you close all macro-capable Office 2013 programs and restart. Some other settings don't take effect until just Word is closed and restarted. Let's start with four commandments. These represent elevated stages, so try them in order:

1. **When you make a change to Word's macro security settings and do not see a change in Word's macro behavior, close all instances of Word that are running and try again.**

2. **When closing and restarting Word doesn't change Word's macro behavior, close all Office 2013 programs and try again.**

3. **When changing a security setting and closing/restarting Office 2013 doesn't change Word's macro behavior, use Windows Task Manager to make sure all Office applications are really closed, and if not, close them and try again.**

4. **When none of the above changes Word's macro behavior, check whether the recalcitrance is caused by a different security setting.**

Confirming Office is really closed with Task Manager

For many users, Windows Task Manager is an essential tool. They could not get through a day of computing without it. Many others need Windows Task Manager but simply don't know about it.

To start Windows Task Manager, press Ctrl+Alt+Delete and click Task Manager. If pressing that key combination frightens you (even though it can't reboot or shut down Windows), right-click a blank area in the taskbar and choose Task Manager instead. You also can select the Search charm, scroll right, and click Task Manager under Windows System. One of these methods should start the Windows Task Manager.

> **NOTE**
>
> In Windows 7, you select right-click the taskbar and click Start Task Manager; there is no Search charm in Windows 7.

Look first in the Applications tab in Windows 7. Even if no Office applications show up there, it's possible that one or more are still running but unable to close due to an unseen problem. Click the Processes tab in the Windows 7 Task Manager. In Windows 8, click More details and then the Processes tab. Figure 32.11 shows the Processes tab in the Windows 8 Task Manager. (The Windows 7 Task Manager looks slightly different.) Click each Office application process to stop, and then click End Process (Windows 7) or End task (Windows 8). In Windows 7, you will see the startup command name rather that the program name listed among the processes. Look for the following processes, and end them:

- WINWORD.EXE (Word)
- ONENOTE.EXE (OneNote)
- ONENOTEM.EXE (OneNote Launcher)
- OUTLOOK.EXE (Outlook)
- EXCEL.EXE (Excel)
- MSACCESS.EXE (Access)
- POWERPNT.EXE (PowerPoint)
- MSPUB.EXE (Publisher)
- SPDESIGN.EXE (SharePoint Designer)

Close the Task Manager after you finish closing the processes. With some Office applications, such as Outlook, forcing it to close can result in data loss and possible damage to your Outlook data file. Try starting Outlook normally, wait until it is fully open, and then click the Outlook window's Close button to close the program. Wait two minutes to see if it has now disappeared from the list of running processes. If not, try signing out of your Windows session and then signing back in. When you sign out, this forces all programs in the current session to close.

FIGURE 32.11

Use the Processes tab in Windows Task Manager to determine whether you have running instances of Office applications.

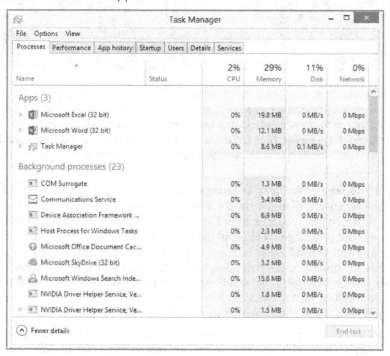

Macros and security

Word's macro behavior is governed by a number of different settings, most of which are covered in Chapter 31. When Word appears to be unresponsive to changes in security settings, it's likely due either to a need to close all of Office for the change to take effect or to layers of security that are affecting things from multiple directions. Security settings that affect whether macros run are found in Word Options at File ⇨ Options ⇨ Trust Center ⇨ Trust Center Settings. The tabs and their key settings are:

- **Macro settings:** A frequent problem is that the Disable all macros except digitally signed macros option is selected. If you need to leave this option selected, the workaround is usually digitally signing all the macros, and then closing and restarting Word. Moving the template or file containing the macros into a trusted location can also solve the problem.

> **CAUTION**
>
> When given a choice between putting a document into a trusted location versus designating the document's location as trusted, unless the location contains just that one file, it's almost always safer to move the document into a trusted location. If you set a storage location that you use often as "trusted," it's too easy to inadvertently save untrustworthy files to that location. Moving files one at a time, however, requires more thought and attention, and accidents are less likely.

- **Trusted Locations:** You can use the Add new location button to add another folder that you want to designate as a trusted location. A common problem is that this setting often is forgotten, so efforts to prevent a certain set of macros from running fail. Moving the file that contains them to a nontrusted location usually solves the problem. Better still, it solves the problem without having to close and restart Word or Office.

- **Trusted Publishers:** You may be prompted to add a publisher to the list of Trusted Publishers when you install or load an add-in. In other cases a Security Alert may appear, in which case you can click Trust all documents from this publisher or Enable all code published by this publisher before clicking OK to continue opening the file and add the publisher to the list of trusted publishers. There are typically two other options in the Security Alert: The Help protect me from unknown content (recommended) option rejects the publisher, and content will not be run. The Enable this add-in for this session only option allows you to run the current content but does not add the publisher as a trusted publisher.

- **Add-ins:** You can control whether add-ins must be from a Trusted Publisher. Check Require Application Add-Ins to be signed by Trusted Publisher to tighten security.

- **Message Bar:** A common problem is that the choice of whether to enable content in a document with macros isn't presented because the Message Bar is disabled. If you want to take advantage of the prompt to enable content, you must enable Show Message Bar in all applications when active content, such as ActiveX controls and macros, has been blocked.

Macro Storage

Macros can be stored in macro-enabled document templates or in macro-enabled documents. Word 2013 has four different native file formats:

- **.docx:** Ordinary Word file that cannot contain macros
- **.docm:** Macro-enabled document file
- **.dotx:** Plain document template that cannot contain macros
- **.dotm:** Macro-enabled document template file

When you record or otherwise create a macro and instruct Word to store it in a .docx or .dotx file, Word doesn't balk at that point. When you save the file, however, Word now tells you that you cannot save the VBA project in a macro-free document, as shown in Figure 32.12.

FIGURE 32.12

VBA projects can be saved only in .docm or .dotm files.

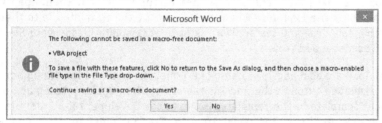

To save the macros, choose No. Word then opens the Save As dialog box. Open the Save as Type list, choose either Word Macro-Enabled Document (*.docm), as shown in Figure 32.13, or Word Macro-Enabled Template (*.dotm).

FIGURE 32.13

You can save macros only in macro-enabled documents and templates.

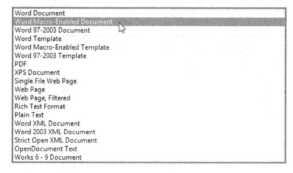

Global add-Ins

If you choose to store your macros in Normal.dotm, they are automatically loaded when you start Word. Any shortcut keys or Quick Access Toolbar tools assigned to run macros will run just fine, assuming that the macros and shortcuts are stored in Normal.dotm.

When a template or other add-in is available throughout the Word session, it is known as a *global* template or add-in. Normal.dotm by default is a global add-in. Other global add-ins can be loaded in one of two ways. They can be stored in Word's Startup folder, in which case they are loaded when Word starts, or they can be explicitly loaded using the Template and Add-ins dialog box.

To copy a file to the Startup folder, you first need to determine where that is. Choose File ➪ Options ➪ Advanced ➪ File Locations (under the General section). Click Startup ➪ Modify. Use Look in to determine the path where Startup is located. Then, open Windows Explorer (Windows 7) or File Explorer (Windows 8) and copy the template file to that location. The next time you close and restart Word, any Word template files in your Startup folder are loaded as global add-ins.

The other way to load a global add-in is using the Templates and Add-ins dialog box, shown in Figure 32.14, displayed through the Add-Ins tab of the Word Options dialog box or by clicking Document Template in the Templates group of the Developer tab. Under Global templates and add-ins, any templates loaded from the Startup folder appear, along with any that you have added here previously. When you open Word, only templates in the Startup folder are loaded. Other templates you've loaded in past sessions are listed, but are not checked. Place a check next to any unloaded templates you want to load. To load a template not listed, click Add. In the Add Template dialog box, the starting location is Trusted Templates. If the template you want isn't there, navigate to its location, select it, and click OK. Note, however, that depending on your macro security settings, if the template is *not* in a trusted location and isn't otherwise permitted, its macros will be disabled when you try to access them.

FIGURE 32.14

You can add and remove templates using the Templates and Add-ins dialog box.

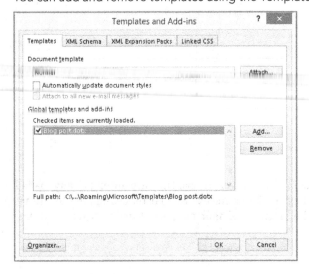

One option is to designate a .dotm file other than Normal.dotm as your main storage location for macros, and store that file in Word's Startup folder. That way, your macros are loaded when Word starts. Moreover, if Normal.dotm becomes corrupted (which, unfortunately, is altogether likely at some point in your Word career), your task of rebuilding won't be quite as onerous, because you won't have all of your eggs in one basket, so to speak.

> **NOTE**
>
> If you choose to store your everyday macros in a .dotm file other than Normal.dotm, while the macros themselves are not stored in Normal.dotm, any key assignments or Quick Access Toolbar assignments that access those macros must be stored in Normal.dotm in order to work.

32

Automatic Macros

In designing document templates, as well as in setting up the Word editing environment, it sometimes is useful to perform setup or housekeeping chores. To facilitate this, Word has a collection of reserved names you can use to create automatic macros:

- **AutoExec:** Runs when you start Word. AutoExec works only when it is stored in Normal.dotm.

- **AutoOpen:** Runs when you open a document based on the template that contains it. If an AutoOpen macro is stored in Normal.dotm, it runs any time a document based on Normal.dotm is opened but not when a new document based on Normal.dotm is created. A popular use for AutoOpen is to set the desired zoom or other view-related settings when documents are opened. Another popular purpose is to update certain fields.

- **AutoClose:** Runs when a document based on the template that contains it is closed.

- **AutoExit:** Runs when you exit from Word. AutoExit works only when it is stored in Normal.dotm.

- **AutoNew:** Runs when a document based on the template that contains it is created. This is a popular kind of automatic macro to use when creating active document templates. An AutoNew document can populate a new document with content, prompt for a file name or other information, insert the current date as static text, and so on.

Macros by these names do not exist until you create them. For example, if you have a set of startup chores that you perform every time you start Word, the next time you start Word, before you do your startup chores, start the macro recorder, and name the macro **AutoExec**. Then perform your startup chores. Stop the macro recorder when you're done. The next time you start Word, your AutoExec macro will perform your startup chores for you.

Visual Basic for Applications: Quick and Dirty Answers

You've already learned a bit about Visual Basic and the Visual Basic Editor. In this section, you learn only what you need to know to get started—quick and dirty, as they say. The best way to gain an understanding of Word macros is by recording a macro and then looking at the resulting Visual Basic code to see how Word translated your actions into code.

All you really need to know

Visual Basic can be intimidating, as can the Visual Basic Editor. Understanding what's happening can help disarm its intimidating quality. On the other hand, too much too soon can be overwhelming, and you might never want to come back. Following are the top 10 things you need to know.

1. Starting and toggling the Visual Basic Editor

You can start the Visual Basic Editor any time you want by editing a macro or simply by starting the editor, without any particular macro in mind. To edit an existing macro or to create one, just press Alt+F8. If you see macros listed, click one, and then click Edit. If you don't see any, type a name and click Create.

To open the Visual Basic Editor with no particular destination in mind, press Alt+F11. Note that once you're in the Visual Basic Editor, Alt+F11 now returns the favor, and goes back to the Word document editing window. Hence, you can use Alt+F11, effectively, to toggle between the Visual Basic Editor and Word.

2. Project Explorer and code windows

The two main sections of the Visual Basic Editor you need to know about are the Project Explorer and the Code window, shown earlier in Figure 32.6. The left side, the Project Explorer, works like any tree structure in Windows. Click + to expand; click - to collapse. Double-click to select a macro, which is then displayed in the Code window. If the Code window is ever replaced by something else, try pressing F7 to bring the code back into view.

3. Running macros directly from the Visual Basic Editor

You can run macros directly from the Visual Basic Editor. While it's true that this works best if you have two monitors—one for showing the Visual Basic Editor and another for showing the Word document window—it's not essential. In the Windows taskbar, click the Visual Basic icon, and then Ctrl+click the icon for the Word window. Right-click either selected program and choose Tile Horizontally. Now you should be able to see both windows at the same time.

With the macro you're testing displayed in the Code window, click the Run button, also shown earlier in Figure 32.7. It's available in either the Standard or the Debug toolbar. If you run into an error, click Reset, fix the error, and try again. To run the macro one line at a time, click Step into.

Additional Run-related commands are contained in the Run menu. You can also run a macro by pressing F5, but the Visual Basic Editor window must be active for it to work. If the Word window is active, the F5 activates the Go To tab in the Find and Replace dialog box.

4. The Visual Basic Editor reads your mind

When you type a Visual Basic object name, the editor knows what "could" come next and shows you a list of the possible methods, properties, and more that you can add next, as shown in Figure 32.15. Use the Down arrow key to move down through the choices, and when you see what you want, press the Spacebar to insert it. Sometimes Word shows you a list; other times, Word shows you the syntax.

5. The Visual Basic Editor wants to help

If you want more information about a command, click it and press F1. The Object Browser window opens so that you can browse to explore the various commands and object relationships.

FIGURE 32.15

When you follow a Visual Basic object or keyword with a period, the editor shows you a list of what can come next.

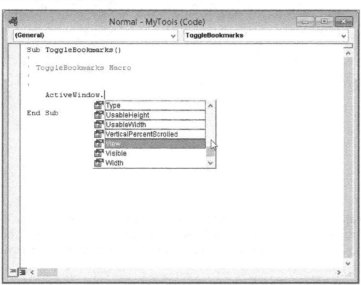

6. If the Visual Basic Editor window doesn't respond...

If you try clicking somewhere in the Visual Basic Editor window but nothing happens, it's usually because a dialog box is open in Word itself but isn't displaying on top of the Visual Basic window. The two application windows might look independent, but they're not. Close Word's dialog box and try again.

7. If the Visual Basic project is "locked," change security

If you try to expand the tree in the Project Explorer but it says that the project is unviewable, the quickest solution is to close Visual Basic and Word, move the template that contains the macros to a trusted location, and then try again.

If that doesn't work, however, it's possible that the project really is locked. In the Project Explorer window, right-click the top level of the project (identified as Normal, Project, TemplateProject, or a name corresponding to a global add-in), and choose Project Properties. In the Protection tab of the Project Properties dialog box (Figure 32.16), remove the check next to Lock project for viewing; supply the password, if needed; and click OK. Reverse the process to lock and protect one of your projects.

FIGURE 32.16

Projects can be locked for security reasons or because the project was explicitly locked by the user.

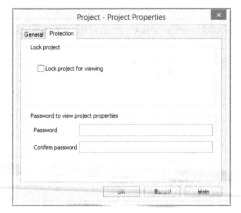

8. The larger context

When you see commands listed in the code window, you're usually not looking at the entire command. Because you're within Word, Visual Basic saves space by not including the entire name. For example, consider the following brief macro, which types *Hello* at the insertion point:

```
Sub Hello()
  Selection.TypeText Text: = "Hello"
End Sub
```

`Selection.TypeText` is an abbreviation for `Word.Application.Selection.TypeText`. Because both Word and Application are assumed, however, you don't need either of those for the command to work.

9. Watch macros as they're being recorded

When you start recording a macro, immediately click the Pause Recording button in the Developer tab. Press Alt+F11 to display the Visual Basic Editor, and navigate to the macro being recorded. Arrange the Word window and the Visual Basic Editor window so you see both. Press Alt+F11 to return to the Word window, and click Resume Recording.

Now as you record your macro, you'll see the corresponding commands appear in the Visual Basic Editor. This is a great way to get a sense of what does what, and what kind of Visual Basic commands correspond to actions in Word. You'll also discover that some things cannot be recorded. If you watch your macro as it's being recorded, you'll know what is left out and have a better understanding of what kind of editing the macro requires in order to work properly.

10. Now you know why it's a good idea to prompt to save Normal.dotm

When you're experimenting with macros, there are a lot of things you'll do that you won't necessarily want saved as part of `Normal.dotm`. Choose File ➪ Options ➪ Advanced. In the Save section, click Prompt before saving Normal template to check it.

For more information

The *Microsoft Word 2013 Bible* is a lot of things, but it is not a book about how to program using Visual Basic for Applications. For that, you need other resources. A good place to start is the Visual Basic for Applications online Help. Open the Visual Basic Editor, and press F1 to launch your Web browser and display the Word 2013 developer resources on MSDN. Once you're more involved in Visual Basic for Applications, you'll find the *Word Object Model Reference* to be invaluable.

You can find free online resources for learning and using Visual Basic for Applications at the following:

- `www.mousetrax.com/techpage.html#autoforms`
- `http://word.mvps.org`

> **TIP**
>
> The Microsoft Developer Network website (msdn.com) has excellent VBA resources, even for beginners. Search the site for "VBA." I also recommend searching for these articles: "Getting Started with VBA in Word 2010" and "101 VBA Samples for Office 2010." Even though they are written for the prior versions, the syntax and techniques still apply in Word 2013.

Summary

In this chapter you've gotten your feet wet with Word's brand of VBA (Visual Basic for Applications). You've seen how to record a macro and test it. You've also learned a little about how to edit macros to make them do things that the recorder can't make them do. You're now also basically familiar with the Visual Basic Editor, and you should be able to do the following:

- Record a macro, and assign it to the Quick Access Toolbar or a keyboard shortcut
- Manage Visual Basic projects by creating new modules and copying new macros to them
- Manage your macros by storing them in global templates other than `Normal.dotm`
- Digitally sign your Visual Basic project

Command-Line Switches for Controlling Word Startup

IN THIS APPENDIX

Reviewing what command-line switches do

Learning the available command-line switches

Y̶ou learned in Chapter 1, "Taking Your First Steps with Word," that one option you have for starting Word 2013 is to create a shortcut for it on the Windows Desktop, as detailed in the section "Creating a desktop shortcut and shortcut key." As shown in Figure 1.2, you can work with the entry in the Target text box of the Properties dialog box for the shortcut to control exactly how Word starts up or to perform certain tasks. This appendix details the command-line switches you can use when starting Word.

> **TIP**
>
> If you start Word using the Command or Run dialog box in either Windows 7 or 8, you also can use a command-line switch there.

Command-Line Switches

When you are using a command-line switch, note that they each require a space after the trailing quote that follows the file specification for the Word executable file, and before the backslash (\), for example, `"C:\Program Files (x86)\Microsoft Office\Office15\WINWORD.EXE"`[space]`/a`. There is no space, however, between the / and the character that follows it. Note also that when a file path specification or filename itself contains a space, the entire name must be enclosed in quotes.

In the Target text box of the shortcut's Properties dialog box, the entire startup file and path name appears enclosed in quotes. You should add the space and the startup switch *outside* the quotes (after the second quotation mark). For example, `"C:\Program Files (x86)\Microsoft Office\Office15\WINWORD.EXE" /safe` starts Word in safe mode. This appendix shows the switches listed with a forward slash.

> **NOTE**
>
> The path `C:\Program Files (x86)\Microsoft Office\Office15\WINWORD.EXE` is for the 32-bit version of Word 2013. For the 64-bit version, the path is `C:\Program Files\Microsoft Office\Office15\WINWORD.EXE`. Vary the path according to your version when entering startup switches.

> **TIP**
>
> Sometimes getting the command-line specifications right involves a fair amount of trial and error. To save time and effort, create a full-function Windows shortcut for starting Word. Open the Properties dialog box and make your change(s) to the Target field. Click OK, and then test the shortcut.

/a

The `/a` switch prevents Word from automatically loading global templates (including your version of `normal.dotm`) and add-ins. It also prevents Word from loading some of the settings in Word's Data key in the registry. The `/a` switch often is used as a diagnostic tool for isolating problems with Word. Hence, if adding the `/a` switch "solves" whatever problem you're having, then the problem is located in a global template or an add-in.

> **NOTE**
>
> The `/a` switch in Word 2013 does not suppress changes to the QAT. It also doesn't prevent the display of files in the Recent Documents list when you click the File button.

Using the `/a` switch is not as drastic or complete as starting Word in safe mode, because add-ins and global templates can still be loaded manually when you use the `/a` switch. An interesting quirk about the `/a` switch is that sometimes running Word just once with it is enough to fix certain registry corruption problems. In contrast, starting Word in safe mode does not modify the registry.

/laddinpath

This switch starts Word and immediately loads a specific Word add-in — for example, `/l"c:\program files\stat\statpak.dll"`.

/m

This switch prevents Word from running any AutoExec macros. It is sometimes used in troubleshooting as well as to prevent damage to documents from unexpected AutoExec macros.

/mcommandname

This switch starts Word and immediately runs the indicated command or macro name. For example, `/mfile1` starts Word and immediately runs the `File1` command, which tells Word to open the first file listed in the Recently Used Files list. Or, if you want to start Word and display a new file, use the /mfilenew switch. If you want to start Word and see the legacy Word 2003 New dialog box for selecting from a handful of basic document templates rather than the Word Start screen, use /mfilenewdialog.

/n
This starts Word without opening a new blank document.

/pxslt
This switch starts Word and creates a new XML document based on the indicated XSLT (Extensible Stylesheet Language Transformation)—for example, /p"c:\XML\formatted.xsl".

/r
The /r switch forces Word to rewrite the registry entries. This is often used to fix problems with corrupted registry entries. Only the registry entries are changed, and Word opens and closes quickly.

/safe
This switch starts Word in safe mode. This is the same as starting Word while holding down the Ctrl key and then clicking Yes. The full specifications of what safe mode does in Word 2013 are not available as of this writing. They will be similar to those for Word 2010, however, which are available at http://support.microsoft.com/kb/210565.

/tfilename
This switch starts Word and opens the single document file specified—for example, /tBrochure.docx or /t"C:\ Users\Lisa\Documents\Brochure.docx".

/ttemplatename
This switch starts Word and creates a new document based on the indicated template—for example, /tBrochure.dot or /t"C:\Program Files (x86)\Microsoft Office\ Templates\1033\Brochure.dot".

/u
This switch merely prevents Word from loading. If you're a system administrator, you could temporarily disable users' ability to run Word using this switch.

/w
This switch starts a new instance of Word with a new blank Document window. The new document will not appear as an option in the View ⇨ Window ⇨ Switch Windows list of other open instances of Word.

path\filename

Specifying a path and file name causes Word to open that file. This method works best when you want to open multiple files when you open Word. If the path is missing, the file must be located in Word's default document folder. For example, to create a shortcut for Word to open a document named `C:\Users\Lisa\Documents\Resources.docx`, I might use the following target specification: `"C:\Program Files (x86)\Microsoft Office\Office15\WINWORD.EXE" C:\Users\Lisa\Documents\Resource.docx C:\Users\Lisa\Documents\Editors.docx`.

Note that both the program specification and the full path and name of the startup command is inside quotes, but the file paths and names are not. As noted earlier, when the path and file name don't include any spaces, you can leave the quotes out. In practice, it's a good idea to be in the habit of using them so you don't forget them when needed, so I often include them even when not strictly called for. The switch will still work with quotes around the file name and path.

Index

A

Index